Bryant, Donald Cross
Fundamentals of
Public Speaking.

FUNDAMENTALS of PUBLIC SPEAKING

Donald C. Bryant
THE UNIVERSITY OF IOWA
Karl R. Wallace
UNIVERSITY OF MASSACHUSETTS

FUNDAMENTALS of PUBLIC SPEAKING

fourth edition

APPLETON-CENTURY-CROFTS
EDUCATIONAL DIVISION
MEREDITH CORPORATION

New York

629–1

Library of Congress Card Number: 74–77531

PRINTED IN THE UNITED STATES OF AMERICA
390–14915–2

Contents

Appendices

Preface

In this fourth edition of *Fundamentals of Public Speaking,* we preserve the chief characteristic features of prior editions. One such feature is the provision of practical materials and advice. So again we offer a working textbook for the college student and his teacher. Systematic instruction in speech communication is not yet generally woven into the texture of high school education, and consequently most college students do not know what is involved in developing sound habits and standards of public speaking and discussion. Concerning the selection of subjects for speaking, the finding and organizing of materials, the methods of developing materials where the clear communication of information is at issue, the foundations of style and appropriateness in language, the psychological and physical conditions of delivery, and variant strategies in the presentation of speeches—these we continue to discuss in considerable detail and we offer specific counsel on them. Our treatment is, we hope, sufficiently clear and full to permit the mature and well-motivated student to become virtually his own instructor. We make no apologies for retaining the ABC's of bodily movement and gesture and the description of general reference resources available in a library. These appear as Appendices A and B. We also retain early in the book a brief introduction to the basic unit of discourse, which the student may use readily in his first speeches.

Another feature of former editions is reflected in our assumption that the mature student should know what lies behind effective and ready utterance. Ability and skill in speaking are not enough. Sound knowledge of principle and theory should illuminate and undergird practice. So in this edition we maintain the position that the processes involved in systematic communication are encompassed in the arts and sciences of verbal communication. The parent art and science was called rhetoric. Although it was—and is—an autonomous art, some of its materials and certainly its social functions necessarily give it political and ethical colorations. These relationships we explore primarily in the early chapters and in the chapter on ethics and *ethos.* Much, if not all, of what lies behind the habits and skills of speechmaking is revealed in the model or basic concepts of an art. The model embraces the creator, his ends (or purposes), materials, media, and forms. The model is reflected in Chapter 2. By systematically comparing public speaking with other arts, one may see sharply both its creative and its communicative aspects, and one may see clearly what he is doing as he prepares and delivers a speech. Preparation and delivery are two aspects of a functional whole, for phrasing and uttering are but the final stages of a creative act. In part the model is reflected in the organizing categories of the book, which call attention primarily to the materials and forms of a speech. As a consequence, facts and evidence are regarded as materials existing independently of speaker and listener. They are discovered among the observables of a communicative situation; hence, we treat evidence in the chapter devoted to the finding of materials rather than discuss it later in the chapter on proof.

We continue to treat linguistic utterances as the meaningful and public forms of human experience. The statement, the "sentence," is the objective, the observable, unit. So it seems to be both practical and sound to view speaking as a sequence of statements. Accordingly, we keep our established point of view toward the basic operations involved in making both informative and persuasive speeches. The informative speech is seen in terms of statements and their development, so managed as to achieve clearness and interest. The "logical" dimension of the persuasive speech is treated entirely in terms of statements, the meaning of these statements, and the interdependence of their meanings and their logical forms. Thus we gain the advantage of linking the presentation of patterned statements directly with the logical analysis that yields them. The effect is to correlate realistically, for the elementary student, logical and semantic aspects of language with communication. We trust, also, that our point of view has the effect of tying style more integrally to communication than is usually done. After all, style is the body and form of utterance, and for both speaker and listener it is manifest only in utterance.

Some novel features of this edition, we think, are significant. They lurk in the background throughout, but they appear pointedly in Chapter 3, "The Basis of Communication," and in Chapters 17–19, which deal with those materials of persuasive utterance that reside within the speaker and the audience. The essential requirements for linguistic response are seen to be attention—a psychological mechanism—and the material conditions with which the mechanism works. Viewed broadly, the material conditions are revealed in two sources: interests and values, which are products of growing up in one's culture; and facts and evidence, which are the objective materials of the communicative setting and external to the participants. Interest as something distinct from attention seems to be a product of values. Interests and values, in turn, are determinants of attitudes. To categorize thus and to associate the components of communicative utterances are not only theoretically sound but also practically advantageous to the student. He sees that to make a statement is to attend to the conditions that produce it. He sees that to reason with statements, to be logical with them, is to be aware of the ways in which they are formally related to one another. The student sees that to listen is to direct attention to statements that may hold interest and value for him. An act of communication brings speaker and listener together on grounds perceived to be of value to both.

Other new aspects of this edition should be noted. The ethical problems of both speaker and listener are shown to arise from the choices that are made, and must be made, in communicative situations. So we discuss more realistically and more thoroughly the ethical bases of persuasion than was possible in the third edition. We have treated *ethos* as one of the ethical problems of the communicator, for the kind of portrait the speaker presents is largely within his control. He can choose the features of the self-image he wants his audience to see.

Another departure from earlier editions is evident in the handling of outlining. Formerly we devoted separate chapters to outlining the informative speech and the persuasive speech. Now, partly in response to our helpful critics, we treat outlining in a single chapter, "The Basis of Outlining." There are, indeed, forms of relating and organizing statements common to both informative and persuasive speeches. These are presented first, followed by forms peculiar to each type of speech.

This fourth edition continues to reflect our conviction that mature students in their first speechmaking course should study speeches as well as build them. Often it is easier to detect the processes and procedures of oral communication when the utterance is somebody else's. Obviously, it is easier to criticize and evaluate another's utterance than one's own. A communicative utterance, informal or formal, is the response to the context that evokes it. A speech, then, has a history of its own, and some speeches, like some literature, are preserved as part of the record of man's life. Not only do speeches reveal what men thought and felt—and how they saw fit to cope publicly with their ideas and feelings—but they are among the social forces that influence men and action. So in Part VII we again present a method for analyzing speeches. Added are illustrative analyses of John F. Kennedy's Inaugural Address, one from *The New Yorker* magazine, one by Professor Bryant. Eight of the sixteen speeches for study in Chapter 25 are new to this edition.

In scores of ways and places we have been influenced by our colleagues and students. In particular, Professor Kenneth Burns has kept us on the track here and there, and Professor Robert W. Smith of Alma College has strengthened our thinking about the ethics of public speaking. The knowledge and long experience of Professor Richard Smith of the University of Illinois Library are reflected in the description of reference materials in Appendix A. To our assistants, Katherine Anderson, Ray Dearin, and Sheryl Etling, we are especially grateful.

D. C. B.
K. R. W.

I

Introductory Principles

1
The Study of Public Speaking

Public speaking in a collegiate setting is in the tradition of the liberal arts and sciences. It includes both learning and doing. It involves both principles and practice, study and performance, knowledge and experience. It is directed toward helping students to understand speechmaking—one of the most characteristic and persistent activities of men in society—and to improve their own ability to speak effectively. Drawn from the practice and experience of hundreds of speechmakers in the ancient Greek world, principles of public speaking were first formulated and organized into textbooks over 2,400 years ago. These principles have been transmitted down through the centuries, always being altered and added to. Changing political and social conditions, for example, have created different roles and values for public address and have prompted new styles and habits of public speaking. The conditions of modern society likewise have affected standards of communication. Modern speechmakers, through their accumulated experience, continue to add to our knowledge; and students of public address, employing the methods of history, criticism, and scientific experiment, also provide new information year by year.

Traditionally called *rhetoric,* or the art of practical popular discourse, the principles of public speaking aid in the adjustment of people to ideas and ideas to people. Hence the practice of public speaking has ever been helpful to the individual in his professional and community life. And as a mode of public discussion it is indispensable to the vigor and well-being of a free society. Indeed, these are the basic reasons why public speaking is worthy of study.

The Tradition

Persons who undertake a serious study of public speaking usually want to become better speakers. A student will not be excited, perhaps, to learn that he is pursuing almost the oldest systematic study in the annals of education. Nevertheless, he may find some assurance and pride in realizing that his study and practice are built on experience which is ancient as well as modern. The word *communication* has an up-to-the-minute ring; yet much of its meaning has deep roots in words such as *rhetoric, poetics, language, speech, oratory,* and *literature.*

Ever since about 450 B.C., when Corax, a teacher and scholar in the city of Syracuse in Sicily, wrote the first book on rhetoric, generation after generation of civilized men has devoted much of its time and the talents of some of its greatest teachers and scholars to the principles and practice of public speaking. In ancient Greece and Rome, *rhetoric* was, in fact, the theory of prose composition, because almost all ancient prose was *oral.* Since ancient times the term *rhetoric* has taken on other narrower meanings, until today it is often understood to mean merely grammar and the rules of written composition. Though we now have no single term to mean what the Greeks and Romans meant by rhetoric, the study of oral public address still thrives.

Among those who have written on the principles of public speaking are many of the most prominent men in history: Plato and Aristotle, the greatest philosophers and teachers of ancient Greece; Cicero, one of the two foremost public speakers of the ancient world; Quintilian, the Roman teacher whose treatise on the education of the public speaker, *Institutes of Oratory,* is one of the basic educational works of all time; Tacitus, the Roman historian; St. Augustine, one of the fathers of the Church; Erasmus of Rotterdam, the eminent Renaissance scholar; Thomas Hobbes and Francis Bacon, two of the greatest English philosophers; Fénelon, the French bishop; and John Quincy Adams, the American scholar, teacher, and President. Each age has had many good teachers and writers on the subject, and in every age the study of public speaking has had a place in education—often a prominent place.

Of course, the teachers and the doctrines in the textbooks have not always been the same in kind and quality. Like all other social phenomena, public speaking has changed with fashion and with the needs and interests of times and countries. The theory and the practice of public speaking have been good and they have been bad, as have the theory and practice of politics, medicine, ethics, and poetry. In ancient Athens, for example, the so-called Sophists endorsed a shallow and irresponsible theory and practice of public speaking in the law courts and in exhibitions. Plato became so disgusted with the abuses of the Sophists that at one time he wrote eloquently against the whole art of rhetoric, claiming that, like flattery, adornment, and cookery, it did as much to make bad things seem attractive as to make good things appealing. At a later time he stated principles for sound and useful public speaking, which many people still subscribe to as their ideal. Aristotle, his great contemporary, directly countered the impression that public address and chicanery had become synonymous. Rhetoric, he said, is not evil because it is put to evil uses by evil men, any more than is a knife, which can be used to murder a man or to perform an operation that will save his life. Furthermore, Aristotle established the principle that the best public speaking is not founded on the glibness of tongue and baseless appeal to ignorance and emotion of which Plato accused the Sophists. It is founded on knowledge and sound thinking, though it is supported by eloquence and uses emotion for greater effectiveness.

Modern Values

As the study of public speaking has enjoyed dignity and importance in all the ages of Western civilization, so it is important today when the demands upon the spoken word and the facilities for transmitting it are so much greater than ever before. Today, of course, in the running of our society, we have the additional aids of tremendous quantities of all sorts of printed matter and of wide dissemination of information and argument through television and radio. But because of the extent and the increased complexity of our social, economic, and political life, there is not less but more demand for oral communication.

Modern society associates important values with public speaking. Some are personal; some are social. Some are self-evident: self-improvement, personal success, and confidence. Others are less evident because they are connected with such values as social responsibility and the welfare of others.

Personal values

Among the personal values, confidence is the one most frequently mentioned by students who elect a course in public speaking. Perhaps the more accurate word is *self-confidence,* for they want to feel that they can talk readily and surely to others. They know that they can acquire and strengthen such trust in themselves through practice in speaking to others and through learning the principles and conventions of good speaking, under the guidance and encouragement of a teacher. They know what everybody knows, that confidence is built through knowledge and experience.

Next to confidence is a value that people refer to vaguely as *skill in speaking.* By this they seem to mean the ability to speak clearly and interestingly and to demonstrate a certain fluency and readiness with words. By *skill* some persons also mean the ability to persuade others to accept ideas and arguments. Such abilities are associated with success in life—with achievement in one's occupation, business, or profession.

The belief that skill in oral communication is an asset in business, professional, and public life is well founded. The good speaker has always been prized in the field of law, and students preparing for the bar are often advised to elect some courses in public speaking. In the law school itself, instruction in trial practice and the moot court gives greater emphasis to communication than was the rule a generation ago. In the life of the clergyman, the ability to speak well is indispensable. Some seminaries today are giving more attention to the art of preaching than they have for many years. The armed forces in their officer-training programs include units of instruction devoted to oral communication. In political life, of course, skill in public speaking, if not absolutely essential, enhances the influence of the politician, statesman, and administrative official, whether he serves on the local, state, or national scene. We expect our public men to speak well; if they do not, they disappoint us. In these days, curricula in engineering, agriculture, and architecture often include formal instruction in public speaking.

In the last four decades, commerce and industry have become more alive to the values of communication than they have been at any previous time. The size and complexity of mass production and distribution, the intricacies of organization, marketing, and selling, the emphasis on public relations—all have combined to make skill in writing and speaking more important in our economy than ever before. Many industries, General Motors and DuPont for example, have training programs in discussion and speechmaking which are offered primarily to employees who show promise of becoming executives. Recently some fifty presidents of America's largest corporations testified to the values of effective communication in industry. An analysis of their views reveals these significant opinions: Breakdowns in industrial communication are definitely related to labor disputes and strikes. The major causes of breakdown can often be traced to "lack of communicative ability on the part of management," to "inadequate use of communication media," and to "inadequate training programs in . . . communication." Many presidents believed that all important policies should be transmitted and explained orally as well as in writing. Many of them thought that all persons in managerial positions should be trained in communication.[1] It has long been held that "the first function of the executive is to develop and maintain a system of communication."[2] A conservative interpretation of such opinion suggests that the ability to speak well (and, of course to write) does not hurt a person's chances of success in the world of business and industry.

Some students who wish to develop their abilities in oral communication plan to become teachers. Teacher-training programs often specify a course in public speaking. Our society, alive to the technological gains in other societies, and all they imply, seems determined to improve our educational system. Among other things, the teacher's role has assumed new significance, whether he remains in the conventional classroom or moves to the TV screen. Since his profession is enjoying greater prestige than it has had in over fifty years, the direct relationship between the skilled teacher and the person skilled in

[1] The opinions are drawn from a pamphlet, *Business and Industrial Communication from the Viewpoint of the Corporation President,* by P. E. Lull, F. E. Funk, and D. T. Pierson (Lafayette, Ind.: Purdue University, 1954).

[2] Chester I. Barnard, *The Functions of the Executive* (Cambridge: Harvard University Press, 1938), p. 226.

oral communication cannot be stressed too strongly. The good teacher is a master at translating new information into terms the learner can understand. He is aided by written materials, textbooks, syllabi, and the like; nevertheless he must supplement such materials with oral explanations, with examples, illustrations, and familiar experiences. He is ready with the right word at the right time. Possibly there is but one marked difference between the expert speaker and the expert teacher. The teacher, by test and examination, is able to find out how effectively he has communicated with his audience; the speaker ordinarily cannot test his hearers.

Social values

The personal values and goals associated with public speaking are close to every student. The social values are more remote. Yet in the long run they are not less significant to the welfare of our free society than our more self-centered interests. Social values are many. Here we single out the preeminent social value that is directly related to communication: the success of the democratic process.

Democracy is a way of life in which ultimate power and responsibility reside in and are shared by the people. To share power and responsibility is to believe all men are competent to understand the goals and methods of representative government and are capable of learning its skills and of taking part effectively in its processes.

A democratic society makes two assumptions which bear critically upon communication. First is the assumption that democracy will not work unless there is a general communication among men—a constant and effective interchange of both fact and opinion. The point is made by George Sabine, one of the ablest historians of political theory:

> The fundamental difference in point of view between the philosophy of liberal democracy and that of either communism or national socialism is that democracy always believed in the possibility of general communication. Whether in terms of universal natural rights or the greatest happiness or the common good, its theory . . . [held that] men of reasonable intelligence and normal good will could communicate . . . and could reach by negotiation as much understanding and agreement as was needed to serve the purposes of a limited public authority. For this reason a democratic social philosophy conceived a community not as a constellation of impersonal forces—either racial or economic—but as a complex of human beings and of human interests.[3]

Human interests are always in need of adjustment and readjustment, and communication as a means of adjustment is more characteristically human

[3] *A History of Political Theory,* rev. ed. (New York, 1950), p. 907.

than force. As we have remarked already, rhetoric may be fruitfully thought of as the process of adjusting ideas to people and people to ideas.

A second assumption made by a democratic society is that if communication is widespread and *free,* knowledge will prevail over ignorance, and truth over falsehood.

> In discussion truth has an advantage. Arguments always tell for truth as such, and against error as such; if you let the human mind alone, it has a preference for good argument over bad. . . . But if you do not let it alone, you give truth no advantage at all; you substitute a game of force where all doctrines are equal, for a game of logic, where the truer have the better chance.[4]

The implication here is of the utmost importance. There must be free competition among ideas if knowledge and truth are to win the contest. Men must be free to say what they will, restrained only by rules which they themselves recognize and abide by. Under this condition it is possible to have a game of ideas, which goes on day by day, year by year, age after age. But the game of ideas is changed into a game of force whenever one dictator compels me to say one thing and another dictator compels my friend to say another thing. In this state of affairs, the competition is between dictators. My ideas and my friend's do not count; they cancel each other out; only in this sense are they "equal." The game is won by the dictator who can wield the greater power and the bigger club. In this kind of game, men cannot choose between truth and falsehood or between good and evil; they can choose only between forces.

The game of ideas is slow and endless. We talk interminably. An astute commentator on our modern democracies, E. L. Godkin, estimates that half of our talk is waste, but that "the other half certainly tells. We know this from the change in ideas from generation to generation. We see that opinions which at one time everybody held became absurd in the course of half a century—opinions about religion and morals and manners and government." In one period men believed in witches and in a flat earth. In another period they laughed at such absurdities. Godkin concludes with this conviction:

> But there can be no doubt that it is talk—somebody's, anybody's, everybody's talk—by which these changes are wrought, by which each generation comes to feel and think differently from its predecessor. No one ever talks freely about anything without contributing something, let it be ever so little, to the unseen forces which carry the race on to its final destiny. Even if he does not make a positive impression, he counteracts or modifies some other impression, or sets in motion some train of ideas in some one else, which helps to change the face of the world. So I shall, in disregard of the great laudation of silence

[4] Walter Bagehot, "The Metaphysical Basis of Toleration," *The Works of Walter Bagehot,* ed. Mrs. Russell Barrington. (London, 1915), IV, 222.

which filled the earth in the days of Carlyle, say that one of the functions of an educated man is to talk, and, of course, he should try to talk wisely.[5]

In considering the values of public speaking today, we are not thinking primarily of fine eloquence and oratory—the oratory of Cicero, Burke, Webster, Robert Ingersoll, or William Jennings Bryan. Those men were great public speakers who used styles of speaking adapted to the manners and fashions of their countries and ages; but their styles were not the only modes of effective speaking even in their own days. We are concerned in this book with fundamental principles of public speaking rather than with special styles of utterance. A sanitary engineer discussing an improved water purification plant before a city council in the manner of Cicero accusing Cataline, of Burke impeaching Warren Hastings, or of Webster replying to Hayne, would be utterly ridiculous. But no less than Cicero, Burke, and Webster, the engineer is confronted by a problem of public speaking. He must be clear and intelligible; he must be easy to follow and reasonably pleasant to listen to; he must be able to hold the attention of his listeners to the thing in hand and to interest them; he must persuade them to accept his proposal, and he must achieve his ends primarily through language. These also were the problems of Cicero, Burke, and Webster. The basic principles for solving these problems are much the same, though tastes and fashions of presentation may have changed.

Perhaps as we discuss the social values in public speaking, we should notice the mistaken faith many persons seem to put in inarticulateness. Anyone who seems to do anything too well or too easily is distrusted. "He sounded too good, he was too smooth, he must be a scoundrel" is a criticism as basically unsound as it is frequent. We have become victims of the feeling that only the evil or false can be pleasant, that the greater the truth and the sounder the teaching, the more unpleasant must be their expression! Throughout history some sensitive people have sought that pseudo-Platonic refuge. If powerful, pleasant, or fluent speech can make falsehood, deceit, and intellectual emptiness seem to the unwary like truth, honesty, and solid sense, how much more attractive may not the same qualities of utterance make the good, the desirable, the real? If Hitler rose to power through his speeches, so did Paul, St. Augustine, Samuel Adams, Lincoln, and Churchill. A halting, embarrassed inarticulateness has never been a guarantee of deep thought or of excellence in any profession. In a society supported as substantially as ours is by speech, the most lamentable fact is not that audiences are gullible and easily led and that many speakers and commercial and political hucksters exploit fear, greed, and sex without sound ideas and make the "worse appear the better reason." The sadder fact is that more of the intelligent, able, and

[5] *Problems of Modern Democracy,* 3rd. ed. (New York, 1898), pp. 222–224.

honest people do not take the trouble to equip themselves to be critical members of audiences and better speakers. Virtue and goodness of themselves may be sufficient for the successful maintenance of the Kingdom of Heaven, but they apparently need mighty support if they are to govern the nations on earth. Educated men may well ponder Francis Bacon's advice: "The business of rhetoric is to make pictures of virtue and goodness, so that they may be seen."

Furthermore, every thoughtful person is opposed to the absurd exhibitionism of so-called elocution, to the hollow bombast and the slick effrontery and falsehood of high-pressure salesmanship. The terms *elocution* and *oratory* have been badly victimized by being popularly attached to oral monstrosities. At their best, these currently unacceptable kinds of public speaking once satisfied the fashions and tastes of a day that is gone. At their worst, they were spectacular nonsense. It is a mistake to suppose that public speaking should be damned because some of its manifestations are strange or outmoded. Good public speaking does not demand a special manner and vocabulary to set it apart and make it different from ordinary talk. It is ineffective and useless so far as it seems to be engaged in for itself. It must be communication fitted to the manner and fashions of the persons talked to, and it must not be out of harmony with the ideas and feelings the speaker is trying to communicate. Elocution, oratory, or, for that matter, much of the advertising talk we hear on the air is not bad because it is public speaking; it is bad because its language, content, and manner of delivery are ridiculously out of harmony with the nature and worth of the thing being talked about, the person doing the talking, and the basic good sense of audiences.

The principles of public speaking that must be adapted to life, work, and society today must be explained in terms of today. We propose to present these principles in current terms.

The habit of critical listening

Training in public speaking should not only help one become a better speaker; it should also make one a better listener and should facilitate a critical and intelligent understanding of those social processes in which public speaking plays a prominent role. In former times the art of listening was a widespread necessity. In the earlier stages of our society, public speaking was practically the only means available for the large-scale dissemination of news, information, ideas, and opinions. But with the invention of printing, the rise of literacy, the appearance of the newspaper, and the simultaneous growth in the size and complexity of our social and political organizations, the printed word became the chief means of reaching great masses of people. As a result, skill in listening seemed less essential than skill in reading. Since the rise of radio and the development of television, however, the spoken word competes with the newspaper in reaching great audiences. We get our news now as much by radio and TV as by newspaper; our political leaders address us as much by radio and TV as by newspaper; our advertisers sell us goods by TV and radio in greater quantities than they ever did through the press or personal solicitation.

Under this modern barrage of words which deluges us everywhere, we have not as a people acquired the attitude of the judicious critic. We do not *habitually* weigh and consider; rather, we respond impressionably. If a speaker can interest and entertain us, we listen with approval; if we like a speaker because of his reputation or his political allegiance, we approve of what he says without much resistance; if we dislike a speaker, we indiscriminately condemn his message. Extremely valuable in modern society, then, is the ability to listen with discrimination. As he becomes a more skilled, a more accomplished, in short, a better speaker, a student should also become a more critical listener—less gullible, stabler, wiser, and clearer minded, better able to distinguish the solid from the hollow, the forthright from the dishonest, the real from the fake. The audience is as vital a part of public speaking as the speaker. The analytical and critical study of public speaking, such as that undertaken in this book and conducted in public speaking classrooms, will usually result in an individual's becoming a better listener and a better member of an audience.

Learning Public Speaking

A course in public speaking is offered—not infrequently required—in most colleges, and textbooks like this one are written because of time-tested experience. Skill in public speaking can be learned through systematic study and practice. Comments like the following, which one hears from time to time, need not detain the student from study. "I'm not cut out to be a speaker." "I distrust glib speakers, and I don't want to be one." "Some speakers, like the advertisers and hucksters, sound affected and insincere." "A lot of speakers today, like the politicians, aren't saying anything worth saying." "Yes, I'd like to speak well, but I don't think I can discover the secret which will make *me* a good speaker."

To become a public speaker obviously requires talent and desire. As Quintilian observed long ago, to suppose that a person without native ability can be given ability by study is nonsense. For most persons, on the other hand, native ability, without instruction and intelligent practice, has never been enough for the development of their full potential. The ancient prescription "Nature, instruction, and practice" is still the soundest prescription for all—except, perhaps, for the few special "geniuses" whom we envy but seldom see. Given a reasonable portion of brains, almost anyone can learn to be an acceptable public speaker if he is willing to work intelligently and persistently. Few persons in any generation have the mind, soul, talents, genius, physical endowments, and opportunity to become public speakers like Cicero, Burke, Churchill, Franklin Roosevelt, or even Hitler; and few people have the need for such ability. The mechanical engineer or the physician or the shop foreman or the college student who for a few months will devote the same energy to the study of public speaking that he gives to his specialty can learn to speak acceptably.

Students sometimes mistakenly suppose that one may learn to make speeches without learning to say something worth listening to—something profitable to the listener. Public speaking is sometimes a fine art, creating artifacts to be contemplated in part for themselves. But first it is a useful art, a practical art, whose products are to be valued for what they do before they are valued for what they are. The principles of good speaking, therefore, are never entirely separate from the materials and purposes to which they are being applied. Needless to say, many words are uttered in public—even harmoniously—which convey no idea, information, or worthy sentiment; and doubtless these performances may be called public speaking. They cannot, however, be said to be *good* public speaking, which is what we seek to achieve.

Accordingly, the public speaker or the student of public speaking must have something of consequence to say. The man who knows most about most things and most people—he who has thought most, has read most, has experienced most, has observed most, has become most familiar with the minds and hearts and manners of his fellow men, and has retained most completely the knowledge and insight thus gained—this man, if he has also learned the principles of public speaking and has cultivated the will to communicate, will be the best speaker. Of course, most good speakers, even college professors, fall somewhat short of these ideals. Nevertheless, no matter how restricted the area of subject matter within which we may choose to speak, it is our duty as speakers to know our subjects well and, in addition, to acquire a store of knowledge of human beings and a store of available ideas by which we can make our subjects clear, interesting, and convincing. Only thus will we have something worth saying and the means of communicating it successfully to others who do not know it or have not thought it already.

All except the dullest of us gain some knowledge and some experience from the mere process of living, and the more we are subjected to education, the greater our knowledge and experience become. Much of what we acquire is common to others like us, but each of us has some store, however meager, of knowledge and experience more or less peculiar to himself. This stock of common and special material serves very well as a start for most beginning speakers and students of public speaking, but unless it is rapidly and deliberately augmented it soon begins to get thin and shopworn. Subjects upon which we want to talk and can talk become hard to find, and our reserve of the common ingredients of good speaking becomes sadly depleted. If you want to speak well, then, the answer, and the only answer, is: *Learn more, observe more, think more,* not only when you have a speech to make, but between times. If a student's time and effort in the study of public speaking are well expended, he will learn not only to speak but to speak *about something.* He will learn how to discover and use the resources that he already has; and he will learn to increase those resources and keep on increasing them.

FURTHER READING

ARNOLD, J. W. *The Symbols of Government.* New Haven, Conn., 1935.

BASKERVILLE, Barnet. "The Place of Oratory in American Literature," *Quarterly Journal of Speech,* 39 (December 1953), 459–464.

BERELSON, B. "Democratic Theory and Public Opinion," *Public Opinion Quarterly,* 16 (Fall 1952), 311–330.

BERLO, David K. *The Process of Communication.* New York, 1960.

Bibliography of Speech Education. Comp. by Lester Thonssen, Elizabeth Fatherson, and Dorothea Thonssen. New York, 1939. *Supplement: 1939–1948.* New York, 1950. Lists all sorts of books and articles on all aspects of Speech, historical, critical, and experimental, up to 1948.

BROWN, Charles T., and VAN RIPER, Charles. *Speech and Man.* Englewood Cliffs, N.J., 1966.

BRYANT, Donald C. "Aspects of the Rhetorical Tradition: Emotion, Style, and Literary Association," *Quarterly Journal of Speech,* 36 (October 1950), 326–332.

———. "Aspects of the Rhetorical Tradition: The Intellectual Foundation," *Quarterly Journal of Speech,* 36 (April 1950), 169–176.

CHASE, Stuart. *The Tyranny of Words.* New York, 1938.

GARDINER, Sir Alan. *The Theory of Speech and Language.* 2nd ed. Oxford, 1951.

HAYAKAWA, S. I. *Language in Action.* Rev. ed. New York, 1949.

NILSEN, T. R. "Free Speech, Persuasion, and the Democratic Process," *Quarterly Journal of Speech,* 44 (October 1958), 235–243.

REDDING, W. Charles. "The Empirical Study of Human Communication in Business and Industry." *The Frontiers in Experimental Speech-Communication Research,* Syracuse University Press, Syracuse, N.Y., 1966. Contains a large number of references to many aspects of communication problems in industry.

STEVENS, Leonard A. *The Ill-Spoken Word: The Decline of Speech in America.* New York, 1966.

WALLACE, Karl R. "Rhetoric, Politics, and Education of the Ready Man," in *The Rhetorical Idiom,* edited by Donald C. Bryant. Ithaca, N.Y., Cornell University Press, 1958.

WILSON, John F., and ARNOLD, Carroll C. *Public Speaking as a Liberal Art.* Boston, 1964. Chapters 1–2.

2

Definition and Scope of Public Speaking

Public speaking we define as systematic, practical, verbal communication which is basically oral but involves gesture and other audiovisual supplements, intended to enlarge or alter listeners' knowledge or comprehension, or to influence their attitudes and behavior.

Public Speaking as a Special Kind of Communication

First, how is public speaking like any act of communication? Every act of communication has five elements: Who is saying What to Whom through what Medium with what Effect? Public speaking, belonging to the family of communicative arts, possesses the same elements as any other act of communication. Public speaking specifically involves a speaker who builds his speech for listeners who are capable of responding to language and gesture in ways that are consistent with his intentions. We can illuminate our definition further by considering how public speaking differs from the other communicative arts, such as literature, painting, music, and theatre.

The listener

The audience gives to oral communication a sense of directness which is felt more intensely and more urgently than in music, painting, and literature. One reason, of course, is that listeners and communicators, in the circumstances of public speaking, usually confront each other face to face. As a result, a speaker not only abstractly recognizes the presence of his hearers; he feels their presence. (Even in radio and television, speaker and listener have some feeling of immediacy.) The poet and musical composer, on the other hand, never face their audiences, unless they themselves read aloud or play their own compositions.

Another condition that gives directness to oral communication is less apparent to the student speaker than to the veteran communicator. A speaker is not merely in the presence of listeners; he faces an audience that is definite, specific, and real. Listeners gather at a definite time and place—at 8 P.M. in the school auditorium. They are aware of what is going on in the world about them—the current crime wave, crop controls and food prices, space missiles, the troubles of Vietnam, and Middle East tensions. They want to hear the speaker on his subject, or are willing to listen to him. Thus, factors of time and place and subject combine to give concreteness and personality to an audience. The speaker plans for this specific audience and occasion. On the other hand, the writer's audience, as compared with the speaker's, is remote and vague. Authors whose pieces appear in national journals and magazines, like *Harper's* or *The New Yorker,* cannot touch their readers directly. It is said that such writers aim at "educated American adults," ages twenty to sixty-five. Even more distant and formless than the reader of *Harper's* is the audience of the novelist, poet, and painter. So amorphous is this unseen audience that writers, even when discussing timely practical problems, tend to become more interested in their subjects than in their readers. A writer who succeeds in talking directly to us from the page has probably forgotten all about the vast "public." He is communicating with a few persons like himself, perhaps real persons with whom he has talked and debated, who have raised questions and objections that needed answers, whose interest and boredom have made him sensitive to others. In some such manner, a hazy, generalized "public" can assume flesh-and-blood characteristics. The sense of remoteness and impersonality may easily come to dominate a writer, especially in a course in writing. Hence, perhaps, the recent revival of interest in rhetoric in the teaching of English. Teachers of composition wish their students to consider definite readers, even when they write compositions that only the teacher will read.

The student in a class in public speaking is not so liable to the sin of detachment. He will gradually discover the best example of a specific audience, that is, an audience whose interests, abilities, and opinions he will learn much about. It is, of course, his classroom audience, ever present and ever real. He must not be misled into thinking the class situation is either solely or primarily artificial. Both listener and speaker are studying and practicing the art of oral communication and are self-consciously aware of doing so. And in the classroom, as a rule, listeners do not invite their fellows to speak to them—the instructor does that! But in all other respects, the communicative environment is real. The speaker faces real persons. He faces the same audience often enough to learn a great deal about its "personality." (Indeed, unless he becomes a clergyman or a trial lawyer, he may never again as a speaker know an audience so well.) By accepting his classmates as they are—and speaking to them rather than to some remote imaginary group—by trying to make them understand, to interest them, or otherwise to influence them, the speaker can help himself acquire a lively sense of *direct* communication.

Effect

When we consider the effect of a speech upon its hearers, we are talking about potential response. Viewed broadly, the responses to speaking are practical and instrumental, and are of three main kinds. To see this is to recognize first that hearers respond to a speech as a whole.

We can profitably regard a speech as an artifact, an object made by the skill and ingenuity of man, as contrasted with a natural object like a rock, a tree, or a goat. Artifacts, in turn, can be classified into two general groups: discursive and nondiscursive. Examples of the nondiscursive are automobiles, buildings, pictures, words, and phrases–anything that registers upon us instantaneously. The discursive unfolds through a period of time; it has a beginning, a development, and an end. Familiar examples are a football game, a journey, a novel, a poem, a symphony, or a speech. None of these affects us as a whole until it is completed. To consider the effect of a speech is to think of the response to the speech as a whole.

If we regard the speech as an artifact, we can understand why speechmaking, in contrast to the fine arts such as music, painting, and literature, is a practical, instrumental art. The respondent views some artifacts as more or less useful than others. We can employ artifacts to learn something or to do something. If we want to write, a pen or pencil is obviously a useful instrument; if we want to build highways or upholster furniture, any relevant information or knowledge is practical. In other words, the instrumental artifacts are means to some end. On the other hand, some artifacts seem to be ends in themselves. We respond to a painting, a play, or a sonnet with little thought of its utility. We regard it as satisfying, pleasing, aesthetically exciting. But a speech has practical consequences to a respondent. Unless he is merely a critic, he listens, not because he wishes to contemplate the speech as an artistic performance but because he expects it to be profitable in some way. In this sense, speechmaking is practical. The proper response to a speech is not *at* the speech or *to* the speaker, but is in line with what the speech is intended to accomplish. The correct response is well illustrated by the Athenian audience who, after hearing Demosthenes urge war against Philip, went away saying "Let's fight the Macedonians." The wrong response is represented by the Athenians' reaction to Aeschines' oratory: "What a wonderful speech!"

The different responses to a speech correspond to three kinds of effects. (1) The effect may be that of knowledge and understanding. The listener is able to say "I see," "I know," or "I understand." His knowledge has gained breadth or depth. (2) The effect may be some change (including strengthening or weakening) in the listeners' opinions or attitudes, and the shift may be in different directions. This response is well illustrated in a classroom audience that hears a speech contending that alimony in divorce cases is justified only when the wife or the children need support. Some listeners who already hold this view find their beliefs reinforced and intensified. Some who held no opinion on the subject accept the speaker's belief. Still others, in disagreement with the speaker, report they are less strongly opposed, even uncertain. (3) The effect may be some type of action, ranging from polite hand clapping to enthusiastic applause to doing what the speaker suggests or directs.

These are the main types of responses to speeches (and to any practical discourse), although on rare occasions there are speeches to which we respond only with interest, pleasure, or amusement. It is important only to recognize that there is always some kind of response to a communicative artifact, and that the response consists in whatever the audience thinks and does in consequence. Sometimes the response is immediate and observable, as when a man buys insurance after a sales talk. More often the response is remote and unrecognized, as when one day we find that we have a new attitude toward Orientals and are unaware that past information and argument, absorbed through forgotten speeches, articles, and discussions about Far Eastern problems, have brought about the change. Such gradual changes illustrate Godkin's point that talk, anybody's talk, anywhere and anytime, may be responsible for creating or changing belief.

Kinds of Speeches. The responses to speechmaking and to practical discourse in general furnish the basis for classifying speeches into types, or kinds. For the purposes of this book, we shall consider two broad types, the informative and the persuasive. Differences in function or purpose of a speech, or intended response to it, do not necessarily in themselves create sharp differences in type. A speaker, for example, may wish his audience to accept certain facts and circumstances that, because of bias or prejudice, its members have refused to consider. Is his speech persuasive or informative? Differences in materials and methods do not always indicate differences between the two types of speeches. For example, the materials of persuasion in the hands of a man like Thomas Henry Huxley often consisted almost entirely of explanatory and narrative information. Like other writers on speechmaking, however, we have found that a broad classification of discourse best serves the purposes of teaching. We therefore discuss and emphasize some matters in connection with the informative speech, some with the persuasive speech.

The *informative speech* is intended primarily to impart knowledge or to illuminate a subject. Its materials consist of facts and data, on the one hand, and the principles, laws, and explanations of facts, on the other. The informative speaker uses the materials that form the basis of the various fields of study—engineering, home economics, physics, accounting, medicine. Hence, a common type of informative speech is the lecture. The listener is a learner and the result of his learning is knowledge.

The *persuasive speech* is intended to influence the opinion and behavior of an audience. Its materials are drawn from problems about which men hold differing beliefs and opinions—controversial matters that call for decision and action. The problems may be very general: In what ways can public school education be improved? They may be quite specific: Should the high school graduate be able to speak a foreign language? Very broadly considered, the persuasive speaker is an advisor. Technically, the materials of persuasion are the facts, data, laws, principles, and explanations that furnish the informative speech, plus the opinions, arguments, and circumstances bearing on a problem that calls for decision. The speaker says or implies that the audience should accept this view or act in ways consistent with it. The listener is the judge. He accepts, rejects, or doubts the view. He may or may not act on the view when he has the chance.

The persuasive speaker is always telling hearers what they ought to believe or do. We ought, for example, to support our community chest. An informative speaker, in contrast, does not ask his audience to accept one belief rather than another, or to act one way rather than another. He always says, "Here are the facts and ideas as seen and understood by persons in a position to know them; these are the ways the facts are interpreted and explained by such persons." Accordingly, an informative speaker would not argue whether his hearers should contribute to the community chest, but he might explain the way the chest is organized and run and how it handles its funds. The informative speech is descriptive, explanatory, and diagnostic; the persuasive speech is prescriptive, directive, and advisory.

The classification of speeches into two kinds, informative and persuasive, may be extended or narrowed. Some writers on practical discourse, for example, recognize the speech of entertainment, whose chief effect is that of interesting or amusing its listeners. Often classification is extended by naming some speeches after the special occasion or condition which prompts them. Such, for instance, are the political speech, the eulogy, the speech of introduction, and the after-dinner speech. In Chapter 22 we discuss some of these special forms. To a student of public speaking, however, the ability to recognize the elaborate classifications of discourse is not so important as the understanding of what speeches do to listeners. And as we have remarked, speeches function to extend information and knowledge, to influence attitude and belief, and to direct conduct. The understanding of these potential functions will help the student properly to consider his objective when he prepares a speech.

The speaker

In what ways is a speaker like any other communicator or creator? In what ways is he unique? In comparing the speechmaker with other creators, we are now concerned with what creators are doing when they make artifacts.

Without going into detail, we can isolate their principal operations. First, they decide upon their purpose—the response they want from their audience. Second, they consider all the resources which may accomplish their purpose—all the materials, ideas, and meanings which seem to bear upon the task at hand. Third, from their available resources, they select whatever seems best to serve the purpose, and they reject everything else. Fourth, they arrange their materials into a whole; that is, they settle upon the form and structure of the object. Finally, they fill in the details, adjusting and polishing them, until the object is ready for the audience.

To be able to single out such operations is to recognize also that the process of creating something can be treated methodically and systematically. A person who has become expert in his art, of course, may not always follow the operations in order, nor may he at certain times be conscious of following them at all. Indeed, the ability to work efficiently without being aware of the governing rule or formula is one of the marks of the master craftsman. The learner, however, should be conscious of what he is doing. If he is wise, he tries to work methodically and to avoid depending primarily on trial and error, stumbling about blindly, wasting time and motion.

Like any creator, the speechmaker intends to secure some kind of response from his audience, and he builds his speech with a purpose in mind. He undertakes operations that are similar to those of any maker of artifacts. In the history of speechmaking the work of finding ideas, materials, and arguments and of surveying one's resources was called *invention*. Originally a technical term in rhetoric and literature, the word is now more often associated with science and technology, with the discovery of special techniques, new machines, and gadgets. Psychologically speaking, invention is closely related to *search* and *inspiration*. A second operation, the work of selecting, arranging, and giving form and structure to a speech was called *disposition*. The speaker was thought of as choosing his main ideas and information for the occasion, laying them out logically for the purpose at hand, and deciding upon the broad outlines of the speech. The further processes involved in managing the details of the composition were designated by the term *style*. Since the speaker's mode of transmitting ideas is embedded in language, style was conceived of as the manner of selecting and handling the details of language in ways that communicated the speaker's intended meanings. Style included the amplification and filling-out of the logical structure by comparison, illustration, figures of speech, and the like, as well as the managing of sentences. In a word, the speaker was considered a stylist when he was completing, adjusting, and readying the details of his composition to meet the needs of communicating with a particular audience. Modern speakers go through the same operations, though advances in the fields of logic and psychology enable them to know more about the operations than ever before.

The public speaker differs from other creators in two important ways. In the first place, his process of creation overlaps his act of presentation. We appreciate this difference when we look at the three modes of delivery speakers commonly use. In the fixed-text mode the speaker reads aloud the text he has written or reproduces the text word for word from memory. At the other extreme is the impromptu mode. The speaker is asked—or is prompted for some reason—to talk on the spur of the moment. He has had no chance to prepare for the speech. The third mode is that of extemporaneous delivery, in which speakers build their compositions prior to presentation, but coin their language in the act of speaking—just as we all do when we converse. The extemporaneous speaker's preparation is often very extensive and painstaking; as a rule it entails making of an outline, sometimes the writing of the entire speech, and much oral rehearsal. Yet the final expression of his ideas the speaker leaves to the occasion, because he knows that if he is not chained to a fixed sequence of words, he can alter details, if necessary, during delivery. If his hearers look puzzled, he can stop to restate an idea, add an illustration, make a comparison, or define an ambiguous phrase. Thus the extemporaneous speaker, sensitive to the immediate responses of his audience, does not freeze his language prior to delivery. His style is given its final mold during the act of utterance.

The circumstances of delivery, then, demonstrate that the speaker is in part creating his speech as he delivers it. Sometimes, as in the impromptu mode, he builds his entire speech as he talks. In fact, in every impromptu speech (as well as in most conversations), creation and presentation are simultaneous. No other artist, not even the actor or musical performer, builds his entire work in front of his audience. More often, as in the extemporaneous mode, the public speaker undertakes most of his composition prior to delivery, expecting that the occasion of utterance will prompt some adjustment of details and set the final style of his language. Less often, as in the fixed-text mode of presentation, the speaker reads his composition, and when he does he may be considered, with other artists, to have completed his product before offering it to the audience. Even so, it is instructive to distinguish between the "completion," of the speech as a composition and its final realization. Strictly construed, a speech that is built for delivery to a specific group of hearers is not realized—it does not *live* or exist—until it is spoken. Thus the oft-repeated truism that a speech lives but once.

The public speaker differs from other creators in a second important respect. In no other art do the personality and character of the communicator register so directly upon the audience and so immediately influence the effect of communication, for, as we have already remarked, whenever a speech is made to listeners, a speaker must be delivering it. The speaker cannot, like a painter, complete his composition, hang it in a gallery, and go away. Nor can he, like a writer, finish his composition and abandon it to whatever audience may find it. In oral communication, the speaker as a person wields direct influence.

Some qualities of personality and character that are critically important in communication are revealed through our ideas and opinions. Our words reflect such values as truthfulness, humor, knowledge and competence, accuracy of statement, sincerity and consistency of belief, respect and sympathy for others, or their contraries. Personal qualities are evident whenever we use language, particularly in writing and speaking. Some, however, are signaled most directly by the inflections, intonations, and qualities of the voice. Our ears, for example, instantly recognize notes of friendliness, sympathy, humor, modesty, and respect, or the reverse. They at once sense the ring of conviction and truth and detect as readily tones of insecurity, sarcasm, and falsity. Our eyes, observing the gestures of face and body, take in at a glance the signs of friendliness, liveliness, and directness; and they also derive impressions from appearance and dress. Thus the speaker, as do any of us in our everyday conversations, draws his own portrait swiftly and surely. The novelist's personality and character are usually in the background and must be searched for; the person of the speaker is in the foreground and revealed in everything he says and does.

A student will probably speak extemporaneously more often than he reads or speaks in an impromptu manner. But whatever his mode of presentation, the speaker belongs in the company of creators. Although he is practicing a useful rather than a fine art, he will gain experience in the processes fundamental to both types of art. He can learn, moreover, to handle these processes methodically, for he can look ahead to his speaking date, take early stock of his resources, add to them as soon as possible, set aside time for organizing and outlining his materials, and reserve definite periods for oral rehearsal. Intelligent planning and work bring gratifying results; one doesn't need to be a genius to speak well. Recognizing these advantages, a student can rapidly develop a great deal of confidence in his abilities. Furthermore, through his speeches he can win respect and influence as a person. He can offer useful knowledge and information to his classroom listeners. He can present opinions that are well-reasoned and well-grounded. He can prepare thoroughly and speak as clearly and as accurately as possible. He can respect his hearers and treat their interests in a direct and friendly manner; and by having their welfare at heart, he can create the right impression.

Definition and Scope of Public Speaking

Media, speech, and gesture

We have observed that a communicator makes contact with a respondent only through some physical medium. Any systematic, conventional, and persistent combination of verbal symbols we will consider as a language. There are hundreds of languages, classified into families, subfamilies, and dialects. A language is basically speech, although many languages have visual counterparts, written characters. Thus, language may be regarded as conventionalized speech sounds and, in this sense, as a medium of communication.

Similarly, gesture is a medium of communication. Common gestures are the smile, the grimace, the lifted eyebrow, the shrug of the shoulders, and the shake of the head. The arts of pantomine and dance have elaborated and classified a large number of movements, often called the language of bodily movements. And elocutionists in days past worked out intricate systems of gestures. We, however, maintain the distinction between language and nonverbal systems.

Thus, the two media of oral communication are speech and gesture, and they help to distinguish public speaking from all the other arts, which use different media. For example, literature is presented to us primarily through the medium of written characters. The fine arts employ lines, spatial shapes, and colors; music, tones; dance, bodily movement; and mathematics, symbols of quantitative relationships and geometrical figures.

The public speaker is not directly concerned with the physical events of speech unless they are defective in some way. Consider, for a moment, the chain of events involved in the act of speech. The first event is physiological and consists of all movements that produce voice and articulate vocal sound into intelligible speech. When voice and articulation meet the requirements of the speaking situation, the result is adequate loudness, flexibility, and distinctness. Moreover, when the speaker's language reflects the basic conventions of correct usage, the result is acceptable pronunciation and grammar. Most students of speechmaking meet such requirements. But when they do not, they must give special attention to that medium. Furthermore, when gesture fits the communicative situation, the result is spontaneity and ease of movement. Students who inhibit gesture need to learn respect for the resources of ready movement. Chapter 14 and Appendix B provide basic information for those who need to improve their media of communication.

The second link in the chain is acoustical and visual. The ear picks up our speech and the eye registers our gestures. Defective vision is never a problem for the student speaker unless his reading is unduly slow or inaccurate and thus hinders his rapid search for written materials. Defective hearing becomes a problem for the speaker only if it impairs the intelligibility of his speech. The ear can monitor only what it can respond to, and if over long periods it has not heard some of the sounds of speech, the result may be handicap of voice and articulation.

The final link in the chain is neurological. What the ear and the eye as sense organs can respond to is transmitted to the brain. With neurological events, the public speaker is not immediately concerned.

Language and meaning

Language is more than a sequence of events. It is a *symbolic* experience and hence synonymous with *meaning.* Language, because it possesses meaning is inseparable from *idea* or *thought.* Linguistic and gestural behavior, a physical manifestation of thought, is thus the outward form or shape given to thought at the moment of utterance.

The nature of meaning is a subject that belongs properly to the science of semantics, but the student of public speaking should be reminded that he is concerned with meaningful behavior that is communicative, not merely expressive. He is especially concerned not merely with the denotative meanings of a language but with meanings that are important and significant in the communicative situation. In a word, as we explain in Chapter 3, the public speaker is concerned with values.

In his concern with meaning and ideas, the speechmaker is no different from any other creator. Nor is the listener, in his concern with meaning, any different from any other respondent. To the extent that the arts entail communication from one person to another, they employ media that have acquired meanings through long usage among human beings. The speechmaker is unlike other creators, in part, because of the ways in which he uses his media —speech and gesture—to transmit meaning and idea in achieving his purposes. The accepted ways of handling media and meaning are his *methods* and *techniques.*

In elaborating our definition of public speaking, we have come full circle. A speech is brought into being by an audience—a *specific* audience that joins directly speaker and listener. The conjunction of speaker and listener is purposeful and practical, for the speaker builds a speech intended to convey information and knowledge or to influence the beliefs and attitudes of the audience about something of mutual value to him and them. A speech, the product of systematic effort, entails creative operations usually, though not invariably, undertaken prior to delivery, and bears direct impressions of the speaker's personality and character. The speech lives and communicates through the verbal and gestural behavior of a speaker during delivery.

Much of what we have been saying in this chapter can be schematized in a simple "model." Figure 1 represents the act of communicating, that is, a speaker and listener, both of whom are aware of a communicative context, that is, of some problem or subject that creates a specific communicative situation for bringing them together. The speaker responds to what he has seen and read and heard that is relevant to the situation. His responses are his interpretations and evaluations, the meanings of the situation to him. In communicating, his meanings become symbolized in language and gesture and thereby generate a message for the listener to attend to. On his part, the listener responds to the message. His responses are his interpretations and evaluations, his meanings. During the dialogue between speaker-listener and listener-speaker, the behavior of each may reveal attentiveness, boredom, understanding, puzzlement, incredulity, approval, disapproval, and the like. This kind of information is continually fed back from one to the other. As he deems it necessary and desirable, each adjusts his message appropriately. Figure 1 refers only to what occurs during communication. It does not indicate the practical success or effect of an exchange of messages beyond the communicative situation.

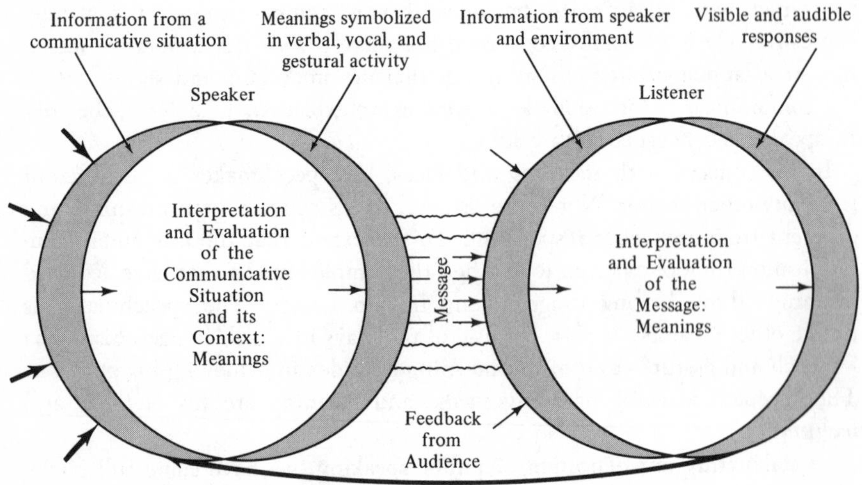

Figure 1. A COMMUNICATING ENTITY

FURTHER READING

Berlo, David K. *The Process of Communication.* New York, 1960.

Bryant, Donald C., "Rhetoric: Its Functions and Its Scope," *Quarterly Journal of Speech,* 39 (December 1953), 401–424.

Bryson, Lyman (ed.). *The Communication of Ideas.* New York, 1948.

Campbell, James H., and Hepler, Hal W. *Dimensions in Communication: Readings.* Belmont, Calif., 1965.

Carroll, John B. *The Study of Language.* Cambridge, Mass., 1955. Chapter 4, "Linguistics and the Social Sciences."

Cherry, Colin. *On Human Communication.* New York: Science Editions, Inc., 1961. Chapter 1.

Ewbank, H. L., Sr., Baird, A. C., Brigance, W. N., Parrish, W. M., and Weaver, T. T. "What is Speech?—A Symposium," *Quarterly Journal of Speech,* 41 (April 1955), 145–153.

Greene, T. M. *The Arts and the Art of Criticism.* Princeton, N.J., 1940.

Langer, Susanne K. *Philosophy in a New Key.* Baltimore: Penguin Books Inc., 1948. Chapter 4, "Discursive and Presentational Forms."

Schramm, Wilbur (ed.). *Communications in Modern Society.* Urbana, Ill., 1948.

Weaver, R. M. *The Ethics of Rhetoric.* Chicago, 1953. Chapter 1, "The Phaedrus and the Nature of Rhetoric."

Wellek, René, and Warren, Austin. *Theory of Literature.* New York, 1949.

3

The Basis of Communication: Attention, Interest, and Values

We have seen that a speech is an artifact to which an audience responds and that the two main kinds of response distinguish the informative speech from the persuasive speech. We have observed, also, that the speech is a discursive artifact. It begins, unfolds, and ends minutes or an hour or so later. The interval between beginning and end is filled with language and gesture that convey meanings and ideas. In addition, we have remarked that the speaker's methods and techniques are his ways for selecting, managing, and controlling what he says and how he says it.

Methods and techniques of speechmaking may be looked at from two points of view. First, one may examine the methods that aim to accomplish the purpose or effect of the speech. Of necessity one must then distinguish between methods appropriate to the purposes of the informative speech and methods appropriate to the purposes of the persuasive speech. Some methods, however, may be common, in whole or in part, to both kinds of speeches: for example, methods relating to finding, surveying, and selecting ideas; to organizing and structuring ideas; to adjusting details of language; and to presenting or delivering the speech. The bulk of this book deals with these methods as well as the distinctive methods of each kind of speech.

Second, one may scrutinize the conditions and principles that underlie and provide the basis for all methods. In this chapter we will approach speechmaking from this latter point of view.

The principles of public speaking derive from the conditions that govern attention and interest. A speaker presents a statement or a sequence of statements to his listener, who receives the statement or chain of statements. The process poses two problems for a speaker; first, that of directing attention to the physical events of utterance, that is, to the sounds of speech and to bodily action and gesture; and second, that of sustaining attention to the entire sequence of statements, to the speech as a whole. The first problem must be solved if the speaker is to be intelligible and clear, as he must be if his language is to convey the meanings he intends. The second problem must be solved if the speaker is to secure and maintain interest. Claiming attention in ways relevant to the goals and function of the speech makes it *possible* to be meaningful; claiming and holding attention makes it *possible* to be interesting. To these statements we add but one other observation. Being meaningful and being interesting are the preconditions of securing belief and action; if a speaker wishes to persuade he must present a speech that is both meaningful and interesting to his audience.

The speaker directs his hearers' attention to the verbal and visual stimuli and to the language and bodily action that he presents to his audience. If he is to be successful he must apply certain psychological principles of attention to the management of what he says. In what follows we present these principles and indicate also the ways they operate in speechmaking.

Control of Attention

Principle of intensity

Among competing stimuli, the stronger, more intense stimulus is preferred to the weaker.

A voice clear, firm, and strong enough to be heard with ease by everyone helps to hold attention. A weak voice loses attention. Not only is it weak and uncertain as a source of stimulation, but it puts an extra burden on the speaker's verbal stimuli, his language.

Language that evokes images of experience, images of objects and events, readily claims attention. Words, phrases, and passages that paint pictures are more intense and stronger than those that do not enlist the imagination. *Mustang* is better than *auto; it's like a bouquet of freshly cut spring flowers* is better than *it's lovely*. The speech that makes liberal use of specific language, specific examples and illustrations, comparisons, and contrasts has gone a long way toward holding attention. The speech that consists of little but abstract language and broad generalizations places too great a strain upon attention.

Principle of size

Among stimuli that vary in size, the larger is preferred to the smaller.

This principle, as applied to stimulus conditions in communication, may be restated as follows: A stimulus taking up more space than another is preferred, and a stimulus lasting longer than another is preferred. In each condition there is a marked difference in energy and strength.

A speaker's full vocal and bodily response creates a stronger stimulus than a small, inhibited response. The fully developed gesture, the extended movement, holds attention better than the small, restricted gesture. The facial expression that is broad enough for all to see, like the smile or the frown, is better than the facial expression that is dim, uncertain, and fleeting.

The principal statements and ideas of a speech when given adequate development claim attention better than they do when they are left undeveloped. In communication the process of developing an idea, or point, is called *amplification.* Some common methods of amplification are *repetition, restatement, illustration,* and *quotation.* In fact, all types of development are ways of enlarging an idea.

Principle of activity

Among competing stimuli, the moving one is preferred to the one at rest.

The flexible voice, the voice that "moves," commands attention more surely than the inflexible, flat, changeless voice. The trained voice moves through an astonishing range of changes—changes of pitch (inflection), changes of loudness (intensity), changes in timbre, and changes in rate. All speech shows such changes, but the trained voice reveals a greater range of movement than the untrained voice. A person who does nothing to improve his weak, unresponsive voice is asking his language to take on an extra burden in communication. Similarly, the speaker who pooh-poohs and neglects gesture denies himself a powerful source of stimulation, for bodily movement and gesture help keep attention. Bodily activities direct the listener's attention to what a speaker is saying and reinforce meaning.

Language that stirs listeners to *images of action* claims attention easily. The moving picture is preferred to the still picture.

Principle of pattern and organization

Among two or more collections of stimuli, the group that is organized has preference over the group that is disorganized; a unified whole is preferred to its separate parts.

The whole must be organized if the listener's attention is to sort out sequences of verbal stimuli and focus easily and swiftly uopn them. The law explains why a speechmaker must devote much of his own attention to the organizing of his speech.

Three factors determine what one's attention can form into a pattern.

Contiguity. *The items in a stimulus-field must be near enough to each other to be taken in as a whole.*

Since the language of a speech unfolds moment by moment and the end of the speech is minutes—sometimes many minutes—from its beginning, the problem of holding a speech together is a major one.

Some of a speaker's language serves to direct attention to the *structure* of his speech. The central idea of a speech and its supporting main heads must be seen in relation to each other and must dominate the details of amplification. One can look at a photograph and get a unified impression of it almost at once. But a listener cannot secure a unified impression of a speech until it is completed. So the speaker takes special pains to show how his main ideas are connected and thus aids the hearer to grasp his speech as a whole.

Attention is helped greatly by signpost language: by announcement of the central idea or of the purpose of the speech, by clear indications of subideas (*points* or *heads*), by transitional links and summaries from part to part, and by a concluding summary. Such pointing devices help secure focus and reeval the pattern of the speech.

The effect of language devices that bind the parts of a speech together is suggested in Figure 2. The function of signpost language is indicated by the solid lines, the parts of a speech by broken lines.

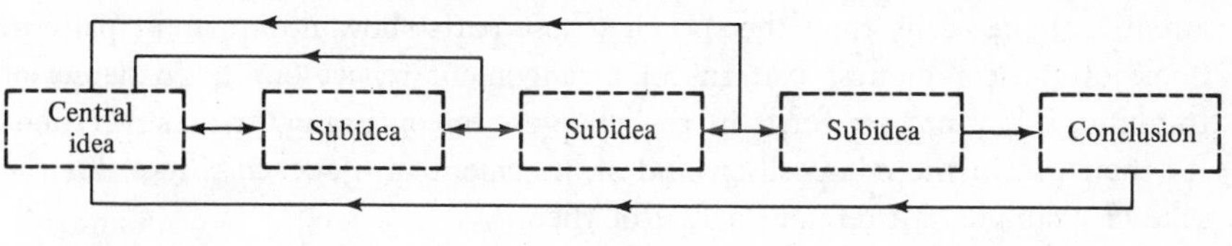

Figure 2

Similarity. *Similar items in a stimulus-field are preferred to dissimilar items.* The classification or grouping of words and of words-in-a-sequence is possible because in our past experience the words have something in common. Consider the "groups" below:

A		B	
book	pipe	green	yellow
auto	window	blue	violet
idea	theatre	red	color
speech	agriculture	spectrum	orange

After looking at each group, consider these questions: Upon which group did your attention linger and focus? To which group did you first bring a meaningful response? What do the items in A have in common? The items in B? Answering these questions will illustrate how attention prefers stimulus-ideas that have something in common.

The speech that is organized into systematic groups of related ideas holds attention better than the speech that is disorganized.

The principle of similarity provides a special case, the principle of singularity, or contrast. In a stimulus-field of similar items the one item that is dissimilar may command attention: the red marble among the blues ones, the mispronounced word in otherwise standard speech, the raised eyebrow in an otherwise placid countenance.

Order. *Orderly items in a stimulus-field are preferred to items without order.*

Through living and learning, we have not only formed habits of classifying similar experiences and ideas together, we have also formed habits of ordering them in one way rather than another. The influence of order on attention can be illustrated thus: color spectrum–red-orange-yellow-green-blue-violet–the order in which colors appear in the rainbow. This arrangement has become so familiar that we find it easy to attend to and remember. It invokes the principle of familiarity (see below) as well as the principle of order.

The speech whose parts reveal typical patterns of arrangement controls attention more easily than the speech whose parts show no apparent pattern. Some of the commonest patterns of arrangement reflect our basic habits of thinking. They are set forth in the chapters on outlining, with suggestions for their use in the composition and arrangement of a speech. Here, for the sake of example, we refer to a few of them.

The pattern that moves ideas from the *general to the specific* is effective because we have learned that the general implies the specific. Hence, *houses* may lead one to think of one's own house. Similarly, a cause implies an effect and much of our thinking is arranged in *cause-effect* patterns. Either part of a *comparison* implies the other. A *problem* implies a *solution,* and a *purpose* implies *means.* The pattern of *generalization* implies that what is true of a number of similar events is true of all of them. And the reverse of this arrangement, the pattern of *deduction,* implies that what is true of all things in a class is true of one of them. These patterns are some of the ways in which our experience is given structure and order. The speaker who can arrange the materials and ideas of his speech into standard patterns gains a powerful hold over the attention of his listeners.

Much is written about "generating" ideas.[1] As they work over their materials and ideas, both speaker and writer are delighted when they discover that one idea gives rise to a second, which prompts a third, and so on. What is happening is an association among the materials of experience which have been stamped into the individual's memory. Ideas and words follow one upon another partly because of the resemblances in structure and order among materials long since learned.

[1] See, for example, the Christensen article cited at the end of this chapter.

Principle of familiarity

Among two stimuli, one familiar and the other strange, the familiar one is preferred.

As applied to speaking, this principle is of great importance. It underlies the basic methods that govern the selection and treatment of the materials for any kind of speech. First, in an explanatory situation, new information and factual materials are best grasped when the speaker explains their relation to what is already familiar and understood by the audience. The novel exercises a strong pull on attention, but brings a response only if seen through familiar experience. To a child who had never seen a zebra, a factual description would do little, but much would be accomplished if the description were woven around the statement "A zebra is a striped horse." Accordingly, comparisons, contrasts, examples, and definitions invite attention because they bring together the familiar and the unfamiliar, the old and the new.

In the communication of information, the object is to maintain an appropriate balance between the familiar and unfamiliar, the old and the new. To try to offer something "strictly" new is to be unintelligible, for the absolutely novel thing can evoke no response at all. Audiences—and for that matter, any of us—prefer only as much of the new as can be tolerated. That which is perceived as different is that which carries information. That which is the same—the merely familiar—conveys no information, and is indeed dull and boring. Psychologically speaking, complex cues in the field of attention are preferred to simple ones as long as the result is not confusing or tiring.

Second, in the persuasive contexts, the principle of familiarity governs attention and response in two ways. The speaker's proposal must be understood by the audience, and understanding comes when the listeners grasp the new and strange in terms of the familiar experience. The proposal, moreover, must win acceptance by the audience. Acceptance is won most readily when the facts, arguments, and appeals that support the proposal are built around values and opinions already shared by the hearers.

Acceptance appears to involve what is intellectually and emotionally consonant to us. We avoid dissonance among the patterns and habits of experience as we shun discordant sounds; in fact, dissonant materials of experience, if they persist for long periods of time, become the condition for disturbing frustrations. Behind every effective piece of persuasion is its unexpressed strategy: Accept this proposal because it is in keeping with the familiar, fundamental facts of experience; it is consistent with your motives, your emotional experience, your attitudes, your values.

Perhaps the clearest short illustration of this strategy is seen in G. W. Curtis's speech "Liberty Under the Law," in Chapter 25. Note how skillfully Curtis touched on the loyalties and attitudes of each national and religious group in his audience, how he bound them all together by evoking the emotion of patriotism, how he associated patriotism with respect for law and order, and finally how he identified his proposal with law and order. His hearers responded at every moment as he wished; and after the speech they acted as he wished.

Set, or expectancy

When we speak of *set*, we are referring to a temporary state of being ready to focus on a stimulus. Indeed, we are so ready that if the stimulus is not presented we feel let down, or disappointed. We expect something, but we are not rewarded; we anticipate, but we are not satisfied.

Expectancy is roused by a specific occasion and its accompanying circumstances. When we read of a murder, we are set to learn what caused it. When we learn that a famous speaker or musician is to appear on the campus, we anticipate his arrival. When we go to hear a speaker whose announced subject sounds interesting, we expect him to talk on it and not on something else. In the classroom, expectancy is always at work whenever a speaker talks on a familiar subject. His hearers expect some new information or a new opinion. So it is that expectancy may be roused by the condition of the moment and we are ready to respond when the right stimulus appears.

Emotion. Emotions are internal experiences that influence attention. Listeners in a gay mood find it hard to attend to a sober sermon. Listeners in a sad, depressed mood cannot laugh at a joke and perhaps do not even "hear" it.

Emotion, which is a condition of the body, involves the body as a whole and is commonly described by such words as *tense, stirred-up, agitated, exhilarated.* Such behavior is reflected in our clichés, *hopping mad, fit to be tied, madly in love, livid with anger, rocking with laughter.* Emotional experience is often closely linked with goals and values we consider desirable. Love, for example, is usually associated with pleasure, and the resulting experience may have sustaining strength and depth. Love and affection give meaning to the duties and obligations of family life, and pride often sustains the desire to succeed and to be esteemed by others.

Some emotions appear to serve the survival needs of the individual: *sexual love, anger* and *indignation, fear,* and *hate;* some appear to reflect social needs, the more civilized aspects of the human being: *pride* and *shame, sympathy* and *pity, friendship* and *enmity, grief* and *humor.*

For the speaker, the relevance of emotion and attention is illustrated in the introduction and the conclusion of a speech. A function of the introduction is to allay feelings hostile to favorable attention and to rouse feeling that is friendly to attention. A final emotional appeal to one's audience, if such be appropriate, can be made in the conclusion.

Attitude. Another component of internal experience which influences attention is attitude. An attitude is a response that signals aversion or repulsion, favor or disfavor, like or dislike, toward an object or fact. Our attitudes are reactions to the features we find attractive or unattractive in a stimulus.

People acquire a large number of attitudes about a large number of things, such as objects or words. If one has had an unfortunate experience with dogs, he will be repelled when he sees a dog or hears the word *dog*. Persons in our society find the word *democracy* attractive; they dislike the words *dictator, tyrant,* and *communism.*

Attitudes are certainly aspects of what we regard as our beliefs and opinions. Indeed, an opinion can be described as a verbalized attitude. A belief is a statement which we embrace with greater confidence than we do an opinion. If a belief is well grounded in fact and experience, we are prone to call it a *conviction.* This condition of belief is well illustrated in the wisdom of the law courts. Ideally, a jury is not supposed to find a person guilty, that is, to convict him of an act, unless the twelve good men and true are satisfied beyond reasonable doubt.

But, no matter how much confidence may be built into statements of belief and opinion, the psychological ingredient of attitude—the feeling of liking or disliking, of favoring or disfavoring—is always present. Hence, when a speaker triggers attitudes favorable to his purposes, he is working not only with a condition of attention but with a condition of belief as well. To influence attitude is to influence belief. Students of persuasion know this truth well. Later, in Chapters 16 and 19, it is reflected in our view of the persuasive speech and of its methods and techniques.

Conditions of Interest

For both the speaker and listener, the conditions that control interest grow out of the speaker's awareness of the importance and significance of his speech. The speaker judges what aspects of the occasion concern him most, and this kind of judgment directly indicates importance. The importance of our public utterances, like the importance of anything we say or do, springs out of our sense of values. We acquire a large number of values, which become guides for our judgments, that is, for the choices we make and the decisions we arrive at. But in making a particular choice, say, a political candidate or an automobile, we find that all values do not apply with equal appropriateness and force. A candidate may appeal because of his moral strength, an auto because of its usefulness to one's business or because of its status value. So the speaker, in judging what concerns him most, applies the values he considers most appropriate to that occasion. For the purposes of practical discourse, we do not need to distinguish between values and interests. We need only recognize that whatever people find valuable they also find interesting. This statement is of special significance to the speaker, for whenever his explanations and reasonings reflect matters of importance to his audience, his speech is interesting—indeed, to both him and his hearers.

Values are learned and become part of every individual's experience and makeup. They are acquired from his family and from his social and cultural environment; hence they reflect the behavior patterns—usually and for the most part the dominant ones—of a society. Scholars who specialize in the psychology of personality and in the study of ethics usually refer to these patterns as the *rules* and *norms* of a society, as social *practices* and *conventions,* and as social *ideals* of behavior. So fundamental are values to human behavior, to our thought as well as our conduct, that they shape our behavior in the same way that axioms illuminate constructions in geometry. They are the foundations of social living and of every individual's personality and character. They so permeate our whole beings and become so stable that it is possible to classify them and arrange them on scales.

One such scale is presented by A. H. Maslow.[1] In an adapted form it is presented here by way of illustration, because it will throw further light on the nature of values.

Individual Needs

- I. Satisfaction of Physical Needs
  - A. Hunger
  - B. Thirst
  - C. Conditions of health
  - D. Sexual urges
- II. Satisfaction of Needs for Security
  - A. Safety from physical danger
  - B. Safety from emotional dangers
  - C. Protection from uncomfortable surroundings
- III. Satisfaction of One's Need To Belong
  - A. Being loved by family
  - B. Being accepted by peers
  - C. Being accepted by superiors
  - D. Having a mate
- IV. Satisfaction of Needs for Esteem
  - A. Being respected by one's inferiors
  - B. Being respected by one's peers
  - C. Being respected by one's superiors
  - D. Respecting oneself
- V. Exercise of One's Capabilities
- VI. Self-Actualization: Becoming, Maintaining, and Developing Oneself

[1] *Motivation and Personality* (New York: Harper & Row, 1954), Chapter 5. See also below, p. 43.

A need acquires value. In the scheme above, needs are ranked according to their power and their priority in satisfying the individual as he grows and develops. First, as we know, are the desires for food and water, needs so primitive that they are regulated internally by the body's homeostatic mechanisms, which provide the conditions of health and fight disease. Next in power are needs for rest and sleep and for sexual activity. Following these in the order of priority is the desire for security, first manifested in the child, who, once his biological needs are cared for, wants to be comfortable and safe. He is satisfied by an orderly, predictable world. The child's need for safety become the adult's need for security, though perhaps better defined and more various. The man usually prefers jobs with good benefits and seniority or tenure, opens savings accounts, and buys insurance. Next in the order of needs are the desires to belong and to enjoy affectionate relations with others. With these desires met as well as may be, the individual becomes increasingly aware of himself and how others regard him. He wants self-respect and the respect of others. He enjoys strength and power, achievement, confidence, and independence. He prizes his reputation, whether it depends upon status and position or upon esteem. He becomes aware, too, of what he can best do in the world of work. All such needs are recognized by every civilized individual, and they must be satisfied in some degree and in some combination if an individual can say that he has become his best, his highest, self. Self-fulfillment, so Maslow and others believe, is the ultimate goal in life. "What a man *can* be, he *must* be."

Such needs an individual refers to when he evaluates his decisions and actions. When asked to explain or to justify one of his acts he inevitably draws upon his values for relevant "reasons." Among the reasons he recognizes, some he judges more important and interesting than others.

Speakers who must decide what is important not only to themselves but also to their audiences should recognize two other features of values. Norms, conventions, and ideals cut across all aspects of a person's experience and become features not of one part of his being, but of his whole self. Some students of human behavior speak of experience as consisting of knowledge (what we can be said to know), emotions, motives, desires, feelings, and attitudes. Some students of learning behavior consider experience in terms of cognitive behavior, conative behavior, and affective behavior. But a value judgment may reflect any one of these types of experience, and it may reflect more than one kind. A person decides to go fishing simply because it pleases him. The value involved is pleasurable feeling. A young man decides that he should go to college. This judgment brings to focus, and results from, a number of segments of his experience. He may think that college means a better job in the future than he could get without a college education and thus be motivated by financial reward and the desire to achieve position and status. Or he may genuinely enjoy learning for its own sake.

Perhaps he is attempting to keep the respect and approval of his closest friends who expect him to attend college. Anyone's "reasons" for going to college may be compounded of other motives, desires, and feelings as well. Each person's compound of values, his reasons for behaving as he does, belongs to him.

The valuative aspect of experience, moreover, as embedded in speech and language behavior, is indeed a part of what we mean by the meaning of words. Professor Charles Osgood and his students have found that most words show an evaluative feature; they bear connotations of what is considered good and bad. The adjective *heroic,* for example, in addition to its obvious meanings, connotes something that is strong and desirable. *Cowardly* implies something weak and repugnant. Probably no word, no utterance, is completely neutral, cold, and impersonal. Language not only labels objects and classifies our experiences; it announces our feelings and attitudes about them. So in making choices, in expressing preferences, and in making judgments, we are announcing what is important to us. From Gordon W. Allport we derive a popular definition of values as *meanings* important to us when we make a particular choice or decision. In any communicative situation, values are the meanings, and only the meanings, that both speaker and audience perceive as important and significant to them.

If a speaker is to control the interest of his audience, he must be concerned with what is important not merely to himself but to his hearers as well. He must be concerned not only about his self but about other selves; that is, his image of himself includes his image of others and his estimate of what others—his audience—think of him. Communication inevitably places demands upon the social self, especially in public speaking and public address and discussion in all of their forms and settings. Accordingly, in his preparation and planning, a speaker cannot think exclusively of his own interests and purposes. For this reason we present a view of values that invites communicators to think like communicators.

In the following outline our sketch of things desirable (I) reflects in part Maslow's scheme of needs. Our view, however, goes beyond Maslow's, for, in recognizing the categories of the obligatory and the commendable, we incorporate some of the chief values of political life and ethical action. In rhetorical discussion and theory the ultimate justification of information and argument is grounded in political and ethical ideals. Though we may rarely measure up to them fully in practice, they mold and define our fundamental interests and ideals.

A Survey of Values

I. The Desirable
   This class of values includes *goals, ends,* and *motives* of thought and conduct.

A. Satisfaction of physical well-being
   1. Maintainance of food supply and drink
   2. Maintenance of health
B. Satisfaction of pleasurable tensions and feelings
   1. Sexual activity
   2. Venturesome activity, involving risk and suspense
   3. Novel activity, involving interplay of the old and new
   4. Playful activity: humor and laughter
C. Action in one's own interests
   1. Wages and salary
   2. Property
D. Action in the interests of others: good will
E. Achievement
   1. Personal
      a. Realization of one's capabilities
      b. Production and creation of something
      c. Possession and discovery of knowledge
      d. Power: being in a position to exercise control
      e. Physical attractiveness in dress, speech, and action
   2. Social
      a. Status: occupying a position respected by others
      b. Esteem: personal achievement respected by others
      c. Belongingness: being liked, loved, and accepted by others
F. Freedom: a condition permitting satisfaction of desires under minimal constraints
G. The useful: the means of achieving one's desires and ends

II. The Obligatory

Refers to the *expectations* of others, often regarded as social norms, or frames of reference, established by a society. They are essential to cooperative action. They are among the general conditions of acceptability and persuasion.

A. Duties: behaviors specified or expected because of one's membership or position in a recognized group
   1. Family
      a. Obligations of parents
      b. Obligations of children
   2. State: national and local
      a. The lawmaker's concerns
         (1) Conditions and rights securable through law for the realization of individual desires: opportunities
         (2) The general welfare of citizens
         (3) Justice in the application of law
      b. The citizen's concerns
         (1) Respect for his own rights
         (2) Respect for law and the rights of others
   3. Economic: duties required by a business, company, and corporation

4. Religious: conduct specified and sanctioned by church or creed
5. Educational: the ideals and practices of schools, colleges, and universities
6. Professional: the principles, methods, rules, and conventions specified by persons who are committed to an art or science
7. Special clubs, fraternities, and so on

B. Truth telling

C. Promise keeping

D. *Mores:* the rules, practices, and conventions observed by a culture, typically recognized in customs of speech and dress, in folk sayings and maxims, and in manners generally

III. The Commendable

This term may be applied to any behavior regarded as desirable and obligatory, but it is used specifically and properly to refer to very general *kinds* of desirable conduct that have become stable and predictable. The labels below are descriptive ones. When applied to an individual they function as signs that he has shown such behavior or that he can be expected to show such behavior under similar circumstances. An individual, for example, who has habitually acted honestly is expected to continue to act honestly. Hence the labels also refer to states of being or "character," which in part are productive of the kinds of responses described. Other labels often used are character traits and virtues.

A. Conscientiousness: behavior in keeping with one's self-image and obligations

B. Kindliness

C. Fairness

D. Courage

E. Magnanimity

F. Honesty

G. Prudence

H. Tolerance

I. Persistence

J. Sincerity

This classification of values is not necessarily the only one, nor the best one for every purpose. We present it because it is sufficiently general and close to human interests, needs, and motives to suggest the sources of materials and arguments that speakers must consider if they wish to interest their listeners, that is, if they wish to reveal what is important and significant about their explanations and proposals. As speakers gain experience in their art, they may discover a scheme of values more appropriate to their vocational and professional needs than this one.

If each of the entries in the outline above is expressed as a statement, it is evident that each becomes a basic belief, or axiom, of our thought and conduct. For example:

> A desirable goal in life is the experience of pleasure.
> (Or: The experience of pleasure is desirable.)
> A desirable goal is having a position that is respected by others.
> It is desirable to exercise freedom of choice under as few restraints as possible.
> Caring for their children is a duty of parents.
> Protection of its citizens is a duty of the state.
> Educating its citizens is an obligation of the state.
> Fairness is commendable.
> (Or: It is commendable to act fairly.)

Values as fully expressed as these are sometimes stated directly in a speech. More often they are not enunciated explicitly; they are implied or are alluded to by word or phrase. Yet they inevitably emerge on any occasion in which speaker and audience are sensitive to things of mutual importance and interest. In his Inaugural Address (pages 420–422), John F. Kennedy all but explicitly stated that it is a government's duty to protect the country: ". . . only when our arms are sufficient beyond doubt can we be certain beyond doubt that they will never be employed." The address is rife with allusions to freedom as a desire of our nation and a goal of subject peoples. He referred to a global ideal: "The belief that the rights of man come not from the generosity of the state but from the hand of God." He did not let the citizen forget his obligation to his country: "Ask not what your country can do for you—ask what you can do for your country." In the speech Kennedy had prepared to deliver at Dallas on the day of his assassination, he used facts to express the inequality of opportunity that hinders Negro achievement.

> The Negro baby born in America today . . . has about one-half as much chance of completing high school as a white baby born in the same place on the same day, one-third as much chance of completing college, one-third as much chance of becoming a professional man, twice as much chance of being unemployed, about one-seventh as much chance of earning $10,000 a year, a life expectancy which is seven years shorter. . . .

The values that emerge from an occasion and from the problems that *make* the occasion are usually plain enough to a perceptive speaker.

To ponder a value system is to become aware of the utility of values in communication. First, our values constitute one of the two sources of materials relevant to a speech. One source is found among the *facts*, the special items of information, that have given rise to the occasion; and these in turn always reveal a background and history that the wise speaker seeks to grasp. From the other source of materials—our values—come the conceptions that we apply to the occasion and its facts. In making the application, a speaker is in truth interpreting the occasion, the information it affords, and the audience he faces in terms of his experience and that of others. This is what John F. Kennedy did in the passage cited from his Dallas speech. In the facts of the Negro's condition, he saw evidence of unequal opportunity.

The application of values to a communicative situation involves two questions that lead the speaker to the import and significance of things:

1. What values are relevant to the situation?
2. Among relevant values, which ones have priority?

The speaker's answers to the first question produce *a survey of the possible materials* relevant to the rhetorical situation. The answers to the second question produce materials that are inherently interesting. They are interesting, because when a speaker assigns priorities to the materials relevant to a particular occasion he is in effect saying, "These are important to me and to my purpose, and they may also be important to my audience."

In the second place, different occasions and subjects bring different values to the fore. Hence, the priorities of one occasion may not be effective on another occasion. What is important at one time and place may not be significant at another time and place. Peace seems more important when we are threatened with war than when war is not in prospect. Higher wages, always at issue in negotiations over a new work-contract, may seem less important to labor during a recession than during a period of economic prosperity. Freedom, self-rule, and education to a people subjected to dictatorship may take priority over questions of more food and better health. To the conscientious objector, religious convictions are more important than community esteem. If it be true that self-interest always rules us, it is equally true that what we believe serviceable to our self-interest—that is, what appears important to our welfare—varies from occasion to occasion, circumstance to circumstance.

In the third place, speaker and audience may not hold the same priorities on the same occasion. During the Civil War, the North wanted England to respect the trade embargo against the South and to remain strictly neutral. But for England and her textile workers trade was more important than neutrality or hatred of slavery. The Federal Government sent Henry Ward Beecher to England to explain and defend its position. He had to recognize the priorities of both countries and seek lines of argument for accommodating both. This he did most successfully in his famous Liverpool Address. Like Beecher, most speakers have to recognize the audience's paramount interests as well as their own, and to employ these interests in exposition and argument. Speakers who are inventive and imaginative enough to do so have little trouble in controlling attention and interest; often they are persuasive as well.

This book is built upon the idea that the control of interest involves locating and using the priorities that speakers and audiences assign to the facts and values emerging from a particular occasion. To a remarkable degree, the materials of interest are also the materials of argument and persuasion. They originate in the same sources: the facts of the occasion and subject, and the interpretation of the facts that men supply out of the enduring features of their experience, that is, their values and the meanings that these values have in communicative contexts.

The same idea and the same features of experience govern our discussion of the interpretation and criticism of speeches. A speaker in effect says, What features do I find in the occasion, subject, and audience that are important and significant enough to cause me to make a speech? A listener in effect says, What do I find in the speech and speaker that are important and significant to me? The critic in effect says, What in the speech is important and significant, from which other speakers and other audiences may learn?

Attention and Interest of the Speaker

The speaker is like the listener in that he experiences the same kinds of stimulation and responses and is subject to the same conditions of attention.

First, the speaker's effective stimulus is the audience. No audience, no speech. Of course, a person might prepare a speech for fun, but considered logically his efforts would be pointless if he were not going to deliver the speech or publish it in some manner. And, in a larger sense, the student of public speaking may be stimulated by certain private motives, such as the desire to build confidence or to speak well, to which his work in a speech course is a response. But for each actual, specific speech the audience remains the stimulus that sets off the chain of events in the speaker's *preparation* and gets him "set" and ready to speak.

Second, the process of preparing a speech (perhaps we should say in all strictness, preparing *for* a speech) involves attention to one's own experience: searching it, extending it, organizing it, and bringing it within the experience of one's listeners. The speaker explores his past experience for a subject, focuses upon a number of possibilities, and decides upon one. His *choice* of subject is his response. If his choice reflects what is valuable about the subject—that is, what is important and meaningful to him—he has found the source of interest that will sustain both him and his audience. Once satisfied that he himself understands, he turns his attention to the kind of response he wants to elicit from his hearers in the time allotted him. The response he finally decides upon becomes his statement of purpose. He then engages in another series of explorations, this time seeking and selecting ideas and materials that are consistent with the purpose of the speech and that will bring his experience with his subject within the interest of his hearers. He asks himself, What will my audience consider valuable about this subject? The classroom speaker will not go far wrong if he reasons that what claimed his attention and his interest will similarly interest others. With his materials selected, the speaker turns to the process of building his outline, arranging ideas to make them contiguous, similar, and orderly. At this stage of his preparation, the speaker realizes that the better his outline the more easily he will attend to and remember it. In his effort to control the attention of others, he is learning to control his own attention; and in developing the details of his outline, he is sharpening his own attention. Examples, comparisons, contrasts, and specific illustrations help to strengthen and intensify his experience, and thus help him to remember it. Ideas and materials associated with values, emotions, and feelings may stir him to enthusiasm, so that on the platform he will be a dynamic, colorful person rather than a listless figure speaking a piece. In brief, the preparation of a speech is a process through which the speaker directs and controls his experience by sharpening, deepening, molding and disciplining it. He creates a state of readiness to which he responds during rehearsal and delivery with speech and gesture.

Third, the delivery of a speech is a chain of responses. The speaker steps before his audience and gets set. The audience triggers his initial words and starts him going. Once he is started, the experience gained in his preparation takes over. He is responding to the experience—reliving it. The language that fills mind and mouth at any moment may or may not be identical with the language of preparation and rehearsal. But by and large it will *correspond* with what has been bound into his prior experience. He may or may not be aware that he is repeating language, for as he responds to his experience he is simply thinking creatively and communicatively again.

The speaker who thus responds during delivery will be as spontaneous, genuine, real, sparkling, and dynamic as he is in his liveliest conversational moments. After all, our conversation is triggered by the other fellow—his presence or his remark—and our reply is the instantaneous response to him and to our inner experience. The speaker who has such an experience during the moments of delivery is also experiencing *communication.* As he responds, he is saying in effect to his listeners, I hope you are getting my meaning. The speaker's language and gesture are his meaningful response to his preparation for his audience; and his language and gesture in turn become stimuli for the audience's meaningful response to him. So, if the speech is effective, speaker and listener share meanings. In this sense communication is communion. It is a satisfying and rewarding experience.

FURTHER READING

ALLPORT, Gordon W. *Becoming: Basic Considerations for a Psychology of Personality*. New Haven: Yale Paperbound, 1961.

BREMBECK, W. L., and HOWELL, W. S. *Persuasion: A Means of Social Control*. New York, 1952. Chapter 15, "Attention."

CARROLL, John B. *The Study of Language*. Cambridge, Mass., 1955. Chapter 2, "Linguistics and Psychology."

CHRISTENSEN, Francis. "A Generative Rhetoric of the Paragraph." *College Composition and Communication*, 16 (October 1965), 144–156.

GRAY, G. W., and WISE, C. M. *The Bases of Speech*. 3rd ed. New York, 1959. Chapter 6, "The Linguistic Basis," Chapter 7, "The Psychological Basis."

LEPLEY, Ray (ed.). *The Language of Value*. New York, 1957. In particular, "The Language of Values," by Willis Moore.

MASLOW, Abraham H. *Toward a Psychology of Being*. Princeton, New Jersey, 1962.

MILLER, G. A. *Language and Communication*. New York, 1951. Chapters 8–11.

SMITH, B. L., LASSWELL, H. D., and CASEY, R. D. (eds.) *Propaganda, Communication, and Public Opinion*. Princeton: Princeton University Press, 1946.

WINANS, J. A. *Public Speaking*. New York, 1917. Chapter 3. "Principles of Attention."

4
The First Speeches

Getting started right

Long before the student of public speaking has time to study the substance of the textbook and to advance far in his mastery of the principles of speechmaking, he will begin preparing and delivering speeches. Near the beginning of his study, therefore, firm guidance in the application of sound operating principles and procedures is needed. Then the student, even in his first speeches, will be prepared to proceed systematically in the use of principles which he will later study more fully, one at a time. He will avoid having to unlearn procedures and to break bad habits which he had begun to fix through random practice.

In his earliest speeches a learner's principal problems may appear to be breaking the ice and getting a little experience in talking on his feet. Experience in teaching indicates, however, that almost from the first the student may overcome the worst of his initial hesitancy and timidity and gain some confidence before an audience, even as he learns to crystallize, clarify, and develop ideas according to sound and systematic principles. As a matter of psychological fact, the speaker who feels reasonably sure that he has something clear and intelligible to say and who is concerned with communicating it clearly and intelligibly to his listeners usually does not have much time to be concerned with himself, his feelings, or his effectiveness. In other words, the more he focuses on his message and on communicating it to his audience, the less liable he will be to focus on himself.

This chapter presents certain fundamental patterns for the first speeches. The important matter from the start is the conscious application—the use—of sound principles, patterns, and procedures, which should become the speaker's *habitual* ways of thinking for speaking. Then many of the problems which plague beginning speakers will disappear.

There are times, of course, when one has the impulse or the obligation to speak but has nothing particular to say. Then the first problem is finding a subject and material. Most students, after very little consideration, will find their accumulated resources quite equal to the demands of their initial short speeches. Besides, in school and college they have usually had considerable experience in finding subjects and materials for written exercises in English composition. They have learned something about utilizing their reading and a good deal about taking stock of their own knowledge and experience in order to write interestingly. Those same resources will enable them initially to find the substance for speaking interestingly to others. The problem of finding a subject and materials, therefore, we will defer for the time being (see Chapters 5 and 6).

Managing substance

The problems of advantageously managing the substance of speeches, however—the problems of making statements and filling them out—may properly occupy more attention at this point. Most college students and educated adults are more experienced and better prepared in this phase of speechmaking than at first they may be aware. The ways of careful, thoughtful conversation are also the ways of good public speaking. Consider the following responses to conversational situations.

I think I understand what you mean, but say it another way so I can be sure.

That sounds like a sensible statement. Can you back it up with facts and information?

What do you mean by saying people seldom do anything much better than they have to? Are there such people? Give me an example or two.

I would not be surprised if you have something which may be useful in your new method of determining public opinion, but I don't really understand it. What is it like?

I believe you mean what you say, and I respect your opinion, but it is only your opinion. Who else says so?

The Basic Pattern

Each of the preceding requests for information points up the prime principle of systematic, orderly discourse. Each involves crystallizing an idea, an opinion, a judgment, or an inquiry into a statement and enriching, supporting, reinforcing, and amplifying—in short, developing it.

Each situation illustrates the basic operating pattern of thinking for speaking and of organizing speeches—an arrangement of *statement* and *development* for the statement. The concept of *topic sentence* in the study of written composition somewhat resembles the pattern underlying good speeches. And anyone who has considered the various methods of developing a topic sentence into an effective paragraph has begun his initiation into the methods of giving form and development to the substance of his first speeches. The problems of theme writing and speechmaking are by no means the same, but their methods of giving order and movement to their materials are certainly comparable.

As Aristotle asserted long ago, and as practice still demonstrates, a good speech and each of the basic units which together make up a good speech consist essentially of two elements: (1) a *statement* and (2) a *development* which explains or reinforces the statement.

The statement

For our present purpose a *statement* is a declarative sentence formulating an idea, a feeling, a judgment, an opinion, or a matter of inquiry that needs *development* through particularization, illustration, concretion, interpretation, reinforcement, or support of some sort if it is to convey its intended meaning and force to the audience to whom it is addressed. Each of the demands and queries on page 45 occurs because some declarative statement has been made or implied, the meaning of which is not clear enough or full enough for the listener. The speaker, in replying to the query, would probably make the statement again and then would satisfy his listener with the kind of developing material asked for.

Development

By *development* we mean the sum of such methods, materials, and language as should serve, with the particular listeners involved, to make intelligible, to make concrete, to reinforce, to enliven, to support, or otherwise to fill out the meaning and significance of the *statement.* Anything a speaker says, then, which tends to prove his point, explain his idea, or make his statement clear, vivid, or attractive to his audience is considered development.

There are many possible sources and methods of development, most of which we will discuss in our later chapters. In his first speeches, however, the student should try consciously to become aware of perhaps four or five obvious means of development and should concentrate on using them. These means are indicated by the queries on page 45. In answer to query (1) what is needed is a *restatement* of the same thing that has been said; in answer to (2) the speaker will give *factual information;* in replying to (3) *examples* should clear up the uncertainty; in order to satisfy the inquirer in (4) the speaker will have to make *comparisons;* and for (5) the speaker will offer *testimony*.

Developing Material. For first speeches the most common and most useful kinds of development may be identified in the following ways.

Restatement. Restatement is largely a matter of language. By recasting a statement in other language or other form or both, a speaker not only adds emphasis but often hits upon terminology and phrasing which will strike his listeners as clearer, fuller, more familiar, or in some way more understandable or forceful than the language of the original statement.

Factual information. When we say that a speaker knows what he is talking about and has the facts on his subject, we usually mean that he has filled out and supported his contentions with plenty of verifiable information, factual data, figures and statistical material, and firsthand information.

Example. Whether as the short, undeveloped specific instance or as the longer, fully developed illustration, example is the detailing, sketching, narrating, describing, or otherwise setting before the audience of typical circumstances, characteristic cases, or particular instances which help to make clear, vivid, or credible the statement that the speaker wants his audience to accept.

Comparison and contrast. Comparison and contrast are closely related to example. They are concerned with showing likenesses and differences among objects, ideas, and situations. The former puts stress upon illuminating similarities; the latter on dissimilarities.

Testimony. Simply described, testimony is the say-so of someone other than the speaker, in support of a point or in explanation of an idea. One very common form of testimony is quotation, including quotation from men and books of the past.

Such, in brief, are the five most common and useful methods and materials of development which the student should begin using at once in his first speeches. We will discuss each more fully under the general topic of amplification in the informative speech in Chapter 7, and under the topic of support in the persuasive speech in Chapters 18 and 20. Now we will proceed to illustrate the use of these materials of development in characteristic patterns of the short speech.

Putting the Speech Together: Pattern

We have remarked that some arrangement of statement with development of the statement comprises the basic operating pattern for a speaker's thinking and for organizing speeches. That is, when one thinks most efficiently for speaking, one habitually thinks of truths or opinions one wishes to communicate, and one thinks of them in connection with material that might develop them. These elements may come to mind as idea first, followed by developing matter; or as concrete facts and examples first, leading to the idea; or as some of the potential material first, then a version of the idea, followed by more developing matter. The order is largely dependent on habit and circumstances and will vary with the speaker and the occasion. But for all speakers the habit of joining the two basic elements into regular patterns of movement is important. The formulation of an idea should result immediately in the movement toward material with which to develop it; and the apprehension of facts, events, similarities, and so forth, should lead to an idea of what they signify—to a relevant *statement.*

These patterns in the speaker's own thinking serve him as patterns for organizing his material into speeches, or units of speeches. The three common patterns may be represented schematically as follows:

Pattern 1

STATEMENT TO BE DEVELOPED
    DEVELOPING MATERIAL

Pattern 2

    DEVELOPING MATERIAL
STATEMENT TO WHICH IT LEADS

Pattern 3

    DEVELOPING MATERIAL
STATEMENT BEING DEVELOPED
    FURTHER DEVELOPING MATERIAL

The diagrammatic arrangements above are intended to illustrate two facts: (1) Development materials may precede the statement they support, or they may succeed the statement, or they may both precede and follow. (2) No matter what the time order of the statement and its developing ideas, the development is always logically subordinate to the statement, and the statement is always logically superior to the development. In the diagrams this relationship is suggested by placing the statement to the left of its developing materials.

We observe in passing that these patterns also illustrate possible nuclei for the speech outline, which is the plan, or blueprint, for the construction of the speech. Like the blueprint for a house or a jet-bomber, it is most useful if it is prepared before final construction is begun. Full consideration of the speech outline will be given in Chapters 9 and 10. For the present we will concern ourselves only with the basic patterns in their simplest forms. We will employ the several kinds of development and the three patterns of statement-development.

Patterns of the short speech

1. The most usual pattern of the short speech on a simple, expository theme may be illustrated by the following scheme. The governing *statement* is made at the beginning and is developed through information, example,

testimony, and restatement. No doubt, in such a speech comparison or contrast also might profitably have been used.

STATEMENT

The development of the transistor has opened new vistas for the portable radio receiver.

DEVELOPMENT

The transistor has eliminated the heaviest and the most fragile parts of the radio. (*Information*)
The transistor requires only small flashlight batteries for power. (*Information*)
The transistor replaced the vacuum tube. (*Information*)
It has made really tiny radios practicable. (*Information*)
Radios with strong, clear tone and wide range may measure no more than 3″ x 4″ x 1″. (*Information*)
Our postman says that his transistor radio, which he carries in his shirt pocket, has taken most of the monotony out of walking his rounds each day. (*Testimony*)
The radio we use while hiking and boating we keep in the glove compartment of the car along with the camera. (*Example*)
In a world of TV, the transistor radio has established a secure place of its own. (*Restatement*)

Observe that in the brief speech of this sort, restatement may serve as conclusion as well as additional development.

2. A simple speech can be chiefly developed through the use of information. This sort of pattern and development might be more likely to appear as one of the basic units of a complex speech, but it is sometimes effective for the simple, short informative speech.

STATEMENT

The summer weather in this city is neither excessively hot nor excessively humid.

DEVELOPMENT

The average mean summer temperature is 75°.
The average number of days from June 1 to October 1 when the temperature rises above 85° is 14.
The average number of days during the same period when the temperature does not rise above 75° is 50.
The normal humidity in summer is 50%.
The average number of days in summer when the humidity rises above 70% is 15.
The "discomfort index" shows fewer than 10 days in the "very uncomfortable" range.
(*Information*)

The preceding figures are provided by the United States Weather Bureau. (*Testimony*)

3. The pattern for the short speech in which the development precedes and leads to the statement is illustrated in the scheme below for a speech employing example exclusively. The speaker plans to cite briefly several specific instances, then to clinch his idea with extended illustration. With this speech the audience would probably get a special satisfaction out of the explicit appearance of the statement at the end, where the statement would serve as a neat conclusion as well.

As we have sketched it, this speech would be intended principally for entertainment through a kind of ironic humor. If the speaker's purpose were more serious, if he were addressing the university administration and advocating some improvement at registration time, he would probably want to use additional kinds of materials for development, especially information and comparison. He might give figures, perhaps collected by the student newspaper, showing just how long the average student spends in getting registered, at which department's table he has to wait the longest, and at what hours the congestion is worst. The speaker might also wish to offer some comparison with registration in other universities, and some testimony from individual students and faculty.

DEVELOPMENT

As we begin our college year, we have to stand in line (*Specific Instances*)
at the registrar's to get our cards,
at each department's table in the field house to register for our courses,
at the treasurer's to pay our fees,
at the health center for our physical examinations,
at the bookstore to buy our supplies,
at the cafeteria counter to get our dinner.

Let us follow Jack Waller from 6:00 A.M. to 7:00 P.M. of registration day of his freshman year. (*Illustration*)

STATEMENT

Obviously, getting into college and staying in college are largely matters of standing in line.

4. A special kind of short speech developing an idea (stated or implied) by offering one extended example, or *illustration,* usually of the narrative or story sort, may be most interesting and effective in pointing a moral or enlivening an idea. Such, for example, is Jesus' parable of the Good Samaritan (*Luke* 10:30–37).

STATEMENT

(*Your neighbor is he who needs your help.*)

DEVELOPMENT

> The story of the man who went down from Jerusalem to Jericho illustrates what it is to be a neighbor.

Observe that the *statement* in this little speech is not the question which was asked of Jesus, "Who is my neighbor?" It is the *answer* to that question. That answer never appears as a formulated statement in the speech. Hence we place it in parentheses in the scheme above. Nevertheless it is the governing proposition, implicit in the story, and must be included in the scheme.

All the details of examples need not be included in the scheme or outline, but there should be a separate descriptive heading for each example. The student might consider how one would phrase the statement for the parable of the Prodigal Son (*Luke* 15:11–32), and for the parable of the Talents (*Matthew* 25:14–30).

In a speech about registration, like the one already sketched, the speaker might well limit himself to one narrative example of his own experience, such as the one concerning Jack Waller, including all the appalling (or amusing) episodes and either formulating the statement explicitly at the end or suggesting to the listeners that they form their own conclusions. This also would be a speech of one extended *illustration.*

5. *Testimony* alone seldom provides adequate development when a proposition of any consequence is to be explained or supported (though some tournament debaters seem to think that quoting authorities is all that is needed to win). Even the writers of advertising, who are the most flagrant users of testimony, do not regularly rely on it exclusively, except for very brief, quick impact: "Buy Kleen Kine Milk. Babe Ruth approved of milk; the Bible associates milk with honey; and we all know the phrase, 'the milk of human kindness.'" Advertisers usually couple testimony with something which is intended to seem like information: "Kleen Kine Milk is up to three times more nourishing for up to 15 percent less." (More and less than *what* is seldom indicated.) Though easily abused, testimony may be very well and effectively used in conjunction with other kinds of supporting material, especially example and information.

The following scheme illustrates development by testimony. It also serves as an example of the pattern in which the statement is both preceded and followed by development.

DEVELOPMENT

> "A man's a man for a' that," said Robert Burns. (*Testimony*)
> Edmund Burke said that he did not know how to draw up an indictment against a whole people. (*Testimony*)

STATEMENT

A man is best judged for himself, not for his race, class, nationality, or religion.

DEVELOPMENT

The Constitution of the United States recognizes no qualitative categories for judging men. (*Information*)
Records of crime show that native-born Americans commit as serious crimes as do immigrants. (*Information*)
There is no reliable evidence of the inherent intellectual or moral superiority of the white man over the Negro. (*Information*)
"The fault, dear Brutus, is not in our stars but in ourselves. . . ." (*Testimony, serving as conclusion*)

6. The following scheme suggests the development of a statement through the use of comparison and analogy.

STATEMENT

The government of the U.S.S.R. is based on an ascending concentration of power, from the local soviets to the Supreme Soviet.

DEVELOPMENT

It may be called a pyramid of power. (*Metaphor*)
It is like a large business organization, where each of the minor executives has several supervisors reporting to him, and he in turn reports to a superior who reports to a superior, and so on. (*Comparison*)
It is like the English system of privy councils under Elizabeth I. (*Analogy—to be extended*)

Every flea has little fleas
  Upon his back to bite 'im
And little fleas have lesser fleas—
  So on *ad infinitum.*
(*Testimony, as illustrative comparison*)

The schemes just given illustrate the speeches simplest in form and plan: speeches in which only a single statement requires development. Most speeches are not so simple. Nevertheless, the best speeches, however long and complex, consist of basic units of statement-and-development such as we have been examining, combined into larger patterns. The structure and outlines of such speeches, as we have said, will be the business of Chapter 9. Until the student has studied those later chapters, he will do well to concentrate on developing his skill with *statement* and *development* in the simple structure of one or two units.

Introductions and conclusions

We have said little or nothing in this chapter about introductions, conclusions, connective and transitional material, and the sort of filling-in with words and sentences that transforms the bare structure into the neat, shapely speech. These elements deserve full consideration. Later chapters will be devoted to them. All we wish to say now is keep introductions and conclusions in the first speeches brief and simple. An introduction need consist only of a statement or two which will get the attention of listeners and at the same time lead into the ideas that follow it. The conclusion of a short speech, as we have suggested in the scheme on page 49, often consists simply of *restating* the idea expressed in the statement.

The following speech is a fine example of a good first speech.

HOWARD E. SCHMITZ

The Old Crank Next Door

This speech was delivered by a young college graduate, a chemist, in an adult evening class in public speaking. His audience was composed of a variety of men and women from many businesses and professions, having in common chiefly their desire to improve their speaking. The speech was intended to fulfill a regular assignment of a 3-to-4-minute speech of simple structure.

All of us have a conscience and each of us has a pretty good idea of what a conscience is. I am not concerned, therefore, either with proving that you have a conscience or with explaining what I think a conscience is. What I want to do this evening is to point out three things which I think are important to keep in mind if we are to understand and get along with our consciences.

In the first place, the only thing that conscience does is to punish us. Its nature is clearly shown by the words used to describe it: "strict," "stern," "harsh," "pricking," "scolding," "nagging." Even "guilty," when used in this connection, refers not to the conscience itself, but to the way that it makes us feel. On the other hand, who ever heard of a "kind," "generous," or "forgiving" conscience?

Secondly, we can subdue our conscience but never escape from it, as evidenced by the story about Mr. —— which we all read in the papers two weeks ago. Here was a man who in a period of fifteen years embezzled something over $200,000 from the bank for which he worked. To me, the amazing thing about the story is not that he was able to embezzle so much money successfully, without even his wife's knowledge, but that he was caught by his own word. Not only did he admit his guilt without being accused, but he continued to volunteer a great deal of information about what he had done—information which might not have been found out even by close cross-questioning. I think it is plain that although his conscience had been by-passed for fifteen years, it finally caught up with him.

The last important thing to remember is that the punishments handed out by conscience are often much too severe for the crime committed. For example, think of the normally moderate drinker who goes to an especially good party one evening and has three or four too many drinks. He soon begins to feel pretty good and does and says things that he ordinarily would not, much to everyone's delight. But he finally goes home and goes to sleep, and by morning his drugged conscience will have regained full strength. You can rest assured that no one who was at the party will feel as ashamed of his behavior as he himself will, and it will probably be some time before he will be able to square himself with his precious conscience.

Thus we can see that although the conscience is often called "a little voice inside," it acts more like "the old crank next door." It never has a good word for us, is always looking for trouble, and when it finds it, often makes the punishment outweigh the crime. As with the crank next door, the best we can do is to understand its nasty disposition and try to give it few things to complain about.

II
Subjects and Materials

5
Selecting Subjects

Interesting subjects for speeches arise from the situations that prompt speaking, that is, from the occasions and circumstances calling for speeches, from the relations of audiences to those occasions and circumstances, from the audience's assessment of the importance of the circumstances, and especially from the speaker's feeling of the importance and value of occasion and audience to him.

Appropriateness to the Occasion

Occasion is a rhetorical concept referring to all the circumstances that in combination bring a speech into being. A speech is a response to a rhetorical occasion. In the full context of a rhetorical situation, one finds the cause, or causes, of a speech. The principal factors that constitute an occasion are time and place, audience, speaker, and subject. When one says that a subject is good, he means that it is fitting, or appropriate, to the other factors of the occasion.

Thus, the occasion often dictates the subject of the speech and restricts the speaker's range of choice. At his press conference, the President of the United States knows that reporters will ask him about the important news or rumors of the moment; hence, his subjects are cut out for him. At an automobile dealers' meeting to learn about the new models, the company speakers have their special subjects designated. Some occasions, then, create expectations speakers cannot ignore.

Specific time and occasion

Is the occasion a regular quarterly meeting of an employees' association of a department store? And does the meeting fall early in January? If the president of the association were to speak, what might he talk on? Might the occasion suggest both the subject and the purpose? Would he, for example, want to entertain his hearers with an account of incidents of the recent Christmas-shopping madhouse? The audience might well be in a mood to respond favorably to humor. On the other hand, if one of its prominent members had recently died in an auto wreck, it might be in no mood to hear an entertaining speech. Would he explain what they must do about completing their income tax returns? Or would he try to persuade them to attend meetings more regularly and to recruit other members? In brief, an audience meeting at a particular time has ideas and feelings about recent or coming events; a speaker should be aware of these when he chooses his subject and general purpose.

However, the persons for whom we intend this chapter are the numerous speakers who enjoy considerable freedom in choosing their subjects. We have in mind especially the classroom situation, where the student has the major responsibility for selecting his subject.

The classroom occasion

Most readers of this book should give special consideration to circumstances of place and time in the classroom. True, they confront the same group of people session after session; they speak under the same general conditions; the general purpose—to inform, to amuse, to persuade—is often prescribed by the instructor; but the circumstances of the classroom, fortunately, are not always the same from day to day. Because the same general situation recurs, one may forget two important aspects of the occasion. The first is the specific time at which the student speaks. He may be the first to speak in that class. If he is, he should not forget that his hearers may have just come from other classes, and their minds may still be turning over ideas from those classes. Or they may be still thinking about what they were reading or studying in the library the hour before. Some "listeners" may be set to carry on some late preparation for their next class while the speaker labors, and others may want to read the newspapers they have just picked up. Some may still be in the throes of a lively discussion, and some may be thinking primarily about the free afternoon ahead or the evening date. On the other hand, if the speaker has been preceded by another, he should not forget that his hearers may be still weighing the preceding speech and the class's discussion and criticism of it. As the new speaker steps to the platform his hearers' attention is not on the ideas of his speech; their interest is elsewhere. If he recognizes this inevitable aspect of the classroom audience in choosing his subject, he will want to pick a subject that he can readily associate with their interests, one that is so interesting it can drive out competing ideas.

The second aspect of the classroom situation that beginning speakers often fail to face squarely is that the class itself—the audience—is a real, flesh-and-blood group that can be interested in what a speaker has to say, as well as in how he says it. True it is that in a public speaking class students have the impression that practice in speaking is the main thing, and the audience merely furnishes a chance for practice, and that the set-up, in short, is an artificial learning situation. Although circumstances are somewhat artificial, the speaker should not make the situation even more artificial. For example, it is a mistake to suppose that by imagining your class to be the Young Men's Business Club and selecting a subject appropriate to that group you can make your speech more genuine. The speaker who fancies the class members to be something other than they really are virtually ignores his listeners. They quickly realize the neglect and rightly conclude that if they are to be interested at all they must be concerned with skill, technique, and presentation. If in selecting a subject a student sidesteps his audience in the classroom, he cannot expect to secure attention for his ideas. Classroom audiences often become interested in what is said. After all, both students and instructors are human beings to be dealt with as an audience or as a series of audiences. We have our interests, our feelings, our experiences, our enthusiasms, our share of ignorance, our prejudices, and our wrong ideas. We can stay awake or go to sleep. We can be interested or bored. Our ignorance can be removed, our opinions changed. And we are probably as sympathetic an audience as a speaker will ever address. The good student speaker will speak in his own person to us in our own persons. Our natures are various enough so that his problems will be sufficiently real as long as he stays with us. "Interest *us*, inform *us*, persuade *us*," we say. "Never try just to make a speech; it can't be done." The student speaker should consider his audience in the classroom as he would anywhere else.

Influence of time limit on subject and purpose

In the occasion and circumstances of any speech, the time allotted to the speaker must greatly influence the choice of specific subject and purpose. The time factor is especially important in the short speech. Once the proper subject is chosen, the problem becomes how to limit and restrict it so as to leave a single impression with the audience.

A *personage*, asked to speak before the East End Kiwanis Club or the students of Central High School because they want to hear him, regardless of what he speaks about, has the whole responsibility of choosing the subject —both the general subject, "Education," for example, and the particular delimitation of that subject, for instance, courses in safety on the highway. An authority on South America, asked to speak before the St. Andrew's Men's Club but not given a subject, will, no doubt, choose to speak on South America; but he will have to decide what limited aspect of the subject to explore in his twenty-minute speech. Perhaps he will choose some new evidences of the success or lack of success of the Alliance for Progress in Brazil, as most proper for audience, occasion, and time available. Even if one is asked to speak to the chapter of Sigma Beta on the founders of the fraternity, he still has the problem of defining just what part of that subject he will try to cover. Whenever anyone speaks, unless he is merely delivering a canned speech written and arranged for by someone else (as sometimes happens in political campaigns), he will have the problem, if not of choosing the general subject, at least of defining it—often both.

Delimiting the general subject into a specific subject of such size and simplicity that it can be handled fully enough in the time available is not always easy, but it must be done in order to avoid the skimming speech, the speech of too-little-about-too-much. Where the alternative lies between listing in five to seven minutes as many as possible of the proposals for handling traffic in the rush-hours and presenting with interesting and informative fullness the plans of one or two organizations, the speaker should choose, for example, to discuss what the citizens' committee has proposed. It is what the audience remembers that matters, not what the speaker thinks he has presented; and listening audiences, even more than reading audiences, remember a few ideas that have been vividly and fully amplified, whereas they retain almost nothing from a large collection of undeveloped statements—a rapid sequence of pellets of information or ideas.

No speaker, for example, no matter how "full of his subject" he may be, can say anything adequate on all the phases of television, in from five to ten minutes. He must, therefore, select some unified phase or segment of the subject which will meet the knowledge and interests of his particular audience and limit himself to that. Instead of casually dipping into the subject of bullfighting for five minutes, he might better explain fully some of the terms used in describing bullfights; or instead of trying to present hurriedly all the reasons why shippers should prefer railroads to trucks, he might well concentrate on the one or two reasons that will touch his present audience most closely.

In deciding how to limit his ideas and supporting material, the speaker might construct a potential test of the knowledge or behavior which he would expect from his audience as a result of the speech. If his objective were to impart an understanding of flower arranging, for example, he might expect his listeners to answer correctly a question concerning the proper balance of heights of flowers. To answer any question, the listener must have received the information in a form interesting enough to listen to and clear enough to understand. Formulating such a test will help the speaker focus on the essential aspects of his topic—the ones that he hopes the audience will retain.

Limiting the subject must be a process of *cutting down,* not *thinning out.* Strange as the advice may seem, experience shows that most student speakers need to say *more about less,* not less about more. They need to say *enough about something* rather than too little about everything.

Since the mistake most often made by speakers in settling upon specific subjects is saying too little about too much, we shall suggest two helpful expedients in choosing a limited view of a subject and of making a single impression upon hearers. We shall assume a brief speech is from four to seven minutes. We shall assume, too, that the audience is interested in collective bargaining and that it has a good deal of information about it.

1. *Determining and phrasing concisely the specific purpose will often limit the subject satisfactorily.* Is the audience to be firm in its support of collective bargaining? But for whom? Public employees? A particular class of public employees such as firemen? Or teachers? Or policemen, if the right to strike is not included? In particular kinds of situations? The speaker should phrase his specific purpose accordingly: To show that people are right to support collective bargaining for industrial workers; or to show that it is right to exclude domestic help from collective bargaining. To state the purpose in a general way is not enough: "To explain why collective bargaining exists"; "to argue against collective bargaining"—these are far too broad in scope, even for a ten-minute speech.

2. In developing the ideas that will accomplish the purpose, it would be well to *plan to use at least two one-minute illustrations.* If there isn't time for two detailed illustrations, the purpose and subject are probably still too broad to make a single vivid impression on the hearers.

Appropriateness to the Speaker

In looking for a subject that arises out of the occasion and is also fitting for him, a sensible speaker will consider his own immediate resources:

His life and experience.
His vocation, business, or profession.
The work of persons he knows.
Information he has gained from reading, watching television, listening to public speeches.
His reactions to movies, plays, exhibitions, sporting events.
The current affairs, events, and problems of his locality, his city, his state, his nation, and the world.

Knowledge and experience

The notion is much too common (much more prevalent in public speaking classes than in ordinary social intercourse) that nothing that one knows, believes, wants, or has done can be of interest to other people. We all, to be sure, have many of the same experiences and the same thoughts. We also have many of the same interests, and we often enjoy nothing more than proving to each other that we have common experiences. Witness any gathering where people talk about their ailments and operations. One's own mind and one's own experience are the first good sources of subjects; and no subject is really good until, in the broadest sense, it has become one's own. One doesn't have to be a real estate operator or a builder, to have just gone through the experience of buying property and building a house. The information gathered and the problems faced are full and fresh in the speaker's mind and will prove interesting to his audience, whose experiences and information are at best scantier and more remote than his. What an individual knows more about, what he understands more fully, what he has thought through more completely than most people—therein lie subjects for speeches. If he doesn't know enough, though he knows more than most people, he can learn more.

Taking note of conversations should prove lucrative in finding subjects for speeches. What do we and our friends talk about? What questions do we ask? What do other people talk and ask about? Answers to these questions give fairly good notions of what people are interested in and curious about.

Occupation and profession

Everyone is to some extent a specialist. He knows his own job more intimately than other people know it, and he is better acquainted with the jobs that go on about him—in his shop, in his department, in his plant, in his industry, in his neighborhood, or in his home town—than are strangers. We all, of course, know a little something about the work of a secretary, a bookkeeper, a file clerk, a salesman, a crane operator, a head usher, a filling-station attendant; and if a speaker tells us, in general terms, only what everyone knows, he will not interest us. If, however, from his own concrete experience, he distinguishes his job as a secretary to the vice-president of the Chow-Chow Mills, or as file clerk in the U.S. Inspector's Office from other such jobs, we will be interested. What does it take to be editor of the campus newspaper, manager of the basketball team, server of hot foods in the cafeteria, assistant telephone operator, laboratory assistant in zoology? What does one do? What does one have to know?

Reading and listening habits

Let the speaker searching for a subject ask: "Have I read a book, an article, a piece in the paper lately which seemed informative, interesting, provocative of ideas? Have I thus run across a fresher or newer or better outlook on something that stirs my interest anew? Perhaps it is worth explanation or interpretation. Perhaps I can recommend that my hearers read it." Of course the speaker's job will be to explain the book or article to the audience, not merely to indicate that he has read it; to show his audience that they will enjoy the book, not merely to tell them so. This means the use of much vivid, specific detail.

"What have I heard on the radio or television that provoked ideas or gave me interesting or valuable information my audience may have missed?" If a speaker listens for subjects he will find many possibilities.

Selecting the Subject

Courses of study

For students in school or college, reading and listening are likely to be largely connected with courses of study, from which may come many good subjects for classroom speeches.

As we have suggested in Chapter 3, the aspects of ideas that people find attractive and interesting are the new, the familiar, and the systematic. Consider the student who explained what a chemical solution is. He drew his subject from his chemistry course in quantitative analysis. One-third of his listeners were taking the same course with the same instructor, yet the speaker did not bore them; nor did he speak over the heads of the rest of his audience. All found the speech intensely interesting. Why? Because he was wise enough (1) to take a subject that everyone knew something about and was to a greater or lesser degree familiar; (2) to amplify the information he had heard in class and had read in the textbook by consulting other books on the nature of chemical solutions and by asking his instructor for further information on one matter that was not clear to him, thus gaining and presenting information that was new to his audience; and (3) to present the results of his thinking so clearly and systematically that the order and structure of his ideas made listening easy and pleasant.

What this student speaker did, others can do—if they have the wisdom, the imagination, and the energy to add new information to the old, to find a new "slant," or point of view, and to work over their ideas until they can deliver them clearly. There are great potentialities for subjects in courses in science, the social sciences, English literature and language, engineering, law, and medicine. One of the most practical steps to take toward finding subjects is to thumb through notes and textbooks, with these quesions in mind: What topics need further clarification and illustration? Which ones may be especially interesting and timely? Perhaps this is a neat formula for a short speech: Add new information to old, include new illustrations for old information, and present everything so clearly that it cannot be misunderstood.

Current affairs

Current affairs constitutes a source of subjects for speeches that is most often, and rightly, turned to by students of public speaking. The dangers are, however, that students will turn to it too exclusively and will conceive of it too generally. There are many small subjects as well as large ones in these areas. It is not necessary to discuss a public question in all its aspects in order to speak on it. One does not have to tackle the whole subject of open housing in order to discuss profitably the joint use of municipal recreational facilities. Nor does one need to be a national authority on state governments in order to make himself well enough informed on the legislative article of the proposed new state constitution to talk profitably upon it to a general audience.

People are often poorly informed on current affairs and problems, except those few that strike them immediately, personally, and deeply. We all, however, are eager to be told. Otherwise there would be far fewer analysts and commentators on radio and TV, and in the press. Any speaker who will inform himself with reasonable thoroughness on a public question, or even on any phase of such a question, will have several good subjects for speeches. People with technical specialties, too, may find subjects adapted to their special knowledge in current events. For example, one engineering student noticed in the newspaper the account of the collapse of a new Mississippi river bridge in a high wind. The event prompted him to look into the history of similar accidents, and his investigations resulted in a very good speech on the current collapse, others like it, and the probable cause.

Current problems and questions are often only the immediate versions of problems and questions that are always with us, the discussion of which is always pertinent and potentially interesting. Religion, love and marriage, divorce, health, education, taxation, war and peace, race relations, good government—all these are subjects that are unlikely to be exhausted for many years to come. Though they are old subjects, phases of them may be made new by a speaker who will restate them in a new way, give them fresh illustration, adapt them to current conditions.

The Speaker as Learner. Many students have made excellent speeches simply by following up subjects about which they were curious and wanted to learn more. Engineering students frequently find that their public speaking class provides them with the opportunity, which their full schedules would not otherwise permit, of reading (for credit!) materials outside their field. They often pick subjects on which they have little knowledge but a lot of curiosity. Two years ago a young woman won a universitywide speech contest, speaking on the plight of the ignored American Indian. Her curiosity had first been piqued by a plane conversation with a lawyer who represented an Indian reservation. Later she made her speech class the occasion for informing herself fully. She specialized in the subject and made one of the best speeches in the class.

Appropriateness to the Audience

What are audiences interested in? First, more often than not, they can be interested in what others know about and are interested in. Especially is this true of the classroom audience, and many of these possibilities we have pointed to already.

Second, they are interested in what all human beings are fundamentally interested in. They are attracted by new light on what is already familiar to them, that is, "news"—news about the current campus notable or some public figure; about the latest thing in airplanes, automobilies, medical techniques, engineering procedures, clothing styles, accident insurance, computers. Or, the old and familiar presented in a new and unusual way. Or, a fresh point of view or a new interpretation. Not only do new facts and data claim attention; new ways of looking at the established, familiar facts also are often effective. Detective stories almost always illustrate this truth. The facts are put before the District Attorney, the slow-witted police sergeant, the sharp detective, and the reader, and each supplies his own interpretation. Each interpretation usually produces a different murderer, and each is interesting, although eventually there is but one correct solution.

Third, people are interested in familiar ideas and facts presented systematically and clearly. We often enjoy seeing familiar facts brought together and given structure and continuity, so that we recognize the whole and its parts all in neat order. A student might discover, for example, that after the class had read this chapter he could hold their interest on the topic "How to Find Speech Subjects" if he did nothing more than to present an orderly concise review.

Subjects too difficult for oral presentation

Though many more kinds of subjects are available than some student speakers realize, it is true that certain subjects are unadaptable to successful oral presentation, and still others require the use of facilities usually not available to a speaker. In one phase of the instruction intended to improve the effectiveness of employees in an industrial plant, the leader of a group of foremen first described fully and carefully how to tie the fire underwriters' knot. He then asked members of the audience to tie the knot—but no one could. Next he explained and demonstrated, but still no one could tie the knot. Until he guided an individual several times through the actual performance, the instruction proved ineffective. Here was a subject unadapted to effective oral presentation. The audience learned from the speaker's words that there was a knot to be tied. He might also successfully have informed them of the uses of the knot, and possibly why the knot was better than others for certain purposes. He could not make them understand the knot itself.

Subjects of the following kinds are likely to be very difficult or impossible for unaided oral presentation:

> Subtle or complicated processes, the explanation of which requires the accurate visualization by the listener of a long series of actions and the correct remembering of them.
>
> Technical subjects requiring the mastery of specialized concepts and vocabulary, and the pursuit of close reasoning which demands reviewing and slow working out through study. Many papers read at scientific and learned gatherings, even before specialists, result only in the audience's realizing that some investigation has been done and some conclusions reached by the speaker, the account of which it will be necessary to read over and study carefully later on.
>
> Subjects requiring the detailed understanding of large quantities of figures and statistics. (If, of course, only the conclusions and the fact that statistics have been used to derive the conclusions are important, then these subjects are quite usable.)
>
> Subjects which involve the discussion of intimate or personal material which people would read alone without embarrassment or discomfort, but which they would be reluctant to listen to in a group.

The value of a good subject

A speaker who is satisfied with his subject, whether in the classroom or elsewhere, enjoys important initial advantages. A good subject is especially advantageous to a learning speaker, for it livens both his desire to do business with his audience and his manner of presentation.

When a speaker senses that his subject fits the occasion, the audience, and himself—is important for his audience and for him—his delivery benefits markedly. A good subject sharpens the speaker's sense of immediacy and enhances his sense of direct communication with his audience. If the subject really fits the audience and matters to the speaker, and if he thinks that he knows more about it than the audience does, or that he has a new slant on it, he will be eager to address his listeners. Both his voice and manner will reveal those intangible clues that indicate to an audience "This speaker has real business with us." The speaker's voice inflection has greater variety, greater force and energy, and directly commands attention. Words come more easily, and his rate of utterance shows greater flexibility.

The speaker who likes his subject invariably puts the stamp of his own personality on his speech. Although he may have picked up ideas from a number of sources, *he* reacts to them in *his* own way; he turns them to *his* use and for *his* purposes; he combines them in *his* manner and gives them *his* emphasis and *his* own peculiar coloring. As a result, his speech is a new combination of ideas, a compound that bears the impress of his own judgment, imagination, and personality. It becomes a speech that only *he* can produce. Although his speech may reflect in part old and familiar notions, it is a new, *individual* product.

Important as a good subject is, one word of caution is in order. Searching or waiting for the perfect subject is a waste of time. There is no such thing. If the student speaker can persuade himself that what he values his fellow students ought also to value, if he understands his subject and attempts to make his audience understand or accept it, he will go a long way toward making a good speech.

To conclude: Good subjects for speeches arise from the occasions and factors that create speeches, and from a sense of what speakers and audiences consider as significant, worthwhile, and valuable to communicate. The intrinsic worth of a subject may be less important than what the speaker does with it—what he makes of it for his classroom audience. An adequate subject chosen early is much better than an excellent subject chosen too late to be developed well.

6
Finding and Handling Materials

When a speaker has chosen his subject, or at least has a possible subject in mind, he can proceed to work efficiently. Conscious of his subject and beginning to live with it, he finds it attracting ideas from many sources and often at unexpected times. Awareness of one's subject seems to prime one's brain, put one on the alert, and sharpen one's perceptions.

What is a speaker looking for? He wants to find two kinds of materials: (1) reliable facts, and (2) authoritative interpretations and opinions. These constitute the basic material for both informative and persuasive discourse. Sometimes these spring readily out of the memory and experience of the speaker; more often they have to be searched for.

Kinds of Materials

Facts

In the communicative situation, facts consist of verifiable data that are held to be true independent of the speaker's use of them. Such data are reported directly to us by our sensory apparatus; hence they may be thought of as perceptions, bits of experience, or events and happenings. When these data appear in informative communications, they can well be called *information.* When they occur in persuasive communications and in arguments, they are properly thought of as *evidence.*

The difference between fact and interpretation can be illustrated in this way. Suppose some persons are playing bridge when they hear a piercing scream in the street. They rush to the window and behold a woman yelling in the road, a car passing by, a man running in one direction, and a dog running in another direction. These events are facts observed by each person. Now suppose one observer says, "The man hit her"; another, "The car hit her"; another, "The dog bit her." These statements are interpretations of the data by three different persons. Suppose it becomes important to decide which interpretation is to be accepted. Each statement, each interpretation, becomes doubtful. A doubtful statement is known technically as an opinion. In looking for information, then, facts should not be confused with interpretations, nor interpretations with opinions.

The first type of fact is the single, isolated fact or event, historical or present. The X Corporation will spend a quarter of a billion dollars on new machinery in 1960. James's grade last semester in History 777 was "B." Franklin was present at the Constitutional Convention in Philadelphia in 1787.

The second kind of fact is statistical data. We need to recognize simply that one function of statistics is classification of a number of facts for whatever purpose the investigator has in mind. The Acting Director of the University Honors Program was interested in knowing how well the James Scholars, academically superior high school students, had performed in the University. These bright students had been grouped according to their rank in their high school class and according to their achievement in the honors program. In the speech printed on page 488, Professor Dora E. Damrin reported:

> In 1959 we admitted 137 students [into the James Scholar Program]. This group had a mean high school rank of 93.8. By the end of their freshman year 36 percent—or one out of every three students—had been dropped. Last year, September 1963, we admitted 289 students. The mean high school rank for this group hit an all-time high of 94.7. By the end of their freshman year 49 percent—or one out of every *two* students—had been dropped.

In newspapers and magazines we always encounter statistics. To get some idea of the many ways data are classified statistically, inspect *Information Please Almanac* and the *Statistical Abstract of the United States.* (See these and other bibliographic resources in Appendix A.)

A third kind of fact is represented by scientific laws and principles. Like statistics, they are ways of describing and classifying a large number of single related events. From our knowledge of elementary economics, we have all learned that in a free market the greater the supply of a commodity, the lower the price; in other words, the more oranges, the lower their price. This is the old law of supply and demand. From our first encounter with electrical phenomena, we learned that like charges of electricity repel, unlike attract, and electricity flows from the negative pole to the positive pole; and from psychology we know that every stimulus has its response, every response its stimulus. Indeed, all our sciences and disciplines have established principles and laws. They may be considered general statements of fact, because they describe the behavior of many individual events under conditions of controlled observation. The events have been noted and verified time and again. Hence, the principle derived from the events is considered to be verified, to be true, until someone makes an observation which calls it in question. Our textbooks on any subject contain scores of up-to-date examples of such principles and laws.

Opinions

In making their explanations and enforcing their arguments, speakers, like all of us, often have to rely on the opinion of others. This is certainly the case when facts are unobtainable. We seek and trust opinions in which we have little doubt and considerable confidence. We tend to honor the opinions of scientists and technologists on technical matters. The courts of law make much of "expert" opinion and testimony. We may find ourselves believing that fraternity hazing often results in physical injury because a dean of students says that bones have been broken at his university. He should know, and unless we have other grounds of belief or disbelief, his statement carries weight.

Reliability and trustworthiness of facts and opinions

In gathering materials, a speaker must, of course, evaluate what he reads and hears, for other facts, evidence, and opinion are checks on the reliability and trustworthiness of his sources.

Are the Sources of Evidence Reliable? Who observed the fact or compiled the statistics? Is there any reason to suspect that the observer was influenced by more than ordinary bias? The facts about lung cancer and cigarette smoking are many and various. One puts more trust in those coming from an independent laboratory than in those originating in the laboratory of a tobacco company.

The reliability of authoritative opinion must be weighed with special care. Is the person expressing the opinion in a special position to know the facts from which his opinion is derived? A dean of students is presumably in a position to know about hazing practices and their results. But would he be as acceptable an authority on hazing in other universities as some national agency that had compiled information on the hazing practices of all fraternities?

Furthermore, does the person expressing the opinion have a reputation for good judgment, that is, for making conservative and valid inferences from the facts that are behind his opinions? Is he free of prejudice? A practical way of deciding these questions is to discover whether the authority enjoys the respect and confidence of others who know of him and his work. Has the book from which the speaker has drawn the opinion been favorably received by those who can pass upon its worth? (A convenient source of evaluation is the *Book Review Digest,* where many reviews of recent books are brought together.)

Finally, does the opinion run counter to the author's natural interest and bias? If so, it can be given great weight. When Wendell Willkie, a Republican campaigning for the presidency against Franklin Roosevelt, a Democrat, publicly endorsed Roosevelt's foreign policy and his treatment of the war, the endorsement was especially significant because it was contrary to Mr. Willkie's interests to express an opinion that would help the Democrats and which they would use as a campaign argument.

Is the Evidence Sufficiently Inclusive in Scope? Are there other witnesses to the same fact, and do they make the same report? Agreement among a number of witnesses is an excellent check on accuracy. The single evidential fact seldom carries much weight. The law usually insists on more than one witness to a fact.

If a speaker relies on the opinions and judgments of others, he must be sure that a number of authorities hold similar opinions on the same matter. This gives a check on the *consistency* of opinion, as well as on its scope.

If the evidence is statistical, what do the statistics really mean? Does the observer or reporter indicate for what purpose they were gathered? Does he state the method of investigation used? Do the statistics cover a large number of cases? If statistics are valuable in influencing his and other persons' decisions, the speaker should be able to explain the data clearly in his speech.

Is the Evidence Recent? In using the opinions of authorities, the speaker should become date-conscious and should prefer the reliable opinion that is most up-to-date. Authorities, like any of us, do change their minds. And the speaker should check whether the witness who is reporting an event cites a specific date.

If one can find it, evidence may be used to support almost any statement. In truth, most of our arguments find their sources in facts and opinions. We discover an argument in the first place when some experience, condition, or opinion is interpreted. One person will see the significance of grades in one way, another in another way. When the meanings clash, argument is created. In this way argument springs from evidential fact and opinion. It leads us *away* from evidence into the methodical and systematic exploration of its controversial significance. If argument becomes idle and futile, it is in part because its basis—facts, evidence, and opinions—has been lost.

Exploring for Materials

Anyone who wants to prepare speeches efficiently should write down ideas the moment he gets them. If he merely resolves to record the idea later, or tells himself he couldn't possibly forget *that,* the chances are that he will not have the idea when he wants it.

Economy of effort in speech preparation is the result of working methodically. Because no two minds work exactly alike, there is, of course, no single method of working that is equally effective for everyone. And because there is no rigid universal formula, the young speaker in particular should develop a profitable method of his own. His good sense should tell him to avoid aimless and frantic activity, which is sheer wastefulness.

An awareness of the following general conditions that underlie creative activity should help the student speaker to work out his own procedures for creating a speech that is characteristically his and nobody else's.

Much out of much

The mind is like a storehouse. If much is in it, much can come out; if little is in it, little can come out. Ten items of information can be grouped in thousands of different ways; three items can be grouped in only six. "Inspiration" seems to be directly proportional to the abundance of one's information and to the extent and depth of one's experience. The preparation of a speech is basically a matter of rapidly increasing one's materials on a subject —of working them over and stirring them around until a satisfying product is produced.

Like attracts like

Unlike the elementary law of electricity that like charges repel each other, an idea supported by a motive attracts similar ideas and repels dissimilar ones. We see what we want to see and do not see what we do not want to see—unless someone forces us to. To stack the cards intelligently in his favor, the speaker should keep subject and motive in the forefront of his consciousness. Then, without deliberate effort, he will find himself picking up related ideas out of his past experience and his current studies and conversation with others.

Listening and talking

Listening and talking, together with observation and investigation, are the most direct methods of extending knowledge and experience about one's subject. We may find some ideas and information through casual conversation and discussion with our friends; but we cannot depend solely upon casual contacts. It is profitable to seek talk with others on the subject, to plan interviews with informed persons, and to steer the conversation in the right direction. Especially in college circles can we find such persons—both students and instructors. The great virtue of conversation is that it not only tells us what we do not know and what we need to verify and clarify but it also strengthens and intensifies what we do know and gives us practice in talking about it. Furthermore, the questions other people ask, as well as the information they disclose, tell us what they do not know and would find interesting. So conversation provides clues that may reveal the state of information and interest of an audience. Political speakers know this, and when they go into a strange community for a speech, they like to talk first with the local newspapermen.

Observing and investigating

If his subject makes it possible, the speaker should look as well as discuss. If he were speaking on the functions or the problems of the local school board, he could well observe a session of the board. If he were condemning the tactics of the justices of the peace, he could easily go look at the local justice in action.

The special boon of observation is that it makes experience vivid and intense. Because it registers sharp impressions, it lengthens memory—and it yields firsthand examples for speeches.

Reading

Conversation, observation, and direct investigation are the preferred ways of knowing what one is talking about, but for most speakers at most times, these methods are extremely limited and uneconomical. Students especially do not have the time and opportunity to travel, and being young they have limited experience. So reading remains the fastest and most practicable avenue for the extension of their knowledge.

The student can read up on a speech subject efficiently if he will distinguish between focus and perspective. Remembering that the focus is the specific subject, the student can go directly to the relevant source materials in the library or elsewhere. Indeed, he may have acquired a number of foci for his subject—through conversation and in other ways—that he needs to extend or verify. At any rate, he can read as a hound hunts, with nose on the trail.

Gaining the perspective on a subject entails reading not only on the subject but around it. The more we can learn about the history and background of the subject, the better. Any special subject is closely related to more general ones. For example, if he plans to talk on the best method of reviewing for examinations, a student would soon be led to the principles of learning and memory. He should be especially sure to read anything on his subject that his audience is very likely to have read or to know about. Otherwise the listeners may well react "Doesn't he know we know so-and-so and are thinking about this-and-that?" Finally, in working on a controversial subject, it is best not to take sides firmly until after one has read widely and considered fairly the best arguments on all sides. The speaker in controversy needs as much perspective as possible.

How much reading? No one can say for sure. But a few trusted rules of thumb may help to decide. In general, read as much as time will permit—and then a little more. The extra article adds to confidence. For an informative speech, reading should be extensive enough to enable the speaker to answer a relevant question from anyone in the audience. For a persuasive speech, we can be reasonably sure we have not missed the important arguments if we read until the arguments begin being repeated.

Read Critically. The person who is determined to disbelieve everything he reads is usually as badly off as the person who swallows everything whole. One should read to learn and to understand, or as Bacon said, "to weigh and consider," not to approve or disapprove. The speaker should decide on approval or disapproval, if either is involved, only after he knows the subject. He should also read with skepticism about the source and authority of the material. When reading opinion and argument, and even when reading primarily informative, factual material, he should determine, if possible, who wrote it and why it was written, being careful, also, to notice when and where it was published. Who a writer is, what his basic beliefs and assumptions are, and the purpose for which he is presenting his explanation or his argument may tell much about the value of the material for present purposes. One can learn a good deal about an author by consulting the sources of biographical information listed in Appendix A.

Read Accurately. Enough misunderstanding, misinformation, and misrepresentation are everywhere already. A careful investigator and an accurate communicator guards against creating more. He understands not only what the source says but what it means. One's first reading of a book or article may be swift to get the general drift. But thereafter one should read only as fast as he can with understanding. Moreover, it is essential to consider statements, ideas, and information in the contexts in which they occur. A statement often means one thing in its context and something different when it stands alone.

Finding Information in Print

The library is to the speechmaker what the laboratory is to the scientist. It is the speaker's place of search and research. A full discussion of sources for reading material is ordinarily found in any good book on composition and rhetoric. Furthermore, the reference librarians in any school or public library will gladly introduce a student to the many guides to reading matter. For the convenience of the student whose memory needs jogging, Appendix A includes a brief mention of some of the most important bibliographical aids.

To save time in searching for material in print, the student should first consult the experts and specialists available to him. If he wants a modern biologist's view on evolution, for example, he may ask a teacher of biology to recommend a book or article. The instructor will be delighted to have him show interest. If the speaker has had a college course related to his subject, he should consult his notes and reference lists. Then when he enters the library he can look directly for the material. The student can resort to the sources mentioned in Appendix A to amplify his information.

Taking Notes

Perhaps workable techniques of note taking are as numerous as readers. Yet in developing his own methods, a student should be aware of the standard timesavers and conventions.

Index cards, 3″ x 5″ or 4″ x 6″, or half-sheets of paper are better than full pages for taking notes. Cards and half-sheets are faster to handle and sort when one gets to the stage of grouping one's ideas.

In general it is best to restrict each card to a single idea or topic, whether the idea be general or highly specific. A card could well contain but a single fact or a single example with its appropriate head. Card 2 cites a single object having many meanings. Other cards might have as their headings other objects and might list their meanings. The heading of Card 1 points out two ideas, but they are so closely related that the note-taker put them together.

When one starts reading, often he does not know what specific ideas, facts, examples, or quotations he will eventually use in his speech. He obtains likely looking books and articles and explores them. He proceeds wisely to summarize, as briefly as he can, each article, book, or important section thereof, on a single card. Card 3 is an example of such a summary. In shaping the ideas of his speech at a later date, he may suddenly realize that a certain book is relevant. He can then use its card to recall its content and whether it contained usable facts and illustrations. A summary card, then, guides one back to a source and to pointed research for special items. Summary cards are valuable in another way. Reviewing several cards together may suggest to the speaker the central idea of the speech or some of its leading ideas.

Card 4 refers to an author, or an authority note. The speaker records only the information he needs to identify the person for his audience and to show the author's connection with his subject. The words in parentheses may reflect the speaker's idea of a possible main head or topic within his speech. If so,

Note Cards

Extent and Effectiveness of Strikes (foreign countries)

On April 1, 1958, a 24-hour strike in France involved 1 million public workers.

"Transportation was brought to a virtual standstill throughout the country. . . ."

The World Almanac (1959) and Book of Facts, p. 99.

CARD 1

Meanings of *cross*

Objects, like words, carry meanings. For example: *cross.*

Says Suzanne Langer: It is "the actual instrument of Christ's death, hence a symbol of suffering; first laid on his shoulders, an actual burden, as well as an actual product of human handicraft, and on both grounds a symbol of his accepted moral burden; also an ancient symbol of the four zodiac points, with a cosmic connotation; a 'natural' symbol of cross roads (we still use it on our highways as a warning before an intersection), and therefore of decision, crisis, choice; also of *being crossed,* i.e., of frustration, adversity, fate; and finally, to the artistic eye a cross is the figure of a man. All these and many other meanings lie dormant in that simple, familiar, significant shape."

Philosophy in a New Key (Baltimore, Pelican Books, 1948), p. 231.

CARD 2

"Reason and Morality," by Kai Nielsen. *Journal of Higher Education,* XXVIII (May 1957), 265–275.

Theme: Morality is a kind of activity that regulates our desires and interests and guides us to rational choices among them.

1. It helps one to realize his individual desires when to do so does not hurt others.
2. It is the exercise of practical wisdom in human conduct; it involves right and wrong choices in particular cases.
3. It is not scientific knowledge, for this gives us information about what *is* and does not tell us what we *ought* to do.
4. Science, by supplying knowledge about nature and about ourselves, can help us make choices and justify them.
5. Choice is not an arbitrary or capricious decision; it is rational and can help reduce or avoid frustrations.

CARD 3

Fermi, Laura C. (Peaceful Uses of the Atom)

Wife of Dr. Enrico Fermi, winner of Nobel Prize in Physics for 1938 and University of Chicago professor before his death. Mrs. Fermi was familiar with her husband's work on uranium, as shown in her *Atoms in the Family,* 1954.

Appointed by the U.S. Atomic Energy Commission to attend the International Conference on the Peaceful Uses of the Atom, Geneva, 1955. Her book, *Atoms for the World,* records her impressions of the Conference. The New York *Herald Tribune* said of the book: It "combines domestic detail with a careful presentation of the problems . . . we must face as a result of the opening up of a vast new field of energy."

Current Biography (1958).

Card 4

another card, or cards, would bear the same heading, "Peaceful Uses of the Atom," and would record appropriate ideas, materials, and examples.

Reference cards should always show the source, the date, and the page of the material—accurately. To have to go back for these facts is a woeful, but very common, waste of time.

How many note cards? A good rule is, many more than at the moment seem necessary. Later on in building the speech, it is a lot easier to eliminate superfluous cards than to make additional trips to the library for further reading. It is comfortable and efficient to have too much material at hand rather than too little.

Handling Materials

Possibly after beginning to think over the subject and beginning to collect information, and certainly after completing the reading and note-taking, a speaker needs time to contemplate what he has been putting into his mind. So an efficient and productive workman begins his speech preparation early and spaces it at planned intervals. In these intervals he thinks consciously about his subject, reads, takes notes, converses, reviews his materials, groups and classifies his ideas, adjusts his subject to meet the time limits of his speech, and anticipates the actual building of the outline. These are his moments and hours of deliberate thinking. But much of our most productive, creative thinking goes on subconsciously between periods of deliberation. Our minds cook, stew, boil, and mix the ingredients of our experience when we are entirely unaware of the process. Psychologists sometimes refer to the process as the "incubation" period of thought, and out of it springs the unexpectedly bright idea whose appearance seems so mysterious and inexplicable. In his preparation, an intelligent speaker provides intervals of incubation periods between his periods of deliberate thought and effort. He "rests," and when the bright idea flashes out, he jots it down to consider later. So a speaker should schedule periods of preparation, lay them out methodically to give his mind a chance. He should try being a philosopher in the sense of the German boardinghouse keeper's definition, "A philosopher is a man who thinks and thinks and thinks, and when he gets tired of thinking, he thinks over what he has thought." After some intervals of deliberation and incubation, it is time to build the outline.

Originality

We have described briefly how the speaker saturates himself with a subject —by conversing about it, investigating it directly when possible, reading up on it, and assimilating it into his system during intervals of deliberation and incubation. The speaker who goes through such an experience will create an original speech, though he probably will not be the first person in the world to have spoken or written on the specific subject. He will produce an original speech because, first, his product will differ from any one of his sources. It will be a compound formed from diverse ideas and materials. It will not be a copy of somebody else's product, nor will it be a weak imitation in the shape of a digest or summary. Second, as his peculiar reaction to the many sources of material to which he exposed himself, the speech will reveal his individuality.

Whatever is original contains elements of a new experience. Change or movement gives rise to our notions of what is new or old, for without change every experience would be old and familiar; all would be monotonous. Suppose a student of speech hears a lecture or reads an article about the frontier and plans to make a speech on that subject. Will his speech be significantly different from the lecture he heard? Will he make his speech "new" by adding materials and ideas to those of the lecture or by presenting the lecture's ideas in an appreciably different order and style? An original speech, from the speaker's point of view, is a product that differs significantly from the impulses and sources that occasioned it. The report, the summary, the digest, and the précis do not differ appreciably either in substance or in treatment from their originals; they are imperfect copies. Indeed, in making a report—an activity valuable as intellectual training—a speaker does not intend to make his product significantly different from the original; rather, he tries to adhere closely to the thought and structure of the original. The reporter merely wishes to act as transmitter of another's ideas, which he endeavors to transmit as faithfully as circumstances will allow.

An original speech reveals something of the speaker's individuality; it bears his stamp or trademark. It is the way that only he can react to the impulses that gave birth to his speech. Three persons may be asked to read a certain article, "In Defense of Politicians," and to make a speech based on it. Each of the trio will react differently to the article and will give three different speeches—different in point of view, type, and treatment of ideas. Each person will react according to his past experience and bring something different to bear on the article. Hence, an original speech differs significantly from its sources and bears the imprint of its maker's personality.

Ethics of acknowledging sources

Although a person knows his speech is original, he must not sidestep explicit acknowledgment of his sources. Reference to his sources, of course, enhances the speaker's *ethos,* his *image.* It gives the speaker personal authority and prestige with his hearers, for they infer that he has paid them the compliment of preparing carefully and that he is more widely informed than they. The speaker also has a moral obligation to acknowledge his indebtedness. A man who has exerted effort to make information available or who has expressed an idea with striking effectiveness has some right to be recognized. It is not only right but courteous to recognize a man's labor and inventiveness.

Although it is not easy to know when to acknowledge sources, the following general suggestions should be observed scrupulously. (1) A speaker should cite the source of any quotation or close paraphrase which he uses. To use the ideas and phraseology of another without acknowledgment is plagiarism —literary theft. (2) An unusual idea or an exceptional fact that has increased a speaker's knowledge or has set him thinking, or an effective and unusual expression that he knows he has derived from a definite source, he should acknowledge. He should try to cultivate some awareness of the difference between out-of-the-ordinary ideas and those that are the common stock of everyday conversation or those that he has assimilated so thoroughly that their original source is beyond his recall. Obviously one cannot pay respects to a forgotten source; and common ideas and expressions on a situation or a problem need not be acknowledged, for such materials belong to everyone.

Phrasing Acknowledgment. Without special rehearsal the speaker will find making references awkward and stiff. But with a little oral practice in referring to sources, a speaker can learn to make swift and smooth acknowledgments. Some common ways of managing references follow.

Early in the speech, in the introduction wherever convenient and relevant, refer to the principal source or sources. Then, no additional acknowledgment is necessary. For example:

> In discussing the influences that made Robert E. Lee a kind and honorable man, I have been greatly helped by Douglas S. Freeman's four volume biography of Lee, and by the same author's first volume on *Lee's Lieutenants*. Professor Wilkes suggested in history class last week that Lee's sense of honor was not derived from tradition merely. The remark set me thinking.

Work in acknowledgments wherever they can be put conveniently and logically. Usually the "spot" acknowledgment concerns a fact, a particular idea, a quotation, or a striking phrase or figure of speech.

It may precede the reference:

> Goethe expressed his advice on the acknowledgment of source materials in this way: "The most foolish error of all is made by clever young men in thinking that they forfeit their originality if they recognize a truth which has already been recognized by others."
>
> Goethe has said that "the most foolish error. . . ."
>
> According to Goethe, "the most foolish error. . . .

The reference may be dropped neatly into the middle of the quotation or the idea being expressed:

> "The most foolish error of all," said Goethe, "is made by clever young men. . . ."
>
> "This machine," so the American Match Company states in a recent pamphlet, "turns out 5,000 matches every minute."

Acknowledgment may follow the reference:

> "An idea is his who best expresses it," Bacon said.
>
> "The most foolish error . . . recognized by others." In those words Goethe expressed his conviction.

Where the trustworthiness or the recency of information is important, make the reference explicit and as complete as necessary to be accurate. For example:

> As to the proper method of pronouncing foreign place names, W. Cabell Greet, in his 1944 edition of *World Words*, says that a good rule is "to adopt the foreign pronunciation insofar as it can be rendered by customary English sounds in the phrasing and rhythm of an English sentence."

Rarely in a speech is it necessary to cite volume number and page. Nor is the popular habit of saying "quote" and "unquote" necessary or graceful. Voice and manner of speaking can usually distinguish quoted matter. If not, then plain statements are best: "I shall quote," "That is the end of the quotation."

Form of References. When a reference list is called for, it should accompany the speech outline and is usually placed at the end. The following form of arrangement, punctuation, and capitalization represents standard practice:

I. References to One's Own Experience, to Conversation, and to Lectures
   A. Briefly describe the experience:
      "My experience as a department store salesman."
   B. Briefly describe the conversation, interview, and lecture. Be as *specific* as possible:
      "Conversation with students."
      "Interview with Professor A. F. Jones."
      "Lecture notes in American history."

II. Reference to Books
   Marckwardt, A. H. *Scribner Handbook of English.* New York, 1940.
   If a book has two or more authors, treat them thus:
   Jones, R. F., and Black, J. S. . . .

III. Reference to Articles
   A. Magazine articles:
      Wilson, J. "Handling the Apostrophe," *The English Journal,* XXI (June, 1923), 187–200.
   B. For articles appearing in books:
      Hazlitt, William. "On Going on a Journey," in R. S. Loomis and D. L. Clark (eds.), *Modern English Readings.* New York, 1942, pp. 117–122.
   C. For articles appearing in general reference books:
      "Rhetoric." *Encyclopaedia Britannica.* 14th ed.; London, 1929.
      In citing any *Britannica* since 1932, it is preferable to use the date of printing; thus: "Rhetoric." *Encyclopaedia Britannica.* 1952.
   D. For citation of newspapers:
      1. For the signed article and editorial:
         Steinbeck, John. "The Attack on Salerno," *The New York Times.* September, 1, 1943, p. 32. (If the paper has numbered sections, alter the citation thus: . . . November 1, 1943, sec. 3, p. 32.)
      2. For the news article and unsigned editorial or article:
         "Moscow Conference a Great Success." *The Washington Post.* November 5, 1943, p. 1.

IV. Reference to Pamphlets Where No Person Is Cited as Author or Editor
   Colonies and Dependent Areas. Boston: World Peace Foundation, 1943.

III
Informative Speaking

7

Development of Materials in Informative Speaking

When the speaker is satisfied that he is filled with his subject, he is ready to construct his speech. He *manages* his stock of ideas; he forms and shapes them into an intelligible whole. Management consists principally in the speaker's developing ideas in keeping with the purpose of his speech. An audience's ignorance of a subject is the stimulus for an informative speech. The speaker desires to supply the knowledge the audience lacks. Because the acquisition of knowledge involves two psychological activities, perceiving and understanding, the general purposes of informative speaking are intelligibility and understanding. To perceive and to understand are to know.

An informative speech can answer three basic questions: What? How? Why? What is to be understood? What is its nature, that is, how and why did it become that way? If what is to be known is the operation or function of something, we ask: How does it behave and why does it behave as it does? This book, for instance, may be regarded as an example of informative discourse, for it presents answers to these questions: What is public speaking? How does one build a speech? Why is it thus built? Most speeches, of course, are not as long as a book. Yet they may be long enough to answer all three questions. A thirty-minute speech on the United Fund, for example, may explain what the organization is, how it functions, and why. Most classroom speeches, however, are short. Although he knows a great deal about the United Fund, a classroom speaker might wisely concentrate only on how the United Fund spends its money. But whatever the scope of the informative speech, its materials are regarded by both speaker and audience as settled and demonstrable, calling for understanding rather than belief.

Methods of Understanding

The speaker secures understanding in two basic ways: by presenting an organized whole, and by developing the statements of which the whole consists. The result is satisfactory when the listener can grasp the central idea and perceive its relationship to the parts of the speech. For the speaker organization is accomplished by building an outline. The procedure for constructing it is presented in Chapter 9. In this chapter and the next, we concentrate on means and methods of development.

Development—often called amplification in the history of rhetoric—is the process of enlarging upon a statement, or upon some part of it, in order to clarify its meaning for the hearer. For example, the hearer may find the statement strange and unclear, so that the speaker must enlarge upon it by translating it into familiar language. Or the hearer may recognize the language of the statement without being able to understand it immediately. When this is so, the speaker has to extend the statement until it registers.

A single broad principle underlies development: Understanding is secured by associating the new and the strange with the old and familiar. The speaker himself understands when he brings the new within his own experience. The audience understands when the speaker translates his understanding into the experience of his hearers.

Factual information and its use

The basic materials of communication, discussed in Chapter 6, are facts, evidence, and opinions, which the speaker finds in his own experience and observations, and in those of others. From these materials he selects those that he will find useful, even essential, in developing the statements of his outline. Not all statements in an informative speech can be developed by factual information, but whenever possible the speaker should enlarge his statements with facts. Reliable facts and authoritative opinions promote not only the listener's understanding but his respect for the speaker.

Statistical data should be presented as simply as possible without sacrificing essential accuracy. For the popular audience, round numbers are usually sufficient. Unless the difference between 974,232 and 974,251 is vital, it is better to say "over 974,000." An accountant may demand that the national debt be expressed down to the last dollar and cent, but for the layman a statement to the nearest million, or probably to the nearest billion, would be adequate. In a reference to the tolerance in a bearing in an airplane engine, an aeronautical engineer would appreciate the difference between .0016 and .0018 of an inch, but most of us would find an approximate figure of 1/500 of an inch easier to grasp and as useful as the more exact figure. Hence, unless minute accuracy is called for, the round figure is enough.

Furthermore, simplicity can be gained by a visual presentation of the statistics. In a speech where considerable data are necessary, speakers are coming more and more to use charts and graphs flashed on screens. The ear often needs the help of the eye.

In handling statistics, the speaker may make facts meaningful and vivid by bringing them within the experience of the audience. A reliable way of doing so is through comparison. To say, for example, that a class has a grade average of 80 may be true and exact, but the isolated fact gains meaning and force if the speaker adds that the average of last semester's class was 83. Also, a standard of comparison helps most persons to visualize linear and cubic dimensions. Describing a new building as 330 feet high will probably be less effective than stating, "If laid on its side, the building would be longer than a football field." Most popular writers, like Stuart Chase, who is quoted on page 166, are masters of such swift comparisons.

Accuracy in using factual materials is critically important at all times but especially when the information is common to both speaker and audience. A speaker at the University of Illinois was comparing the effects of increasing enrollments on the large university and the small college. He referred to the enrollment at Illinois as about 20,000 students. Just a week before, the student newspaper had reported the official figure as 17,780. At the conclusion of his speech, his listeners' first reaction was, "Don't you know what our enrollment really is?" Most of the audience knew the exact figure, and the error not only distracted their attention but hurt the speaker's reputation. The speaker who is at all sensitive to his audience's scope of knowledge realizes that persons do read newspapers and magazines and are more or less familiar with certain current facts. Student groups, in particular, often have in common textbooks, courses, lectures, and basic information. Such common basic facts, though they occupy but a small portion of a speech, must be presented with strict accuracy. Trusting to the audience's ignorance is dishonorable and unskillful.

Finally, whenever factual information is introduced, it is sound practice to name the source and date. If the speaker is dealing with the newest development in textile fibers, he should be up-to-date and make his listeners aware that he is. If he is treating an old and traditional subject, he should take advantage of the latest information. In explaining the ground plan of ancient Athens, he will want to know what archeologists have discovered in recent years. On most subjects for popular audience, it is sufficient to state the year or the month and year. The day of the month becomes important only when new information on a subject is published frequently. For the past year, for example, we have had a stream of news reports and articles on the presence of insecticides in foodstuffs and animals. It would then be important to know that Professor X had reported so-and-so on February 10, 1969, and that Dr. Y had found so-and-so on February 23, 1969.

Naming the source of information is highly desirable. Facts have a greater significance when the hearer is given some sense of their reliability. In a speech on the rising costs of college education, one could simply state the illustrative fact:

> At Harvard in 1937 tuition was $400; in 1967 it had risen to $2,000.

Or one could introduce the fact thus:

> The U.S. Office of Education has gathered information from colleges and universities about their tuition costs over a thirty-year period. As reported in *Time* in June, 1967, Harvard's tuition was $2,000. In 1937 it was $400.

In the latter illustration we learn the source of the fact, the date of the statistic, its scope, and for what purpose it was collected. Such items lend weight to the single fact of tuition cost. The speaker should not take easy refuge in the lame words "Statistics show. . . ." unless he is prepared, upon questioning, to tell when and by whom they were collected, and for what purpose. The informative speaker is like a scientist or a historian; he not only knows his facts but he knows whether to trust them. An audience shares the same attitude. It appreciates facts and likes to know that they are reliable.

Example

An example cannot be understood by itself. It must always be an example of something. In speechmaking (and in all discourse), the something is the statement to be developed. The example extends the meaning of the statement by supplying a particular case or circumstance:

> One function of advertising is to remind people of the product over and over again.
>
> In my town the Methodists still ring their church bell every Sunday morning.

A particular instance is thus used to exemplify a more general idea. Accordingly, the example, by definition, is a particular case, incident, or circumstance of the more general idea expressed in the statement that it amplifies.

Kinds of example. Examples are generally classified as short or long, real or invented.

The short example is the *instance,* a particular case the speaker sets forth as briefly as he can without losing the listener's understanding. If the instance is chosen so that the listener can grasp it immediately, it needs only the barest mention. Such an instance is the ringing of the church bell every Sunday.

The long example is the *illustration.* It builds up and fills out the particular case by giving it a setting and supplying narrative and descriptive details. The example thus becomes a sort of compact story or a thumbnail sketch of the circumstances. The illustration is the example *illuminated.*

The illustration is especially useful in two types of situation. In the first, it is employed in place of the instance when a speaker wants simultaneously to be vivid and to give the hearer a sense of action and reality. Bruce Barton developed the church bell example into an illustration:

> . . . a member of my profession, an advertising man, . . . was in the employ of a circus. It was his function to precede the circus into various communities, distribute tickets to the editor, put up on the barns pictures of the bearded lady and the man-eating snakes, and finally to get in touch with the proprietor of some store and persuade him to purchase the space on either side of the elephant for his advertisement in the parade.
>
> Coming one day to a crossroads town our friend found that there was only one store. The proprietor did not receive him enthusiastically. "Why should I advertise?" he demanded. "I have been here for twenty years. There isn't a man, woman, or child around these parts that doesn't know where I am and what I sell." The advertising man answered very promptly (because in our business if we hesitate we are lost), and he said to the proprietor, pointing across the street, "What is that building over there?" The proprietor answered, "That is the Methodist Episcopal Church." The advertising man said, "How long has that been there?" The proprietor said, "Oh, I don't know; seventy-five years probably." "And yet," exclaimed the advertising man, "they ring the church bell every Sunday morning."

The example offered as an instance would have taken about ten seconds; the illustration probably took about a minute and a half. Characteristic are the swift narrative setting, the dialogue which heightens the impression of a real event, the careful ordering of details to lead to the point—and the touch of humor.

In the second situation, when the content of the example is not instantly intelligible to the listener, or its information is novel and technical, the illustration is almost indispensable if the speaker is to give his listeners time to understand.

To an audience that did not know much about filibustering in the United States Senate, a classroom speaker used the illustration with telling effect. Quoting from the dictionary, he defined the filibuster as "delaying tactics employed in parliamentary debate and usually involving long speeches on topics irrelevant to the subject." He amplified immediately:

> You are all members of some organization—your literary society, your lodge, your farm club, your church, your young people's society. Now, as you know, such an organization holds a business meeting once in a while—called a deliberative meeting. If you were governed by the present Senate rules, it would be possible for any member of the organization to stand up and talk just as long as he wanted to on any motion that was brought before the house. In fact, he would not have to talk straight to the point all the time, either. He could start by making it appear that he was going to talk about a certain point involved in the motion, and then he could say or read anything he pleased. He could recite poetry, or read a novel, or give a lot of dry statistics from some

departmental report a hundred years old. He could do anything he pleased to kill time, and the rest of the members would have to let him keep right on for at least two days and perhaps much longer unless they could get two-thirds of the members together to put through a device for stopping him. Of course, you would not all have to listen to him, for you could go out and eat and sleep and do anything you pleased. But, in the meeting, that member would have the floor, and nobody could take it away from him.

Today most people hold science in high regard, and many popular speeches and articles draw some information from the results of scientific experiments. In presenting such information, the illustration is perhaps the best way of securing understanding. To present the result of an experiment only as an instance in a single sentence either baffles a listener or gives him but a glimpse of its exact meaning and significance. Hence, whenever an experiment is used as an example in a speech, it is wise to handle it as an illustration. In ordering such an illustration, the speakers will find it convenient and natural to follow a typical arrangement: (1) name of the experimenter, place of experiment, and date reported; (2) purpose of the experiment; (3) the setup and conduct of the experiment; and (4) the result, which is the point of information that he wants the listener to comprehend.

Suppose a person is talking about the kinds of emphasis useful in speechmaking and one of the statements to be amplified is, "Giving special emphasis to a point helps make it effective." He might follow up with this idea:

> For example, a statement accompanied by a gesture is better remembered than the same statement without the gesture.

Now suppose that in place of that sentence the speaker says:

> Professor Ray Ehrensberger, when he was teaching public speaking at Syracuse University, completed an experiment in 1937 on the various modes of emphasis, later publishing the results in a research journal, *Speech Monographs.* Among other things, he wanted to find out whether gestures helped or hindered the ideas they accompanied. He designed a way to find out. He constructed a short speech on a subject strange to the audience. Then six skilled speakers delivered it to twenty-one student classroom audiences, matched according to intelligence. With certain statements the speakers used gestures half of the time; the other half of the time the speakers delivered the same statements without gestures. At the end of each speech, the listeners responded to a questionnaire designed to test what they remembered. The statements with gestures were better remembered than the same statements without gestures. Ehrensberger concluded that gesture is an effective means of emphasizing an idea.[1]

[1] For a full account of this early and significant experiment on modes of emphasis in speechmaking, see "An Experimental Study of the Relative Effectiveness of Certain Forms of Emphasis in Public Speaking," *Speech Monographs,* 12 (1945), 94–111.

The illustration gives us time to appreciate the essential information. By briefly identifying the experimenter, stating his purpose simply, and swiftly telling how he worked, the speaker gets us ready to grasp the point at once. Even the bare narration of the experiment lends an air of weight and reality. For popular consumption, only the *necessary* details have been included. Omitted are the refinements of the experiment, the complete description of the experimental situation, the mass of data collected, the statistical computations, and the tests showing that the results of the experiment are not due to chance.

In handling experimental information, the most rigorous selection and the most careful ordering of ideas are imperative, if one is to avoid diffuseness, cluttering, and confusion. As in the treatment of statistics, the last decimal place is not important so long as the statement is basically accurate and so long as the speaker can provide additional details if someone asks for them.

Examples are not only short or long; they are also either real or invented. The real example is real in the sense that its content is actual. It is an event, a case, a situation that has happened. All the examples we have so far included in this section of the chapter are real.

The invented example, often called the hypothetical or fictitious example, is precisely what its name implies. Drawing upon his imagination and judgment, the speaker makes up an example. He does not relate what has happened; he offers what might have taken place. A football coach explaining the theory of the off-tackle play explained that, more than most plays, it depends upon perfect timing. Each man, he said, must do precisely the right thing at the right moment, and if he does, the play always gains yardage. The coach knew his faculty listeners could not be relied upon to remember an off-tackle play they had seen; so he did not use an actual instance. Nor did he feel he could take the time to describe such a play with a factual detailed illustration. And he had at hand no film of the play. So he amplified by saying, "Now if you were to execute the off-tackle play as it should be done, you would do . . . and . . . ." In two minutes he made his audience see a perfect play through his invented illustration. The hypothetical example, then, amplifies an idea by presenting something that might be, or might have been.

Young speakers sometimes hesitate to use fictitious examples. Their reluctance in part is well grounded, for in preparing to speak on most subjects, one can usually find examples of past events, and the historical instance or fact always has the ring of truth. Nevertheless, for purposes of amplification the invented example is superior to all others when one is trying to explain the theoretical or the ideal condition. The ideal state of affairs can have no real example; the communicator must construct one. No ideal house exists, for a particular house represents a series of adaptations to the owner's pocketbook and his idiosyncrasies of taste. Yet the architect is guided by his notions of the ideal house, just as the football coach had his idea of the perfect off-tackle play. Similarly, all of us have our ideals of conduct as compared with what we actually do. Indeed, we are guided by the ideal in every field of endeavor—in engineering, in agriculture, in the sciences, in government, in industrial production and organization, in dress design, in hotel management, and the like. The ideal is always an abstraction, and the only way a speaker can turn it into a concrete, vivid picture is through an invented illustration.

Through the invented example the speaker may give rein to his imaginative powers and he may create not only fictions nearer to perfection than actuality can provide but fictions more real, more engaging, and perhaps more amusing than actuality. The poet and the dramatist in the speaker may come out to good advantage. It never occurs to us to care whether Christ was reporting an actual case of robbery on the Jericho road when he told the illustrative story of the Good Samaritan. That tale has engaged more interest and has illustrated a point better and longer than any newspaper story ever written. Plato used myths to clarify the more difficult of his philosophical and ethical ideas. Myths are fictions which draw the reader or the listener pleasantly and surely into a grasp of the ideas. The myth of the chariot, for example, in the *Phaedrus,* illuminates Plato's idea of the struggle of spiritual love and sensual love in the soul of man. What Christ or Plato did, and what good speakers have always done, the student with a spark of inventiveness can attempt with profit.

Selection of Examples. Certain important considerations should govern the selection of examples.

Emphasis. In a speech the most important statements and points—those which would be fatal to clarity if the listener did not understand them—deserve examples. Furthermore, the speaker wants his audience to *remember* important ideas, and the illustration with its specific, vivid details is the longest-lived reminder of an idea. When minor ideas are to be exemplified, the short example—the instance—is usually preferable.

Relevance to statement. Although it is obvious that examples should be directly relevant to the statements they develop, speakers are constantly tempted to squeeze and torture an example to try to make it fit. Perhaps they have found fascinating illustrations; so they feel that they ought to use them somehow. It's worth the trouble to find an example that is relevant, or to invent one. Straining an example into a bad fit only puzzles an audience. Like the funny story dragged in by the skin of its teeth, it may be interesting, but it always distracts from the main thing.

Relevance to the listeners' experience. A number of examples so selected that they will touch the different interests and experiences of the audience are effective in developing an important idea. Examples drawn from country life will strike the imaginations of some listeners; those drawn from city life, others. Examples from mechanics and science will clarify ideas for some people; those from business and the arts will appeal to others. Very few examples will be equally effective for everyone in general audiences. There was a time when examples from the Bible were familiar to almost everyone. Today no single source of examples seems to be effective with all audiences. The wise speaker, therefore, learns as much as he can about the experience of his audience and chooses his examples to fit the main areas of its experience.

The particular, recent experience of his audience is a good source of examples. For instance, is there any connection between his subject and the highway or airplane accident nearby, a strike in a local industry, Saturday's football game, the latest murder or divorce, or the current lesson in algebra, history, or zoology?

In order to make use of immediate familiar events, the speaker should equip himself as well as he can with knowledge of current and local circumstances. To avoid serious misfiring of his references to local and immediate interests, however, he should be sure that he knows his ground thoroughly, does not arouse feelings which will operate to his disadvantage, and does not discredit himself by incorrect or incomplete knowledge of the situation. A member of the League of Woman Voters made excellent use of her knowledge of local circumstances when she explained to an audience in another city the merit system for the selection of civil servants. The city had recently suffered great and serious damage from a fire, because of the ineptitude and incompetence of the local fire chief, a political appointee untrained for his job. Without any apparent reference to local circumstances, the speaker mentioned fire and police officials among those whose jobs require special competence. The audience responded immediately and enthusiastically, and their interest in the speech at once became very keen. The speaker had associated the merit system with something that her audience was most interested in at the moment.

Infallible and comprehensive rules for the successful use of recent familiar events cannot be given, for a speaker can be given no substitute for a keen, retentive, active mind. Useful as current and local circumstances may be, the speaker must not force them into association with his ideas or distort them to his uses. They should appear to be related plausibly and naturally, or they should not be used at all.

Interest value of examples. As we have said, examples activate the laws of attention and, therefore, tend to add interest. In selecting his examples, the speaker will enhance their capacity to stimulate interest if he associates them with some of the fundamental human values. Any of the materials of development may be associated profitably with values and interests, but examples, because they are specific and concrete, are especially effective when they touch such springs of interest as sex, health, wealth, humor, personal achievement, status, and esteem.

In connection with our study of persuasion we will be concerned with the basic values and impelling motives as the springs of action. Even when no particular action other than participation in the experience of the moment is at issue, motives, goals, and values may work very effectively as sources of attention and interest. The speaker should use them for that purpose whenever appropriate.

Love, marriage, procreation, and the beautiful human form are components of the most universally interesting stories. Anything that is associated with the relations between the sexes is a perennial source of interest. A picture of a beautiful woman is often a valuable part—sometimes the only part—of advertisements intended to interest men and even women. In the London subway stations an advertiser pictured a beautiful blonde in a bathing suit climbing out of a swimming pool. To enhance the sale of a patent medicine, he sought to transfer the interest in sex aroused by the picture to his product, "Bile Beans"! A resourceful speaker will not neglect the discreet, fitting, and honest use of this source of interest in his examples.

Likewise, people's normal goals are the things that preserve life, health, and well-being, and promote wealth. That is, people have a built-in set to respond, at least initially, when such matters are brought to their attention. The speaker should, therefore, associate his examples with these goals when he can. For example, workers in a factory never listen with so much ready interest to a lecture on safety methods as they do just after one of their fellows has injured himself through careless handling of the machinery. "There's a right way and there are many wrong ways to write a check," says a speaker who is cashier in a bank. "Only last week we paid a check for ninety-three dollars against the account of one of our depositors because he had been careless in writing a check for three dollars." Here the pocketbook interest, with the added interest of the concrete example, is associated with instructions on how to write a check.

People also value things affecting their pride in achievement, and this pride may be stimulated through examples. The competitive interest in grades in school can often be converted into an interest in the subject matter of study. Again, examples touching the glories of the old Alma Mater interest loyal alumni; those that call up memories of the "old gang" interest most people; and except in times of the utmost cynicism, reminders of our affection for our country interest all of us.

The principle of the moving stimulus, of activity, should also influence the speaker's choice of examples. In the explanation of a process or a machine or a maneuver in football, tennis, or war, for example, the interesting speaker will not stop with the essential details of bare exposition. He will show his audience someone performing the process or will show an article of manufacture going through the process; in his explanation he will have the machine running, and if possible someone running it; he will describe armies or players maneuvering or men fighting battles.

We are all interested in what people are doing and saying. Whenever practicable, therefore, a speaker should associate his topic with people. To interest an audience in the technique of lip reading, for example, a speaker could hardly do better than to describe a nurse, herself stone-deaf, writing replies to the spoken questions of a child lying in a hospital bed who has just found that he has lost his hearing. This introduction of human interest brings together the imaginative appeal of the concrete example, the positive value placed upon good will, and the abiding interest of people in achievement—and attaches them all to the science of lip reading. The university photographer, wishing a picture that will interest the public in the new power-press in the mechanical engineering laboratory, poses two or three engineering students with hands on the levers and controls of the machine. He is giving a human touch to what otherwise might have been a dead, inhuman picture.

Interest in personality, like any other valuable avenue of access to people's minds and feelings, can be overworked, cheapened, and discredited by the uses to which it is put—from advertising useless facial preparations and patent medicines to exploiting the ephemeral marriages of movie beauties. The perennial, irrepressible interest of man in his fellow man, however, may be as readily directed to the worthy and the important.

Humor and the example. Humor is undeniably one of the most valuable sources of interest in examples. What we have just said about emphasis and relevance, and our advice below on appropriateness, apply with special force to the use of the humorous example.

Not everyone who can appreciate a joke has a talent for telling one, and the person who is a poor raconteur generally is not likely to shine in telling a humorous anecdote. Inexperienced debaters trying to enliven their statistics with funny stories (usually at the expense of their opponents) are often so clumsy in their narratives that they make themselves ridiculous instead of enlivening or enlightening the subject. Perhaps the infrequency of the talent for humor among politicians, rather than its impropriety in political discussion, was principally responsible for the uproar from the opposition over the wit in Adlai Stevenson's Presidential campaign speeches. The student speaker, nevertheless, should experiment with humor in his examples. Perhaps, guided by the principles of relevance, propriety, and freshness, he will cultivate a real talent.

Stories and anecdotes, of course, may be funny independently of any context in which they are told, but unless they are relevant to the speaker's ideas, the audience's interest in the stories will stop and not extend to the ideas. A speaker does not drag stories into contexts to which they have no appropriate relation unless he is so desperate for the audience's attention that he must have it whether or no; and he shouldn't say "That reminds me of a story . . ." unless there is something in what he is discussing which really should remind him of the story. The spurious relevance which speakers sometimes invent in order to avoid the trouble of finding really relevant humor is likely to be more harmful to their message than would a frank "time-out for us to be amused together."

On the matter of *propriety,* let us add a word from Cicero. Humor, he said, should not be "too frequent, lest it become buffoonery; nor . . . of a smutty nature, lest it be low farce; nor pert, lest it be impudent; nor aimed at misfortune, lest it be brutal; nor at crime, lest laughter take the place of loathing; nor should . . . [it] be inappropriate to the speaker's own character, to that of the jury, or to the occasion; for all these points come under the head of propriety."[2] In short, when in doubt, don't!

The freshness of a humorous story depends, of course, upon who is telling it to whom, when, and how. The story that went very well in the freshman history lecture (for everyone has to hear a story for the first time!) may be pretty stale fare at the senior banquet. Nevertheless, on some after-dinner or sportive occasions a speaker, especially if he has the reputation of being a wit, can amuse with almost any threadbare wheeze or feeble pun. People laugh, at such times, simply because they want to laugh and are waiting for an excuse. Most of the time, however, audiences want fresh humor or fresh applications of old humor. An inexperienced speaker, at least, will avoid thumbing through joke books and anthologies of wit and humor, not because the contents of such books are not amusing (or at least were not amusing originally), but because they are everyone's property. Similarly, retelling stories and jokes published in such popular magazines as *Reader's Digest* and in the comic strips is not always as effective as the speaker might expect. The humor may have been very good when published, but most of the audience has already read it and has heard others repeat it again and again since its publication. In spite of the habits of the locker room and the smoking car, a speaker cannot escape from the consequences of his stale joke by merely changing the characters or by prefacing it with "Stop me if you've heard this." (See "Triteness," pages 215–217.)

An old story, in order to be effective, should be given a new twist, a new application, or a disguised setting. Then the audience may be interested in recognizing the essentials of the story and be pleased at the surprise elements. The following two versions of the same story illustrate the use of new setting

[2] *Orator,* trans. by H. M. Hubbell (Cambridge, Mass., Harvard University Press, 1942), p. 371.

and new emphasis in an anecdote of the surprise ending or "plug-line" sort. The first version was intended to illustrate a certain conservative attitude toward the Holy Scriptures in rural New England in the generation of our great-grandfathers.

> In the fall of the year, after the crops were in, a certain itinerant schoolmaster in New England approached a well-known farmer, who had a large family of small children, with the proposal that he be engaged to conduct the family's education for a few months. "Well, mebbe," said the farmer. "What kin ya teach em?" The teacher replied that he was prepared to teach arithmetic, spelling, writing, reading, geometry, and Latin. "Good," said the farmer, "That's all sound learnin'—except the Latin. None of that! If the English language was good enough for Moses and the Apostles, it's good enough for my children!"

The second version was adapted many years later to illustrate what the speaker thought a harmful attitude toward educational expenditure:

> At an open meeting of the school board to consider improvements in the offerings at the Township High School, it had been proposed to authorize the hiring of an additional teacher in order to reduce the size of the English classes and to make it possible to offer French, Spanish, and perhaps beginning German. When it began to look as if the proposal might pass, one of the older members of the board, who exercised considerable influence because of his wealth, rose to his feet in protest. Looking squarely at the taxpayers, he declared that the new teacher was not needed and that he wanted to keep the school tax down. Then he finished with the following clincher: "No Sir. I'm against bringing these foreign influences into our school and our community. If the English language was good enough for Moses and the Apostles, it's certainly good enough for our children."

We conclude, then, that in managing his examples the speaker will do well to consider the factors of interest and to associate what he wants to make interesting with what is already interesting to audiences in general and to his audience in particular.

Appropriateness to subject and occasion. Tact and taste are not easily subject to rules. Should one use humorous illustrations on a solemn occasion? Does copious use of fictitious examples indirectly tell an audience that the speaker does not know enough to discover factual examples? It all depends on whether a speaker enjoys the respect and confidence of his hearers. Within very wide limits examples may properly be drawn from any areas of common knowledge or common experience. A speaker should exercise care, however, that in his choice of examples he doesn't depart widely from the tone and spirit which the occasion demands and his purpose requires. Extreme cases of faulty taste may easily be cited. In a speech honoring Washington's Birthday, it would seem incongruous for a speaker to couple Washington's conduct at Valley Forge with Benedict Arnold's at Quebec in illustration of the various kinds of courage evinced by a great hero. It is impossible to lay down rules for good sense and tact in choosing examples, but inexperienced speakers should err on the side of caution.

Appropriateness to speaker. Many examples that seem proper to the subject and the occasion may offend a particular audience or may seem to that audience unbefitting a particular speaker. An audience composed largely of churchgoers may be antagonized by an illustration from a lay speaker suggesting the liability of the clergy to err; yet the same audience would probably take no offense at the same example used by a clergyman. The trouble with the example would not be irrelevance to the speaker's idea, but its tendency to raise distracting and competing ideas in the listeners. College students speaking before audiences of businessmen sometimes make the mistake of choosing their examples, however pat, from areas of business about which they themselves seem too young and inexperienced to know anything. The natural response of their listeners is not, "We see the point; he hits the nail on the head," but, "What does that youngster know about business?" A speaker cannot expect his listeners to concentrate on his point if he sets them to criticizing his choice of examples.

Handling Details of Examples.

Order of details. No detail should be introduced before its proper place in the structure, nor should it be delayed beyond the point where it fits the story. Examples and illustrations are picture-forming, and the pictures will be formed once the speaker has set the audience's imagination working, whether he provides the ingredients or not. Hence, if the speaker does not provide details at the proper time, the audience will invent its own details, which may not be the ones the speaker wanted. Very seldom can repair work be done afterwards, no matter how often the speaker inserts, "By the way, this house I am speaking of was built on sand." The audience already has built it on granite, and there it will stand. Of course, the speaker has the picture already formed for himself; so any details he mentions, in whatever order, may seem satisfactory to him. But his audience has to form its image from what he suggests or fails to suggest, in the order in which he suggests it.

Number of details. Examples, and particularly illustrations, should include enough details for clarity, but unessential details should be edited out. The speaker has to judge how much knowledge and experience his audience brings to bear on the example. If his listeners have much knowledge he need suggest few details; little audience knowledge will demand more detail from the speaker. If he were talking to a city audience and drew an example from farm life, he would have to use a larger number of descriptive details than he would if he were speaking to a rural audience.

Speakers who draw illustrations from their personal experiences are tempted to include too many details, some of which are completely unnecessary. How often do we hear the exuberant storyteller interrupt himself with "Oh, that's not important anyway," or with some other parenthetical self-correction such as, "No, I believe that it wasn't Wednesday, the third; I think it was Thursday, the fourth." Overdrawing and overloading an illustration with detail confuses and breaks up any impression of movement and pace.

Comparison. As means of development, comparisons extend the statement by pointing out its likeness to another idea, object, or situation. A concise expression of likeness is often a simile or a metaphor. When the likeness is developed at some length, it is usually called an analogy. As an instance of the short comparison, Joseph Wood Krutch compared protoplasm with jelly. He asserted that protoplasm is the simplest form of life, and amplified the idea immediately with the statement, "it is a shapeless blob of rebellious jelly." Much of our conversation is filled with comparisons, and much of our slang consists of metaphors. The special virtue of comparison is its power to make an idea strong, sharp, and intense as well as larger through the addition of information.

The short comparison mentions only a single point of likeness. The analogy, or long comparison, recognizes a number of points of likeness between objects or situations. One of the masters of analogy in the popular lecture was Thomas Henry Huxley, who often tried to make ordinary English workingmen understand what a liberal education is all about. One of his favorite statements was that education consists in learning about Nature. Then, knowing that his audience knew something about chess, he would say that learning about Nature is like learning to play chess. The world is the chessboard; the phenomena of Nature represent the pieces; and the laws of Nature are the rules of the game. Education, then, is mastering the rules of the game of life.

In pondering this example of analogy, observe the precise points of likeness. First is the controlling idea of the comparison: learning is to chess what learning is to Nature. Then this idea is amplified by three points of similarity: world and chessboard, phenomena and pieces, laws and rules. Successful use of analogy depends upon seeing precisely the points of comparison and of stating them clearly.

Analogies, like examples, may be either real or fictitious. When the analogy is real, it is called literal analogy. When fictitious, it is a figurative analogy. To distinguish the one from the other, a person needs only to recognize that most objects and actions can be grouped into logical classes, such as animal life and plant life, animate objects and inanimate objects, voluntary acts and involuntary acts. Such classifications and subdivisions are almost endless. The literal analogy always draws comparisons within the same class of things; it compares man with man, flower with flower, game with game, machine with machine. So Jones's behavior can readily be compared with Smith's, city government in St. Louis with that in Detroit, one farm with another, one dress with another, and so on. Within a class of things, there are always many points of correspondence. Hence, a speaker has a rich mine of comparisons when he can liken his subject, say the sports program at X university, with a sports program his hearers know about.

The figurative analogy compares objects and events that fall into unlike classes. Strictly speaking, it states an identity of relationship between two unlike contexts. The short figurative comparison is a *simile* or a *metaphor.* William James observed, using a simile, that a gas jet was like the moon. In days when gas was used for illumination, gas jet and moon could be thought of as identical in function, the gas jet lighting up a room and the moon lighting up the earth. Huxley was using a figurative comparison when he likened the game of chess to the game of life. Successful chess playing and successful living are two quite different orders of things, yet with respect to the act of learning he found a number of similarities. In speechmaking, the analogy is especially useful, because one can always compare one's subject—no matter what it may be—to something else in order to associate the strange with the familiar. Any two ideas or objects may at first seem entirely unlike, yet upon probing they may reveal a similarity in function, purpose, materials and qualities, cause, or effect. At first glance, for example, race horses and athletes may appear to have nothing in common, but if we consider their treatment and training, we can discover some interesting comparisons.

Familiar illustrations of the analogy are the Biblical parables of the Sowers and of the Wise and Foolish Virgins, and Aesop's fable of the boy who cried "Wolf!" Another well-known example is Lincoln's comparison between Blondin, the tightrope walker, and the position of the Federal Government during the critical days of the Civil War.

> Gentlemen, I want you to suppose a case for a moment. Suppose that all the property you were worth was in gold, and you have put it in the hands of Blondin, the famous rope-walker, to carry across the Niagara Falls on a tight rope. Would you shake the rope while he was passing over it, or keep shouting to him, "Blondin, stoop a little more! Go a little faster!" No, I am sure you would not. You would hold your breath as well as your tongue, and keep your hand off until he was safely over. Now, the government is in the same situation. It is carrying an immense weight across a stormy ocean. Untold treasures are in its hands. It is doing the best it can. Don't badger it! Just keep still, and it will get you safely over.[3]

[3] Carl Sandburg, *Abraham Lincoln: The War Years* (New York, 1939), II, 125.

The figurative analogy may serve admirably (as may the fictitious example) to modify the tone of an exposition that runs the risk of becoming too serious and sober and consequently dull. Thomas Huxley wished to exemplify the notion that the laws of scientific induction and deduction come within the scope of everyday experience. To underscore his point he drew a figurative comparison, not from his own invention but from literature:

> There is a well-known incident in one of Molière's plays, where the author makes the hero express unbounded delight on being told that he had been talking prose during the whole of his life. In the same way, I trust that you will take comfort and be delighted with yourselves, on the discovery that you have been acting on the principles of inductive and deductive philosophy during the same period.

Contrast

As a method of development, contrast is the opposite of comparison. It carries out the idea of a statement by showing how it is unlike another idea. Basically contrast involves two objects, conditions, or ideas that in some way are opposed to each other. Contrast therefore always entails some degree of difference.

In deciding whether to amplify a statement by a contrasting idea, the speaker should be aware of two types of contrast: (1) that which reveals minimum, yet distinct, difference, and (2) that which states maximum difference. When I say that the Athletic Manufacturing Company in my town is owned by its many stockholders, but that the Ever-Ready Grocery Store is owned by one man, I am expressing a significant difference in ownership. When I say one employs a manager and the other does not, one makes a profit and the other shows a loss, I am expressing differences which are at opposite ends of a scale. These are polar opposites, often referred to as antipodal or antithetical.

An example of plain, but not radical, contrast comes from a speech by the late Secretary of State, John Foster Dulles. Speaking to the American Federation of Labor in New York City, he used contrast simply and effectively to underline what a production worker's time was worth in New York and in Moscow:

> To buy a pound of butter in New York, it takes 27 minutes of work; in Moscow over 6 hours of work. For a pound of sugar, 3½ minutes in New York, 8 minutes in Moscow; for a quart of milk, 7 minutes in New York, 42 minutes in Moscow; for a dozen eggs, 25 minutes in New York, nearly 3 hours in Moscow; for a cotton shirt, nearly 1 hour in New York, 22 hours in Moscow; for a man's suit, 3 days in New York, 47 days in Moscow; for shoes, 1 day in New York, 13 days in Moscow; and for a woman's wool suit, 22 hours in New York, 22 days in Moscow.

The antithetical contrast is exemplified by a college lecturer who distinguished between the fields of organic chemistry and inorganic chemistry. The organic chemist, he said, is interested in all living things, the inorganic chemist in nonliving substances. The former helps us to understand the cell, the latter the atom. The one works side by side with the biologist and the physician, the other with the physicist and the engineer. The one is inside life, the other outside it. Yet, he continued in summary, neither chemist can ignore the other. The inorganic scientist must know something about life to understand nonliving matter, and the organic scientist must know enough about material forces to reinforce his study of living things.

A special use of contrast is *definition by negation.* Novice speakers find it particularly effective in pinning down the meaning of a fuzzy word or concept and in making clear the purpose of a speech. In partial explanation of the old notion that man is a rational or reasoning animal, one student said:

> When I refer to man as a *rational* being, I do not mean that he is distinguished from other animals because of his ability to reason—at least they *learn,* and learning often calls for reasoning. Nor do I mean to set man off from animals because he can generalize and discover principles, for the dog will show much "generalizing" behavior, based on analogy, when he stops chasing skunks. He may have chased two or three with unfortunate results; so he "reasons" that all skunks will give him pain, and he keeps his distance thereafter. No, man is not rational, in contrast to other animals, if we mean only that he learns, reasons, and generalizes.

Besides the use of negation in helping to explain an ambiguous word, a speaker frequently finds it applicable in explaining the purpose of his speech, particularly when he thinks his purpose may be misunderstood. A student who talked on the process of flue-curing tobacco felt that his audience might think he was going to deal with other ways of curing tobacco or with the steps in production that immediately preceded and succeeded the process. He, therefore, gave emphasis to his special purpose as follows:

> Perhaps I should say that I am going to speak only about flue-curing tobacco. Interesting as the process of sun-curing tobacco is, I am not concerned with it now. Furthermore, we shall assume that the tobacco has been harvested and has been brought to the flue shed ready for hanging. Also, we shall stop with the process as soon as the curing has been finished and the tobacco is ready to be taken down and carried to market.

Whether contrast proceeds by stating minimum degrees of difference between two like contexts, by antithesis, or by negation, it is a means of amplification that builds up the meaning of an idea by increasing its precision and accuracy. Contrast enhances precision because it helps prevent ambiguity and misunderstanding. Comparison promotes understanding in a positive way, for the listener is told that his experience applies to the idea. He is helped to grasp new or strange information by adding the old and familiar. Contrast, on the other hand, enhances understanding in a negative way. The listener is asked to set aside his experience, to rule it out as not being applicable at the moment. The difference in the psychological effect of comparison and contrast is compressed in this example: My house is ranch-type, but it is not L-shaped. Comparison helps us see a statement in the right light; contrast prevents our seeing it in the wrong light.

Selecting and Arranging Comparisons and Contrasts. A comparison or a contrast presents two ideas, one of which must be familiar to the listener. If the speaker tries to elucidate a new idea with a new idea, the result can only be darkness, mystification, and confusion. Indeed, the speaker defeats his purpose in comparing and contrasting.

In handling the two parts of a comparison or a contrast, the speaker should keep them as close together as possible. Close proximity is especially desirable when comparing, as informative speeches often do, the advantages and disadvantages of a mechanism, process, or operation. For example, one might be explaining a method of study and pointing out its virtues and drawbacks. It would be easy and natural to proceed like this:

Advantages
- I. ________________
- II. ________________

Disadvantages
- I. ________________
- II. ________________

If each of the items required a minute of explanation, the four blocks of ideas would be far enough apart to put an unnecessary burden on the listener's memory. The comparison would be easier to remember and more sharp and clear if an advantage were immediately followed by the disadvantage most closely related to it:

Advantage I. ________________
Disdvantage I. ________________
Advantage II. ________________
Disadvantage II. ________________

In general, then, the closer together the items of comparison or contrast, the better.

Causes of effects

Another means of development is explaining an effect by its cause. If the statement calling for amplification asserts some condition or event to be accounted for, a curious person would want to know why it came about. So it is natural for a speaker to follow such a statement with a discussion of the cause or causes of the condition. For example:

> States seem reluctant today to make large increases in funds for educational uses. [Why?]
>
> The burden falls principally upon property taxes in most states.

Effect refers to some present or past condition, event, or situation which we have experienced, read about, or otherwise have become aware of. Furthermore, out of our experience we have learned that when one event is often, or always, followed by another, we suspect some sort of influence or connection between them. If the influence is not by chance or coincidence, we hold that the second event has been "caused" by the first. From our knowledge of the sciences we are well acquainted with forces which produce effects, or as the phrase goes, with events which are closely "correlated" with one another. And from our knowledge of human behavior and social events, we are ever aware that these two mutually influence one another. So in the example above, the first statement calls attention to a condition that is widely recognized today—the reluctance of state governments to vote money for educational purposes. The second statement singles out one of the causes which may account for the reluctance. Of course it is but one of many causes, and a speaker might want to amplify further by discussing other causes as well.

To explain an effect by its cause or causes is an important and fundamental way of extending information. We are ever curious, always asking why. It rains—why? The temperature soars to 100 degrees—why? One substance we may eat is nourishing, another poisonous—why? Uranimum 235 is more readily fissionable than other atoms—why? One person is an "A" student, another a "C" student—why? Almost any state or event or condition we think about or learn about can be regarded as an effect, and when it is so regarded we inquire into how and why it came about. Students of communication, particularly students of speechmaking, should reflect that they are right in the middle of cause-and-effect relationships. We say that a speech is effective. What is its effect, or effects? What were the causes?

The amplification of effects by their causes is useful in informative speeches and for a wide variety of subjects. Hence in preparing for their speeches, students do well to keep a sharp eye out for materials that help to explain the events and conditions they are dealing with: in particular, relevant principles and laws, especially the general principles of natural phenomena that the natural and social sciences deal with and that the audience may be familiar with or have at least heard about. For example, in explaining the operation of the vacuum tube, one would draw upon the familiar law of electricity: like charges repel, unlike attract. The improvement of one's tennis game involves the application of the familiar laws of learning. Wages and prices depend, in part at least, upon the economic law of supply and demand, and the maintenance of health and avoidance of disease upon principles of exercise and nutrition. A felony or a crime, juvenile delinquency, and divorce reflect habits and principles of human behavior, of motivation and social status. It would be hard to find a subject, even for a short speech, that would not lead the speaker to consider effects and their causes.

Two words of caution are in order. First, any effect may have not one cause, but several. Hence, a statement that asserts an effect may be amplified by a number of statements, each pointing out a cause. How many causes should a speaker present? How complete should he be? There are no pat answers. In the short speech to a popular audience, probably he does best to point out and discuss the single cause that in his judgment seems most important. He knows superior intellect has something to do with an "A" record, yet in talking to an audience of average students he might appropriately emphasize habits of hard persistent study. The old rule of action applies here: Do one thing well rather than three things superficially.

Second, the speaker, like any sound reasoner, must beware of finding cause where the evidence establishes only correlation. Two events that seem always to occur together or in succession need not be related as cause and effect. The fallacy known as *post hoc, propter hoc* is always tempting. Two events, for example, may each be caused by a third. The speaker must convince himself that the alleged cause *could* produce the effect and that there was no other possible cause operative that would be more likely to produce it.

Logical definition

As a method of development, logical definition illuminates a word or an idea in a statement by first placing it within its class and then by distinguishing it from its class. The method combines comparison and contrast and through them makes clear the special meaning the speaker is attaching to the word. In discussing the nature of religious experience, a speaker said that "it always involves faith. And faith," he added promptly, "is belief which cannot be verified scientifically." Thus he swiftly put faith into the classification of beliefs and then pointed out that it differed from some beliefs because it could not be proved scientifically. Later he tried to distinguish faith from superstition and prejudice. Another speaker, talking about a new kind of synthetic rubber, defined rubber as an elastic substance—a kind of substance having the power of resuming its shape after being compressed. Thus he implicitly compared and contrasted rubber with other substances in order to point up its striking characteristic, elasticity.

Requirements of Definition. In using definition, speakers should be aware of four requirements.

1. Definition should cover all cases or instances of the word, idea, or thing being defined. If *elasticity* is said to be a property belonging to all rubber objects, it must be true that every rubber object is elastic. If the use of language is said to distinguish man from all other animals, then it must be true that every man uses language.

2. The definition of the word or idea must *exclude* all else not bearing the same name. Can *elasticity* properly distinguish rubber, if other substances are elastic? If the use of language really distinguishes man from other animals, then it cannot be characteristic of any other animal. By observing these two requirements, a speaker can do much to make his meanings accurate and precise.

3. The word or idea being defined should be amplified in language that is familiar and clear to the audience. To say that a conservative politician is one who rarely thinks beyond the *status quo* would not be so clear to most persons as to say that he is one who prefers whatever is settled and established and who distrusts what is new and untried.

4. The definition should be as brief as is consistent with accuracy. In a short speech there is rarely time to define exhaustively. Instead the speaker picks out the essential defining idea, which he can do if he observes rules (1) and (2) above. He omits the less significant characteristics. This Jonathan Swift did in defining style as "proper words in proper places." There are other characteristics of style, but in the context in which he was using the word, he was content to name but one of its essential features.

Restatement

We have set forth various methods of development: factual information, example and illustration, comparison, contrast, causes of effects, and logical definition. These are ways of expanding a statement by adding significant substance and information to it. In turning attention now to other means, we shall deal with three basic ways of enlarging upon a statement, not by adding information, but by repeating the idea of the statement itself. The principle is that of *restatement:* making the statement again in different language.

An example of saying the same thing in different words occurred in a student speech explaining how an architect goes about his work:

> Before he can start to draw at all, he must have a design in his head. He needs a plan. He must have something to aim at.

Obviously the second and third sentences are repeating essentially the same idea announced in the clause, "he must have a design in his head." For an example of restatement involving a shift in the form of expression, observe this simple case:

> He must have a design in his head. A design or plan he must clearly have in his mind.

Repetition of this sort occurs frequently in extemporaneous speaking and in our conversation. We can scarcely avoid it, for we feel that the hearer must fix his attention on the idea and grasp it firmly before he is ready to hear it discussed and amplified in other ways.

If not abused, restatement is of real advantage in speechmaking. The use of different terms often gives a statement a new and fresh slant. Furthermore, restatement may touch a familiar chord in the listener which the original words failed to arouse. Variety in the language in which important ideas are expressed, like variety in examples, helps a speaker to reach the experience of his various hearers. Some will readily understand one word, some another. As we are all painfully aware, however, repetition can be easily abused. Persons who will not take time to prepare their speeches thoroughly, who try to get by on bluff and a gabby front, and who think that audiences have not the intelligence to appreciate solid facts and information nor the acumen to detect guff—such persons are tempted to substitute repetition for content and firm substance. When they do, they only succeed in deceiving themselves and insulting or at least boring their hearers. Who has not become impatient, perhaps at times disgusted, with the endless over-and-over, around-and-around of the TV commercial? Restatement does not move an idea forward. Properly used, it halts an idea, replaying the thought just long enough to let the hearer seize its meaning clearly.

No doubt, as some propagandists and advertisers believe, incessant repetition of a statement produces acceptance or consent, provided that competing statements are excluded. The honorable speaker, however, wishes to illumine matters for his audience, not to stupefy it.

In using restatement, the speaker should keep firm guides in mind. First, as soon as the most important statements of the speech appear, he should restate them: that is, the statements of the purpose and the central idea or theme, and the main head which leads off a unit or block of ideas, a unit corresponding roughly to a written paragraph. Then should follow substantial amplification. Second, the speaker can close a unit of closely related ideas with a version of the statement that started the unit. If the unit began with "An architect has in mind a design from which he works," it might end with the restatement, "An architect tries to settle upon a clear design for a house before he does anything else." Third, restatement finds a ready place in the conclusion of a speech if one summarizes by repeating the substance of the central idea and of each main head. (An example of such a summary is on page 174.) The speaker must respect repetition of idea and employ the technique wisely. He should not expect every audience to understand a statement just because he has stated it once.

Synonym

A synonym makes a strange word intelligible by associating it with a familiar word that has the same, or nearly the same meaning. Restatement is worked through synonyms. Although the semanticist may be right in maintaining that no two words have precisely the same meaning, no good speaker or writer ignores synonyms. They are his fastest way of rendering the strange familiar.

The use of the synonym probably springs from the desire to be precise. The technical vocabulary that is adopted in a specialized field of study uses words, or other kinds of symbols, having one and only one meaning. So there need be no synonyms in a technical vocabulary. Hence, when a specialist communicates with another specialist in the same field, when expert speaks to expert, both the communicator and the receiver respond in the same way. When the chemist says *Carbon 14* to another chemist, both respond alike because Carbon 14 means only one thing. But such is not the state of affairs in popular communication where one word of ordinary language may have a dozen meanings or responses.

An informed speaker regards himself as an expert on his subject. He is related to his hearer as an expert is to the layman. And as a result of his study and experience, he has acquired exact and precise ideas. He respects these and takes pride in them. So he desires, quite rightly, to use the precise word in his speech, although he knows it will be strange to the hearer. What must he then do? He has two courses. He can employ the exact word and immediately follow it with synonyms. If, for example, he were explaining the chief ways people respond to other people, he might say: "One of the typical ways of responding to another person is with aversion, a feeling of dislike, a sort of running away from the person and avoiding him." Thus *aversion,* the special word of the psychologist, is associated swiftly with the more familiar words, *dislike, running away,* and *avoiding.* If the speaker does not resort to synonyms, his other alternative is that of logical definition, which was discussed above.

Etymology

Etymology is a means of explaining the significance of a word by citing the original meaning of the word. We can use the technique to illuminate swiftly the meaning of *etymology* itself. The word is Greek in origin, stemming from *etymos,* meaning *real,* or *true,* and *logos,* meaning *word, thought,* or *speech.* Thus *etymology* means either speech and discourse about speech, or the study of the original meanings of words.

It is evident that etymology as a technique of explanation is closely related to synonym, for when one looks for the original usage of a word, he often finds it associated with terms that are simpler and more familiar than the word in question and that mean nearly the same thing. Perhaps there is no more rapid way of developing a feeling for synonyms, of distinguishing the closely related meanings of a word, than to consider its original usage. The first recorded meaning of a word is often a sort of core from which later meanings have radiated.

When does a word need clarification by synonym? There are no formulas a speaker can follow. He simply must develop a feeling for his audience, compare its knowledge and experience with his own, and never forget that it does not know as much about his subject as he does. We shall make but two pointed suggestions. First, technical words and terms have to be brought within the orbit of the familiar. To the extent that the engineer, chemist, artist, or economist draws upon the specialized vocabulary of his field in addressing a popular audience, he must swiftly explain each strange word or phrase the first time he uses it. If, for example, he were explaining the work of an MIT research group that is trying to discover the conditions that stimulate persons suddenly to conceive original ideas, he might use one of their coined words, *omphaloskepsis.* However, he had better add instantly that it means "a state of relaxed contemplation" or lazy daydreaming about a bothersome problem. The truly strange word bears no meaning at all to the audience and cries out for explanation. Second, the fuzzy-familiar word may require focus. This is the word the hearer recognizes without being able to attach a clear meaning to it. A speaker was explaining some of the niceties of sailing. At appropriate spots in the speech he employed the terms *vector, acute angle, velocity,* and *perpendicular.* The majority of his hearers had encountered these words before, but they suffered moments of confusion, nevertheless. Their former experience with the words was so remote that they could not recall meanings on the instant. What was needed for each word was a reminding synonym. The speaker carefully defined the technical terms of sailing, but he was insensitive to this fuzzy-familiar vocabulary.

Such vaguely familiar words are all about us. Many of them, derived from our studies, have special meanings which, like *acute angle,* have for us become weak and dim. Others we have picked up higgledy-piggledy through occasional usage and have never bothered to define. Often fuzzy-familiar words are abstract, rather than concrete and specific—words such as *democracy, mind, art, duty, good, truth, virtue, compound, atom, expedient, judicial, beauty.* Such words can never be tied to a particular object in the way that a concrete word, such as *tree*, can point to an object. They can be understood only when they are related to more familiar terms and experiences, usually by synonyms and logical definition, sometimes by example. One of the marks of a firstrate communicator is his sensitivity to such abstractions. Keenly aware of them, he clarifies them as he goes along. Hence a sensitivity to these abstractions is related to a sensitivity to the means of making them definite to a particular audience. At any given time two audiences may have rather different senses of the word *discrimination*.

Quotation

Viewed as means of development, quotation is simply restatement through the use of a statement by somebody other than the speaker. In discussing some of the problems of intercollegiate athletics, suppose one said,

> Planning a program of intercollegiate athletics and carrying it out is a complex business.

The idea could be restated by quotation, thus:

> In making a general appraisal of organized athletics in the United States, Harold Stoke observes: "Most of the larger colleges and universities, private and public, are organized into athletic conferences managed by highly paid commissioners. Through them, complicated athletic schedules are worked out with all the finesse of the international bargaining table, and considerations of finance, publicity, the prospective careers of coaches and even of presidents, are balanced in equations which would baffle electronic computers."

A speaker uses quotation principally because its language expresses an idea better than he can. The superiority of expression may represent a happy marriage of conciseness and clarity. The quotation, to use a slang expression, may say a mouthful in a hurry. For example, one might restate the idea that modern architecture is functional by drawing on Francis Bacon's terse language: "Houses are built to live in, and not to look on." Or the superiority of another's words may rest in some striking quality that rivets the listener's attention. This quality may be evident in a sharp image, a simile or metaphor, an antithetical contrast, or some neatly balanced language. In other words, the quotation may have some literary excellence the speaker wants to take advantage of. If, for instance, he were to state that authorities on children's literature always remind us that some books are good, some less good, he might follow with another familiar statement from Bacon: "Some books are to be tasted, others to be swallowed, and some few to be chewed and digested."

In handling the quotation, it is well to avoid the barbarous, distracting device of introducing it with the words "Now I quote" and concluding it with "Unquote." Of course, the speaker must make clear that he is using the language of another. But he can manage the acknowledgment more deftly by naming the author. He can preface the quotation with a quick phrase, "As Francis Bacon said. . . ." A short sentence giving the setting will also work well before the quotation, such a sentence as "Francis Bacon expressed the idea in this manner." Note above how the quotation from Harold Stoke has been introduced. Furthermore, naming the author is not only a good way of signaling the quotation; it also gives the effect of authority. (See page 80.)

Development

The methods of development are not only ways to clearness and understanding. They involve also ways of controlling attention and maintaining interest. The speaker who observes them need not worry about being uninteresting if he will but keep in mind the basic principle of interest—the association of what is novel with what is familiar—will respect the need for variety, and will identify the values inherent in the occasion.

Novelty and familiarity

The novel and the familiar may be combined in two ways. A speaker may first present what he thinks is new to his audience and then immediately relate it to something familiar, or he may offer the old idea and then show its new application. To Americans of recent generations, assembly-line methods of manufacture are familiar, and shipbuilding is an old and well-known process. What made Henry Kaiser's procedures interesting during World War II was his application of assembly-line methods to the building of large ships; the familiar principle had been put to new use. An architect's blueprint is completely uninteresting to many persons until the person who is trying to explain it says, for example, "Here is the kitchen, here is the door to the basement, here is the window under which we will put the sink." Then the listener becomes interested because he or she has found something familiar in the unfamiliar.

Variety

Effective in maintaining attention is the application of the principle of change. As we have seen, action and movement help to control attention. But movement must be varied if it is to be effective. Monotonous action will be as deadening as inaction. Hence, as his speech unfolds, a speaker should endeavor to give his ideas variety. Two ways of providing variety should be especially noted: (1) variety in the *kinds* of development used, and (2) change in the *point of view* from which the audience looks at the materials presented.

1. Examples, we advised, should be chosen from a variety of fields. The principle of variety should be extended to all kinds of development. A chain of explanatory statements, for instance, should be varied by the introduction of example or testimony or comparison. The presentation of information, especially of statistics and figures, should be varied by offering examples of the significance or of the application of these figures. Statistics offered to show that rise in position in the business world is accompanied by increase of vocabulary should be followed or preceded by specific measurable cases of vocabularies of men at various levels of salary and authority. A presentation of the specific benefits to the central states from the creation of a Missouri Valley Authority should be varied by the citation of opinions of persons known to be familiar with the needs of the Missouri Valley and with the Tennessee Valley Authority. Furthermore, examples should be presented of the way the MVA would help a farmer in Kansas or a rancher in Montana; and comparisons should be made with the benefits obtained in the Tennessee Valley.

2. Variety in point of view as the speaker develops and amplifies his ideas is also highly desirable. In describing the campus of the university, the interesting speaker might take his listener on a verbal walk along the campus paths. Before the listener is weary of walking, the speaker might put him in a car and whisk him over the campus roads and around the outskirts. The speaker might then take him up the library tower or to the top floor of the administration building and let him look out over the campus, or he might give him a bird's-eye view from an airplane. In explaining the new state constitution, the speaker who wished to avoid wearying his audience might turn from description of the executive department to the effects the revision would have on farmers. From farmers he might turn to urban property-owners, and then to labor, business, and education. In short, a speaker should maintain one view long enough to fix it clearly in his audience's mind, but not so long as to stupefy his audience with monotony. He will beware of the habit of Washington Irving's Wouter Van Twiller, who always conceived a subject on so vast a scale that he had no room in his mind to turn it over and look at all its sides. This device of varying the angle of vision has been developed so far in the movies that any scene photographed from the same spot and at the same angle or distance seldom lasts longer than 50 or 60 seconds. There must always be order in the variety, however. Otherwise interest will give way to jumble and confusion.

Values

What are interesting above all, as we elaborated in Chapter 3, are the things men value. In planning for a particular occasion, the speaker who is sensitive to the materials that are important and significant to both himself and his audience will have little trouble in sustaining interest. Doubtless it is easier to find basic values in situations that evoke argument and persuasion than in occasions calling for explanation, definition, and the exposition of causal forces. The informative speaker needs to be particularly inventive and imaginative in making his speech significantly meaningful.

Conclusion

In conclusion, we remind the informative speaker that his speech consists of a series of statements, the most important of which cannot be understood without development. In preparing his speech, the speaker must consider each important statement and ask himself, "What methods of development can I use to make this idea clear to my audience?" From his resources he must select the methods he thinks will be most effective. Only rarely can a statement be enlarged satisfactorily by a single method. Usually the speaker must use several methods if his hearers are to understand him and if he is to be interesting.

8
Visual Materials

In employing facts to develop statements, speakers have long recognized the advantages of visual aids. *A visual aid* is material that a speaker may present for his hearers to see. Because most persons are more eye-minded than ear-minded, visual materials serve the speaker in two ways: they promote clearness and they are a powerful source of interest.

Visual materials make for clear impressions because they make the meaning of spoken words tangible and "real." Language alone, even when words are most specific and concrete, at its best can only stir up images; and when precise communication is desired this may not be enough, because the hearer's image may not be the same as the speaker's. An image, moreover, as a sort of inner picture, seems to lack substance. But when the speaker refers to a model, a chart, or illustrative object, his words relate to something a listener can see directly. His words, furthermore, *point* to an object, and they obviously refer to that object rather than to another. Thus, words take on meanings which are solid and precise. As a student once exclaimed, "You can't get away from a model or a snapshot. It's *there*." Attention, and hence retention, are usually greater, the more senses the receiver employs.

Visual materials in a speech are interesting chiefly because they involve a change from one activity to another, from hearing to seeing. Usually, also, their use requires the speaker to gesture and change his position more than he would without them; and movement, as we know, helps to control attention.

About the invention, selection, and use of visual aids, experts have written many books, some of which are mentioned at the end of this chapter. We shall limit ourselves, however, to the information and suggestions that most speakers can put to use without having to call on the technicians who specialize in making motion pictures, filmstrips, lantern slides, artistic drawings, and elaborate layouts.

Kinds of Visual Materials

Although visual materials are of many kinds and may be classified in different ways, we shall group them as simply as possible. Each group has its principal advantages, proper uses, and common abuses.

Blackboard diagrams and sketches

Blackboard diagrams and sketches are best used when a speaker needs to build his sketch, step by step. He draws the first feature and explains it, draws the second, and so on, until the illustration is fully developed. The device is especially adapted to the explanation of processes and procedures (if they can be stripped down to their essentials) and to simple operations and machines.

The great advantage of the step-by-step diagram is that the listener can see only what is being talked about at the moment. He does not suffer the temptation to explore other features of the illustration before the speaker wants him to, as he does when a single, complete diagram appears before him early in the speech. The serial diagram, then, controls attention economically. It also creates anticipation and interest, for the audience is curious to see what the next features will be.

Preliminary planning and methodical rehearsal make the blackboard sketch effective. First, the prospective speaker should see the diagram as a whole. Then he should determine how many separate parts are needed and in what order to present them. Finally, he must make the diagram part of the language of the speech by incorporating it into the rehearsal period. In rehearsal, indeed, there is no substitute for a blackboard. It allows one to judge how large one can make each feature and still complete the picture without crowding. It shows one how best to work and not unduly block the view of his audience. Above all, this kind of practice gives the best chance of learning to look at the audience as much as possible.

The ineptitude of some blackboard speakers needs only the briefest mention. Who has not seen—sometimes in his teachers—a person who addressed his blackboard rather than his audience? Who has not seen a speaker cover up his drawing, thus forcing the listener to crane his neck, to peer and squirm, and finally, to resign himself to confusion? Has anyone escaped blackboard work that was too small or too faint to be seen easily, or so badly planned that repeated erasures were necessary before some feature was just right? Have we not all endured wasted periods of flat silence with speakers who never learned to talk and draw at the same time? Persons need not be so unskilled if they remember that effective blackboard illustration needs planning and practice, and if they actually plan and practice until they can proceed with assurance.

Models and objects

A model is a materialized example. It is a three-dimensional representation of an object, small enough to be displayed in place of the real object or large enough to be seen when the object would be so small as to be invisible.

The small-scale airplane and railroad, miniature furniture, the tiny house with its landscaping, and the stage set are familiar illustrations of models reduced in size. Oversized models are often used by the anatomy teacher in his discussion, for example, of the heart, the ear, and the larynx. Occasionally, also, some models may be taken apart and reassembled in order to show the innermost parts of an object, or the parts may be moved about to show how they work or how they appear in different positions. A student used very effectively a model of a living room with scale furniture to show the principles of arranging furniture in a house. Sometimes, of course, models may not look much like the real thing, for they may be designed to show the structural relationships between the parts of an object. Chemistry teachers, for example, use models of various kinds of atoms and molecules which resemble tinker-toy constructions more than they do their unseeable counterparts.

Another kind of model is the mock-up, used with great success by teachers in the sciences, in engineering, and in the armed services. It usually consists of real objects, or parts of objects or machines, mounted on a board to illustrate how the parts function. For example, light bulbs, wire, a dry cell battery, and switches are often arranged to show the fundamental principles of electric circuits.

Occasionally a speaker finds he can employ objects themselves. In demonstrating the fundamentals of the golf swing or of tennis strokes there is no substitute for the club or the racket. In recent years student speakers have displayed disassembled ribbon microphones, a baseball cut in half, the parts of a shoe, a cutaway carburetor, a book in the various stages of binding, the chief parts of a small generator, a knocked-down electric drill, a thermostat, a silent mercury light switch, magazine advertisements, musical instruments, and drawing materials. One can readily guess from the objects displayed what purposes the speakers had in mind.

The great advantage of the object and the model lies in their three dimensions. A solid object represented on a plane surface, even when drawn in perspective, is not easy to visualize. But the object itself or a model is readily perceived as solid no matter how a speaker handles it. Visually, the difference between a model and a diagram is the difference between a picture of an airplane and a model of one. Another special advantage of the model is that a speaker can move the thing and its parts about in any way he wishes at any moment to exhibit precisely what he wants to show. Whereas he might need three or four diagrams to demonstrate the parts and operation of a rotary pump, and consume valuable time to sketch on a blackboard or to draw on charts, the pump or a model can be manipulated swiftly. The model is maneuverable; it is dynamic. The speaker who finds himself with a subject that involves three-dimensional objects should face this question again and again during the early stages or preparation: Can I secure—or make—a simple model?

In learning to use models skillfully, speakers should (1) rehearse with the model until it can be handled easily and surely, with each part being introduced precisely when needed; (2) point out with a pencil or in some manner each feature and part as it is introduced. *Identify it unmistakably.* Naming the part is not enough; the connection between the name and the thing must be made visually; (3) keep their eyes on the audience as much as possible, rather than on the model; (4) make the model large enough to be seen by everyone. An object too small to be easily seen is worse than no object at all; it only irritates the audience.

Charts

A chart is a drawing, a sketch, or any arrangement of lines and colors on paper or cardboard prepared prior to the delivery of a speech and exhibited during the speech as the speaker needs it. Since charts are extraordinarily useful for presenting all kinds of information in many different forms, speakers representing business and industry have long used them widely. Student speakers should employ them more often than they do. Some of the kinds of charts, easily and inexpensively prepared, are mentioned and illustrated below. All of them show how rather difficult ideas, such as those dealing with the structure and arrangement of clubs, societies, and institutions or those dealing with data and statistical information, can be made concrete and clear.

Organization Chart. Figure 3 shows how a speaker, wishing to explain the basic organization of a university, might visualize its structure. Note that the chart is functional, for each group (enclosed in blocks) has duties and purposes which distinguish it from every other group.

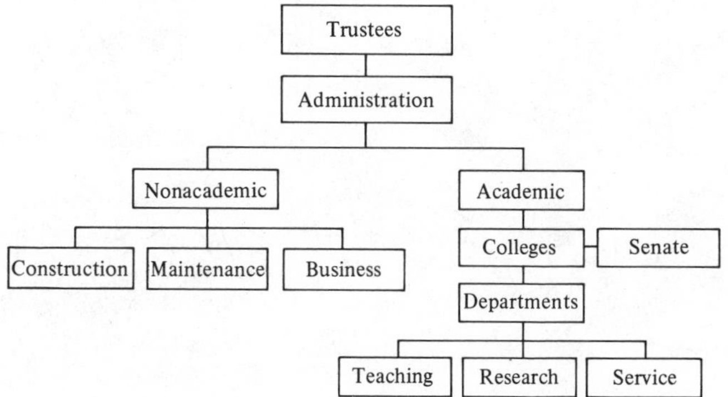

Figure 3. ORGANIZATION CHART
The Structure of a University

Piece O' Pie. The piece o' pie (Figure 4) is a common, easy way of presenting simple statistics so that their relative size may be appreciated.

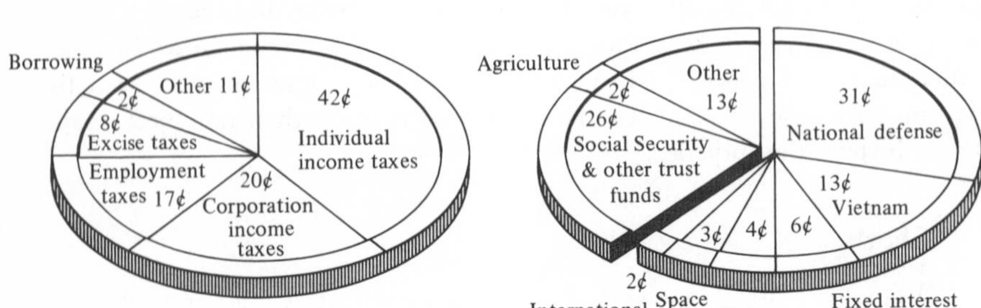

Figure 4. PIECE O' PIE
The Federal Government Dollar, 1968

Cutaway

Figure 5 is a neat illustration of the cutaway technique, which permits one to show essential aspects of the interior of an object. Observe that the sketch is designed to make clear the *spatial* arrangement and *positions* of one part with respect to another.

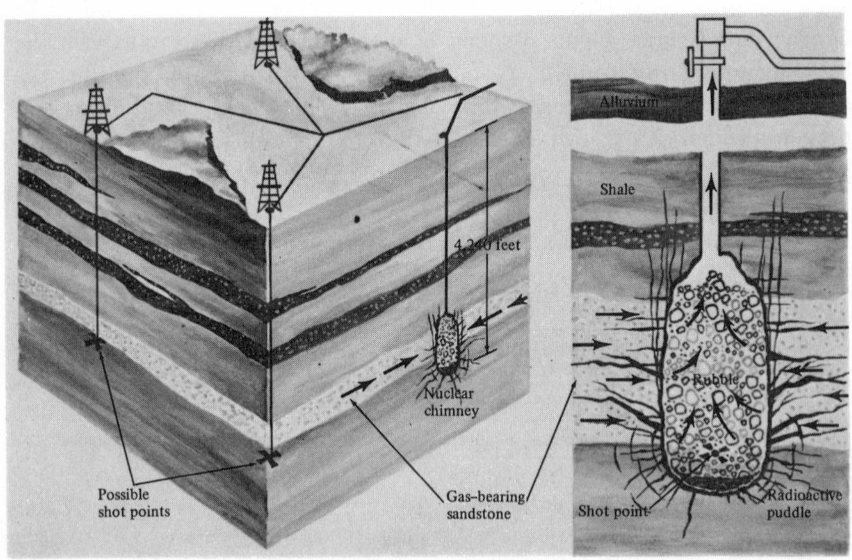

Figure 5. CUTAWAY
Nuclear Mining

Observe, too, how uncomplicated a complicated setup can be made to appear when only the barest essentials required to reveal basic parts and their operations are selected. The result for both speaker and audience is simplicity and clarity. Animated cutaways have come to be used often on TV programs, both for serious exposition and for advertising.

Maps

A map is designed to show certain features of land and sea. The map-maker includes only the features that serve his purpose. In producing road maps, for example, he assumes that the prime purpose of a motorist is to get from place to place without getting lost and to drive on the best available roads. A speaker, similarly, makes a map to suit only *his* purpose. He includes only the essentials, uncluttered by useless and irrelevant details. Our example, Figure 6, is a map designed to accompany an article dealing with the westward shift in the location of the center of the population in the United States.

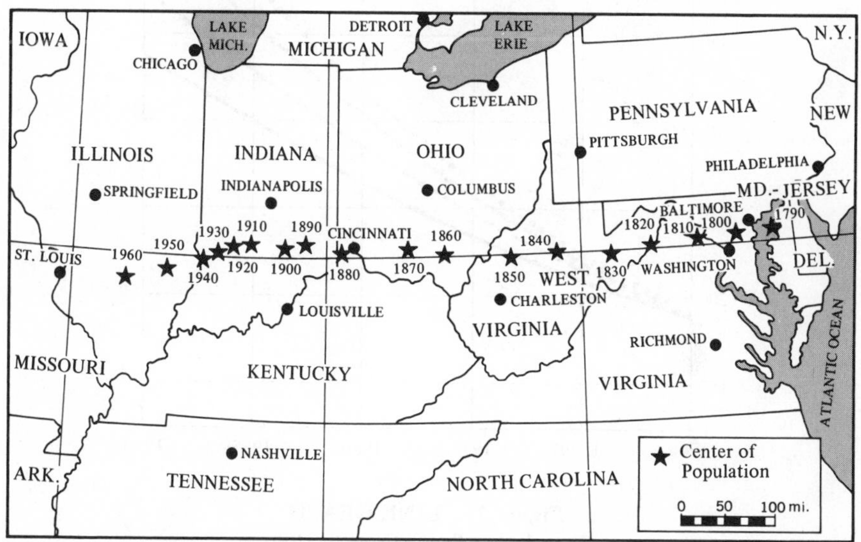

Figure 6. MAP
Center of Population for Coterminus U.S., 1790–1960

Graphs. The charts we have mentioned are devices for visualizing factual materials whose functions, operations, structures, and positions must be seen to be understood. The arrangement of charts to illustrate these factors would be impossible without our notions of time and space. The graph, however, is a visual device for presenting facts generally involving number and quantity in relation chiefly to time. The graph is the eye of statistics. We will briefly consider the commonest kinds of graphs, those that speakers themselves can readily construct from data they discover in their reading and investigation.

The *line graph* is best adapted to showing how related sets of facts change and develop according to some common measure of reference—usually that of time. The graph in Figure 7, for example, shows the projected growth of

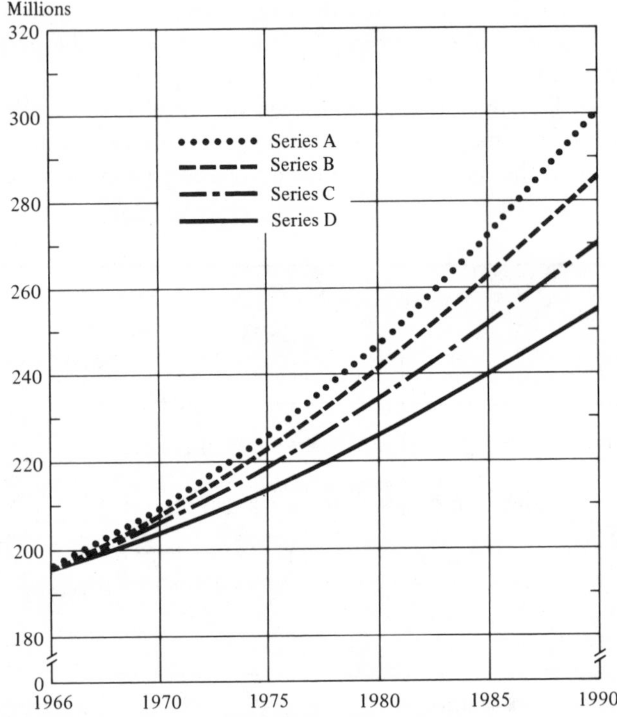

Figure 7. LINE GRAPH
Population Projections to 1990

the nation's population over almost a quarter of a century. The *profile graph* is the twin of the line graph, and can be used to present the same data. By shading or coloring the area under the curve, the effect is made sharp and dramatic as in Figure 8, which shows the growth and distribution of United States investment abroad.

The *bar graph* is also a device for presenting two facts in comparison with each other, but unlike the line graph it does not usually show how the facts

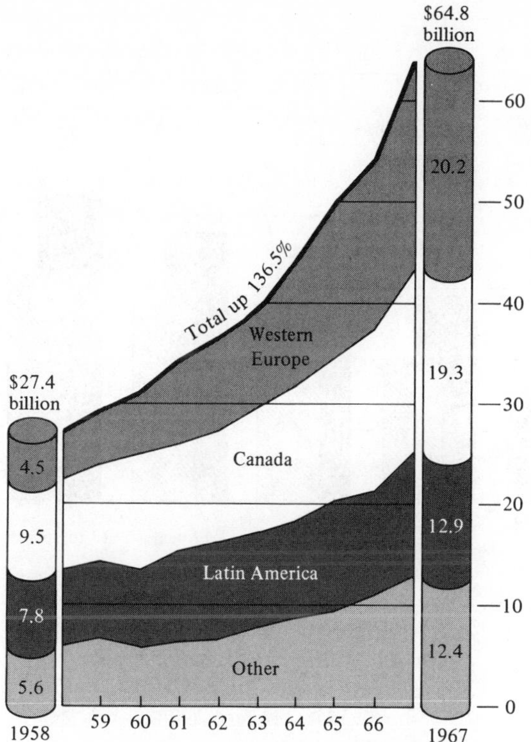

Figure 8. PROFILE GRAPH
U.S. Investment Abroad (book value)

change over time. Instead, the bar graph simply confronts one fact with another, one set of results with another set. It presents the final results, the end product, without trying to show the intermediate data. Observe that the bar graph in Figure 9 is concerned only with the comparative incomes of white and nonwhite families.

The *pictograph* is designed to present and compare numerical facts by using a simplified picture or pictorial symbol, as in Figure 10. The symbolic picture, moreover, is directly associated with the objects, events, or situations to which the statistics refer.

Advantages of the Chart. The chart has four distinct advantages over the blackboard sketch or diagram. It can be used faster in the speech than the blackboard can, and accordingly, makes possible a swift-running speech. Even when a speaker employs a series of charts, he can display the right one at the right time, say what is needed about each, and move on. The chart also makes it relatively easy for a speaker to keep his eyes on his audience; the blackboard, on the other hand, requires him to attend to it as he draws, rather

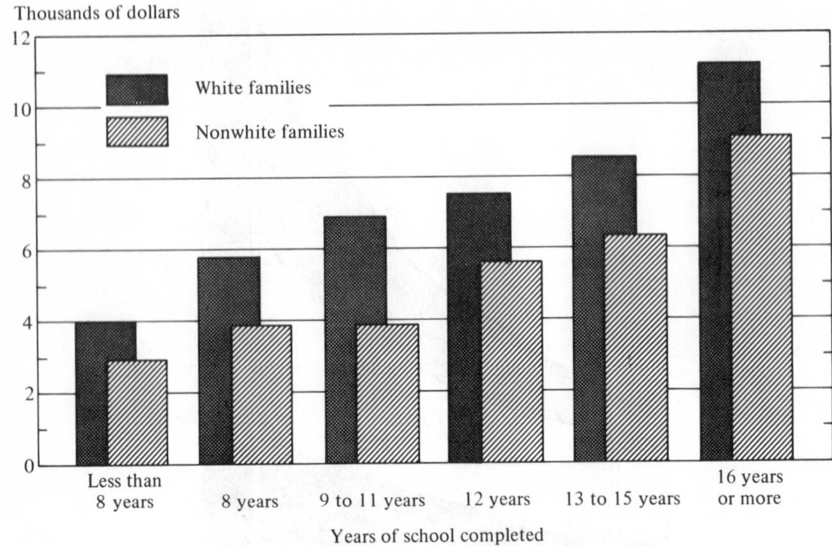

Figure 9. BAR GRAPH
Median Money Income of Families, by Education and Color of Head, 1965

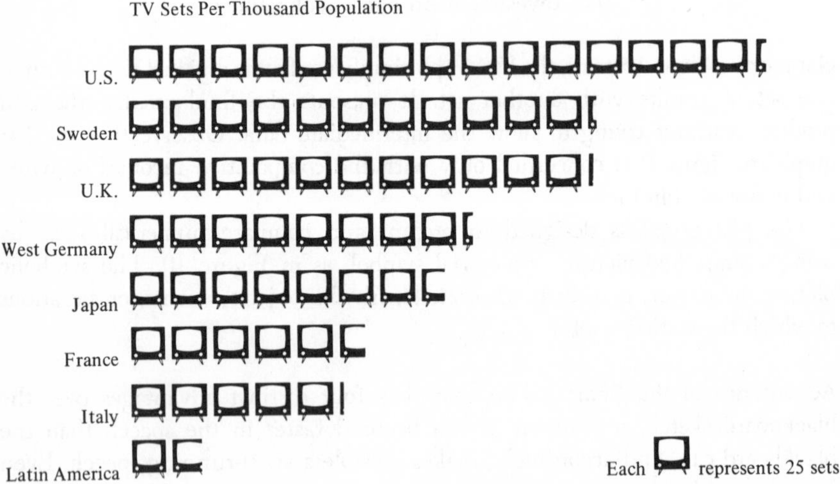

Figure 10. PICTOGRAPH
The Television Standard of Living

than to the audience. The chart, furthermore, can be more readily used in rehearsal than the blackboard. Few speakers have available a sufficiently large blackboard when they are ready to rehearse, and student speakers cannot always find an empty classroom to rehearse in when they want it. Finally, charts give opportunity to use color and lines of different breadth. Contrasting colors can be employed to secure both emphasis and interest; heavy lines can be used to outline prominent features, light lines for subordinate details; shading and cross-hatching can be put in to suggest thickness. Such refinements add variety and interest, as well as promote clearness.

In the classroom student speakers sometimes are troubled about where to place a chart—whether to thumbtack it to the blackboard frame or desk edge, to prop it upon a desk, or to pin it to some nearby handy surface, such as a curtain. Wherever a special stand for holding charts is not available, the best solution is for the speaker to manage the size and material of the chart so that he can hold it in front of him when he wants it. For this purpose, the largest practicable dimension seems to be about 24 x 30 inches. The material need be only stiff enough to support itself. A chart like this, if its features are bold and uncluttered with unnecessary detail, can be easily seen by a group of fifty persons. A speaker can readily learn to glance down at his chart from above and point out its features with a pencil.

The blackboard sketch or diagram, the model, the object, and the chart all hold great possibilities for securing both clearness and interest in a speech. Speechmakers often use other types of visual aids, such as photographs, lantern slides, filmstrips, and motion pictures. We have restricted our suggestions here to the aids which student speakers themselves can manufacture without technical assistance and can use without special projectors and darkened rooms. Of course the photograph is often employed effectively, but in our experience the student speaker has found its merits outweighed by its drawbacks. Most photographs are too small to be seen, even by an audience of fifteen persons. They must be enlarged, and enlargement is costly—far more expensive than the materials for a chart. Unless originally taken for the special purpose of the speech, moreover, the photograph usually contains more features and more detail than are needed. Thus the audience, if not confused, is often distracted from the business at hand. In fact, the more unskillful the speaker the more his hearers will welcome any excuse to explore a picture for features which recall familiar pleasant associations.

Using Visual Materials

When introducing each kind of visual device and discussing its special advantages, we have offered some suggestions for its use. For emphasis, we restate—and add other suggestions which apply to *all* kinds of visual aids.

Size: Whatever kind of visual material is used, it must be *large* enough for everyone to see clearly and easily. Don't guess; be sure.

Details: Include only those features and details which are *essential* to clearness. Above all, avoid useless labels and names on a chart or graph. If labels are to be seen, their lettering must be large, and many labels will therefore give a cluttered effect.

Artistry: Any chart or sketch, no matter how simple, must be *precise* and *neat.* An impression of carelessness and sloppiness reflects unfavorably on the speaker. Furthermore, a chart that is elaborate with extra decorative touches of line and color is as ineffective and inefficient an aid to verbal communication as is muddy drawing. Even if a speaker happens to be superior at picture-making and draftsmanship, his job is to communicate ideas, not tell his hearers what a fine artist he is.

Eyes: The audience's eyes, not the speaker's, are to be kept on the visual materials. The speaker's eyes should not stray from his hearers longer than is absolutely necessary.

Setting: Any visual device needs a verbal setting when it is first displayed, just as a verbal illustration or story needs a setting if its point is to be understood. Perhaps the best swift setting is secured when a speaker follows this formula: (1) state first what the device is intended to show; (2) point out next its *main* features, so that the listeners have some grasp of the whole. It can be helpful also to ask the audience some leading questions before explaining the visual aid. The questions will get the audience to participate at once.

Pointing: Use a pointer, pencil, or finger to *locate* the specific feature or detailed part being talked about at the moment. Even some veteran speakers assume that a properly labeled, clear chart held prominently before an audience is sufficient and that all eyes will spot each feature as the speaker refers to it. But because any sketch, chart, or graph is found to contain more than a single item, spectator's eyes roam over the illustration; they are visually curious. To control roaming and to direct focusing, pointing is necessary. But when the spot is located, the speaker should look at the audience.

To use or not to use visual materials

Many earnest persons who take their speechmaking seriously find it easier to organize ideas, to manage details, to present them orally—in other words, to apply the methods and techniques of speaking—than to judge what ideas and materials are the most appropriate and effective for a particular audience and occasion. The problem of selecting the right idea, right phrase, right word for the right time and right persons is not easy. Nor is it easy to decide in a particular speech whether to use visual materials. Two fundamental principles, however, may help a speaker make his decision. Helpful, too, may be a list of some of the kinds of subjects for which usually—but not invariably—a speaker should appeal to the eye as well as to the ear.

Visual materials should be used when speech is not likely to secure clearness and understanding without them; this is the principle of effectiveness. Visual devices should be called upon when speech alone takes considerably more time to achieve clearness than would be necessary with visual aids; this is the principle of efficiency.

The following kinds of subjects usually cannot readily be made clear through speech alone, and visualization is almost always a requirement for audiences who are hearing about them for the first time:

The how-something-is-done subject. *Examples:* laying out a garden; planning a house; conducting a laboratory experiment.

Explanations of operations, machines, physical and natural events. *Examples:* commercially separating cream from milk; the carburetor; drilling an oil well; the universe of an atom; the vacuum tube; development of the human embryo; transmission of nerve impulses.

Subjects dealing with the structure or organization of something—how one part is related to another. *Examples:* The Chicago Board of Trade; county manager form of government; the Red Cross; the university players club; the X Chemical Company; the Illinois Central Railroad.

Subjects requiring much information in the form of statistics and demanding summaries of factual material. *Examples:* The law of supply and demand; income tax versus sales tax; purchasing power of the dollar—1969 versus 1938; steel profits and wages; crop rotation and yields; grades as related to intelligence; pure metals versus alloys.

Through observation and experience we know that some factual materials, in both the informative and the persuasive speech, may be communicated more swiftly and efficiently by visual devices than by speech. In a few seconds the eyes may see and comprehend what the ears might require two minutes for. Suppose, for example, that a speaker were arguing that the Federal budget should be reduced. If one of his supporting points were that "the proportion of national income needed to pay the federal bill has become uncomfortably large," he might wish to amplify as follows:

In 1930, out of each dollar of income, the government took 6 cents; in 1935, 10 cents; in 1940, 12 cents; in 1945, 30 cents; in 1950, 33 cents.

This would not be unclear, when expressed orally, but the full force of the comparison might not be instantly grasped. So, to secure greater emphasis and make attention easier, the speaker decides he will try to put the ideas this way:

> In 1930, out of each dollar of income, the government took 6 cents; twenty years ago each one of us paid to Uncle Sam 6 percent of every dollar we received. In 1935, five years later, we paid 10 cents, or 10 percent. In 1940, we were contributing 12 cents, and by 1945, because of World War II, the 12 cents had more than doubled—it had become 30 cents. In 1950 we were supporting our government with 33 cents. In twenty years, our government bill multiplied over five times.

The second statement is less compact, easier to follow, and probably more effective communication than the first. The speaker realizes, however, that he is devoting over twice the time to the same material. He has other similar passages in the speech. Must he stop speaking on time? He doesn't want to cut the evidence or an entire section of his talk. Therefore, he decides to appeal to the eye, and with the first passage uses a bar graph:

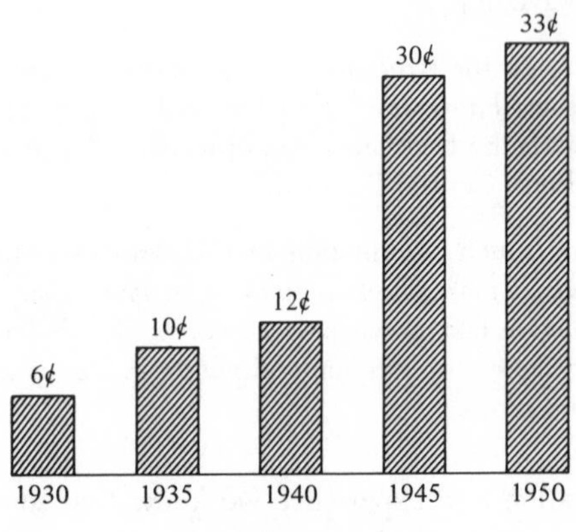

Figure 11

He produces the graph as he starts the passage and by the end of the passage he has used only a little more time than he would have used had he spoken without the graph. He has made his hearers' eyes do what in the second passage he had to do through restatement and some diffusion of language. In brief, through a visual aid he has become more efficient.

The speaker must judge whether or not to use visual means of presentation. He must decide for the speech at hand whether he can use them and whether by using them he can better secure understanding and can attain higher efficiency than he would without them.

FURTHER READING

Arkin, Herbert, and Colton, R. *Graphs: How to Make and Use Them.* Rev. ed. New York, 1940. A full practical treatment.

Brinton, Williard C. *Graphic Presentation.* New York, 1939. Containing hundreds of examples of all kinds of charts and including suggestions for constructing them, this book seems designed primarily for persons and business firms with special facilities for preparing graphic aids. Nevertheless, an hour's time with this book will suggest almost infinite possibilities to a speaker who wants to visualize part of his speech and has not discovered how to do it.

Carskadon, Thomas R., and Modley, Rudolph. *U.S.A.: A Measure of a Nation: A Graphic Presentation of America's Needs and Resources.* New York, 1949. A fine example of visual materials in use.

Dale, Edgar. *Audio-Visual Methods of Teaching.* New York, 1946. Chapter 4 classifies visual materials according to their "distance" from the real objects of experience.

——— (ed.). *Display for Learning.* New York, 1952. Part Two, "Materials for Display," contains many suggestions and illustrations useful to the speaker.

Kinder, James S. *Audio-Visual Materials and Techniques.* New York, 1950. Chapter 7, "Graphical Visual Materials," contains many detailed suggestions that apply to the speaker as well as the teacher.

Rose, L. A., Bennett, B. B., and Foster, E. F. *Engineering Reports.* New York, 1950.

Weaver, G. G., and Bollinger, E. W. *Visual Aids: Their Construction and Use.* New York, 1949. Chapter 4, "How to Make, Display, and Use Charts."

IV

Forming and Ordering Materials

9

The Basis of Outlining

The speaker who has collected a good deal of information on his subject, and who has begun to mull over his material—defining, illustrating, comparing, and contrasting—with a view to making his information clear and acceptable to his hearers, discovers that many items and separate bits of fact and information are understandable by themselves. But at about this point he realizes also that the separate items will not have much meaning for either him or his hearers unless he orders and arranges them into a significant pattern, with every item in its right place. He reminds himself of what we pointed out in Chapter 3: any mind prefers organized ideas to disorganized ideas; and audiences, accordingly, find it exceedingly difficult to hold isolated and unattached information in mind for any appreciable length of time. Nor can audiences readily backtrack and fit into what has already been said information that the speaker forgot or neglected to give at the proper time. Hence, a speaker soon realizes, either as a result of his own experience on the platform or as he confronts increasingly complex problems and begins to make more complex speeches, that he must not present information and argument until he can put it into its natural place in an organized structure. Nor dare he omit detail that will keep intact the significant and consecutive pattern of his thought. One of the surest ways of confusing an audience is to say, "Oh, I should have mentioned earlier. . . ."

The principles and techniques of building speech outlines for informative and persuasive speeches are much the same. In any context the planning, organizing, and shaping of materials involves two operations, analysis and synthesis; that is, dividing and composing. These operations reflect our experience with, and our recognition of, logical relationships among ideas. We group ideas and put them into language according to meanings perceived as principal or subordinate.

Analysis is the process of investigating a subject or problem to see what it involves, resolving it into its constituents, and discovering how the parts relate to the whole and the whole to the parts. This process goes on when, with a possible speech subject in mind, one reviews his experience and ideas and begins to see what the subject involves. It continues more intensively and with more complexity as one reads, talks, and investigates; as one sees the background of his subject, its main problems, and the ramifications of its parts. Analysis, then, is an essential step in speech preparation. About analysis we will say little now except for what we have already suggested: collect information and evidence on the subject in all sorts of ways; see the essentials of the subject or problem; perceive clearly by defining, comparing, and illustrating; and understand the main arguments in a controversy. We will now explain the synthesis of materials for a specific speech.

Synthesis is putting the materials of a speech together for the purpose one has in mind. In building a speech, synthesis involves three principal steps. (1) Determine the specific purpose. If a speech is to be short, its purpose may be quite limited; accordingly, one will reject some, perhaps many, of the ideas turned up through investigation and analysis. (2) Decide what materials are relevant to the specific purpose, and what do not belong. (3) Organize and pattern the relevant ideas so that both speaker and audience can perceive them clearly and remember them easily. The last step requires three actions:

1. Formulating a central idea or a governing theme that stands as the main statement of the speech. In the informative speech it seems best to call it the *subject sentence,* in the persuasive speech the *proposition.*
2. Phrasing main heads that relate to each other and to the central idea. In informative speeches, main heads directly support, develop, and explain the subject sentence; in persuasive speeches they are reasons for accepting the proposition.
3. Planning and ordering subheads and details so that they directly amplify and develop the meanings carried by the main heads. Always a part of explanation and argument, subheads are at the level of example, illustration, evidence, and descriptive detail. They are likely to be a prime source of interest. The visual product of forming and ordering the materials of a speech is a speech outline.

Practical suggestions

After one has collected his materials and has satisfactorily analyzed them, it is wise to begin synthesis by pinning down the specific purpose of the speech in conjunction with the subject sentence or the proposition.

The specific purpose is best thought of as the response the speaker wants to elicit from his hearers. In some situations it can be regarded as the goal of the speech, or as the immediate or ultimate effect. So one tries to decide precisely what he wants from his audience and phrases it in a way that represents the desired response or goal. For example:

Response desired: Understanding what arbitration is.
Specific Purpose: To explain arbitration.

Response desired: Belief in the effectiveness of the United Nations to solve international disputes.
Specific Purpose: To convince my audience of the effectiveness of the United Nations to solve international disputes.

The subject sentence of an informative speech is a statement that epitomizes the ideas used to accomplish the specific purpose. It is a statement that to the speaker as master of his subject says it all; if the speaker were his own audience, the subject sentence would be the *one* statement that he could accept as being a general and accurate explanation of his subject. But from the uninformed hearer's point of view, the subject sentence is the one statement that through amplification becomes so meaningful, so enveloped and enriched with the ideas used to extend and support it, that it works upon the hearer as an extended stimulus sufficient to bring about the desired response. Other names for the subject sentence are *central theme* or *thesis statement.* For example:

Response desired: Understanding what arbitration is.
Subject Sentence: Arbitration is an arrangement that settles a disputed matter out of court.

In an informative speech, the subject sentence also defines or characterizes the subject materials. It classifies and differentiates the subject so accurately that the resulting statement cannot be applied to anything else; that is, the resulting statement is *peculiar* and *distinctive.* Suppose, for example, one wished to define briefly the nature of man. One might say, "Man is a symbol-using animal." Man is thus put into the familiar class of animals and at the same time is designated as a particular kind of animal, the symbol-using.

In the persuasive speech, the proposition is an evaluative statement or a proposal that the speaker desires the audience to accept or to act upon. It is the speaker's conclusion about some aspect of the problem at hand. In capsule form, it is the best advice he can recommend.

Response desired: Belief in the United Nations' ability to cope with international disputes.
Proposition: Public opinion to the contrary, the United Nations has been effective in settling international disputes.

Stating the subject sentence

The subject sentence of an informative speech is usually a statement of fact. It is either a definition or a swift characterization of the materials the speaker has selected and is forming around the specific purpose. To help in coining a subject sentence we offer three suggestions:

1. *Try to formulate a* limited *definition.* The subject sentence can point out *one important way* in which the subject—whether it deals with an object, a play, a novel, a process, a mechanism, a word, a person, or an institution—is distinguished from other closely related subjects.

Boys' Town is an institution for training in citizenship.

The Constitution of the United States was the result of an economic movement.

Elihu Root's career was governed, not by political expediency, but by principle.

Silas Marner is the story of a man redeemed from greed by the love of a child.

Behrman's play *End of Summer* is the portrait of a woman without a mind.

A distinguishing feature of the University of Virginia is its honor system.

2. *Formulate a* full *definition.* In the subject sentence state *all* the peculiarities that set the subject off from closely related subjects.

Burglary is breaking and entering the dwelling-house of another in the night time, with intent to commit felony in the same.

Polo is a game played on horseback, usually with a light wooden ball and with mallets having long flexible handles, with four players on a side, whose effort is to drive the ball between their opponents' goal posts at the opposite end of the field.

A cooperative store is a "store or shop belonging to and supported by a cooperative society, with the purpose of supplying its members with goods at moderate prices, and of distributing the profits, if any, among the members and regular customers."

A great help in coining a full definition, especially when one is dealing with a process, a mechanism, or an operation, is this procedure. Divide a sheet of paper into three columns: Purpose of Process, Materials Used, Manner of Handling Materials. With the process in mind, jot down ideas appropriate to each column. Then study them carefully and write a single concise sentence that incorporates the ideas.

Suppose one wished to explain the manufacture of plain linoleum; here are the columnar data:

PURPOSE OF PROCESS	MATERIALS USED	MANNER OF HANDLING MATERIALS
Floor covering	Linseed Oil	Mixing machines
Will be waterproof	Rosin (ground)	Pressing cork into burlap
Won't dent easily	Cork	Oxidizing
Will outlast wood	Burlap	

The resulting sentence might be, "The manufacturer of plain linoleum is accomplished by mixing linseed oil, ground rosin, and cork, pressing the mixture into a burlap foundation, and allowing it to oxidize, thereby making a floor covering that is resilient, durable, and waterproof."

One of the great advantages of such a statement is that the main heads of its development are clearly implied:

I. The purpose [or function] of the process is. . . .
II. The materials are. . . .
III. The manner of using the materials is. . . .

3. *Name the principle, or principles, on which the explanation of the subject depends.*

> A modern reformatory operates on the assumption that vocational training, good food, and proper environment can make a bad boy into a good citizen.
>
> The jet engine applies in a new way the laws governing the behavior of gases under pressure.

In determining and phrasing the subject sentence, take special pains to avoid loose ill-considered statements like these: "Polo is a unique game"; "A holding company is not as complicated as it seems." Such statements do not point out the distinctive features of their subjects. Almost always, they are signs that the speaker has not thought long enough to decide what he really is talking about.

Stating the proposition

The proposition in a persuasive speech will usually be one of two types.

1. *An evaluative or critical statement.* This reflects the speaker's belief about an issue arising out of the arguments that have clustered around a problem. The statement is his stand or position about something in controversy. If one were interested in foreign aid, his main criticism might be: The U.S. has not found effective ways of aiding underdeveloped countries to help themselves. Or one might be concerned with a specific condition: The U.S. is not giving India enough money for her economic development.

2. *A statement of policy.* This is the speaker's view of the way a problem is solved. There are two main kinds of policy statement, one specific, the other general. The specific policy statement passes judgment on a particular proposal which is being discussed as a solution to the problem at hand. For example:

Students should support the proposal to build a new field house to be financed by an increase in student fees.

Any candidate for a national office should be permitted to speak on the campus.

Students should attend the rally for the Michigan game.

Instead of advocating a specific solution, the general statement of policy simply calls for a change—any change. It says, in effect, that the audience ought to get ready to consider or to do something. For example:

Colleges and universities ought to construct some needed buildings by increasing student fees.

Leading politicians of any party should be allowed to speak on the campus.

Athletic rallies should be better supported.

A value proposition reveals the speaker's assessment of the various aspects of a problem; it may point out that one aspect or one issue of the problem is more important than another. It may also express his dissatisfaction with some state of affairs about which he thinks his hearers should be as dissatisfied as he. A policy proposition, on the other hand, offers a particular solution of the problem. The speaker proposes to resolve the controversy in some way. He may advise what is the best thing to believe or do. Or he may advise his hearers to do nothing and argue that the difficulties besetting them are not as bad as the reformers claim. In any case, the accent of a policy proposition is distinctly different from that of a subject sentence. Its accent is on the future—what ought to be believed or done.

Patterning main heads

The selection and phraseology of the main heads of a speech involve two problems: choosing heads that are directly *relevant* to the subject sentence or proposition; and patterning the heads so clearly that one head suggests other related heads.

The problem of relevance is easily solved. A main head directly amplifies a subject sentence or proposition if it and main head make sense when *for*, *because*, or *in that* is used as a connective between them. For example:

Subject Sentence: The gaseous content of a city's smoke blanket impairs health. (for)
I. It irritates sensitive membranes.

The second problem, that of organizing main heads into a pattern, is more difficult. Yet to both speaker and audience its solution is absolutely essential if clarity of idea and ease of utterance are to be attained. First, a pattern is an arrangement of ideas or things into a system so that any one item in the system suggests and implies other items and so that all essential items have been included and all unessential and irrelevant items have been excluded. Note in the example that follows that (1) each head implies the other, and (2) the parts of the whole take in all the classes of people implied in the subject sentence.

Subject Sentence: Group hospitalization insurance is designed to spread costs of hospitalization so as to benefit everyone.

I. It benefits the patient.
II. It benefits the physician.
III. It aids the hospital.
IV. It benefits the community.

Patterning of ideas is essential, in the second place, because systematic arrangement of ideas gives a speech a clarity that can be achieved in no other way. A pattern of ideas, finally, makes both attention and memory easy for the speaker during delivery. If one looks once more at the example above he will discover that the four main heads have (1) continuity, that is, the first leads to the second, and so on, (2) similarity, that is, they are governed by the same subject and are relevant to the subject sentence and to each other, and (3) inclusiveness, that is, all the items in that particular pattern are present. The observant student may recall here that among stimuli bombarding the mind from without, preference is given to organized, patterned stimuli rather than to unsystematic, chaotic stimuli. He may remember, too, that systematic stimuli will always reveal three conditions—continuity, similarity, and inclusiveness—that help to make them systematic. Accordingly, the better the pattern of main heads in the speech, the easier it is for the speaker to recall and react swiftly to ideas as he talks.

Only after organizing a number of speeches will one discover patterns with some ease. Practice at making ideas systematic gradually builds up a habit of logical arrangement; and when the habit has once been formed, organizing materials is easy and rapid. In forming and fixing the habit, however, one must go through the whole process, no matter how obvious some of it may seem at first.

Though some subjects almost automatically fall into obvious patterns, there are times when the obvious divisions do not serve the speaker's purpose so well as other divisions would. A speech on healthful menus would divide itself almost without help into breakfast menus, luncheon menus, and dinner menus. If the speaker, however, were mainly concerned with balanced meals (whether breakfasts, luncheons, or dinners), he might wish to emphasize his purpose by making his basis for main divisions the different essentials of diet, such as fats, starches, proteins, vitamins. He might then *subdivide* his main divisions according to breakfast, luncheon, and dinner menus.

Standard patterns

Through long experience, speakers and writers have found that a comparatively few plans or patterns of analysis serve satisfactorily for breaking down the majority of subjects. The novice speaker learns to use these patterns and to recognize the kinds of subjects to which each is well adapted.

The Time Pattern. Narrative details and such expository speeches as involve the explanation of a process, for example, or instructions on "how to do it," are more or less naturally chronological. One item comes before another in the speech because it comes before it in the process. For such a speech, the speaker should try to find a limited number (two or three in a short speech) of time divisions into which to group the many chronological items of his material. He should avoid many main divisions. Grouping helps him remember and helps his audience to grasp the entire speech. For example:

Subject Sentence: There are four literary landmarks in the history of free speech in England.

I. Peter Wentworth was tried by the Star Chamber for calling for freedom of speech in Parliament in 1576.
II. John Milton wrote the speech "Areopagitica" in behalf of liberty for printing in 1644.
III. Thomas Erskine defended Thomas Paine's right to publish *The Rights of Man* in 1791.
IV. John Stuart Mill, in his essay *On Liberty,* 1858, argued that liberty of thought and action should be curtailed only when it directly harms others.

Subject Sentence: Ballet had its origins in the Italian Renaissance and it spread rapidly to other European countries.

I. The first ballet performance took place in Tortona, Italy, in 1489.
II. Catherine de Medici introduced ballet to France in 1581.
III. The English Masque evolved into a form very similar to the French during the reign of Henry VIII.
IV. Ballet was well established in Russia by the time of Catherine the Great, in the early eighteenth century.

In using the *time* pattern, it is not necessary, of course, to maintain the chronological sequence. The reverse of the chronological would equally represent a time *relation,* or a speaker might start with one period of time and move on to what came before that time and then to what came after.

The Space Pattern. The division on the basis of *spatial* relations is natural and obvious for some kinds of subject matter. For instance, most newscasts are so divided: international news, Washington news, other national news, local news. Besides geographical subjects, others may profitably be organized to proceed from front to back or back to front, top to bottom or bottom to top, inside to outside or outside to inside, near to far or far to near. For example:

Subject Sentence: The Sea of Cortez (the romantic name for the Gulf of California) is a fisherman's paradise.

I. In the northern end of the gulf totuava, grouper, and pompano are plentiful.
II. In the midriff region the waters abound in yellowtail, roosterfish, skipjack, and black sea bass.
III. La Paz, in the south, is noted for its billfish: sailfish, marlin, and swordfish.

Subject Sentence: The atmosphere, or the sea of air which surrounds our planet, has several distinctive layers.

I. The part of the atmosphere in which we live and in which our weather occurs is the troposphere.
II. Above the troposphere is the stratosphere in which the temperature is constant.
III. In the mesosphere temperatures first increase with height and then decrease with height.
IV. In the ionosphere, temperature increases with elevation reaching almost 200° F.

Subject Sentence: The control panel of the powerhouse is arranged for greatest convenience of the operator.

I. Close in front of him are the instruments that he uses most often.
II. Farther away to the sides are the less-used dials and levers.

Because many persons are strongly visual-minded and are likely to connect things they wish to remember with places, the *space* pattern of analysis has another distinct advantage. In listening to the explanation of a process, for example, if the listener can visualize part of the process going on in one place and part in another, he often finds it easier to keep track of details and to remember them.

Topical Pattern. Any speech in which the heads spring from the natural or conventional divisions of the subject itself is topically organized. The broad divisions in medicine, for instance, are based on *structure* and *function;* in matter and in science, on *animate* and *inanimate;* in law, on *civil* and *criminal.* Narrow specific subjects break into logically appropriate divisions also. Accordingly, the forms of the topical pattern are greater in variety than those of other patterns. The following samples further illustrate the qualities of the topical pattern:

Subject Sentence: The United Nations is made up of three basic parts.

I. The General Assembly is made up of all member nations, each of which has one vote.

II. The Security Council is made up of fifteen members.
   A. There are five permanent members.
   B. The other ten are elected by the General Assembly for two-year terms.
III. The Secretary-General is the chief administrative officer.

Subject Sentence: The North Pole is not necessarily the cold, snowy, stormy place you think it is.

I. Winter temperatures are only slightly lower than North Dakota's, while the climate of some regions could be called "tropical" in the summer.
II. We think of lots of ice and snow, but when the snowfall is converted to inches of water, an average winter yields only eight inches.
III. The Arctic is one of the least stormy large regions of the world—violent gales are extremely rare.

One kind of *topical* pattern, so often useful that special attention should be given to it, analyzes the material on the basis of *the persons, groups, or categories of people affected.* For example:

Subject Sentence: The daily newspaper provides something for each of many kinds of readers.

I. It serves those persons who want information and opinion on public affairs.
II. It provides for those who wish to be entertained.
III. It guides the shopper.
IV. It serves the businessman.

The speaker is most likely to discover various "natural" divisions of his subject through reading. Accordingly, even if he is working on an expository subject that he knows intimately through personal experience, he would do well to dig up a book or article related specifically or generally to the topic, and to read enough to become aware of the author's divisions and classifications.

Causal Pattern. In dealing with events and their forces, one can often use a pattern like the following:

Subject Sentence: A run on a bank has many causes.

I. Its ultimate cause is lack of confidence in the ability of the bank to honor deposits.
II. A contributory cause may be a financial depression.
III. An immediate cause may be rumors that the bank is in danger of bankruptcy.

Subject Sentence: Race rioting is one of the products of a society of unequal opportunity.

I. A feeling of despair and hopelessness is often at the basis of riots in our big cities.

II. Inferior schools, few job opportunities, and slum housing contribute to the hostile attitude of rioters.
III. Despair and hostility build up until a relatively minor incident precipitates a riot of enormous proportions.

Purpose-Means Pattern. This is especially useful in arranging the essentials of a process or an art.

Subject Sentence: Flower arrangement is an artistic endeavor.
I. There is an attempt to present a pleasing picture.
II. There is an attempt to apply the principles of visual harmony and balance.

Subject Sentence: Arbitration is an arrangement settling a disputed matter without taking it to court.
I. The purpose of an arbitration board is to find a compromise between the positions of the disputants.
II. Both sides present their arguments to a three-man board that they have selected and whose decision is regarded as final.

Question Pattern. Here the system of main heads *answers* the four questions: What is it? What is it not? In what manner? Why? For example:

Subject Sentence: In ancient Rome, rhetoric was the art of speaking well.

(What it is)	I. Rhetoric included all those operations which were thought necessary for speaking well. A. It included the invention of ideas. B. Etc.
(What it is not)	II. Although associated with poetics, rhetoric was not identified with it.
(In what manner or what way)	III. Much emphasis was given to the manner of presentation, particularly the style and delivery.
(Reason why or cause)	IV. Audiences were expert in judging the quality of oratory. A. Roman education always included much training in speaking. An educated man was an orator, and vice versa. B. They listened to many fine speakers.

Patterns for persuasion

There are, in addition, some ways to pattern main heads that are better adapted to the speech that is primarily persuasive. In speeches whose propositions are statements of policy, for example, three patterns are useful:

Problem Solution.

Proposition: A job-training program should be instituted for unskilled workers.
I. There are few jobs available for unskilled workers.
II. There are numerous unfilled positions requiring skilled labor.

III. Training programs for unskilled workers would make them available for these positions.

Theory–Practice.

Proposition: Narcotics addicts should be committed to civil institutions for rehabilitation.

I. The rehabilitation of addicts of all kinds is a slow, painstaking process that can only succeed in an institution designed for that purpose.
II. The rehabilitation of narcotics addicts would work out the same way.

Desirable-Practicable.

Proposition: Urban renewal can meet the problems of big-city slums.

I. Neighborhoods can be kept intact.
II. Revitalization of old buildings is technologically feasible.

Patterning the essentials of argument

We present now a number of ways of patterning argument and evidence in the persuasive speech. The symbol x stands for a main head or for any other level of head occurring anywhere in a speech.

Simple Deductive Arrangement. Here the main head is regarded as the conclusion of a deductive inference, and the subheads are treated as the premises.

x. He is in an unpleasant mood, for
1. Doubt is unpleasant. (*General Premise*)
1′. He is in doubt. (*Specific Premise*)
a. ______________________________
b. ______________________________

When the speaker is conscious that he is outlining a bit of deductive reasoning, (*a*) he must decide whether his audience needs to hear both the general and the specific premise, and (*b*) he should realize that most of the proof will be in support of the more specific statement.

General Statement to Typical Example.

x. Outlining helps the student to think, for
1. John Jones found that it did, and
1′. He is a representative student.

When the audience is likely to question the typicalness of a single example, the speaker must be able to defend his choice of example. He can outline the defense as in the example below.

x. Automobile tire advertisements often appeal to fundamental human desires and motives, for

1. The Goodyear tire gives that "margin of safety," and
2. The appeal to safety is typical of tire advertisements, for
   a. ______________________________
   b. ______________________________

Causal Pattern. When a main head is an *effect,* it may be supported by a cause as the first subhead and a defense of the cause as the second subhead.

x. The suicide rate among bachelors is greater than among married men, for
   1. Bachelors have little sense of responsibility to deter them.
   1′. This is the most important cause operating to produce the effect.
      a. ______________________________
      b. ______________________________

Observe that the arrangement below comes naturally from the problem-solution aspect of any controversial problem.

x. The present situation is deplorable.
   1. There are evils (conditions we don't like).
   2. They are due to certain causes.
y. My solution is desirable.
   1. It calls for a definite change from the present.
   2. It will remove the causes that produce our present ills.
z. My solution is the best solution.
   1. It is more desirable than other solutions.
      a. It will cure our ills better than other solutions.
      b. It will not introduce as many new ills as will other solutions.
   2. It is more practicable than other solutions.

Notice that this pattern is really the familiar problem-solution scheme extended somewhat.

Comparison.

x. An honor system would work at *X* University.
   1. It works at *Y* University.
   1′. The two universities are alike in those respects that make an honor system successful.

Observe that the analogy here is literal and has the force of argument.

Contrast.

x. A persuasive speaker, unlike a divine prophet, must exhibit tact in his choice of ideas and in their expression.
   1. The prophet can ignore the weaknesses and foibles of his hearers.
   1′. But the speaker must ever consider the prejudices and attitudes of his audience.

Refutation.

x. The argument that Jones is wise because he has a good education is unsound, for
   1. A good education does not always confer wisdom on a man.

When the speaker seeks to refute or to meet the objections of others, whether in formal speaking, in discussion, or in conversation, he should always do two things: First, state explicitly and fairly the essence of his opponent's view and his objection to it. Second, explain or prove the contention. Observe that the preceding form does the first, and opens a way for the second. *Caution:* Notice particularly that the preceding form is a schematic way of writing the basic thought. In a speech as actually delivered, or in conversation, a more tactful, less blunt, manner of expression is ordinarily imperative. For example, "Can it be that Jones is wise because he has had a good education? After all, education and good judgment are hardly identical."

Admissions and Concessions.

x. Although we may agree that the New Deal had proper objectives, we can hardly praise its methods.
   1. Class feeling was stirred up.

Observe that this construction places the conceded matter in a subordinate position, and the point which the speaker intends to discuss comes last, where he can easily proceed to expand it.

Evidence–Testimony Pattern. A convenient scheme for remembering a sequence of supporting arguments proceeds from the particular idea to the supporting general idea, on to the evidence, both factual and opinion.

x. In the early 1950's, the correspondent for the Associated Press in Moscow had little chance to learn of the true conditions in Russia. (*Particular Idea*)
   1. Correspondents had no access to the sources of information. (*General Idea*)
   2. The correspondent had not been outside of Moscow once in fifteen months. (*Factual Evidence*)
      a. Eric Johnston says that correspondents had seldom been allowed to travel. (*Opinion Evidence*)

In studying these patterns for handling the specific arguments and details of a persuasive speech, students should observe that these patterns may aid in phrasing and expressing arguments, both in the speech outline and in the speech as delivered. Accordingly, *where one cannot phrase structural patterns clearly and readily, we strongly urge the adoption of similar forms.* Do not hesitate to use the forms as models. Remember, the connection between a conclusion and its supporting statements must be clear.

Making the Speech Outline

With the broad pattern of the speech decided upon, the speaker is ready to construct his speech outline. It contains all the ideas he plans to use and in the order in which he wishes to say them. The speech outline should be his guide in rehearsal and oral practice.

Rules of form and arrangement

1. The speech outline should show five distinct parts: Title, Introduction, Subject Sentence, Development, Conclusion.

Outline Form

TITLE

INTRODUCTION

Attention Material __________
____

Orienting Material __________
Including Specific __________
Purpose __________
____

Subject Sentence or __________
Proposition __________

DEVELOPMENT

I. Main head __________
  A. Sub-head __________
    1. __________
      a. __________
        (1) __________
        (2) __________
      b. __________
    2. __________
  B. __________
II. __________
  Etc. __________
III. __________
  Etc. __________

CONCLUSION

Summary and *suggestion* __________
and/or *appeal* __________
____

2. The relation between heads, subheads, and so on, must be indicated by a consistent set of symbols and by indentations: I, A, 1, *a*, (1), (*a*).

3. Each item down to the level of illustrations or specific detail must be a complete sentence.

I. A Chemical solution is not a mixture.
  A. Turbid water is not a solution.
    1. Pieces of matter are in suspension.
      a. Dirt thrown into beaker and stirred illustrates this.
        (1) Note particles.

Rules of logical structure

1. Each head should be a simple sentence which expresses a single idea only; avoid compound and complex sentences.

Wrong: 1. Since they feel they are being charged extra, patrons do not like tipping.
Right: 1. Patrons do not like tipping.
  a. They feel that they are being charged extra.

2. The subject sentence or proposition should state clearly and completely the governing idea of the speech. It will normally appear in the outline between the introduction and the development, will be labeled Subject Sentence or Proposition, and will not be numbered. When the speaker wishes to indicate that he will postpone his governing idea until he has presented some or all of his development, he may place it in the outline at the point where he wishes to introduce it. It will still be labeled, carried out to the left margin, and not numbered.

3. A main head should be a statement that directly supports the subject sentence or proposition. Words that will test for proper subordination are *for, because, in that,* and *to be specific.*

Subject Sentence: Napoleon was a greater general than Caesar. (for)
DEVELOPMENT
1. He was the greater tactician.

Proposition: Cities should adopt a program of exterminating rats in the slums. (for)
DEVELOPMENT
1. Rats are injurious to human health and welfare.

4. The main heads when viewed together should show a logical pattern, division, or classification of the ideas used to develop the subject sentence. Avoid overlapping main heads.

5. Subheads and all subordinate details should develop the main heads directly and unmistakably. Tests for proper subordination are as follows: (*a*) When a subordinate head follows a main head, the two should be related by such connectives as ***in that, for, because, to enumerate.***

I. Social settlements are down-to-earth, practical agencies for relieving poverty in slum areas. (for)
   A. Their staff of professional men and women live in tenement neighborhoods. (because)
      1. In these neighborhoods the needs of working people can best be seen.

(*b*) When a subordinate head precedes its main head, the two should be related by using such connectives as ***therefore, thus, hence, as a result, consequently.***

      1. In tenement neighborhoods the needs of working people can best be seen. (hence)
   A. A Social settlement's staff of professional men and women will live in the tenement neighborhood. (thus)
I. Social settlements are down-to-earth agencies for relieving poverty in slum areas.

Use of Speech Outline

The speech outline is designed to give a complete sequence of ideas, arranged in the order in which they are to be presented in the speech; it is the path or trail the speaker pursues from beginning to end. Accordingly, he should use it in rehearsal.

In the first speeches one should try to make his presentation follow the path of the speech outline as closely as he can. Do not try to memorize the items, but through practice and repetition become so thoroughly familiar with the ideas that they are readily put into language during the moments of utterance. Try to avoid consciously and deliberately burdening the mind with arbitrary associations; for example, avoid associating a main head with its symbol or with its special place or spot on the page and avoid memorizing sequences of words as such. In other words, try to make the association of ideas natural and logical rather than arbitrary. The speaker should dominate the outline; the outline should not dominate him.

Students will do well to follow the method of rehearsal that has been outlined in Appendix B; it is designed to help the mind associate idea logically and naturally, rather than arbitrarily.

Specimen outlines of informative speeches

The seven outlines in these pages represent some of the best work of student speakers. Most of them reflect some revision. The speeches based on them ran from seven to twelve minutes.

The first two outlines below illustrate what can be done in organizing the materials of processes and procedures.

The Classification Procedure of the Selective Service

INTRODUCTION

A. Attention Material
  1. Do you feel a draft?
  2. I am speaking of the United States Selective Service System draft.
     a. If you're a male between the ages of 18 and 35, you probably know about this draft.
     b. If you're a girl with a brother or boy friend of draftable age, you, too, are probably concerned about it.

B. Orienting Material
  Specific Purpose: to explain the procedure used by the Selective Service in classifying draft-age men.
  Subject Sentence: This procedure involves an initial classification on the basis of a completed questionnaire, with a further classification on the basis of a physical examination and the claim of conscientious objection.

DEVELOPMENT

I. The initial classification is made on the basis of the information obtained from a questionnaire sent out by the local draft board.
  A. It contains information about occupational, educational, and marital status, and physical disabilities.
  B. Registrants are now placed in a subclass of one of four main classes.
    1. Men placed in Class 4 are specifically deferred by law, unfit for military service, or conscientious objectors.
       a. Those placed in class 4–F are physically, mentally, or morally unfit.
       b. Conscientious objectors are classed as 4–E.
       c. Ministers and divinity students are in Class 4–D.
       d. Non-declarent aliens are classed as 4–C.
       e. Officials deferred by law are classed as 4–B.
       f. Veterans are classed as 4–A.
    2. Men placed in Class 3 are deferred because of dependents.

3. Men placed in Class 2 are deferred because of occupational and educational status.
    a. Students are classed as 2–S.
    b. Those necessary for the national defense are classed as 2–B.
    c. Those necessary in their civilian activity are classed as 2–A.
4. Men placed in Class 1 are available for immediate service.
    a. Men who have reached age 26 are classed as 1–H.
    b. Members of the armed forces are classed as 1–C.
    c. Those fit only for limited service are classed as 1–B.
    d. Those fit for general military service are classed as 1–A.

II. The second classification is on the basis of a physical examination and the claim of conscientious objection.
  A. A physical examination is given to those in Class 1 and those claiming conscientious objection.
  B. Non-objectors are classified according to their physical examination results.
    1. Those physically and mentally fit are placed in Class 1–A.
    2. Those fit only for limited service are classed as 1–B.
    3. Those unfit for any service are classed as 4–F.
  C. Conscientious objectors are screened and, if accepted, are classed as 4–E.

CONCLUSION

This, then, is the procedure used to classify eligible men in each of the 4,000 local draft boards throughout the country. According to the Selective Service System Report for May 1, 1966, the overall picture of the 18 million draft-age men in the U.S. shapes up like this: Class 4, those unfit for service, deferred by law, or conscientious objectors, accounts for about 5 million men. Class 3, those deferred because of dependents, accounts for about 3 million men. Those in Class 2, with student or occupational deferments, number slightly less than 7 million. However, only about 1 million of these men are classed 1–A—available for immediate induction. The Selective Service goes to great lengths to insure that each individual is given the proper draft status. The classifications are on the basis of (1) information obtained from the questionnaire; and (2) the physical exam or claim of conscientious objection. President Johnson has stated about the classification procedure, "We don't want just a system, we want a just system."

BIBLIOGRAPHY

"Are Changes Coming in the Draft?" *U.S. News and World Report,* 60 (June 13, 1966), 46–47.

Baldinger, Milton I. *The Constitutionality and Operation of Certain Phases of the Selective Service System.* Washington, D.C.: School of Law, Georgetown University, 1941.

Hershey, Maj. General Lewis B. "Stepping up the Draft: Who Will Go Now," *U.S. News and World Report,* 51 (Sept. 4, 1961), 62–67.

U.S. Selective Service System. *Information Concerning Occupational Classifications.* Washington, D.C.: Government Printing Office, Aug. 16, 1943.

U.S. Selective Service System. *Selective Service Regulations.* Washington, D.C.: Government Printing Office, 1944.

A Simple Digital Computer

INTRODUCTION

A. Attention Material
   1. The University of Illinois has the Illiac on its engineering campus.
   2. The Illiac is an example of a digital computer using the binary notation.

B. Orienting Material
   Specific Purpose: Today, I would like to explain in a simplified manner what happens in a digital computer using the binary notation.
   Subject Sentence: A digital computer is the combination of a denary-to-binary converter, a binary calculator, and a binary-to-denary converter.

DEVELOPMENT

I. The difference between denary notation and binary notation should be understood.
   A. There are ten digits in the denary notation—1, 2, 3, etc.
   B. There are only two digits in the binary notation—1 and 0.
   C. The value of a digit in a denary number increases as powers of ten (1, 10, 100, etc.) as they move to the left.
   D. The value of a digit in a binary number increases as powers of two (1, 2, 4, 8, etc.) as they move to the left.
   E. The total value of a number in either notation is found in the same manner—the individual values of the digits are added to find the total value.
      1. A graphic illustration will show this.
         [Now that we have some idea of a binary number, I will proceed with the basic plan of the computer.]

II. The first operation is converting the incoming denary numbers to binary numbers.
   A. A graphic illustration will help show what is accomplished.
      1. The denary number is expressed in bushels of grain.
      2. This amount of grain is then expressed by a binary number.
         a. A series of boxes holding 1, 2, 4, 8, 16, etc., bushels of grain are to be filled completely or not at all.
         b. All of the original grain is to be used.
         c. The full boxes corresponds to the digit "1" in binary notation; the empty ones, "0."

3. The resulting binary number represents the same value—bushels of corn—as the denary number.

B. The digital computer uses an electronic circuit for converting denary numbers to binary numbers.
[Next, we proceed to the main part of the computer.]

III. The second step is the manipulation of the binary numbers by the calculator—the heart of the digital computer.

A. Explaining the simple operation of adding binary numbers will help show what this stage of the machine does.

1. When "1" is added to "0," the sum is "1."
2. When "1" is added to "1," the sum is "10."
   a. When a number is added to itself, the number has been doubled.
   b. According to binary notation, to double a number is to move it one place to the left.
   [Several problems will be worked on the blackboard.]

B. The manipulation of the binary number is done by electronic circuits.

C. The binary system is more convenient than the denary system in this part of the computer.

1. The electronic circuits are simplified.
   a. In the denary system, there are ten digits.
   b. In the binary system, there are two digits which can be expressed by two entities—
   (1) positive or negative,
   (2) conducting or not conducting,
   (3) magnetism or no magnetism.

[Now that we have the results in the binary notation, they must be changed to the denary notation.]

IV. The last step is converting the results in binary numbers to denary numbers.

A. A graphic illustration will explain what happens in this process.

1. Whenever a "1" appears in a binary number, a chain corresponding to its position is pulled.
2. A series of bins release 1, 2, 4, 8, 16, etc., marbles respectively when a chain is pulled.
3. The marbles fall into a chute which runs them through a counting machine.
4. The denary number is obtained in this manner.

B. Again, an electronic circuit handles this maneuver.

CONCLUSION

The digital computer is essentially a machine that converts denary numbers to binary numbers, manipulates these binary numbers, and then converts the results back into denary numbers.

SOURCES

A course in computer theory and considerable experience working with computers in the Control Systems Laboratory.

This outline illustrates how a speech can be built around a definition. Observe that the speaker explicitly referred to his chief source materials in the Introduction, and felt no need to cite them more fully in a reference list.

What is a "Solution"

INTRODUCTION

A. Attention Material
   1. Many of you are now taking qualitative analysis.
      a. Last week you heard Professor X explain the nature of a solution.
      b. If you don't understand what a solution is any better than I did, perhaps I can help you.
   2. I talked with Professor X for half an hour and then read a special article on solutions in the *Journal of Chemical Engineering.* I believe I now know what a solution is.

B. Orienting Material
   Specific Purpose: To explain the meaning of *solution* as the chemist sees it.
   Subject Sentence: A solution is a body of homogeneous character, whose composition may be varied continuously within certain limits.

DEVELOPMENT

I. Homogeneity is an essential of all true solutions.
   A. *Homogeneity* means "identity or similarity of kind or nature."
   B. Salt in a glass of water is a good example. (Demonstrate by mixing salt and water in a beaker.)
      1. Neither by eye nor microscope can different physical states be detected.

II. The composition of true solutions may be varied continuously within certain limits.
   A. This is illustrated by the addition of salt a little at a time to a glass of water.
      1. The salt dissolves for a long while.
      2. Then finally it settles to the bottom and the limit of the process has been reached.
   B. In certain cases the limit may be infinity.
      1. Water and alcohol will dissolve each other in any given quantities.

III. True solutions are differentiated from other mixtures.
   A. Turbid water is not a solution. (Stir soil and water in a beaker and hold to light.)
      1. It is merely a suspension of pieces of matter.
      2. It is not homogeneous in character.
      3. The solid will settle to the bottom eventually.
   B. The mixture of milk and cream is not a true solution.
      1. Cream is merely a mass of fat globules suspended in the water of the milk.
      2. Suspensions of one liquid in another are called emulsions.
   C. Metal particles suspended in water although they show little tendency to settle out cannot be classified as true solutions.
      1. This type of mixture is intermediate between the dispersion of the solution and that of the suspension.

CONCLUSION

It's all very simple, you see. A solution is a homogeneous body whose composition may be varied within certain limits.

Specimen outlines of persuasive speeches

The next four outlines illustrate speakers' responses to three typical aspects of persuasive situations. In the first outline, the speaker has centered on the importance of a problem; in the next two outlines, on the solution of a problem. In the last, the speaker calls for action.

The Problem of LSD

INTRODUCTION

A. Attention Material
   1. Lysergic acid dyethylamide has many characteristics.
      a. It has no color.
      b. You cannot taste it.
      c. It has no odor.
   2. LSD can be bought on the black market for three to five dollars.
   3. It can be made in a college chemistry lab from a parasitic fungus on rye heads.
   4. The main advocator of LSD is ex-Harvard professor, Timothy Leary.

B. Orienting Material
   Specific purpose: I plan to show how LSD has become a great problem.
   Subject Sentence: No longer a psychological research tool, LSD presents a threat to health, official research projects, and innocent users as well as to others.

DEVELOPMENT

I. LSD is a threat to health.
 A. The facts concerning LSD show that it can drastically alter psychological make-up.
  1. When under the influence of LSD the mind is in a state of disorganization.
   a. It is often impossible to distinguish one's body from one's surroundings.
   b. It has been described as an experience in which earthly realities evaporate.
   c. The user undergoes a psychological death.
  2. LSD is a hallucinogen.
   a. Hallucinations are based on something real; a stick becomes a writhing snake.
   b. A Harvard student thought he was God.
   c. Another believed himself to be only six inches tall.
   d. Still another thought he was an orange and the moment someone touched him he would turn to orange juice.
  3. Dr. Sidney Cohen, author of the popular book, *The Beyond Within,* says: "Many people are doing what we would never do experimentally. Someday their brains may wind up in the laboratory and give us the answers."
 B. LSD also causes physiological changes, although they are not as drastic as the psychic ones.
  1. The blood sugar goes up slightly.
  2. Blood pressure rises.
  3. Nausea occurs.
  4. The user experiences chills, irregular breathing, sweating of the palms, and trembling of the extremities.
  5. Sleeping and eating are impossible.
  6. The pupils of the eyes are so widely dilated that one must wear dark glasses even at night to keep out the glare.
  7. There is evidence that there may be long-range effects on the brain.
  8. It is hypothesized that LSD may cause mutations in chromosomes, resulting in deformations and hereditary deterioration.

II. The spread of LSD is causing problems in official research and medical projects.
 A. The only legal distributor has been the Sandoz Pharmaceutical Company.
  1. It recently cancelled all distribution.
  2. It had been accused as being responsible for the illegal spread of the drug.
  3. Laboratory investigators using the Sandoz permit must now obtain permits from the FDA.

B. Many doctors shy away from useful work of controlled experiments.
   1. Experiments had been done with control of pain and alcoholism.
   2. There is talk of cutting off some projects.

C. Doctors and organizations have let it be known that a problem exists.
   1. According to a NIMH report, "Acid heads seek out bootleggers, but legitimate research projects now have trouble getting patients who might be helped by the drug to accept it."
   2. Dr. Ralph Banay, medical director of the Civic Centers Clinic in New York, says: "The black market in LSD will soon have its effect on scientists. Because of illicit use of the highly dangerous hallucinatory drug, research with LSD is going to be very difficult."

III. Most important, the use of LSD poses a threat to innocent people.

A. There is nothing furtive about the acid scene.
   1. Leary calls it the psychic revolution of man.
   2. In New York, or San Francisco, a girl just off the bus from Boise can find it faster than the YWCA by merely asking for a trip.

B. Many children and other innocent people may become the victims of the LSD craze.
   1. "When my husband and I want to take a trip together," said the psychedelic mother of four, as quoted from the *Post,* "I just put a little acid in the kids' orange juice in the morning and let them spend the day freaking out in the woods."
   2. Five-year-old Donna Wingenroth found a sugar cube in the refrigerator of her family's Brooklyn apartment and thinking it was candy, swallowed it.
      a. It had been soaked with LSD and stashed there by her eighteen-year-old uncle.
      b. She was rushed to the hospital alternately laughing and screaming hysterically.
      c. After a stomach pumping and days of intravenous feeding she recovered with no apparent brain damage.
   3. In 1966, in the famous Kessler case, a man slashed to death his fifty-seven-year-old mother-in-law while under the influence of LSD.

CONCLUSION

LSD is a threatening problem today. Its appeal is far-reaching—on college campuses and in teen-age groups. Innocent people are affected and the users themselves may face grave psychological and physical dangers. In conclusion I would like to read a quote by a Los Angeles author using the pseudonym Jane Dunlap.

> I became an angel floating delightfully through space . . . every cell in my body in a frenzy of joyous vibration. I became a Chinese coolie . . . a

fat Turkish sultan . . . silkworms . . . a cobra. I became great streaks of lightning cutting sheer splendor into the skys. . . .

Maybe this is how it is—maybe not. Sure, you can fly now, but what later?

REFERENCES

"Dangerous LSD?" *Scientific American,* 214 (February, 1966), 54.

"Dangers of LSD," *Time,* 87 (April 22, 1966), 52.

"Illicit LSD Traffic Hurts Research Efforts," *Scientific News Letter,* 89 (April 30, 1960), 327.

Kobler, John. "Dangerous Magic of LSD," *Saturday Evening Post,* 236 (November 2, 1963), 30–32.

"LSD: Control, not Prohibition," *Life,* 60 (April 29, 1966), 4 [Editorial].

Rosenfield, Albert, and Farrell, Barry. "Spread and Perils of LSD," *Life,* 60 (March 25, 1966), 28–33.

Education for the Gifted

INTRODUCTION

A. Attention Material
 1. Michael Grost is receiving a special education.
  a. He is an eleven-year-old student at Michigan State University.
  b. He is learning more than if he were in a regular program.
 2. Michael Grost is exceptional.
  a. He has an extremely high IQ.
  b. He is very well adjusted emotionally.
 3. Other gifted children could be helped through special programs.

B. Orienting Material

Specific Purpose: to show that the present programs for the gifted are not enough, and to present my plan for improved education for this group.

Proposition: More provision for developing individual abilities than exists at present should be made for our gifted children.

DEVELOPMENT

I. Acceleration and complete isolation of the gifted is not the best solution.
 A. Acceleration is not the answer.
  1. Professor Leta Hollingworth warns that often there are physical and social maladjustments.
  2. The student may miss fundamental knowledge and skills.
  3. The new curriculum is still aimed at the average student.
 B. Complete isolation is not the answer.
  1. The child is not always superior in all subjects.
  2. The student may not be socially or physically mature enough.
  3. Dr. Leonard H. Clark says, The evidence does not show that ability grouping has been successful."

(Since these practices have not been successful to develop the full potential of the gifted, I suggest the following ideas.)

II. Giftedness should be identified as soon as possible to allow for full development of the child's abilities.
   A. Gertrude Hildreth's book, *Educating Gifted Children,* says that parents could be trained to identify giftedness in their children.
   B. Children could be placed in an environment that would encourage early development.
   C. Special training could then be given to gifted pupils to improve study and work habits.

III. Students should be classified in special classes on the basis of their abilities in particular subjects.
   A. A child might be placed in a special math or science class.
   B. He might be placed in a regular English class.

IV. Better students should tutor poorer students.
   A. This helps the superior student's understanding of the subject.
   B. This brings out the leadership quality.
   C. This allows a feeling of communication between the two groups.

V. Grade groupings should be abolished.
   A. A gradeless system is working at Melbourne High School in Melbourne, Florida.
      1. A student may take sophomore English, junior math, and senior French.
      2. The student may move up or down as his case warrants.
      3. Principal B. Frank Brown says, "Flowers have been blooming all over the place."
   B. A gradeless system is also working at Woodrow Wilson Junior High in Elizabeth, New Jersey.

CONCLUSION

In short, I think you can see that the present practice of complete separation of the gifted child is not doing the job. I hope that you will agree that early identification of giftedness, classification by special ability, opportunities for superior students to tutor poorer students, and the abolition of grade groupings would greatly improve our educational program for gifted children.

BIBLIOGRAPHY

Hildreth, Gertrude H. *Educating Gifted Children.* New York, 1952.

Pritchard, Miriam C. "The Contributions of Leta S. Hollingworth to the Study of Gifted Children." *The Gifted Child,* edited by Paul Witty, Boston, 1951.

Pollack, Jack Harrison. "Should We Separate Smart and Average Kids?" *Parade Magazine, Chicago Sun Times* (January 3, 1965), 4–5.

The Way Out of the Dropout Problem

INTRODUCTION

A. Attention Material
  1. During each school year, nearly one million students leave school with no desire to complete their education.
  2. These students, branded dropouts, have been described as a great national tragedy.
  3. I feel we should do something to alleviate the harmful social and economic consequences of this problem.

B. Orienting Material

Proposition: We should adopt a threefold national program to solve the school dropout problem.

(Here the word "solve" means both to decrease the number of dropouts and to help those who do leave school to become a productive segment of our economy.)

DEVELOPMENT

I. The solution to the dropout problem should include testing, curricular revision, and employment.
  A. First, schools would increase and improve their testing and counseling programs to discourage would-be dropouts.
  B. Second, curricula designed on a study-work basis would be set up.
  C. Employers would be encouraged to hire those students who do drop out of school.

II. Experience shows the program as feasible.
  A. Counseling and testing are useful in spotting and helping potential dropouts.
    1. The student's interest or lack of interest in school shows up in this way.
      a. A sample testing program sponsored by the federal government in 1962 discovered nearly 13,000 potential dropouts.
      b. Individual guidance can often spot a dropout and help him stay in school.
    2. Testing and guidance can direct a student to classes that hold a special interest for him.
  B. School-work programs would help the potential dropout.
    1. Seldom does a dropout's interest lie within a purely academic field.
      a. He sees no purpose in studying English literature or trigonometry.
      b. He often does not have the ability to study straight academic courses.
      c. He often does better to pursue clerical or vocational work.

2. The program has proved effective in several pilot attempts.
   a. According to the *North Central Association Quarterly,* the New York City Work Experience Program was effective.
      (1) In this program, 30 percent of dropouts returned to school.
      (2) Another 30 percent continued to work at the same job after graduation.
      (3) Another 24 percent were either in other private industry or were in the armed forces.
   b. The School to Employment Program has had much the same effect.
   c. Chicago's school-work plan has also been highly successful.

C. Employment in private industry would help the students who will inevitably drop out.
   1. It should be recognized that a high school diploma is not absolutely necessary for obtaining a job.
      a. According to *The Reporter,* March 26, 1964, fifty years ago very few of the employed population had a high school education.
      b. The service jobs have not changed to such a degree that the non-graduates are incapable today of holding such positions.
   2. We will make these people a productive segment of our economy by giving them jobs.

III. The plan as a whole would eliminate the major problems associated with the dropouts.
   A. It would decrease juvenile delinquency and other social problems connected with dropouts.
      1. It would keep many potential dropouts in school.
      2. It would give useful employment to those who do drop out.
   B. It would alleviate the economic problem connected with the dropout.
      1. Those who remain in school will likely get a better job upon graduation.
      2. Those who do drop out would be given gainful employment.

CONCLUSION

In summary, then, my proposal would do more than just show mercy to the dropout. The dropout now gets all the mercy he wants. What he needs is to have his dignity restored. He needs to become a productive segment of our economy. I feel the plan that I have just presented is the first step to restoring his dignity.

BIBLIOGRAPHY

Birkmaier, E. E. "What's to be Done with the Dropout When He Drops Back In?" *North Central Association Quarterly,* 38 (Spring 1964), 301–308.

Brandes, E. M. "Manpower Planning and the New Pariahs." *The Reporter,* 30 (March 26, 1964), 17–19.

Kennedy, J. F. "Dropout Campaign: Exchange of Letters between President Kennedy and Commissioner Keppel." *School Life,* 46 (October 1963), 2–3.

Let's Stop H.R. 4671

INTRODUCTION

A. Attention Material
  1. "Dam it," says Secretary of the Interior Udall; "dam it," says the Bureau of Water Reclamation.
  2. "It" here refers to one of the greatest scenic wonders of the world, our own Grand Canyon.

B. Orienting Material
  1. Legislation to initiate the damming of the Grand Canyon is now before the Interior Committee of the U.S. House of Representatives as H.R. 4671.
  2. The supporters of this bill justify the desecration of the Grand Canyon by maintaining that "it will be instrumental in bringing water to the arid states of the Southwest—primarily Arizona."

Specific Purpose: To persuade my audience to protest H.R. 4671.

Proposition: The proposed bill would needlessly desecrate our Grand Canyon and use our money to do it.

DEVELOPMENT

I. The Grand Canyon dams are planned to make money rather than to provide water for the Southwest.
  A. The proposed dams will not provide one drop of water for Arizona.
  A′. Instead, they will provide money to buy water.
    1. Hydroelectric power plants will be built on the two Grand Canyon dams.
    2. Expected revenue from these power plants will be used to pay for an aqueduct bringing water from the Columbia River.
  B. Supporters of H.R. 4671 look at the Grand Canyon dams only as "cash registers" to pay their debts.

II. The bill would desecrate one of the world's scenic wonders and destroy rare wildlife and invaluable, irreplaceable geological records.
  A. The Marble Canyon Dam is expected to back water up 55 miles while the Bridge Canyon Dam is expected to back water up 93 miles filling the canyon halfway up to the ridge.
  B. The water rise would destroy plants, birds, and wildlife.
    1. The bighorn sheep habitat would go under water at Bridge Canyon.
    2. The wild burrow and deer habitat at Marble Canyon would be destroyed.

C. The damage to geological specimens would be enormous.
   1. Edwin D. McKee of the National Park Service and the U.S. Geological Survey says, "The geological features lost to the dam project would be overwhelming. The Grand Canyon is the most revealing single page of Earth's history anywhere open on the face of the globe."
   2. Rep. John Saylor of Pennsylvania, a member of the House Interior Committee says, "The complete immersion of the inner gorge would destroy a unique geological record and the river which helped to write it."

III. Money to pay for water could be raised more economically and efficiently by building a nuclear power plant near an urban area of high power demand.
   A. I agree with Alan P. Carlin, a Rand Corporation economist, who said that neither Marble Canyon Dam nor Bridge Canyon Dam would be as efficient as a nuclear power plant combined with a pumped storage plant.
      1. The plant would use the same water repeatedly by pumping it from a lower to an upper storage basin and running it through the turbines at hours of peak demand.
      2. The plant would be cheaper to build.
      3. The transmission costs would be lower.
      4. A TVA nuclear generator costs half of the proposed cost of the two Grand Canyon dams.
   B. The nuclear power plant would make more money to pay back the government loan.
      1. Nuclear steam plants in the East are expected to deliver power at the price of four mills per kilo hour.
      1′. This could compete with the prices of private power concerns.
      2. The Grand Canyon dams would sell power at 5.3 mills per kilo hour.

CONCLUSION

What can we do about this threat to our property? We can write letters and send telegrams to our Congressman telling him we want this bill stopped. I appeal to you to do this. Remember, it is not a choice between water for the Southwest and an unspoiled Grand Canyon. The Grand Canyon dams are looked at only as "cash registers" to pay for an aqueduct system that would bring water to the Southwest. These dams would not bring in enough money, however. The best solution is to build a nuclear power plant near the dry cities to pay for the aqueduct. This is your Grand Canyon; and it can never be replaced. Theodore Roosevelt once said "Ages have been at work on it. Man can only mar it." I don't think we want any man or group of men to mar our property needlessly. I have here a letter ready to be sent to my Congressman asking him to stop H.R. 4671. I appeal to each of you to do the same. This is the only way our Grand Canyon can be saved and the time is now.

BIBLIOGRAPHY

Carter, Luther J. "Grand Canyon Debate." *Science,* 152 (June 17, 1966), 1600–1605.

Richter, R. "Ruin for the Grand Canyon?" *Audubon Magazine,* 68 (July 1966), 62–63.

Staveley, G., and East, B. *"Last days of the Colorado?" Outdoor Life,* 138 (July 1966), 24–27.

Stewart, B. "Think Big." *Harper's Magazine,* 221 (August 1965), 62–63.

FURTHER READING

BAIRD, A. Craig. *Rhetoric: A Philosophical Inquiry.* New York, 1965. Chapter 9, "Structure."

CHRISTENSEN, Francis. "A Generative Rhetoric of the Paragraph." *College Composition and Communication,* 16 (October 1965), 144–156.

CROWELL, Laura. "Building the 'Four Freedoms' Speech." *Speech Monographs,* 22 (November 1955), 266–283.

MUDD, Charles S., and SILLARS, Malcolm O. *Speech: Content and Communication.* San Francisco, 1962. Chapter 8, on outlining.

WALTER, Otis M., and SCOTT, Robert L. *Thinking and Speaking.* New York, 1962. Chapters 9–10.

WHITE, Eugene E., and HENDERLIDER, Clair R. "What Harry S Truman Told Us About His Speaking." *Quarterly Journal of Speech,* 40 (February 1954), 37–42.

10

Framing the Speech and Highlighting the Essentials

The basis of outlining, as we have said, lies in the choice of specific purpose and subject sentence or proposition, and the selection of relevant explanatory materials and chief arguments that can be effectively developed within the time limits of the speech. To do these things during speech preparation is not only to help one's memory but probably also to help satisfy the audience's sense of the logic of one's position. But a speaker cannot be content solely with the logic of his ideas. Logic, which is abstract and difficult to grasp even in the best of oral circumstances, cannot be absorbed in large doses by most audiences. There is, then, always the problem of getting an audience to listen to one's position and to recognize it for what it is—an explanatory whole or a case to be considered. The position is framed, its boundaries indicated, and its essentials highlighted. In getting an audience to listen and in directing attention to essentials, a speaker becomes concerned with certain specific tactics and a master strategy. We turn now to tactics, and in the next chapter consider strategy.

Introductions

The first tactic must provide a way of getting the audience to listen. This is a problem of claiming attention and of doing it in a way that leads into the subject matter of the speech. On occasions when a speaker is introduced by his host, the problem is not so demanding as when he must make his own way without assistance. In any event, the speaker must dominate the scene. In the moments prior to his speech, listeners may be concerned with thoughts of friends who are present, with the latest news or gossip, with some feature of the auditorium or of the speaker's dress or manner. Listeners may be turning over preconceived ideas about the speaker, perhaps guessing at the slant he may give to his subject. They may be friendly or hostile or apathetic. In these respects a classroom audience is no different from a "real" audience. The need to secure favorable attention is evident.

Getting attention

Familiar Ideas and References. As we have seen in Chapter 3, the familiar and the novel aspects of a stimulus-situation exert a powerful pull on attention. The familiar idea in a new setting, the novel idea in an old setting, and the novel way of stating a familiar idea, all are effective ways of getting started in any speech, particularly in the informative speech.

Reference to the occasion or the place. Is there any relationship between the subject and the date of the speech? A scientist lecturing on meteorology at Charlottesville, Virginia, on Jefferson's birthday might well refer to Jefferson's interest in recording data on the weather.

Observe Woodrow Wilson's recognition of the occasion and place in his address on "The Meaning of the Declaration of Independence."

> We are assembled to celebrate the one hundred and thirty-eighth anniversary of the birth of the United States. I suppose that we can more vividly realize the circumstances of that birth here than anywhere else. The Declaration of Independence was written in Philadelphia; it was adopted in this historic building by which we stand. I have just had the privilege of sitting in the chair of the great man who presided over the deliberations of those who gave the declaration to the world. My hand rests at this moment upon the table upon which the declaration was signed. We can feel that we are almost in the visible and tangible presence of a great historic transaction.[1]

Reference to the special interests of the audience. What is the connection between the subject and the hearers' vocational and professional interests? Their political affiliations? Their local and community problems?

St. Clair McKelway, speaking many years ago to the National Society of China Importers on the topic "Smashed Crockery," connected his theme, "Opinions, like china, break and change," to the business interest of his audience:

> The china I buy abroad is marked "Fragile" in shipment. That which I buy at home is marked "Glass—This Side Up With Care." The foreign word of caution is fact. The American note of warning is fiction—with a moral motive. The common purpose of both is protection from freight fractors and baggage smashers. The European appeals to knowledge. The American addresses the imagination. The one expresses the truth. The other extends it. Neither is entirely successful. The skill and care of shippers cannot always victoriously cope with the innate destructiveness of fallen human nature. There is a great deal of smashed crockery in the world.
>
> You who are masters in the art of packing things and we whose vocation

[1] J. M. O'Neill, *Models of Speech Composition* (New York, 1921), p. 554.

is the art of putting things, both have reason to know that no pains of placing or of preparation will guarantee freight or phrases, plates or propositions, china of any kind or principles of any sort, from the dangers of travel or from the tests of time. . . .

If, however, the ceramic kingdom is strewn with smashed crockery, how much more so are the worlds of theology, medicine, politics, society, law, and the like. No finer piece of plate was ever put forth than the one inscribed: "I will believe only what I know."[2]

Reference to a recent incident or to a familiar quotation. To start with a reference to a local or national event that has made a deep impression on the community and to link it logically with the subject makes a very easy and effective opening. This type of approach, however, cannot often be used, for only rarely will a speaker be presented with an event that falls in neatly with his subject and the occasion. The beginning speaker in particular must guard against the temptation to stretch an event, to squeeze and torture a happening or a quotation, in order to show a connection between it and his subject.

Good use of the local incident was made by a student in an oratorical contest at Evanston, Illinois. Four days before the contest, the Assistant State's Attorney had been machine-gunned. The student, speaking on the breakdown of the home as a cause of crime, was thus presented with a fitting event that he turned to his benefit. This was his opening sentence:

> The murder of your prosecuting attorney, last Wednesday, has made my subject an unusually timely one for this audience, for beginning with the first recorded human crime—the murder of Abel by Cain—and coming down to this murder in your city day before yesterday, the perplexing question of crime has baffled society.[3]

Reference to what a preceding speaker has said. Where several speakers appear on one occasion, as at banquets, conventions, and in the classroom, an alert speaker can often take his opening remarks from something that has already been said. This means of approach is particularly effective because the reference is fresh in the hearers' minds and it gives some sense of spontaneity to the speech.

At least two possible ways of managing the reference should be considered. One can start with a swift report of what an earlier speaker has said, and then:

1. Explain how his subject fits into the earlier speech, by stating that he will develop a different aspect of the subject.

[2] *Ibid.*, pp. 649–650.

[3] M. G. Robinson, "The Eleventh Commandment," *Classified Speech Models*, W. N. Brigance, ed. (1928), p. 19

At a meeting of small-home architects, one man spoke of new plumbing layouts, and later in the afternoon another speaker alluded to the earlier topic and added that he was going to report on a new type of valve that regulated water pressure.

2. Show a plausible association between his subject and the previous one.

In a round of class speeches which lasted for a week, a speaker on the first day talked on the proper design of a fireplace. Later in the week an aspiring geologist spoke on how to find water. His approach was in this vein:

> A few days ago my friend Mack Taylor told you how to build a fireplace that wouldn't smoke. Now I'm going to speak on something that's far more fundamental than designing fireplaces. It's right important if you should sometime decide to build a home in the country, and you'd better look to it long before you worry about fireplaces. In fact, you'd better look to it before you even decide just where you're going to put that house.
>
> What I want to do is to tell you where you can find water. The method used is recommended by up-to-date geologists. It is . . . , etc.

The Novel Idea or Striking Means of Expression. Also effective in beginning a speech is novelty in thought or expression. Novelty appeals to us because it it represents a *change* from familiar ideas and experience. The change may consist of a new and different fact or idea, an addition to the substance or stuff of our experience. Or the change may consist primarily of a different way or new manner of presenting an old notion.

Stuart Chase illustrated the use of the novel fact as he began his description of Grand Coulee Dam:

> In a desert in Egypt has stood for six thousand years the most massive structure ever built by man. In a desert in the State of Washington a new champion arises. The Great Pyramid weighs some 7,000,000 tons—say 120 Queen Mary's spiked together and squashed solid. The Grand Coulee Dam on the Columbia River already exceeds this total. When it is finished it will weigh 23,000,000 tons, over thrice the heft of Cheops.
>
> One of these masses is built of cut stone, the other of poured concrete. One took 50,000 men twenty years to build, the other will take 5,000 men six years, in a task not only three times greater but vastly more complex and dangerous. Both structures relied on the labor of those who would otherwise have been unemployed. Egyptian peasants in the off season built Cheops; American workingmen and engineers shelved by a great depression are building Grand Coulee.[4]

[4] From *Idle Money, Idle Men* (New York, copyright, 1940, by Stuart Chase). By permission of Harcourt, Brace and Company.

The unusual way of putting an idea is perhaps best demonstrated by the *epigram,* a terse, pointed, even witty, manner of expression. Observe how Edwin Slosson, once Director of Science Service, put an old idea as he opened a speech on methods of manufacturing a new synthetic:

> Science consists in learning from nature how to surpass nature. The chemist in particular is never content till he can do something that his teacher can't. In the field of fabrics he has made dyes more brilliant than any to be found in the three kingdoms of nature, animal, vegetable and mineral, and now he is inventing new textiles to tint with them.[5]

The novel and striking beginning is liable to three dangers. (1) It may degenerate into sheer sensationalism—the scare headline that leaves the hearer at one moment bug-eyed, at the next fooled and let down. (2) Occasionally, it is difficult to make the rest of the speech as interesting as the smash opening. A student speaker built a talk on Hume's epigram, "Happy is he whose circumstances suit his temper, but more excellent is he who can suit his temper to his circumstances." He led off with the quotation, with impressive effect, but nothing he said afterwards had as much punch and interest as the epigram. (3) To drag in the unusual statement when it is not quite appropriate and relevant is a temptation. Upon one occasion a college dean delivered a lecture whose purpose was to contrast the simple structure and organization of the small college with the complex structure of the large university. His opening statement was, "At the large college, the student may go through more college, but at the small college, more college goes through him." One listener reported that he never quite saw the connection between the epigram and the rest of the speech, despite the speaker's brave attempt to supply a bridge.

If the student speaker can avoid these three dangers, he will find the novel expression an effective means of riveting attention.

The Emotional Approach. Especially useful are two emotions: pride and humor. The former can be touched off by sincerely complimenting the audience, as did Henry Grady in addressing the New England Society of New York City in 1886. His opening words below, although somewhat extravagant to our ears, leave no doubt as to Grady's sincerity:

> Let me express to you my appreciation of the kindness by which I am permitted to address you. I make this abrupt acknowledgment advisedly, for I feel that if, when I raise my provincial voice in this ancient and august presence, I could find courage for no more than the opening sentence, it would be well if, in that sentence, I had met in a rough sense my obligation as a guest, and had perished, so to speak, with courtesy on my lips and grace in my heart. Permitted through

[5] As quoted by W. P. Sandford and W. H. Yaeger, *Business Speeches by Business Men* (New York: McGraw-Hill Book Co., 1930), p. 519.

> your kindness to catch my second wind, let me say that I appreciate the significance of being the first Southerner to speak at this board, which bears the substance, if it surpasses the semblance, of original New England hospitality, and honors a sentiment that in turn honors you, but in which my personality is lost, and the compliment to my people made plain.[6]

In praising a group two pieces of advice are in order. First, the surest guide to the use of the compliment is whether the speaker *feels* impelled to praise his audience. A sincere compliment is always appreciated; a forced, manufactured one only embarrasses a group and hurts the speaker's reputation. Second, the speaker should be sure he can express the compliment with neatness and dispatch. Deft phrasing is at a premium, for no compliment, no matter how genuine, can stand up in the public situation under awkward, hesitant, fumbling expression.

Humor, of course, speakers have always regarded as a good method of ice-breaking. The humorous story or anecdote as a means of introduction is extremely effective if three conditions are always respected. (1) The story must be in point and not dragged in. The test for relevance is simple: could the story be used as a supporting example for a main head or a subhead? If so, it belongs in the speech and one can lead off with it if he wishes. (2) The mood or temper of the occasion must not be inimical to humor; an anecdote is out of place when the occasion is solemn or dignified. (3) The story must not take up more time than it is worth. The expository speaker, since he deals with facts rather than with matters in controversy, does not need to conciliate his hearers. If he has selected his subject well, if it is reasonably appropriate to his hearers, he should get to the heart of his speech as fast as his audience will let him. The extended anecdote often wastes time.

For an example of a humorous story properly used as an introduction see Bruce Barton's speech "Which Knew Not Joseph," which is printed in Chapter 25.

Imagery. The strong, intense stimulus boldly claims attention; and one of the strongest stimuli possible through language is the *image*. The extended image or series of images is particularly effective in the introduction, especially when the images come through description or through a detailed illustration.

Arousing Curiosity. Stirring the audience to curiosity is sometimes called the conundrum approach. Edward A. Filene used this kind of approach in a speech at Boston in 1935:

[6] "The New South," December 22, 1886. The complete text of the speech and a description of its setting are conveniently found in Raymond B. Nixon, *Henry W. Grady: Spokesman of the New South* (New York: Alfred A. Knopf, 1943), pp. 340–350.

Let me mention just a few of the stirring events which are now happening in Boston. To begin with, there is the Italian-Ethiopian War and the sanctions which the League of Nations has been trying to apply. Then there is the new economic crisis facing Hitler, the recent grab of Northern China by the Japanese, and the ever-present question of what is really happening in Russia.

You may say, to be sure, that these things are not happening within our city limits; but that is rather beside the point; for our community, we must have noticed, no longer has any limits. Whatever is happening anywhere in these days is happening here. Why, for instance, is there so much unemployment in Boston? It is because there is so much unemployment elsewhere—that is all. If people elsewhere were employed, they would be buying more of our products, and Boston industries would boom. Once we supposed that we could study poverty by studying the poor in Boston. Now we know, or we ought to know, that we can't understand poverty in Boston unless we study poverty throughout the world.[7]

Often, questions can be used to stir curiosity at the outset of a speech. For example:

Suppose you were a mediator in a dispute between the management of the Acme Paper Box Co. and its unionized employees, and suppose the union served notice that it would call a strike within 24 hours if its demands concerning wages, hours of work, and vacations with pay were not met. Where would you hold the meeting at which you would try to secure an agreement? How would you proceed in the meeting? Should management present its case first? Or should labor? Which would be the best topic to discuss first—Wages? Hours? Or paid vacations? And on what grounds would you decide which topic should take precedence?

These are some of the more important problems that a mediator, sent out by the U.S. Conciliation Service, has to deal with. I wish to tell you something of the principles that guide him in solving them.

Reference to the Significance of the Subject. Perhaps this is the most rewarding means of approach for the novice speaker to master. It can be used for most speeches on most occasions and for persuasive as well as for informative speeches. And this kind of approach not only stands a good chance of claiming the hearer's attention; it is also likely to stir the speaker himself to greater energy, alertness, and interest than most types of introduction.

The method is simple. Let the attention section of the introduction be developed around this *implied* theme: My subject is important to *you,* at this *time* and on this *occasion.* In other words, the speaker tells his listeners *why* they should listen; he refers to values and motives important to them.

In planning to use this scheme, the speaker should note, first, that he does

[7] As quoted in Sarett and Foster, *Basic Principles of Speech* (New York, 1936), pp. 415–416.

not actually state his subject is important; to do so would probably result in a colorless, trite statement. Second, he chooses two or three reasons why the subject is significant; he states these and amplifies each, if necessary, until he sees the audience react favorably and knows he has won its attention. He can then move on to his purpose and point of view.

The success of this approach depends entirely on whether the speaker really believes there are excellent reasons why his audience should listen to him on his subject at that time. If he has good reasons, then his subject is truly appropriate to both his audience and himself. If he enjoys success with this method, it will be due primarily to two factors: (1) The reasons he picks—if they are significant rather than trivial—will usually reflect the motives and values which direct our lives and partially govern what we attend to and perceive. The responses touched off may well be strong and deep. (2) Since he gives the reasons that led him to settle on this subject rather than some other, he is likely to respond strongly himself. He becomes interested, energetic, alert, and direct; he remotivates himself. Any speaker who is slow to warm to his speech should try this approach.

One of the classic short approaches of this kind is that employed by Jeremiah S. Black when he argued the right of trial by jury before the Supreme Court, in December, 1866. A Federal military court martial had tried and sentenced to death one Mulligan and two associates, all of them civilians. Mulligan appealed; and before the Supreme Court, the military tribunal maintained that it had the power to try civilians during wartime even when the civil courts were open, and, furthermore, that the civil courts were powerless to prevent the military from acting. In the face of such a contention, Black's approach was not overdrawn:

> I am not afraid that you will underrate the importance of this case. It concerns the rights of the whole people. Such questions have generally been settled by arms; but since the beginning of the world no battle has ever been lost or won upon which the liberties of a nation were so distinctly staked as they are on the result of this argument. The pen that writes the judgment of the court will be mightier for good or for evil than any sword that ever was wielded by mortal arm.[8]

(Observe the basic values to which the speaker referred: *rights, liberty,* and *the good.*)

A student interested in insurance once spoke to a class of boys as follows:

> Perhaps you don't like to be bothered by life insurance salesmen who are always trying to sell you a policy. Forget the men and consider the thing. For

[8] O'Neill, *op. cit.*, p. 84.

the young unmarried man, insurance can be a means of saving. Upon his marrying, he finds that he has a way of protecting his wife and family from financial worries if he should die. Insurance can also be a means of building up a retirement income that will give a man comfort and security in late life.

I propose this morning to explain the advantages and disadvantages of three kinds of life insurance.

In making his speech outline, the speaker does well to block in the materials he uses to claim attention. For example:

INTRODUCTION

Attention Material

1. What does a college aim to do?
   a. Our college newspaper recently carried an article by Professor Dabney, saying that colleges should aim to produce "intellectual aristocrats."
   b. Last Monday in this class Mr. Kushner defended the not-too-serious purpose of the average student.
2. Many are the attacks on college education; and some colleges have met the criticism by various reforms and new schemes. Examples are,
   a. University of Chicago plan.
   b. St. John's College plan.
   c. Antioch College plan.

Orienting the audience

Satisfied that he knows how he is going to try to claim the attention of his hearers, the speaker turns to his next tactic. He decides how to frame his ideas. This involves orienting the audience to the order and structure of his plan. Most speeches include the types of materials mentioned below, but the number and treatment of these materials depends upon the audience's state of mind. Is the audience well or ill informed on the subject? Is it well disposed toward the speaker and his position? Is it emotionally upset? Is it strongly biased one way or another? Such questions point to the kinds of problems the speaker must face in deciding how directly and how extensively his audience is to be oriented.

Specific purpose

Announcement of purpose is a minimum sign of structure, and an explicit statement of purpose appears in almost all speeches. For example, "I shall attempt to explain how a professional dress designer works." Or, "I wonder whether you can always approve of the behavior of organized agitators." Sometimes no more orientation than this is needed, and the speaker can proceed at once to his first main head. But usually fuller orientation is required.

The subject sentence or proposition

Many speeches fully state the subject sentence or the proposition and often immediately restate it. The object of this repetition is to dwell on the main idea until it registers. Often the subject sentence of an informative speech is abstract, even a bit complicated and profound, and an audience cannot grasp it without restatement.

Order of development

Speakers still announce with profit where their expositions will begin and where they will end. They present a capsule sketch of the order of their chief ideas. The classical name for this kind of orientation is *partition.* For example: "In explaining how domestic roquefort cheese is made, I shall first mention the ingredients, and then take you step by step, from the beginning of the process to the finished product ready for boxing and shipment."

Background information

A bit of history often helps hearers to see a speaker's point of view. A particularly interesting kind of background sketch is that which reveals how the speaker arrived at his purpose or his proposition. For example: "A friend of a friend of mine," said a student speaker, "was thrown into Cook County Jail for three days for smoking marijuana. The conditions he described are horrifying." The young lady continued, saying swiftly that she personally checked into conditions, interviewed a warden and a judge whom she knew, and began reading on prison conditions generally. Then she said: "I want to assure you that the shocking behavior permitted some prisoners in Cook County Jail can be matched elsewhere in this country. When I lay out the facts I think you will agree."

This kind of orienting introduction often springs out of a speaker's sense of what is important and significant to both him and his audience. One is led to use background material when it interestingly explains his purpose or when it illuminates his stand on a problem. A narrative sketch is sometimes essential, as it is in law court speeches, where the issues upon which the judgment of guilt or innocence depend always emerge out of a specific set of circumstances. The background sketch should be placed in the introduction wherever it will fit in easily and logically.

In making the speech outline, orienting material is blocked in as part of the Introduction. For example:

Orienting Material

1. It is the Antioch plan that I think will interest you.
2. Founded by Horace Mann, in 1853, who left upon the college this motto: "Be ashamed to die unless you have won some victory for humanity."
3. Dr. Arthur E. Morgan, known as "Roosevelt-baiter" or "ex-TVA" Morgan, was president of Antioch from 1920 to 1936.
   a. As an engineer he had seen the failure of technical education to produce educated men.
      (1) Culture and skill didn't seem to go together.
   b. Dr. Morgan decided they could be brought together.

Conclusions

So strong is our sense of orderliness that we feel anything having a definite beginning must have a definite end. This feeling gives rise to another tactic to underscore the structure of a speech. All kinds of speeches in all sorts of circumstances close with a signal meaning "end." Sometimes the only signal will be vocal, for in impromptu utterances the speaker's awareness that he is coming to the end is revealed in his intonation. He "says" he is concluding without saying the words. But in most cases the conclusion is signalled verbally as well as vocally. The commonest form is the summary, or what the journalist calls the "recap."

The summary

Summaries may be formal and concise or informal and somewhat discursive. In either case, the summary can be managed by *restatement*—recurrence of old idea in different words—rather than by *repetition*—recurrence of old idea in the same phraseology. Accordingly, the shortest possible recipe for a summary is, Restate the ideas expressed in the subject sentence and in the main heads.

To illustrate the summary, suppose the subject sentence and main heads were as follows:

> The control panel of a powerhouse is arranged for the greatest convenience of the operator.
>
> I. Close in front of him are the instruments which he uses most often.
> II. Farther away to the sides are the less used dials and levers.

The formal summary might be this:

> In short, the instruments that control the machinery of a powerhouse are arranged on a large panel to suit the convenience of the operator, the instru-

ments most used being in front of the attendant and ready to his hand, the instruments least used being at the extreme sides of the panel.

The less formal summary might run something like this:

> To conclude, then: If you were to visit the control room in Urbana's powerhouse, you would see Mike Williams, on the night shift, seated before the large control panel—a panel that is arranged like most control panels in powerhouses. Immediately in front of him, and easy to reach, are the instruments he may need five or six times during the night. At the far sides of the panel are the dials and levers that may be used once a week, or even less often.

The effect of summarizing can often be obtained tersely in short speeches by stating only the subject sentence or the proposition. This tactic works best when the speaker during delivery is aware of the progression of his ideas. He knows he is moving from point to point, from main head to main head, his awareness of progress being heightened by the use of well-planned verbal transitions that carry him and his hearers from head to head. He aims at and he builds up to his most important and climactic logical idea—and then states it. The tactic is useful when the subject sentence is complicated, as it sometime is in good exposition. It is omitted from the introduction and appears fully stated only in the conclusion. It may be good tactics, too, in some persuasive situations when a speaker may think it unwise to state his proposal until he has carefully laid the foundation for it.

In preparing the speech outline, it is good practice to lay out carefully the ideas appearing in the conclusion. For example:

CONCLUSION

> We see, then, that Antioch College, which Dr. Eliot of Harvard once referred to as one of the most significant experiments in American education, succeeds by correlating technical and cultural studies on the one hand, and study and life on the other.

Details of Emphasis

The tactics mentioned so far should be considered in deciding where to place materials and ideas that point up the overall structure of the speech. Now we direct attention to more elementary tactics, to ways of signalling the main ideas and parts of a speech in order that listeners may easily grasp the progression of meaning and not be puzzled and distracted along the way. Ideally, listeners should not recognize structure, which must always serve meaning. But even to approximate this ideal, the novice speaker or writer has to use tactics that at first seem obvious and wooden. Some of these devices seem to shout their purpose, yet with practice in their use a speaker can deftly build up a meaningful whole.

Transitions

Among the devices to underscore main heads are transitional phrases and sentences.

Signposts are words and phrases that introduce main heads and indicate their order. They should appear in sets, as *First, Second, Third,* etc. Variants are *In the first place,* etc., *The first step,* etc., *The first matter we shall discuss is,* etc., *Let us first consider,* etc.

Parallel Structure in Main Heads. Through experience and "conditioning" we have come to regard things similar in structure and size as equal in value and having equal claims on attention. Hence, if the speaker phrases head II exactly as he worded head I, a listener senses that both heads are coordinate in value. He reacts similarly when he hears heads III and IV. Parallelism of structure, accordingly, connects main heads. An example of four parallel heads follows.

I. On the north side of the quadrangle are the dormitories.
II. On the east side of the quadrangle are the science halls.
III. On the south side of the quadrangle are the administration and classroom buildings.
IV. On the west side of the quadrangle is the great auditorium.

The Flash-Back and Preview. This device consists in alluding at the major points of the speech to what has just been said and to what will follow. Although there are many ways of managing such a transition, perhaps the *not only–but also* formula is the swiftest and easiest to handle. In the example below, the material supporting each main head has been omitted.

I. Antioch combines cultural and practical studies
(Antioch not only combines cultural and practical studies; it also joins study with practical experience.)
II. Antioch combines academic study with work in the business world
(Antioch has done more than combine cultural and practical studies and join study with experience; it has found that its system works.)
III. Antioch's plan has been successful.

A consistent set of conjunctive adverbs can be employed to introduce subheads. A workable list of such words includes *moreover, also, furthermore,* and *finally.*

The same set of words used to tag main heads must not be used to designate subheads. There's no surer way of confusing listeners, than to cross them up by inconsistent labeling. The rule of thumb is this: Use one set of labels for main heads, another set for subheads. In all cases avoid, if possible, the useless, undiscriminating connectives, "and another thing," and "then too."

The speaker who experiences difficulty in managing deft transitions ought to write his transitions out and include them in his speech outline in parentheses, as is done in the example above.

Proportion

Carefully proportioning the main divisions of a speech helps to maintain the due weight of each part. A hearer adds up a speech much as a viewer adds up a scene or a picture. There are foreground, background, and details; the relative size and value of each feature is seen. Thus, all of them fall into perspective when the perspective a hearer gains of a speaker's intentions and meanings is within the control of the speechmaker.

In the informative speech, it is particularly easy to let the main divisions—Introduction, Development, and Conclusion—slide out of focus. The beginning speaker will often discover that half his speaking time has elapsed before he has completed his introduction and is ready to produce the meat of his talk. Sometimes his introduction is so short that he is well into his development before his hearers are ready to listen; and occasionally he finds that his time has run out before he arrives at his conclusion.

It is necessary, therefore, that the divisions of the speech be carefully proportioned. For the speech (say 4–10 minutes), a good general guide is this: Introduction—10–12 per cent of the total speaking time; Conclusion—4–5 per-cent of the total time; Development—the remainder of the time. If a speech were to last four minutes, this would mean an introduction of about 24–29 seconds and a conclusion of 10–12 seconds, thus leaving well over three minutes for the heart of the speech. Of course, these proportions can, and should, be altered upon occasion. In the informative speech, frequently it may be necessary to offer a relatively long background of preliminary explanations to "set" what comes after; and sometimes, as in a short speech that follows a time order pattern, a formal conclusion is omitted. Furthermore, in the persuasive speech, as we shall see later, the length of the speech divisions may vary considerably. Nevertheless, the proportions recommended above may be relied upon for the great majority of speeches.

11

Strategies of Organization

The student of speechmaking who has learned to be clear to others—and perhaps also to be interesting—is in a position to experiment with strategies of organization. It is well and good to know that one can speak—and write—clearly, to know that one can outline the materials he intends to present, can use effectively the tactics that indicate structure, and can recollect, rethink, and speak from the materials of preparation in language and gesture which are meaningful to others. In a word, it is good to be able to form one's experience into a speech, to make oneself intelligible as a communicator.

But there are forms of discourse other than those that conventionally serve the needs of clearness. The forms reflect strategies serving the ends of interest and persuasion. They reflect a communicator's desire to adapt and accommodate his message to the requirements of a particular audience and occasion. As the materials of a speech reflect the speaker's purpose, the nature of his audience, and the occasion, so do the forms. If every sentence is unique, as a professor of linguistics has maintained, so is every speech unique. Sometimes the form and structure of a speech reflect primarily the speaker's desire to be original. More often the order and progression of ideas reflect the demands of a special audience situation. Form then becomes a means of persuasion.

A strategic form is a plan of presentation that the speaker judges to be most appropriate for his purpose and the condition of his audience. The study of many speeches by many speakers over many years has yielded a variety of strategic plans. We present twelve of them here.

Proof, Proposition, and More Proof

This plan of presentation entails but a small change in the conventional pattern. The speaker is to talk on a problem that has been much discussed and explored. His audience is more or less familiar with the principal issues and arguments. But he has found what he thinks to be a strong argument that he can develop appealingly. Knowing that with fairly well-informed hearers the first argument is more impressive than the last, he begins with his argument and develops it completely. Then, lest his listeners start wondering where he is going, he orients them with care, stating his proposition and making the necessary explanations and definitions. Following the orientation, the speaker moves through the rest of the proof in the customary manner. His outline looks like this:

TITLE

I. (The strong argument stated clearly and developed)
______

A. ______

1. ______
2. ______

B. ______

(Transition statement or phrase to Proposition)

ORIENTATION

Proposition: ______

(Definitions and explanations outlined here)
______
______

(Transition to Point II)

II. ______
______

III. (etc.) ______

CONCLUSION

______
______

Deductive Arrangement

The speaker discovers that he can treat his proposition as the specific premise of a syllogism. So he begins his speech with a general premise that is in agreement with a belief or value his audience accepts. This general premise needs no proof, although the speaker may want to restate it. In effect, the speaker reminds the audience of something it approves without question. He next presents his proposition, or specific premise, asserting that it falls within the meaning of the general premise. Then he offers proof and evidence in detail. The speech ends with a statement that is the formal conclusion of the syllogism. An example of this type of plan is the Declaration of Independence:

General Premise: Whenever any form of government becomes destructive, the people have a right to alter or abolish it.

Specific Premise: This English colonial government has become destructive.
Conclusion: These united colonies are, and of a right ought to be, free and independent states.

In the document, King George's misdeeds constitute proof of the specific premise and occupy about two-thirds of the Declaration.

The deductive plan is readily applicable to the problem stage of a state of affairs that the speaker believes may become serious enough to warrant action. So the general premise reminds the audience that besetting evils and intolerable conditions cry for a remedy. The proposition is that certain conditions are becoming, or in fact are, intolerable; it is supported by citation of evils and explanation of their causes. The conclusion is simply, Something ought to be done.

Inductive Arrangements

There are a few situations in which hard facts and their straightforward presentation appear to influence attitude and belief. An audience may not know or care to know that a problem exists. Or it may know of a problem situation and have become accustomed to living with it in apathy. Both situations are illustrated at a certain university by the perennial financial plight of the campus YMCA. We have heard a number of good classroom speeches in which speakers, starting with no mention of the empty coffers of the Y, have presented information and fact in a vivid manner and have concluded by saying the Y manifestly needed help or by asking members in the audience to pledge financial aid. Purpose or proposition was withheld until the facts had made their own appeal.

Or in another setting an audience may hold a specific belief that rests on weak and insufficient evidence. Once a dean of men banned radios in a dormitory because he received complaints about their noise. Students (for some reason!) did not wish to risk a frontal attack on the dean's opinion. They collected evidence on the matter, presented it at a meeting of administrative officers without comment until at the end they phrased their points concisely. The ban was lifted.

The progression of materials and ideas in the inductive order can be illustrated thus:

TITLE

Attention Material

____

____

(Transition to first facts)

FACTS OF THE SITUATION

I. ______________________
  A. ______________________
  B. ______________________
II. etc. ______________________

CONCLUSION

(What do the facts mean?)

I. ______________________
II. ______________________
  Proposition ______________________
  ____
  ____

In the inductive arrangement, the student needs to take special note of two factors which will promote clear and skillful presentation:

1. The facts-of-the-situation section must itself be clearly arranged and ordered, so that both speaker and audience can readily keep the factual material in mind; in other words, the facts must be *patterned.* Perhaps the easiest way of systematizing the facts is to group them according to the main heads that they imply, but do not state.

First, draw up a sketch of basic ideas.

Specific Purpose: To prove that the Dean's ban on radios in Dormitory X is unwarranted.

Proposition: Radios in Dormitory X are not a nuisance.

  I. During the day they are rarely used.
  II. At night they are not on except at the designated hour.
  III. At no time are they on loud enough to disturb others.

Second, prepare the speech outline with the main heads in mind but do not phrase them as such.

AN UNJUSTIFIED BAN

Attention Material ______________________
____

(Accordingly, I made a survey of the habits of radio users in Dormitory X)

I. During the day radios were used during these hours:
  A. ______________________
  B. etc. ______________________
II. At night radio owners reported the following:
  A. ______________________
  B. ______________________

III. As to how loud the students kept their radios, the survey showed this:
  A. ____________________
  B. etc. ____________________

CONCLUSION

I.
II.
III. } as in Sketch.

Proposition as in Sketch.

2. In a short speech, the proposition can sometimes be omitted. If the presentation has been clear, the audience will take pleasure in drawing its own conclusion.

Before trying the inductive plan, one would do well to read closely two speeches that illustrate it in action. One is the work of a student, C. Glen Haas, "I Was a Jockey," *Year Book of College Oratory,* E. E. Anderson, ed., IX (1937), 251–266. The other is Thomas Henry Huxley's famous lecture, "On a Piece of Chalk," which may be found in any collection of Huxley's works.

Expository Plan

The expository plan is like the conventional layout for an informative speech. The purpose and subject sentence appear to be simply informative in nature, as do the developing materials. But all has been planned for a persuasive purpose. Evidence and arguments have been decided upon beforehand. The speaker, however, decides to transform argument into explanation. His method, tone, and role become those of the historian, scientist, or reporter, rather than those of the persuader, exhorter, or pleader. In effect, his whole mien says, "Just let me explain things for your benefit."

The decision to persuade by fact and explanation is prompted by a number of factors. Both speaker and audience may be tired of discussing a persistent problem in the argumentative way. So both welcome a fresh approach and method. Or a speaker may find himself with a good collection of facts and testimony on one aspect of a problem, which he feels can be presented more easily and interestingly if it is worked into an expository package rather than into an argumentative case. Or a speaker, faced with stubborn, resistant, hostile listeners, may feel he can win a better hearing as reporter than as advocate. The plan is applied readily in certain situations.

Advocating a specific program or solution

When the discussion of a problem has settled down to the workability of rival solutions, often it is effective to explain how one of the solutions has worked in comparable circumstances. The person who has the relevant information has little to do beyond organizing and clearly presenting a set of facts. If, for example, an audience of college students disagreed as to the best method of student counseling for their college and someone believed that the procedure in use at Illinois was superior to other schemes, he might decide to make a speech with this purpose: to explain the student counseling system at Illinois. He would then build his entire speech on this purpose and from beginning to end would organize and present his information as he would in any informative speech. In short, he would enter the controversy as a historian or reporter, not as an advocate, and he would let the audience make the inference, this is the plan we should have at our college.

On one occasion in class a speaker "explained" the manufacture of the Write Well fountain pen. He arranged his materials under three heads, Design of the Pen, Materials Used, and Assembly of the Parts. He had worked in both the Write Well factory and the Superior factory which made a rival pen. Under the first two heads he contrasted the design and materials of the Write Well with those of the Superior pen. The contrast was so clear that at the close of the speech his hearers were all set to buy a Write Well the next time they needed a fountain pen. Entirely from facts, they acquired a favorable attitude toward the Write Well product.

Circumventing resistance and prejudice

In the early 1930's much widespread criticism of the government's policy of regulating agricultural production to keep up the prices of beef, pork, and wheat, especially when the "little pigs" were killed to keep down the supply of pork, caused agricultural officials to feel called upon to defend the policy. One individual appearing before a rural audience in the Middle West met the criticism by clearly explaining what the Agricultural Adjustment Act was intended to do and how in a few instances it had worked. He did not try to meet the heated criticisms of the moment, nor did he say literally that the act was good and had been effective in some cases. He merely explained; that is, he made a straightforward expository speech. A few hearers told him afterward that until he spoke they had not understood what the act really was. Thus opposition, if not entirely removed, was at least softened. When opposition is the result of ignorance, exposition is a wise method of persuasion.

Exposition often works well, too, when a person or idea is unpopular and a speaker wishes to secure a more favorable attitude toward the individual or idea. At one college the President fell into disfavor with the students. A classroom speaker addressed himself to this purpose: to relate how students rooming in the President's house felt about him. His proposition was, "They find the President humane and friendly." The bulk of the speech consisted of five or six well-planned incidents that illustrated the President's kindliness. In this talk, the speaker sounded like a storyteller, for each incident was a little story in itself.

Persuasion through exposition seems to be gaining in favor. This strategy fits in nicely with the scientific, technological mood of our age in which the solid fact, be it data or law, is highly respected, if not worshipped. Information is emphasized in the advertising campaigns sponsored by conservative corporations—the public utilities, steel and electrical appliance manufacturers—and school systems selling new programs and bonds. A large number of students ought to try persuasion through exposition. They resist because, so they argue, this method means more work. One must first make an outline for a persuasive speech and then construct its expository counterpart! Both operations are necessary for the first trial or two if one is not to confuse one's hearers. The strategy, it should be remarked, is not inherently misleading or deceitful. As a means of persuasion, it appears in the context of persuasive situations; and the American people have become so alive to the selling of products and ideas that it is a rare person indeed who cannot evaluate the motives of a communicator.

Narrative Plan

In purpose and method, the narrative plan of presentation is much like the expository plan. The speaker aims to persuade, but his role is more like that of historian or storyteller than expositor. His materials are descriptive and imageful. He selects and manages them in keeping with his purpose. Like a good reporter, he interprets facts and events as he sees them, but his interpretations place less emphasis on causes and conditions. The expositor will imply, "I'm explaining things so that you may understand." The narrator will imply, "I'm telling you the facts and describing their background as I see them."

The strategy of narrative persuasion is very common in politics and in certain types of courtroom speaking. The speaker for the party in power finds his best persuasion, often, in the chronological account of the successive achievements of his administration after the succession of misfortunes which occurred while the other party was in power. Many of Franklin D. Roosevelt's most effective speeches were little more than descriptions of the unhappy condition of the American people during the Great Depression, followed by an account of the measures which the New Deal had taken, one after another, to bring back happiness and prosperity. In his legal practice, it is said, Abraham Lincoln, when he had finished his narrative of the events of the alleged crime, would often be stopped by the people and his opponent given the floor, so convincing had been Lincoln's narrative argument.

The effectiveness of vivid narration in securing action can be striking when an audience's enthusiasm for an old cause has waned, or when people are tired of hearing the same old thing. A veteran of World War I, invalided home, was enlisted to speak in support of the various Liberty Loan drives and went about uprging people to buy bonds and more bonds. He met with small success in using direct argument, but his sales jumped when he made his speeches a description of the combat experiences of himself and his comrades. The direct plea, "We are doing our part; you do yours," with its relevant arguments and appeals, didn't work well; but stories that implied the same message did.

The best recent illustration of the narrative plan is to be seen in Abba Eban's speech, printed on pages 440–459. After the six-day war in June, 1967, in which Israel completely defeated her Arab opponents, the Foreign Minister of Israel put his country's case before the General Assembly of the United Nations and the world in a long, detailed, heavily documented narrative of the struggle of Israel to survive and prosper in spite of the hostility of her neighbors. Beginning with the founding of the state of Israel in 1948—and even before—Mr. Eban developed a vivid and moving narrative of the succession of events leading to the lightning war of 1967, such that Israel's occupation of the conquered Arab territories should seem both just and necessary. His strategy was not directly to argue the plight of a small nation among its enemies, a pawn in the game of the big powers, but to select verifiable events and to weave them into an affecting story so that "the facts should speak for themselves." The effective counter to this sort of narrative persuasion, of course, is not simply the enraged denial, but the seemingly objective construction of a parallel account of equally verifiable events, or of the same events "more correctly" interpreted, which the audience can see as more probable than the opponent's account.

Single Illustration as the Entire Speech

This plan presents a single argument, or a number of arguments, by translating them into a detailed, vivid illustration of the proposition. It is often appropriate for the two- to three-minute speech. The proposition itself may be stated (usually at the end), or it may be hinted at deftly, or it may be omitted entirely.

To see this plan at work, read some of the parables of Jesus, especially those in Matthew XXV: 1–13, 14–30; Luke VII: 5–8 and 11–15; Luke X: 30–37; Luke XIV: 15–24; Luke XV: 11–32; and Luke XVI: 19–31. The Parable of Bridesmaids (Goodspeed's translation) follows:

> Then the Kingdom of Heaven will be like ten bridesmaids who took their lamps and went out to meet the bridegroom. Now five of them were foolish and five were sensible. For the foolish ones brought their lamps but brought no oil with them, but the sensible ones with their lamps brought oil in their

flasks. As the bridegroom was slow in coming, they all grew drowsy and fell asleep. But in the middle of the night there was a shout, "Here is the bridegroom! Come out and meet him!" Then all the bridesmaids awoke, and trimmed their lamps. And the foolish ones said to the sensible ones, "Give us some of your oil, for our lamps are going out." But the sensible ones answered, "There may not be enough for us and you. You had better go to the dealers and buy yourselves some." But while they were gone to buy it, the bridegroom arrived, and the ones that were ready went in with him to the wedding banquet, and the door was closed. Afterward the other bridesmaids came and said, "Sir! Sir! Open the door for us!" But he answered, "I tell you, I do not know you!" So you must be on the watch, for you do not know either the day or the hour.

Plan Based on Contrast

Here the speaker develops his ideas through contrast. Sometimes the contrast is engineered to fit into the conventional plan; it may also be worked out in the inductive plan.

There are three ways of handling the contrasting materials:

1. The contrasting ideas may be presented as a chain of short, compact contrasts that are balanced. Part of Claude Bowers's keynote speech at the Democratic National Convention at Houston in 1928 exemplified the method:

> They [the Republicans] frankly base their policies on the political principles of Hamilton, and we go forth to battle for the principles of Thomas Jefferson. The issues are as fundamental as they were when Jefferson and Hamilton crossed swords more than a century ago. To understand the conflicting views of these two men on the functions of government is to grasp the deep significance of this campaign.
>
> Now, Hamilton believed in the rule of an aristocracy of money, and Jefferson in a democracy of men.
>
> Hamilton believed that governments are created for the domination of the masses, and Jefferson that they are created for the service of the people.
>
> Hamilton wrote to Morris that governments are strong in proportion as they are made profitable to the powerful, and Jefferson knew that no government is fit to live that does not conserve the interest of the average man.
>
> Hamilton proposed a scheme for binding the wealthy to the government by making government a source of revenue to the wealthy, and Jefferson unfurled his banner of equal rights.
>
> Hamilton wanted to wipe out the boundary lines of States, and Jefferson was the champion of their sovereign powers.
>
> Hamilton would have concentrated authority remote from the people, and Jefferson would have diffused it among them.
>
> Hamilton would have injected governmental activities into all the affairs of men, and Jefferson laid it down as an axiom of freedom that "that government is best which governs least.". . .

> Why, you cannot believe with Lincoln in democracy and with Hamilton against it.
>
> You cannot believe with Lincoln that the principles of Jefferson are "the definitions and the axioms of a free society," and with Hamilton that they are the definitions of anarchy.
>
> You cannot believe with Lincoln in a government "of the people, by the people and for the people," and with Hamilton "in a government of the wealthy, by the influential and for the powerful."[1]

2. The contrasting ideas may be presented in successive sections of the speech, the first part of the contrast being developed at length in one section, the second part in the following section. This places the contrasting ideas in separate blocks. Had Bowers elected to handle his contrast in this manner he would have put all of Hamilton's political philosophy together in one section; then he would have turned and developed all of Jefferson's philosophy in the next section.

The contrast plan is most readily used in developing rival solutions to a problem. First the speaker deals fully and completely with the advantages of his solution; then he presents what appears to him to be the disadvantages of the rival solution.

3. The contrast can sometimes be managed to secure climax, especially if the factual material is presented as a narrative, as in the Parable of the Good Samaritan:

> Then an expert in the Law got up to test him and said, "Master, what must I do to make sure of eternal life?"
>
> Jesus said to him, "What does the Law say? How does it read?"
>
> He answered, "You must love the Lord your God with your whole heart, your whole soul, your whole strength, and your whole mind, and your neighbor as you do yourself."
>
> Jesus said to him, "You are right. Do that, and you will live."
>
> But he, wishing to justify his question, said, "And who is my neighbor?"
>
> Jesus replied, "A man was on his way down from Jerusalem to Jericho, when he fell into the hands of robbers, and they stripped him and beat him and went off leaving him half dead. Now a priest happened to be going that way, and when he saw him, he went by on the other side of the road. And a Levite also came to the place, and when he saw him, he went by on the other side. But a Samaritan who was traveling that way came upon him, and when he saw him he pitied him, and he went up to him and dressed his wounds with oil and wine and bound them up. And he put him on his own mule and brought him to an inn and took care of him. Then next day he took out a dollar and gave it to the innkeeper and said, 'Take care of him, and whatever more you spend I will refund to you on my way back.' Which of these three do you think proved himself a neighbor to the man who fell into the robber's hands?"

[1] J. M. O'Neill and F. K. Riley, *Contemporary Speeches* (New York, 1930), pp. 508–509.

He said, "The man who took pity on him."
Jesus said to him, "Go and do so yourself!"

The contrast plan is particularly effective because it makes the rival ideas more intense; like contrasting colors, each part enhances and gives force to the other.

Final Appeal

The speaker here proceeds as in the conventional plan, but the last section of the development is reserved for a forceful appeal to one or more fundamental motives or values. Sometimes the appeal may take the place of a formal conclusion, and a review of one's arguments can be omitted.

Good examples of this plan are G. W. Curtis's "The Leadership of Educated Men," and "The Puritan Principle, or Liberty Under the Law." The former may be found in *Modern Eloquence;* the latter appears in this book on pages 547–550.

Massing of Admitted Ideas

The speaker starts by stating, and sometimes briefly discussing, the ideas and arguments that his hearers will accept. Then he proceeds to show that these ideas logically support his own view—his proposition. Schematically, the procedure is this:

INTRODUCTION

In discussing this question (state the question), we can all agree on certain beliefs:

A. Belief 1
   1. ______
   2. (etc.) ______
B. Belief 2
C. (Etc.)

DEVELOPMENT

What are the consequences of these beliefs for one who holds that arbitration should be compulsory in all labor disputes? (The proposition is thus brought in.)

I. Belief 1 is consistent with compulsory arbitration, for
   A. ______
   B. (etc.) ______
II. Belief 2 is consistent, etc. etc.

CONCLUSION

______

______

Repetition Formula

This is a device of presentation more than it is a strategy of organization. It capitalizes on the fact that repetition not only aids clearness but lodges an idea firmly in memory.

Repetition of a rhetorical question

The speaker follows the conventional order or arrangement, but he clinches the discussion of each point with a rhetorical question to which the hearers will nod assent. The same question is repeated each time. It has a binding effect and makes good use of suggestion. It is particularly effective when used at the close of a section in which an objection is answered. Observe Shakespeare's use of the device, combined with irony, in Mark Antony's speech, the first part of which is cited here:

> Friends, Romans, countrymen, lend me your ears;
> I come to bury Caesar, not to praise him.
> The evil that men do lives after them,
> The good is oft interred with their bones;
> So let it be with Caesar. The noble Brutus
> Hath told you Caesar was ambitious;
> If it were so, it was a grievous fault,
> And grievously hath Caesar answer'd it.
> Here, under leave of Brutus and the rest,—
> For Brutus is an honourable man;
> So are they all, all honourable men,—
> Come I to speak in Caesar's funeral.
> He was my friend, faithful and just to me:
> But Brutus says he was ambitious;
> And Brutus is an honourable man.
> He hath brought many captives home to Rome
> Whose ransoms did the general coffers fill:
> Did this in Caesar seem ambitious?
> When that the poor have cried, Caesar hath wept;
> Ambition should be made of sterner stuff:
> Yet Brutus says he was ambitious;
> And Brutus is an honourable man.
> You all did see that on the Lupercal
> I thrice presented him a kingly crown,
> Which he did thrice refuse: was this ambition?
> Yet Brutus says he was ambitious;
> And, such, he is an honourable man.

Repetition of proposition

Again the speaker follows the conventional plan of arrangement, but he clinches the discussion of each point, not with a rhetorical question, but with the proposition itself.

In the presidential campaign of 1928, Alfred E. Smith in a speech at Boston criticized his rival for being ambiguous on the question of government ownership of natural resources. Mr. Hoover, in setting out the Republicans' stand on the development of waterpower, had said he would "use words to convey meaning, not to hide it." In reply, Mr. Smith took the position that Mr. Hoover had "used words to hide meaning, not to convey it." He examined each contention of Mr. Hoover's, commented on it to show its ambiguity, and ended each comment with, "Mr. Hoover has here used words to hide meaning not to convey it." Thus a refrain was set up in the speech with telling force.[2] Alfred E. Smith also used the proposition as a refrain in his "Cooing Dove" speech, which appears on pages 520–526.

Especially telling is repetition in the form of a catchy slogan or epigram. In his Atlanta Address, Booker T. Washington couched his main appeal in the phrase, "Let down your bucket where you are."

A simple excellent method of introducing the slogan is to place it in, or derive it from, a vivid illustration that expresses the sense of the opinion. Many a sermon on charity, friendliness, or helpfulness has started off with the Parable of the Good Samaritan, has used as the controlling idea, "Pass not by on the other side," and has repeated the injunction at appropriate intervals.

The Problem-Solution Plan

In this form of presentation, the speech is divided into four major parts: (1) the Attention Step, (2) the Problem Step, (3) the Solution Step, and (4) the Appeal Step. The first step tells the hearer that all is not right with the world—there really *is* a problem to be faced. The second step defines, explains, and diagnoses the problem precisely, looking especially to its nature and causes. The third step brings forth the solution and demonstrates that it will not only remove the causes that give rise to the problem, but will be the *best* solution possible. The final step seeks to paint the solution in the most attractive and compelling light possible, usually by associating it with the desires, wishes, and ideals of the audience.

A variation of this four-division arrangement is that proposed by Alan

[2] For the complete text of Smith's speech, consult J. M. O'Neill and F. K. Riley, *Contemporary Speeches* (New York, 1930), pp. 536–551.

Monroe in his *Principles and Types of Speech*. Monroe recognizes five steps: (1) *attention;* (2) *need*—this enumerates and establishes the evils and difficulties of the present situation; (3) *satisfaction*—here the speaker shows how his proposal will satisfy the needs; (4) *visualization*—this vividly presents the proposal in action; (5) *action*—the speaker suggests what the audience can do.[3]

When an audience has been well exposed to a problem and its possible solutions, the problem-solution strategy fits in nicely. The speaker, of course, wants to emphasize his own solution. He tries to make his audience see that it emerges logically from the full context of prior discussion of the subject. Usually this strategy takes time and does not meet the demands of a very short speech.

The Classical Plan

From Cicero's time to the present, the classical arrangement of a speech has been this: (1) Exordium, in which the purpose is to win attention and allay prejudices or hostile feeling; (2) Narration, or sketch of the background and origins of the subject and statement of the proposition, together with any definitions, concessions, or other explanations; (3) Partition, or an explicit declaration of points to be proved; (4) Proof; (5) Refutation of the opposing arguments and objections; and (6) Peroration, or a summary together with a final vivid plea for action or acceptance.

The classical strategy is suited to the speaker who needs and desires to discuss the proposition fully. It has been most often used in deliberative assemblies, in senates and parliaments, when in the closing hours of debate a speaker presents the entire case for his party. A good example is Edmund Burke's "Speech on Conciliation with America." The classical plan reminds the student of speechmaking of the possibilities which would arise if he were to treat his problem and subject exhaustively. Like the problem-solution strategy, the classical arrangement can serve as a master plan from which the speaker derives hints for arranging the materials of a speech with a limited point of view and length made to an audience ready for open "logical" discussion.

In closing this chapter, we remark that strategies of structure and presentation are to be considered in any kind of communicative situation, by both speaker and writer. The strategy of form is always a matter of prime concern when one considers how best to adapt and accommodate ideas and arguments to the state of mind of a particular audience.

[3] As an example of a speech that follows these steps, see Bennett Champ Clark's speech, "Neutrality—What Kind?" in Monroe's *Principles and Types of Speech*, rev. ed. (New York, 1939), pp. 340–345.

12

Style: The Language of the Speech

Throughout the long history of systematic writing on the principles of public speaking—that is, on rhetoric—the part of the subject which most writers have treated at greatest length and in most detail has been style, or as it was called traditionally, *elocutio*. This emphasis is understandable. Speeches, first and foremost, are tissues of words, words carried and conditioned by voice and utterance and modified by bodily expression, but principally words. Words are the common counters, the standard coinage, with which we conduct our transactions in communication, whether in speech or in writing and whatever the particular purpose. The words of an utterance also are the external signs of a speaker's internal, mental activity. Language, then, rather than other symbols and signals, finally makes a speech—or a letter, or a poem, or any other verbal composition—the thing it is. Language gives ideas existence and makes them live; language brings experience from something conceived and potential in the mind, feelings, and imagination to something actual and dynamic in human relations.

Another reason why so much attention centers in language is that the speaker's vocal and gestural signs during delivery create the listeners' first and quickest impressions of the message, of the sort of person the speaker is, and of the tone and mood of the occasion. Furthermore, in the long run, the way an idea or an opinion is cast into language (and in speeches, of course, spoken language) determines *precisely* what that idea or opinion is. Finally, memorable language often remains in listeners' minds and represents for them what the whole speech means. Whatever Lincoln intended in his Gettysburg Address, for over a hundred years it has meant to Americans the ideal of "government of the people, by the people, and for the people." Probably the grandeur of Sir Winston Churchill's language and the strength and stability suggested by his stately sentences had as much to do with sustaining the English in their resistance as had any particular messages he gave them.

Definition and Qualities of Style

There can be no doubt, therefore, of the importance of the speaker's skillful use of language, and hence of what is called *good style*. Broadly conceived, of course, style probably cannot be separated from other factors in the meaning of a speech. It involves, as the Frenchman Buffon observed, "the order and movement which we give to our ideas." In that sense style comprehends much that we have already discussed. In this chapter, however, we shall attend more particularly to style as *that factor in the dynamics of speaking which results from the selection and management of language.*

We recognize, of course, that the texture of speeches as presented, as distinguished from their texture as preserved in writing or in print, is an oral texture. The language, therefore, is oral language, the basic meaning of which is modified and supplemented by the qualities and resources of the media of communication—vocal sound, pronunciation, enunciation, and the visible adjuncts of speaking. The student will realize, therefore, that the whole of our discussion in Part V is immediately relevant to the discussion of style. For practical purposes of instruction, however, we separate consideration of the verbal from the vocal and visual.

The foregoing definition of style has certain important implications. In the first place, it implies that style is always present in discourse. Though in common parlance people sometimes say that a speech or a man had style or had no style, our definition implies that style is not limited to good speaking or to certain persons. Style will be good, bad, or indifferent depending on what language a speaker selects to reveal his thoughts to others, and how he manages that language. A second important implication of the definition is that style depends upon the qualities of the words and upon the manner in which the words are worked together and are made to function in connected speech.

Obviously, whether as words or as connected passages, the speaker's language should serve efficiently the purpose of speaking. That is, good style will assist the speaker in getting the audience to (1) understand his meaning, (2) believe in him, (3) remember his message, and (4) wish to accept his ideas. To promote these ends good style will be (1) clear, (2) appropriate, (3) interesting and attractive, and (4) impressive. These four qualities of style do not correspond exactly, of course, to the four purposes which the speaking may serve. Roughly, however, we may observe that to be understood a speaker must be clear; that if his language fits the subject, audience, occasion, and himself, his audience is most likely to respect and believe him; that interesting and attractive language tends to make listening easy; and that impressiveness tends to secure memory and motivate action. The *minimal* qualities required of any satisfactory speaking style will be *clearness,* so that the message may be understood, and *appropriateness,* so that language will in no way discredit the speaker.

In accordance with the definition of style and the desirable qualities of style, we will discuss (1) the speaker's selection of language, his vocabulary, and (2) his management of language in connected speech, with reference to the four principal qualities which we have mentioned, and (3) desirable methods for developing good style.

Selection of Language—Words

"Proper words in proper places make the true definition of a style," wrote Jonathan Swift to a young clergyman just beginning his career of preaching. We shall begin with the choice of proper words.

Clearness

Clear language is language that is meaningful to an audience as it is spoken. This means, of course, that speakers need a reliable sense of what language audiences of various sorts are likely to understand instantly or to find confusing and strange. Through experience in speaking and through knowledge of his hearers a speaker develops a feeling for clear and easy expression. Nevertheless, even though there is no substitute for experience, a speaker can do much deliberately to improve his clearness by selecting language that carries the qualities of familiarity, concreteness, specificity, and action.

Familiar words

Words in current general oral use which have live meanings to most people in the society in which the speaker is talking are to be preferred to more strange or more "elegant" words. People may well have some sense of what is signified by *fallacious reasoning,* though normally they do not use the expression. Nevertheless, the speaker before a general audience who wants to be sure that he is clear will probably say *false thinking* instead. *Pernicious precedent* may be the most exact expression and in some ways the most preferable, but a speaker had better say *bad example* unless he is absolutely sure that his audience knows the meaning of both pernicious and precedent. The skillful speaker might say, "This legislation will constitute a pernicious precedent; such laws will leave a bad example for future congresses to follow."

Strange words

Strange words, of course, may arouse the curiosity of hearers, and if used sparingly, as Aristotle observed, they may help create a tone of impressiveness; nevertheless, they almost always hinder understanding, and speakers must learn not to depend upon them. Even such relatively innocent usages as *cinema* for *movie,* and such slightly foreign expressions as *holiday* for *vacation,* and *motorcar* for *auto* may delay comprehension. Yet unfamiliar words seem to enhance the audience's respect for a speaker; they are regarded as signs of the expert.

One may find statistical accounts of the relative familiarity, based on frequency of occurrence, of various classes of English words. The speaker may find such accounts suggestive, but he cannot be governed by them. He must speak in the language which he can command, but he should ask himself again and again, "Am I sure that my audience will know this word or will understand it as I understand it?" "Is there some more familiar word which would convey my meaning and would not arouse irrelevant feelings or ideas in my listeners?" In using familiar language, however, a speaker should beware of seeming to talk down to the audience. Whatever language a speaker uses, he should use as if it were the natural and obvious thing to do.

Technical words

The use of specialized and technical terminology or of a restricted vocational jargon also presents problems of familiarity. As we suggested in discussing definition, a speaker must not expect an audience to understand technical language just because he does, or because, as offenders sometimes say, "Anyone who keeps his eyes and ears open ought to know what that means." Most people receive only the vaguest and most remote impressions from the special langauge of an occupation or profession or social climate other than their own. On many college campuses, for example, the term *grade-point average* has a definite meaning and is immediately clear. To unacademic persons, however, it has only the most nebulous meaning, if any. One cannot even safely expect a general audience to have an exact idea of what is meant by such common commercial expressions as *inventory, trial balance, requisitions, flow sheet, form letter,* or such frequently used political expressions as *autonomy, self-determination, log rolling, unicameral.* Terminology of this sort should be used wherever necessary, although many times when it is used a more common expression would serve the purpose just as well. When it is used, however, it should be accompanied unobtrusively by explanation, or it should be used in such a context that its meaning cannot be mistaken. The problem of technical or pseudo-technical vocabulary in the common phases of experience is increasing as the terms of the social and psychological sciences creep into popular parlance. Such words as *fixation, psychosis, complex, Freudian slip, culture, statistical significance* have a spurious currency which the speaker who would be clear must beware of. Such terms are likely to mean no more to the general audience than that the speaker wishes to be thought a well-informed fellow, not necessarily that he *is* one.

Perhaps a good aid in checking one's vocabulary for familiarity is developing a healthy respect for the capacity of people to *misunderstand* and to be puzzled by the out of the ordinary. Hence one should cultivate the habit of asking oneself often, "Do these words seem familiar to me because I am the person I am, with certain special knowledge and special experience, or because they are current in the general usage of people such as those I am addressing?" Some conscious attention to this question will soon result in the habit of distinguishing between language that is clear to oneself and language that is clear to one's listeners.

Concrete and specific words

The concrete, specific word carries a clear and definite meaning to listeners because it points to real objects and real events and is associated with them in objective experience. Consequently, for most purposes concrete terms are better than abstract, and specific terms are better than general terms. When abstract language is necessary, it should be defined or otherwise explained swiftly. If the abstract or technical term is the most accurate for the purpose and is, therefore, necessary, it cannot be left undefined without producing fuzziness in the minds of the audience.

Democracy is abstract, *the government of the United States* is concrete. *Creature* is abstract, *horse* or *man* or *pussycat* is concrete. *Honesty* is abstract; *refusing a perfectly safe opportunity for cheating on an examination* is concrete. *"Depart from evil and do good"* is abstract; *"Thou shalt not covet thy neighbor's wife"* is concrete. Abstract language like abstract thought has great values. Some of the best philosophical and scientific writing in the world would be impossible without it. With the subjects, however, on which most of us talk most of the time, the more abstract the language we use the less memorable will be our speech. Undoubtedly there are important meanings in such common abstractions as *virtue, goodness, sin, liberty, social equality, discrimination, profit, justice,* but in themselves they hardly produce clearness of idea or intention.

A certain Middle Western city is general; *St. Louis* or *Chicago* or *Toledo* or *Topeka* is specific and should be used instead (unless there is some special reason for not mentioning the name). *Extracurricular activities* is general; the *campus newspaper,* the *yearbook,* the *French club,* the *debate team,* the *student senate* are specific. At times, of course, speakers wish to be general or vague, expecting their audiences to supply, as suits them, the concrete, specific ideas which the speakers avoid. At such times the speaker, obviously, is not being clear and definite, and his style shows that he is not. Under most circumstances of public speaking, however, although we may express our ideas at first in abstract and general terms in order possibly to get preliminary and vague general acceptance of them, not until we become concrete and specific do we really come to grips with the minds, feelings, prejudices, and preconceptions of our audience and succeed in convincing or informing them. The clearness of meaning which comes with concrete, specific language stands out notably in the following sentence from Booker T. Washington's Atlanta Address (see pages 540–546). He wished to say that the progress which the southern Negroes had made in the thirty years since freedom had not come without struggle and difficulty. Observe the familiar, concrete, specific words he chose.

> Starting thirty years ago with ownership here and there of a few quilts and pumpkins and chickens (gathered from miscellaneous sources), remember that the path that has led from these to invention and production of agricultural instruments, buggies, steam-engines, news-papers, books, statuary, carving, paintings, the management of drug-stores and banks, has not been trodden without contact with thorns and thistles.

In connection with concrete and specific language, see the discussion of the language of factual statement on pp. 86–87 and of the citation of statistics on pp. 87–88. The speaker who would be clear will ask himself, "How can I bring my ideas down to cases?" "Can I name names and mention specific items to replace or supplement my abstractions and generalities?" "What expressions which I am using seem specific and concrete to me but may seem general and abstract to my audience?"

Action words

In Chapter 3 we pointed out that stimuli in motion are more compelling than stimuli at rest. People almost always prefer the moving picture to the still picture. Accordingly, whenever a concrete word or phrase also suggests movement and activity, it enhances clearness.

A speaker can take at least a few practical steps to make his language act. First, he can watch for opportunities to use action words in place of words which do not suggest movement. To say that a machine *runs* is better than to say that a machine *functions;* to say that something *stands up* suggests more activity than to say something *resists rough use* or *assumes a vertical position;* to say that the council *debated and passed* an ordinance is probably superior to saying that the council *considered and approved* an ordinance. The general rule, then, is to use words, particularly verbs, that tend to conjure up momentary action pictures. Second, speakers should prefer verbs in the active voice, which present the subject of a sentence as performing the action indicated by the predicate. It is better, for example, to say, "The gunner drops the shell into the mortar," than to say, "The shell is held over the muzzle of the mortar," or, "The shell is dropped into the mortar by the gunner." "We know we should act" is better than "It is thought that action should be taken." "Congress created a committee to investigate the problem" is superior to "The problem is to be investigated by a committee set up by Congress." "Action by the committee is desired by the chairman" represents a kind of reverse English compared with "The chairman wants the committee to take action." "We ate our lunch quickly by the pasture gate" does not leave the meaning in doubt as does the passive form "Our lunch was eaten by the pasture gate." The active voice, in brief, almost always creates a sense of movement; the passive voice, even when clear, stops movement. Still water is less dynamic than running, rushing, turbulent water.

Appropriateness

A speaker's words may be very clear and yet unfitting and inappropriate to him, to his audience, to his subject, or to the occasion.

To the Speaker. When language is inappropriate to the speaker, he is usually either straining for elegance or impressiveness and achieving only inflation or is mistakenly trying to speak his audience's language, to be one of the boys, and managing only to be silly and substandard. When the agent of the light and power company, whose customer has asked to have the electricity turned off, inquires, "Were you contemplating changing your residence?" he is trying for elegance and achieving foolish pomposity. Had he asked, "Are you thinking of moving?" he would have done his business in not only the most unobtrusive but the most efficient language. When the college graduate, who is assumed to be a person of some education, affects the defective grammar and semiliterate vocabulary of the uneducated, he is not (as he may claim) getting on common ground with his audience. He is insulting his audience, as did Patrick Henry when he talked to backwoodsmen using their dialectal and ungrammatical expressions. Most listeners recognize the inappropriateness of such vocabulary. They understand simple correct language, even if they do not habitually use it themselves, and they expect a man to speak to them in that language if he is the sort of person to whom it should be normal.

A speaker should also be cautious in using the special terminology or jargon of a particular set of people or of an occupation not his own. When a college debater, discussing socialized medicine before a group that included physicians, endeavored to meet the physicians on their own verbal ground, he confused *diagnosis* with *prognosis*. He did not find out until later why some of the medical men smiled. If a speaker is to use a specialized idiom, he must use it with complete assurance and accuracy. He must realize that any audience would rather hear him speaking fluently and clearly in the language which he can command than hear him blundering cheerfully in an idiom in which he is not at home—unless he intends to be funny at his own expense.

Language of the Speaker as a Person and as a Speaker. The speaker's language, therefore, first of all must seem to belong to him, to be becoming to him, as a person and as a speaker. What language belongs to him as a special individual, what is his private habit of speech, bears upon the fitness of his language; but most of the time listeners are not personally and intimately acquainted with the speaker. They know him as a kind of person—an educated businessman, a labor leader, a clergyman, a college student—and what seems becoming to him in that role and in his role as speaker, taken together, will be fitting and appropriate.

The sense of what qualities of language become a man as speaker over and above what fit him as an individual is a delicate sense. That there is a difference has been recognized from Aristotle's time to our own. The subtlety of the difference has led to many mistakes. On the one hand, it has trapped people into adopting a special "speaking style," (and tone of voice) which can readily degenerate into the ridiculous. On the other, and by revulsion from what is called "oratorical" language, it has led to an exaggerated ordinariness, a deliberate debasing of language below what a self-respecting person would use in careful conversation.

Language Superior to Casual Talk. The most desirable language for public speaking will maintain a nice balance a little on the careful side of good conversation. The language which is normal in offhand, informal conversation does not seem natural in public speaking. Therefore the advice of the late Professor Winans is excellent, ". . . public speech does not require a low tone, or a careless manner, or undignified English. . . . Give your thoughts fitting garb; to plain thoughts plain expression, to heightened thoughts heightened expression." In a word, the language of a good public speaker is the language of a "gentleman conversing," whatever the prevailing, accepted characteristics of a gentleman may be.

It is impossible to provide samples of the language that all speakers should use in all situations so that their language will seem so normal to listeners that it will not be conspicuous. That language will be somewhere within the scope of the following rough-and-ready prescription: language which is barely usable in the offhand talk of ordinary conversation, because of its informality and casualness will appear debased when it is elevated to the speaker's platform. Language which seems a little too formal in conversation will seem on the platform just enough elevated or enlarged to be in the proper perspective. The learning speaker who keeps a gentle pressure (but only *gentle,* without forcing) on himself to tone up his language will usually improve satisfactorily.

Language of the Educated Person. Most of the users of this book are educated people or are on the way to becoming educated people. They are among those people, therefore, who will be expected to use language that is not defective in grammar, usage, or pronunciation. Their language should not raise their hearers' eyebrows or divert the attention of the "judicious," as Hamlet told the players. Bad grammar and faulty pronunciation, of course, are not moral offenses. Nevertheless, because on most occasions they conflict with what listeners expect of educated speakers, they draw attention away from intended meaning by adding an unintended meaning—that the speaker is somehow deficient in his education. It may be true no longer that, as Ruskin wrote a century ago, "a false accent or a mistaken syllable is enough, in the parliament of any civilized nation, to assign to a man a certain degree of inferior standing forever." Nonetheless, such grammatical errors as *like I said, if I would have known, everybody has their own opinion,* widespread as they may be, do a speaker no good. Nor does he gain by such false elegancies as the *usage* of a new gadget rather than the *use* of it, *in lieu of* for *in place of*, and *media, criteria* and *curricula* as singulars.

The educated speaker, however, is no prude, and his example does not justify the ostentatious display of vulgarity with which some popular demagogues try to distinguish themselves from their educated, civilized opponents. As Nicholas Murray Butler told a graduating class at Columbia University half a century ago, the educated man "knows the wide distinction between correct English on the one hand, and pedantic, or as it is sometimes called "elegant" English on the other. He is more likely to 'go to bed' than to 'retire,' to 'get up' than 'arise,'. . . . to 'dress' rather than to 'clothe himself,' and to 'make a speech' rather than to 'deliver an oration.'" Today, would he perhaps "give a talk" rather than "make a speech"?

In general, an audience expects a public speaker to use language that is superior to what he would employ in his casual, off-the-cuff conversation. The speaker who aims "to speak better than he thinks he can" will probably satisfy this expectation of his hearers. His language will help to hold attention; at least his language will not distract attention.

To Audience, Subject, and Occasion. Much of what can be said profitably about appropriateness to audience, subject, and occasion in the choice of words is implicit in our discussion of clearness and of appropriateness to the speaker. We will discuss the matter further in connection with appropriateness in connected discourse. Two or three points may be specially fitting here, however.

Obviously, audiences differ, occasions differ, and subjects differ; but these three elements interlock so closely that when one is changed, the others change in some respects. Adlai Stevenson, in his speech on the educated citizen to the senior class at Princeton University in 1954, at the height of the national frenzy known as McCarthyism (see Chapter 25), would not use the same language he would use in a speech on the same subject before the National Education Association in a less embittered year, when time, occasion, and audience would have altered the subject and the language appropriate to it. Because audience, occasion, and subject are interrelated, one cannot lay down self-operating rules and formulas for making language appropriate. Perhaps we should merely quote again a sentence of the late Professor Winans, "Give your thoughts fitting garb; to plain thoughts plain expression, to heightened thoughts heightened expression." The plainness and heightened quality of the thoughts are determined in part by the qualities of the audience and the occasion. Probably, therefore, the most one can do is to encourage taste and a feeling for fitness of language. In particular, a speaker should consider the appropriateness of slang, jargon, and the language of extravagance.

Slang and Jargon. In considering the appropriateness of language to audiences, the speaker should be cautious about using slang, although the temptation to use it is strong. Slang is often vivid, sharp, and telling; it seems like a common bond between audience and speaker; and because it is familiar and readily recognized, it seems to be a natural, easy means for promoting clearness. Nevertheless, speakers should also be aware of the pitfalls of slang. First, slang is slippery and ever-changing; its vocabulary goes out of date faster than popular songs and slogans. Consequently, the slang expressions which seem familiar and clear to the speaker may be Greek to his audience. The speaker, therefore, must be sure that his colloquialisms are also his hearers'. Second, the flavor of informality and casualness in slang is jarring on many occasions and from many speakers. Rarely is slang suitable on formal occasions or from a speaker who is not well known and well liked by his audience. Third, the use of slang even when accurate may suggest that the speaker is just trying to be a good fellow or is talking down to his audience. In brief, if slang, like humor, can sweeten a speech; like humor, it can sour a speech.

The observations about the use of slang apply also to the use of the special terminology and jargon of, let us say, sports writers and commentators, of the entertainment world, as represented in the publication *Variety,* and of such cults as the Hippies and the discotheque enthusiasts. A speaker, of course, may show off in any of these idioms, but by the criteria of clearness and appropriateness it takes very special audiences and very special speakers to make such language desirable.

Extravagance. The language of exaggeration, of *super,* so dear to the tongues and pens of our advertisers, involves basically the problem of propriety. Perhaps we should not be concerned with this fantastic vocabulary, which we as listeners may tend to discount automatically. We hear so much of it, however, that we can hardly help allowing it to creep into our speaking on serious and significant occasions unless we are consciously careful. The common trouble with TV and radio commercials is not that they are uningenious and ill executed. Far from it. The trouble is that they are likely to be couched in such exaggerated language and to be delivered in such hyperthyroid excitement that they are all out of proportion to subject, speaker, audience, and occasion. We cannot dress up commonplace matters such as breakfast cereal and laundry soap with false enthusiasm and inflated diction without seeming absurd and ridiculous and without losing the respect and confidence of judicious listeners. After all, in a vocabulary where *supercolossal* describes the normal, usual condition, what does one say to express unusual approval?

The Type of Speech. Finally, two broad considerations may help the speaker judge the appropriateness of language. The first is the kind of purpose which subject and occasion have given rise to. A scientist seeking to impart information at a meeting of scientists will inevitably emphasize the language of fact. Figurative vocabulary will be at a minimum; so also will be the emotionally loaded and picturesque word. A scientific or technical subject planned for a popular audience—the lecture occasion—will demand the common language of the layman, the diction of definition, example, comparison, and contrast. It will keep a reasonable balance between technical, strange words, on the one hand, and familiar, concrete, and vivid language, on the other. But, if the subject is controversial, touching necessarily upon the opinions, attitude, and prejudices aroused by the occasion, the diction of emotion will come into play. For the political speaker urging his hearers to throw the rascals out of Washington, the language of fact gains strength from the language of appeal, exhortation, and power. MacArthur defending his Korean record before Congress, Lincoln debating Douglas or honoring the Union dead at Gettysburg, Henry Grady appealing to the Yankees to understand the New South, Johnson and Goldwater campaigning for the Presidency, the student earnestly dealing with racial prejudice—none can escape language which moves men's emotions as well as their minds, and none need escape.

Significance of Subject and Occasion. The second broad consideration is the importance and significance of subject and occasion. Language, to be appropriate, must correspond to the value with which speaker and audience regard the subject. Or as Aristotle tells us, unless we are trying to be funny, "we must neither speak casually about weighty matters, nor solemnly about trivial ones." Is urging your student audience to attend the torchlight procession for the football team, or urging them to join the protest march to Selma more important? The answer depends upon how one weighs the occasion that one as a speaker is preparing to meet. Under the circumstances, which subject is the more pressing? The decision depends also upon one's perspective. If the occasion is not urgent, which subject should matter most to one and one's hearers? The decision taken will color the language of the speech from beginning to end. The language will either ring true or sound hollow; it will be either in tune or off key.

Interest, attractiveness, impressiveness

Individual words, quite independently of their use in connected passages, may be interesting, attractive, or impressive. The concrete, specific word is not only more clear but more interesting than the abstract, general word. No doubt the concrete word is clearer because it is more interesting. The active voice of verbs is more interesting than the passive. Some words have special or peculiar attractiveness, are particularly pleasing, either from association, sound, or some more mysterious cause. One is reminded of the elderly lady who told a speaker that she had enjoyed his speech because he had used that blessed word which she loved, *Mesopotamia*. Most of us would agree, further, that more dignity and impressiveness are inherent in the words *constitutional convention* than in the headline writer's equivalent *code parley*. The one word *peace* has served to focus the whole message of Christian preachers on many notable occasions, and more recently it has become one of the favorite catchwords of the propagandists of the Communist world. Furthermore, perhaps some words are beautiful and others ugly simply because of their sounds. It is hard, however, to isolate the beauty or ugliness of words as sounds from the beauty or ugliness they have acquired through association and meaning.

These qualities, however, are most significantly associated with words in connected discourse. We shall, therefore, discuss next the aspect of style involving connected language. Again, we shall treat language as clear, appropriate, interesting, attractive, and impressive.

Management of Language—Words in Combination

Clearness

Let us recall Swift's definition of style, "Proper words in proper places." We have been discussing the proper words; now we will look at the proper places—and first at the management of words for clarity. Usually, clearness is the result of casting familiar, concrete, specific, active words into familiar, direct, uncomplicated sentences and larger thought-units in which the structural and logical relations are easily visible and are marked with connecting and relating words. Declarative sentences in the active voice which are not too long to be spoken easily in one breath will usually be clearer than the longer, more oblique sentences. Observe the relative clarity of the following two versions of the same passage:

> If waves are watched rolling in and striking the iron columns of an ordinary pier, it is seen that although the larger waves are not much obstructed by the column, but are merely divided briefly and joined again, as a regiment of soldiers is divided by a tree, the short waves are blocked and scattered by the columns.
>
> Imagine that we stand on any ordinary seaside pier and watch the waves rolling in and striking the iron columns of the pier. Large waves pay little attention to the columns. They divide right and left and reunite after passing each column, much as a regiment of soldiers would if a tree stood in their road. It is almost as though the columns had not been there. But the short waves and ripples find the columns of the pier a much more formidable obstacle. When the short waves impinge on the columns, they are reflected back and spread as new ripples in all directions.

Neither passage is *notably* unclear, at least to a reader. To a listener the first passage would undoubtedly be harder to grasp and to recall. There is little in the words or the structure to focus attention and thus facilitate understanding.

The use of familiar rather than strange sentence structure promotes clearness, as does the sharply constructed paragraph or basic unit in which the *statement* is easy to recognize and the *development* is marked by guide-post words and phrases: *let us take an example, for instance, another bit of information, consequently, on the other hand.*

Clearness, as we have observed, is partly, perhaps largely, dependent upon attention, and attention is much the same as interest. The qualities that make style interesting, therefore, will be of much help in making it clear.

Appropriateness

As we shall observe again when we discuss the means of improving one's language and of cultivating style, style in speaking and style in writing are closely akin. Excellence in written style, which registers chiefly through the eye, is best when it exhibits the qualities we have been discussing: clearness, appropriateness, interest, and impressiveness. Thus the basis of good style in writing is the same as the basis of good style in speaking. Yet the difference between the circumstances of listening and of reading accounts for certain important differences between oral and written style. Certain elements and qualities are appropriate to the direct, face-to-face, personal encounter between speaker and a particular audience which do not fit so well the more remote relationship between writer and general reader, or even particular reader. Furthermore, the great versatility of voice and bodily gesture in grouping, emphasizing, contrasting, and structuring language as it is spoken perhaps makes appropriate to speaking a less stringent discipline in the selection and management of language than is required in good writing. In brief, though the essay and the speech are blood relatives, the essay is not simply a written speech, nor is speech an essay standing on its hind legs.

Oral Style. Let the speaker never forget, therefore, that he is directing his language to a specific audience and not to the general reader. Therefore, the working language of a speech will usually differ in some respects from that of an essay or theme or article.

Directness. First, some elements of language will reveal direct, speaker-to-hearer communication. The language of direct oral discourse is more plentifully sprinkled with *I*, with *we, our,* and *us,* than is most written discourse except the personal letter. It is marked, also, by a more copious use of the question than most readers would tolerate. Indeed, the use of interrogation and the first and second person pronouns show unmistakably that audience and speaker are face to face in immediate communication.

The interrogation is easy to use, once a speaker really thinks of himself as a speaker, and once he finds that talking to an audience is no different from elevated conversation. He should realize, above all, that the question is one of the best ways he has of making hearers respond. The two main kinds of question, the open and closed, both elicit response. The first simply invites hearers to consider what is coming next and usually introduces a point or main idea. Thus it "sets" hearers and rouses a kind of expectancy. The closed, or rhetorical, question contains an invitation to say Yes or No and is often used to tie up an argument.

Both kinds are illustrated in Albert Beveridge's speech which opened the Republican campaign for Charles Evans Hughes in the fall of 1916. Beveridge was attacking Wilson's and the Democrats' handling of the Mexican Incident. A hearer might have responded much as we indicate in brackets.

> Have we been kept out of war with Mexico? [I can't say immediately, it depends on what war is.] What is war? [I'll listen—what is it?] Merely a declaration? [Possibly not this, but—] Our naval war with France was waged for two years without a declaration. Japan struck Russia without a declaration. War means offensive and deadly acts. We invaded Mexico and withdrew; but fighting took place and American marines were killed. Our territory was invaded by Mexicans who were driven out; but again Americans were killed. We invaded that country once more and to-day our military forces, with siege guns, are intrenched in the heart of Northern Mexico. They have fought with uniformed Mexicans and soldiers of both sides have fallen. Almost the whole of our effective military forces are kept on the border and lines of communication established with Pershing's men. Our War Department has held officially that a deserter from our army must be punished as in time of war. The government's censorship of all news from Mexico is more rigid than that of the European belligerents. If all this is not war, what is it? [I wouldn't know right now.] If

such a state of things existed between ourselves and any other nation, what would we call it? [Well, war I guess.] What would the world call it? [War.]

Profuseness. Second, oral language is more profuse, more repetitious than written language. It is more inclined to pile up words rather than trust to the discovery of the single exact word. A student speaker, roused by a local crime wave, was not satisfied to express a chief point only once. Early in his speech he said,

> The gangsters warred against each other.

Then, following a few statistics and an example, he put the same idea this way:

> The racketeers killed racketeers. The mobsters of the Capone days rarely molested ordinary people. Murder was just an "occupational hazard."

A *writer* might be content to state the idea once, feeling that the reader's eye and mind would take it in instantly—or if not, that rereading would be easy and automatic. But the *speaker,* keenly aware of his listeners, made sure through restatement that they would understand. The same speech affords an illustration of the piling up of words, words that are near-synonyms, overlapping in meaning:

> The hoodlums today are the mugger, the knifer, the rapist, the strangler, the brute attacker.

In the pressure of extemporaneous utterance, eager to insure clearness, emphasis, and force, the speaker did not revise his list of hoodlums, as might the writer, to secure a neat, logical classification of gangsters. Written language at its best is more compact than this, is more often content with fewer synonymous terms and amplifying phrases.

Informal constructions. The language of extemporaneous speech, in the third place, often reveals sentences whose construction is less traditional and formal than would be proper for the eye alone. The eye must depend upon the signs of punctuation and capitalization and upon the careful placing of sentence elements, such as qualifying phrases and clauses, if the reader is to avoid confusion and distraction. The ear, however, can depend upon the tremendous resources of voice and gesture to set sentences straight. Inflection, pause, pace, and emphasis are the oral signs of punctuation; they tell the listener how sentence elements are related to each other. A participle that dangles to the eye may not dangle to the ear! Furthermore, in speaking there is greater variety in the length of sentences. A succession of short, terse sentences which would bother the eye may not hinder the ear. A long sentence (Robert Ingersoll once spun a perfectly clear sentence six pages long) that the eye would reject is often acceptable to the ear, probably because the voice can handle it as a related sequence of short or relatively short sentences. In brief, language constructions which are appropriate to listeners may not be appropriate to readers.

Thomas DeQuincey's advice on oral style is in point here:

> Every mode of intellectual communication has its separate strength and separate weakness. . . . In a book one can turn to a past page if anything in the present depends upon it. But, return being impossible in the case of a spoken language, where each sentence dies as it is born, both the speaker and the hearer become aware of a mutual interest in a much looser style, and a perpetual dispensation from the severities of abstract discussion. It is for the benefit of both that the weightier propositions should be detained before the ear a good deal longer than the chastity of taste or the austerity of logic would tolerate in a book. Time must be given for the intellect to eddy about a truth and to appropriate its bearings.

The following brief passage from a speech of President Halsey to the students of the University of Bridgeport exhibits many of the qualities characteristic of the oral style of direct address. It is dignified but sufficiently intimate and is readable as well as listenable.

> We in colleges, both faculty and students, must keep this goal of freedom clearly in view, because it is principally from the students in college that our leaders come. You who represent the student body of the University of Bridgeport, and your fellow students in other colleges throughout the land, are a highly selected group—you are one in five of all people your age. Therefore, upon you rests a greater responsibility in this matter of freedom because you are being given greater opportunities. As the potential leaders of people in a free country, you must help us to help you toward an education for freedom.
>
> And so, I would say to you today as we open this twenty-first year of our college, that each and every one of us must keep this goal forever before him. And to the members of the faculty I say specifically that regardless of what we teach, how we teach, or whom we teach, education for freedom must be the ultimate objective.

The following passage, from Emerson's *American Scholar*, though taken from a speech, suggests the attitude, perhaps, of meditating before an audience rather than addressing oneself directly to listeners.

> The actions and events of our childhood and youth are now matters of calmest observation. They lie like fair pictures in the air. Not so with our recent actions, with the business which we now have in hand. On this we are quite unable to speculate. Our affections as yet circulate through it. We no more

> feel or know it than we feel the feet, or the hand, or the brain of our body. The new deed is yet a part of life, remains for a time immersed in our unconscious life. In some contemplative hour it detaches itself from the life like a ripe fruit, to become a thought of the mind. Instantly it is raised, transfigured; the corruptible has put on incorruption. Henceforth it is an object of beauty, however base its origin and neighborhood.

Oral style, in sum, is the manifestation of the fitness of the language of discourse to the speaking situation: to speaker, to audience, to subject, to the special dimensions which voice, pronunciation, facial expression, and gesture can add to language, and to occasion as interrelated elements in a face-to-face oral event.

Interest and attractiveness

His language is potentially the speaker's most versatile resource for enhancing his audience's attention, interest, and pleasure. Through a skillful management of language, a speaker can gain special effects which appeal to our preference for action, to our curiosity, and to our senses of humor and of beauty. Sometimes, even when a speaker hasn't much of importance to say or a listener does not want to attend to his speech the speaker's flow of language and his vocal performance may be enough to give his audience a gratifying experience.

Activity

The language of action promotes interest, not only by action-words and by verbs in the active voice, but by sentences which move. Lively movement is suggested by short, quick clauses or sentences. For example:

> We can't wait for the last straggler. We must not listen to the faint of heart. Looking back takes our eyes from our path, and complaining of the cost confuses our purpose. We shall make no major mistake. Let us act now and correct any minor errors as we go.

Longer sentences of several clauses may suggest slow, wandering, easy movement.

Another way of suggesting both action and scene is to turn indirect discourse into direct discourse. Not this: "I was told the other day that interest in the honors program is increasing." But this:

> One day last week, as I was sitting down to lunch at the only vacant table in the cafeteria, Professor Williams came by with his tray and joined me. The new honors program for undergraduates is really his special baby, so I inquired, "How are your honorable honors students stacking up for next year,

> Mr. Williams?" "Stacking up is right, Charles. Last year we had to apply a little gentle pressure to fill our honors classes for Freshmen, though we had plenty of qualified students. Now for next fall we have them standing in line to get in—half as many more than we can handle."

Here are human beings in action—and the language is concrete and specific as well.

Curiosity

One of the important factors which stimulate attention and interest is the special set or readiness to respond. In solving a mathematical problem or a puzzle or a riddle, it is the hint that leads to the correct answer. It is the getting set for a race. If this getting-set stage stops short of tension and excitement, it is curiosity; if it brings with it tense excitement, as in the movie, the play, the novel, the detective story, and sometimes the final examination, it is suspense. Both curiosity and suspense are useful in helping the speaker control attention and hold interest, and both may be promoted by astute management of style.

The building-up of concrete detail in description may stir curiosity. This building-up may be promoted by stylistic devices of accumulation. For example:

> A wedding is about to take place in North Africa. The natives are gathering in their best attire, their dark faces contrasting sharply with their white, sheet-like garments and the light walls and sands. As the ceremonies are reaching their climax, the bride and groom suddenly postpone the rest of the celebration while the whole party gathers around a World Health Organization truck and eagerly forms in line, chattering and laughing happily. Is it for bread, or for soup, or for Point-Four technical advice on weddings, or for foreign economic aid? No. It is for delousing with DDT.

Curiosity is aroused, a touch of humor infused, and the speaker proceeds to his subject.

The effectiveness of the story or anecdote, whether humorous or not, in arousing curiosity is universally recognized. Just as widely recognized is the value of stylistic qualities in the telling of a story to enhance or dampen curiosity, both within the story itself and in its application to the speaker's point. Skillful use of curiosity at both points is illustrated in the following passage spoken by Booker T. Washington to an audience of Negro children:

> There is a way for us to work out of every difficulty we may be in. There is a story told of two unfortunate frogs who in the night had the misfortune to fall into a jar of milk. Soon afterward one of the frogs said, "There is no use to make any effort; we might just as well sink to bottom and have life over with." The second frog said, "That is not the way to look at it. Where there is a will

> there is a way. I am going to get out of this milk." So the second frog began to kick and he kept kicking until three o'clock in the morning, when his kicking had turned the milk to butter, and he walked out on dry land. Now I am on the side of the kicking frog every time, and I believe there is a way for us to kick out of every difficulty in which we find ourselves placed as a race.

Earlier in the chapter we mentioned the characteristic function of the question in helping to create the sense of direct conversation in style. The question may serve also as a direct bid for curiosity. The open question sometimes serves well in starting off a whole speech, or in introducing a main point. It opens the way for an answer which the speaker immediately supplies. For example, "Do you know what is the biggest business in the world? The United States Government." Sometimes a speaker may use a series of questions effectively, as did Patrick Henry in his "Appeal to Arms" speech:

> Has Great Britain any enemy, in this quarter of the world, to call for this accumulation of navies and armies? No sir, she has none. They are meant for us; they can be meant for no other. They are sent over to bind and rivet upon us those chains which the British ministry have been so long forging. And what have we to oppose them? Shall we try argument? Sir, we have been trying that for the last ten years. Have we anything new to offer upon the subject? Nothing. We have held the subject up in every light of which it is capable; but it has been all in vain.

Perhaps the best formula for finding good questions is this: Frame the question that a hearer would ask if he were to interrupt, and place it at that point in the speech where he might logically ask it. This Patrick Henry did in the passage just quoted.

Humor

In connection with amplification through example, we said something about the use and place of humor in speechmaking. Stories or anecdotes, though excellent sources of humor within the reach of most speakers, are often not the most effective humorous vehicles for producing interest. Some of the best and most relevant humor lies in style: in the turn of phrase, the use of an amusing simile, surprise in the presentation of detail, application of a familiar quotation to a context for which it was not originally intended, and other devices which appear as integral parts of arguments, ideas, and explanations. An idea is shaped for a humorous effect. Thus did the famous Samuel Johnson score a point against certain pompous and pedestrian scientists by referring to them as "those stately sons of demonstration who are at great pains to prove that two and two can be found to equal four." At another time Johnson disposed of women preachers by the surprise use of a comparison. "A woman's preaching," he said, "is like a dog's walking on his hinder legs.

It is not done well; but you are surprised to find it done at all." And Robert M. Hutchins, reviewing ten years of his administration in a speech to faculty and trustees just after the University of Chicago had been attacked by a notably unrestrained newspaper columnist, made an amusing combination of items: "Apart from fire and pestilence we have had about everything happen to us that could happen in the past ten years. Yesterday we had a robbery, today we have Westbrook Pegler." Someone who wished to break the news humorously to a famous actress commented, "Madame, your show is slipping." A speaker once defined a dilettante as a man who goes about announcing the discovery of lands which have long since been explored and mapped.

Humor is interesting, but it should be used to transfer the interest to the ideas or materials which the speaker wishes his audience to attend to and remember. Hence it is bad practice to haul in gags, vaudeville fashion, or string together wisecracks at the opening of a speech without regard to their relevance. It is the part of a clown or of an emcee on TV. A student speaker used original humor very successfully and relevantly in the opening of a speech on the coming uses of the new lightweight, stainless metals. He reminded the audience of what they had heard about other wonderful household aids. "Automatic washing machines which will wash the clothes, blue them, dry them, iron them, fold them, and put them away—all without any help from the housewife; and electric stoves which will prepare, cook, flavor, garnish, carve, and serve roasts while the host and hostess sit with their guests on the patio." This good-humored exaggeration and the surprise detail got the audience quite ready and eager for what the speaker was going to offer them.

Impressiveness

We say that language is impressive when expression is memorable. Words and idea have been compounded so effectively that they stick in the listener's memory. The listener's experience has been so intense that when he recalls the idea, he recalls the exact language in which he heard it expressed. Style which is impressive in this sense is also interesting, for what sticks in the memory has held attention. It is worthwhile, however, to distinguish roughly between what is pleasant and engaging to listen to while it is going on and what also stays with us and is often intensified as time pauses.

Speakers and listeners alike know that the commanding sentence, the lively word, the apt phrase, the vivid metaphor, the amusing epithet, of all the elements of a speech, often make the most immediate and most enduring impression on listeners. Franklin D. Roosevelt's label "horse-and-buggy," which he attached to the economic ideas which he wished to reform, served efficiently for many people to summarize the gist of a series of his speeches.

A generation earlier Woodrow Wilson had coined a slogan which summarized the purposes he had proclaimed for our participation in World War I and our part in the peace settlement. Most Americans know the slogan "Make the World Safe for Democracy." A happy figure of speech also may serve to focus the whole force of an argument. Thomas Paine, the American patriot and friend of the French Revolution, summed up with such a figure his contempt for Edmund Burke's argument against the French revolutionists: "He pities the plumage, but forgets the dying bird."

Further examples of impressiveness come to mind in abundance: Winston Churchill's tribute to the Royal Air Force, "Never in the field of human conflict was so much owed by so many to so few," and his splendid affirmation of the stamina and will of the English people, "We shall fight on the beaches, we shall fight on the landing grounds, we shall fight in the fields and in the streets, we shall fight in the hills, we shall never surrender"; Lincoln's "government of the people, by the people, and for the people"; Franklin D. Roosevelt's coinage, born of the panic days of the Great Depression, "We have nothing to fear but fear itself"; Homer's "wine-dark sea'; Christ's "Render unto Caesar the things that are Caesar's"; William Jennings Bryan's condemnation of the gold standard as "crucifying mankind upon a cross of gold"; the countless folk sayings, such as "The race is not always to the swift"; and sharp word inventions like "The inhibited don't mind being prohibited."

Speakers prize coinages like these. Consequently, they strive to invent some of their own, and failing, they may be fortunate enough to discover usable ones as they read and talk. They select memorable phrases appropriate for the speech at hand and use them as short quotations. Late in the rehearsal stage of preparation, they may spend considerable time practicing these borrowed phrases to make sure that they can speak them with complete spontaneity. There is, alas, no recipe for constructing impressive expressions. But if a speaker recognizes some of the main types of impressiveness, he may be stimulated to invent effective expressions of his own and certainly he will discover such phrases more readily in the language of others.

Imagery and the Metaphor. Impressiveness in style is greatly enhanced by the vividness which comes with good imagery. Imagery takes advantage of the intensity and force of a stimulus or idea in promoting swift and ready response. Imagery in the speech involves the selection of words that make the listener use his sensory apparatus as if he were actually in the presence of the things being referred to. Imagery gives the listener a substitute for actuality, or a new and more vivid kind of actuality. One of the characters in a novel by J. B. Priestley attends a concert in which, for the first time, he hears a "modern" symphonic piece. The author describes the effect of certain passages upon the conventional, conservative sensibilities of the listener: "Tall, thin people were sitting around sneering at each other and drinking quinine, while an imbecile child sat on the floor and ran its finger nails up and down a slate." Thus the speaker who wishes to give force and intensity to his ideas tries to turn his abstract and general ideas into concrete and specific images. He is a sort of translator, like the poet, who takes his audience from the abstract to the earthy, and he discovers in the process of translation that he gives clarity as well as impressiveness to the new experience.

Though it is impossible to teach image making, through the ages books on style have devoted a great deal of space to the classification and description of images and figures of speech, to remind speakers and writers of the possibilities. A seriously interested student may find some profit and amusement in glancing through such a treatment. We suggest, for example, the Latin *Rhetorica Ad Herennium,* translated by Harry Caplan for the Loeb Classical Library. We have neither space here nor inclination for an extended treatment. We would remind the student, however, of the various kinds of imagery which are available to him:

Visual:	red carpet	*Gustatory:*	bitter tea
Auditory:	fire siren	*Tactile:*	sandpaper beard
Olfactory:	burned toast	*Motor:*	jumping a hedge

Kinesthetic: lifting a weight, pushing a door

All the other senses listed probably call up visual images as well.

Introduce any of the unitalicized items above with the word *like,* and one has a figure of speech, a simile. Omit the expression of likeness from a simile, leaving an identification, and one has a metaphor: "Rommel, the desert fox." A metaphor is what Henry Ward Beecher called "the window in an argument," because it lights up reason. The metaphor rouses an image, a flash picture or sensation; its concentration brings attention into a fast sharp focus and its image gives strength and intensity. Metaphor, as Aristotle observed centuries ago, though the most distinguished ornament of the speaker's style is the least teachable because it depends upon a talent for seeing significant resemblances. Nevertheless, a speaker may foster his talent for metaphor. As the literary critic J. Middleton Murry wrote, "A metaphor is the result of the search for a precise epithet. Try to be precise and you are bound to be metaphorical." Perhaps this is the sense in which the great British speaker Edmund Burke was said to reason in metaphor.

Antithesis and Contrast. Antithesis is a compressed contrast which brings close together words whose meanings are at opposite extremes. "The educated man has no monopoly on knowledge; the uneducated man has no monopoly on ignorance." Usually, as in this example, the structure of the expression is parallel and strictly balanced. Thus pattern and thought reinforce each other and carry the punch of a well-aimed blow. For an illustration of an extended antithesis with repeated blows resulting in great force, see the passage beginning "Hamilton believed in the rule of an aristocracy of money, and Jefferson in a democracy of men" on page 185. Study of the passage will show that antithesis can be effective even without strict balance. It will show, also, that such thought and expression are not sudden inspiration, exploding into being during the heat of delivery. Like all truly impressive effects, they are carefully planned and worked over until language and idea become indistinguishable. Observe the extended development of a number of contrasts in antithetical stylistic structure in the following paragraphs from an opening address to the students and staff of the University of Toronto, by the President, Dr. Sidney Smith. In the second paragraph especially, the balanced, periodic structure of the sentences is particularly notable. Style of this sort is the result of the greatest care in the selection and management of language to embody precision of thought in forceful structure.

> You have freedom of choice, and by inescapable equations your choices will bring you profit or loss. If you choose to work, you will pass; if you don't, you will fail. If you neglect your work, you will dislike it; if you do it well, you will enjoy it. If you join little cliques, you will be self-satisfied; if you make friends widely, you will be interesting. If you act like a boor, you will be despised; if you act like a human being, you will be respected. If you spurn wisdom, wise people will spurn you; if you seek wisdom, they will seek you. If you adopt a pose of boredom, you will be a bore; if you show vitality, you will be alive. If you spend your free time playing bridge, you will be a good bridge player; if you spend it reading, discussing and thinking of things that matter, you will be an educated person.
>
> If you have come here for social prestige, you can get what you are after, but you may not like it much when you have got it; you would really have done better to concentrate on debutantes' parties. If you have come here to learn to make money, you can get what you are after, but you run the risk of finding yourself unhappy in your goal; you would really have done better to get into the building trades or the stock market. If you have come here to be a personality kid and win friends and influence people, you might get what you are after, but it would have been quicker and cheaper to take a course in salesmanship. If you have come here to learn to serve your fellowmen as a member of one of the learned professions, you are in the right place. If you have come to study the most important ideas that mankind has evolved, you are in the right place. If you have come to penetrate the fascinating mysteries and powers of nature, you are in the right place. If you have come to learn of the cultural and intellectual heritage of the past, so as to stand on the giant's shoulders and see farther, "to follow knowledge, like a sinking star, beyond the utmost bound of human thought," you are in the right place. You may never get what you are after, but in the trying you will become what you could never otherwise have been, and these next few years that you spend here will be the keystone of the arch of your experience.

The following sentence, with contrasting balance, effectively communicates the main point of the student speech on pages 53–54. It also distills an image which gives a title to the speech. "Thus we can see that although the conscience is often called 'a little voice inside,' it acts more like 'the old crank next door.'" Perhaps the most felicitous call to patriotism of our generation rang in President Kennedy's Inaugural epigram: "Ask not what your country can do for you, but what you can do for your country." There is nothing unusual in the choice of words. The impressiveness comes from balance and contrast, from the reversal of subject and object from one clause to the other, and from *Ask not* instead of *Do not ask* at the beginning. That opening structure, through the sense of antiquity and the echo of Biblical language in it, suggests, perhaps, the sacred dignity of service to country.

Novel and Unusual Expression. Any out-of-the-ordinary twist to language which puts an idea compactly is likely to secure a striking effect. The novelty of the expression makes it fresh and lively; the terseness gives it intensity and sharpness. Sometimes the unusual turn springs from an apparent contradiction: "The situation was so bad that it was bound to yield some good." A well-known senator is said to have one of the best minds in the Senate until he has to make it up. The play on words, whether a pun or not, is another source of the novel turn, as may be seen in Edison's assertion that "genius is ninety-nine per cent perspiration and one per cent inspiration." Somebody has given this a different twist: "Lazy persons never learn that inspiration comes from perspiration." A debater once advised his opponent, whose bombastic delivery could not conceal barrenness of thought, to put less fire into his speech and more of his speech into the fire. Coinages like these are epigrammatic.

A ready source of novel and terse expression is the epithet, which substitutes for the proper name of a person or thing, a word or phrase which suggests some distinctive trait or quality of the object. In castigating the men behind the oil scandals of the Harding Administration, Claude Bowers soon dropped the names, Fall, Sinclair, and Doheny, and referred instead to the "Powers of Privilege and Pillage" and the "Powers of Darkness." Later in his speech Bowers called Privilege and Pillage the "Gold Dust Twins," making a pun on a then familiar pictorial ad for a washing powder. The greedy and furtive methods of the oil plotters were tagged as "Addition, Subtraction–and Silence." Because one of the scandal's key figures habitually carried a black briefcase, journalists were quick with the epithet, "the Little Black Baggers," again alluding to a familiar label for political adventurers, "Carpet Baggers." Similarly, the alleged mess of the Truman Administration became known in opposition oratory as "Government by mink coat and deep freeze." James G. Blaine, a handsome crusading politician of the 1890's, was known for a time as "the Plumed Knight." A political party, clearly split into conservative and progressive groups and showing a dual personality, recently has been dubbed "schizophrenic." A more recent coinage, associating young nonconformists with the opponents of the war in Vietnam, is "Vietniks." Such happy mintages are hard to come by, it is true, and are soon worn out; nevertheless, if the speaker can coin but one or two such expressions, they are worth his time and imagination. When he says them he can see his listeners almost snap to attention. Such coinages are prized and exploited endlessly by advertisers.

In order to invent an effective phrase, state the governing idea of the speech in the most concise and accurate way possible. Do the same thing for the chief supporting ideas and for the conclusion. Summarize the entire thought of the speech in twenty words. More often than not, as we have said, the effort to be both compact and precise results in vivid figurative language. And if the main ideas of a speech can be expressed in striking language, the listener will grasp and remember essentials rather than details, as in Churchill's statements quoted on page 211. They are brief compressions of entire speeches. We still remember them. Similarly, Lincoln epitomized a speech with, "A house divided against itself cannot stand." Expressions like these do for a speech what slogans do for advertisers, who often pay handsomely for new coinages.

False Impressiveness—the Trite and Shopworn. Throughout the history of instruction in style, whether for writing or speaking, it ever seems to have been easier to be specific about bad style than good, about the ways speakers and writers go wrong than the ways they go right. The reason may be that we notice the things which we don't like, while good style seldom attracts attention to itself. Again the governing principle seems to be appropriateness, adherence to the fitting. Perhaps in the long run the best one can do for a speaker is to help him clear from his linguistic habits the disfigurements and obstacles in his style, and leave him free to create the stylistic excellences which his taste and talent direct.

Let us call attention, therefore, to one of the common sources of pallor and dullness in style, and one of the easiest for a speaker to fall into—triteness. Triteness may be defined roughly as saying the same old thing in the same old way at the wrong time. Triteness completely violates the principles of attention and interest. We know that the new in the familiar, and the familiar in the new, are interesting. The totally familiar and the totally new, however, are both completely uninteresting.

When the touring political candidate begins "My Friends [or Fellow Americans], it gives me a very real sense of personal pleasure to pay another visit to your fair city in this great state," he wishes to appear especially direct and genuine. In fact, he is pompous in as trite a way as possible. Each of his presumably friendly and elegant expressions, is a cliché so shopworn from thousands of repetitions by hundreds of candidates as to sound utterly perfunctory. True, his opening may have the familiar ring of candidate-beginning-standard-speech, but the words are so much a routine that they convey little more. He might have surprised and interested his audience, at least for the moment, had he begun simply, "Ladies and Gentlemen: I'm pleased to be here again."

Most trite expressions are so, not because they are in themselves inadequate or inaccurate or because they have been used many times. They are trite because they are used as if they were new or special. Old metaphors and other figures of speech, once vivid or ingenious, are used by the addict of the cliché as if he had manufactured them specially for the occasion. The first person who said "pretty as a picture," no doubt called up a vivid image for himself and his listener. That expression today is little more than a routine compliment; the simile has long since ossified. One who describes himself or someone else as "sick as a dog" is probably exaggerating, and he has probably never visualized the image.

As we have said, fresh imagery is a speaker's great resource for vividness. Stale imagery, however, is often no more than meaningless or slightly disappointing filler. The woman who remarked that Shakespeare is nothing but a collection of old quotations was responding to the overworking and misapplication of some of the most imaginative language in English: *her infinite variety; how weary, stale, flat, and unprofitable; bestride the world like a colossus; lend me your ears; to be or not to be.* Polonius, whose speech to the departing Laertes may be the most often quoted portion of Shakespeare, is Shakespeare's special portrait of the trite, cliché-ridden old man, who thinks that he is being profound and original. When a speaker hears himself beginning to sound like Polonius, he had better take a new look at his habits of language!

A modest degree of triteness is normal and necessary in most circumstances. It gives an ordinariness and naturalness to everyday speech. People expect familiar ideas to be expressed in familiar ways—within limits. The impressive speaker, however, is the one who uses the trite and commonplace as background, not as the staple of his discourse. The speaker, on the other hand, who is so afraid of the cliché that he never says anything in the usual way, succeeds only in being difficult and strange, not impressive.

For the young speaker to develop a reliable sense of what is trite and what is not, is no simple matter. Such a sense can come only from much experience with language and sensitive observation of it. After all, everyone has to encounter an expression for the first time, and then it is new and fresh to him. If the speaker is aware of the subtle danger of the cliché, however, he is on the way to controlling it. He will look out for such automatic expressions as *last but not least, blast-off, not the heat but the humidity, not the money but the principle of the thing, that's just politics.*

Many writers discuss triteness, often very tritely. Two who discuss it amusingly and pointedly, with many embarrassing examples, are Gelett Burgess and Sir Arthur Quiller-Couch. Burgess's "*Are You a Bromide?*" published sixty or so years ago, illustrates very amusingly the behavior of the blissfully trite person who is each of us, at least part of the time! Some of his examples are dated, but most are perennial. Quiller-Couch, in his "Interlude: On Jargon," in *The Art of the Writer* (1916), makes profitable sport of the leaning which we all have towards the hackneyed on the one hand and the strange on the other. Any speaker who would like to clear some of the trash from his language, and have fun doing so, might well read Burgess and Quiller-Couch.

Rhythm and Harmony. So far our discussion of impressiveness has emphasized the impact of image and conflict, the gem of expression, the distillation of idea into the compact and powerful expression. Another source of impressiveness, however, no less important, is more difficult to characterize quickly and to exemplify neatly: the impressiveness which derives from the movement and sound of a sustained passage. Early in the Christian era, the critic called Longinus, speaking of the kinds of grandeur in style, contrasted Demosthenes and Cicero, both of whom he admired greatly. Demosthenes, he said, strikes like a thunderbolt, whereas Cicero consumes all before him like a great conflagration. From Demosthenes nothing can be taken away; to Cicero nothing can be added (observe the antithesis). Today the massiveness of Cicero has little appeal to listeners in the Western world, though when they have listened to Winston Churchill, perhaps they have felt something of the grand swell. The rhythm and harmony of fine oral style, however, joined with an important message on a significant occasion, can still impress American audiences. Few of us can achieve distinction of this sort, or even define it, though we can recognize it when we hear it and miss it when we do not. All, however, who would accomplish more than the ordinary, will measure their own language by the sense which comes from familiarity with the best, and they will not hesitate to try to rise at times above themselves, in choice of language and in that "other rhythm" of prose.

In the following sections we discuss reading and writing as ways of acquiring sensitivity to the fine rhythms and harmonies of good style. In a short space we can give no better instruction. The following passages, however, supply two touchstones for what fine style in sober public speaking can be. The first is from Edmund Burke's speech "On Conciliation with the Colonies."

> The question with me is not whether you have a right to render your people miserable, but whether it is not your interest to make them happy. It is not what a lawyer tells me I *may* do, but what humanity, reason, and justice tell me I *ought* to do. Is a politick act the worse for being a generous one? Is no concession proper but that which is made from your want of right to keep what you grant? Or does it lessen the grace or dignity of relaxing in the exer-

> cise of an odious claim, because you have your evidence-room full of titles and your magazines stuffed with arms to enforce them? What signify all those titles and all those arms? Of what avail are they when the reason of the thing tells me that the assertion of my title is the loss of my suit, and that I could do nothing but wound myself by the use of my own weapons?

The second comes from Abraham Lincoln's Second Inaugural Address.

> Neither party expected for the war, the magnitude, or the duration, which it has already attained. Neither anticipated that the *cause* of the conflict might cease with, or even before, the conflict itself should cease. Each looked for an easier triumph, and a result less fundamental and astounding. Both read the same Bible, and pray to the same God; and each invokes His aid against the other. It may seem strange that any men should dare to ask a just God's assistance in wringing their bread from the sweat of other men's faces; but let us judge not that we be not judged. The prayers of both could not be answered; that of neither has been answered fully. The Almighty has His own purposes. "Woe unto the world because of offenses! for it must needs be that offenses come; but woe to that man by whom the offense cometh." If we shall suppose that American slavery is one of those offenses which, in the providence of God, must needs come, but which, having continued through His appointed time, He now wills to remove, and that He gives to both North and South, this terrible war, as the woe due to those by whom the offense came, shall we discern therein any departure from those divine attributes which the believers in a living God always ascribe to Him? Fondly do we hope—fervently do we pray—that this mighty scourge of war may speedily pass away. Yet, if God wills that it continue, until all the wealth piled by the bondman's two hundred and fifty years of unrequited toil shall be sunk, and until every drop of blood drawn with the lash, shall be paid by another drawn with the sword, as was said three thousand years ago, so still it must be said "the judgments of the Lord are true and righteous altogether."

Improving Style

Speaking often

Speaking often is one of the obvious ways of learning to use language well. Much speaking, however, may intensify bad habits as well as create good ones. Judicious and critical practice and experience, therefore, are necessary. The speaker, especially while he is a learner, should try out each speech aloud several times before he presents it to his final audience. This procedure we have recommended in our discussion of delivery (Chapter 3). Several rehearsals may well be devoted to experimenting consciously with the different ways of putting ideas into language. A speaker also will covet opportunities to speak on the same subject before different audiences, changing his language to make it more effective each time. Probably everyone has had the experience of telling to many different audiences some favorite exciting or humorous anecdote. If he is a good narrator, interested in the maximum effect from his story, not only has he tried different ordering of the details, but from one telling to the next he has been consciously seeking to improve the clarity, the fitness, the force, and probably the humor of the language in which he told the story. This sort of exercise is very good for one who would speak well. For greatest profit, obviously, the speaker must be keen to the listeners' response to his language as he goes along, noticing what is puzzling, what is amusing, what is clear, what is dead, and accordingly altering his technique. Most of what we advise in Appendix B about the process of rehearsing a speech, directed toward effectiveness of delivery, is equally applicable to the improvement of style. The speaker, however, must be critically sensitive to his own performance or his practice will be useless—if not harmful.

Listening and reading

Perhaps as fundamental as speaking often is reading and listening. One does not come instinctively to a sense of clearness and fitness in language. One has to cultivate it. Through extensive and frequent exposure one has to absorb a sense of what good language is. There are only two sources of this experience: one is hearing good oral discourse, the other is reading.

There is much good oral discourse to be heard in the world, on the air, from the pulpit, from the public lecture platform, and even in the college and university classroom. Furthermore, good recordings of speaking are more and more easily obtained. Not always, alas, are these specimens easy to find, and they are even more difficult to find when one wants them. Therefore reading good prose and poetry is the speaker's best resource for exposing his mind and ear to excellent use of language.

Imagery, the soul of poetry, has always been a vital force, as we have said, in good public speaking as well. Imagery in example, in illustration, in narrative, is perhaps the more easily noticed. Imagery in language is more subtle but just as effective. The two illustrations which open Bruce Barton's speech (pages 526–531) build up ready pictures for us, but a terse reference to "the ruthless politician who roared and clawed his way to power" less obviously evokes an image of the lion. Since poetry is alive with metaphors—compact, precise, and piercing—the reading of poetry sharpens perception and develops a feeling for metaphorical language. Imagery is likely to be neglected by the learning speaker as he tries to improve, but a little effort here will yield good results. His early attempts may appear feeble and trite, but he will learn—though not unless he experiments. The feeling for rhythm, which is enlivened by the reading, especially the oral reading, of verse, may also have good effects on a speaker's style.

The generations of English-speaking people who progressed from the cradle to the grave in almost daily contact with the oral and silent reading of the King James version of the Bible were fortunate indeed. The language of the English Bible, of course, is not the only good English, nor is it even the best for general use in our present world. Nevertheless, the generations who knew the Bible intimately could never be so completely adrift in the sea of language, without direction and without a basis of selection, as those today who have no firm common background of excellent oral and written discourse. Woodrow Wilson attributed his command of language to years of hearing the Bible read aloud and to reading it aloud himself. The usual objection, of course, is that a speaker or a writer should develop his own best language rather than imitate the language of others, however good. If the case were as simple as that, the objection would no doubt be sound. But any language has its norms, and these norms over a period of years will come from the best of written language modified by live, oral, contemporary usage, and touched with happy individuality. Since we are not born with language but have to learn it, we have to learn it somewhere. Since as speakers we are expected to be better users of language than the untaught and the uncultivated, we should take as our models the best that our culture has to offer, both past and present, not the worst, however popular, or even the ordinary, run-of-the-mine, half-effective speech of trivial conversation.

For improving the use of language, no one can overestimate reading aloud. We learned to speak because we heard and talked long before we learned to read and write. Accordingly, hearing and speaking remain the most effective avenues leading to improvement in our command over speaking. To hear and to read orally a vocabulary wider and more precise than our own is to enhance our own oral vocabulary; to hear and mouth language that is constructed better than ours, is more rhythmical and impressive, is to improve our own oral patterns. The earnest public speaker, therefore should read aloud—and read aloud as much as he can. He will find courses in oral reading (or oral interpretation of literature) helpful not only because there the models of language will be exemplary but because a teacher can help him to listen accurately and critically to himself. But if courses are not available, he can do much if he selects good materials and strives to read as if he were communicating with a listener.

Writing

Writing and speaking need the corrective influence of each other if either is to attain its maximum excellence. A careful writer often tests his sentences by reading them aloud, either to himself or to someone else. Thus he seeks to modify any unnecessarily complicated structure and to shorten sentences which would otherwise require a reader to carry too much detail in mind before he gets to the essential action words. A careful speaker will examine critically his extemporaneous utterance. From a recording of his speech, or a stenographic copy of what he said, he can criticize his own language—discovering, moaning over, and repairing the fragmentation, needless repetition, and inept expression. He can write in, for future reference, those coinages he wished he had used, but didn't!

Writing is at its best only when it permits that lively flow of thought which is characteristic of good speaking, only when it conveys the vitality—the lifelikeness—of spoken language, only when it exploits the best lanes of approach to its audience. Conversely, speaking is excellent when it is governed by some of that discipline which controls the best writing: (1) when the speaker has so developed his usable vocabulary that the most accurate and appropriate language which the audience will respond to springs readily to his tongue; (2) when something of shapeliness and grace appears in the speaker's normal mode of talk; (3) when sentences take on without rigidity or complexity some semblance of structure, of subordination and coordination, clear evidence that some things come before or after others by design rather than by chance.

Write, rehearse, revise

The value of practice in writing as a means of improving the use of language in speaking is attested by the wisest teachers and by the practice of the best speakers. We will cite for examples only one of each.

Quintilian's Testimony. In the tenth book of his *Institutes,* the greatest Roman textbook on education of the public speaker, Quintilian calls to his aid Cicero, whose *De Oratore* is a great speaker's analysis of what makes the ideal orator:

> . . . as regards those [aids] which we must supply for ourselves, it is the pen which brings at once the most labour and the most profit. Cicero is fully justified in describing it as the best producer and teacher of eloquence, and it may be noted that in the *De Oratore* he supports his own judgment on the authority of Lucius Crassus, in whose mouth he places this remark. We must write as much as possible and with the utmost care. . . . Without the consciousness of such preliminary study our powers of speaking extempore will give us nothing but an empty flow of words, springing from the lips and not from the brain. It is in writing that eloquence has its roots and foundations, it is writing that provides that holy of holies where the wealth of oratory is stored, and whence it is produced to meet the demands of sudden emergencies.

Through writing, Quintilian knew, we not only impress into our minds carefully chosen language which will then come more easily to our aid while we are speaking, but we work out and secure for our future use thoughts and ideas which will be the more readily at our command when we want them.

How should this writing be done? "At first," he continues, "our pen must be slow yet sure."

> We must search for what is best and refuse to give a joyful welcome to every thought the moment that it presents itself; we must first criticize the fruits of our imagination, and then, once approved, arrange them with care. For we must select both thoughts and words and weigh them one by one. . . . We must frequently revise what we have just written. For besides the fact that thus we secure a better connection between what follows and what precedes, the warmth of thought which has cooled down while we were writing is revived anew, and gathers fresh impetus from going over the ground again. [*Inst.* X, iii. 1–6]

So wrote the teacher of public speaking. Let us look now at the practice of one of the greatest of the English parliamentary speakers, Edmund Burke.

Burke's Practice. We have long known that the author of the speeches "On Conciliation with the Colonies," the "Impeachment of Warren Hastings," and the great argument "Reflections on the Revolution in France" toiled over his published works and revised the manuscripts and even the page proofs again and again before he would permit them to be published. Until very recently, however, we had little useful evidence of how Burke prepared for speaking. Now stores of Burke's manuscripts and papers, never before available, are accessible to students. These papers range from small scraps less than half the size of this page, to large, double-folio sheets, covered with notes and partial texts of Burke's ordinary, day-to-day speeches in Parliament. They show that though Burke never read a speech to the House, he almost always found time to write out and to revise again and again in thought and language, what he intended to say. Even when he was the most accomplished orator in the House of Commons, he rehearsed in writing before nearly every speech—days, hours, or minutes beforehand—whenever he knew what he would probably want to say. Other speakers were often more agile than Burke in debate, more fluent in utterance. No one was more powerful, more excellent in language. He wrote incredible quantities, and his speaking profited.

It follows, we think, that after a speaker has begun to feel really at home in the speaking situation, in the experience of a lively sense of oral communication with an audience, has achieved a full realization of the force and content of thought at the moment of utterance, he should take to writing as a regular, substantial part of his preparation. After planning and outlining and after some oral rehearsal such as we advise in Chapter 9 and Appendix B, the student should write out his speech, or much of it, just as he would speak it to his audience. He should set the written text aside for a few hours or a few days. Then he should retrieve it, read it aloud critically, and revise the language and the sentences as better or more fitting words come to him and as he discovers sentences which are clumsy or not so clear as they could be. Once more, he should read the new version aloud to a tender and critical ear (his own).

Depending upon how much time and trouble and effort a speaker is willing to devote to his practice, and therefore depending on how much and how rapidly he wishes to improve his language, he will repeat the process, that is, he will throw away the first written speech, and rehearse several times aloud from the outline or from memory of the outline, without trying to recall the written text at all. Then he will write out, lay aside, revise, and reread again. And so on. At last, when time for preparation has run out, he will be sure that the written text is out of sight and out of conscious mind. It will have done its work on the speaker's sense of the language which best promotes his purpose. If now, from habit, he does not use the best language he has previously written or spoken, or language just as good, the cause will lie somewhere other than in his preparation.

We say that writing to improve language is mostly for the speaker who is in the middle and later stages of his education and his career in public speaking. Of course, it will be beneficial, if properly controlled, from the beginning. Dangers surround the first speeches, however, which make it better to defer conscious striving for improvement in language until the best basic habits of thought and platform behavior are on the way to being formed and confirmed.

We know, of course, that life and time are short, hurried and full—that the busy college student may think the achievement of excellence perhaps not possible in the economy of his career. But this book is for the man or woman who would go all the way, as well as for him who would start in the right direction. There is profit in working toward the best, even if one must stop short of it.

Maintain an oral attitude

One danger arises because of previous education. Most of the instruction and guided practice which American school boys and girls receive in discourse is devoted to writing—themes in English class. Therefore, as they advance in years and education, and as they first face the composition of speeches, they naturally resort for precedent and help to their recollection of the only kind of deliberate composition which they have been taught. They should realize that the primary precedent in the study and practice of speaking is oral discourse—the relating, explaining, describing, and arguing—which they have been resorting to, perhaps incidentally and without rule or criticism, in school and out, for many years. Thus the need of the beginning speaker is to develop an oral attitude toward speechmaking. He must come to think of speaking as a kind of planned discourse parallel to and related to writing, but not the same. He cannot progress well in speaking if he continues to think of a speech, even a classroom speech, as a talking theme, an essay read aloud.

For this reason the main object of our attention from the outset of this book is the planned but extemporaneous speech—not the speech which is written out and read aloud or memorized. And for this same reason there is little in the earlier chapters which gives special consideration to language. Thinking for communication and in communication is the first consideration. If there were to be only one consideration, that would be it. We all come equipped with a usable enough stock of language to get well started. Thinking and speaking-writing, however, are so much parts of the same process—thought is so completely dependent upon symbols—that improvement in the one is impossible without improvement in the other. Furthermore, the language of words, rather than thought itself, is amenable to direct study. Consequently it is impossible to get far in the purpose of improving speaking, which we have called "applied thought," without seeking to improve the use of language.

We come around, then, to the conclusion that the maturing public speaker who would rise above the ordinary, the commonplace, the good-enough-but-undistinguished in his language will speak often, will read silently, will read aloud, and will write. All these activities he will engage in critically, with intent to profit.

Force, vividness, memorableness, the qualities in language which give speechmaking clearness, aptness, interest, and impressiveness, are the ones most seriously missed when language falls below what the audience expects, what the subject demands, and what the occasion and the speaker's personality justify. These qualities taken together effect that fitness of the speaker's language to the speech as spoken discourse which must be the good speaker's object. Let the speaker remember that in public speaking the audience must not only understand but see. The philosopher, the moralist, and perhaps the scientist need only make us understand the truth; the popular speaker must make us realize, make us see, make us want to make the truth actual in practice. This is still the basic necessity even when the philosopher and the speaker are the same man. The language of clarity vitalized by the language of force, vividness, and memorableness is an indispensable ally of the public speaker.

SIR JAMES JEANS

*Why the Sky Looks Blue**

The following explanation of a common phenomenon, by one of the world's greatest physicists, is about as perfect an example as one could find of the use of analogy in exposition, the relating of the unfamiliar to the familiar. The selection expresses a single idea which is amplified through analogy.

Imagine that we stand on any ordinary seaside pier, and watch the waves rolling in and striking against the iron columns of the pier. Large waves pay little attention to the columns—they divide right and left and re-unite after passing each column, much as a regiment of soldiers would if a tree stood in their road; it is almost as though the columns had not been there. But the short waves and ripples find the columns of the pier a much more formidable obstacle. When the short waves impinge on the columns, they are reflected back and spread as new ripples in all directions. To use the technical term, they are "scattered." The obstacle provided by the iron columns hardly affects the long waves at all, but scatters the short ripples.

We have been watching a sort of working model of the way in which sunlight struggles through the earth's atmosphere. Between us on earth and outer space the atmosphere interposes innumerable obstacles in the form of molecules of air, tiny droplets of water, and small particles of dust. These are represented by the columns of the pier.

The waves of the sea represent the sunlight. We know that sunlight is a blend of lights of many colours—as we can prove for ourselves by passing it through a prism, or even through a jug of water, or as Nature demonstrates to us when she passes it through the raindrops of a summer shower and produces a rainbow. We also know that light consists of waves, and that the different colours of light are produced by waves of different lengths, red light by long waves and blue light by short waves. The mixture of waves which constitutes sunlight has to struggle through the obstacles it meets in the atmosphere, just as the mixture of waves at the seaside has to struggle past the columns of the pier. And these obstacles treat the light-waves much as the columns of the pier treat the sea-waves. The long waves which constitute red light are hardly affected, but the short waves which constitute blue light are scattered in all directions.

*** From Sir James Jeans, *The Stars in Their Courses* (Cambridge, Eng., 1931), pp. 23–24. By permission of the Cambridge University Press.**

Thus, the different constituents of sunlight are treated in different ways as they struggle through the earth's atmosphere. A wave of blue light may be scattered by a dust particle, and turned out of its course. After a time a second dust particle again turns it out of its course, and so on, until finally it enters our eyes by a path as zigzag as that of a flash of lightning. Consequently the blue waves of the sunlight enter our eyes from all directions. And that is why the sky looks blue.

FURTHER READING

ARISTOTLE. *Rhetoric.* Trans. by John Henry Freese. Cambridge, Mass., Loeb Classical Library, 1939. Bk. III, Chapters 1–12.

BAIRD, A. Craig, and KNOWER, Franklin H. *General Speech.* New York, 1949, Chapter 10, "Language."

BORCHERS, Gladys. "An Approach to the Problem of Oral Style," *Quarterly Journal of Speech,* 22 (1936), 114–117.

BLANKENSHIP, Jane. *Public Speaking: A Rhetorical Perspective.* Englewood Cliffs, N.J., 1966. Chapters 6–7, on style.

COOPER, Lane (ed.). *Theories of Style.* New York, 1907. See Swift, "A Letter to a Young Clergyman," Buffon, "Discourse on Style," Spencer, "The Philosophy of Style." Republished as *The Art of the Writer.* Ithaca, N.Y., 1952.

GIBSON, Walker. *The Limits of Language.* New York, 1962. See especially Chapter 12, "A Note on Style and the Limits of Language."

GRIMES, Wilma. "The Mirth Experience in Public Address," *Speech Monographs,* 22 (November 1955), 243–255.

LANGER, Suzanne K. *Philosophy in a New Key.* Baltimore: Penguin Books, Inc. 1948. Chapter 5, "Language."

LEE, Irving J. *The Language of Wisdom and Folly.* New York, 1949.

———. "Four Ways of Looking at a Speech," *Quarterly Journal of Speech,* 28 (1942), 148–155.

MURPHY, Richard. "The Speech as Literary Genre," *Quarterly Journal of Speech,* 44 (1958), 117–127.

MURRY, J. Middleton. *The Problem of Style.* Oxford, 1925. Chapters I, IV, and VI.

PARRISH, W. M. "The Study of Speeches," in W. M. Parrish and Marie Hochmuth (eds.), *American Speeches.* New York, 1954.

POTTER, Simeon. *Our Language.* Baltimore: Pelican Books, 1950. Chapter 10, "Authority and Usage," and Chapter 11, "Slang and Dialect."

READ, Sir Herbert. *English Prose Style.* New edition, 1952. Boston: Beacon Press, 1961.

Rhetorica ad Herennium. Trans. by Harry Caplan. Cambridge, Mass.: Loeb Classical Library, 1954. Bk. IV.

RICHARDS, I. A. *The Philosophy of Rhetoric.* New York, 1936. Lecture V, "Metaphor."

SAPIR, Edward. *Language*. New York: Harvest Books, 1949.

SEBEOK, Thomas A. (ed.) *Style in Language*. New York and London, 1960.

SUTHERLAND, James R. *On English Prose*. Toronto: University of Toronto Press, 1957.

THOMAS, Gordon L. "Oral Style and Intelligibility," *Speech Monographs*, 23 (March 1956), 46–54.

V

Delivery

13
Principles of Delivery

Delivery and style are the aspects of the process of oral communication through which a speaker's conceptions become actual to him and his audience. "Ideas" and meanings become available only through physical means—through words and word structures and their audible and visible shapes. A speaker's participation in a communicative situation is partly internal and partly external. Through delivery and style his internal activity—his "thinking"—is both completed for him and manifested to others. Hence there are both physical and psychological aspects of delivery and style. In Chapter 12 we dealt with one of the physical aspects: words and language. In Chapter 14 we shall deal with the other physical events, voice and pronunciation, as the carriers and shapers of language. Their dimensions are those of sound: pitch (including the dominant pitch or key of speech), loudness, quality or timbre of voice, and rate of utterance. In this chapter we direct attention to the psychological qualities of utterances and gesture that reveal the speaker's own attention to his conceptions and meanings.[1]

The psychology of delivery is grounded on a single basic principle: conceptions and meanings dominate utterance and bodily behavior. Meanings dominate the listener. They dominate the speaker. In delivery that is judged good, listener and speaker fully attend to meanings during moments of utterance. In delivery that is less than good, some competing stimulus—an irrelevant idea, for example—prevents the speaker or the audience from concentrating on the relevant idea. One cannot fully concentrate on any statement on this page if he is at the same time thinking about going to the movies.

The principle is derived from observations of the mind at work in lively direct conversation. Of course we cannot see the mind at work; we can only make our best guesses. A speaker can come close to achieving the realization

[1] For the philosophically minded reader, we observe that *conception* includes for us the cognitive, conative, and affective aspects of internal states of being. Strictly speaking, the symbolic or meaningful aspects of experience are responses to conceptions. Hence a communicator speaks out of his conceptions through symbols and signals to the conceptions of others.

of meaning of utterance, by minimizing the kinds of stimuli which distract his attention and compete for the dominance of idea.

From our experience in conversation, almost any of us can point to stimuli which divert us as listeners from the message being spoken. They may be some unusual features of dress or of the face which momentarily command attention. Or some mannerism of posture, movement, or gesture. Or some bothersome trait of speech, such as long pauses, frequent pauses, rapidity of utterance, indistinctness of speech, novel pronunciation, *uhs* and *ers*. Or some sign of indirectness of communication, such as dullness of tone, immobility of face or body, averted eyes. Or some quality of voice or gesture which we interpret as insincerity, affectedness, or lack of interest in us. Or perhaps the diverting stimulus is an unrecognizable word or phrase. These are a few of the distractions. In conversation when we are attending only to what is said, we are being dominated by ideas and nothing else.

In formal, public speaking situations, the listener may be subject to the same distractions that he encounters in conversation. But they may strike him more forcefully and be more bothersome because the speaker plays a more prominent role than he does in conversation. Furthermore, we do not expect irrelevant stimuli from a good speaker. We expect him to claim our attention utterly and hold it; we expect to think with him.

Like the listener, the speaker is dominated by ideas during utterance when other stimuli do not compete for his attention and divert him from concentrating on meaning. Some of the competing stimuli are primarily emotional, such as nervousness, anxiety, and (in extremely rare instances) stage fright. More often the stimulus is a feeling of inadequacy, springing from inexperience in public speaking, from a sense of having nothing worth saying, or from insufficient preparation (such as poor organization of materials and inadequate rehearsal). Hence the struggle to concentrate gets in the way of thinking itself. When the speaker is talking in the absence of distracting experiences, he is living ideas and meaning.

As is evident, it is difficult to describe in words what is entailed in "full realization of meaning at the moment of utterance." One knows through having the experience—and the experience is very common. It permeates all lively direct conversation.

The Requirements

In keeping with the basic principle, the psychology of delivery should meet four requirements. (1) The audience should be unaware of the physical aspects of delivery. (2) The speaker should be concentrating on meaning during his moments of utterance. (3) The speaker should experience a sense of communication with his audience. (4) The speaker's bodily action should reflect meaning and serve the needs of communication. James A. Winans was the first writer to call the last three of the standards, taken together, "the conversational quality" in delivery.

Inattention to physical events

The speaker's object is to stir his audience to thought, not to invite his listeners to speculate about his pitch, loudness, timbre, rate, and gesture. A speech is not a performance and the speaker cannot afford to let his audience regard him as a performer. If at the conclusion of a speech, a listener responds with such comments as "What a wonderful speech," "His voice was squeaky," "What silly mispronunciation," "His gestures were lovely, but such an awkward stance," the speaker knows that his hearers have been distracted by the manner of his presentation. If, on the other hand, the audience is talking about what was said, if the hearers respond with discussion and questions, with objections and arguments, the speaker knows that he has stimulated thought. A good practical test of delivery under any circumstances, even in the classroom, is, "Did the audience forget that I was making a speech?" The beginning speaker will be wise to ponder an apparent paradox: If nobody notices delivery, it is good; if delivery is talked about, whether in praise or in censure, it is bad.

Realization of meaning during utterance

The speaker during delivery should be as fully responsive to conceptions and their meaning as he is in good everyday conversation. Now what happens when a person speaks in everyday situations? He gets an idea, he says, and he just utters it. Precisely. He doesn't get the idea, frame a careful sentence that is grammatically correct and beautifully balanced, and then utter it. He doesn't decide that a particular sentence requires a downward inflection of the voice, that he must say it one way rather than another, or that he must pause at one place for one-tenth of a second, at another place for two seconds. Not at all. He gets an idea, or the germ of an idea, and starts speaking. He thinks as he speaks; and the vocal inflections and gymnastics, often incredibly intricate as sound patterns, are at one with his meaning. Utterance, accordingly, is genuine and spontaneous, and if his acquired habits are good, so is his utterance. The listener is not even aware of it as utterance unless it is in some way peculiar and therefore distracting. We call that mental activity which results in genuineness and spontaneity of delivery, vivid-realization-of-idea-at-the-moment-of-utterance. It is perhaps the most desirable aspect of delivery.

As we speak before a group for the first time, do our minds behave as they would in private conversation? Perhaps they do; if so, we are fortunate.

Most of us, however, realize that we are no longer engaged in private, informal colloquy; the "platform" is a new situation and our minds have not been at work there. Consequently, in the face of some self-consciousness and perhaps a touch of fright, we go ahead, and by gaining experience in the speaking situation, we become accustomed to it. That is, we learn to think and talk on the platform as the occasion and circumstances demand. Actually our minds do not behave in a new and strange manner; they are only learning to adapt, to function freely in a new and different situation.

If vivid-realization-of-idea-at-the-moment-of-utterance is a most desirable aspect of delivery, most undesirable is its opposite, absent-mindedness. Listen to the child who is just learning to read, or the adult who in reading aloud merely mouths a string of words, or the speaker whose delivery sounds memorized, parrotlike, and canned. True, the speaker is pronouncing words in a sequence, but the utterance does not sound like speech impregnated with meaning. It is flat, lifeless, monotonous, and singsongy. Meaning and idea are quite literally absent; the body is present, but the spirit is elsewhere. This distemper of delivery is to be avoided.

Almost as undesirable as absent-mindedness, and certainly as unfortunate, is a mechanical and artificial quality in delivery. Some elocutionists in days past, eager for a shortcut to good delivery and anxious to manage the voice as if it were a man-made musical instrument, invented systems of rules by which a speaker could learn to manipulate his voice artificially. The beginning speaker will do well to avoid mechanical tricks on the platform. His attention must be centered on ideas from start to finish. If his attention is on a rule, if he thinks "my voice must fall here," obviously he cannot at the same moment be concentrating on his message. Attention cannot focus fully on two different stimuli (or ideas) at the same time, and when a speaker tries to focus simultaneously on a rule and on the idea to which it is to be applied, he is only asking his mind to do the impossible. He must avoid setting up mental hurdles. The time to attend to the process of utterance is in rehearsal periods when one is concentrating on improving habits.

There is, of course, a proper time and place for mechanical rules and drills. After he has gained some experience on the platform and his mind has begun to function in the new situation as it does in the old, a student may find, upon consultation with his instructor, that his voice and speech are in need of special training.

Sense of communication

The speaker on the platform should have a keen sense of communication with his hearers. By a sense of communication is meant a feeling or awareness that two or more minds are engaged in mutual action and reaction. The feeling is evident in almost every conversation. Both parties to a live conversation are well aware that two people are engaged; neither is talking at a stone wall. Furthermore, in addition to some mental interaction, the feeling of communication, of being with another, is helped by the conversationalists' confronting and looking at each other. It is this identical relationship between speakers in normal conversation that must also be evident in the public situation between speaker and audience. Recognition of this relationship led Emerson to say that public speaking is only an enlarged conversation, and that the speaker is a gentleman conversing.

Like learning to think vividly during the moments of utterance, learning to feel with the audience means learning to do in the audience situation what may already be normal in the private situation. The task is adjustment to larger circumstances, and the adaptation comes about chiefly through experience on the platform. Although a student may have to make a number of speeches before he feels in close touch with his audience from the beginning of the speech to the end, he may have moments of direct contact even in his first speech. Looking at the audience (and seeing them), makes a speaker aware that the hearers are looking at him rather than shifting their eyes restlessly about, or fixing them on the pages of a covertly placed textbook or newspaper. He may discover that their faces are alive with interest, and no longer bear that stony mask of polite attention. Or a frown, a grin, a nod or shake of the head, may be the sign that some idea has struck its mark. Perhaps there is no greater personal satisfaction in speaking than the feeling that hearers are responding to one's ideas.

If a sense of communication is to be cultivated on the platform, its opposite, soliloquizing aloofness, is to be removed. The delivery of the public speaker must not be marked by the remoteness of the preacher in prayer, or of Hamlet as he ruminates to himself. The speaker talks to others; or, to express the communicative quality of delivery in its strictest sense, the speaker talks to and with others, not at them. Speaker and hearer know that they are in touch with one another.

Gesture and meaning

Body and mind are so closely linked that an idea vividly experienced prompts not only speech but gesture also. The mind, as Robert Louis Stevenson once suggested, is not locked within the body as in a dungeon; it dwells ever on the threshold with appealing signals that we not only hear as speech, but see as action. In fact, so strong is the connection between idea and action that gestures of the face, arms, and body are spontaneous. They are wrapped in the fabric of meaning. But gesture does not break through into meaning, it cannot aid communication, unless the body is free to respond to idea. Being in a bodily condition to respond freely is called poise. Hence, poise is necessary if the speaker is to gesture spontaneously.

Basically, poise simply describes bodily behavior that is efficient; it is movement that fits a particular situation with economy and without obtrusiveness; it is, in brief, activity that is fully adaptive. Like good speech, poise in behavior is never noticed. Like poor speech, behavior without poise is conspicuous because of its inadequacies; it may be random, needlessly repetitious, gratuitous, or awkward. Good platform behavior, accordingly, is bodily activity that fits the communicative situation.

Freedom to Gesture. Learning to become bodily expressive on the platform does not mean becoming a pantomimist and an actor. Action must not usurp the role of speech. Nor does it mean deliberately inventing gestures and planting them wherever may seem appropriate. There is no place on the platform for studied, mechanical, artificial gesture, because such gesture is likely to be just as distracting to the hearer as mechanical management of the voice. The hallmark of good gesture, like good speech, is its apparent genuineness and spontaneity. The effect is precisely that noted by one who regularly listened to Henry Clay's speeches. Clay's action, he remarked, was "the spontaneous offspring of the passing thought." "He gesticulated all over. The whole body had its story to tell, and added to the attractions of his able arguments."

Learning to become physically responsive involves, in the first place, getting the body free to respond to the meanings of the mind. For most of us, the face and body respond with considerable ease and freedom in private colloquy. Accordingly, the beginning speaker seeks to maintain his normal freedom of action on the platform. In learning to gesture, then, the process is one of adaptation to the new situation through guided experience and practice. The beginner learns, accordingly, to handle himself so as not to inhibit bodily responses that ordinarily accompany vivid and vigorous thought. First appearances on the platform usually inhibit such normal activity as an individual possesses, and if he wants to regain freedom of action, he will not fall into positions that will defeat gesture rather than encourage it. In Appendix B we outline a procedure for encouraging bodily action.

Discipline of Gesture. Learning to become bodily communicative on the platform, in the second place, implies discipline of gesture. After the speaker has become bodily alert and responsive, he is not utterly free to behave as his old, everyday impulses dictate. He must recognize that because he is standing before others, or otherwise assuming a more prominent place than is customary in conversation, his position has become emphatic. Consequently, some behavior that is inconspicuous and proper in daily intercourse may become glaringly evident on the platform. Such, for example, are mannerisms, or repetitious behavior which are peculiar to the individual. In fact, they are so distinctive of the individual that his friends and associates have come to accept them as part of his personality. Hence, by a man's friends his mannerisms escape notice or are charitably tolerated. On the platform and in the presence of strangers, they yell for attention. What is natural and acceptable in one environment is no longer natural and acceptable in another. Accordingly, under the guidance of his instructor and his classroom listeners, the student may need to eliminate certain mannerisms. They may be such habitual quirks of behavior as stroking one's hair, pulling one's collar or nose, adjusting one's tie, waving one's hand, rubbing one's knuckles, smoothing one's dress, or fussing with one's necklace or earring. Whatever they are, they compete with meaning for the hearer's attention.

Beyond the discipline required to eliminate mannerisms, most beginning speakers must undertake some training to smooth out gesture, to iron out roughness and awkwardness that may distract attention. The training is begun after the speaker finds that his body is responding with considerable ease and freedom. Only after action on the platform begins to be spontaneous and habitual can the novice afford to be self-conscious about his gesture. In the early speeches the important first steps are (1) handling one's body so as not to inhibit action, (2) responding freely to all impulses to activity, and (3) eliminating distracting mannerisms of behavior. Refinement of gesture comes later in the speaker's development.

In the adjustment of ideas to people and people to ideas, it is the meaning and the man which count. The acts of delivery serve them.

Delivery as a Habit

The delivery of a speech is a fairly complex mode of behavior. Nevertheless, it does not differ essentially from the act of speaking in any situation. In every speaking situation, there is a stimulus that calls forth the act—essentially a person-to-be-spoken-to. What he says or does provokes utterance. In every speech situation there is a response—vocal sounds and gestures of face and body. Furthermore, the response is immediate and habitual. Similarly, speech on the platform is vocal and bodily response to an audience. One steps to the platform. There is an audience-to-be-spoken-to, and in response to it, one speaks. "Ah!" but one says, "I am not in the *habit* of speaking to an *audience*." That is precisely the point. The speaker recognizes that platform speaking presents a new situation to which he has not learned to respond habitually. His efforts, consequently, will be devoted to the acquisition of a new habit.

Method and practice

If the speaker is to work intelligently to acquire the habit of public speaking, he needs to realize what happens when one sets out to build a habit efficiently. In the first place, the process is methodical, rather than hit-and-miss. It involves knowing the goal; one must understand what he is after. A swimmer cannot learn the Australian crawl unless he knows what it is. Similarly, one cannot acquire a good delivery unless he understands its principles, the first of which have already been presented in this chapter. Nor, for that matter, can one learn to construct a good speech unless he knows the principles of speechmaking. Habit formation is methodical, also, in that it involves practice and repetition. The importance of practice in acquiring good delivery can hardly be overestimated. It is, in fact, so fundamental that if one were forced to resort to only three rules of speechmaking, they might well be these: practice, practice, practice. Although the student may have frequent opportunities to speak to a classroom audience, he will discover that preliminary rehearsals are extremely helpful. Later we shall recommend a procedure to be followed in rehearsal.

As important as practice is, however, it will not by itself build a good habit. First, there is some danger of practicing the wrong thing. The adage that "practice makes perfect" is a great truth, but it is two-edged. Practice alone will perfect undesirable behavior just as readily as desirable behavior. Hence, anyone who sets out to acquire a new habit must see clearly what the new habit is. Certainly if this is essential in forming relatively simple habits like running the 100-yard dash, it is doubly essential in forming a complex habit like public speaking. Just standing-up-and-saying-something, then, is not enough; one needs and should encourage the criticisms and comments from both instructor and listeners who should help to keep one on the right path. The learning speaker, therefore, performs instructional routines exactly, such as full outlining according to form, which may seem needless to the experienced speaker, who already has the habits which the learner should be acquiring.

Motivating and sharpening experience

In the second place, the process of acquiring a habit is always facilitated by one's mental set and experience during learning. If practice is made a fetish, there is danger of overlooking two conditions of learning that are just as important as practice. One is *motivation;* the other is *intensity* of perception and understanding. The results of experimental studies on learning agree that the desire to do a thing helps in the doing. To one who expects to acquire a good delivery this leads to a great axiom: the desire to speak to this audience on this subject is a powerful stimulus to facility, fluency, and variety of utterance. Experimental studies suggest, also, that the more intense an experience is, the readier and longer the retention of the experience.

This knowledge applied to delivery means that the clearer and sharper one's ideas are as he works them over in preparing, framing, and rehearsing his speech, the easier they come back to him on the platform. Indeed, if the student can learn to work methodically in preparing a speech, if his ideas can be marshalled into an unmistakably clear pattern and sequence, and if he can make them *vivid* and intensely meaningful to himself, he will discover that for the most part they will spring from him spontaneously and easily; he will not have to remember them, consciously, deliberately, and painfully. This is the difference between remembering ideas by rote and assimilating them until they are part of experience. Acquiring a good delivery, then, is far more than putting in time in rehearsal; it involves learning to handle, to govern, and to control one's own thinking by getting oneself emotionally set for speaking and by sharply appreciating ideas in a sequence. A speaker's mind on the platform is a free-running machine, not a machine that needs laborious and frequent priming and restarting.

Public speaking not instinctive

In the third place, as the student goes about building a habit of good delivery, he should not confuse habit with instinct. A habit is learned behavior that meets the needs of a situation; an instinct is unlearned behavior in response to a situation. Experimental psychologists seem to agree that there are at most only three situations that call forth instinctive behavior: fear is the unlearned response to falling; fear is the instinctive reaction to loud noise; and cooing, smiling, and similar manifestations of "love" behavior always attend the caress. These responses are evident at birth or shortly thereafter. If the psychologists are right, then, all other behavior is learned. There is, consequently, no instinct to speak; we must all learn to speak, as indeed we do, slowly and haltingly, over some three or four years in early childhood. Speaking, then, becomes one kind of response to communicative situations. As communicative situations multiply in number and diversity, speech responses become more complex and diversified. There is, further, no instinct to speak on the platform or in the "public" situation, and assuredly no instinct or unlearned capacity to speak there with fluency and ease and appropriateness. A man must learn to adapt to the stimulus of the "public" situation, and in order to make the adaptation efficient, he seeks to make it habitual, rather than random, uncertain, and self-conscious.

Miracles don't happen

Accordingly, if effective utterance on the platform is not instinctive, there is at least one important corollary for him who would learn: Don't expect miracles. One can learn only through doing, by handling himself mentally and bodily as the situation demands. One person may adapt rapidly; another may adapt slowly and through error. But whatever happens, after delivery is over one should check up and seek to know why he succeeded, why he failed, and handle himself accordingly in the next speech. It is too much to expect an instructor to find some special formula or touch some hidden spring that will render the learning speaker instantly and invariably at ease and will release a flow of brilliant, clear, and fitting language. An instructor can only act as friendly guide and sympathetic critic. Imagine what he would have to do, or, better yet, what a speaker would have to do, if adaptation were to be instantly perfect and invariably successful. He would have to construct a situation that fitted himself to perfection. The audience would have to be selected so as to fit his special information, desires, and emotional and mental idiosyncrasies. The audience might have to be specially coached, so that it would respond each moment in a way that would encourage him. It would have to assemble at a place where he felt perfectly at home. Finally, it would either have to be primed and prepared to overlook his peculiarities of delivery, or else the members of the audience would have to possess or approve of those peculiarities. In other words, if without training the speaker were to speak well he would have to tailor his audience to fit him rather than to tailor himself to fit his audience. In a democratic society such tailoring is, of course, absurd. In a tyrannical society, perhaps the speaker, like Hitler and Mussolini, can handpick his listeners, govern their applause, and stage-manage the setting.

As the student endeavors to build a habit of speaking in the audience situation, he should recognize, in the last place, that the acquisition of a habit always involves some initial self-consciousness. Trying anything for the first time makes a man aware that he is doing something new, and trying to do something according to principles and directions makes him aware that he is trying to control his conduct. Accordingly, as the student speaker seeks to adapt to the audience situation in the first speeches and as he endeavors to conform to the first requirements of delivery, he may not escape some feeling of self-consciousness. But as he continues to make speeches, he will discover a comforting fact: As a result of practice and experience, self-consciousness disappears when the mind is fully occupied with meaning.

Full mental responsiveness to ideas at the moment of utterance and a keen sense of communication and appropriate gesture are probably most evident and are most readily achieved in what we call the extemporaneous and the impromptu modes of delivery. The training and experience of the young speaker will be primarily in these modes.

Emotional Problem in Delivery

Before concluding the discussion of the psychology of delivery, we advise students not to confuse normal behavior with behavior that may be abnormal.

Much of the feeling that is labeled nervousness and worry is as normal as roses in June. It is always evoked by any new situation to which we want to respond appropriately and successfully. Furthermore, because we are only human beings and not machines, we know that we can never be certain that we will behave as we would like to. For example, if a student applies for a scholarship and is asked to an interview with the dean, he may be quite rightly concerned over saying what needs to be said and making a favorable impression. The delivery of a speech presents the same kind of situation. We want to do well; we care about making a good speech, but we are not sure we will be completely successful. So we stew and worry, fuss and fidget, just as we do over any task we really care about. Some veteran speakers about to face an audience on an important subject don't sleep much the night before! Such feelings are quite different from true fear.

Nervousness and worry are often accompanied by tension. Unless tension is so extreme as to freeze one into a state of immobility, it is desirable and useful. Indeed, it is as useful to the speaker as it is to the athlete. Just as a runner does his best when set, spring-like, to be off, so a speaker is at his physical and mental best when keyed up to his task. In fact, there is considerable experimental evidence to show that no one does his best at a task unless he regards it as a challenge, a challenge sufficient to cause some concern, some flutter, some fuming. The man who takes public speaking in his stride as a routine job will make a routine speech. Hence, a speaker should welcome the toned-up intensity of feeling. It will help him speak better than he thinks he can.

True stage fright, on the other hand, is a special kind of fear response that will inhibit the speaker. First, it is a withdrawal or retreat response. Although the everyday fear experience may be marked by running away or otherwise avoiding the object of fright, stage fright is often marked by trembling, knee shaking, rigidity and immobility, and fast irregular breathing prior to the speech or during delivery. Furthermore, the suffering speaker finds himself in a situation where he cannot run away without publicly admitting failure and thus damaging his pride. Consequently, his response on the platform is not ordinary avoidance behavior, such as running away or simply avoiding speaking, but tautness, rigidity, and immobility of both body and mind. Second, the basis of such behavior, as in any case of fear, is twofold: (1) the situation means harm and danger, and (2) this danger can be avoided by flight and withdrawal. To the speaker, danger means failure, failure to remember, to do well, to say the acceptable thing, to behave acceptably.

It should be clear, therefore, that if stage fright is this kind of experience it can be attacked in three ways: (1) by minimizing the appearance of danger in the situation, (2) by dispelling the idea that danger can be met only by withdrawing and running away; and (3) by not running away. A speaker may be able to attack at all these points, but if he can attack at only one point he will experience less fear and apprehension. What he should do is to analyze the experience as frankly and completely as he can (here his instructor may be of great help) and try to discover what point to assault and what tactics to employ.

Minimizing the hazard

The novice speaker has effective ways of coping with emotional problems rationally and objectively. First, he should recognize that speaking to an audience does not differ greatly from speaking in private; public speaking is but an enlarged conversation. Thus public speaking may become less formidable and be associated with what he may already do well.

Second, he should rapidly build up a feeling of familiarity about public speaking. This he does through experience, an unsurpassed teacher, and also through the study of principles and through listening to speeches and reading them. Knowledge of what makes a good speech and of what is expected of speakers in the way of information and interest, composition and organization, presentation and behavior, in both informative and persuasive speeches, does much to take the danger out of the situation. It is the new and strange, we think, that may cause harm, and once the situation is experienced and understood one possible cause of harm is removed.

Third, the classroom speaker should realize that his fellows are with him, not against him. Since all are engaged in the same enterprise, the classroom audience is not so critical of his endeavors as he may think; it is as sympathetic and as helpful an audience as exists anywhere. It is quick to praise and admire good work because it appreciates, infinitely more than does the casual, outside audience, the sweat and labor behind a good speech.

Finally, he can capitalize upon the advantages of beginning preparation early and of preparing thoroughly. Thorough preparation brings with it four psychological aids: (1) a speaker knows that he is ready to meet the situation; (2) he knows that he is better equipped to cope with any last-minute adjustments to his audience than if he were not well prepared; (3) he knows that good preparation means less chance of forgetting; and (4) he gains confidence.

Confronting the hazard

The starting point of fear, as we have seen, is perceiving that a situation is harmful and that harm can be escaped by retreating. It is possible to perceive danger and not judge it as something to run from. Indeed, we do this when we get angry, for the source of anger is danger plus awareness that there is something to be attacked and destroyed. It should be evident, then, that what we see or think of as dangerous need not cause fear. This fact has important application for the anxious speaker. He can deliberately interpret the hazardous situation as something to be confronted squarely, to be faced positively and directly—like a foe to be conquered, not to be fled from. Thus, he induces or adopts the attitude of determination toward his task. In effect, he says to himself, "I will speak; I will continue to speak; I will welcome every opportunity to speak; I will keep at it." He knows full well, moreover, that if he quits even once and runs, he has let fear get the better of him and the job is much harder.

Replacing fear by another emotion

If the hazards of speaking are something to be overcome by positive attack, the student speaker stands an excellent chance of replacing fear with some other emotion. We cannot experience two emotions simultaneously. Accordingly, acute stage fright can sometimes be overcome if the speaker can work on a subject he feels keenly about. Perhaps the most serviceable subjects are those which will rouse indignation, humor, pity, and sympathy.

Sometimes the emotion of pride can overcome partially if not entirely the fear of speaking publicly. Most students want to make good speeches and to be recognized by their classmates as good speakers. The reward they seek is not merely a grade, but pride, prestige, and reputation. Accordingly, a speaker may feel real pride during the stages of his preparation, and if he feels pride he can nurse it along and encourage it. When he can pat himself on the back, there isn't much room left for extreme worry.

The person who is emotionally upset because public speaking is new to him will soon discover that he has no cause for fear. He should look at the problem rationally, reduce its newness to familiar terms through study and experience, and along the way test any positive measures of control which seem applicable to him. He should not, however, expect or desire to be rid of all nervousness, worry, and tension. In the proper degree, these aspects of the speaking experience work for him, rather than against him.

Emotional conditioning

In a few unusual instances, stage fright may be traced not to apprehension over the new and unknown, but to unfortunate experiences in the past. It is learned behavior and may represent emotional conditioning and emotional conflict.

An individual may have made three or four speeches and with each speech he suffered real fright. As a result, the fear experience becomes closely and intensely conditioned to speechmaking. Then the mere prospect of having to make another speech and face another audience evokes fear.

When stage fright is thus learned, the individual employs two direct approaches. The first makes use of this idea: No two speaking situations, even in the classroom, are, strictly speaking, precisely the same. If Situation

1 was accompanied by fright, then Situation 2, different in some respects from Situation 1, need not evoke fright. Consequently, one seeks comfort by clearly recognizing in what ways his next speech will differ from his last. Is the *occasion* different? the *subject* different? the *treatment of the subject* different? the *audience* different in some respects? the *speaker* himself changed? The second approach is to recognize and to emphasize the pleasant and successful aspects of one's speaking experience, and thus build up positive, attractive associations. Has the speaker been commended for being clear? Informative? Interesting? Direct and communicative? For effective platform behavior? Usually a speech deserves praise in some respect, and praise stimulates the feeling of pride. Accordingly, as one faces successive speeches, one should take inventory of successes; the pleasant associations thus secured will soon counterbalance, then overbalance, unpleasant associations.

Emotional conflict

Some psychologists hold that stage fright is a symptom of two conflicting desires: craving for an audience and for the approval of others, and fear of an audience and of the disapproval of others. The speaker wants an audience and he doesn't want an audience, and the resulting conflict knots him up physically and mentally.

Where such conflict is evident, the general method of reducing it consists in making one desire dominant so that the other desire loses much, if not all, of its power to compete. The speaker strengthens his desire for an audience by making himself keenly aware of any favorable associations with it. He finds good reasons for speaking to the particular audience, at the particular time, and on the particular subject. He makes an inventory of his past successes as a speaker. He isolates the special reasons why his audience may be, or should be, kindly, sympathetic, and respectful toward him. Then he sets about to *make* his speech interesting to his hearers. In brief, he does everything he can to strengthen his connection with an audience and to make prominent all favorable associations with it.

Much has been written about stage fright, its causes and remedies. Yet we possess little exact knowledge about the phenomenon, and there appears to be no general medicine for every case. Perhaps, after all, the wisest advice comes from a veteran teacher: "One can't be abnormally self-conscious if he gives first place to the welfare of others. So put your audience first. Plan everything you do for your hearers. Interest them. Their welfare is the thing, not your ego."

Guide to improvement

If a person is to meet the standards of delivery set out in this chapter, he must handle himself intelligently. Most people, if they are to acquire and develop good habits of speaking to an audience, must do more than just speak to audiences. They must practice, deliberately training themselves in those skills in which they are deficient. Some will need one kind of practice, some another, and some several kinds. In Appendix B, therefore, we include a variety of routines and exercises which, on the basis of his own diagnosis or his instructor's, any student may use with profit—that is, if he has time and wishes to become really expert in speaking before an audience. Of course, there will be some persons who, after grasping the principles presented in this chapter, will find themselves adapting readily to the platform situation. Let none, however, be hasty in deciding that for *him* practice and drill would not be worth the bother!

Excellence in delivery: Concentration and memory

By meeting the standards and applying the methods we have been describing, virtually any student of speechmaking can acquire habits of delivery which would be regarded as adequate and acceptable for most occasions. Yet there will be a few students, perhaps for professional reasons, who will want to set higher goals. They will not be content with adequacy of delivery; they will want to aim at excellence. They will wish to appear at their mental and vocal *best* on the platform, they will want to have sure powers of concentration and memory, language whose style is distinguished, a voice having all the inflection and melody it is capable of, and bodily action which is fully expressive of idea and emotion.

There are two main roads to excellence in delivery. One way, too specialized to describe in this book, is training the voice and body to become increasingly responsive to meanings. The other way lies in training oneself to concentrate *intensely* on language and its meanings and to engage often and regularly in writing and speaking. The essence of this method lies in intensity of linguistic experience and its frequent repetition. We cannot here present the theory of the method, nor describe it in detail. We can offer only a program which provides direction for the effort.

The program rests on two principles:

Language and meaning are indissolubly connected. Hence, the sharper and stronger the idea, the more easy and ready is the word.

The stronger, deeper, and more vivid the idea, the easier it is remembered.

In studying the program, one will discover that in some respects it extends some of the suggestions made earlier in this chapter and in the chapter on the basis of oral communication. The program represents a fairly complete and systematic guide to follow in conjunction with speech preparation. A person who can discipline himself to pursue it rigorously and conscientiously can markedly improve his ability to concentrate upon ideas during utterance and to recall them readily. He will also enhance his command over language.

1. Make strong and intense the ideas and images that constitute the background of the speech and the speech itself.

a. In the early stages of preparation, read in two or three good sources, rather than skim over many. Read them slowly; reread, getting the exact meaning of every word, phrase, and figure of speech. Then outline the structure of the article, much as one would outline a speech, noting the central idea, main heads, and principal subheads. The aim is to drive ideas and images into one's being. This is the intensest kind of impression—far more intense than most students give to course assignments.
b. Take notes of the ideas likely to be useful in preparing the speech outline. Writing helps impression; writing is one way of repeating the ideas that may reappear in the speech, and both expression and repetition aid memory.
c. Talk over one's reading; discuss, argue, report, and explain, even if one gets on tangents that don't lead directly into the speech. Talk keeps ideas churning, helps impression, and amounts to repetition in speech.
d. As the speech outline is built up in detail, make the ideas interesting and memorable for the audience. In seeking to drive ideas into others, one drives them more deeply into himself.
e. Write the speech in full.

In rehearsal, *after* securing some command over the stream of ideas, practice separately the vivid, *imageful* parts of the speech:

a. Comparisons and contrasts.
b. Illustrations and extended examples.
c. Figures of speech and all effective turns of phrase.

Further, repeat passages that have prompted gestures, and extend the gestures; here language, action, and idea all unite to make the most powerful impression.

2. Tighten one's grasp on the *structure and pattern* of the speech.

a. Heighten the sense of the *whole*.
Repeat in order the following: purpose of the speech, subject sentence, main heads. This may best be done during the late stages of rehearsal.
b. In the final rehearsal, view the conclusion as a goal to build up to; or, to change the figure, regard the conclusion as a target to shoot at. This awareness of the logical goal, lurking always in the fringe of attention as one speaks, gives *direction* and *movement* to ideas.

Pay special attention to the *parts* of the speech and to the way they are *related* to each other.

a. Be sure that there is a consistent set of verbal signposts for each group of heads.
For main heads, *first, second, third,* and variants of these.
b. Run through the heads with their signposts, first practicing the main heads and then working with each set of subheads.
c. Where transitional sentences are used to link the major parts of the speech, practice these. If one can associate a transition with bodily movement (such as gesturing or changing position), the idea is easier to recall.

Adopt a key word or a vivid phrase with which to associate each main head and subhead. (Most of the widely advertised memory systems lean heavily upon this kind of association.)

3. Work deliberately to experience helpful emotions and attitudes; remember that emotion and attitude when associated with ideas promote their recall and give energy and variety to voice and gesture.

In early rehearsals, cultivate the feeling of *wanting* to speak to a specific purpose. In late rehearsals, practice *separately* any passages that evoke:

a. Such attitudes as *concession, admission:* "You are quite right . . . ," "This is familiar to you," "Here is something new," "This is especially significant."
b. Such emotions as *sympathy, indignation, irony, sarcasm, humor, fear* (warnings and cautions).

4. Learn to overcome distractions which require special efforts in concentration. Either sympathetic friends or the classroom audience can be instructed to heckle with questions and remarks that one must stop and reply to at the moment, returning later to the course of the speech with an appropriate bridge.

Hecklers might use questions and comments such as the following:

I don't understand that; will you clarify?

I can't agree with that point; here's my objection. . . .

How do you know that; what's your authority?

That argument is weak; what's your evidence?

You're being too abstract; can you cite an illustration?

I don't see that what you've just said has any relation to your main idea; is it relevant?

I'm lost; where are you?

5. Keep up interest in the speech, and to avoid going stale do something *new* to the speech. Even a small change will revive interest not only in the

change made, but in the entire speech; interest spreads from the part to the whole.

a. Insert new *details:* a new illustration, a fresh quotation, two or three figures of speech.
b. Rehearse in a new place and new surroundings.
c. Work in some new pictorial gestures—the kind that picture an idea.
d. Shift the *order* of ideas in one section of the speech. If, say, you have been developing a section by starting with general ideas and going to specific illustrations, reverse the order.
e. Experiment with a different introduction.

When one applies these suggestions to successive speeches, he will appreciate that they aim to strengthen the perception of ideas and meanings by making ideas sharp and vivid, by repeating them, and by enhancing their structure and pattern. At the same time, he will observe that the program aims to strengthen the association between the perception of ideas on the one hand and their language expression on the other.

FURTHER READING

Caton, Charles A. (ed.) *Philosophy and Ordinary Language.* Urbana: University of Illinois Press, 1963. Chapter 8, "The Theory of Meaning" by Gilbert Ryle.

Parrish, W. M. "The Concept of 'Naturalness,'" *Quarterly Journal of Speech,* 40 (December 1951), 448–454.

Winans, J. A. *Public Speaking.* New York, 1917. Chapter 2, "Conversing with an Audience."

Some recent information on stage fright:

Clevenger, Theodore, Jr. "A Synthesis of Experimental Research in Stage Fright," *Quarterly Journal of Speech,* 40 (April 1959), 134–145.

———, and King, Thomas R. "A Factor Analysis of the Visible Symptoms of Stage Fright," *Speech Monographs,* 28 (November 1961), 296–298.

Eisenson, Jon, Auer, J. Jeffery, and Irwin, John V. *The Psychology of Communication.* New York, 1963. Chapter 18, "Psychology of Stage Fright."

Lerea, Louis, "The Verbal Behavior of Speech Fright," *Speech Monographs,* 23 (August 1956), 229–233.

Paivo, Allan, and Lambert, Wallace E. "Measures and Correlates of Audience Anxiety ('Stage Fright')," *Journal of Personality,* 27 (March 1959), 1–17.

14
Voice and Pronunciation

Voice and pronunciation as physical aspects of delivery, as the carriers of spoken language, can receive but scanty treatment in a course or book devoted to public speaking. Voice and speech improvement rest upon exact knowledge of the speech and hearing mechanism, of the anatomy and physiology of breathing, of voice production, and of hearing. Such knowledge can barely be presented in a special course, to say nothing of one dealing with the processes of speechmaking. Voice training, when undertaken to improve the vocal qualities of speech, requires much time and concentrated practice. The labor is long even for the person with a normal voice. It is even longer for a person whose voice shows certain abnormalities which require the skill of corrective specialists. The improvement of articulation and pronunciation, when desirable and necessary, also is time consuming. A knowledge of phonetics and the behavior of speech sounds underlies intelligent and permanent improvement, not to mention hours of persistent practice. The student in his first course in speechmaking finds little protracted time for such knowledge and practice. Nevertheless, if his speech shows serious defects, he must find the time to correct them, either in a special course or under the guidance of special teachers. This he would do, not merely to become a better speechmaker, but to improve his everyday speech.

Although the student speechmaker's habits may be acceptable for everyday conversation, he must realize that the demands of public speaking are usually more severe. He may need, therefore, to learn to use his equipment better than he does ordinarily. He will need to speak loud enough to be heard easily, and speak distinctly. He can often improve vocal quality, and sometimes he can secure greater flexibility and variety of vocal sound. In working for such gains, it is extremely important to realize that the guides for improvement must be in harmony with the natural behavior of the vocal mechanism. To work with Nature is better than to work against her; to work against her sometimes does damage to the voice. In this chapter we shall briefly describe the mechanism of voice and offer some suggestions for improving voice and articulation.

Sound is produced by a vibrating body which sets into motion air waves which strike the ear and are interpreted by the brain. The vibrating material may be air itself, as in the organ pipe; or it may be strings, as in the piano and the violin; or it may be a reed, as in the clarinet; or it may be flesh, such as the lips of the mouth (as in cornet playing) and the vocal lips or bands of the larynx. Obviously, a vibrating body cannot set itself into motion; it must be struck, plucked, or agitated in some manner. So it is with the vocal bands; they cannot vibrate by themselves. They are set into vibration by breath under pressure, and the amount of pressure varies from soft tones to loud tones, and from low-pitched sounds to high-pitched sounds. For most speakers, control over the breath is needed in order to secure adequate loudness.

Anatomy of Breathing

The vocal bands are set in a group of cartilages, of which the most evident is the wedge-shaped thyroid cartilage at the front of the neck, which is popularly called the Adam's Apple. This group of cartilages, known as the larynx, stands on top of the windpipe which goes down to the lungs. Located in the upper region of the chest, the lungs are, so far as voice production is concerned, an intricate system of interconnecting air sacs. Although they are somewhat elastic and will spring back into shape after being compressed, much as a squeezed sponge does, they cannot act by themselves. They are not made of muscle at all, and no muscles are attached to them. This is an important fact for the speaker, because control over breathing has nothing to do with control over the lungs. Control, as we shall see, is secured elsewhere.

Just below the lungs is the diaphragm, partly muscular, partly cartilaginous, a dome-shaped partition which divides the lungs and heart above it from the abdominal organs below it. Surrounding the lungs in the walls of the chest are the ribs, which are equipped with muscles which raise and lower them. Surrounding the viscera are the muscles of the abdominal walls. It is these three sets of muscles—the *diaphragm,* the *rib muscles,* and the *abdominal muscles*—which work in conjunction to press upon the lungs and to provide air pressure against the vocal bands. To see in brief how these provide pressure is to understand the few principles that underlie the control of the breath stream.

The Breathing Cycle

When one inhales and then expels breath, these events occur. (1) The diaphragm muscles contract and thus flatten out the diaphragm's dome. This creates a partial vacuum in the region above the diaphragm. The rib-raising muscles may also contract—especially in deep breathing, such as is needed in violent exercise—and the consequent rise of the ribs also helps to create a vacuum. In response to lowered air pressure in the lung region, air rushes in from the outside through the nose, mouth, and windpipe, and inflates the lungs. This entire process constitutes *inhalation.* (2) The pulling-down of the diaphragm causes a squeezing of the organs below and this in turn causes the abdominal muscles to distend. Most of the distention takes place in the region at the front of the body, between the belt line and the inverted V formed by the ribs. (3) The diaphragm muscles relax; the ribs lower, permitting the chest walls to press against the lungs; and the abdominal muscles push the viscera up against the diaphragm and thus bring pressure from below against the lungs. With the squeezing of the lungs, air is expelled. In this manner, *exhalation* is accomplished.

Vocal Sound

When the vocal bands come together and the air stream from below is forced between them, the bands vibrate and sound waves are produced. The waves move up the throat passage, most of them emerging from the mouth and some of them going out through the nasal passages. These sound waves, set up by the vocal bands, are reinforced by a combination of resonators. Some of the resonators—notably the bony structure of the upper chest and of the head—act as sounding boards, and others—principally the throat passage, the mouth cavity, and the nasal passages—act as air-column resonators. As a part of speech, accordingly, the human voice is a complex set of sound waves, initiated by breath agitating the vocal bands and reinforced by resonators.

The sound made thus has all the characteristics of any sound: *pitch, loudness,* and *timbre* (or quality). Some notion as to what these characteristics involve may be gained from the table below, which calls attention to two important aspects of sound: its *physical* properties (behavior of the vibrating body and waves), and its *psychological* properties (interpretation of the sound waves by ear and brain).

	AS PHYSICAL PROPERTIES	AS PSYCHOLOGICAL PHENOMENA
Pitch	Frequency or rate of vibration of vocal bands.	Interpreted on a scale from *low* to *high.*
Loudness	Intensity. Relation between amount or distance traveled by vibrating bands and frequency of vibration. *Amplitude* is the distance that a wave impulse oscillates.	Interpreted on a scale from *soft* to *loud.*
Timbre	Relation between the native character of the vocal bands, the degree of complexity of vibration, and action of the resonators. The complexity of a wave's form.	Interpreted as what makes a voice recognizable and distinctive, and pleasant or unpleasant.

The public speaker is interested in his voice for two fundamental reasons. (1) He wishes to avoid those voice qualities that distract his hearers' attention from what he is saying—such qualities as harshness, shrillness, nasality, hoarseness, sameness of pitch, and sameness of loudness. All these invite attention to themselves. Many of these distracting qualities constitute special individual problems, and in most cases where they are present, a speaker would do well to secure special counsel from his instructor or from an expert on voice. (2) The speaker desires to make his vocal instrument as flexible and as responsive to meanings as is possible. He should realize that the sound he makes, quite apart from what he says verbally, is a powerful stimulus to his hearers; and like any stimulus, the more change and variety and color it has, the easier it holds attention and compels interest. In securing maximum flexibility of his voice, the speaker should undertake intensive training and exercise, a program too specialized to present in this book. Nevertheless, he can appreciably and rapidly help himself by applying the following suggestions.

Breath control and loudness

The way to increased loudness, when needed, is simple. One applies extra pressure against the lungs. He does a little more of what comes naturally. First he makes certain that he knows what his abdominal muscles and chest are doing during exhalation. Some persons will discover that the main movement is in the chest region, others in the abdominal region. Still others will find that chest and abdomen move simultaneously. But whatever one's habit, one should follow it. Second, along with the exhalation movement one applies a little additional pressure in the same direction. The result is increased air pressure against the vocal bands. They travel a greater distance, thus sending out stronger sound waves to the listener's ear. The sound heard is louder than it would be if no additional pressure had been applied. The process is easy, yet the speaker who needs to talk louder must establish conscious control over the process until it becomes habitual.

Increased loudness for the speaker also entails more air and somewhat deeper breathing than he uses in ordinary conversation. So in *inhalation* he takes in somewhat more air than he needs otherwise. Yet at the same time he must not take in too much air, nor gulp it in suddenly with an obvious heave. Deep inhalation often causes a quick release of excessive air, producing a burst of loudness inappropriate to meaning. The effect is like a quick sigh. When repeated over and over, one hears a downhill loudness pattern, ranging from too loud to not loud enough. When one gulps a large amount of air, he feels compelled to get rid of most of it instantly. Gulping, too, often gives a breathy quality to the voice.

When one increases loudness, he breathes oftener than ordinary conversation requires. The rule is to breathe as frequetnly as one needs to, using enough breath to increase loudness, but no more. To get the knack of speaking louder, some students will need a brief coaching session with a teacher.

Improvement of voice quality

The speaker who sets out to improve voice quality must give the throat and mouth maximum opportunity to function as resonators. This is by far the most important single endeavor.

The procedure is to relax the muscles of the jaw, neck, and upper torso until one feels lazy and easy. Stiffness, tautness, and tension must be eliminated, because tension in the muscles of the neck often gives a pinched, shrill, or harsh quality to tone. Some muscles are attached to the larynx; others rest against it. When these muscles are taut, they pinch the voice box unduly, and through a kind of sympathetic action the vocal muscles of the larynx, and the deep, constrictor muscles that constitute the inner walls of the lower throat also become tense and rigid. Furthermore, taut jaw muscles frequently cause a muffled or a harsh quality in the voice, because they won't let the jaw drop enough to allow tone to come out of the mouth freely. The open throat is absolutely essential to good voice production.

Even if a speaker's voice has no distracting qualities, it can become better if the throat and mouth resonators are open and free. This will be at once evident when one realizes that the action of these resonators to a considerable degree influences three components of vocal sound: the pitch we hear, the loudness, and the quality or timbre. First, although the pitch changes of the voice are in part due to the adjustments of the muscles of the larynx—adjustments which determine the tension, thickness, and length of the vibrating bands—the pitch we hear is also due to the voice resonators, for these resonators strengthen some vibrations and damp out others. If the throat, mouth, and nasal passages are free to respond instantly and fully to a wide range of pitches, the key, the inflection, and melody of the voice will be made the most of. Second, although loudness is partly the result of breath pressure exerted against the vocal bands, it is also influenced by the resonators which increase the intensity of vocal sound exactly as does a box resonator upon which a vibrating tuning fork is placed. Finally, although the quality of voice depends in part upon the texture and the complexity of vibration of the vocal bands, voice quality also depends upon the action of the resonators. Their action reinforces some parts of the complex pattern of vibrations and damps out others. It should be clear, therefore, that the human resonators play an essential role in determining the kind of vocal sound we hear. The conclusion is doubtless obvious: To improve voice in any of its aspects—pitch, loudness, and quality—give the resonators a chance to function freely and efficiently. Avoid undue throat and jaw tensions; *relax*.

Improvement of vocal variety

In their delivery, most speakers are capable of greater vocal variety than they exhibit; that is, they are capable of greater inflection (changes in pitch) and greater changes in loudness and rate of utterance. In their private conversations, especially in moments of excitement and keen interest, their voices show all the range that is natural to them. The endeavor, then, is to secure the same range in formal delivery. The fundamental mental condition, of course, is to be as concerned and interested in talking to an audience as one is in his best conversation. Some persons, however, do not experience their full vocal range on the platform because they do not *associate* it with speechmaking. What is needed is to establish the association, to hear and feel what their voices can do in a speech.

One method of working is through deliberate exaggeration of vocal quality during the rehearsal period. After the speech is running along fairly smoothly, shouting the most important ideas will enable one to feel and hear what great changes of loudness he himself can command. Saying the principal ideas with deliberate slowness and racing through a detailed illustration will give a student speaker a sense of what great change of pace he is capable of. Finally, saying the principal ideas first on a fairly high pitch level, then on a very low one will show the range that the voice can exhibit.

The chief purpose of employing exaggeration is to give the individual the sensations of vocal change and to associate the sensations with the presentation of the speech. But although exaggeration may be useful during practice, mechanical manipulation of the voice has no place on the platform. Monotony may be better than artificiality. When the speaker faces his hearers, he must speak as directly and as genuinely as he can. His primary business is to relive ideas; he hasn't time to coach himself with reminders: "I must speak louder here"; "This must go slower"; "This requires a high pitch, this a low pitch." If he has practiced intelligently and diligently, the results will be revealed automatically. He can trust mind and voice to respond correctly.

Mental activity and vocal variety

The public speaker who is in search of variety of voice and who does not need to undertake voice training to overcome monotony must never overlook the intimate relationship between mind and voice. The more sharp, vivid, and intense mental action is, the greater and surer is the vocal response and the greater are changes of pitch, of loudness, and of rate of utterance. The relationships are significant to the speaker who wants to secure the utmost vocal variety he is capable of, for they clearly indicate the method by which he can achieve his goal. In short, he can train himself to react sharply and fully to the communicative situation and to what he is saying as he says it, or in terms of our discussion of delivery in Chapter 13, he can strive to achieve a full realization of meaning at the moment of utterance and a keen sense of communication with his hearers.

Natural key

Both in delivery and in working on voice, one must keep to his own natural pitch-level, or key. This is the pitch that is heard most often—the dominant pitch—which is appropriate and peculiar to one's vocal mechanism. Determined by heredity and the laws of physical growth, the vocal bands and resonators produce sounds which are naturally appropriate to them. A bass voice, for example, is by nature bass and not tenor. The habitual pitch-level of most persons is their natural pitch-level, but a few persons may through habit speak in a key that is higher or lower than their natural key, a practice which should be corrected.

In any speaking situation, one's natural key should prevail. An unnaturally high pitch may cause shrillness. Moreover, a high pitch seriously limits the speaker's pitch range and thus restricts his opportunity of securing variety of inflection. A high pitch gives him little range above it. On the other hand, a person's natural key provides for considerable range above and below it. An unnaturally low pitch often causes hoarseness, gutturalness, and harshness. It too, limits a speaker's vocal range, for there is little opportunity to go below it. Consequently, the speaker should tune his ear to his own conversation, note the dominant pitch-level, and use it on the platform. If he is relaxed just before he starts speaking and then begins with quiet directness, he will probably hit his natural key. Tenseness will usually shoot the pitch up.

One special caution is in order here. If the key is naturally high, do not try to lower it; if it is naturally very low, do not try to raise it. Few people can change their natural pitch-levels without risking damage to their voices. The system of muscles regulating pitch has been built into us; it is determined by the laws of heredity and of physical growth. Its physical character cannot be altered. All a speaker can do is to strengthen and render more flexible his natural mechanism, to make the most of his potentialities.

Pronunciation

The word pronunciation has two meanings for the student of speaking. Taken broadly, it refers to the action of the speech agents in producing speech sounds. It refers to the physical adjustments which modify the breath and sound stream into the sounds of speech. In this broad sense, pronunciation includes *articulation,* a term referring to the positions of the tongue, teeth, lips, and soft palate in forming speech, especially consonant sounds, and to the distinctness and precision of utterance. In its narrower sense, pronunciation refers to the *correctness* of speech, whether the stress and accent of words are acceptable (*re'search* or *research'*), whether sounds have been improperly omitted (*jellm'n* for *gentlemen*), or substituted (*baff* for *bath*), or improperly added (*athaletic* for *athletic*).

Distinctness of utterance

Public speech should be distinct enough to avoid confusing and distracting the hearers; utterance must not interfere with the ready perception of meanings. In judging whether he speaks with adequate precision, the speaker should be guided by three considerations.

In formal communication, first of all, the articulation of consonant sounds needs to be somewhat more careful and precise than in informal conversation. Although most people are intelligible enough in the normal leisurely conversation of their ordinary lives, they are not so adequately equipped for special circumstances: when they speak to an audience, when time is precious, and when confusion and misunderstanding cannot be tolerated. Hence, one who speaks in public should not assume that his everyday utterance is sufficiently clear and precise to meet the demands of the more exacting situation until he has proved that it is. He can learn whether articulation is adequate by enlisting the aid of a competent observer, such as his instructor, and by recording his speech and listening to it. His best friends either won't tell him or are so accustomed to his speech that they don't notice imperfections.

Second, *sloppiness* or *slovenliness* is perhaps the chief fault of articulation. By this is meant what is often called lazy, blurred, or mushy speech. It is somewhat like bad, undecipherable handwriting or a private system of shorthand that can be understood only by the user. One common sign of sloppiness is a slighting and obscuring of consonant sounds in many-syllabled words and at the ends of words, especially the consonants, *t* and *d*, *f* and *v*, *k* and *g*, *p* and *b*, particularly when these consonants are followed by vowels. Examples are *bake* for *baked, wunnerful* for *wonderful, definly* for *definitely, inresting* for *interesting, unnerstan* for *understand, pain it* for *paint it, summarine* for *submarine, couldn'* for *couldn't, wouldn'* for *wouldn't.* Even when slovenly speech is readily intelligible, it lowers the speaker's standing in the opinions of many listeners, even though they themselves may be guilty of the same fault.

Another sign of slovenliness is the telescoping and cluttering of words and sentences. Utterance is so rapid or incomplete that the speaker seems to have a hot potato in his mouth. He says *Unine Stays Gumm't* for *United States Government.* Both the telescoping of sounds and the obscuring of consonants are almost invariably accompanied by the omission and substitution of sounds. An example is *jiss gonna git* for *just going to get.*

Utterance that is overdistinct is as unacceptable as indistinct speech. It is usually as distracting to the hearer as is sloppy speech, for it is likely to strike him as pretty, fancy, elegant, and highbrow. Furthermore, many contractions, omissions, and elisions of the sounds of everyday speech have come to be accepted. A listener is tuned to them, and when a speaker tries to get in every sound, spellingbook fashion, the result is confusion. For example *boy 'n girl* is more acceptable than a carefully pronounced *boy and girl.*

In general, the public speaker is a little more careful in utterance than he is in informal conversation. Student speakers, like student actors, are especially prone to the fault of sloppy diction. They should take special pains to remedy it.

Correctness of pronunciation

What constitutes correct pronunciation is often a difficult and much-disputed matter—difficult, first, because every person has his pet opinions on the subject. Moreover, as a good democrat a person often holds that his pronunciation is as good as anybody's. Possibly he is right, for it may serve his purposes in the circle of his own friends and associates. Furthermore, those who study the behavior of speech sounds—the phoneticians—do not always agree on whether a particular pronunciation of a word is correct. Some, for example, interested primarily in the history of spoken language, will tolerate variant pronunciations because they know that if a new pronunciation catches on and becomes accepted through usage, it will be regarded as correct. And how is one to judge whether a new pronunciation will catch on?

Since it is true that pronunciation has changed, is changing, and will continue to change, how is one to judge whether his pronunciation is correct? Most authorities face the fact of change and say that current, cultivated or educated usage is the measuring stick for pronunciation. A speaker would be wise to accept this standard, for if his pronunciation reflects current usage, his manner of speech will not distract the attention of his listeners.

To help in deciding what current usage is, the public speaker may profit from a few suggestions. They are offered here solely with his needs in mind, and his needs are governed by at least two conditions. (1) Public speaking is as a rule more formal and more careful than is informal and familiar conversation. (2) The public speaker is often addressing hearers, especially if he is on the air, who represent considerable variety of pronunciation, and his own pronunciation can scarcely reveal such variety. Hence we say to the student speaker:

1. *Study the usage of the dialect region to which you belong through long association, and conform to its usage.*

Although there are hundreds of local dialects in the United States, there are three dialect regions: the territory east of the Hudson River, including some parts of New York City and Long Island (Eastern speech); the region south of the Ohio River and Mason Dixon Line, east of the Mississippi and including Louisiana, the eastern portions of Arkansas, Oklahoma, and Texas (Southern speech); the rest of the United States (General American speech, spoken by three-fourths of all Americans). Born and brought up in one of these linguistic areas, or having lived in one of them during your formative years, you will reflect the pronunciation of your regional family.

If some of your pronunciations are peculiar to the narrow locality you have been reared in, listen to the speech of those in your community who are well educated and who have traveled. Such people tend to reflect in their pronunciation the wider usage of the region, and they can be accepted as fair models. Listen also to the network radio and TV announcers and to the speech of movie actors who play straight rather than character parts. Such people use a slightly modified General American speech that is intelligible everywhere. But if you use Southern or Eastern speech, do not try to make it over to conform to General American, for only the expert who knows language behavior and who practices methodically over a long period of time can do a good job, free of the inconsistencies that any person with a normally sharp ear would laugh at as affectation. Unless for some special purpose, such as making your career that of the actor or the announcer or commentator, it is unwise and unnecessary to copy a pronunciation foreign to the accepted usage of a large dialect region. (Even the large broadcasting systems today permit wider usage in pronunciation than they did a generation ago.) Broad, rather than provincial, differences in pronunciation are tolerated, and a listener easily adjusts to them.

Where two pronunciations of the same word occur with about the same frequency, either one is acceptable.

2. *For words used infrequently, consult the pronunciations recommended by a good dictionary.*

For words in constant use, the dictionary is not always a reliable guide. First, as the dictionary makers themselves acknowledge, it takes from ten to fifteen years to get out a new edition, and although the makers do their best to record current usage, the accepted pronunciation of a word may have changed by the date of publication. Constant use modifies pronunciation fairly rapidly, as in the case of the accent on *quintuplet,* which has shifted from the first to the second syllable in the last twenty years. On the other hand, a word used infrequently is subject to little change, and one can usually rely on the dictionary.

The pronunciations in some dictionaries must be followed cautiously, in the second place, because their makers have not always found it possible to indicate differences between the pronunciations of the same word in the major dialect regions. Most dictionaries reflect, for the most part, the usage of the General American area. The only recent exception to this practice we know of is John S. Kenyon and Thomas R. Knott's, *A Pronouncing Dictionary of American English* (G. & C. Merriam Co., Springfield, Mass., 1944). This work records the pronunciation of words as they are used in ordinary conversation in each of the three dialect regions.

As for place names, note where your dictionary lists them—whether in the general text with other words, or in a special section. Their pronunciations may be shown. Observe, too, whether the names of famous people are listed and whether their pronunciations are indicated. For the pronunciations of some 12,000 foreign names and words, consult W. Cabell Greet, *World Words: Recommended Pronunciations* (New York, Columbia University Press, 1944). Note in particular Greet's discussion of pronunciation on pages 1–4 and his excellent advice for the anglicization of foreign words: ". . . adopt the foreign pronunciation insofar as it can be rendered by customary English sounds in the phrasing and rhythm of an English sentence."

Above all, on consulting a dictionary for pronunciation, become thoroughly familiar with the key sounds and symbols it uses to show pronunciation. The symbols are usually discussed at length in a separate section at the front. If you use a dictionary infrequently, *always* consult the key words listed at the bottom of every page. It is easy to forget what the pronunciation symbols mean, and the key words keep you straight.

The pronunciation of the public speaker, then, should be clear and intelligible. It should reflect the best widespread usage of the dialect region to which he is native. In a word, it should be free of localisms and idiosyncrasies of pronunciation that would distract the listener's attention.

FURTHER READING

Anderson, Virgil. *Training the Speaking Voice.* 2nd ed. New York, 1961.

Bronstein, Arthur F., and Jacoby, Beatrice F. *Your Speaking Voice.* New York, 1967.

Denes, Peter B., and Pinson, Elliott N. *The Speech Chain.* Bell Telephone Laboratories, Inc., 1963.

Eisenson, Jon. *The Improvement of Voice and Diction.* 2nd ed. New York, 1965.

Fairbanks, Grant. *Voice and Articulation Drillbook.* New York, 1960.

Fisher, Hilda B. *Improving Voice and Articulation.* New York, 1966.

Gray, G. W., and Wise, C. M. *The Bases of Speech.* New York, 1959. Chapters 2–3, "On Voice and Pronunciation."

Hanley, Theodore D., and Thurman, Wayne L. *Developing Vocal Skills.* New York, 1962.

Potter, Simeon. *Our Language.* Baltimore: Penguin Books, 1950. Chapter 13, "British and American English."

15

Impromptu Speaking, Speaking from Manuscript, and the Public Interview

Throughout the book we give principal attention to extemporaneous speaking, that is, to speaking which is carefully prepared, and preferably rehearsed, but is not committed to final language until the time when the speech is made. This mode of delivery has usually been highly prized, and it is the norm by which other modes are measured. There are occasions, however, when persons must speak impromptu, that is, without advance notice, and there are others when they are expected to read from manuscript. In this chapter, accordingly, we present suggestions for the impromptu speech and the manuscript speech. We give some attention also to a special combination or adaptation of the extemporaneous and the impromptu speech, which, with the multiplication of interview and panel programs on television and radio, is assuming a larger and larger place in the speaking of public figures both national and local.

The Impromptu Speech

Perhaps nothing so satisfies our egos as success in speaking impromptu, in speaking unexpectedly without having had a chance to prepare for the occasion.

Unfortunately, most impromptu speaking is bad because the speaker, surprised in deep water, loses his head and thrashes and flounders. His delivery is halting and hard, and his remarks are usually inane and irrelevant, repetitious and disconnected. In alarm and desperation, he clutches at any idea that pops into mind and without examining it hopes that it will somehow save him. When impromptu utterance is good, it is very, very good. Delivery, in particular, may be excellent; it may exhibit the verve, sparkle, and spontaneity that one struggles to attain in the extemporaneous speech. Possibly there is no student of public speaking who has not observed that his impromptu delivery is at times superior to his prepared efforts. He may recognize that he talks well when the circumstances of communication are just right. When the preceding speaker stirs him to react strongly or discussion starts him thinking, when he springs to correct the speaker's information, to criticize an argument, or to express a different point of view, he has simultaneously an idea to communicate and the impulse to say it—and presto! the job is done with vigor and dispatch. He should recognize, however, that it is the fortuitous combination of circumstances, it is just the right situation, that brings about his effective response. Indeed, when the circumstances are made to order, who can fail?

We are concerned here with the situation in which the circumstances are not perfect, in which a speaker, called on unexpectedly, must, like an aggressive athlete, make his own breaks and take advantage of the opportunity to speak instead of letting it slip by.

In coping with the impromptu situation, a speaker should recognize, paradoxical as the observation may seem, that he is not wholly without preparation. He has a background of experience and information upon which he may be able to draw. The problem is how to make his past work for him. He may be able to enjoy considerable success by attacking the problem in the following ways.

Listen carefully

Careful listening is not difficult if discussion from the platform or from the floor succeeds in claiming a person's interest. But if the speechmaking and the discussion do not readily interest him and if there is the slightest possibility that he may be called upon to speak, he must make a special effort to follow the talk closely. It is the ideas he hears expressed that may touch off information and experience, and thus prompt some kind of reaction. The reaction may be any of these, or others: "The speaker has overlooked an important point"; "I could add an illustration to that point"; "he is being inconsistent"; "that argument is weak"; "he believes so-and-so, but I think the opposite is true (or, but I believe he is only partly right)." When such ideas strike, make a note of them wherever they occur. Make a brief note—only a phrase or two so as not to lose the trend of the speech or the discussion, and to preserve a record of reactions to it.

Control nervousness

If one is called on to speak, he may experience a wild moment. "What shall I say; oh, what shall I do! I can't say anything! I'm caught; I wish I were out of here!" Such a reaction is emotional, and emotion, as we have seen, feeds on itself and makes the experience more intense. The speaker should recognize such an emotional response at once, and cope with it. He can ease himself physically by relaxing and thus reducing muscular tension. He can breathe regularly. With a little practice, he can learn to ease off thus in four or five seconds. Then he can turn his attention to the situation and meet it squarely. Has a specific question been asked that demands a definite answer? If he can answer it, let him start walking to the platform and decide what his answer will be. (If necessary to gain time, he can ask for the repetition of the question. This gives the mind something to do.) The decision will probably prompt a reason or two to back it up or at least suggest an illustration. At this moment he has, whether he recognizes it or not, what amounts to a central idea with which he can lead off, and one or two ideas to follow and support it. He can easily conclude by restating his opening idea. If he cannot reply to the direct question, two roads are open. Either he can decline to speak, excusing himself as graciously as possible, or he can say in substance, "I don't have anything to say to that question, but if I may, I should like to comment on such-and-such a point." Here is where his notes come in handy, for his decision to comment on another point may be prompted by a glance at them. He can use them to recall swiftly his earlier reactions.

If on the other hand, a general question is asked—such as "Would you care to comment on so-an-so's remarks?"—he turns at once to his notes for suggestions. To one inexperienced in impromptu discussion, notes are here invaluable because a general question or invitation suggests no possibilities. It isn't specific enough to give one a mental start, and the review of notes may prompt an idea.

Become thoroughly familiar with useful patterns of thought

So far we have been concerned principally with suggestions that aid the impromptu speaker in selecting something to say. Now we shall present some aids to the rapid organization of his ideas. The impromptu speech, like the extemporaneous speech, requires a speaker not only to have something to say but to say it as clearly as he can. The least to be expected of him is that he will contrive a simple sensible governing statement and support it with an example or two. Anything more he may be able to accomplish is clear profit.

The patterns below, intended primarily to promote clarity of expression, may also serve to suggest ideas. The student would do well to memorize them so thoroughly that they become part of him; he should, in other words, assimilate them completely. They then stand a good chance of coming to his aid, unrecognized and unheralded, in those few moments of preparation in the impromptu situation, to provide form for his thoughts. In classroom practice if the teacher can manage to give the student an extra moment or two before speaking, he can review them deliberately and select the pattern most appropriate to his reply.

1. Lead off with what has been said. Express your reaction. Support it. (*A variant of this*: Start with the question asked you. Answer it in one sentence. Explain or give reasons for the answer.)
2. Lead off with an illustration. Conclude by stating the point it suggests.
3. Say that an important point has been omitted. State it. Support it.
4. Express disagreement with a certain argument. Give reasons for disagreeing.
5. Express disagreement in terms of the problem discussed.
   a. The evils have been exaggerated. State why.
   b. The solution is bad, for
      (1) There is a better one. State it. Give reasons.
      (2) It is impractical. Give reasons.
6. The reasoning in such-and-such an argument is in error, because of
   a. Insufficient or untrustworthy facts. Explain.
   b. Inadequate or untrustworthy testimony. Explain.
   c. Faulty analogy. Explain.
   d. Faulty cause-and-effect reasoning. Explain.
7. The argument shows an inconsistency. Explain.

Impromptu Speeches about Speaking. The formula above will aid greatly in discussing impromptu the content and reasoning of any speech, in or out of the classroom. In the classroom, also, considerable discussion may be directed to speaking as such. Impromptu speaking about speeches has special values for the student. It lays the foundation of good criticism, not only of class speeches, but of all speeches, anywhere. (See Chapter 23.) It affords, moreover, additional training in speech for both parties to the criticism, for the student speaker secures further practice in impromptu utterance and the student criticized learns about his successes and failures from one of his peers. Finally, the speaker, familiar with the standards, methods, and techniques of speechmaking, has knowledge which he can use on the spur of the moment.

The patterns already set out above will be useful in criticizing a speaker's argument; those below will aid in organizing impromptu criticism of other phases of speechmaking.

SPEAKER'S SUBJECT

The subject of Mr. X's speech was appropriate (was inappropriate), for

I. A good speech subject, as we all know, should . . . . (Here you remind your audience of the *standards* by which a subject should be judged. Reference to standards in this pattern and in those following gives you ready material for your opening remarks.)

I′. And his subject meets (does not meet; in part meets) the requirements of a good subject, for . . . . (Here you go on to support your judgment.)

SPEAKER'S INFORMATION AND CHOICE OF IDEAS

X's speech was worth (was not worth) listening to, for

I. A good speech should enlarge our information (or influence our thinking and action)

I′. And I learned something (little) from X's speech (or X's argument on . . . appealed [did not appeal] to me), for . . . .

DELIVERY

X's speech was well (poorly) delivered, for

I. A speaker's delivery should show qualities of . . . .

I′. X's delivery showed (did not show) such qualities, for

A. He was (was not) mentally alert to ideas, for . . . .

B. As for sense of communication, he . . . .

C. As for vocal qualities, he . . . .

D. As for pronunciation, he . . . .

E. As for bodily responsiveness

1. To ideas, he . . . .

2. To the platform situation, he . . . .

An impromptu criticism might well be limited to *one* of the aspects of delivery alluded to in A-E above. For example:

The vocal qualities of X's delivery were acceptable (unacceptable), for

I. Desirable qualities are . . . .

I′. X possessed (did not possess) these qualities, for . . . .

SPEECH ORGANIZATION

X's speech was clear (clear in part; not clear), for

I. Its purpose was (was not) evident, for . . . .

II. Its subject sentence was (was not) evident, for . . . . (If the subject sentence was evident, cite it and thus support your judgment; if it was not clear, try to suggest why it wasn't.)

III. Its main heads were (were not) recognizable, for . . . . (If the heads were evident, cite them.)

IV. The heads were relevant (irrelevant) to the subject sentence, for . . . .

V. It effectively used (did not use) some of the methods of securing clearness, for . . . .

Rarely will an alert individual find himself completely unprepared for the impromptu situation. Although he cannot prepare specifically for the unexpected occasion, he can train himself to listen closely, take note of his reactions, and develop the knack of swiftly arranging his remarks. The more speaking experience he gains, the more resources of idea, information, and illustration he accumulates, the more readily will possible supporting and amplifying material cluster about an idea. A good impromptu speech, with an idea worth remembering, cannot be made from an empty or lethargic mind.

The Public Interview

If nothing satisfies our egos as well as success in impromptu speaking, surely high among the ego-satisfactions is proving oneself in the circumstances of the public interview, the "press" conference, the question-and-answer situation. Some writers on speech, in fact, tend to think of the "speech" as a thing of the past along with the "oration." There is widespread respect for the give-and-take and interaction of the conference, the panel, the interview, and other forms and modes of public "conversation," of interpersonal communication. Characteristic of these freer forms of public discussion are the extemporaneous and impromptu modes of utterance.

Various public affairs programs put on by the television and radio networks (especially on Sunday mornings) are notable specimens of the essentially extemporaneous-impromptu mode of speaking: "Meet the Press," "Face the Nation," "Issues and Answers." The pattern is familiar. A person of current importance or conspicuousness in national or international affairs is publicly questioned for half an hour or so by one or more persons from the news media. The questions may range as widely as the questioners choose, but usually they are intended to elicite or provoke from the "guest" some information, opinion, or argument concerning the matters of public interest with which he is known to be related: Secretary Romney to housing, Mayor Stokes to racial disturbances, the president of the State University to the financial needs of higher education.

Such programs, of course, exhibit major public issues and usually involve experienced professional speakers. They are only enlarged occurrences, however, of a more and more common kind of speaking situation in which any business or professional man, local politician or administrator, labor leader, student protestor, or educated citizen is likely to find himself. The oral interview before the camera and microphone—and hence the public—will become a more rather than less frequent vehicle of public speaking. Therefore, the student speaker will be well advised to learn to adapt the principles and practices of public utterance to the interview.

The oral interview is extemporaneous in that the speaker usually knows—or can guess with reasonable confidence—that he will speak and what he will be asked to speak about. Hence he can prepare as he would for an extemporaneous speech. He can recall and review what he already knows and thinks. He can equip himself afresh with relevant information. He can formulate and organize his ideas. In advance he can find effective examples, comparisons, definitions, explanations, images, values, motives, and other means of amplification and development. And he can even rehearse beforehand units which he is pretty sure will fit, and other little "speeches" on his subject or subjects. In other words, he will review his general experience and knowledge, and will bring himself up to date on new knowledge of the sort which he knows or suspects may be useful. On some subjects and on certain kinds of occasions there may even be advance agreement that certain questions will be asked and others not. Of course, especially on radio, there are programs in the superficial form of question-and-answer or interview, which are really only interrupted discourse read from manuscript by the "expert." Some programs of this sort may work very well, for good scripts as well as poor ones may be written, and performers may be good readers or poor ones. In the next section of the chapter we advise the student on the techniques of reading a script well. For the present, however, we are concerned with the genuinely extemporaneous-impromptu situation.

We have reviewed the ways in which the speaker's performance in the "spontaneous, unrehearsed, live" interview will be the same as in any planned, prepared extemporaneous speech. He will be giving a series of small related speeches, rearrangeable and exchangeable as the program develops, but not without opportunity for preparation.

On the other hand, the ingenuity and skill of the speaker are especially evident in his management of those characteristic techniques of the impromptu speech which we have discussed earlier in the chapter—the speech for which there is neither time nor occasion to take specific thought in advance. Speaking in the public interview is impromptu in that, though the speaker has prepared himself on the subject and may have worked out answers to anticipated questions, he is unlikely to know just when, how, and in what order the questions will be asked and what the further responses of his questioners may be.

In such speaking, therefore, adaptability and versatility in both material and language are at a premium. That speaker will be able to adapt and adjust best to the circumstances who has the confidence of knowing that he has thought through most phases of the problems beforehand, and has talked through them in orderly fashion. He will be thoroughly familiar with the principles of oral communication discussed in this book and in particular with the patterns of extemporaneous and impromptu organization presented in Chapter 4 and in the previous section of this chapter.

The Manuscript Speech

Delivering a speech from manuscript, which nowadays usually means a typescript, is perhaps more common than ever before in the history of public speaking. In part this is due to the influence of radio and TV. In part it is caused by the pressure of business and public life, for many men in industry and government are too busy to take time to prepare well for extemporaneous utterance. In part, too, speaking from a prepared manuscript assists one to speak with accuracy and to avoid the hazards of misquotation. But in large part, the greater use of manuscripts is probably due to the simple truth that fewer men in responsible positions today have had the training in public speaking that their counterparts enjoyed almost as a matter of course three or four generations ago.

Hence although extemporaneous delivery is still the most common method used by speakers, the modern student of public speaking should have some experience in delivering a speech from manuscript. In these times when much communication is by radio and television, most leaders in political, business, and civic life will appear at one time or another before the microphone and camera. For many of these appearances, they will be required or will think it wise to prepare written versions of their speeches and to read them.

Reading

To read aloud well is relatively uncommon. It requires some training and practice. For this reason colleges often devote an entire course to reading aloud, and those persons who expect to read in public, especially those preparing for political and administrative positions, for the law, for the ministry, and for teaching, should take intensive instruction in reading. We do not propose to offer such intensive instruction here; we wish merely to present a few basic suggestions that should set the reader on the proper road.

The goal of all oral reading is a delivery that sounds like spontaneous talk. A reader tries to express *ideas.* He tries *to react to the meanings* of the written words and hold the meaning in mind, concentrating utterly upon it, while he says the prepared language. In brief, his reading should reveal two qualities of good delivery: full realization of meaning at the moment of utterance and a keen sense of direct communication.

Preparation of the written speech

Prepare a Speech, Not an Essay. In planning for the written speech, one should, of course, prepare as thoroughly as for the extemporaneous speech. This observation needs emphasis, for many speakers mistakenly feel that because they can lean on written language they need not give so much care to preparation as they would to the construction of an extemporaneous speech. Often they regard the written speech as an essay. Consequently, they select a subject that is too broad to be treated adequately without using more abstract and general language than an audience can understand. As a result, vivid, specific illustrations and details, and the many other ways of adapting and fitting ideas to an audience, tend to be left out. Frequently a written speech is fuzzy and unclear because the speaker thought he could write before he made a complete speech outline, that is, before he clarified and ordered his mind on the subject. Our advice, accordingly, is this: Plan the speech, outline it, and write it out *in every detail* just as if you expected later to discard the manuscript and talk extemporaneously. If you have the opportunity and facilities, try dictating the speech from the outline. The written speech should in every respect reveal a real person talking to a specific audience on a specific occasion. As the speech is being written, the speaker should visualize himself *talking* to his hearers.

Before preparing the final draft of the speech, the speaker should check the text methodically with these questions in mind:

1. Does the introduction really claim the interest of hearer and establish direct contact with the audience?
2. Is each illustration detailed enough to be clear and vivid?
3. Are there enough transitions and signpost phrases to keep the audience from getting lost?
4. Is the style of direct address used when referrring to people? In general, prefer *we, our, us, I, you,* to *they, people, a person, the reader, the author.*
5. Are there many abstract words and phrases? Can you substitute *concrete* and *specific* words and phrases? (Time spent in inspection and substitution will repay a speaker a hundredfold.)

Eliminate from the Manuscript All Sources of Distraction. Give yourself maximum opportunity to concentrate on ideas by avoiding visual stimuli which will only distract your attention. Accordingly:

1. Type the manuscript on one side of the paper only; this facilitates handling. Triple space the lines, for this reduces the danger of rereading a line or of skipping a line. If you cannot type the manuscript or have it typed for you, write in a large bold hand.
2. Have the copy absolutely clean; do not clutter up the page with last-minute additions between the lines and in the margins. Don't cross out material and transpose word order. Visual clutter distracts attention.

Practice aloud

Handling the Manuscript. A reader may handle his manuscript in one of two ways. (1) He may hold it in his hands somewhat above waist level, high enough so that he can see it easily without bending his head and not so high as to hide his face. One hand should hold the manuscript, and the other hand should be free to shift pages and to gesture. (2) He may place it on a speaker's stand, or on a table, but only if either one is high enough to permit him to consult the paper readily without bending over. If it is on a stand, both hands are free to gesture.

The speaker should check both positions carefully with this fact in mind: The head should be erect, because in this position the eyes can be readily kept on the audience. Bending-over tends to keep the eyes riveted to the manuscript, and the reader needs to do everything he can to keep in physical touch with his hearers. *Let the eyes, not the head, drop to the paper.*

Two cautions should be observed: Do not try to conceal a manuscript (or notes, for that matter) from an audience, do not apologize for reading.

Look at the Hearers. Inexpert reading tends to make delivery indirect; both speaker and audience are usually robbed of any feeling of direct communication, principally because the speaker glues his eyes to his manuscript. Consequently, in practice reading a speaker must spend much of his effort in learning to keep his eyes on the audience. *He should practice until he can look at his hearers 90 percent of the time.* For at least nine minutes of a ten-minute speech he should have his eyes on his audience.

Achieving such directness involves great familiarity with one's manuscript and ability to find one's place unerringly. Both can be accomplished through persistent practice.

Practice in keeping one's place should proceed in this manner:

Take a long look at the words ahead and concentrate on their meaning; then look up and speak them. When the speaker can go no farther, he should drop his eyes to the proper place, take another look ahead, look up, and speak again. This procedure should be repeated again and again.

Practice in this way should continue until the student determines his maximum memory span, until he discovers the longest word groups he can hold in mind before he needs to consult the text for another glance ahead. Let us illustrate briefly. Suppose the opening paragraph is represented by this passage from Huxley:

> Suppose it were perfectly certain that the life and fortune of every one of us / would, one day or other,/ depend upon his winning or losing a game at chess./ Don't you think we should all consider it a primary duty / to learn at least the names and the moves of the pieces;/ to have a notion of a gambit,/ and a keen eye for all the means of giving and getting out of a check? / Do you not think we should look with a disapprobation amounting to scorn,/ upon a father who allowed his son,/ or the state which allowed its members,/ to grow up without knowing a pawn from a knight?

Upon first reading this aloud, the student might discover that he has to pause and look down frequently, perhaps at the end of each thought-unit, as indicated by the slant lines (/). With further practice, he could easily speak each sentence, and therefore would need to consult the text only three times; and with still more work, he could probably speak the entire paragraph. As he works through his manuscript in this manner, he will discover that his memory span will depend on whether the ideas are abstract and general, or concrete and specific; accordingly, the frequency with which he glances down will vary considerably, for sometimes he will be able to hold only one sentence-idea in mind, sometimes a number of sentence-ideas. The object is to practice until he has to consult the text as little as possible. When he has located the spots where he *must* glance down, he may *mark* them with some convenient symbol. (Many students like to use a small circle in red ink.) The marks will guide his eyes and prevent confusion.

Concentrate on Meaning and Idea Rather Than on Words. Cultivate and build up the feeling that you must speak to this audience at this time, that you are in touch with your hearers and they with you. Since you have constructed the speech, you are intimate with its ideas and with the way they are related to each other. You built the speech; therefore you should understand it fully. Consequently, the most practical aid to the re-creation of its ideas is to feel the force of the stimulus that prompts the speech. That stimulus is your audience and the feeling that you have business with it. To experience this feeling and to keep in touch visually with your hearers will do much to prompt you to react to ideas rather than to words merely, and will do much to secure the proper emphasis, loudness, and inflection.

> *Acquire the habit of speaking no passage until its meaning has a chance to hit your mind.*

This means, essentially, that you must learn to *pause,* for it is during the pause that the mind is most active in concentrating and preparing for what is to come. Unskillful readers almost invariably read too fast—so fast that they have little chance to react to ideas; both body and mind are wrapped up in mere utterance—in articulating sounds. Silence in reading is golden.

First, one should recognize how much of the total speaking time is taken up by silence. A practical way of doing this is to try reading the first 125 words of your speech in no less than one minute. Although rate of utterance and pausing depend upon the speaker's personality, his material, and the size of his audience, 125 words for the opening minute will not be far wrong. In experimenting with the opening minute, be careful not to drag out individual sounds and words. Utter them with normal distinctness, as if talking. You will then notice that the total time needed for a given passage is influenced by the number of pauses and by the length of pauses.

Second, having made this observation, let the number of pauses be dictated by the ideas. Pause wherever the sense dictates a pause, wherever there would normally be a pause in speaking the same ideas in the same language in conversation. It will be evident that one pauses oftener than punctuation dictates.

Third, not only pause often enough to appreciate ideas, but also pause long enough to get set for the next idea. *Construct* an idea before uttering it. Don't hurry ahead for the language; wait for its meaning to strike you and then utterance will reflect idea. Where ideas are closely related to each other and follow each other swiftly, pauses may be quite short—a second or less in duration; where a major thought sequence ends and another begins, as at the major divisions of a speech, pauses may be several seconds long. But whether the pause is short or long, the mind is getting set for the next idea.

While working on the pause and trying to subordinate language to sense, the student will find himself substituting new words and phrases for what he has written. Such substitution is in fact a reliable sign that he is reacting to ideas; he is thinking so well that other words naturally come into being to express the same idea. He will brush up on precise phraseology late in rehearsal.

Make Prominent the Structure of the Speech. After the reading begins to sound and feel like live conversation, the student should give special attention in a final rehearsal to the major ideas that reflect the pattern of the speech as a whole. Such ideas will be at least those passages that state or allude to the purpose of the speech, the central idea, and the main heads. These must be given emphasis. The student should not, however, give them prominence by merely reading them louder, for this is likely to be mechanical and artificial. Rather, during the pauses preceding them, he should *realize that they are the most important* of his ideas. Such realization should produce the proper emphasis in speaking them.

In brief, if one has a speech to read, not a general essay, and if one practices assiduously with ideas uppermost in mind, one can usually read very acceptably and often can appear to talk spontaneously. In any event, a speaker should *prepare* to read when he has to stick to a text. There is no excuse for stumbling awkwardly about, for reading like a racehorse, or for dull, lifeless communication.

The near-manuscript outline

Some speakers like to work up outlines which approach the full text of a manuscript. Actually such devices are neither manuscripts nor outlines but are combinations of both. They are most useful when a speaker, wanting to be careful and exact in his use of language and wishing to quote extensively, does not care to read from manuscript. So he prepares something close to a manuscript, to rehearse from.

The example below was prepared by a student for his final speech in a college public speaking class.

We Are Not Alone!

INTRODUCTION

For thousands of years men have gazed into the evening sky, when the stars seemed almost close enough to touch, and have asked themselves, "Is there life on those remote worlds? Do beings like ourselves exist elsewhere in this universe?"

For centuries these questions seemed unanswerable. Only recently has science given us logical answers to these questions.

Yet how many of us had given serious thought to this question? In a poll in class the other day, a few of you thought one way, a few the other, and a large part of you didn't know, or made very hurried decisions. The poll took you by surprise. You had never really given the question of life on other planets much serious thought before.

We read about other civilizations in science fiction stories and see the cartoonists' "Mars Men" in our daily newspaper. Yet, as the men of olden times took it for granted that the sun, moon, and stars all revolved about the earth, I think we, *in our everyday lives,* take it for granted, whether consciously or not, that we are the only intelligent beings in the space about us.

It is my belief that we cannot take this idea that we are "alone," so to speak, for granted.

DEVELOPMENT

I. Life will exist wherever and whenever necessary conditions are present.

A. Sir Harold Spencer-Jones, British Astronomer Royal, says, "Life does not occur because of some unique accident. It is the result of definite processes; given the suitable conditions these processes will *inevitably* lead to the development of life." In other words, the creation of life is not "magic." When the necessary conditions are present, life will form.

B. The "building blocks" of life are basic materials and may be found anywhere.

1. Nobel Prize winner, Dr. Wendell M. Stanly of the Virus Laboratory of the University of California says, "Work on the viruses has provided us with new reasons for considering that life as we know it does not come into existence suddenly, but is inherent in all matter."

2. *The Reader's Digest* reports,
"Chemist Stanley Miller of the University of Chicago put into a test tube what was believed to be the chief elements of the atmosphere two or three billion years ago: methane, ammonia, hydrogen, and water. He exposed them repeatedly to an electric spark. Within a week he had produced three of the amino acids which are the basis

of protein, the very stuff of life. So perhaps the first molecules necessary to life were formed by lightning acting on the Earth's atmosphere."

C. Life on Mars is "living proof" that life will exist when conditions are present.

1. After a series of intensive studies of Mars when it was close to the Earth in 1956, Dr. William M. Sinton, presently at Lowell Observatory, described the suspected life on Mars as "organic and regenerative; that is, living and reproducing."

2. Sir Harold Jones points out, "The fact that primitive plants grow in the thin Martian atmosphere suggests that life of higher sorts could arise, or may have arisen elsewhere in the Universe where conditions are better."

[So if we accept the fact that life *will* develop when conditions are favorable, we must face the question of the probability of all these favorable conditions that we are all familiar with (temperature, water, oxygen, etc.) actually occurring at the same time on a given planet, so as to make life possible there.]

II. The probabilities that favorable conditions exist on a large number of planets are so overwhelming that the existence of life on other planets is undeniable.

A. The modern theory on probability of life on other planets is very close to that held by three authorities:
Dr. Gerard Kuiper, Director of Yerkes Observatory
Dr. Otto Struve, Head of Astronomy Department, University of California
Dr. Harlow Shapley, Harvard University Observatory

1. Dr. Shapley has best presented the argument based on probability: "It is not unreasonable to suppose that one star in every million will have a family of planets. Of these, one star in every thousand might meet the conditions necessary for organic life. Of these again, the chance that one in a thousand might develop highly organized, intelligent beings is only one in a trillion. (1 in 1,000,000,000,000). But, there are thought to be 100 quadrillion stars. This could mean 100 million (100,000,000) planets with beings somewhat resembling ourselves."

CONCLUSION

I would like to conclude with a quotation taken from Sir Harold Jones's book, *Life on Other Planets:*

"We can not resist the conclusion that life, though rare, is scattered throughout the universe. It may be compared to a rare plant which can flourish only when the tempertaure, the humidity, the soil, the altitude and the amount of sunshine are favorable. Given the appropriate conditions, then here, there, and elsewhere the planet may be found."

In concluding our discussion of delivery and its modes, we remind the student that our language as spoken (and written) is the outer manifestation of the inner man. It is utterance prompted by communicative situations. It reflects and completes creative thinking when a speaker makes evident his meaning to serve his purpose. Delivery is dominated by meaning and the sense of communication; the sounds of speech and the gestures of the body are the physical signs and shapes of meaning. Whatever the modes and styles of presentation, all are in the service of meaningful communication.

FURTHER READING

Bacon, Wallace. *The Art of Interpretation.* New York, 1966.

Grimes, Wilma H., and Mattingly, Alethea S. *Interpretation: Writer, Reader, Audience.* San Francisco, 1961.

Lee, Charlotte I. *Oral Interpretation.* 3rd ed. Boston, 1965.

Parrish, Wayland M. *Reading Aloud.* 4th ed. New York, 1966.

Sloan, Thomas O. (ed.) *The Oral Study of Literature.* New York, 1966.

VI
Materials and Forms in Persuasive Speaking

16

Definition of Persuasive Speaking

In approaching the study and practice of persuasive discourse, the perceptive and mature student encounters problems of definitions that as a rule are practical but not final. It is essential only to recognize the chief differences between informative speaking and persuasive speaking in order to see how one may learn to handle persuasive situations intelligently—to see that if a person has some sound notions about persuasion he can proceed more efficiently in building a speech than if he has not. He will be more efficient because where it is possible to draw workable distinctions, he can regard an occasion as persuasive rather than informative, recognize persuasive purposes and goals, and think fruitfully about persuasive materials and methods. He can prepare a speech in an orderly way.

In a book of this kind there is no room to offer a theory of persuasion. We shall simply indicate some of the difficulties in defining persuasion and then suggest a practical definition of persuasive speaking.

If persuasive discourse differs from informative or expository discourse, the distinction is that between promoting knowledge and understanding on the one hand, and belief and action on the other. But if in most cases we may readily perceive a difference between knowing and doing, the distinction between believing and acting is in theory and in practice more subtle and bothersome. Suppose one is asked simply to refrain from demonstrating for civil rights. Would his refusal to act be an action? Or since no activity in the ordinary sense would be involved, is one simply being asked to make up his mind? Would making up one's mind, then, be a matter of belief rather than of action? There was a time in the history of logic and rhetoric when it was quite proper to separate conviction and action, and to hold that argumentative speechmaking, addressed to the intellect, was a kind of discourse generally unlike persuasive speechmaking, which was addressed to the emotions. Or suppose one is told that anything he hears, as may be the case with everything he perceives or learns through any medium of communication, influences him somehow, sometime, whether directly or subtly, whether then or in a far future. There is the story of the commuter, exposed week after week to the advertisements in the subway cars, and his dog. The man took to eating shredded wheat, which he had never dreamed of buying, much less eating.

He tried the same breakfast food on his dog, but the animal persistently rejected it. Would the dog have accepted it, he mused, had the animal been able to read? So, if every experience influences subsequent behavior in some way, then all communication is persuasive. Or suppose a speaker does not intend to influence another's behavior, but does inadvertently, as would be the case if in explaining certain stock market operations he supplied the knowledge and motive the other needed to start buying stocks. Or, finally, is persuasion the attempt to influence the attitudes of an audience, that is, to build up feelings of liking or disliking, favoring or not favoring, some belief, policy, proposition, or line of action? Some experimenters in both psychology and rhetorical communication hold that only rarely is a single speech enough to change belief or impel action. But a single speech may have an effect on an audience's attitudes; it may incline hearers to feel better disposed or less ill-disposed toward a proposal, although they may not immediately believe or act. A particular speech, then, may be one factor among the many which, over a period of time, produce the desired belief or behavior.

Interesting and instructive as the preceding considerations and their refinements may be, the beginning student can proceed profitably if he accepts this definition: *persuasive speaking is verbal communication whose prime purpose or goal is the influencing of attitude, belief, or behavior.* Persuasion certainly involves an effect and the intention to produce it. The situation that prompts a communicator to try to persuade is an audience's quandary about what to believe or not to believe, what to do or not to do. The audience is in a state of doubt; the speaker desires to induce a state of belief, to ask the audience to make up its mind, to take a position, or to act on the matter. Or, from the speaker's point of view, the audience has the wrong attitude; it holds the wrong belief or is about to do the wrong thing. Or the audience has the right attitude and holds the right belief, but has failed to act. A speaker may be concerned about Federal aid to education, the State sales tax, the local traffic problem, health insurance, the current election and candidates, the morals of the latest novel or motion picture, freedom of speech on campus, or open housing laws. Such subjects have their controversial aspects. On any one, he may want his hearers to share his attitude; he may ask them to accept his position, belief, or opinion; or he may intend them to act as he recommends or advises.

In persuasive situations, then, speakers are aware of possible effects. They ask for a change of some kind, or for the maintenance of an attitude or belief. If a change is asked for, it is real and meaningful, definite and specific. Nevertheless, the change need not be a conversion; it need not represent a shift in attitude from favorable to unfavorable, nor a shift in loyalty from one religious sect to another, from one political party to another, nor from believing that lying is sometimes justifiable to the conviction that lying is never justifiable.

Some of the characteristics of attitudes and beliefs illustrate the sorts of change in listeners that persuasive speakers aim at. An attitude may be pro or con, and it reveals an individual's position, his stance, in respect to the matter in controversy. Attitude is reflected in a speaker's purpose and expressed in his proposition. He is for the proposition and tries to persuade his audience to take the same position. A community, let us say, is indifferent to a slum clearance program; so a speaker advocates that action be started by setting up a slum clearance council. It is clear where he stands and what he wants the community to accept. Both attitudes and beliefs, moreover, reveal degrees of strength or intensity. This fact we recognize when we say we have confidence or faith in something. So the effect desired from a speech may be the increase or decrease of the listeners' confidence or faith in something.

This is the case when speakers confront partisan audiences, when in political rallies Republicans address Republicans and Democrats appeal to Democrats, seeking to get out the vote by stirring up enthusiasm for the party and its candidates, when preachers address their flocks Sunday after Sunday, seeking to keep moral and religious values fresh and strong enough to influence everyday behavior. Speeches in these circumstances have been called inspirational. The effect desired is a renewal or a heightening of the state of confidence already existing, a raising of the temperature of belief; hence the affective aspect of attitude becomes prominent and the values brought into play are saturated with feeling and emotion. This was the case when John F. Kennedy made his civil rights speech to the nation, shortly after the turmoil created when two Negroes sought entrance to the University of Alabama in the summer of 1963. "We are confronted," he said, "with a moral issue," so fundamental that it should prompt every citizen to examine his belief in equality of opportunity for all. Do we really believe in this ideal? Kennedy asked. Are we more than apathetic about it? How great is our confidence in it? The time is at hand, he declared, for "every American [to] examine his conscience. . . ."

So students should recognize that the potential effectiveness of a single persuasive speech depends in part upon the nature and extent of the change desired in the audience's attitudes or beliefs; and he should realize that the speaker whose proposition clearly fits the state of belief existing in his audience is most likely to secure the response he wants. More important, as a result of close analysis of an audience's attitudes, values, and opinions, the speaker will understand that a single persuasive effort will elicit specific action, if at all, and make converts when it is one of many speeches, or other factors in a well-designed program, which unfolds over a considerable period. The program may be that of a political party or that of a company with a product to sell or with its reputation and good will to maintain. Above all, we can be confident that communication is essential to persuasion. Without communication there would be no community of belief or of action. If the most casual remark has an effect and a place in human relationships, then the well-conceived speech has its function, even though its precise effect may not be totally identifiable nor measurable.

The Materials of Persuasive Speaking

The characteristic materials of persuasion are to be found in the occasion and audience, in the total situation, to which the speaker responds with his speech. The main sources are three: the facts and circumstances of a situation marked by differences of belief and opinion; the experience of the audience; and the experience of the speaker. These materials combine and coalesce in a way that gives rise to the purpose, or intent, of the speech and to the means employed to achieve the purpose. The means used are of two kinds: material and formal. The materials drawn upon are among those that have prompted the speaker's purpose, that is, the facts of a controversy and the experience of audience and speaker. These we shall discuss in this and the next three chapters. The formal means of persuasion are usually called the forms of proof, and the patterns of structure presented in Chapter 11, Strategies of Organization. The persuasive speaker, like any communicator, is confronted with the problem of finding and selecting materials, and of forming them into a whole that is meaningful and acceptable to his hearers. What dominates these processes is the communicator's sense of purpose or intent.

The time, the trouble, and the thought a speaker gives to determining his purpose are well used. The recognition of his purpose is his response to the factual, material aspects of the problematic situation to which both he and his audience have become subject; hence to try to settle upon the specific nature of one's purpose is to think in terms of one's materials. The students at X University have become restive and critical under the rules that regulate their conduct and they want changes. What is to be done, if anything; and how? In this kind of situation, a student does not have to speak. But if he does speak, what does he want? What is desirable? Practical? Commendable? If he elects to speak, he will discover a purpose, perhaps a number of purposes, as a result of knowing the facts of student unrest and of analyzing his feelings about them. From the study of fact and analysis of his feeling comes awareness of the values that give special significance and meaning to the problem. What any persuasive speaker should recognize is that the impulse to speak and the selection of purpose or goal constitute a union of different kinds of materials: feelings, emotions, values, opinions, and facts. When a speaker finally commits himself to a single dominant purpose, the language in which he phrases that purpose is the product of such materials. His purpose, for example, might be to consolidate student feelings of neglect and alienation, or to gain acceptance of a proposal that students be represented on key university committees.

About the material means of persuasion little need be said at this point. In referring to them concisely as the experience of the speaker and the experience of the audience, we are taking experience to mean the complete texture of feeling, emotion, values, belief, and knowledge that makes up a human being and that has been acquired through learning. Every individual, of course, is unique in the way he has combined his learnings. There is something distinctive about his personality that marks him as being different from other persons. In persuasive communication, however, the important considerations are the ways in which speaker and audience are similar. Some of the central problems in persuasion are these: What experience do speaker and audience have in common? What similarities of experience can be made evident in the speech? To find workable answers to these questions, study is directed to the values the speaker and his hearers share on the occasion and subject. As a result, another problem is perceived to be crucial to successful persuasion: Can the speaker through his language and argument show that the values shared by him and his audience apply to the achievement of his purpose and to the acceptance of his proposal?

Forms of Persuasion

The forms of persuasion are the forms of proof. They are the patterns of reasoning and argument: for example, the deductive pattern, patterns that emphasize cause-and-effect relationships, the pattern of analogy, and generalization from examples. Whether or not one knows their special names, these patterns are familiar to everybody. We use them every day. When we say that "politicians will do anything to get elected," we are expressing a generalization based on the behavior of the two or three politicians we know. If we say that we cannot swallow an argument because the speaker is obviously prejudiced, we use the deductive pattern, whether or not we are fully aware of it. Back of our statement is the notion that prejudiced persons often warp or slant their arguments and cannot be taken entirely at a face value. Our speaker is simply a case in point.

The patterns of reasoning have great value in persuasion. First, they marry two factors of attention, familiarity and pattern; hence, they materially help speakers to keep the attention of listeners. Second, they constitute the verbal framework in which the materials of proof appear to best advantage. Several years ago a student speaker set out to intensify the attitude of his listeners against communism. One point of the speech he started like this:

> Most of us believe that government ought to rest on the consent of the governed. Communism is bad because it cannot ever risk a final judgment from the people. Let me show you why this is so in Stalin's Russia. . . .

The materials of part of the argument consist of two opinions with which the audience was in agreement: "Government ought to rest on the consent of the governed" and "Communism is bad." These became part of the framework for the speaker's point, which he went on to support, that Stalin could not afford to have free elections as we know them. The implicit pattern, which the student perhaps did not see fully and vividly, is, when stated explicitly, something like this:

> Government that does not rest on the consent of the governed is bad.
> Russian communism doesn't so rest.
> Russian communism is therefore bad.

This example illustrates but one pattern, the deductive; nevertheless, the principal points, arguments, and appeals of the persuasive speech combine structure and idea, statement and supporting materials, in similar manner in other patterns.

The principal forms of proof will be discussed in Chapter 21.

Persuasive speaking and informative speaking

In the persuasive speech, one meets both old and new problems. The familiar problems are carry-overs from the informative speech. About his subject, the persuasive speaker must know more or see more clearly than his hearers; he cannot therefore neglect any possible avenues of information—his own experience and the experience gained from others through discussion and reading. (The basic indexes to information may be reviewed in Appendix A.) Certainly, also, his delivery must be as expert, as direct, easy, and forceful in persuasion as in explanation. Furthermore, he will find that in persuasion he must lavish as much care in organizing materials, in rehearsing, and in employing language skillfully as he would in preparation for a speech of information.

Special problems in persuasion

The new problems of the speaker are created by the nature of persuasion. Perhaps a speaker must know his audience more thoroughly to persuade it than to inform it. He must size up his hearers in ways more diverse and more subtle than for the informative speech. The informative talk requires a speaker to gauge mainly the extent of his hearers' *knowledge* of the subject, so that he may select his materials and manage his explanations in keeping with what they know and understand. Persuasion makes the same demand, of course. But it requires also that the speaker develop method and skill in gauging his listeners' attitudes toward his specific goal, toward the chief ideas he selects to secure the response he wants, toward supporting materials, and even toward words, phrases, names, places, and institutions which he may mention or allude to. A speaker keenly sensitive to the experience of his prospective audience will inspect practically every detail of his speech, trying to call out favorable attitude and values, and to avoid giving needless offense.

Even the organization, management, and presentation of the persuasive speech as a whole introduce special problems. Most informative speeches, as we have seen, progress in a straightforward course. They methodically orient the listener, stating the speaker's purpose and the subject sentence, and making needed explanations which square away the subject before the development proper begins. They then march on point by point, detail by detail, until all is wrapped up in a neat conclusion. Their pattern and structure unfold clearly and often symmetrically. But some persuasive speeches do not appear at first glance to march so directly to their goals. Good ones always reveal structure, but the purpose and the proposal may not explicitly appear in the introduction and may not be stated, if at all, until the speaker believes the audience is ready. All depends upon the amount of resistance the speaker thinks he will encounter—whether his hearers are hostile, mildly hostile, skittishly neutral, favorable. He will show his hand only at the appropriate time. In brief, the order and form of presentation in persuasion are often markedly influenced by the audience's attitude toward the speaker's purpose.

The persuasive speech also brings to sharp focus the problem of the speaker's ethics and of personal integrity. Any speaker or any artist eager to please and to gain his goal sometimes must decide whether to compromise his standards in order to achieve his effects. In the next chapter we discuss the ethics and morality of the public speaker.

FURTHER READING

Bettinghaus, Erwin P. *Message Preparation: The Nature of Proof*. Indianapolis, Ind., 1966. Chapter 2, "The Nature of Belief."

Brembeck, W. L., and Howell, W. S. *Persuasion: A Means of Social Control*. New York, 1952.

Campbell, James H., and Hepler, Hal W. *Dimension in Communication: Readings*. Belmont, Calif., 1965. Section Two, "Persuasion."

Lund, F. H. "The Psychology of Belief," *Journal of Abnormal and Social Psychology*," 20 (1925), 63–112, 174–224.

Minnick, Wayne. *The Art of Persuasion*. Boston, 1957.

Oliver, Robert. *The Psychology of Persuasive Speech*. New York, 1957.

Scheidel, Thomas M. *Persuasive Speaking*. Glenview, Ill., 1967.

17

Ethics and Ethos

The ethics of public utterance is perhaps of greater concern today than ever before. Through newspaper, journal, and TV both speakers and listeners have available increasing amounts of information and opinion. On public issues of any importance, they are exposed to a variety of points of view and to special assaults upon their feelings and understandings. So for the person who wants to make up his mind on an issue, the problem is not so much a lack of fact and opinion as it is the evaluation of materials, arguments, and appeals. The problem of evaluation, of what to accept or reject, is made difficult in part by the quantity and variety of information. It is rendered difficult, too, because nearly all communications are partisan to some extent. They are almost bound to be partisan because self-interest rates high on any scale of values. Speakers and advertisers have axes to grind; so have more remote and less visible sources of communications: governmental agencies and bureaucrats, public utilities, industrial companies, entertainment and service corporations, and even philanthropic foundations. Hence in evaluating persuasive discourse, listeners (and readers) must be sensitive to the basic questions: Is the speaker credible? Is he trustworthy? Truthful? Competent? Obviously these questions apply to any communication anywhere, anytime. Less obvious is it that technically they are ethical and moral questions. We shall first briefly indicate how they are ethical and then proceed to examine on what grounds the conduct of speakers can be appraised as good or bad.

Concerning Ethical Problems in General

Our word *ethical* comes from a Greek word meaning character and custom. The Latins translated *ethicos* as *moralis,* from which we have our word *moral*. Today the two words *ethical* and *moral* often bear the same meaning. They refer to a general condition or to a state of mind that in moments of decision leads the individual to prefer good ends to bad ends, right actions to wrong actions. The most general of good ends has been regarded variously from time to time as happiness or well-being or self-fulfillment or the greatest good for the greatest number. The generally accepted means for achieving these ends have been learned and settled states of mind or dispositions called good habits, or virtues. In classical and medieval times the list of virtues included wisdom, or knowledge; prudence; courage, or fortitude; temperance, or orderliness; justice, or uprightness; liberality; highmindedness; friendliness; and truthfulness. These qualities helped to account for men's actions. They still do today. When a man must choose between alternative beliefs or courses of action, such habits applied to the case at hand lead him to prefer the good and the right to the evil and the wrong. Sometimes the choice is dictated immediately by a feeling of obligation; we must give a truthful answer simply because it is right to tell the truth and wrong to lie. Sometimes the choice is more deliberative: we ponder over what is desirable in the circumstances, and we consider whether others will approve our decision or blame us. It is worth observing, perhaps, that in decision-making, the virtues are sources of strength that compel us to choose; they are names for patterns of energy that are built into human experience and that induce us to act in certain ways. Every individual, then, has virtues and vices. The peculiar combination and texture in each person give him his character.

What are the sources of virtue? They are implied by the word *custom* and by the ideals that give rise to the rules, conventions, and *mores* by which a society regulates the conduct of the individual and by which the individual more or less accommodates himself to his society. "Thou shalt respect thy father and thy mother" is a rule reflecting the Judeo-Christian ethic. Other rules reflect the customs and beliefs of other religions and societies. In a political society, laws reflect the rules and practices that citizens are more or less willing to live by. The ideals of citizens, if they are written in any single place, are found in the constitution of the state. That is why Aristotle advised his students of speechmaking to study a country's constitution and its laws if they would know the general character and values of an audience. The highest ideals of many people come from the religion they profess and their efforts to live by its rules, which are the means of achieving the ends of a religious life. In the Middle Ages the goal of almost everyone was immortality, or eternal life.

The source of moral strength, therefore, and the source of the ends and goals of conduct lie in the life and experience of a society. Because societies are many in number and kind, ideals and ends, rules and customs, differ from nation to nation, culture to culture, and group to group. This variety has led many students of ethics to regard moral values as relative, whether the values are expressed in codes and legislation or remain unwritten and revealed only in practice. Accordingly, the standards we apply in making choices and arriving at judgments are those recognized in the rules, conventions, and practices of the society and culture to which we belong. "Slavery is wrong." "It is best to keep one's word." "Thou shalt not steal." "Treat others as you would wish to be treated." Often the standards do not resemble rules so much as they resemble the ideals of an ethnic group or of a national state. The United States, for example, idealizes freedom of speech and religion, and the protection of individual property, and recognizes certain inalienable rights of individuals. When the standards are clearly rules, they are regarded by society as important enough to carry sanctions; that is, they are enforced in some way. If the rule is expressed as a law it is enforced through the courts; if the rule is a fraternity or college regulation it is enforced by threat of expulsion or simply by the unfavorable opinion of the group. When an individual's actions do not meet the standards of his group, he loses esteem. Even the United Nations counts on public opinion to control its members' conduct.

Some rules governing the choice of ends and means are found in the principles and ends of a profession or art. Medicine aims to preserve health or to restore men to health, and in keeping with this end are rules, methods, and practices to which the physician is committed. Painting has its ends and standards. And as we shall soon see, so does the art of speechmaking.

The rules relevant to the selection of ends and means constitute restraints upon freedom of choice. Indeed, constraint is a necessary feature in choosing. To the age-long question, "How free is the individual to act as he desires?" man has never found an answer that permitted the individual to act without being bound in some way by the desires of others. Otherwise we would never feel that there are some circumstances in which we must justify or excuse our behavior.

In general, then, the idea of *ethical* implies situations that require choices which must be made with due regard for the ends involved, for the means and methods of achieving the ends, and for the rules and standards applicable to *all* such choices. The lawyer wants to win his case in court. Shall he tell the whole truth, or not? A young lady is courted by a suitor who admires wealth. Should she appear affluent when she is not? Implied in such situations is another feature of morality: What *ought* to be chosen? What *should* be preferred? Is what should be preferred the same as what one wants or wishes to do? Decisions that emerge from problems like these are called *judgments.* Our judgments, revealed in statements and propositions, imply the distinction between what *is* done and what *ought* to be done. The young lady decided to appear wealthy. Should she have?

One other feature of the ethical is useful to note here. Choosing, justifying, excusing, judging, and evaluating are all rational, not irrational, acts. Ethical judgments call for support; hence they are preceded or followed by "reasons" perceived as relevant and applicable to the situation. The materials of these reasons are based, directly or indirectly, upon values such as those sketched in Chapter 3. Values, of course, appear most concretely in the rules and customs by which a society regulates the conduct of its members. When a speaker is called upon to justify his choice of purpose or of means, his reasons represent an appeal to values and rules. There is no other way of justification, and ethical behavior has often been termed rule-controlled behavior.

One way of easily recognizing ethical situations leads directly to the vocabulary we use in evaluating actions and, specifically in judging speakers and speaking. An ethical situation occurs whenever we apply words like *good* and *bad, right* and *wrong,* to our actions; or when we say or imply that the ends or the methods of our actions are praiseworthy or blameworthy, desirable or undesirable, obligatory or not. In employing such words to describe the ethical quality of a speech, however, one needs to guard against undue ambiguity.

To say that a speech is good can carry a number of meanings: One may mean that the speech or the speaker has revealed the right values and virtues. Or one may be referring to the total impression the speech made on him, to the speaker's purpose or intention primarily, to the correctness of the speaker's factual information, or to the methods and techniques by which the speaker has framed and presented his materials. In these contexts the words *good* and *bad* are evaluative terms that signify general approval or general disapproval. The list of values in Chapter 3 might have been called a list of things considered good. Accordingly, the congressman who speaks for legislation to reduce poverty is praised for his good intentions. If the same man distorted information in order to make his case seem stronger, he would be censured for his bad methods. His choice of method, we would say, is wrong. The same congressman might be judged a particularly "effective" or skillful communicator; hence one could say that he had made a good speech, meaning only that people assign a high value to his skill. So when *good* and *bad, right* and *wrong,* are applied to a speech or to a speaker, one must recognize what is meant—whether the words apply to the speaker's purpose, goal, or intent; to his means or methods; to the quality of his information; or to his skill as an artist.

Concerning Ethics in Persuasion

How does a speaker justify his choices of purpose, materials, and methods? By what standards does a listener judge or appraise the ethics of a speaker? Perhaps it is evident from our discussion of ethical problems in general that not every situation nor every professional activity may have a neat, dogmatic formula which can be confidently applied to every choice and be slavishly, uncritically followed. All we can do is set out some guiding principles for responsible public discourse which speakers must apply to themselves if in our society they wish to be considered good rather than bad. The guidelines reflect two points of view. There is the view that rhetoric as the art of practical or popular discourse is a branch of, and is bound to, the art of politics, the dominant art of mutually cooperative living. And politics in a free society functions in ways that adjust the values of the individual to the values of the many and permit the values of the individual to affect the values of the many. There is also the view of the student of ethics whose business is to theorize about ethical principles and the grounds for their justification. The first view we consider now.

Respect for ends—social ideals

An ethic is built into the art of rhetoric and persuasion because the domain of rhetoric and public discourse overlaps that of politics. The overlap is in the region of ethical values.

To understand that rhetoric and politics share the same ethical values, one must realize that politics, taken in its basic meaning, goes far beyond the everyday associations, some of them unsavory, which cluster about politicians. It refers to the ways of living in a state, or national community. To see that politics is the art of living together in a state is to see at once that political life, like individual and family life, has its goals, values, and ideals. In a free society organized under a representative government which is responsible to the citizenry, the ideals of the political association reflect the ideals of its members. In fact, one needs only to glance at our own constitution to be reminded of some basic American values. We are told that we respect "justice," "tranquility," defense and safety of both the person and the state, "the general welfare," "liberty to ourselves and our posterity," the stability of financial institutions and the protection of property, and freedom of religion, speech, and press. We give allegiance to trial by jury and may not be "deprived of life, liberty, or property, without due process of law." The Declaration of Independence perennially reminds us that "all men are created equal," and that we all possess certain "inalienable rights," such as "life, liberty, and the pursuit of happiness." The language is that of the 1780's, yet it could be translated into a modern vocabulary of motivation.

The art of rhetoric is instrumental to political and social life. It serves the national community and must therefore respect the values of the nation. So the ethical ideals of the public speaker rest directly on the ideals of political life. This base is nowhere more evident than in any mature, fully developed theory of rhetoric. For example, the classical works on rhetoric, concerned almost entirely with persuasion, point out that the substance of arguments comes not only from the facts in a controversy but also from the desires, motivations, and opinions of the audience and that these in turn reflect the values which the audience has acquired from its social and political life.

Those works devote a large amount of their space to ways of discovering arguments whose premises reflect the moral and social beliefs of men.

In brief, the persuader if he be true to his art and if he place the welfare of his audience above his special ambitions has done much to guarantee his own ethical position. He is in a good sense a political moralist.

The thoughtful student of persuasion will not be misled by a certain plausible contention: the belief that rhetoric is a tool and technique, and like logic, has no inherent morality. Whether a skill or a technique is used morally or immorally, it is held, depends upon the character of the *individual* employing it, not upon the nature of the skill. The holders of this view forget that rhetoric, like all the arts, involves much more than skill. Central to art is the power of the artist's conceptions—his ability to select his effects and purposes, to search for available materials, and to choose and mold them to the task at hand. In other words, the power of *invention* is critical to any art. Inventing appropriate arguments and finding appropriate materials are no less critical to speechmaking. Style and delivery are important, but they are by no means the fundamentals of the art.

When one analyzes the moralities of rhetoric and of logic, one encounters no basis of comparison. Logic is a descriptive discipline, concerned with the correct, or valid, *relationships* among words and symbols. For example: If *C* is greater than *B* and *B* is greater than *A,* then *C* is greater than *A.* Or, if John has married his cousin, he will be disinherited. In neither case is any social or personal value at issue. The logician *as* logician is indifferent to whether John married or not and to the consequences of his not marrying his cousin. In brief, logic is concerned not with the value aspects of its symbols but with the *formal* ways in which they may validly be put together. But the rhetorician and the speechmaker, as we have seen, are directly enmeshed in value judgments and social ideals and, in truth, are so bound up with values that they cannot say the same things in Russia as in the United States. We approve of certain political and religious values that the Russians do not. On the other hand, logic as a formal discipline is influenced little, if at all, by any kind of political climate.

In probing for the ethical basis of rhetorical discourse, Professor Richard Murphy has highlighted the problem:

> Rhetoric is an art. It is a way of making things real in its own way. After centuries of opposition, it is now accepted that there is a *poetic* truth unlike any other form of truth. There is a way of presenting materials—a way which has been opposed and even banned at times—which is not factual, not chronological, not historical, but *dramatic.* So we must recognize that there is a way of rhetoric. It is a hazardous method, as all art methods are, for it means selection and arrangement and artistry in appeal. The Gettysburg Address as a piece of rhetoric could not stand the tests of the Institute of Propaganda Analysis.

Yet it has had through the years a basic rhetorical validity that we drawn upon in our democratic faith.[1]

A persuasive speaker should prefer goals and values which he believes are in the best interest of his audience. The purpose of his speech and the proposition he announces may be highly specific; nevertheless, his speech directly or indirectly ought to help the audience to preserve or to realize better the values that correspond to the basic interests of human beings. The speaker must weigh social values in relation to his private and personal desires. He may, of course, wish to speak in order to promote his own prestige, power, and influence, or to secure office and position, or simply to make a good speech and receive a good grade. He should satisfy himself, however, that his own motives are not inconsistent with the welfare of others.

Respect for standards and means

The persuasive speaker may satisfy himself that he serves his audience and not they him. Nevertheless, he encounters a second moral problem: may he use any means to achieve the purpose of his speech? In a broader context, this is the age-old question we have encountered before: does the end justify the means? The answer is not easy, especially when the question arises in our everyday intercourse with others. Does one lie to spare the feelings of his friend? Does the physician refrain from telling his patient that his tumor is malignant? The individual will often have to search his own soul, sometimes without a ready formula to help him. But when one focuses on the public speaker, who unquestionably has special responsibilities and duties to his audience, the answers are in general clear and unmistakable.

For the persuasive speaker, the end alone does not justify the means. The dominant principle has often been stated: "Evil means, even for a good end, produce evil results." The speaker must respect the means as well as the end. For a particular speech, it is the *quality* of the production that counts, not its effect. What matters is how *well* the persuader spoke, how well he measured up to the standards of speechmaking. In any art or profession, the standards in part relate to means and methods of production. They require that the practitioner have knowledge of his art, that he be competent in diagnosing his task, and that he select appropriate materials and use proper methods and techniques in handling them. The standards, of course, are set through long and repeated experience with the art and are perennially scrutinized by teachers, students, and critics. And because the standards have been determined by experience and their effects tested in thousands of cases,

[1] "Preface to an Ethic of Rhetoric," *The Rhetorical Idiom: Essays in Rhetoric, Oratory, Language, and Drama Presented to Herbert August Wichelns*, ed. Donald C. Bryant (Ithaca, N. Y.: Cornell University Press, 1958), pp. 141–142.

the products turn out to be successful far more often than not. This is why the professions think it both safe and proper to emphasize the standard of production rather than the effect. Sometimes a man may not secure his intended effect, although he may have done well. On the other hand, if he feels he must succeed every time, he is open to temptation and may compromise the standards of his profession or his art.

So it is with speechmaking. The standards of speechmaking and the quality of a particular speech are more important in judging the persuader than the success of his effort. Some 2,300 years ago Aristotle suggested the appropriate yardstick:

> The function of speechmaking is not simply to succeed in persuading, but rather to discover the means of coming as near such success as the circumstances of each particular case allow. In this it resembles all other arts. For example, it is not the function of medicine simply to make a man quite healthy, but to put him as far as may be on the road to health; it is possible to give excellent treatment even to those who can never enjoy health.[2]

Good lawyers and good surgeons occasionally lose a case. Good engineers are not always successful in their ventures. Good speakers do not invariably win the applause or the vote. Accordingly, the persuader's morality correlates with the quality of his speech. A speech is good to the extent that it meets proper standards; it is bad to the extent that it does not.

Some Basic Considerations. Most professional persons, as we have shown, are subject to a code of ethics which guides their behavior. A code for the public speaker would in part formulate the standards of speechmaking as unequivocally as possible. In part it would state some "Thou shalt's" and "Thou shalt not's." These would refer specifically to the speaker's motivations and to the breadth and choice of his materials. The fundamental ones we shall present here, observing that they are derived from certain values which the art of popular discourse shares with our political life. The values reflect the *ideals* of a free society under democratic principles.

Political scientists in democratic countries generally agree that the fundamental value in a democratic way of life is caught up in the phrase, "the dignity and worth of the individual." Two theorists confidently assert that the phrase expresses "the supreme value" of democracy.[3] Hence our society values a man as a man. Moreover, it is the dignity and worth, not of all men, not of men in the mass aggregate, but of the *individual* man. Our political

[2] *Rhetoric,* 1355b 9–14, trans. by W. Rhys Roberts in *The Works of Aristotle Translated into English under the Editorship of W. D. Ross,* XI (Oxford, 1924).

[3] H. D. Lasswell and M. S. McDougal, "Legal Education and Public Policy: Professional Training in the Public Interest," *Yale Law Journal,* 51 (March 1943), 212.

life, in mutual recognition of this fact, has been called a "commonwealth of mutual deference." Out of this great value, reinforced through the ages by religious teachings, has come our ideal of mutual self-respect.

Respect for Others' Opinions. The supreme value holds a moral for persuasion. It entails, first, that the speaker respect the views and opinions of his hearers. Those which are important and relevant to his arguments, he should recognize in his speech, either explicitly or implicitly. Views similar to his own will bolster his opinions. Views at variance with his he may be able to counter in ways which seem convincing to him. If he cannot, he should freely admit their force, rather than ignore them. The truth in a controversy is never all on one side.

The failure to recognize strong opposing opinions is usually due to two defects. The speaker is under compulsion to win and feels that he cannot win without ignoring competing views. Poor debaters are victims of this defect; good ones are not. Or the speaker knows that his own position and arguments are weak and cannot stand the light of stronger ones. A victim of shoddy, superficial thought and preparation, he foolishly hopes to cover up by omission. One of the persuader's test questions, then, is this: Have I acknowledged by statement or by clear implication the significant opinions of others?

Respect for One's Own Opinion. The supreme value entails, second, that the persuader respects his own opinion. He should himself be *convinced* of the soundness of his point of view. He is always in the middle of subjects and situations which demand evaluation and decision. He must make up his mind, draw a conclusion, hold an opinion. He must be able to say, "This I believe." Above all, his must be a *considered* opinion.

If one is to hold a considered opinion on any matter, he must expose himself to a variety of opinions and facts. He must survey the field. Unless he does so, he cannot weigh and consider conflicting opinions and arguments, become wise to prejudice and bias, and discover fundamental and relevant facts. An intelligent educated person has no right to an opinion based on ignorance. He cannot be blind or one-sided. He must think about the problem as rationally as he can. Ignorance is incompatible with intellectual integrity. As a professor of literature once declared, "My students understand that they must earn the right to think ill of great literature."

In the commonwealth of speaker and audience, a speaker defers to the well-grounded opinions of others and the audience defers to the convictions of the speaker. Yet neither party will accept compromise at the expense of principle and strong belief. Both will prefer disagreement to appeasement. Mutual respect of divergent opinions is the basis of our toleration of dissent and disagreement.

Fairness. Arising from the belief in the dignity and worth of the individual is the belief in equality of opportunity. Our society holds that each person should have a fair chance of realizing his capabilities, and every person, so far as is possible, should have the *same* chance. From these convictions stems a large part of the meaning we attach to fair play and justice. These convictions also make another far-reaching assumption: that the individual is capable of learning. Hence it is held that the individual must have widest access to information and knowledge, partly to benefit himself and partly to become an intelligent and informed citizen. In a democracy, as we know, the citizen holds the ultimate power. So a democracy must assume that persons can acquire the knowledge necessary to understand its values, its procedures, and its processes, and that they can form considered opinions and test them by means of discussion and action. As a result of such convictions, democracy demands that knowledge be made available to all, rather than to the few. It requires that the sources and channels of communication be wide and diverse, rather than limited and one-sided. It cannot tolerate restriction and distortion of information. Hence it must cherish and protect certain special freedoms: freedom of speech, freedom of the press, and freedom of assembly.

For the persuader's morality, these convictions yield significant corollaries. A speaker is both a source and a channel of knowledge and opinion. He has had special opportunity to explore and analyze his subject and in this way holds an advantage over his hearers. Hence he is obligated not only to express his convictions clearly and frankly, but to show his hearers fully and fairly why he holds them. He offers opinion and information, partly to test his own convictions in the public arena and partly to improve the opinions of others. In short, he himself is a representative of the democratic way of life.

Knowledge. The speaker, first of all, should not only respect information; he should possess it. He should have talked and read widely enough on his subject to know that he has not missed any essential facts and arguments. How can one tell when he has acquired sufficient mastery over his subject? A practical test of competence is contained in this question: Can I answer squarely, without evasion, any question relevant to my subject that a hearer may ask? An affirmative answer should adequately meet the standard of knowledge.

Suppression and distortion. The persuader, in the second place, must not suppress information unfavorable to his case, any more than he should manufacture favorable facts and evidence. We are referring here to material whose exclusion misleads an audience. The material of a speech determines the dominant impression or color of a speech, as red light added to green produces black, or blue pigment added to yellow makes green. By suppressing such material, the speaker stacks the cards in his favor. We recall a student speaker, eager to have his college adopt the honor system, who gave the impression that it was widely used among colleges. To make his argument weighty he named a dozen or so colleges and cited the circumstances and the year in which each adopted the system. Such care and accuracy, coupled with the number of examples, clearly impressed his hearers. But the favorable impression vanished when, under questioning, he admitted that many of the same colleges had abandoned their honor codes. One color became a quite different hue. The person who practices suppression is actually engaging in censorship for his own advantage. He is only somewhat worse than he who engages in censorship for the "good" of others.

Akin to suppression are distortion, warping, and doctoring of facts, opinion, and quoted materials. The persuader must shun distortion like the plague. He cannot allow himself to modify quotations to get the slant he desires, to juggle statistical information to suit a preconceived argument, or grossly to exaggerate facts without letting his hearers know that he is speaking in jest. Indeed, a public speaker, like the fisherman and the Texan, may appropriately exaggerate with humorous intent. But when he is a straight-faced reporter, he must report with *accuracy*. Thus he keeps faith with his audience.

Persons who are willing to practice suppression and distortion usually believe that a good end justifies the use of any means. Such was the belief of the late Senator who was determined to weed out communistic influence in the national government. His methods were sometimes reprehensible, as his senatorial colleagues recognized when they censured him. The student who wants to see examples of suppression and distortion in speechmaking should read the article, "Joe McCarthy: Brief-Case Demagogue," by Barnett Baskerville, in the September 1954 issue of *Today's Speech*. Its author draws upon the work of careful scholars who subjected some of Senator McCarthy's factual materials and quotations to painstaking analysis. In the speeches during one period, for example, it was found that "assertions had been radically at variance with the facts in fifty specific instances." The analyst of two 1952 campaign speeches concluded that they were "a most amazing demonstration of studied inaccuracy." A television speech, in which original documents were shown, yielded "no less than eighteen 'false statements or distortions' in the text which the speaker described as having 'complete, unchallengable documentation!'" It is well to recall the maxim that evil means, even for a good end, spawn evil. It may matter more *how* an audience is persuaded than *what* it is persuaded to do or to believe. The least a public figure can do is to keep the record straight. A speaker before any audience is a public personage.

Motivations of the speaker and of others. Finally, the persuader should help his hearers to evaluate two kinds of sources upon which the strength of his speech depends in part. One consists of the sources from which facts, statistics, and quoted opinions are drawn. The other is the speaker's own character, particularly his trustworthiness.

The speaker will aid his hearers to weigh any special bias, prejudice, and private motivation inherent in source materials. He knows that opinion and fact are unacceptable if their sources are contaminated. As an investigator preparing for his speech, he has had the opportunity of discovering whether private motives, such as those of self-interest, personal prestige, and personal profit, have merely imparted a special flavor to the source or have made it unwise to drink from. Such information he should share with his hearers, thus giving them a chance to evaluate the foundations of argument. Most audiences are competent judges of reasoning and of their own interests. But they cannot weigh the interests of others without the relevant information.

Similarly, an audience deserves some idea of the speaker's own motivations. It is easy for a practiced speaker to sound like an honest man. Unless he is well known to his hearers, they have little chance of telling whether he has their welfare chiefly in mind, or his own, or both. Some years ago a senator from California, both in the Senate and in his public utterances elsewhere, took a clear stand on the ownership of oil deposits lying under the ocean off coastal states. He favored state ownership rather than Federal ownership. Until the Associated Press dug up the fact, he did not reveal that for at least two years a group of California oilmen had paid some of his office bills and political expenses. Doubtless the senator was convinced of his stand, but the concealment of his connection with the oil interests had put his audiences at a disadvantage. When a speaker's private motivations are relevant to the reception of his message, he should make them known. He cannot be like the bad propagandist who conceals any motives that might hurt his cause. If a speaker is in doubt whether or not to include evaluative material, a test question may help him to decide: Would I be omitting information about either my source materials or my own motives which, if revealed, would damage my case? If he can answer *no,* then to that extent his speech will be in the tradition of public integrity.

Right and obligation. From the point of view of the student of ethics, persuasion is seen as a rational activity whose goal is "mutual understanding of the best thing to do." This view is represented by B. J. Diggs, Professor of Philosophy and Ethics at the University of Illinois.[4] As a rule, one does not arrive at an understanding of the best thing to do by intuition and feeling, but through deliberation and good judgment. So, in the first place, public

[4] In what follows we are much indebted to Professor Diggs. See his article, "Persuasion and Ethics," *Quarterly Journal of Speech,* 50 (December 1964), 359–373. Students may profit from consulting Karl R. Wallace, "Rhetoric and Advising," *Southern Speech Journal,* 29 (Summer 1964), 279–287.

speakers should recognize that they have the right to persuade. This right is a requirement established by society which, in effect, considers persuading a form of giving advice and counsel. The prime requirement of an adviser is that he be in a position to advise. He must understand the circumstances of others; he must have the appropriate knowledge; he must possess good judgment. Men in this kind of position have a right to undertake persuasion. But this right does not belong to any individual; it is not a natural right; it is a social right bestowed on persons who are in positions to try to persuade others to some belief or action.

In the second place, public speakers should realize that people have an obligation to speak under certain circumstances. Parents have an obligation to instruct their children and to tell them when and why they are wrong. Friendship obligates friends under appropriate circumstances to advise each other, to share information, or to exhort and plead. Public officials have duties to their public, company officers to their employees and stockholders, and teachers to their students. The obligation is built into the role one takes. Roles may be of several kinds; they may be institutional, as in the law. The prosecutor is bound to make the best possible case against the accused, the defending lawyer in behalf of the accused. Or roles may be established through custom and practice, as in friendship, sportsmanship, and the like. Whatever one's role, it may require him to transmit information or undertake persuasion.

The goal of one's persuasive efforts, in the third place, ought to be the right thing to do. A student speaker wants the support of other students in getting college officials to permit on the campus a chapter of the Du Bois Club, an organization believed to be communistic. Is the speaker's purpose the right one under the circumstances? On what grounds is it desirable or praiseworthy? Suppose the speaker expected to become the president of the local club? Would his task be more or less appropriate than it would be in the absence of such motivation? Suppose one had "convictions" about the war in Vietnam, would he be right in urging others to condemn the war? To resist being drafted? In such situations, obviously, one's good judgment is brought to bear and justification of the goal is not easy.

In some circumstances when one is considering the best thing to do, he may be guided by an appropriate "expert." A young student might consult an older student who has had to make a similar choice. Or he might seek the advice of a faculty member. Parents are guided by the experience of other parents, friends by other friends. Professional men—lawyers and architects, for example—are guided by the codes of their professions, and businessmen have recourse to the standards of chambers of commerce and to better business bureaus. Expert advice may be of great help; yet the final choice must be the individual's.

A speaker, in the fourth place, has to decide whether his means, manner, or mode of persuasion is right. As we have indicated, a speaker may justify his purpose or goal to his own satisfaction and that of others, yet an ethical goal does not necessarily justify the use of any means. The kind of means and methods one uses imparts a quality to one's behavior, a quality that is believed to be good or bad, right or wrong. In this context the notions of *good* and *right* may carry much the same meaning that is associated with the word *appropriate*. So in deciding how one ought to persuade, the circumstances of persuasion become important. Doubtless there are times when the mode of exhortation is appropriate and right. When people believe in something yet fail to act on their belief, exhortation seems to be called for. The smoker is convinced that he ought to stop smoking, but he does not. Obviously, this situation differs from that in which people have not yet made up their minds. Exhortation, then, must differ from deliberation, both in materials and in tone. Exhorting may be more emotional than advising; hence, it may require strong appeals, blandishments, pleadings, warnings, and even the use of commands. The speaking of lawyers in the courtroom is not the same as the speaking of preachers in a church, and what is appropriate to legal and pulpit rhetoric is not right in all ways for the political stump speaker or for the U.S. senator in the Senate chamber. The mode and procedures of group discussion are not those of advocacy; the conventions of private conversation in the living-room are not the same as the conventions of TV speaking, and the customs of public speaking in a republic are not those of a totalitarian state. Fortunately, the young speaker, concerned with the morality of his means, finds that audiences have standards and expectations about how speakers ought to behave in certain types of communicative situations. He can learn and become sensitive to these standards; they are to be respected, to be accepted in practice, and to be departed from only with special justification.

The expert in ethics, in the last place, stipulates that ethical behavior in persuasive situations calls for justification with respect to each of the considerations presented above. To justify is to state, or to be able to state if required, good grounds for the choices one makes. The speaker queries himself: Do I believe I have the right to persuade? Am I obliged to speak? Does my goal represent the best thing I can ask my audience to believe or do? Are my means appropriate to the circumstances? In finding grounds for answering these questions, there appears to be no pat formula. The best thing we can advise a speaker to do is to focus on the values he finds relevant to his communicative situation—values significant and important to both himself and his audience. Critical inspection and thoughtful consideration of such values should yield reasons that justify speaking.

To adapt one's message to an audience is a great art, and to succeed in influencing others gives great satisfaction to a speaker. Indeed, a speaker worth his salt wants to succeed. Nevertheless, on any particular occasion he will want to regard the purpose of his speech as a guide for the finding and selecting of materials, and for organizing his efforts, rather than as a goal to be reached at all costs. Minimally, his endeavor will be to measure up to the standards of the art of popular discourse. He will place these standards above the success of the moment, for by observing them he can preserve his morality and integrity. He may or may not succeed in a particular speech, but if he lives by the standards in each and every speech, he can expect his share of success in the long run.

Responsibility of the listener

Much has been said on the ethical problem of the speaker and communicator. Yet no speaker can be expected to bear the entire responsibility for the decision he tries to persuade his audience to make, or even for the action he may exhort his hearers to perform. Communication is a two-way process in a free society. Listeners are free to believe or not; they can choose to act or not. They are not compelled to follow a persuader's lead—unless the speaker is backed by naked force or no possible reasonable alternative exists. Adult listeners, furthermore, are sophisticated enough to know when they are being subjected to persuasive situations and influences. Few do not know what the advertisers are up to, whether the appeal be to the eye or the ear, whether the methods of influence be blatant or subtle, and whether the product be toothpaste or the reputation of a "public" utility. Is there today a teenager, much less an adult, who does not know that a campaigner for political office wants to influence his belief and mold or soften his attitude toward candidate and party? What reader or listener expects the political officeholder, nobly reporting on his acts or the state of the nation, to be uninterested in steering his hearer's mind or emotion? The man who steps into an automobile salesroom, or reads a newspaper editorial, or turns to an article on the controversial subject of the day places himself in a position to be persuaded. This he knows, and he knows, too, that he is not compelled to look or see. But when he chooses to become a party to the persuasive process he accepts some responsibility for its effects on him. If there is a naive audience, it would seem to consist of children, too young in experience and knowledge to recognize persuasion and its methods. Hence, it is that parents and teachers are held to have a special responsibility for their communications to the young.

Ethos. Embedded in the ethics of practical discourse is what has traditionally been known as the *ethos* of a communicator. It is the feature of speaking and writing which reveals the personality of the communicator. More narrowly and more accurately, however, ethos refers not to the total impression the speaker or writer makes, but primarily to the aspects of personality by which an audience judges a communicator to be worthy of belief. When Emerson told a speaker, "What you are thunders so loudly I cannot hear what you say," he was expressing anew what speakers and audiences have always known—that ethos exerts a strong influence in persuasion. It may indeed wield a stronger influence than other materials of persuasion, such as argument, evidence, and appeal to motives and emotion. When these ingredients are largely absent or when their value is difficult to judge, audiences have to depend entirely, as Aristotle observed, upon their estimate of the speaker's character. Quintilian believed good moral character was an essential element in the art of oratory. No bad man, he reasoned, could possibly succeed long as a speaker. A good man always had a chance of success, particularly if he had enough ability to learn the rhetorical art. So Quintilian defined the orator as a good man skilled in speaking.

Until thirty or forty years ago, rhetoricians regarded ethos in about the same way the Greek and Roman theorists had. Ethos consisted of the dimensions of personality whose union produced the impression of trustworthiness. The sources of trust were three: intelligence, virtue, and good will. The good will of a speaker appeared as friendliness toward the audience. The speaker wanted for his hearers the things a friend would. His virtues, often considered as his "moral character," were those we have mentioned on page 285. One or more of the virtues were bound to come into play whenever a speaker in the spirit of good will had studied a problem important to him and his hearers, and those virtues would be perceived in the arguments and appeals in his speech. The intelligence of a speaker was manifested in his "right opinions," that is, in the reasons and values which a sensible and honest man would be expected to produce under the circumstances.

Modern students of rhetorical methods, especially those who have been able to set up experimental conditions or otherwise to control their conditions of analysis, have been able to refine some of the dimensions of ethos. They speak of one dimension as "respect," perhaps a concept pointing to conditions that make for admiration and prestige. They speak of "likeableness," whose conditions are in part those of friendliness. They talk, finally, of "expertness," or competence to discuss the subject at hand, which refers to conditions external to the speech, such as the speaker's reputation and to the signs of the speaker's knowledge, prestige, and esteem as revealed in the speech.

Ethos has been closely studied because of its influence on the credibility and acceptability of a speaker's message. The higher or better the speaker's ethos as perceived by hearers, the more believable his statements and arguments.[5] Young speakers in particular should realize that listeners form portraits or images of them. A speaker, then, is deeply concerned about the kind of portrait he presents. He wants his image to reveal a creditable and acceptable ethos. To a considerable extent he can control the features of his portrait.

To earn the trust and respect of his audience the speaker will form the

[5] Students wishing to consult some of the research on ethos should read the research articles listed at the end of this chapter.

habits of a responsible speaker. He will know when he has the right to try to persuade others. He will know his subject and the values sanctioned by his hearers. He will be able to justify his goal and his means and methods of achieving it. In a word, he will make commitments to ethical standards and thus develop an image of his rhetorical integrity. This image is a unified set of principles, an ethical entity. This image of himself he applies to each case of communication, and in harmony with it he justifies his choices and procedures. Such a procedure gives his speech an air of conviction and a tone of sincerity, intuitively detected by any perceptive mind and sensitive ear. The effect of his image is often evident in the speaker's language, as well as in voice and gesture. He may say, "I'm convinced of this," "I believe that . . . ," "My considered opinion is. . . ." He may remark, "Now this is fact, not theory." "These facts are especially significant." "Let the facts speak for themselves." "We may interpret the facts in many ways, but they are plain for all to see." "For the sake of accuracy, I'll quote Professor Jones's opinion just as he phrased it." In introducing his purpose or position or proposition, he may explain the grounds that led him to advocate it. Probably it was Cicero who said that no man can speak more truly than he believes.

Another source of trust in the speaker is his accuracy of statement and fidelity to fact. Most veteran speakers will take pains to qualify themselves as good reporters and observers. They will quote rather than paraphrase statements important to their position or argument. They will describe how they arranged to be, or happened to be, in a special position to observe accurately or to form a good judgment. Or they will quote others, whom the audience is known to respect, to attest to their views and doings. If a brief bit of testimony is likely to be misunderstood or misjudged, they will carefully supply its context. The novice speaker should become accustomed to doing these things very early in his education.

The expertness or special competence of a speaker is known to others by repute. Most audiences know something about the speaker they hear. A promient figure has a reputation; indeed he is asked to speak, or is required to speak, principally because of his position and prestige. Local publicists just prior to the speech will remind everyone of the speaker's career and of the respect others have for him. On the occasion itself, someone will "introduce" him to his audience and will again touch on his accomplishments and talents. Young persons, particularly classroom speakers, have (at the outset, at least) no such reputation. Their listeners, of course, assume that they have prepared conscientiously; nevertheless, they have to establish their own expertness and good judgment through what they say. They can demonstrate that they recognize expertness by drawing on the expertness of others. They can quote experts and explain why their opinions and facts are trustworthy. They can use their own direct experience and observations as evidence and examples.

The good will, friendliness, or "likeableness" of a speaker springs chiefly from his attitude. He likes people and he wants to help his immediate audience. He manifests this attitude in part by physical signs. His face is pleasant, and he may smile. His voice is cordial, his manner direct and easy. His physical image proclaims, "He's an attractive and likeable fellow." In part the speaker's attitude of good will is shown in the ideas of his speech—by his purpose and by the position he takes toward the problem at hand. Both the speaker's purpose and position reveal that he understands his audience, and its troubles and its quandaries. He knows and respects his listeners' values and their special interests, though he may not in every case condone them. He may like the audience's local leaders and have good words to say of the community and of the organizations to which the members of the audience belong. The novice speaker will certainly want to do everything he honorably can to present an image of the man of good will and friendly intentions, of one who acts and wants to act in the best interest of his audience.

The primary components of likeableness are evident. There are, however, other less prominent features of the speaker's self-portrait, which are also desirable. These qualities are those which cause the speaker to be recognized as a man of good taste and of moderation. Student speakers, growing confident and often enthusiastic with increasing knowledge and experience, tend to overlook these ingredients of likeableness. For example, one avoids offending the sensibilities of a group by being risqué, by being irreverent toward people it respects or toward religion and God, by using humor when the occasion is solemn, or by attacking cherished ideals and deep-seated opinions by recourse to ridicule and to sustained satire and sarcasm.

An approach like this to the revered authority, the cherished belief or tradition, recognizes the hearer's attitude without condoning it:

> We all respect Thomas Jefferson's views on education and find them especially sound for his day and time. But we should not extend less respect to John Dewey whose mature judgment on modern education leads him to say. . . .
>
> We may all believe that the American Army is the greatest in the world. The opinion is a credit to our patriotism and loyalty. Nevertheless, if we examine the opinion carefully, we may see it in a new light.

One also avoids convicting an audience of ignorance. He presents the necessary information, of course, but he doesn't make the mistake of saying, "You didn't know this, did you?" He does not shrug off an objection to his cherished argument with a smart-alecky, "So what!" Rather he acquires an attitude which causes him to respond in a different way, "Doubtless your opinion is well founded, but my information has led me to a different conclusion."

The immoderate person, the superconfident individual, usually gives the impression of knowing it all. A trial in conversation, he is even more obnoxious on the platform. Signs of his immoderation are especially evident in his flat dogmatic assertions, in his sweeping generalizations, and in his voice and manner which plainly imply "*I* can't be wrong." The cause of such immodesty lies principally in his failure to recognize that he may possibly—just possibly—be wrong once in a while. He fails to appreciate what most educated persons learn: that in pro-and-con matters, neither pro nor con has a monopoly on truth. Our opinions can be possibly true, probably true, in all probability true, but never certainly or universally true. Scientific conclusions and laws probably carry the greatest certainty. The physicist may have proved that all bodies will fall in a vacuum at a uniform speed. But even for this observation he will not claim too much, for he will preface most of his laws with the phrase that admits the possibility of doubt: "*So far as we know,* all bodies will fall in a vacuum at a uniform rate." Why should the persuasive speaker, without the laboratory experiment to test his conclusions, be more certain than the scientist? The speaker is often recommending a policy—a belief or action that applies to the future. How can he, without being immodest, say that what he will prove, or has proved, will hold true in the future "beyond all shadow of doubt"? Even in the law, where most questions are decided by reference to past happenings and can be testified to by witnesses, documents, and so forth, juries are specifically charged to reach a verdict that is "beyond *reasonable* doubt." Doubt, accordingly, can seldom be banished. A sensible speaker knows this—and so does his audience.

So it is well to avoid phrases like "I shall prove conclusively," "No one can take exception to this conclusion," "This is proved beyond question." Let him be more accurate and more modest, with such phrases as "It seems to me," "Probably," "Perhaps we can accept this," "My opinion is. . . ."

The speaker who does not claim too much for his conclusions will avoid another sign of immodesty: exaggeration. He will not say carelessly that "all men are honest" when he really means that "most men are honest"; in other words, he will avoid the sweeping generalization. He will, furthermore, appreciate the value of understatement as opposed to overstatement. A sailor who described his rescue from a torpedoed merchantman concluded by saying that the experience was *pretty rough.* He let his hearers supply the high-flown adjectives, *harrowing, terrible, miraculous, amazing.* Indeed, it should be observed that one value of understatement is that the hearer is often ready to concede more than he would permit the speaker to claim.

In concluding, we allude again to Emerson's belief that what a speaker is may mean more than what he says. We trust students of public address are not reluctant to confront and discuss the problems of ethics and ethos. Choices have to be made and rationally justified. Morality is part of the texture of human behavior. The question before every speaker is not "Am I to be moral?"; it is rather "What is my morality to be?"

FURTHER READING

Baier, Kurt. *The Moral Point of View.* Ithaca: Cornell University Press, 1958.

Brembeck, W. L., and Howell, W. S. *Persuasion: A Means of Social Control.* New York, 1952. Chapter 24, "Ethics."

Garner, J. N. "On the Rationality of Persuading," *Mind,* 69 (April 1960), 163–174.

Hovland, Carl J., Janis, Irving L., and Kelley, Harold H. *Communication and Persuasion.* New Haven, Conn., 1953.

Johannesen, Richard L. (ed.) *Ethics and Persuasion, Selected Readings.* Random House Studies in Speech. New York and Toronto, 1967. In this source, see Sidney Hook, "The Ethics of Controversy."

Minnick, Wayne. *The Art of Persuasion.* Boston, 1957. Chapter 12, "Ethics."

Murphy, Richard. "Preface to an Ethic of Rhetoric." *The Rhetorical Idiom,* ed. Donald C. Bryant. Ithaca, N. Y.: Cornell University Press, 1958.

Nilsen, Thomas. *Ethics of Speech Communication.* Indianapolis, 1966.

Nowell-Smith, P. H. *Ethics.* Baltimore: Pelican Books, 1956.

Oliver, Robert. *The Psychology of Persuasive Speech.* New York, 1957. Chapter 2, "Ethics."

Packard, Vance. *The Hidden Persuaders.* New York, 1958.

Schramm, Wilbur. *Responsibility in Mass Communications.* New York, 1957.

Wallace, Karl R. "The Substance of Rhetoric: Good Reasons," *Quarterly Journal of Speech,* 49 (October 1963), 239–249.

Whyte, William H. *Is Anybody Listening?* New York, 1952.

Some research on ethos

Andersen, Kenneth, and Clevenger, Theodore, Jr. "A Summary of Experimental Research in Ethos," *Speech Monographs,* 30 (June 1963), 59–78.

Greenberg, Bradley S., and Miller, Gerald R. "The Effects of Low-Credible Sources on Message Acceptance," *Speech Monographs,* 33 (June 1966), 127–136.

King, Thomas R. "An Experimental Study of the Effect of *Ethos* upon the Immediate and Delayed Recall of Information," *Central States Speech Journal,* 17 (February 1966), 22–28.

Rosenthal, Paul I. "The Concept of Ethos and the Structure of Persuasion," *Speech Monographs,* 33 (June 1966) 114–126.

18

Basic Materials of the Persuasive Situation

The speaker establishes a moral frame of reference for persuasion in both weighing the ends, intentions, purposes, or goals of a speech, and in observing approved and sanctioned means and methods of winning success. His moral frame of reference should be his first consideration, not his last. His own values are at stake as well as his audience's. Gradually the student of persuasion becomes conscious of the standards and values through which he sees his integrity and by which he judges his communicative acts.

In looking for the basic materials inherent in the persuasive situation, a speaker encounters three questions: What is to be his specific purpose? What proposition is he to recommend to the audience? How is he to make the proposition credible and acceptable? The purpose and proposition emerge from the material and substantive aspects of the subject and audience. The means of supporting the proposition emerge partly from the subject and audience and partly from the forms that are applied to the organization of materials. Both the materials and forms of persuasion gain their meaning and power when the speaker focuses primarily upon a single dominant question: What is fitting and appropriate to the circumstances? The answer, in general terms, is to be found in the factual aspects of the subject which provide the focus of discussion, in the values that both speaker and audience perceive as relevant, and in the relative importance of some of these values as compared to others. As we saw in Chapter 3, values are always present in communicative situations and constitute the chief sources of interest.

For all practical purposes, the speaker's concern is to find out what is important and significant in a particular problematic set of circumstances marked by differences of opinion and belief. When he studies the circumstances that create a problem and suggest its possible solutions, he finds his proposition and information relevant to it. He finds also the values that support it and make it worth talking about.

Analysis of the Subject-Problem

The speaker finds himself and his audience beginning to come together when he discovers precisely what the controversy is all about. There are two methods of dealing with any situation marked by differences in attitudes and beliefs.

Dewey's steps in analysis

In thinking about any problematic situation and attempting to resolve it, John E. Dewey declared, discussion always proceeds through five stages.

1. Problematic situation: awareness of difficulty, confusion, uncertainty.
2. Defining the precise nature of the problem.
3. Discovering possible solutions to the problem.
4. Deciding upon the best solution.
5. Testing the chosen solution by putting it into practice.
   a. Resolution of problematic situation, or
   b. Nonresolution of problematic situation.

The testing process, of course, can be neatly controlled under experimental conditions only in the laboratory. Within the contexts of daily living, a preferred solution becomes a proposal, and this, if accepted, is put into practice to determine whether it will work. Whenever a proposal fails in practice, the failure itself becomes a new element in the original situation and an integral part of the problem. Our legislators as legislators rather than as citizens, are concerned with steps 2 through 4. By discussing, listening to testimony of experts and witnesses, debating, presenting bills, and finally passing laws, they attempt to cope meaningfully with social ills. The measure of their wisdom, or lack of it, cannot be judged until other organs of government apply the laws.

How does a problem arise in everyday affairs? First, some observer-participant gets the notion that he does not like what is going on at present. He becomes aware, more or less acutely, of some difficulty, trouble, confusion, or uncertainty in his present situation. He may not, for example, like the subsidizing of intercollegiate athletics at X College. So he complains about it where he can be heard; perhaps he writes, and has published, a letter of protest to the alumni secretary, or to the president of his college. He may encounter other alumni who have been vaguely disturbed over the matter, and discussion goes on. Second, discussion arrives at the point where criticism makes the problem definite in the minds of past and present students as well as of the faculty and administration. It becomes clear that the trouble in subsidizing athletics does not lie in the awarding of athletic scholarships, but in the awarding of scholarships for athletic ability only. Accordingly, the problem is made clear: "How can athletic scholarships be granted at X College on grounds other than athletic prowess?" Third, with the problem clearly recognized, remedies are suggested; perhaps petitions and proposals are sent to the college's board of trustees. Fourth, out of suggested remedies one proposal is adopted in some form by the college's central administration. Finally, as discussion on this matter subsides, the proposal goes into effect to meet its practical test.

Suppose a student were at X College when the discussion of athletic scholarships was going on. Suppose further that he had some knowledge and grasp of the general sequence of difficulty-problem-solution-resolution, or non-resolution. What could he elect to speak on to a college class? He would do well to select the aspect of the subject that reflected the current stage of thought and action. If the audience vaguely felt that the problematic situation was a real one, then the speech might define the problem and bring criticism to a head; a speaker would not propose a solution, since the audience did not yet understand the situation. Or, if current discussion were beyond the stage of definition and students were discussing alternative proposals, the speech might advocate a specific solution.

In short, Dewey's analytical steps not only help in understanding how problems arise and what happens to them but also in defining what view is the appropriate one to present at a given time to a particular audience. This procedure holds true for all areas of controversy—regional, national, and international. Indeed, difficulties and problems on campus differ from those on the international scene only in being closer to home, more concrete, and less broad in extent.

The traditional scheme of analysis

This method of seeing the essentials of a controversy is not unlike the steps of analysis we have just presented. It is, however, somewhat more detailed, and some speakers in their preparation find it more practical because it directs attention to the cause-and-effect mode of thinking and suggests statements (or their equivalents) that may often be used as the proposition or as the main heads of a speech.

I. What criticisms are made of the present situation? Are there evils—effects or conditions we do not like?

I′. What are the causes (both immediate and remote) that have brought about the criticisms and bad effects?

II. What policy, program, or action would if accepted and put into action remove the criticisms and abolish the evils?

  A. Does the proposal for remedying the evils make a definite and clearly recognized change from the present state of affairs?

  A′. Does the proposed solution specifically recognize new causes and conditions that will counteract the old causes that brought about the bad effects?

III. Is the proposal for change the best possible remedy?

  A. Is it definitely distinct and separate from other solutions offered?

  A′. Is it superior to any other remedy?

IV. Would the proposal if adopted set causes to work whose effects would be as bad as those it would remedy?
   A. What drawbacks has the proposal?
   A′. Would they really be serious and significant evils?
   B. Would the proposal be workable? Could it be put into operation?

Again this method of analysis is useful to the persuasive speaker in the same way as are Dewey's steps. The questions help him survey the possibilities of a problematic situation and help him to decide what aspect would be appropriate to the special audience and occasion. On one occasion he would find it appropriate to concentrate on one phase of the subject, at another on some other phase.

As a result of such systematic analysis, the speaker can locate the aspect, or aspects, of the situation from which comes the belief that is made explicit in a proposition. Because he works in this way, the proposition that emerges will be an appropriate one. It will fit the subject matter of the problem and the speaker's knowledge of the problem. But the proposition may not be appropriate to the immediate audience and occasion; and to decide this possibility the speaker should ask, In what state of mind or condition is the audience? Or, in terms that always have been associated with deliberative thinking, What is the *status,* or position, of the audience to be addressed? Except for questions belonging to the communicator's ethics and integrity, this is the most fundamental question a persuader can ask.

To help students cope with the question of the problem's appropriateness to the audience, there is a set of guides derived from the patterns of analysis already indicated. It directs deliberation sharply and concretely, however, by using the old medical analogy between health of the body and health of society.

1. Is the audience aware of ills?
2. If the audience thinks it is subject to ills, are the ills real rather than fancied?
3. If the ills are real, what conditions are responsible for them?
4. Are the ills remediable, or must they be endured?
5. If the ills are curable, what are the remedies?
6. Is a particular remedy preferable to other remedies?
7. Will the remedy (or remedies) cure the present ill (or ills) without introducing new ills?

There are no other fundamental questions to consider.[1]

The utility of these questions is all but obvious. Each query locates a potential proposition. If the members of an audience believe, for example, that the ghettos of the cities exhibit real ills, there is no point in telling them

[1] The advanced student interested in both forensic and deliberative analysis should consult Lee S. Hultzen, "Status in Deliberative Analysis," *The Rhetorical Idiom,* ed. Donald C. Bryant, (Ithaca, N. Y.: Cornell Univeristy Press, 1958), pp. 97–123.

so; nevertheless a speaker may believe that the ills are not quite what the audience thinks them to be. Or the audience may think the ills are curable, while the speaker disagrees. Or the audience may believe a particular remedy is indicated while the speaker prefers a different cure. So in inspecting each question in the light of what he knows about the problem and of what he thinks is the status of the audience, the speaker is likely to discover an appropriate proposition.

If it sharpens one's thinking to regard problems in terms of ills and remedies, it is helpful also to regard them as goods and evils. Such terms inevitably reflect the values and interests of both speaker and audience. To say metaphorically that the social body is ill and can be cured is to say literally that society exhibits conditions that are regarded as evil or bad or wrong, which can be supplanted by conditions regarded as good and right. So the concepts employed in the analysis of problem situations mirror the values and meanings that the speaker believes are important and significant to both himself and his hearers. The facts of the situation are essential of course, but they are perceived and interpreted in the light of values and interests. And among things desirable, obligatory, and praiseworthy, not all apply to a particular occasion with equal force. The facts of the specific case determine the priority of values. Today one may be interested in taxes for schools because he believes that the best possible education enhances his children's opportunities for success. Tomorrow he may be interested in electing as city mayor the most praiseworthy candidate he knows. So a speaker's proposition will state or imply what is good or bad about something: "It is wrong to prevent students from hearing all shades of political opinion." "To be exposed to all colors of political opinion will in general be good rather than bad."

The proposition and the reasons supporting it

A speaker—or for that matter, anyone—who studies a controversial situation becomes aware not only of his own opinions and judgments but also of the reasons why he holds them. His reasons may rest on data and facts, and they may also reflect values and interests which an audience considers good or bad. Some values lie on the surface of things and are easy to see; but many desires and motives are under the surface, in the causes and conditions that deter, impede, and block the normal realization of people's desires and goals. Because they are blocks, they are tinged with emotion. They function as objects of anxiety, irritation, anger, and fear; they are accompanied by feelings of insecurity, discomfort, unpleasantness, and pain. What is wanted, and what a speaker looks for, are causes and conditions that promise to remove frustrations. To be rid of unpleasant tensions is to experience pleasure. To institute conditions that may be expected to restore confidence, promote security, and permit greater freedom of choice and action is the persuader's business. To look for such conditions in the problem-solution situation is of utmost value to the speaker who wants to meet his audience realistically and to interest it. He will then be on the road to discovering the important, the significant, and the movingly meaningful.

We all desire good health, for example. But we are seldom conscious of this motive unless some condition, usually sickness, blocks it. Yet when we are sick, we are not so immediately interested in good health as we are in getting rid of the sickness. So we ask the physician to banish it. He examines the symptoms and condition and prescribes a remedy. If the remedy works, the condition has been removed which kept us from the path of normal good health. Thus it is that whatever is bad, or evil, or wrong with us—this commands our immediate interest and directs our attention to whatever causes seem likely to remove the evil. Furthermore, we become directly aware of a positive, long-run motive only when we refuse to confront the signs and symptoms of illness. It is then that our friends or the physician may motivate us by saying, "You want to be well, don't you? You want to enjoy good health?"

In these respects, the social body is no different from the human body. It becomes concerned and stirred up when it believes that conditions are bad or evil; then it wants to remove whatever evils interfere with the pursuit of its basic motivations—with the pursuit of happiness, of wealth and economic security, family welfare, freedom of action, and social and religious values. So when the speaker concentrates on the *problem* aspects of a controversy, he takes his reasons from the evils of the situation and their causes and conditions. When he deals with the *solution* of a problem, he selects reasons from those causes and conditions which will remove the evils. His chief thoughts concern a remedy or remedies. He looks for conditions which in all likelihood will make the remedy effective. He may also wish to consider their desirability, their connection with positive motives which provide the long-term strength for belief and action.

For uncovering conditions that relate to values, the following examples may suggest the direction in which to look.

Safety and Security: Is the audience composed of people who are poorly paid and housed? What threatens its economic security? What would enhance its sense of economic welfare? Stability of income? Insurance? Pensions? What of the safety of persons? With respect to accidents? Violence in the streets?

Health: What conditions interfere with the health of the audience or with groups it is interested in?

Wealth: What is interfering with economic welfare? What conditions are hurting wages, salaries, savings, production costs, and prices?

Family Welfare: What conditions are harmful to the security and stability of family life? What is injurious to the opportunity, education, and comfort of children?

Freedom: Who or what is working against our basic freedoms? Is the situation placing unwarranted checks on freedom of speech, action, or worship? Who is being tyrannical and arbitrary?

Opportunity and Justice: What opportunities are being denied to the audience or to groups and persons it is interested in? Who is discriminating against whom? Are conditions in some way unjust?

Reputation and Status: What is damaging to the status and prestige of the audience? The community? The nation? What is insulting to whom?

Conformity: Is any aspect of the situation damaging to some cherished tradition or custom?

Duty: Has any person, business group, labor group, or political group been shirking its social responsibilities, or been reneging on its public promises and commitments?

Honor and Loyalty: Have persons or groups involved in the situation been deceitful or untruthful? Has some group or party forsaken accepted ideals of truth, virtue, democracy, religion, or codes of conduct?

The genuine concern of any audience in a problem and its solution is grounded in such values and in conditions which interfere with the normal realization of them.

Values and emotions

The speaker who thus probes a problem will be more than realistic and interesting. He will also be on the way to acquiring the language of power and emotion. If the circumstances actually *threaten* our values and modes of conduct, there is danger, and we cannot avoid feeling anxious and fearful. In the face of injustice and unfairness, we become indignant. We take pride in our accomplishments, and pride also is the feeling which permeates prestige and coveted status. We feel pride in actions that are honorable and dutiful and we are ashamed of dishonor and unfaithfulness. When we think we can successfully cope with a situation, when we believe that we are ready to solve a problem and when it seems probable that we will, we experience confidence and feelings of security. (What emotions do students experience when they take an examination?) When persons unite, determined to face a problem and sincerely desiring to solve it for the benefit of all involved, they experience feelings of mutual understanding and good will. So the speaker who honestly faces a real problem, who understands it, and who believes that he can help an audience solve it, finds his thought and argument impregnated with emotion, and his language will rightly bear the signs of emotion.

The young speaker often errs in thinking that he must avoid emotion and feeling and the mention of values that stir men emotionally. He may even feel that it is wrong to reason other than "logically." But there is no valid basis for deprecating emotion generally, and there will be no ethical problem if the speaker's view represents his considered opinion. The sincere speaker cannot avoid emotion unless he schools himself against it. He will reveal it in his face, his voice, and his movements. And as he responds to his hearers and they to him, he will often unconsciously refer to "our duty and responsibility," "our sense of fair play," and to actions that are "right" or "good." A casual reference or a fleeting allusion to the football game last Saturday or to the dance of the weekend may rouse his listeners to a momentary sense of pleasure—or perhaps of regret and disappointment. When he asks his listeners to reason with him, to judge dispassionately, he is directly touching off a judicial or critical attitude, and indirectly he is complimenting them by supposing that they can judge critically. Thus he is rousing their pride—perhaps their vanity. If he quotes a well-known passage from the Bible, most listeners will experience a slight feeling of reverence—and so may the speaker, as he quotes it. The sensitive speaker cannot be a machine.

The divorce between logic and emotion, furthermore, is more supposed than real. When one sets out to reason most logically, one may discover that what he says speaks as loudly as its logical form and framework. Suppose one were speaking in support of the annual Red Cross drive and he decided that the effective line of attack was to emphasize the little-known service that the local chapter rendered in putting a serviceman in touch with his family when the normal means of communication had broken down. So he took this as his proposition: "The local Red Cross chapter kept servicemen in touch with their families when other means failed." He knew of a number of instances and arranged his material thus:

I. The chapter did this in the city.
   A. A well-to-do family was put in touch with their son.
   B. A poor family was put in touch with their son.
II. The chapter performed such a service in the rural area.
   A. A well-to-do family, etc.
   B. A poor family, etc.

The speaker concluded after four minutes, most of which was devoted to factual description of the four instances. In such a speech the proposition is a limited generalization that is supported beyond reasonable doubt by four instances, and the instances are meant to be typical because he selected cases from both the rich and the poor. In such circumstances was the audience responding primarily because of the reasoning? Or was the main effect secured through what was said—the ideas used and the associations stirred up directly or indirectly? Might not listeners be responding to their sense of duty and obligation to servicemen, their desire for the soldier's happiness and well-being, their affection for home and family relationships, and their sense of justice (no discrimination because of differences in money and position)? Even ideas themselves control attention by calling up our accumulated experience of motives, emotions, and attitudes.

Perhaps the foregoing illustration shows that the speaker need not be bothered with a red-herring problem that is often raised in persuasion: Should I use the logical means of persuasion or the psychological? A safe rule is that both should be employed—indeed they are employed—in any speech and in any communicative situation. The real problem for the speaker is this: Should I in a given speech emphasize the logical connections between my ideas or emphasize the ideas that will definitely call forth certain of my hearers' motives, emotions, and attitudes? It is a question of which process should be the more prominent.

FURTHER READING

Bettinghaus, Erwin P. *Message Preparation: The Nature of Proof*. Indianapolis, Ind., 1966. Chapter 6, on judgments.

Davison, W. Phillips. "The Public Opinion Process," *Public Opinion Quarterly*, 22 (Spring, 1958), 91–106. Valuable as a recent attempt to describe how an "issue" is created.

Festinger, Leon. *A Theory of Cognitive Dissonance*. Evanston, Ill., 1957.

Fulton, R. Barry. "Motivation: Foundation of Persuasion," *Quarterly Journal of Speech*, 49 (October 1963), 295–307.

Gray, G. W., and Braden, Waldo. *Public Speaking: Principles and Practices*. New York, 1951. Chapters 3–4, "Motivation and Interest"; Chapter 5, "Occasion and Audience."

Gray, G. W., and Wise, C. M. *The Bases of Speech*. 3rd ed. New York, 1959. Chapter 9, "The Semantic Basis."

Langer, Susanne K. *Philosophy in a New Key*. Baltimore: Penguin Books, 1948. Chapter 10, "Meaning."

Merton, Robert K. *Mass Persuasion*. New York, 1946.

Newcomb, T. E. *Social Psychology*. New York, 1950. Chapters 3–7, 14–17.

Pence, Orville L. "Emotionally Loaded Argument: Its Effectiveness in Stimulating Recall," *Quarterly Journal of Speech*, 40 (October 1954), 272–276.

Sherif, Carolyn W., Sherif, Muzafer, and Nebergall, Roger E. *Attitude and Attitude Change: The Social Judgment–Involvement Approach*. Philadelphia, 1965.

19
Materials from the Audience

The speaker who has committed himself to a proposition, or is close to commitment, has of course become well aware of his audience. He has ideas about how much his hearers know of the facts of the situation and he knows where his audience stands with reference to the problem-solution situation. He also knows a good deal about his listeners' values, interests, and emotional states. He will complete his study of his audience by considering relevant characteristics of human beings as individuals and as members of groups. The characteristics reveal values, interest, motives, and emotional states not otherwise uncovered.

Any method of sizing up the characteristics of an audience is useful to the person who is not in the habit of thinking that an audience manifests a kind of personality and that it may be as important as his. The categories suggested here can be applied fruitfully.

Age

Many audiences—certainly the radio and television audience—contain persons who are young, old, and middle-aged. It has seemed axiomatic, at least since Aristotle, that the strength and intensity of one's opinions and motives differ with age. Young persons, for example, are supposed to care less for money, wealth, economic security, than persons in their late years. Yet *Time* magazine in the fall of 1951, having asked ministers and teachers to name the dominant traits of postwar youth, reported that one of their dominant motives was economic security—well-paying jobs.

Life reported in 1967 that despite a small activist element and a normal number of rebels, students were still motivated by financial security. Seniors in particular, said a college dean, think hard about the draft and the moralities of patriotism and war; they look forward to professional studies, to marriage, and to prospects of first jobs. But if most students reveal standard motivations and values, a conspicuous number show special emphases. The militant activities protest against evil and exalt honesty above other virtues; they cannot accept the mixture of both good and evil in themselves or in others. The apostles of love and close friendships (they are called hippies, as we write) are disillusioned with everything but themselves; unmilitant and disorganized, they escape into fantasy and the pleasures of the here and now. Most students have their ideals. Alive to the ills of the present, they want a better world in which there is more freedom, greater opportunities for underprivileged minorities, and greater dedication to fair play and justice. They dislike agitation for its own sake, but they are ready critics and reformers.

In his famous characterization of the ages and fortunes of men, Aristotle thought that youth was more radical, more idealistic, more receptive to change and experiment, than men older than fifty years. He believed that men in their prime—about forty-five years old—standing between youth and old age, do not hold strong opinions and beliefs about anything. Not easily excited, they weigh and consider and make up their minds slowly. Their ideals have been tempered by long experience.

The worth of these generalizations a speaker should consider. The classroom speaker, in particular, does well to realize that the motives and opinions of his fellows may differ at least in intensity and priority from group to group and from those of his elders. If during preparation he discusses his own views with his friends, he will learn something of the campus variation in beliefs and attitudes.

Sex

Are women more susceptible to emotional appeals than men? Do they have few settled political opinions and party allegiances? Are they more concerned with protection and stability of the family, more concerned over opportunities for their children, more interested in beauty and personal attractiveness, than men? Some recent studies of the relative persuasibility of men and women indicate that women are more susceptible to persuasive speeches than men. They seem to be more readily influenced on specific subjects, and they tend to generalize more readily than men from the information they acquire. They tend to forget specifics, but they remember generalities and are good at transferring them to other situations. The research seems to confirm the judgment of a famous psychiatrist. The safest observation he could make about women, he said, was that they had an "almost infinite capacity to adapt" to circumstances. On the other hand, women say they are more practical, more hard-headed, more critical and skeptical than men. Speakers need to be aware of such generalizations and consider their relevance for particular occasions.[1]

[1] For details readers may want to consult Thomas M. Scheidel, "Sex and Persuasibility," *Speech Monographs,* 30 (November 1963), 351–358; Irving L. Janis and Peter B. Field, "Sex Differences and Personality Factors Related to Persuasibility," *Personality and Persuasibility,* ed. Carl I. Hovland and Irving L. Janis (New Haven: Yale University Press, 1959), 55–68.

Economic status

The "Have-nots" are supposed to be more interested in wages and hours and in economic security than the "Haves." They may be deeply concerned with improving their status and alive to opportunities for doing so. They may believe that every American has his chance—or should have; consequently, they may be on the lookout for the main chance, comparatively ready for change and new ideas—"radical" rather than "conservative." Men of means, by comparison, may be "conservative." Enjoying economic security, having position and taking pride in it, they may be eager to protect these advantages and skeptical of change and new proposals. They may also be deeply concerned for the welfare of others, as is shown by the hundreds of philanthropic organizations, foundations, and fellowships now in existence. The speaker, accordingly, should not overlook the "economic man" in his audience, and should try to anticipate what beliefs and attitudes he may hold toward the goal of a speech.

Education

Speakers should be aware of the *extent* and *kind* of education among hearers. Both the high school graduate and the college student will hold opinions on the problems currently being debated and discussed—the inner city, inflation, the coming election, foreign policy, education, athletics, modern art, and the like. Probably college education puts a broader base under an opinion than a high school education. If the top tip of a triangle represents an opinion, the college triangle is a large one, embracing a far greater area of information. A highly technical, professional education may also leave a man with smaller opinion triangles than those built up by a general or liberal education. Accordingly, in dealing with hearers showing distinct differences in breadth and level of formal education, the persuasive speaker, as well as the expository speaker, must carefully consider the amount of explanation, information, and data needed to support his opinion. Furthermore, the college student, because of his relatively large area of information, may be more critical of more things than the high school graduate. In listening to a speech, he may think of more objections; and the speaker, knowing this, may have to meet them, or else expect to leave his hearers with divided attention.

Whether a speaker should meet objections to his arguments or should exclude materials and ideas on the other side of his proposition has been debated perennially among students of persuasion. The advice today from the experts depends directly on the educational level of the audience.[2] With

[2] C. I. Hovland, A. A. Lumsdaine, and F. D. Sheffield, "Experiments in Mass Communication," reported in Carl I. Hovland, Irving L. Janis, and Harold H. Kelley, *Communication and Persuasion* (New Haven: Yale University Press, 1953), pp. 105–

educated persons, it appears to be more effective, under experimental conditions at least, to recognize both sides of an argument rather than to stick to one side, whether the listeners are for or against the speaker's position. The reason is obvious: the educated are aware of the many-sidedness of issues, and often, especially when the problem is timely, have been exposed to conflicting ideas and information. With less well-educated hearers, some feel it is better strategy to present but one side of the controversy, especially when the listeners are in favor of a proposition. A speaker interested in the permanency of his persuasion should know, also, that two-sided presentations sustain those who accept his opinion and prepare them better to protect the opinion when they later encounter opposed ideas. Speakers, then, as a rule do well to prepare their adherents against the opposition.

Group allegiances

We have already seen that the desire to belong is a basic human motive. Persons join Rotary, Phi Phi Phi fraternity, a church of their choice, a political party, a professional society, a labor union, a business or a corporation, a government agency, a farmers' cooperative. An individual who joins a group quickly identifies himself with it and soon accepts its goals, ideals, and beliefs.

The persuasive speaker should find out whether a number of his listeners belongs to such groups. The classroom speaker will know, of course, that his fellow students have fraternity and nonfraternity allegiances. They belong, also, to different religious denominations and to a variety of extracurricular societies. They may even wear the labels *Republican* and *Democrat.* By knowing what groups appear in his audience and by finding out something about the aims and beliefs of the groups, a speaker can decide what attitudes are in harmony or in conflict with his opinion and can select his supporting material accordingly.

To know that a sizeable number of hearers belong to a society often leads a speaker to the most usable information he can get. A professor was asked to talk to a group of his university's local alumni. A sponsor of foreign students on the campus, he decided to combat the skepticism toward the foreign students which he knew to exist among most townspeople. He learned that nearly a third of his audience belonged to Rotary International. From a club member, he obtained a pamphlet, *Facts About Rotary,* and became thoroughly familiar with the section devoted to peace and international friendship. As a result he found that each of his major points could be supported by Rotary's

---

111; William J. McGuire and D. Papageoris, "The Relative Efficiency of Various Types of Prior Belief-Defense in Producing Immunity Against Persuasion," *Journal of Abnormal and Social Psychology,* 62 (1961), 327–337; D. Papageorgis and W. J. McGuire, "The Generality of Immunity to Persuasion Produced by Pre-exposure to Weakened Counter Arguments," *Ibid.,* pp. 475–481.

own beliefs. By identifying his attitude with that of a part of his audience, he helped himself to an effective speech. In the two weeks following the talk, foreign students received more invitations to dine in local homes than they had in the two months previous. Individual members of a group take on the coloring and loyalties of their group.

Attitudes

One can view an audience, then, as consisting of persons whose opinions and attitudes are influenced by age, sex, education, economic status, and group allegiances. Another profitable way of viewing hearers is to classify them as *partisans, neutrals,* and *opponents.* This kind of grouping depends upon listeners' attitudes toward the speaker's specific goal.

Such a classification has special merits. First, it focuses the speaker's attention on *attitude.* His own attitude is revealed in the proposition he wants accepted. His hearers' attitude toward his proposition gives him the set of his audience and thus he can view his task concretely. A proposition, it should be observed again, represents the speaker's belief, and, as we saw in Chapter 3, every belief reflects an attitude. Indeed, belief and attitude are so intertwined that a proposition can be considered a verbalized attitude. Like beliefs, attitudes have certain dimensions: direction, degree, intensity, consistency, and salience.[3] The *direction* or stance of a partisan is toward the proposition, and perhaps toward the speaker as well; the stance of an opponent is away from the proposition; the stance of the neutral is doubtful. The *degree* of partisanship, neutrality, or hostility can range from slight to vehement. For example, the attitudes among persons in favor of a proposition will range in intensity from weak to strong. It is useful to know, particularly in small audiences such as classroom groups, whether one has a strong supporter with him—or a strong opponent against him. Then among persons whose attitudes reveal direction and degree, it is helpful to gauge the *salience* of their disposition: Are they more or less ready, more or less disposed, to accept one's proposition, or to act in keeping with it? Finally, the attitude of a hearer toward a proposition suggests his attitude toward related ideas and values. Attitudes show *consistency,* and the man who is against slum clearance may care little about the poor and much about his pocketbook. His opponent will feel some kinship for persons who favor better housing for the underprivileged and some hostility for those against. To look closely at the attitudes revealed by an audience is to develop a sensitivity to others that is difficult to acquire in other ways. During preparation for a speech, one's feelings for the appropriateness of idea and language is sharpened, and during delivery a speaker's sense of communication is enhanced.

[3] The terms are those of Otto Klineberg. See his *Social Psychology,* rev. ed. (New York, 1954), pp. 489–490.

There is another good reason for determining the attitudes present in an audience. When a speaker knows whether his audience is predominantly partisan, neutral, or hostile, he can seek answers to the most practical question of all: *Why* does this audience hold this attitude (or these) toward my proposition? What causes, conditions, and influences have made them respond this way? His answers give him valuable clues for the selection of his supporting materials and arguments, even for the selection of words and phrases. He can estimate the *quality* of attitudes and related beliefs. For example, are his partisans' attitudes the result of thoughtful consideration of the problem? Do his supporters believe strongly because of personal experience and observation? Are they the kind of people who have kept abreast of the problem through discussion and reading? In a word, are they judicious partisans? Or is their partisanship due to haphazard exposure to the problem? Are they indifferent or tepid in their partiality? Or are they in favor of the proposition because they have long been associated with the problem or with related problems and ideas, and have been conditioned by family or group allegiances? Can they be regarded as prejudiced or stereotyped partisans? Is the neutrals' doubt grounded on thoughtful analysis of the matter, or is it due to insufficient information, or to habitual reluctance to make up their minds? Many persons can't bear doubt and simply run away from it. Can the neutrals, then, be classed as judicious doubters? Ignorant doubters? Chronic conflict-avoiders? Can the attitudes of one's opponents be described as those of the judicious minded? The indifferent? The stereotyped? Using these groupings, it is interesting to describe a television audience listening to the President of the United States, or taking in a soft-sell advertisement.

Trying to gauge the attitudes of hearers usually reveals that all kinds of attitudes are represented—favorable, undecided or doubtful, and unfavorable. Rarely will a speaker find an audience solidly partisan, or neutral, or in opposition. True, there are situations in which speaker and audience share attitudes toward a vague concept or phrase. At a political rally of the Democrats, for instance, a party speaker will find all his listeners sharing his favorable attitude toward Democrats, but toward his special view—say, price support for agricultural products—he will not encounter unanimity.

Because an audience ordinarily will show a variety of attitudes toward the speaker's proposition or subject, it is not easy to advise him what to do. Should he plan his main attack on the neutrals? The opponents? Can he neglect the partisans? A safe answer—and a true one—is that all depends on the subject, the audience, and the occasion. There are no sure-fire formulas, tried-and-true recipes. The speaker's own judgment, common sense, tact, and imagination are at a premium here. Nevertheless, in order to be as practical as we can and at the risk of oversimplification, we shall offer some controlling considerations that may prevent the beginner in persuasion from stubbing his toes persistently.

Influencing Neutrals

The neutrals, whether well informed and judicious or ill informed, haven't made up their minds, and a speaker has a real chance to guide them. In general, these people are the so-called independent voters whose decision to vote one way or another—or not at all—decides elections. If they have had too little information to enable them to commit themselves, they will welcome information. It is therefore easier to cope with neutrals than with opponents, a fact that political campaigns invariably recognize. The election campaign aims at two things: to hold the interest and support of partisans and to swing into camp those who are vacillating. Three strategies should be considered.

1. *Select the primary objection (or objections) that has prevented decision, and answer it with the best evidence and argument available.* Often we vacillate because there is one aspect of a situation or problem that bothers us most. We say, "Yes, so-and-so and so-and-so is true, but there's one matter I'm still doubtful of." Some judicial doubters want to be sure on all important aspects of a problem, and if one aspect bothers them, they will reserve decision and refrain from action.

One of the commonest objections raised by conservatively minded people is this: "In theory," they say, "your idea is all right and we're for it, but you simply can't put it into practice—it won't work." Consequently, if the speaker can show how his proposal has actually worked elsewhere, or if he can draw a vivid sketch of how it might work, with enough detail to make the plan seem alive, he can often win favorable response. A sketch of the idea in action is vivid; it is a strong stimulus helping to govern attention and perception. Hence the greatest virtue of the public speaker has often been considered his power not only to make people *understand* but to make them *see*.

2. *Give special emphasis to one aspect of the problem or to one solution, and subordinate or omit other sides of the question and other solutions.* Frequently judicious neutrals find no great objections one way or another, but all sides and alternatives look equally attractive; at one moment they lean one way, at the next moment, another. Consequently, the speaker makes his solution look as attractive as possible by great concentration upon it. Of special importance here will be motives and attitudes that will give force and strength to argument and evidence. The attempt should be to keep attention undivided and to exclude competing, unfavorable ideas. This is not deception unless the speaker is dishonest; it is merely sensible economy.

3. *In addressing the judicious element, use as many facts and as much evidence as is appropriate.* Thus a speaker will tend to satisfy those neutrals who are undecided because of insufficient information. If one has a chance to discuss his subject with potential members of his audience, he should watch for such responses as "I don't know" (a sign of inadequate information?), "I just can't make up my mind" (a sign of vacillation?), and "I agree, but there's one thing that. . . ." (a sign that a special objection is hindering decision?).

Neutrals and Partisans

In addressing the neutrals, one cannot afford to ignore partisans. Two strategies are promising:

1. *Make the entire speech as interesting as possible.* Some of the ideas used to address the neutrals—perhaps all of the ideas—will be old and familiar to the judicious and informed partisan. One avoids alienating supporters by boring them.

In being interesting one is employing good tactics on the indifferent partisan whose indifference and lethargy keep him from active partisanship. Furthermore, by including information for the ill-informed neutrals in the group, one also appeals to the tepid partisan, for his lukewarm attitude may be the result in part of his not having had any real knowledge and argument on the problem. One must be interesting if conflict avoiders are to be roused.

2. *Avoid ideas that will alienate the partisans.* Suppose a speaker were arguing that longer vacations with pay would be a boon to labor and to the country, and some of the hearers were generally sympathetic to labor but didn't like James Hoffa. To mention his name or to cite him as an authority would hurt both the speaker and his argument. Let sleeping inhibitions lie unless there is a real reason for awaking them. This is especially true in addressing prejudiced partisans.

The speaker need not appeal to or condone the prejudice of the irrational partisan. The attitudes that feed his prejudice—such as loyalty to his class and social group—are likely to be so broad that he will apply them automatically to almost anything said or implied.

Influencing Partisans

Often a group is already persuaded of the truth of an idea or of the desirability of an action. The audience is overwhelmingly partisan. A speaker accordingly will concern himself with one of two goals: (1) to impress upon his hearers the old truth and thus encourage them to act upon it whenever the opportunity comes; (2) to urge them to undertake a definite and specific action immediately or in the very near future. In either case the speaker seeks *to intensify* attitude. Most preachers seek to accomplish the first purpose; they try to keep the virtues of right conduct and of religion bright and appealing to a congregation whose presence indicates sympathy and respect for religion. The advertiser and the salesman ordinarily have in mind the second purpose.

For sharpening the impression

The general method is to give the old theme new interest. Accordingly those stimulus-ideas and methods that elicit imagery and enliven the old idea with new information and interpretations are especially valuable. Two tactics are standard.

1. *Associate the old with the new.* Seek a new angle or point of view; use novel illustrations; build up vivid and sharp images.

A good illustration of a speech to impress is Bruce Barton's "Which Knew Not Joseph," printed in Chapter 25. Mr. Barton spoke of the value to business of persistent advertising, of the wisdom of being always sincere, and of the need for being warm and friendly—all old stuff to his audience. Especially effective were his illustrations—the humorous story which has real point, the familiar story of Joseph given a new interpretation, and examples drawn from personal experience.

2. *Apply the old truth to the present situation.* For example, what does the old Christian maxim, "Do unto others as you would that they should do unto you," mean to modern business (if one were addressing a businessmen's club)? To student relationships (if one thought it appropriate to talk on this to his class audience)?

For securing action

Again the speaker's primary job is to keep his listeners' undivided attention on the conduct desired, and avoid ideas that suggest alternative action. An idea of an action, keenly perceived and understood, tends to result in the action.

Of particular value in moving listeners to action are the following methods:

1. *Making the hearer imagine himself doing what is desired.* If one would get a friend to shove aside his books or beer stein and go to the movies, one might say, "Just think of that cool, comfortable theatre. Remember the last Disney we saw? There's another one on. And you know how gorgeous Racquel Welch is—not to mention Al Hirt taking off on the 'Basin Street Blues.' Just think, man!—comfort, Hirt, and music out of this world!" Of

course, pleasure and sex are effective motives here, but it is the imagery so chosen as to put the hearer imaginatively into the action desired that does the real work.

2. *Awakening the confidence of hearers by showing them that the action is practicable.* Perhaps nothing so promotes confidence as showing that other groups, similar to your audience, have acted as you propose and have enjoyed *success.* On an occasion when an all-fraternity council was considering whether to recommend requiring a "C" average for initiation into a fraternity, the strongest appeal was made by a student who took five minutes to explain that the adoption of the measure at X University had been a signal success. Concern and worry were replaced by confidence and considerable enthusiasm.

3. *Enlisting the pride of hearers.* Pride is an emotion centering on the self and is stimulated chiefly by the high regard in which others hold the self. Consequently, we cherish our reputation, are cordial to admiration, and expand under anything that enhances our prestige and self-importance. One can enlist pride by showing that the desired action will enhance or protect the reputation and prestige of hearers.

The speaker reminds his audience that others—individuals or groups—have regarded them as progressive, men of good will, or men of honor, and suggests that in the face of such regard they will not want to refrain from acting as suggested. A speaker who engineers an appeal to his hearers' reputation must always take two steps: (1) logically associate the action desired with one or more basic motives and values, and (2) definitely indicate that other persons respect the audience for holding the attitudes.

Prior to a local election, a housewife well illustrated both steps. A citizen of Brown Township, stumping for the bond issue that would finance a new school building, she reminded her hearers that they had always supported measures which preserved and enhanced the educational opportunities of their children. "In fact," she said in substance, "you have a reputation for guarding the opportunities of our youth. The *Record* [the newspaper of the neighboring county seat] last month said this about us: 'Some persons are asking whether Brown Township will pass the school bond proposal. We think its people will. They not only can afford it, but more than the people in most districts we know of, the citizenry of Brown Township are mindful of the educational welfare of their children.'"

4. *Making the audience face squarely the arguments—and especially conditions and facts—that call for the desired action.* Here the speaker briefly reviews the reasons that have led his hearers to accept the idea of the action that they have not yet taken. In particular he gives great emphasis to the facts —unpleasant though they may be—and to the excuses and evasions that have led his audience to side-step action. One of the weaknesses of human nature is to forget, to put out of mind, unpleasant evils that cry for remedy. We don't like to think of the deplorable conditions in the slums or the poverty

and malnutrition in underprivileged countries. We sometimes excuse our failure to hold an opinion as "having an open mind," our shady business deals as being "good business," our laziness and procrastination as fatigue or illness, our own destructiveness as students' fun, our dissipation as evidence of being a good fellow, and our cheating on examinations as a sign of cleverness rather than of immorality and ignorance! There are times when a speaker can and should speak bluntly and plainly; such a time is when people fail to act as they should because they shut their eyes to facts that demand action and indulge in conscience-saving evasions.

One of the most direct and telling examples of making an audience face the facts of a situation occurred in the course of Clarence Darrow's argument to the judge who was to determine the sentence of two college students, both confessed murderers. Darrow sought life imprisonment for the defendants, rather than execution. He said:

> Your Honor, it may be hardly fair to the court, I am aware, that I have helped to place a serious burden upon your shoulders. And at that I have always meant to be your friend. But this was not an act of friendship.
>
> I know perfectly well that where responsibility is divided by twelve, it is easy to say:
>
> "Away with him."
>
> But, your Honor, if these boys hang, you must do it. There can be no division of responsibility here. You can never explain that the rest overpowered you. It must be by your deliberate, cool, premeditated act, without a chance to shift responsibility.[4]

Influencing Opponents

Conditions

Ordinarily it is futile to try to make converts out of opponents in a single speech. People usually reverse their attitude toward a subject, or modify their beliefs, if at all, over a considerable period of time. The process of radical change is almost always slow and requires substantial education and exposition and persuasion, many speeches and books and articles, and much discussion. The process of change, too, is usually indirect, and the opponent hardly realizes that his attitude has undergone change. If he does sense the change, he cannot tell just when he began to lean in the new direction, or precisely what idea or event marked the line between opposition and partisanship. Accordingly, he who would turn opponents into converts, an unfavorable attitude into a favorable one, would do well to plan a long campaign.

[4] Defense of Richard Loeb and Nathan Leopold, Jr. In W. N. Brigance, ed., *Classified Speech Models of Eighteen Forms of Public Address,* (New York, 1928), p. 141.

The zealous speaker, nevertheless, need not feel discouraged about his chances with the opponents in his audience. First, even in the single speech it is always possible to lower the temperature of the opposition by a degree or two, that is, to change a strongly unfavorable attitude to a mildly unfavorable attitude, or a mildly unfavorable attitude to one that is neutral. Merely to soften opposition in a single effort is a positive accomplishment, and the veteran speaker, as well as the beginner, should regard it as such. Second, converts can sometimes be made on a subject toward which opponents do not respond emotionally and which does not deal with fundamental economic, social, or political questions having wide implications. One would be foolish to try to convert conservative businessmen and industrialists to state socialism, or even to persuade them to take a limited step toward socialism, such as to accept government ownership of public utilities. But on less touchy and fundamental questions, there is fair chance of success. The auditing of the finances of extracurricular societies, changing the grading system, shortening the Christmas holidays, altering rushing rules and the regulations governing parties—to mention only a few campus perennials—do not involve social upheavals. These are limited in their social implications, and opponents who are not strongly prejudiced can sometimes be brought to the advocate's view in a single speech.

There is another time when shift of attitude is quite possible: it is at that stage in a controversy in which discussion concerns *means* and *methods* of change, rather than the desirability of change. When almost everyone agrees that there are deplorable evils, that the disease has reached a point at which something must be done, discussion turns to the means of cure. Since most people have recognized the need for change, there is a big area of agreement. Hence, there is a favorable attitude toward solution of some kind, and this promotes rational consideration and choice of the best cure. Such an atmosphere even permits acceptance of a cure that is not perfect. For example, the United States Senate accepted the United Nations Charter, an imperfect instrument of world peace.

In the third place, one's success with opponents will depend in part upon how wisely he can shape his view to minimize opposition and in part upon whether the audience thinks that the subject is appropriate for the speaker and occasion. This is true especially when his view relates to a general concept or subject area toward which people have firm attitudes reinforced by emotion. We think emotionally on the "integration" of the schools.

Suppose one were to make a speech before strongly prejudiced students to promote a more neutral attitude toward the Negro. Instead of advocating a sweeping proposition, such as "You ought to treat Negroes on equal terms," he could work toward his purpose obliquely and maintain his integrity by speaking to this statement: "Negroes have made valuable contributions to our campus life." We cannot overestimate the wisdom of modifying a view so as to sidestep, circumvent, and otherwise minimize emotional opposition. Against strong emotion and prejudice, logic is of little use unless it be the logic of tact. In practice, then, one can be guided by this general rule:

> Take a position that does not require hearers among whom are influential opponents to make a radical change from their habitual conduct and attitude; select a proposition that requires but little reorientation of habits of action and belief. Be moderate rather than extreme.

Methods

The Judicious Opponent. There are four strategies to consider.

1. *Meet the chief objections of the judicious opponent, so far as they can be discovered through discussion and reading.* The judicious opponent has weighed and considered the question under discussion and, in all probability, has looked at it from all sides—at least he believes so. Since he has reasoned to a conclusion and respects reason, the speaker can meet him directly on rational grounds. He can recognize his objections and reason with him directly about them.

In meeting the objections of opponents, consider carefully the following:

> *a.* Can a major objection be handled early in the speech? Can it be worked in so that it is logically relevant to the development of the first point?
> *b.* Can one admit the truth of a main objection or opposing argument without hurting the main arguments—without being inconsistent?

An admission has two psychological advantages: it recognizes and removes a strong competing idea from an opponent's mind and thus allows him to listen; it compliments an opponent to be told that he is right, and thus enlists pride for the speaker instead of against him.

If a strong opposing argument cannot be admitted as true, is it possible to weaken the objection by showing it rests on:

> Inadequate information and facts? (If so, clearly assert this, and proceed with the new and better facts.)
>
> Unacceptable authority and testimony? (If so, definitely assert this, explain why, and if possible cite a better authority.)
>
> Unsound inference? (If so, state precisely what is wrong with the reasoning and explain why.)

2. *New facts and new conditions may lead an opponent to reconsider his opinions.* The judicious opponent is usually willing to consider any and all

material that is relevant to the problem. He has tried to overlook nothing important in making up his mind. Yet often on problems that keep recurring in different form, such as the best kind of taxation, he has been unable to keep up-to-date and hasn't fully realized that fact. For instance, if he were a great believer in a tax on personal property and if in preparing to argue against such a tax or in favor of a better tax a speaker discovered that the personal property tax recently had been yielding less and less revenue to the state or locality imposing it, the figures showing such a decrease might well be an effective wedge in getting him to reconsider the problem.

3. *Use ideas and opinions shared by speaker and opponent.* Those experienced in conciliation and arbitration techniques say that conflict is intensified when contending parties emphasize their disagreements and that opposition is minimized when agreements are clearly discerned. Consequently, a speaker would be wise to determine what he and his opponents have in common and briefly but clearly to review the common ground early in the speech, probably in the introduction.

Look for agreement particularly in the following areas:

> In the areas through which the controversy and discussion have already passed. If one is concentrating on a particular solution to a problem, presumably all parties agree on certain evils that call for remedy. If everyone agrees that a solution is practicable, presumably there is some agreement that the solution is desirable and holds positive benefits.
>
> In those motives, emotions, and values that are relevant to the subject. All may agree that the solution must be *just* to all parties affected, that it should foster rather than injure our economic welfare, that taxation without representation is tyranny, and so on. Humor may furnish a mutual emotional experience, and the mention of mutual interests may have a unifying effect.

Although emphasizing the grounds of agreement is perhaps most effective with audiences containing important opponents, it is also effective with neutrals and with partisans from whom enthusiasm and action are desired. Indeed, it is so generally useful that Henry Ward Beecher, after getting the idea from the sermons of the Apostles, made it a rhetorical "must" for most of his own sermons. Beecher's words tell of his discovery and of his delight over its success:

> . . . I studied the sermons until I got this idea: That the apostles were accustomed first to feel for a ground on which the people and they stood together; a common ground where they could meet. Then they heaped up a large number of the particulars of knowledge that belonged to everybody; and when they

got that knowledge, which everybody would admit, placed in a proper form before their minds, then they brought it to bear upon them with all their excited heart and feeling. That was the first definite idea of taking aim that I had in my mind.

"Now," said I, "I will make a sermon so." . . . First I sketched out the things we all know. . . . And in that way I went on with my "You all knows," until I had about forty of them. When I got through with that, I turned round and brought it to bear upon them with all my might; and there were seventeen men awakened under that sermon. I never felt so triumphant in my life. I cried all the way home. I said to myself: "Now I know how to preach."[5]

4. *Preliminary explanatory material often minimizes opposition and aids in finding common ground.* Unnecessary disagreements often arise because contending parties don't understand exactly what they think they disagree about, as in an informal discussion which suddenly takes this turn: "You say that Professor Blank gives hard quizzes. What do you mean by a 'hard quiz'? Oh, if you mean that he emphasizes details, I quite agree." As soon as a common ground of understanding is reached, differences of opinion may disappear, or at least speaker and audience rapidly get on to the real issue—the essential point of difference that must be fully discussed.

Accordingly, always consider using material that will accomplish the following:

a. Definition of the language of the proposition. All the resources of definition should be considered here; one should review what has already been said about definition in chapter 7. Especially valuable in persuasion is definition by negation—telling hearers what one does *not* mean—for this method sometimes removes indirectly a critic's objection.

b. Exclusion of nonessential matters. To exclude ideas that are not essential to the purpose and to the argument has the same value as definition by negation. It widens the area of agreement and narrows the area of disagreement and conflict. Two ways of ruling out nonessentials are always worth considering:

Use of admissions. The principle, already referred to earlier, is this: Admit the truth of an opposition argument whenever you can. Otherwise, hearers may infer that the speaker thinks the truth is all on his side, that he is stupid and narrow-minded. Indeed, they might be right, for the person who has no admissions to make usually has not looked into the problem far enough to find the truth on the other side.

Exclusion of irrelevancies. Omit what is logically irrelevant to the proposition. Recently a student spoke on this statement: "Labor unions have given

[5] *Yale Lectures on Preaching* (New York, 1873), I, 10–11.

labor a chance to compete with organized employers." He not only defined what he meant by "labor union" and "organized employers," but before going on he carefully pointed out certain ideas relating to the larger problems of capital and labor relationships with which he was not concerned. He said, in effect: "I am not concerned this morning with whether labor has used its new power wisely, nor do I wish now to discuss whether labor was pampered by the New Deal. Nor shall I consider whether labor is justified in often insisting on a closed shop. I am interested now only in whether the organization of labor has helped to balance the power and influence of the large employer." Such elimination of what is irrelevant to the speaker's special purpose encourages listeners who have prejudices and opinions for or against labor and capital to set them aside and to consider the particular problem that the speaker thinks is appropriate.

The Casual Opponent and the Prejudiced Opponent. If a study of an audience reveals that judicious opponents are in a minority, the speaker does not have an insuperable problem. First, the casual opponent—he who has happened to hear more against the speaker's opinion than for it—probably lacks information. Consequently, the reasoning and information designed for neutrals will be fairly effective for him. Secondly, since a speaker is not likely to make a convert out of a prejudiced opponent, his job is simply to avoid rousing his prejudices and increasing his opposition. A speaker cannot disregard and neglect the prejudiced listener; he takes care not to offend him by a careless remark or phrase.

Stability of belief

In trying to understand audiences, one runs into what can be termed hard-core beliefs or stereotypes, marked by emotion and strong feelings of like or dislike. They resemble prejudices, for their strength is in part emotional; they have the color and feel of respectable opinions, for some of them have the weight of personal history behind them. Others when verbalized will have the force of widely sanctioned value statements. They will range from the highly personal, "It is wrong for me to criticize my family (or church)," to a social ideal, "Promises ought to be kept." They have been born through daily talk and reading in our formative years. We have been conditioned to them through family associations, our early studies, and the company of our peers. So in contemplating his hearers, a speaker should try to decide not only what among their beliefs may be relevant to his proposition and to the problem situation it reflects; he should also try to decide what beliefs are hard-core. We cling longest and hardest to such beliefs. They are unassailable, except through the forces of social attrition, unnoticed, over a long period of time. Once the hard-core beliefs are identified, the speaker should avoid those unfavorable to his cause. He can, on the other hand, select those favorable to him and through them identify his proposition with his audience's most deep-seated values.

FURTHER READING

ALBIG, William. *Modern Public Opinion.* New York, 1956. Chapters 15–16, about groups and group methods.

BACON, Francis. *The New Organon and Related Writings.* Ed. Fulton H. Anderson. Indianapolis: The Liberal Arts Press, 1960. For Bacon's account of the Idols of men's minds, see pp. 47–66.

DOOB, W. W. *Public Opinion and Propaganda.* New York, 1948.

EISENSON, Jon, AUER, J. Jeffery, and IRWIN, John V. *The Psychology of Communication.* New York, 1963. Chapters 5–8.

HALL, C. S., and LINDZEY, G. *Theories of Personality.* New York, 1957.

HOLLINGSWORTH, H. L. *The Psychology of the Audience.* New York, 1935. Chapter 3, "Types of Audiences."

KATZ, Daniel. "The Functional Approach to the Study of Attitudes, *Public Opinion Quarterly,* 24 (1960), 163–204.

LIPPMANN, Walter. *Public Opinion.* Baltimore: Pelican Books, 1946. On conditions and methods of influencing the mass audience.

MASLOW, Abraham H. *Motivation and Personality.* New York, 1954.

MERTON, Robert K. *Social Theory and Social Structure.* Glencoe, Ill., 1957.

OLIVER, Robert. *The Psychology of Persuasive Speech.* New York, 1957. Chapters 9–12, on modes of appeal.

WINANS, James A. *Public Speaking.* New York, 1917. Chapter 8, "Influencing Conduct."

20

Selection of Materials and Strategies

It is from a problematic set of circumstances, from the facts and values inherent in it, and from the status of the audience with respect to it, that the materials of persuasion are uncovered. Useful as it is for a speaker to become fully aware of the available materials of persuasion in any particular case, it is obvious that not all materials can be employed, or should be. Not all of them will be found to be equally appropriate, for reasons of time, taste, probable effectiveness, and other limiting conditions. So the speaker must select, choosing the materials and strategies he thinks will best serve his purpose and proposition.

In making his choices, he will rely chiefly on the good judgment and good sense he has gained through knowing as much about himself, his subject, his audience, and his art as he possibly can. We are, it is true, gradually learning a good deal about specific persuasive effects and their causes when specific conditions of persuasion can be manipulated and controlled. Students of the communication process have asked questions like the following: What means or stimulus-condition produces what change in a particular belief or attitude of a person or audience in what circumstances? But specialized studies have not yet been numerous enough to provide us with many widely applicable rules. By and large, the man who engages in public discussion and public discourse—of which public speaking is but one form—must depend on principles drawn from practical experience. We must be content here with suggesting some general means of persuasion, hoping that they will assist student speakers develop a sense of the appropriate and fitting.

Attention

One of the means of persuasion is through attention (see pages 27–43). Prerequisite to any influencing of belief and attitude is awareness by the audience of what change in its opinions and feelings it is being asked to make. The proposition and its context must ordinarily be clear and certainly must be meaningful if credibility and acceptance are at issue. So the fundamental task of a communicator is to win attention and keep it. This is something more, however, than merely directing attention to the speaker and what he is saying. It involves the focusing of attention in ways that are favorable to the proposition and that keep interest undivided and undistracted from the business at hand. It may have been William James, one of this country's great psychologists, who first maintained that action and belief in specific cases follow upon undivided attention. Rivet attention, keep it, and the desired response follows—at least for the immediate future. One of the foremost modern teachers of public speaking, James A. Winans, based his principles of persuasion on William James's teachings:

> It should be borne in mind that in persuasion we are seeking more than attention in the ordinary sense; we must win favorable attention to our proposals. Just to keep people listening is, after all, comparatively easy. It can be done by stunts, by literally or figuratively standing on one's head, slapping the auditors in the face, or being "funny" in any sense of the word. But some methods attract attention to themselves rather than to the ideas expressed, and some arouse unfavorable attention. If in urging a man to vote my ticket I call him a fool for resisting, I shall gain his lively interest, but hardly his favorable attention to my plea.
>
> Whatever means we employ we . . . are seeking to induce our hearers to give their minds wholly to our proposal, and to keep out, or drive out, of their minds objections, doubts, hostile feelings. . . .[1]

Consequently, the speechmaker should survey his materials with deliberation and consider which seem most likely to secure fair, favorable, and undivided attention. In considering materials, he should remember that attention and interest go hand in hand. To touch upon the interests of hearers is to win their attention. And we remark again that to interest an audience is to draw upon the values and meanings that both the speaker and his hearers regard as important and significant to the situation that unites them.

Attention, emotion, and values

Few conditions so completely absorb attention mechanisms as do emotional states and values closely linked with them. In selecting and using emotion-impregnated materials, speakers should be aware of two strategies: direct presentation of the ideas, in which the emotion or value is named and becomes a manifest ingredient of the argument; and indirect ways of presentation, in which the materials appear in descriptive and narrative frames. The appropriate strategy depends on the audience and occasion and the speaker's sense of effectiveness.

In the direct appeal the motive or value is named and may even be identi-

[1] James A. Winans, *Speech-Making* (New York, 1938), p. 263.

fied or defined briefly; then the speaker explicitly applies it to his point. The process is simply one of applying the general to the particular:

Tipping is unfair to the recipients, for

1. Any situation in which competitors do not have equal opportunity is unfair (and)
2. This is the situation when workers compete for the customer's favor.

The general statement (1) definitely reminds the hearer of what unfairness is. Sometimes it may be amplified by an apt illustration so that the hearer fully appreciates what the value involves. The specific statement (2) directs attention toward the point to be made and thus brings the value to bear directly. This, too, may be amplified and discussed as much as is necessary. If the speaker *omits* the general statement and its attendant ideas, the appeal is less direct.

One way of managing an indirect but strong appeal is by describing through the use of details or illustration the situation that provokes the desired emotion. The following narrative passage is from the speech of a student who had worked in a large department store and who tried to move his hearers to buy intelligently and to support Federal legislation for the standardization of goods.[2]

> My counters were stacked with goods—some good, some excellent, some poorly made, some shoddy, some shopworn. The store made extremely high profits on its shoddy merchandise, and I was told that I would receive a commission whenever I sold some of it. Of course, the store wanted particularly to sell this shoddy merchandise because it was high-profit inferior goods. So my job was to sell a customer a shoddy shirt rather than a good one. Then the store would get its high profits, and I would get my commission. What the customer got—well, that was nobody's business. But at least I would keep my job. For if I didn't sell this shoddy material—and lots of it—I not only would not get my commission—I would be fired. Each evening I was to turn in a special report of just how much of it I had sold during the day.
>
> Now, I soon learned that customers are particularly likely to buy if they think that goods are *on sale*. So my job was to make a customer believe that our regular three-for-one-dollar socks were ordinarily fifty cents. Then maybe she'd take a dozen pairs rather than three. Incidentally, on one occasion these socks, that were always regularly three for one dollar, were advertised as being regularly seventy-nine cent hose selling, for tomorrow only, for fifty cents. And on this occasion the boss humorously remarked that they cost the store only four cents a pair!
>
> A customer approaches me. Am I crazy, or is she a fly, and *am* I a spider, and *is* she coming into my parlor. She wants to buy a shirt. Immediately I think of the poor-moving, shoddy, high-profit shirts. There is one type of shirt

[2] *Prize-Winning Orations,* ed. E. E. Anderson. *Year Book of College Oratory,* IX (New York, 1937), pp. 252–254.

on which I receive a thirty-five cent commission. Besides, the boss is watching. I must sell her one of these. I place three shirts on the counter—this one is one of them. I point out that the shirt (on which incidentally I receive the commission) has all the latest features, that it will give that "swank" appearance, that it is far superior to the other two shirts, that only yesterday I bought six of them myself because they are such fine bargains at this price, that Robert Taylor wears them exclusively. The customer takes five of the shirts. She wants to buy some ties to go with them. Now, I really want to give her a "break." But the boss is still watching. The ties on which I receive a twenty-five cent commission are beautiful, even if I have nightmares on occasions just from selling them. After I have pointed out that these ties really are the latest fall fashion, that they *really have* just come in, that it *really was* one of them that Clarke Gable wore in the second scene of his last picture—after I have pointed out these things to her, the customer takes one for each shirt and also one for Uncle Lem who will have a birthday soon. Poor Uncle Lem! As a matter of fact, these ties have a very poor lining and because of the poor quality of the material out of which they are made, will never tie correctly. The shirts are of a very poor quality. They have a variable thread, making for very poor wear, and have a very poor finish which, when the customer inquires about it and complains about it, I tell her is the famous new "Krinkleweav" which every one is now wearing.

A special sale day comes. Much advertising appears in the newspapers. The city is blanketed with special sixteen-page circulars. Mrs. Van Gotrox, society matron, is persuaded to make a statement. She says, "I will spend *my* day tomorrow purchasing the splendid bargains at the Super Deluxe Department Store." Two-fifty and one-sixty-five shirts are advertised as being one dollar for tomorrow only. Two-fifty pajamas are to be one-sixty-nine. Now, the night before the sale, great preparations are made. True, a few of the shoddy one-sixty-five shirts are placed on the counter at one dollar—the shoddy ones. Then several thousand cellophane-wrapped, glittering, special-shipment, variable thread, poor finish, *always one dollar* shirts are placed on the counter. These are the two-fifty and one-sixty-five shirts which are one dollar for "today only." Today only, these are the shirts that will give that "swank" appearance; today only, these are the shirts of which I bought five yesterday myself; and, thank heavens, *today only,* Robert Taylor wears them exclusively.

Observe that the speaker did not say that he regarded such business and sales as dishonest; he implied the idea. Nor did he say that such methods should rouse the indignation of his hearers; he selected his facts and presented them to rouse indignation. Nor did he tell his audience that such methods hurt their pride; again he let the facts tell his hearers that as buyers they're suckers. When listening to such material a hearer is primarily concerned with the literal facts; yet suggestion is at work, for indirectly from the literal facts the hearer is led to draw three conclusions on points that the speaker could have stated directly, but didn't: Some high-pressure business is dishonest; such business tactics as I describe should make you angry; you ought to be ashamed to be a sucker. (Is there another implied point that touches off a motive?)

Sometimes a speaker can work into his narrative of events and facts a word that either names the attitude or emotion he desires to rouse or is so closely associated with it as to secure the same response. Compare the following passages from Webster's summation speech at the Knapp-White Murder Trial.[3]

A

The deed was executed with a degree of self-possession and steadiness equal to the wickedness with which it was planned. The circumstances are now clearly in evidence before us. Deep sleep had fallen on the destined victim and on all beneath his roof. A healthful old man to whom sleep was sweet, the first sound slumbers of the night held him in their soft but strong embrace. The assassin enters through the window already prepared, into an occupied apartment. With noiseless foot he paces the lonely hall, half lighted by the moon; he winds up the ascent of the stairs, and reaches the door of the chamber. Of this he moves the lock by soft and continued pressure, till it turns on its hinges without noise; and he enters and beholds his victim before him. The room is uncommonly open to the admission of light. The face of the innocent sleeper is turned from the murderer, and the beams of the moon, resting on the gray locks of his aged temple, show him where to strike. The fatal blow is given! and the victim passes, without a struggle or a motion, from the repose of sleep to the repose of death. . . . The deed is done. He retreats, retraces his steps to the window, passes out through it as he came in, and escapes.

B

Let me ask your attention, then, to the appearances on the morning after the murder, which have a tendency to show that it was done in pursuance of a preconcerted plan of operation. What are they? A man was found murdered in his bed. No stranger had done the deed, no one unacquainted with the house had entered. There had obviously and certainly been concert and co-operation. The inmates of the house were not alarmed when the murder was perpetrated. The assassin had entered without any riot or any violence. He had found the way prepared before him. The house had been previously opened. The window was unbarred from within and its fastening unscrewed. There was a lock on the door of the chamber in which Mr. White slept, but the key was gone. It had been taken away and secreted. The footsteps of the murderer were visible outdoors, tending away from the window. The plank by which he had entered the window still remained. The road he pursued had thus been prepared before him. The victim was slain and the murderer had escaped. On the face of the circumstances it was apparent, therefore, that it was a premeditated, concerted murder; that there had been a conspiracy to commit it.

[3] As quoted in Winans, *Speech-Making*, pp. 18–19.

Observe that in passage *A,* Webster inserted into the description of the murder words like *wickedness, assassin, innocent, aged temple.* This passage, spoken early in the speech, was designed to rouse in the jury sympathy for the victim and indignation and revulsion against the murderer. Passage *B,* spoken late in the speech, used the same set of facts; but here Webster dissociated his facts from emotion because they served a different purpose, to prove conspiracy. These parallel passages, as Professor Winans suggests, merit close study by the student of persuasion, for they show how the same ideas can serve different purposes and secure different effects, the one emphasizing the emotional significance of the events, the other the logical significance of the facts.

One emotional spectrum is often associated with the circumstances giving rise to a problem and its solution. From fear at one end, this spectrum grades off to the less severe emotions of worry, anxiety, apprehension, nervousness, and uneasiness. A problem and its difficulties or symptoms are recognized because we feel uneasy and apprehensive about some state of affairs, especially if it concerns safety, security, and health. If the conditions persist and become important, we may scent danger, and then apprehension may become anxiety and even fear. World peace is threatened by the Communist menace. Our prosperity is threatened by rising prices and wages, symptoms of inflation. So persuaders have always roused attention and have argued the gravity of a problem through fear appeals. They have also argued that failure to accept a desirable solution or to take remedial action is fraught with dire consequences. Are appeals to fear effective in changing beliefs and attitudes and in producing action? A number of investigations built around propositions relating automobile safety and seat belts, cigarette smoking and cancer, seem to indicate that appeals to fear succeed. Indeed, indications are that the more intense the appeal the more certain is the desired response, provided the fear argument is perceived to fit the circumstances. Materials drawn from the fear spectrum seem to work partly because they rivet attention and partly because they are constituents of the problem being argued about.[4]

Identification

One of the oldest and also the most modern means of persuasion is the phenomenon of *identification,* a psychological term developed by Kenneth

[4] Some recent reports of experiments dealing with fear appeals are H. Leventhal and P. A. Niles, "A Field Experiment on Fear-Arousal with Data on the Validity of Questionnaire Measures," *Journal of Personality,* 32 (1964), 459–479; H Leventhal, R. Singer, and S. Jones, "Effects of Fear and Specificity of Recommendations upon Attitudes and Behavior," *Journal of Personality and Social Psychology,* II (1965), 20–29; C. A. Insko, A. Arkoff, and V. M. Insko, "Effects of High and Low Fear Arousing Communication upon Opinions towards Smoking," *Journal of Experimental Social Psychology,* I (1965), 256–266.

Burke. Anciently it was held that speakers and audiences mutually influenced each other when they recognized common ideas, interests, and values. Through analysis of subject and audience, a speaker found *topoi,* or topics, or "places" of agreement between him and his audience. Currently, an important means of influence is based on the well-known tendency of an individual to identify himself with someone he admires. As accommodated to the speaker-audience relationship, the phenomenon works in two ways. Hearers find in the speaker traits of personality and character they admire, and they believe his message because they esteem him. The rhetorician's name for this kind of influence, discussed in Chapter 17, is *ethos.* The other way of identification is through what the speaker directly says. The speaker tries to make his proposition acceptable by pointing out ways in which it conforms with, or is consistent with, interests, values, and beliefs to which his audience already subscribes. Burke called this strategy *consubstantiality,* that is, the sharing of the same kind of experience. Winans spoke of persuasive strategy as one in which speaker and hearer found a common ground of purpose, of idea, and of feeling and emotion. Perhaps the most concise description of the method is offered by Burke: In the simplest case of persuasion, he said, "You persuade a man only insofar as you can talk his language by speech, gesture, tonality, order, image, attitude, idea, *identifying* your ways with his."[5]

Modern students of persuasion have become much interested in identification phenomena. Their studies emphasize that identification is a fundamental trait of human nature which every novice communicator should take to heart. People tend to perceive what is consistent with their experience, with their settled ideas and opinions, their feelings and attitudes. They tend not to recognize—or if they recognize they tend to evaluate incorrectly—what is inconsistent with their experience. They tend to believe a statement they see as related to a statement they already believe, and they tend to reject a statement that is at odds with a cherished belief. Why? Such dissonance creates unpleasant internal tensions set up by conflict and doubt. There may be pleasure in learning and in discovering the new and different; yet the new idea can have unpleasant consequences. As Francis Bacon observed, in writing of the ingrained habits of the human mind, man tries to escape this kind of unpleasantness by regularly preferring the positive aspect of things to the negative. As a rule he wants to find the good rather than the bad. He is by nature an optimist, not a pessimist; he is Pollyanna, not Cassandra. Seeking harmony rather than disharmony, man applies these general tendencies to reduce specific dissonances.

That people want to agree if given half a chance poses a special problem for the persuader. Unless he is reassuring an audience or stirring a partisan group to enthusiasm, his position, if a real one, is bound to be in some way

[5] *A Grammar of Motives* (New York, 1945), p. 55. Burke's ideas on rhetoric are well illuminated by Marie Hochmuth [Nichols], "Kenneth Burke and the 'New Rhetoric,'" *Quarterly Journal of Speech,* 37 (April 1952), 133–144.

different from that of his hearers. So his strategy lies in minimizing his disagreement, by making his position agreeable. This he does by likening his proposition to opinions and values that in some way harmonize with it. He finds human nature on his side. Yet with a quite different problem he finds human nature against him. He wants his audience to confront a position that is definitely unpleasant. He wants smokers, let us say, to acknowledge the evidence against them. He then must do battle with the tendency for people to believe what they want to believe, to rationalize each new conflict by thinking it is not really a conflict, and to run away from the new idea by converting it into their cherished idea in new dress. Speakers face a similar habit of mind whenever audiences are reluctant to see the problem at hand—to recognize that there *is* a problem and that it is not about to go away. What then is the strategy of persuasion? Probably it consists in bringing to bear all the resources of attention, evidence, emotion, and obligation. There are times when a situation has to be seen for what it is, when it is appropriate to call a spade a spade.

One of our professional colleagues compares identification with the behavior of two tuning forks when one is set into sympathetic vibration with the other. The two must be capable of responding at the same frequency. When one fork is set vibrating and brought close to the other, the second too will vibrate. There appears to be a similar relationship between speaker and hearer when they respond to each other, when they are in rapport or in resonance with each other.[6]

Kind of appeal

In many persuasive situations, and in particular those in which the speech must be short, the speaker has to choose among a number of values, all of which are relevant to his proposition. But which values are likely to be strongest? If there is a general rule, it is probably this: Give an audience the opportunity of responding to its social ideals and obligations as well as to its immediate self-interests. Men's desires and their personal needs and ambitions provide the basis for compelling appeals, yet most men do not like to have their fellows think that they are motivated to believe or act solely by pride, prestige, and pocketbook. Why do men and women volunteer for military service? Primarily on grounds of self-interest? Fear of social disapproval? Love of adventure and the appeal of the novel? Or are there certain ideals at work also: loyalty and duty to country? Preservation of democratic ways? Protection of one's own rights and the rights of others? Doubtless our motives, particularly in wartime, are cloudy and mixed, as hinted in the slogan, "Buy a bond to help win the war and build your future home." Yet idealism, as well as

[6] Thomas M. Scheidel, *Persuasive Speaking* (Glenview, Ill.: Scott, Foresman and Company, 1967), pp. 72–73.

egocentrism, is often present. Why do some young men refuse to be drafted? Because they fear for their safety? Because they believe war to be immoral?

When Henry Ward Beecher in his Liverpool Address in 1863 sought to turn the tide of English feeling from the Confederacy to the Union cause, he spent much time arguing that recognition of the Union would result in better markets for English goods; but he also appealed to his audience's love of freedom and hatred of slavery, to justice and the good of humanity. He brought self-interest and moral attitudes together in the statement that "pence and pounds join with conscience and honor." It is sound practice, then, not merely to associate a proposal with hearers' self-interests but also with their higher values. If the speaker is a cynic, he can assume his hearers are better than he thinks they are!

Suggestion

Suggestion refers to processes through which persons respond more or less uncritically to stimuli. The response may follow the stimulus immediately, or it may be delayed. The respondent may know that he has behaved uncritically, or he may not recognize what controlled his behavior—if indeed he is aware that he has responded at all. To students of verbal communication, the stimuli involved in suggestion are the meanings associated with language behavior and its features. So in verbal suggestion a listener is responding uncritically to statements and utterances.

The nature of suggestion may be shown in a number of ways. There is the common remark, "Don't say it, or he will do it." Or simply, "Don't suggest it to him." Or more positively, "Go ahead. Suggest it and maybe he will accept it (or do it)." Such remarks imply that the person in mind is on the verge of acting. They imply also that he will probably respond; he will accept the suggestion or will act upon it.

Suggestion rests upon the same assumption as does the phenomenon of attention: a statement understood or accepted will produce the intended response unless inhibitory stimuli intervene. To keep attention fully on the desired response, it is usually necessary to inform, to explain, to argue, to meet objections, and to communicate in ways that have been described in this book. In other words, deliberation normally intervenes between proposal and response. But in suggestion, response follows idea without deliberation. The idea itself, without elaboration, works directly.

The phenomenon of hypnosis throws light upon another feature of suggestion, namely, the relationship between the person suggesting and the person responding. The suggestor is dominant, the respondent submissive; the former controls, the latter does not. In hypnosis, the respondent willingly submits to the conditions that produce a trance. Once in the hypnotic state, he accepts suggestions without resistance provided they do not conflict with deep-seated norms of conduct. In ordinary persuasive situations listeners are rarely submissive. Yet they are subject to suggestion. The suggestive stimuli may or may not be under the speaker's control, and the listener may or may not be aware of them. Let us see why.

Stimulus-fields are organized by respondents in much the same way a picture is organized. There are foreground and background features. The mechanism of attention focuses on foreground features and takes in background features marginally. In oral communication, a listener's perceptions are chiefly aural and visual, and they too are responses to fields of stimulation revealing foci and margins. At the focus of the listener's attention are the dominant meanings carried by the words of the message. In the margin of the attention field are stimuli that work in two ways. They reinforce or enhance the dominant meaning of the foreground. They work as parts of the whole. Marginal stimuli, however, do more than function as integral parts of a picture. They carry their own messages, more or less independent of the dominant meaning. In speech, marginal stimuli are responsible for the nuances of meaning that reside in the structures and forms of language itself and in the subtle changes of voice and gesture. A child says he will come straight home from school, yet his voice may suggest some doubt about it.

In their *Basic Principles of Speech,* Lou Sarett and William Trufant Foster offer a fine illustration of suggestion.[7] A certain professor, when bidding a guest good-bye at the door, often starts a lively conversation. At what he judges to be the "right moment" during the dialogue, he offers a cane to the guest, who takes it, starts out the door, and sometimes gets out on the porch before he is aware of the cane. Then, to his embarrassment, he returns the object. The practical joke has been a success. How is this suggestion? First, the primary stimuli that dominate the experience are the ideas of the conversation. Second, the secondary stimulus operating in the margin of the experience is the cane. Third, the guest responds to both types of stimuli. Throughout, he is pretty much aware that the verbal stimuli of talk are directly dominating the experience, and he is not aware that the offering of the cane has led him to accept it; indeed, he responds to the offer without knowing that he has responded. During a speech, a listener responds to stimuli from a speaker in the same way the guest responded to the professor's talk.

The pervasiveness and subtlety of forces operating through the margins of attention are well illustrated by habits of language behavior and habits of mind. The basic forms of the English sentence are so thoroughly learned by the child that as an adult speaker he is bound to use them. We can say, "I went to the opera last night," but we cannot say, "Night last I opera the to went," and expect to be instantly intelligible. In fact, except for a special purpose, we cannot say the words that way at all. We are bound, too, by the

[7] (Boston, 1946), p. 525.

rhythms and sounds of American speech. Our mental habits become no less firmly fixed than our linguistic habits, as may be seen, for example, in the mechanisms of perception and attention we have been talking about. The items in a stimulus field must become ordered and graded; they must have focus and fringe if they are to be meaningful. Attentive behavior cannot be otherwise.

In suggestion the respondent may be able to detect fringe stimuli and know what influenced him. The departing guest upon discovering the cane in his hand remembered that the professor had thrust it upon him. But the respondent may be incapable of isolating some of the stimuli operating in the fringes of the attention field. He must therefore remain unaware of their influence. He may suspect their effect but cannot detect their source. Such stimuli have been called subliminal; they remain below the level of awareness. For the persuader they introduce a problem in ethics, as we shall see later. We remark now that there are circumstances in which suggestion is appropriate and legitimate, for there are occasions when the time for new facts and further deliberation and argument is past. One says in effect to his hearers: "You are ready to believe, now believe; you are ready to act, now act." The widely recognized methods of suggestion we present next.

Authority

Authority works through suggestion in part because the authoritative statement carries weight almost independently of its plain meaning. Students of persuasion have given us much evidence for this generalization: communicators who are perceived as having prestige are more effective in influencing belief and attitude than communicators with little or no prestige. This statement reflects the value we bestow upon *status*. An authority occupies a position of respect relative to the belief to be accepted or rejected. Because of his position he is thought to possess appropriate knowledge and to be capable of sound judgment. What he says or does carries weight not only because of its plain message but because *he* said it.

In using authorities, the speaker can take pains to *enhance* their impressiveness. Use of the authority's *name* carries more weight than the weak phrase, "authorities (or experts) agree that. . . ." By a phrase or at greater length the speaker can establish that the authority, if unknown to his hearers, *is* an authority. Otherwise the suggestive influence of testimony is lost.

When the speaker has a choice between two equally trustworthy authorities, he should use the one best known to his audience, since attention is sharpened by the familiar stimulus.

Strength is gained also by preferring authorities to whom the audience is favorably disposed. An unfavorable association set up by an authority the hearer does not like—for whatever reason—will weaken, even destroy, the force of the soundest fact.

The speaker's own authoritativeness should not be neglected. A speaker not known to his audience as an authority on his subject should let his hearers know what he has seen, what he has read, and with whom he has talked. If he suffers from false modesty, he can make the reference unobtrusively like this: "When I ran this machine for two months last summer. . . ." "A patrol was sent on this job, and I was picked to go along." "In a meeting of the Student Council last night, which I attended, Jones said. . . ." A speaker, moreover, who has a broad understanding of his subject should tell his hearers that he has knowledge of the forest as well as of his special tree. He can do this at the outset of the speech by indicating that he is aware of the broader aspects of his problem. For example:

> Whether we are to have a little theatre in the proposed Student Union is of real concern to us all. It would give students and townspeople a chance to see good plays that they don't have a chance to see now. It would give students an opportunity for better training in dramatics and would encourage more students to study and major in dramatics. Furthermore, the Building Committee says that there is enough money appropriated to cover the cost of a theatre. We don't have to worry ourselves about the money, therefore. It seems to me that now we ought to be more interested, not in whether we will get the theatre, but whether we can have a theatre that can be used for many purposes rather than for plays alone—for lectures and movies, for visiting dance groups, and the like—and I would like to show you why.

This student, speaking in substance what we have reported, clearly indicated that he recognized the many-sidedness of the question and related his particular view to the larger discussion.

Imagery

Imagery functions in part through suggestion because images that are sharp and vivid enhance the intensity of perception. Many images, furthermore, carry emotional associations. Detailed images are often employed to describe the action desired by the speaker. Those who appreciate the force of imagery will seek opportunities for using concrete and specific language, rather than abstract and general. They will be on the watch for specific examples and detailed illustrations. They will recall that a direct forceful delivery carries greater impact than an indirect weak manner.

Emulation

A powerful means of suggestion utilizes our tendency to do what others do. In persuasion, particularly when one is trying to get lukewarm partisans to act, it is often effective to point out that another person, group, or institution has already taken the desired step. "If The University of Iowa can stage a big rally for the football team, then Iowa State University can," a student once exclaimed in trying to stir up enthusiasm for a pregame rally.

It should be observed that imitation is only effective when the person or group to be imitated meets two conditions: (1) When the person is respected by the audience and the conduct asked for is regarded as possible and reasonable, not farfetched. To ask a student to achieve high grades by holding up to him the example of a member of Phi Beta Kappa is likely to provoke, "So what?" But to show him the record of another boy of his own intellectual calibre may spur him on. (2) When rivalry is involved, imitation gains great force. A Harvard student doesn't want a Yale man to excel him; and competing business firms, motion picture companies, and TV programs emulate each other. In brief, the speaker shows the audience that another respected individual or group is already doing what he urges or has already endorsed his proposition.

Reduction of conflict

One of the fundamental motivations of human beings is avoidance of conflict. To reduce conflict and disagreement with others, people tend to conform to norms of belief; they are influenced by what others do.[8] Recognizing this fact of human nature, persuaders often seek ways of identifying their interests with the interests of others, as we have observed earlier in this chapter. By enhancing the sense of group solidarity, persuaders also utilize the tendency to conform and to belong. Members of the audience are reminded or informed that others, either present or elsewhere, hold the same opinions as they or are behaving as they do.

The sense of solidarity is facilitated when members of an audience respond openly together. Most organizations recognize this fact. Most of them—including the church—employ a *ritual* that requires everyone to sing, to read responsively, to salute, to wear the same badge or uniform. Applause has a unifying effect—if a speaker can get it! So does laughter, and a show of hands.

The speaker can suggest solidarity by touching off motives, emotions, and interests that are *common* to all groups in the audience. A striking example of this achievement is George William Curtis's speech, "The Puritan Principle," delivered when feeling ran high over the Hayes-Tilden election controversy in 1876. Responsible thoughtful people were so sharply divided over the election that they spoke openly of resorting to arms to settle who should

[8] The influence of others' behavior on individual performance extends even to judgments as to length of lines, weight of objects, and the like. Laboratory experiments show that when one individual knows that his fellows have judged one line longer than another, one weight heavier than another, his judgment is influenced in the same direction.

be President. Before about four hundred influential Americans gathered in New York, Curtis advocated that Congress should set up machinery whereby "a President, be he Democrat or be he Republican, shall pass unchallenged to his chair." He brought his listeners close to him and his proposition and at the same time closer to each other by touching deftly on the ideals of their forefathers, to which no one could take exception, by awakening the loyalty which each national group—the Irish, French, English, and German—felt for its home country, and he directed that loyalty to a higher patriotism—love of America, the adopted country. Thus loyalty and patriotism crowded out feelings over sectional and party differences and united everyone.

The *common purposes* of various groups represented in an audience help build solidarity. For example, in an audience gathered to hear a plea for more vocational training in high school, students, faculty, and the general public alike may well have the same purposes and ideals; all want good teachers, good buildings and equipment, the best type of training that will prepare young people for life. To touch upon these aims early in the speech creates a community of feeling and materially helps secure a favorable hearing for the specific question of how much and what kind of vocational training should be added to the school curriculum.

Group consciousness is enhanced by mentioning others who have subscribed to or acted upon the speaker's proposal. The sense of being together—group consciousness—is not limited to those meeting in one room on a particular occasion. A hearer may very well be aware that he is part of a larger local or national group not actually present. A speaker may awaken this consciousness by naming other groups and individuals who believe and act as he wants his audience to believe and act. He leaves the impression that *many* others have endorsed, say, the open-housing bill, and the listener feels the weight of numbers and of public opinion and doesn't want to be left out of the crowd. If the Gallup Poll has taken the temperature of the country on the speaker's proposition, or on a question closely related to it, and a definite majority are in favor, he cites that fact to his hearers. Maybe some committee or some organization has overwhelmingly or unanimously endorsed the proposition. Even to cite a number of individuals who are favorably disposed will create some impression that many people are concerned.

A special caution is in order:

> A person should not give the impression that "public opinion" is with him unless it really is.

Misleading—and sometimes vicious—is the journalist's phrase that "informed sources," or "Washington opinion," believes so-and-so. The phrase too often means that the reporter has talked with only one "informed" person or someone he regards as representing "Washington opinion."

The directive

This is a method of suggestion in which a speaker explicitly tells his audience which idea to accept or reject, and which conduct to follow or avoid. He may give the directive in two ways, directly or obliquely.

In asking for the acceptance of an idea, he can do so obliquely by such phrases or statements as, "I believe we all agree that. . . ." "We can accept this as fact." "Certainly we can accept the authority of the Federal Trade Commission on this point." Or he may tell his hearers how much weight or importance should be attached to an idea, by such phrases as, "We now come to the most important step of all." "This point is crucial (or especially significant) (or fundamental)." "The objection that some people raise is merely a detail (or of no great concern) (or need not be taken too seriously)." Such oblique suggestions are often effective. On the other hand, in asking a listener to accept an idea, the forthright directive usually boomerangs and should be used only when the speaker is sure his audience is ready for it. Its usual form is the *command:* "Accept this." "Reject that." "Don't believe this for a minute." Frequently we respond to the command in the manner just opposite to that intended. To "Accept this," we are prone to say "Why should I?" or "I'll do no such thing." To the overconfident, dogmatic assertion, "This is the gospel truth," we may react with "Is it? You've got to show me." The command, in short, sometimes invites a listener to be perverse, stubborn, and unduly critical; thus it backfires on him who uses it indiscriminately.

As an oblique directive, the rhetorical question works well. In *Julius Caesar,* Shakespeare has Mark Antony cite general examples to show that Caesar was not ambitious, as Brutus had charged (*Julius Caesar,* III, ii: 75–98). After each example, Antony exclaims, "Was this ambition?" Occasionally a speaker can use, with ease and smoothness, a pattern that at once summarizes a chain of argument and evidence and clinches the point with a rhetorical question: "If we may accept so-and-so, so-and-so, and so-and-so, can we not accept the view that . . . ?" It is worth observing that this means of suggestion has a peculiar force, for a hearer who is led to supply the *yes* answer himself really commits himself to the idea without quite realizing it and is loath to go back on his commitment. A salesman usually tries to get his prospects responding with *yes's* before he puts the proposition.

In asking for action from an audience, a speaker uses the directive in much the same way as he does in securing acceptance of his belief. The command is especially effective when an audience is ready to act. A speaker can quite frankly say "Go and do so-and-so." A student once interested a class in reading *The Grapes of Wrath* and at the end of his speech offered an explicit direction:

> All you need to do now, if you are interested in Mr. Steinbeck's book, is to go to the library during the next vacant hour you have and fill out the call

card. The call number of the book is PN6167 S112. There are six copies available, and in three minutes you have the book. If you have no class next hour, go at once and be sure of a good book you can start reading this afternoon or tonight.

The oblique form of the same suggestion would have been "I think you will want to read the book at the first chance you get." Or, "Isn't this book sufficiently interesting to be read at the first opportunity?"

The beginning speaker should remember that when an audience is ready to act and wants to act, he should supply explicit directions. If he can rouse real interest and enthusiasm for the proposal—as he very often can with the partisan audience—he can give the hearers something definite to do. If he wants them to sign a petition or endorse a resolution, he should give them a chance to sign as soon as possible. If he wants them to write their senator or congressman, he should give them definite directions and information so that they can. Supply his name and address, and perhaps suggest what they should say. When a speaker fails to capitalize on the readiness of his hearers to act, he blocks and frustrates them. There are few disappointments so great as to want to do *something* and not to know just what to do or not to be able to do it.

Recurrence

The recurrence of an idea at intervals not only promotes clarity; it also encourages the acceptance of the idea. Recurrence seems to exert a cumulative or piling-up effect in the fringe of attention, and we are for the most part unaware that the reinforcement has influenced our response. Competing ideas and stimuli are subordinated or fail to register at all; they are driven out of mind.

The recurrence of an idea can take two forms, repetition and restatement. The slogan, particularly the advertiser's slogan, is perhaps the commonest example of repetition. Almost anyone may be able to name a half-dozen slogans at once; and if he can, this is evidence that they have done their work so well that he was never conscious of having "memorized" them. Both the idea and the wording flash up without effort: "The Great Society," "The Good Neighbor Policy," "The Forgotten Man," "Progress is our most important product."

A speaker will do well to ponder the statement of his proposition with a view to making it as concise as is consistent with accuracy. A concise statement can readily be repeated verbatim at intervals through the speech, especially at the "clincher" moments at the end of sections or divisions and at major transitions. Furthermore, in striving for conciseness, he will become aware of different wordings of his proposition, and if he thinks repetition too obvious and bald to be effective, he can restate his proposition at intervals.

A speaker will do even better if he can experiment with his proposition—and his main heads, too—until he discovers pithy striking ways of phrasing them, of giving them a vivid, unusual, and catchy twist. Shakespeare gave Mark Antony's slogan "Brutus was an honorable man" an ironic twist. Claude Bowers, in his Keynote Speech at the Democratic National Convention (1928), chose to emphasize what he regarded as the sorry record of the Harding and Coolidge administrations, playing up especially the graft and corruption of the Teapot Dome scandal. He characterized the era as one dominated by the "Powers of Privilege and Pillage" and the "Powers of Darkness."

The position of argument

Often the position of an argument affects the strength of the impression it makes. A persuasive speaker learns to grade his arguments as those that are most important to him and those that will seem to be most important to his hearers. For centuries the rule has been to place last the argument likely to strike the hearer as strongest. Thirty years ago some experimental evidence suggested that in the short speech the strongest argument should take precedence, and the final argument should be strong but not the strongest. The initial point was remembered longer than the others, not because of any intrinsic value, but because first impressions were stronger than others. Today it seems that the effective location of one's points depends in part upon the information and interest of the audience in the controversy. Giving the strongest argument first place is preferred in speaking to audiences that have great familiarity with the problem and a high degree of interest or involvement in the controversy. Last place appears to be the better place for the key argument when audiences are not well informed and not very concerned.[9]

Important as the position of a particular argument may be, some of its effectiveness can be due to its "size." A strong argument is normally developed to a greater extent than a lesser argument, and thus is given more time and space.

Ethics of suggestion

Are there strictures on using the methods of suggestion we have discussed? Whether to use suggestion in a particular case should cause a speaker

[9] Some relevant studies: R. E. Lana, "Familiarity and the Order of Presentation in Persuasive Communications," *Journal of Abnormal and Social Psychology,* 62 (1961), 573–577, "Controversy of the Topic and the Order of Presentation in Persuasive Communications," *Psychological Reports,* 12 (1963), 163–170; R. L. Rosnow, *Opinion Change and Order of Presentation in Persuasive Communications* (unpublished Ph.D. dissertation, American University, Washington, D.C., 1962).

no greater difficulty than he finds with his other ethical problems. Sometimes the deliberate use of suggestion is warranted; at other times it is not. Through long experience with the practices of advertisers and salesmen, many adult audiences are aware of indirect influences upon them, of methods of appeal that short-circuit reason and judgment. Children may not recognize the subtler ways of suggestion. Parents know this and act upon this knowledge in various ways. The ghetto audience seems to be highly suggestible, especially to direct emotional appeals. Certainly no persuader should adopt the policy of relying solely upon suggestion. As a rule, communicators should justify suggestion in the same way they justify other means of persuasion.

The controlled use of buried, unidentifiable, subliminal stimuli caused much criticism when experimenters planted them in television advertisements. It was held improper and unethical to influence a human being intentionally when he has no chance of knowing the kind and source of the influence. When denied knowledge of the forces influencing him, the individual cannot be in a position to choose freely whether to respond one way or another. It is apparent, then, that subliminal influences create a special problem for the speaker or for any communicator. All kinds of stimulation are presented in human speech, whether or not the speaker intends them, and the listener's mechanism of attention will respond to all, the subliminal stimuli as well as to the apparent stimuli. What then does a speaker do? He can avoid the deliberate use of buried stimuli. Nevertheless, their unintended, quite uncontrollable appearance in his voice, manner, and gesture, their presence in the inevitable biases of men's opinions and preferences, and their revelation in the nuances of linguistic meaning he must accept as facts of human behavior. The student of persuasion will recall Thomas Carlyle's rejoinder to a stubborn lady long perplexed by the manifold complexities of life and the world about her. "Mr. Carlyle," she said finally, "I have decided to accept the universe." "By gad, lady," he exclaimed, "you'd better." Francis Bacon's counsel seems still to be sound. When one cannot alter the built-in mechanisms and fixed habits of man, he can circumvent them. Aware of subliminal influences, he can partially offset them by using and emphasizing the means of persuasion that he and his hearers are sophisticated about. A speaker may suspect that his rich, resonant, and flexible voice bears messages he knows not, that his flashing eyes reveal his spirit and touch the spirit of others, and that his dynamic manner and gesture testify to the energy and force of his ideas and the strength of his convictions. (Are there speakers today so superbly equipped?) If he deplores such "natural" advantages of influence, he will not, of course, depend upon them exclusively, as the glamor personality sometimes does. Glamor alone, as we know, does not wear long. Rather, the speaker may wish to give more than ordinary weight to evidence and to conditions that affect its soundness. He may want to emphasize the logic of his arguments and their truth and validity.

FURTHER READING

Adorno, T .W., and others. *The Authoritarian Personality*. New York, 1950.

Allport, Gordon W., and Postman, Leo. *The Psychology of Rumor*. New York, 1947.

Annis, A. D., and Meier, N. C. "The Induction of Opinion Through Suggestion by Means of Planted Content," *Journal of Social Psychology*, 5 (1934), 65–79.

Minnick, Wayne. *The Art of Persuasion*. Boston, 1957. Chapter 15, "Suggestion."

Oliver, Robert. *The Psychology of Persuasive Speech*. New York, 1957. Chapters 6–8, on attention, suggestion, and identification.

Rokeach, Milton. *The Open and Closed Mind*. East Lansing: Michigan State University Press, 1960.

Saenger, Gerhart. *The Psychology of Prejudice*. New York, 1953.

21

The Proposition and Logical Forms

When a speaker considers logical patterns and structures, he deals basically with the forms with which we have learned to think. Structures are habits of organizing our inner experience in outward language. They are fundamental to success in controlling attention. Some structures, technically called arguments, influence belief. By becoming conscious of thought patterns as arguments, a communicator can learn to inspect them critically, to improve his own use of them, to avoid their pitfalls, to lay particular emphasis upon them when he confronts critical listeners, and to gain a reputation for respecting straight reasoning and sound evidence.

In persuasion and in the discussion of public affairs, arguments are indispensable. "We must try to think out arguments," Aristotle wrote, "by keeping our eyes on the actual facts of the subject we have to speak on . . . for the more actual facts we have at our command, the more easily we prove our case; and the more closely they bear on the subject, the more they will seem to belong to that speech only. . . ." This method is so central to public speaking that Aristotle once said flatly, "There is no other way."

The Proposition

In persuasive speeches the dominant logical structure is reflected in the proposition and in the proof or arguments that support it. We turn first to examine briefly the source of propositions and then to a discussion of patterns of argument.

The proposition above all else represents the belief the speaker is asking an audience to accept. If the audience accepts, the speaker has satisfied his purpose.

The proposition, moreover, reflects one of two conditions which are inherent in any persuasive situation. As we have seen, persuasion is prompted by a problem—a state of dissatisfaction over some apparent condition. We are bothered, let us say, by the large number of divorces. Dissatisfaction yields two kinds of propositions: statements about the circumstances of the problem itself and statements about the solution to the problem. As for the first, we may wish in a speech of some length to discuss the entire problem, perhaps in terms of the proposition: "The divorce problem merits our serious consideration." Or in a shorter speech which reflects our special emphasis and the most immediate interest of the audience, the proposition reflects *one* aspect of the problem. For example, "Divorce is made too easy in most states." Here we would discuss a specific condition or cause of divorce. Or perhaps our statement would be somewhat more broad: "Divorce presents a real problem today." Here we would be concerned with defining and explaining the problem as such and showing that it is real, not fancied and ephemeral, and significant, not trivial and empty.

The other kind of proposition represents some sort of solution, either general or specific, again depending on the length of the speech and the interest of the occasion. A person aware of a number of causes of divorce might advance a general remedy which he believed would remove most of them or reduce their effectiveness. For example, "Every high school student should be required to take a course in the responsibilities of marriage and family life," or "Alimony should be granted only to wives with dependent children." In fact, many propositions deal with causes, that is, with the conditions that create or shape a problem. Other types of propositions that relate in some way to a solution are those which argue whether a solution is practical or not, whether one solution is better than another, and whether any solution would not introduce difficulties which would be as bad as the conditions creating the problem. Hence it is evident that a proposition will either define a problem and the conditions giving rise to it or present a solution and evaluate it.

A proposition is something else, too. It is the logical *conclusion* of the arguments that support it. No matter where it may be placed in the speech, whether early or late, all ideas and information support it. Some ideas are statements which are directly linked to the proposition. Other ideas are hooked indirectly to it and work through other statements back to the proposition. The net effect is a systematic arrangement of statements which *taken together* constitute the proof of the proposition. The proof itself consists of a number of arguments.

Logical proof in a speech cannot be thought of as absolute demonstration, such as we find in a geometric theorem. The propositions we offer in speeches are seldom capable of that kind of demonstration. Proof in speeches, however, is what makes our propositions seem sound to men of reasonable mind. Proof, then, operates as the logical support of the proposition, the conclusion. Through proof the speaker aims to secure the intellectual acceptance of his proposition.

The systematic interlocking of ideas and statements may be visualized as follows:

Proposition (*Conclusion*) ______________________________(because)
I. Statement ______________________________(because)
A. Statement ______________________________(because)
1. Statement ______________________________(because)
a. Statement ______________________________
2. Statement ______________________________
II. Statement ______________________________(because)
A. Statement ______________________________
B. Statement ______________________________(because)
1. Statement ______________________________
2. Statement ______________________________(because)
a. Statement ______________________________
b. Statement ______________________________(because)
(1) Statement ______________________________(because)
(2) Statement ______________________________(because)
(*a*) Statement ______________________________(because)
((1)) Statement ______________________________

I and II above are intended to support the proposition directly, with no intervening step. All other statements are more remotely linked to the proposition, some more remotely than others. Note, for example, how far away is ((1)). Yet in well-constructed proof, in a series of interlocking arguments, it would exert its influence up through other statements to II and through II to the proposition.

Proof and Argument

The basis of logical structures

Before looking at the logical patterns which may be used to support the proposition of a persuasive speech, we must secure a preliminary understanding of what is involved when statements are treated logically.

Two or more statements may be connected logically when they meet two general requirements: (1) The meaning of one statement entails the meaning of another statement in such a way as to suggest a third meaning. The linkage between the statements depends entirely on meanings being included in each other, or excluded from each other. (2) The meanings of two statements reflect events or conditions which always or usually accompany each other as cause and effect. To these requirements we now turn.

The Mode of Classification. Classification involves bringing the meaning of one statement within the meaning of another. The process excludes meanings irrelevant to each other.

First, the meaning of one statement may simply overlap that of another. For example:

Cheating on examinations is bad.
We believe that cheating of any kind is bad.

Cheating of any kind overlaps in meaning *cheating on examinations.*

Second, since overlapping ideas have something in common, it is always possible that the two ideas are related to each other as a part is to a whole. When this is so, it is always possible to assert that what holds true of the whole is also true of the part. So, as in the example above, we "reason" that if cheating in general is held to be bad, cheating on examinations is bad. The statement whose meaning carries the notion of a whole or a general condition is called a *general premise.* The statement bearing the notion of a part—the less general or even a particular instance—is called the *specific premise.*

Third, the combination of a general premise and a specific premise yields a statement which is regarded as the *conclusion.* Their common meanings are applied and extended to produce a third and distinct idea. For example:

Faculty observers should not be allowed in the Student Senate. (*Conclusion*)
They hinder freedom of discussion. (*Specific Premise*)
Whatever hinders freedom of discussion in the Senate should not be allowed. (*General Premise*)

Aided by Figures 12 and 13, we can see what is going on in the example. The general premise connects two very general ideas. Observe that the subject-idea is included within the meaning of the predicate-idea, but is not co-extensive with it. The shaded area of Figure 12 shows this. Next, the specific premise asserts that a specific condition expressed as its subject-idea is included

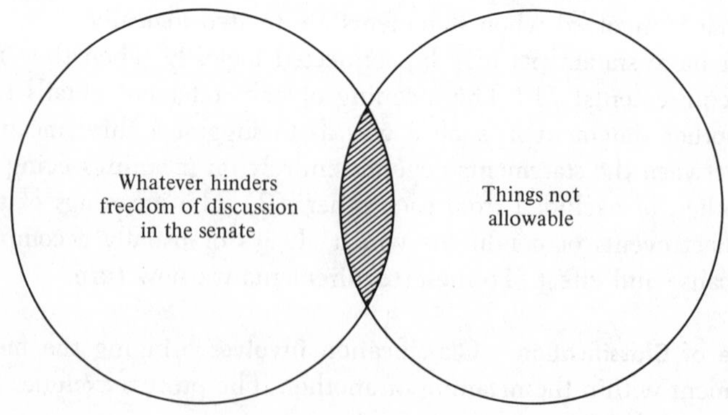

Figure 12

within the predicate-idea. Then the conclusion simply asserts that the specific condition shares, but is not co-extensive with, the meaning which is common to the two premises. Figure 13 visualizes this fact. Thus, a conclusion is said to *follow* from its premises because it shares a common area of meaning in the premises.[1] Much of reasoning is of this character; it declares connections among related meanings.

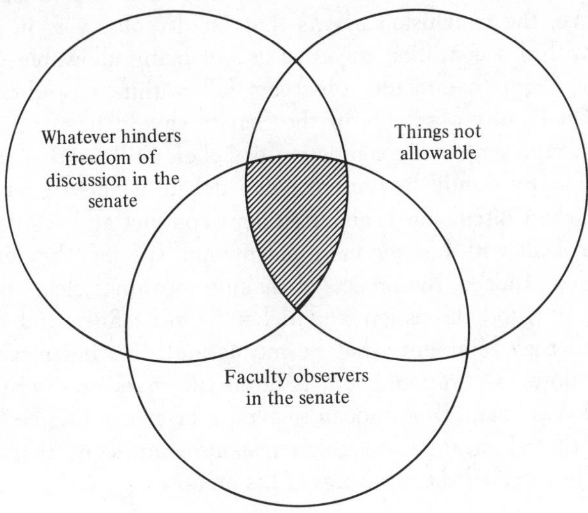

Figure 13

Finally, bringing an idea within the meaning of another idea also is involved when a number of related, *particular* statements are combined into a general statement, or *generalization.* For example:

Most students observe habits of regular study. (*Conclusion*)
  Student *A* does. (*Premise*)
  Student *B* does. (*Premise*)
  Student *C* does, etc., etc. (*Other premises*)

[1] Most teachers and some students will remember that the logic textbooks arrange the propositions of deductive reasoning in this order:

All men are mortal. (*General Premise*)
Socrates is a man. (*Specific Premise*)
∴ Socrates is mortal. (*Conclusion*)

The examples of deductive reasoning in this chapter follow the order and indentation of the speech outline. So, for the illustration above the outline convention is this:

Socrates is mortal. (*Conclusion*)
  All men are mortal. (*General Premise*)
  Socrates is a man. (*Specific Premise*)

The process of generalizing works in part through enumeration. In part it works through an assumption that what may be said of a number of particular events or conditions of the same kind or class may be said of all of them.

The processes we have described above illustrate one fundamental mode of relating meanings to one another. We are always saying that some meaning may be included within another or that it may not, or that it may be included in a certain context or under certain conditions and not in others. In the example above, the conclusion asserts that faculty observers in the Student Senate fall within a condition regarded as *not* being allowable. But another person might claim that faculty observers fall within a condition which *is* allowable, that faculty observers in the Senate should be permitted. A conclusion, then, represents one's conviction or belief. Still another person might believe that faculty should be present when debate is about educational matters but not when discussion is about student conduct and regulations. Thus the meanings dealt with become more narrow and specific; they exclude more and include less. Indeed, the process of making meanings clear and explicit is characteristic of *good* discussion and debate. One refines and explains his premises until they represent what he means and does not mean. Then his conclusion follows. Definition, then, is often the mark of careful argument. How often do we hear, "If you mean so-and-so, of course I agree." Or, "Oh, I didn't mean that; I meant this." Such responses are signs that the speaker had not clearly specified the meanings of his premises.

The Mode of Causation. The second basic way of logically combining statements reflects a relationship called cause and effect. This method becomes critically important whenever we try to apply the methods of scientific reasoning to the solution of human problems. Often we are interested in whether human events, as well as physical events, are associated with one another by chance or by necessity. Our interest is not primarily whether one event or idea may be properly included in another; it is whether one event *controls* and *accounts for* another. One event or condition is said to control a second event or condition when they accompany one another *invariably* and *necessarily*. In animals the action of the heart always accompanies life and its action is necessary to life. Although invariability and necessity represent the ideals of "causation" in the physical sciences, we often have to settle for something less in human behavior. We are content when the connection between two events is "usual," "habitual," and "almost always." The more wheat produced the lower the price; the less wheat produced the higher the price. The necessary principle is said to be the law of supply and demand. Yet the principle has to be modified somewhat when the government buys wheat, removes it from the market, and thus restricts supply. So the principle holds true in most times and cases, or under conditions of a free market. Human events are not so controllable as we might like them to be.

Effect to cause. Causation takes two directions, from effect to cause and from cause to effect. Statements can reflect either direction.

Wilson's poor grade in Course 100 is due chiefly to low intelligence. (*Conclusion*)
He has a low intelligence quotient. (*Specific Premise*)
Low intelligence is connected with poor grades. (*General Premise*)

The conclusion recognizes an effect—Wilson's poor grade—and singles out one cause as primarily responsible. The conclusion would be supported by establishing the fact that Wilson's intelligence *is* limited and by bringing to bear the general idea which connects the fact with the effect. Thus causal reasoning pays special attention to the principle which *connects* two events. If there were other causes or conditions which were held to account for Wilson's grade, they would be stated in a similar pattern:

Wilson's poor grade in Course 100 is due to his poor study habits. (*Conclusion*)
He has poor study habits. (*Specific Premise*)
Poor study habits are connected with poor grades. (*General Premise*)

Cause to effect. Statements may take the direction of cause to effect. The direction is a *prediction*. We hold that some future event is likely to occur because in the past the causes of that event have produced it. We make the powerful assumption that the forces which have worked effectively in the past will continue to operate in the future. We believe that in most significant respects, history will repeat itself. We have confidence that over short periods of time, human behavior is more uniform and regular than not, and that over long periods of time it will be stable unless unforeseen events and forces modify it. Of the "A" student in high school we say, he should be able to make good grades in college; of the "A" student in college we say, he should be able to do well in his profession. In other words, when we know that a particular cause has accounted for a particular effect, we expect the cause to be accompanied by a similar effect in the future:

Jones will do well in college. (*Conclusion*)
He did well in high school. (*Specific Premise*)
Good performance in high school is connected with good performance in college. (*General Premise*)

If one sees how the meanings of statements are properly related by inclusion-exclusion and by cause and effect, he is well on his way to the proper handling of logical proofs. He needs to grasp but two other fundamentals: (1) the formal structure of related meanings depends to a large extent on how *clear* and *precise* the meanings are; and (2) the truth or falsity of a conclusion depends in part upon what the premises *refer* to and in part on how they are *connected.*

Unambiguous Premises. A conclusion gains acceptance or assent because of two factors: (1) the *meanings* involved in the premises are perceived to be *related* to one another; and (2) the *formal* arrangement or connection between related meanings is made evident. Our response of assent comes about partly through the meanings of subject-ideas and predicate-ideas carried by the language of the premises and partly through the meaning *bound into* the combining operation. There is a sort of content meaning on the one hand and a formal meaning on the other. The difference is critical and may be illustrated as follows:

> If *A* is greater than *B* and *B* is greater than *C*, than *A* is greater than *C*.
> If John is taller than Mary and Mary is taller than James, then John is taller than James.

Observe closely that the formal arrangement of the two statements is precisely the same. Note, too, that the content of the "nouns" in the two statements is radically different. *A, B,* and *C* have no content. *John, Mary,* and *James* do have content, for they stand for, or point to, definite persons. There is, then, a basic fact about all of our reasoning when we carry it on in language: into a single formal pattern we may insert hundreds of different meanings. The persuasive speaker uses very few forms of logical support, but the meanings he puts into them are as many as are imbedded in the subjects he talks about.

Because in conversation and in popular discourse we reason through language, the handling of meaning presents a special problem. A conclusion correctly follows from its premises partly because their meanings are clear and *unequivocal.* The milkman, enrolled in an evening course in public speaking, may claim that he devotes plenty of time to the practice of delivery. He rehearses his speech three nights a week and delivers milk every morning. The wobbly meanings here are obvious; we may smile but never be misled or convinced. We encounter real difficulties, however, when premise statements are abstract and their precise meanings depend upon precise distinctions. For example:

> Society should treat juvenile delinquents with sympathy. (*Conclusion*)
> They are not solely responsible for their actions. (*Specific Premise*)
> Persons not entirely responsible for their conduct should be treated with sympathy. (*General Premise*)

How can one interpret the language of this example with any degree of precision? Exactly what idea is included in (or excluded from) the meaning of what other idea? The language is littered with ambiguities. Is society (itself ambiguous) implied in the general premise? Is *juvenile delinquent* used only in the legal sense or the popular sense, or both? Is *solely* equivalent in meaning to *entirely, actions* equivalent to *conduct?* What is meant by *responsible?*

"Men imagine," says Bacon, "that their minds have the command of language; but it often happens that language bears rule over their minds." One cannot connect related meanings to one another in straightforward manner unless the meanings are precise. Within a logical pattern, a particular meaning must remain single, not double.

Hence, both in the construction and the presentation of logical patterns, one recognizes that such ambiguities are inherent in language. When we use abstractions and generalities—and we cannot abolish them entirely—we are simply relating the meaning of one *word or phrase* to the meaning of another. We cannot always talk about concrete, specific objects and events. The consequence is that a good reasoner declares the meanings of his premises; he explains and defines them until it becomes possible for his hearers to grasp the meanings he intends. Once they grasp the meanings, hearers can see the connection between meanings and can experience the force and strength of the formal pattern.

When language is used unequivocally, two of the commonest errors in reasoning are avoided. One is the error of *irrelevance,* or reasoning beside the point. For example, we would argue that speeches ought to be plain, in the sense of being *clear and perspicuous.* But we would be beside the point if we were to infer from that statement that speeches should avoid ornaments of style such as metaphors. We would be confusing effect and cause. There are many ways of securing the effect of plain speaking, and metaphor is one of them. A second common error resides in a different kind of ambiguity. One often fails to observe how *widely* or *extendedly* a general word or statement is intended to be taken. If we were to infer that the college student as a young person preferred economic security to economic risk on the ground that young persons today express such a preference, would the college student, logically speaking, fall within the meaning of "young persons"? All depends on how wide is the territory covered by "young persons." *Some* young persons? *Most* young persons? *All* young persons? If *all* young persons, the college student would logically fall into place; if *some* or *most* young persons, the college student might or might not belong to the group being talked about. The meanings of statements, then, have a quantitative dimension.

Logic, Belief, and Truth. We are now in a position to confront the all-important questions: Why do we believe in a statement? Why do we assent to an argument? We believe because we trust, or have confidence, in the speaker or in someone he trusts. This is a function of the *ethos* of a communicator, as we saw in Chapter 17. We believe, also, because we have learned that statements under certain conditions are probably true and correct.

There are three conditions to take note of. Statements are true if their meanings—their references—are grounded on verifiable evidence. Consider this example:

Most young persons prefer economic security to economic risk. (*General Premise*)
College students are young persons. (*Specific Premise*)
College students prefer economic security to economic risk. (*Conclusion*)

The general premise would be true on one condition: if its meaning rests on verifiable facts and evidence. In other words, it is true if its meaning corresponds to a "real" state of affairs, such as it would if one took a poll of a large number of young persons and found that they subscribed to the belief. In this context *truth* means *being in line with* the standard of reality, with verifiable data obtained through observation.

The specific premise would be true if it met two standards. First, it would have to conform to the realities of our knowledge. We probably agree that in the example *college students* falls within the meaning of *young persons*, but if the fact were in doubt, a speaker would have to produce verifiable evidence. In addition, the specific premise would be true or false depending on whether it were correctly connected with the general premise. In the example, may college students be included within the meaning of *most young persons?* (There would be no doubt, of course, if the general premise read *all* young persons.) If they are included, the premise is true because of the correct connection; if they are not included, the premise is false. In a word, there are rules and conventions by which we judge whether statements are connected to yield a proper conclusion.

The conclusion of an argument is true if the meanings of its premises meet the standard of reality and if the meanings are correctly connected.

Such standards of truth are strictly *logical*. If the persuasive speaker lives up to the ethical requirements of his art, he does his best to meet the logical standards of truth. Yet as a persuader he is ever aware of another criterion of truth. It is a psychological criterion by which we measure the *acceptance* of a statement, our *belief* and confidence in a statement, at the moment it occurs. We are continually accepting statements when we do not doubt them, and we do not doubt them when they are *consistent with past experience* and with what we already believe. Hence, in everyday speech we often apply the word *true* to a statement without thought of whether its meaning corresponds to any real state of things. Someone says, "Men try to be honest," and we may respond instantly, "That's true." The statement fits into our experience and values. We see no need of requiring verifiable evidence. For example, the content of the statement, "College students are young persons," is probably acceptable without supporting evidence.

Rhetorical Evaluation of Premises. The speaker who understands the logic of his arguments asks himself: What premises will my audience accept? What premises must I prove?

In applying these questions to individual speeches, a persuasive speaker will soon realize that most of his effort will be spent in supporting his specific premises. His general premises will usually reflect what his audience accepts as true, for these premises will embody general truths, values, and desires—the hearers' social ideals. Indeed, they may be so obviously true that it would be trite to state them formally. Basically, then, the logic of persuasion consists in finding and stating specific premises that assert a connection between what the audience believes and the conclusion the speaker wants supported. With his specific premises selected, a speaker devotes his chief efforts to establishing their truth.

The Layout of Arguments

We have said that the proof of a proposition consists of arguments. In a particular speech, of course, there are usually many interlocking arguments, whose cumulative effect supports the proposition, which is the logical conclusion of the combined arguments. It is instructive to see how the reasoning involved in logical structures can be applied to arguments. In making the application, speakers would be wise to lay out each argument according to a method like that recommended by Stephen Toulmin.[1] This method is especially useful because it calls attention to the connection between evidence and conclusion. (See our discussion of evidence, pages 68–71.) It directs attention to the kind of reasoning involved. The method also reminds a speaker of the qualification and reservations that are almost always necessary conditions of everyday argument. Toulmin, for example, terms a conclusion a *claim*. The word invites one to ask: How much can I realistically claim for an argument?

The simplest layout of an argument is this:

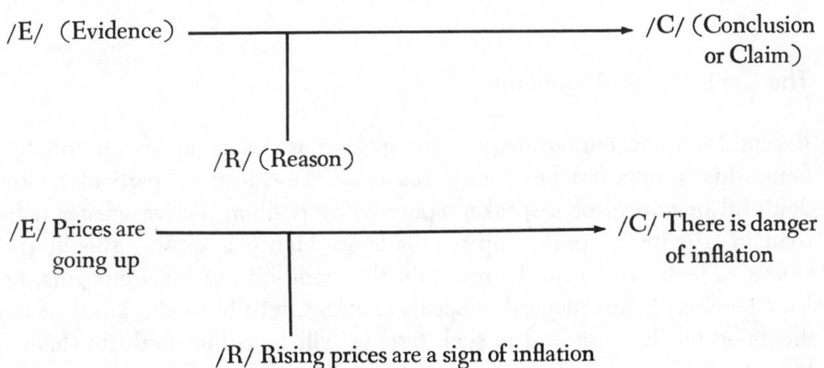
/E/ (Evidence)
/C/ (Conclusion or Claim)
/R/ (Reason)
/E/ Prices are going up
/C/ There is danger of inflation
/R/ Rising prices are a sign of inflation

[1] For the full explanation of the method, see Stephen Toulmin, *The Uses of Argument* (Cambridge: Cambridge University Press, 1958), Chapter 3.

The Reason connects the Evidence with the Conclusion or Claim; hence a reason is said to warrant or to justify a conclusion. Often a reason is a general premise. The argument as laid out above would need no further proof if the audience to whom it was addressed accepted both /E/ and /R/ as true.

Argument is seldom as simple, as neat, and as acceptable as that diagrammed above. A more typical and more complex layout follows:

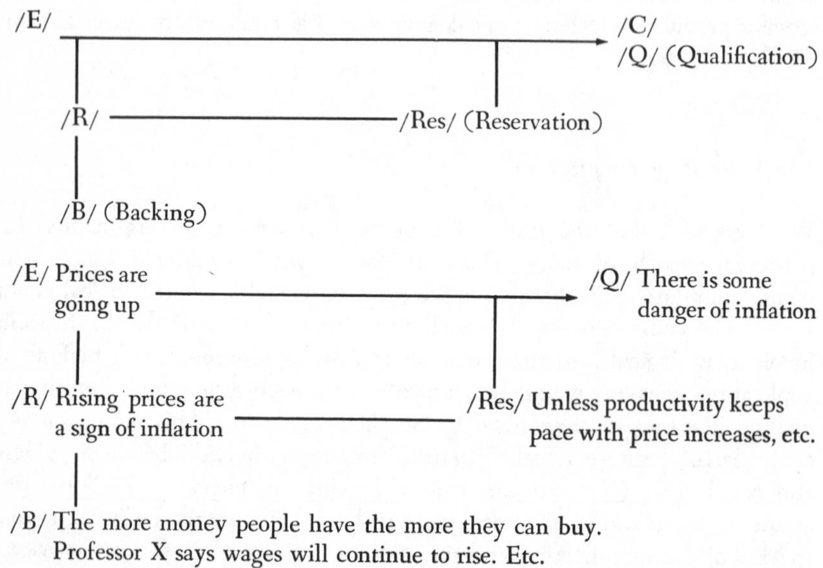
/E/
/C/
/Q/ (Qualification)
/R/
/Res/ (Reservation)
/B/ (Backing)
/E/ Prices are going up
/Q/ There is some danger of inflation
/R/ Rising prices are a sign of inflation
/Res/ Unless productivity keeps pace with price increases, etc.
/B/ The more money people have the more they can buy.
Professor X says wages will continue to rise. Etc.

This layout assumes that the speaker's audience would be likely to accept the conclusion as qualified. It assumes, furthermore, that the audience would find /R/ unacceptable unless /Res/ was pointed out and unless /B/ were provided for /R/.

The Criticism of Argument

Except for some curious reason, no speaker wants to appear unintelligent before his hearers lest he damage his *ethos.* Few hearers, particularly those doubtful or critical of a speaker's purpose or position, derive greater delight than in tripping a speaker up on his logic. Hence a speaker should try to reason as well as he can. To maintain the credibility of his arguments, or at least to avoid being illogical, a speaker looks carefully to the kinds of arguments he has laid out and to such tests as will help him evaluate them. To these matters we turn now.

Deductive argument

Deductive argument is the very common pattern that treats a statement as a conclusion and brings its sense within the meaning of a relevant specific premise and general premise. The specific premise functions as the connecting link between the idea expressed in the general premise and the meaning arrived at in the conclusion. For example:

Room leases should be honored. (*Conclusion*)
  They are contracts. (*Specific Premise*)
  Contracts should be honored. (*General Premise*)

To every instance of deductive reasoning, the speaker applies four test questions:

1. *Are the meanings of the premises unequivocally clear?*

2. *Is the predicate-idea of the specific premise properly included within the subject-idea of the general premise?* In the example above, "contracts" in the general premise is taken to mean all contracts; so the same word in the specific premise is necessarily included within the meaning.

The necessary connection is ideal and a speaker rejoices when he can show one. If there be any condition which he can claim is conclusive, beyond all shadow of doubt, this is it. But in much argument about human problems and behavior as distinct from matters of science, the perfect general premises —the generalizations without exception—are few and far between. General premises are likely to be true almost always, or in most cases. In other words, they are probably true, not invariably true. The perceptive speaker will be cautious about claiming too much for his general premises. If he will employ Toulmin's layout of argument, he will keep in mind an ever-possible qualification, for example, "All contracts should be honored except in unusual circumstances." Indeed, he may want to show, if necessary and if conditions suggest it for the case at hand, that the conditions are *not* unusual or peculiar. We all subscribe to the belief that *no person should lie;* yet there are instances when some high humanitarian motive justifies an exception.

3. *Which premise needs supporting?* In many contexts the general premise is so obviously acceptable to the audience that it barely needs mention, if at all. It is the specific premise which, as a rule, demands support and needs to be established as true.

4. *If a premise is supported by evidence, is the evidence reliable and trustworthy?*

Argument from example

A general statement may be supported by examples. The process is often called generalization from example, or argument from example. An idea that is wider in scope than the example carries the notion of the *many*. The example bears the notion of the *one*. In addition, the connection between the one and the many derives its force from the implication that what is true of the one is also true of the many. For instance:

> Wars are triggered by provocative incidents. (*Generalization*)
> Firing on Fort Sumter started the American Civil War. (*Example*)
> Students gain confidence in public speaking through experience in public speaking classes. (*Generalization*)
> Jones did. (*Example*)
> Tests of vocational aptitude are useful in choosing one's life work. (*Generalization*)
> They were for Jones. (*Example*)

If the argument from example is to be convincing, at least three key questions must be answered affirmatively:

1. *Is a single example sufficient?* Because of their cumulative force, several examples usually carry more weight than a single one. As in statistical inference, the larger the population under observation, the more probable is the truth of the generalization about the population. In numbers there is strength. In a speech, of course, there is not time for anything like an exhaustive enumeration of cases. Yet the lone instance is seldom convincing. The listener is too likely to respond, "But that's only one case; what about others?" The persuaders should keep in mind the distinction between the role of the example in exposition and in persuasion. In explaining a general idea, the example illustrates, and a single one may be enough to secure clearness. In argument, the example is intended to *prove*.

The argument from example is most effective when the instances can be followed by statistical data. To illustrate:

> Most students buy their textbooks at X Bookstore. (*Generalization*)
> Peterson does. (*Example*)
> Rhodes does. (*Example*)
> In our largest dormitory, 11 out of 12 students do. (*Statistics*)
> A survey at X Bookstore last semester showed that 9 out of 10 buyers were students. (*Statistics*)

2. *Are the examples truly comparable and relevant?* A generalization arises out of a number of similar instances and asserts what the instances have in common. Sometimes it is relatively easy to see in what respects examples are similar to each other and to the principal idea expressed in the

general statement. One can readily recognize, for example, a single point of comparison. In the illustration above, there is but a single point of likeness, the buying of textbooks. On the other hand it is more difficult to perceive clearly and to state exactly *several* points of similarity, particularly when they are buried in an abstract word. For example:

> Students in Y fraternity are responsible persons. (*Generalization*)
>
> Barnes of Y fraternity is a responsible individual. (*Example*)

What is entailed in responsibility? Various traits of behavior are associated with it, and one would have to identify these traits before he could know they were common to both the general statement and the example. Upon the presence of the same traits would depend the soundness of any comparison between Barnes and his brothers in the fraternity.

3. *Do the exceptional cases, if any, weaken the generalization?* We recall the old proverb, "The exception proves the rule." It does, in the sense that it *tests* the rule. So any exception must be regarded critically. Is it unusual—so far out of line with other instances that it weakens the force of the generalization? If it cannot be accounted for satisfactorily, a general statement less wide in scope had better be used, or the generalization abandoned entirely.

Argument from analogy

A comparison, as we know, brings together two ideas, objects, or events and makes the most of their similarities rather than their differences. The argument from analogy is built on a number of similarities between two sets of conditions or circumstances. It specifies that one set of conditions has characteristics *A, B, C, D,* and *E,* and that the second set of conditions also reveals *A, B, C,* and *D.* Then it concludes that *E* either is true or will be true in the second set. For example:

> Jones will do good work at X University. (*Conclusion*)
>
> He did good work at Y University. (*Specific Premise*)
>
> X and Y Universities are comparable in ways that affect grades. (*Comparative Premise*)
>
> Both have similar scholastic standards. (*Condition* 1)
>
> Both have similar faculties. (*Condition* 2)
>
> Both place studies ahead of social affairs and campus activities. (*Condition* 3)

Note that the argument from analogy is well named, for it derives its strength and cogency *from* a comparison which is expressed as a premise. Note, also, that the comparative premise is a conclusion with respect to the items of similarity which support it.

Analogical argument is a powerful tool of persuasion if two requirements are met:

1. *The more similarities between two particulars, the more convincing the conclusion.* The conclusion that true-false tests will be successful in elementary economics because they have been successful in elementary physics will increase in soundness as the similarities between the two courses increase. Both courses are designed for freshmen and sophomores; both courses assume that students are of about the same age and have the same academic preparation; both deal with principles and laws that are matters of fact; both aim to impart knowledge rather than skill.

2. *Dissimilarities between the particulars must not be more significant than likenesses.* Do the laws of economics—the law of supply and demand, for example—admit so many qualifications and special conditions that they cannot be tested by a simple true-or-false answer? And are there fewer exceptions and special qualifications in the laws of physics? If the answers are yes, then the single dissimilarity is far more significant than all the similarities noted above.

Effect to cause

As we observed earlier in the chapter, a causal relationship is held to exist whenever one event or condition controls and accounts for the occurrence or behavior of another. In scientific observation and experiment, *events* and *forces* are at issue and are usually distinguished sharply from conditions surrounding them. The falling of a body (effect) is caused by the force of gravity. Yet a coin, let us say, would not fall unless it were in a position to fall and were released from the hand. In other words, there are *conditions,* favorable and unfavorable, which influence the events of causation. Science centers on events. One event is said to produce another when two standards are met: the events must occur together invariably, and there must be a principle or credible explanation for the invariable sequence. The first standard requires that two events must be correlated perfectly; the second says that a law applies and is at work. Both standards must be satisfied. Human sleep, for example, is almost perfectly correlated with darkness at night, yet darkness is not the cause of sleep. It is a favoring condition, but the connection between darkness and sleep is not explained.

In the discussion of human affairs, we are not so well off as the scientist. If he suspects that events are related causally, he can wait and see. He can experiment. But in everyday affairs, people must act. They must make choices and decisions. They cannot wait to determine the real cause of events. The exact cause may be so buried in surrounding conditions that it cannot be located at once. Yet the conditions themselves are so compelling for action and belief that they function like causes. Accordingly, in persuasion and argument, the standards of the physical scientist are modified somewhat. We hold beliefs firmly enough to act with confidence (1) when two events or conditions, or an event and a condition, always or almost always, occur together, and (2) when there is a widely accepted explanation of the connection between them. The causes of war, for example, are combinations of events and conditions. There are conditions of peace. All are well known and widely believed. This is not to say that in persuasion and argument the speaker is excused from making every attempt to ferret out and understand the real causes of the events he is talking about. He is not. Indeed, when his subject takes him into the special knowledge of the natural and social sciences, he should be alive to the principles, laws, and other generalizations which formulate the regular behavior of events. Within this framework, we can direct our attention to the ways of support which recognize effects, causes, and conditions.

In the effect-to-cause pattern, some present or past condition is accounted for by an event or condition which preceded it. The statement to be supported is treated as an effect. The supporting statement, or statements, is regarded as the cause or condition. For example:

> The speeches of politician X are ambiguous. (*Effect*)
> He wants to conceal his real intentions. (*Cause*)
> Persons who conceal their intentions almost always speak ambiguously. (*General Rule*)

Often, as in this example, the credibility of a cause depends upon the credibility of the generalization which is relevant to it. The general rule expresses the audience's knowledge of similar causal conditions and makes the application to the case at hand. In such situations, the cause to be established is an educated guess. It cannot be taken as a fact. Hence, the speaker must be confident that the generalization is acceptable.

In other situations, the speaker is better off. When he can draw on more exact knowledge than that of opinion and belief, when he can pull on the findings of science and experiment, he can establish the fact of the cause. This, combined with the law or general principle, is highly convincing. For example:

> Williams is a dependable student. (*Effect*)
> He always completes his assignments on time. (*Cause*)
> Prompt discharge of commitments always attends dependability. (*Principle*)

Here the statement of cause could be substantiated by enumerating instances and by statistical evidence.

Probably the most convincing situation of all arises when it can be shown that in the absence of the cause there was a contrary effect. For example:

Farmer X produced more wheat per acre than his neighbor. (*Effect*)
He used chemical fertilizer. (*Cause*)
His neighbor did not. (*Absence of Cause*)
Chemical fertilizer always increases the yield of a crop unless some circumstance interferes. (*Principle*)

In selecting a causal argument and in presenting it, a speaker will be guided by a number of questions:

1. *Does the argument deal with events or conditions?* Whenever a speaker can deal with real causes, the argument is more convincing than when he has to depend upon favoring conditions only.

2. *Is the effect accounted for by a single cause or condition?* In locating *the* cause—if there be an only cause—the speaker weighs the possibility of other causes. Human problems are seldom simple. Obviously forest fires, high grades, world peace, radiation effects, and high prices cannot be explained in terms of single causes.

3. *How* direct *is the connection between cause and effect?* To consider this question is to see the difference between an immediate, or trigger, cause and a more remote but compelling condition. The immediate cause of a forest fire may be a lighted cigarette thrown from a car, or an unextinguished campfire. The more remote condition is a habit—carelessness.

4. *In the* absence *of the cause, would the effect be as probable?* Too often we confuse coincidence and chance with cause and effect. Few people today believe that carrying a rabbit's foot, crossing the fingers, or knocking on wood will keep away bad luck. But some athletes still wear lucky socks and lucky numbers. And some persons say that the atom bomb tests are responsible for the outbreak of unusually violent storms and floods in many parts of the country for the past few years. As yet we do not know of a connection between storms and A-bomb explosions, but there were similar periods of abnormally bad weather long before the A-bomb was invented. Our friend the basketball coach actually does win some games without wearing his lucky socks.

Cause to effect

This logical pattern involves a prediction about the future. The effect-to-cause pattern, on the other hand, is oriented on the present and past. By the nature of his task, the persuader must employ both patterns. To see why this is so helps in understanding and in using the patterns.

A persuasive task is created by a problem-solution situation. In fact, since we are considering causal relationships, we can now say with exactness that persuasion is *caused* by a problem-solution condition. The characteristics of this condition have been described earlier (pages 305–308), as Dewey's approach to problem solving and the traditional approach.

The logic of the problem-solution state of affairs can be stated simply: either a speaker must address himself to the problem or a particular solution or both. If he talks on the problem, he has these alternatives: He says, "I think present conditions are bad and I want you to think so too." Or he says, "I see what the problem is, and it is of this nature because of certain causes and conditions." If he talks to the solution, he says, "I have a solution, and it will remove the causes and conditions which created the problem." Or—if the audience has reached this stage of discussion—he says, "My solution is better than a rival solution, for the rival solution won't take care of the causes which produced the conditions you complain about." One can see at a glance that causal relationships are inherent in recognizing, establishing, and solving a problem. One can see, also, that the problem-solution circumstances entail two dimensions of time. If the speaker deals with the problem only, he is concerned with present conditions and what has caused them. He looks to the present in the light of the past. If the speaker deals with a solution, he says in effect, "If you accept my proposition and act in keeping with it, the consequences *will be* desirable." He looks to the future. Like a physician, the persuasive speaker is a diagnostician; he recognizes the symptoms of the disease—the accompanying conditions and their signs—and determines their cause. He prescribes a remedy. Consequently, when a speaker talks about a problem and its sources, he is reasoning about solutions, he thinks of his proposition as a cause or condition which will bring desirable consequences. He is then within the framework of the cause-to-effect pattern.

In the cause-to-effect pattern, statements direct attention to a cause or condition and the predicted effect. In the advocacy of a solution, here are two typical kinds of structure:

1. *A single statement may join both cause and effect.*

> Independent audits of labor union funds would eliminate dishonest union officials.

Note that the subject-idea designates the cause; the predicate-idea names the effect.

2. *One statement asserts a condition which entails more than one effect; succeeding statements specify the effects.*

> It would be desirable to have union officials elected by secret ballot.
> The requirement would prevent intimidation of members at election time.
> It would restore democratic procedures to labor unions which have lost them.

In using a cause-to-effect argument, the speaker encounters two questions: Has the causal relationship held true in the past? If it has been true in the past, is there any reason why it should *not* operate as expected in the future? The relevancy of these questions can be perceived from the following example:

> Independent audits of labor union funds would eliminate dishonest union officials. (*Conclusion*)
>
> Independent audits of the funds of any organization discourage dishonesty among officials. (*General Premise*)
>
> Unions do not differ from other organizations in ways which would make an audit ineffective. (*Comparative Premise*)

The general premise is combining two ideas: it implies that (1) a union is an example of an organization in which (2) the cause has produced the effect. Then the comparative premise says that a union, taken as an example of an organization, reveals no condition which would make the cause ineffective. Thus it is apparent that the cause-to-effect pattern involves a prediction whose force depends upon comparable conditions in the present and the past.

The Effect of Logical Pattern. The speaker who is familiar with the five logical patterns and who gains experience in applying them in his speeches will gradually realize the sources of their effectiveness. He will see that they cannot make sense to a reasonable person unless the meanings they carry are clear, stable, and unequivocable. Only when meanings are unequivocable can their *relationships* be grasped with any accuracy. He will see, too, that the force of the patterns depends not only on unequivocable meanings but on the *systematic connections* between them.

It is largely through such patterns that the speaker secures assent to the truth of his proposition and of its supporting statements. He realizes that the truth he aims at is at best *probable,* not scientific. Its probability will depend in part upon individual arguments—upon the weight and quality of evidence he can build into them and upon their clearness, relevance, and consistency. Its probability will depend, also, upon the cumulative and combined effect of all the arguments in the speech. Every argument will not seem equally strong to an audience. Indeed, this fact led Thomas Reid, famous eighteenth-century philosopher and logician, to insist that "the strength of probable reasoning for the most part depends, not upon any one argument, but upon many, which unite their force and lead to the same conclusion. Any one of them by itself would be insufficient to convince; but the whole taken together may have a force that is irresistible, so that to desire more evidence would be absurd."

The effectiveness of logical patterns is in part traceable to some of the phenomena of attention. The *connection* between premises and conclusion is a condition favorable to attention. Review the laws of pattern in Chapter 3 —the laws of proximity, similarity, and continuity. Stimuli and ideas that are sufficiently close together to be grasped as a whole, that show continuity and similarity, and that do not omit essential and relevant parts, we prefer to those that are disorganized. And what inference does is to emphasize the form-and-pattern aspect of ideas. Take, for example, the timeworn illustration of applying the general premise to the specific premise: *All men are mortal; I am a man; therefore I am mortal.* The parts of the ideas in the two premises are brought close together: *I* am similar to men and am therefore classified within the meaning of the term *all men.* The comparison made between all men and me enables the mind to make another comparison, that what holds true of all men (*i.e.*, mortality) also holds true of me, and because of the two comparisons the ideas have continuity. Finally, *all men* gives the notion of inclusiveness and completeness that *some men* would not give. (The student should try to identify other conditions that reinforce the continuity, similarity, and inclusiveness of the whole.) What is true of this example of deductive inference is likewise true of any pattern which allows one to perceive clearly related meanings and the connection between them.

FURTHER READING

Bettinghaus, Erwin P. *Message Preparation: The Nature of Proof.* Indianapolis, Ind., 1966. Chapters 5, 7.

Campbell, Norman. *What is Science?* New York: Dover Publications, Inc., 1952.

Castell, Alburey, *A College Logic: An Introduction to the Study of Argument and Proof.* New York, 1935.

Chapman, F. M., and Henle, Paul. *The Fundamentals of Logic.* New York, 1933.

Cohen, Morris, and Nagel, Ernest. *An Introduction to Logic and Scientific Method.* New York, 1936.

Conant, James B. *On Understanding Science.* New York: Mentor Books, 1951.

Copi, J. M. *Introduction to Logic.* New York, 1953. Especially good on methods of definition.

Frye, A. M., and Levi, A. W. *Rational Belief.* New York, 1941.

Leonard, H. S. *An Introduction to Principles of Right Reason.* New York, 1957.

Minnick, Wayne. *The Art of Persuasion.* Boston, 1957, Chapter 6, "Argument."

Thouless, R. H. *Straight and Crooked Thinking.* New York, 1932.

Toulmin, Stephen. *The Uses of Argument.* Cambridge, England, 1958. Chapters 2–4.

Weaver, R. M. *The Ethics of Rhetoric.* Chicago, 1953. Chapter 4, "Abraham Lincoln and the Argument From Definition."

Winans, James A. *Public Speaking.* New York, 1917. Chapter 9, "Persuasion and Belief."

VII
Special Occasions

22

Speeches for Special Occasions

Most occasions for public speaking call for speeches whose primary purposes are either to inform or persuade. On many occasions, however, the *main* purpose at least is something else—to extend or receive a courtesy or to provide entertainment for an audience. When these special purposes prevail, the principles and practices of effective speaking which are the subject of this book are just as important and should be just as carefully applied as in expository and persuasive speeches. That is, these special speeches should be carefully prepared, audience and occasion should be carefully analyzed, clear plans and outlines should be developed, ideas should be amplified concretely and vividly, style should be appropriate, delivery should be characterized by conversational quality.

In these speeches, as a matter of fact, certain qualities of content and presentation are even more important than they are in other speeches, because the audience is almost always aware ahead of time what the speaker's purpose is and where his discourse will lead. Neatness and clarity of structure; plentiful and vivid example and concrete detail; ease, audibility, clarity, fluency, and liveliness of utterance; propriety and grace of style—a high premium is to be placed upon each of these in speeches of introduction, of presentation of a gift or an award, of welcome and response to welcome, and in after-dinner speeches and other speeches of entertainment.

In addition to the heightened value to be placed in such speeches upon the qualities which we have just enumerated, the purposes and occasions prescribe for the speaker certain basic and essential requisites of content—certain established formulas, if you will—within which he must function. His success depends upon how well he works out his speech without exceeding his function and without violating the accepted rules of the job he is doing. The rules for each kind of speech are few, but they should be followed, and the opportunities for individual variation are many. In these speeches, however, as in all others, there is no adequate substitute for good sense, good will, keenness of mind, and a feeling for the fitting and proper.

Speeches of Introduction

Speeches of introduction are so common and so frequently bad that everyone should prepare himself for the times when he will make them. Many speakers would much rather not be introduced at all than be subjected to, and be present while the audience is subjected to, the "introductions" which they often encounter. Speakers are usually introduced either by friends and colleagues (who may be very poor speakers) who know them well, or by chairmen who know them only slightly by repute but wish to seem well acquainted, or by individuals or functionaries known to the audience but who do not know the speaker at all. This, alas, is a just statement of a dismal situation, and there is not very much we can do to improve it unless those persons who introduce speakers will undertake to improve themselves.

Speeches of introduction are often inexcusably poor in delivery and in substance. The delivery is likely to be either feeble and indistinct or stiff and self-conscious. Introducers often say too much or too little, and too frequently they lack tact and taste. These faults need not prevail, however, if introducers will understand their functions, be content to serve those functions, and take their tasks seriously.

Purposes

A speech of introduction should accomplish, as far as possible, two purposes; and those two purposes accomplished to the best of his ability, the introducer should do no more. (1) It should place audience and speaker on a footing of mutual acquaintance, confidence, and sympathy. (2) It should promote the purpose of the speech. It is no part of the purpose to display the introducer, *his* relation to the speaker, *his* relation to the audience, *his* relation to the subject. Whatever the introducer says should advance one of these two purposes. He must resist temptation to turn aside from them.

Materials

The irreducible minimum of content for a speech of introduction, even when the speaker is thoroughly well known to the audience, is the speaker's *name* and *identity*. Such brevity, however, is ordinarily undesirable, unless the audience has been brought to attention and quiet beforehand, because the introduction, like the first few speeches of the first act of a play, is likely to be lost in the stir of the audience's settling down. Shailer Mathews' famous introduction of President Wilson, which has become the norm for presenting the President, only *identified* but did not name the speaker. His entire introduction consisted of these words: "Ladies and gentlemen: The President of the United States." In further promoting acquaintance and confidence between speaker and audience, the introducer should mention favorably but *moderately* why the speaker is qualified to talk on his subject: his experience, his position, his special capabilities.

In promoting the purpose of the speech, the introducer will not only try to direct favorable attention to the speaker by referring to his qualifications, but he should lead that attention toward the subject. He should remind the audience why the subject is especially important or significant either in general or in relation to the occasion, to recent events, to coming events such as the anniversary of a person or an institution, or to the particular audience. Again the length or detail of such remarks will be measured by the audience's previous acquaintance with the subject and its significance. The introducer should not labor the obvious; he should remember also that the speaker himself may wish to point out the importance and significance of his subject by way of getting his speech under way.

There may be ideas properly suggested to the introducer by the audience itself: compliments which he, rather than the speaker, might pay in the interest of good will. If the audience is large or especially distinguished, the introducer may compliment it for being so. He should not, however, *call* it large or distinguished if it obviously is not. Such remarks infuse an inappropriate tone of humor, sarcasm, or insincerity into the relation of speaker and audience. If the audience is small, it is well not to mention its size or to apologize for a small audience.

Whenever possible, the introducer should consult the speaker beforehand to confirm the accuracy of his information—especially name and titles—and to find out what the speaker wishes to have said and what he wishes not to have said. Then, unless it is utterly impossible, the introducer should respect the *speaker's wishes.*

Warnings about content and language

Be brief and moderate. Use restraint in both length and content. Remember that the introducer is the host or the representative of the host. The audience wants to hear the speaker. It is a safe rule that if the speaker is to talk from *five* to *fifteen* minutes, the introducer should not use more than from *thirty* seconds to *two* minutes, and normally no speech of introduction should last more than *five* minutes.

Use tact and taste. Don't embarrass both speaker and audience by overpraising the speaker. It is very easy, if one is not careful, to let a perfectly genuine wish to do justice to a speaker's excellence get out of control and turn into extravagance. Do not dwell on a speaker's exploits, although you ought to mention those which are relevant. Do not prejudice a speaker's excellence as a speaker by alluding *directly* to his ability. Such remarks as "You will now hear an interesting and inspiring speech" are usually more harmful than helpful to the speaker-audience relation. It is better that the audience should find the speaker exceeding their expectations than failing to approach the quality predicted. By extravagance the introducer discredits himself as he embarrasses speaker and audience.

Though good humor should always pervade a speech of introduction, the use of humor, especially humor involving the speaker or tending to make light of occasion or subject, is questionable. There are some few occasions, however, where the expert use of good-natured humor is proper, as for instance in Streeter's introduction of Dean Jones of Yale at the inauguration of President Hopkins of Dartmouth.[1] When in doubt, omit humor.

Find fresh, sincere, and plausible substitutes for such trite and hackneyed phrases as "it is an honor and a privilege," "a scholar and a gentleman," "a man who . . . , and a man who . . . , and a man who. . . ."

Arrangement of the speech

Place the essential information near the conclusion. This essential information includes at least the *subject;* sometimes the *name.* A sense of anticlimax and an impatience for the speech to begin develop in the audience if much is said after the subject is announced. Even when your speech of introduction is very short, do not as a rule put the essential information in the first sentence. The audience may not hear or understand, because of the disturbance of getting settled or because of unfamiliarity with the introducer's voice and manner. Observe a climactic order, but do not strive for something tremendous.

Delivery

It is best not to read a speech of introduction. Even at the expense of some possible fumbling and hesitancy, it is better that the audience and the guest should suppose the introducer to be sincerely uttering his own genuine sentiments than that he should appear to be the impersonal mouthpiece of a piece of paper. Know the ideas thoroughly; plan and practice. The speech must move. But do not read. Maintain a lively sense of communication so as not to sound mechanical and perfunctory.

Pause to get attention before beginning; then speak slowly, distinctly, and loudly enough to be easily heard and understood by the guest speaker and by *all* of the audience.

Presenting a Gift, an Award, or a Memorial

This kind of speech is very often needed because of the many occasions when, in all kinds of societies and business, professional, and civic associations, we

[1] J. M. O'Neill, *Models of Speech Composition* (New York, 1921), p. 670.

wish publicly or semi-publicly to acknowledge the distinction attained by individuals, groups or institutions, or to commemorate a person or event with some tangible token.

Watches, fountain pens, pocketbooks, or wallets are presented by their fellow workers or by management to faithful employees who have served ten, twenty-five, forty years. We gather at the dinner table publicly to bid good-bye to an associate who is moving on to another and better job and to present him with a briefcase or a set of luggage.

Words must go with the medals, ribbons, plaques, cups, trophies, certificates, prizes, and scholarships which we award to individuals or groups who have excelled in athletics, scholarship, business, industry, virtue, or good works. On the occasions of most such awards the audience and the individual honored feel let down or cheated unless someone accompanies the presentation with words of praise and appreciation.

Likewise the presentation of a memorial in honor of the dead creates a solemn and dignified occasion which is hollow without proper words of praise and dedication. Whether the university's literary club presents to the library a book fund in memory of a deceased scholar, a gift primarily for *use;* or whether the war veterans present a statue to the city in memory of the honored dead; in all such situations we expect speeches of presentation appropriate to the donor, the donee, the gift, and the person or event being commemorated.

Purposes

The purposes of speeches of presentation are (1) formally and publicly to exhibit the worth of the recipient, (2) to heighten the sense of appreciation or satisfaction felt by the donor, or donors, and (3) usually to represent the gift as a token or symbol rather than remuneration.

Materials

The minimum expectation from a speech of presentation is that the speaker will mention—or at least *name*—the award, the person receiving it, and the donor, and that he will indicate why the presentation is being made. In fulfilling these requisites, especially the last, there are several kinds of material which the speaker will be more or less expected to use. These requisites will derive from the fitness of the donee to be honored, of the honor as coming from the donor, and the fitness or significance of the gift itself.

Briefly stated, the speaker will:

1. Magnify, though not exaggerate, the services, deeds, qualities, accomplishments, and excellences of the recipient.
2. Say something of the considerations that governed the choice of the gift if these considerations are complimentary to this recipient especially.

3. Minimize, though not depreciate, the intrinsic worth of the gift.
4. Go beyond the material characteristics of the gift to discover a deeper meaning, perhaps a symbolic significance (the gift is, after all, a token).

If the donee is a person, name and illustrate with reasonable restraint his deeds and the qualities that make him worthy of this distinction. If the recipient has been selected as a symbol of a group or as typical of many other persons, dwell not only on his excellences but on the excellences of others like him. If the recipient is an institution or organization, look especially to the principles and qualities for which it stands.

Especially when the gift is a memorial, the speaker should describe the qualities of the person being commemorated, look to the reasons for his being especially worthy of memory, and mention the qualities and motives of the donor. This last sometimes involves some history of the donor, especially of his relations to the person or event being remembered, and to the donee.

Concerning the gift itself, the speaker should call attention to any special qualities which make it particularly valuable or significant. If, for example, it shows fine workmanship or if it is a rare gift, the speaker should show pride in these qualities. The qualities which it symbolizes or of which it reminds one should be attached complimentarily to the person being honored. If it is intended for use, let the use seem real and seem appropriate to both donor and donee.

Manner of presentation

Like the speech of introduction, the speech of presentation should seem to express the genuine, sincere sentiments of the speaker and the donor. If possible it should be spoken extemporaneously upon a foundation of preparation and practice. It is better if not read from the page. Its special qualities should be clear, simple organization and felicity or fitness.

If the occasion permits, the speaker should look with satisfaction at the gift when he is speaking about it; and he should address the recipient directly and should look at him, at least when the actual, physical presentation is being made. Though on many occasions the speaker is presumed to be speaking only to the recipient, the audience is in fact a real part of the function and deserves to hear and understand. The speaker should, therefore, avoid the appearance of carrying on a private conversation with the recipient and a few persons close at hand. He should throughout speak *clearly, distinctly,* and *audibly.*

Accepting a Gift, an Award, a Memorial

In accepting a complimentary honor, a speaker will seldom offer any ideas or information to the audience. He will, however, be expected not only to *feel* but to *show* appreciation. Sometimes, of course, his "speech" may consist of no more than saying "Thank you." Many situations, however, seem to call for a protraction of the process of acceptance and for gracious amplification of the speaker's appreciation so that a dignity may be infused into or maintained in the occasion and so that the audience may have time to take full satisfaction in the recipient's evident pleasure. Thus the speaker will look for proper and gracious ideas through which to convey his thanks. There are, of course, times when a speaker may genuinely exclaim, "I don't know how to thank you. I didn't deserve it." This formula, however, is shopworn and should be used with great caution. Especially should a speaker avoid introducing an obviously preplanned speech with the statement, "I am speechless; I can't find the words to thank you."

Materials

On any occasion when more than a mere "Thank you" is in order, the acceptance speaker should include, in felicitous sentences, the following materials:

1. Admiration, thanks, and appreciation for the gift or the honor.
2. Expression of appreciation of the kindness of friends.
3. Minimization, though not depreciation, of his own services or merits.
4. Sharing of the honor, where it is possible, with others.

In amplifying these ideas the speaker may draw remarks from his own experience, referring perhaps to his trials and difficulties if he can do so without self-glorification—without featuring his personal successes. Whenever he refers to successes, he should let them appear to be attributable to the assistance he has had from other people. It is proper for him to pay tribute to others—his friends and associates. In referring to the gift, the speaker will tell what it means to him beyond its intrinsic worth or its practical use, what it inspires him to accomplish in the future, what it symbolizes with respect to his past associations and his future aspirations and ideals.

On some occasions, when the spirit of the scene is genial rather than sober or formal, the speaker may admit pleasant humor and jest into his speech of thanks. The ultimate effect of his humor must never be to depreciate the gift, himself, or the motives of the donor. Never make a jest for the sake of the jest and then try to set things right by saying, "And now to be serious for a moment. . . ." While receiving the gift, look at the person presenting it; in admiring the gift, look at it; in thanking the donor, don't ignore his presence.

Let there be no relaxing in such essential qualities of all public utterance as *clearness, distinctness,* and *easy audibility*.

Welcoming an Individual or a Group

Speeches of welcome put a premium upon tact and taste in the choice of material and upon grace and felicity of style and delivery.

Purpose

The purpose of a speech of welcome is to extend a sincere and grateful greeting to a person or to a group—such a greeting as offers good fellowship and hospitality. It serves the same purpose on a public occasion that a sincere greeting does between individuals, or that the opening of a door does when one is bidding a guest welcome.

Materials

The least a speaker should do in such a speech is:

1. Indicate for whom he is speaking.
2. Present complimentary facts about the person or group to which the courtesy is being extended.
3. Predict pleasant experiences.

In all of this he should take pains to *illustrate,* not to argue.

In elaborating his address of welcome the speaker may have recourse to three general types of materials. First, it is likely that the host thinks favorably of the spirit, purposes, and accomplishments of the guest and the group or organization which the guest represents. The speaker may, therefore, undertake to explain or to point up the purpose or spirit of the occasion—to declare graciously why it is appropriate and significant that the host and guest should come together under the present circumstances. This is the sort of thing which most mayors try to do when welcoming to their cities the conventions or representatives of prominent organizations. Thus was the United Nations Conference welcomed to San Francisco in April 1945, and thus was a new president of a metropolitan university welcomed by a spokesman of the Chamber of Commerce.

Secondly, the host may wish to explain or publicly to rehearse the spirit or purpose of the organization or institution extending the welcome. "This is what we are," says the speaker, "and we trust that you will find us good." Thus might the spokesman of a school or college prepare the way for a visitor from another school or college who has come to observe the operation of a well-established system of independent study for undergraduates. The speaker, however, must take care not to seem boastful or to suggest that the visitor is lucky to be privileged to observe the local wonders. If the visitor comes to impart information or to confer some favor upon the hosts, the welcoming spokesman ought perhaps to refer to the visitor's special qualifications and accomplishments. Welcoming a new director for the Boy Scout organization or the artist who is to paint the murals in the new post office, might well call for material of this kind.

In the third place, and perhaps most frequently, the speaker will think it fitting to pay a tribute to the person or organization being welcomed. Dawes' tribute to the Jewish Welfare Board[2] was an example of this method. The faults of this sort of tribute which thoughtless or ill-prepared speakers will commit are generality and extravagance. The speaker should, if possible, praise the guest for specific distinctions rather than general virtues, and he should keep his praise well within the limits of reasonable plausibility.

General characteristics of the speech

The speech of welcome is well organized. The audience is gratified by form and progress as well as by content, is comfortably aware of where the speaker is going and how he is getting there. There is always a central theme which is serious and complimentary. There is usually a definite approach or introduction which leads gracefully to the suggestion of the main theme, and there is a conclusion, brief and dignified.

The mood of a speech of welcome is more serious and exalted (though, we hope, not more stuffy) than the mood of a speech of introduction, for on these occasions the guest himself and what he represents, rather than his speech, will be the main attraction. The mood is more dignified and more suggestive of formality. There may even be a touch of ritual in it, such as the symbolic offering to the guest of the key to the city. And the mood tends to be strongly emotional. The guest expects the language of emotion; the audience demands it. The speaker must, then, get beyond casual coldness, but he must not exceed good sense by extravagance and spoil everything by gushing.

The speech should exhibit taste and judgment. The manner and the material must fit all elements of the occasion: speaker, audience, guest, time, place, circumstances.

In spite of all the "must's," however—and there are few which good will and good sense will not dictate—there is plenty of room for individuality and originality in the speaker. Newness or freshness (not, however, "smartness") in stating old ideas, or the handling of an old topic in a novel way, provides adequate challenge to the ingenuity of any speaker.

[2] J. M. O'Neill and F. K. Riley, *Contemporary Speeches* (New York, 1930), pp. 13–14.

Responding to a Welcome

A speech of response is basically only a speech of welcome or presentation in reverse. Hence the speaker will:

1. Indicate for whom he is speaking.
2. Express appreciation of the kindness of friends.
3. Speak complimentary words about the person or group extending the courtesy.
4. Minimize his own merits, though not depreciate them.
5. Anticipate pleasant experiences.

In the speech of response, as in the speech accepting a gift or award, the speaker does not, at first, have the initiative. He is following another speaker who has set the pace, so to speak, and has established the tone of the occasion. Whether the previous speaker has done poorly, has shown bad taste and little judgment, or has kept the occasion on a high level of propriety and dignity, the responding speaker dare not abruptly change the pace or tone.

Circumstances, therefore, make the speech of response often the most difficult of all speeches of courtesy because it is the hardest to prepare for and because, when you have prepared, it is impossible to be reasonably sure that what you thought of saying will fit the circumstances. In the first place, the speech of response must often be impromptu, and therefore one is tempted to be content with muttering a few general inanities and letting it go at that—like the average "thank you" letter after Christmas. Furthermore, the response may have to follow different kinds of leads which are frequently unpredictable. One may have to respond to the presentation of a gift or token of esteem or of some mark of honor. Or one may be offered a tribute whose content, and hence the resultant position he may find himself in, cannot be foretold. And then one may be tendered a speech of welcome which cuts the bottom out from under most of what he intended to say. One may, for example, have decided to comment on the spirit, purposes, or virtues of the welcoming group, only to find them already displayed beyond his power to magnify. Or one may have elected to characterize the spirit of the occasion, only to hear the preceding speaker steal every last rumble of his thunder. This kind of speech, therefore, must be composed with the utmost sincerity and as much ingenuity as is available.

Purpose

The speech of response to welcome (with or without presentation of a token) has one purpose only, to express *appreciation*. The speaker will do well to let that purpose thoroughly dominate him and to draw his materials according to an understanding of the full implications of what it is to "appreciate." To appreciate is not merely to thank. It is to *value,* to perceive accurately the *whole worth* of a thing, to *understand.* The speaker will ask himself: Why do I value this address of welcome? This gift? This tribute? The people welcoming me? The group I represent? He will then tell his hosts and his audience.

Materials

He will generally evince his appreciation by elaborating one or more of the following themes. He will express appreciation of the significance of the occasion, what it means and will mean to him and to those whom he represents. He will pay tribute to the organization, institution, community, or persons offering the welcome. He will explain the purpose or spirit of the organization for whom he is speaking. He will, as a matter of fact, adapt to his response the same kinds of material which might have been used in welcoming him.

General characteristics

In form, the speech of response is much like the speech of welcome. It always has a theme. There are always some ways of finding excellence in an organization or of praising or paying tribute to a person. The speech will always have an approach and a conclusion. The special problem of the approach will be the neat and gracious fitting of the speaker's own theme into the situation left by the preceding speaker. This at times may be no small problem! The speaker must avoid the impression of ignoring, either in his manner or in the ideas he uses, the speech with which he was welcomed. Here again words may "fail," but he should not say so unless they really do. The audience expects him to talk. As a matter of fact, a speech of response is usually much longer than a speech of welcome.

It is, perhaps, useless reiteration to say that the speech must *fit* the occasion. The material must be appropriate. More, possibly, than others, this speech puts emphasis on content. Therefore the speaker must know whereof he speaks. Vagueness or plain ignorance will not serve. Blunders in taste and judgment are less likely if one is well equipped with information.

In summary, the speaker has been the recipient of formal courtesy. He must show his *appreciation* of that courtesy.

Speeches for Entertainment

There is some legitimate question whether a speech which does not, to some extent, entertain an audience can be fully effective in any purpose. Surely, for most purposes it is easier to inform and persuade a pleased and interested listener than a displeased and bored one. Hence we may take it for granted that whatever makes a speech interesting, vivid, alive, and communicative also works to make it entertaining—if we interpret entertainment broadly, as we should, and do not restrict it to mere enjoyment of the funny, the comic, the humorous.

As there are few good speeches, for whatever purpose, which do not also incidentally entertain an audience, so there are few good speeches whose *sole* purpose or effect is to amuse or entertain. This is not to say that entertainment as the primary and avowed purpose for a speech is low, illegitimate, or undesirable. Everyone knows that much speaking which is done in public and in private is prompted by a wish to provide pleasure and diversion for one's friends or one's listeners, whoever they may be. And everyone knows that an entertaining talker, either at the dinner table at home, at the banquet table, or on the platform is a valuable asset to society. It is normally true, however, that except perhaps in vaudeville routine, a speech is more thoroughly and effectively entertaining if the entertainment grows more or less plausibly out of the development of ideas intended to convey information and understanding.

In discussing the entertaining speech, therefore, the most that we need do is to suggest some of the typical occasions for speeches of entertainment and to indicate the kinds of methods and supporting material which will usually predominate in such speeches.

Occasions

Many public, if not academic, lectures, though they often have informative value, are fundamentally for the amusement and diversion of those who attend. World travelers, explorers, adventurers, renowned hunters or fishermen—whether they describe places or people, experiences they have had or thoughts which have come to them amidst their adventures—speak mainly to entertain their audiences, not necessarily to educate them. When the traveler returns from his trip to Mexico, to the Grand Canyon, or to the airplane factory, or when he reports his interview with the president of Ecuador, he will want usually to improve the *spirits* of his listeners. If he improves their minds also, he will consider that as so much clear profit beyond what he expected.

Likewise various social and semisocial occasions provide natural circumstances for speeches chiefly to entertain or divert an audience. Club meetings, parties, fraternal gatherings, and especially dinners and luncheons call for conversation and speeches that provide a maximum of entertainment with a minimum of weighty thought or systematic information. Many luncheon and dinner organizations, of course, make it a point to have programs provided with serious and important content. Even so, the speaker who would be heard eagerly and would make his subject acceptable will make his presentation also as entertaining as possible. The luncheon or dinner occasion is, of course, the natural habitat of that most popular of discourses, the after-dinner speech, which is given special treatment below.

Characteristics

In materials the speech for entertainment will favor the novel and vivid over the familiar and the exact, the active and lively over the close and concisely logical. Careful, laborious explanation will yield to lifelike impressions and colorful description. High premiums will be placed on the concrete example, the dramatic anecdote, story, or narrative, the striking comparison and contrast, the apt quotation, the effective introduction of direct discourse and snatches of dialogue. Humorous exaggeration, witty and unexpected phrasing and turns of thought, human interest, human peculiarities and foibles—these factors will stand out in speeches to entertain. In short, we are back to the emphasis of our earlier chapters on clarity and interest; and here, as there, we warn that the means of development, the devices of effectiveness, must serve the function of heightening the meaning of a significant, though not necessarily a complicated, idea.

In his *manner of presentation,* the entertaining speaker will be lively, vigorous, good-natured, optimistic, and kindly. He will keep things moving and will resist the temptation to labor for an effect that seems slow in coming or to milk the last thin drop of humor or wit from a situation or from a gag. He will not expect to rival at their own specialties the high velocity comedians on the variety programs, and he will shun the easy assumption that his every remark must be a witty gem and that anything he says must necessarily be funny.

He will use *humor* to the best of his ability, but he will not overrate his ability. He will know that humor is only *one* avenue of entertainment, and though a good one, not always the most appropriate. In his use of humor he will be guided by what we said earlier—that jokes, anecdotes, and wisecracks are not the only sources of effective humor. He will understand that comedy is founded in the incongruous—in a painless disharmony between a thought and its expression, between a person and his acts or his language, between an individual and his pretensions or his opinion of himself. Where injury or pain begins, genuine humor ends. Though genial parody or take-off and other forms of burlesque are useful, an entertaining speaker will not let himself slip into biting satire or sarcasm. Such behavior, though spectacular and tempting, almost always defeats its own purpose and does more harm than good. The end of entertainment is a glow of friendly satisfaction in the listeners—satisfaction with the speaker and satisfaction with themselves. Only the devices that promote that end are legitimate materials for the entertaining speaker who wishes to entertain again. The audience, as ever, is the measure of the fitting and appropriate.

The After-Dinner Speech

Among speeches whose primary purpose is entertainment, the so-called after-dinner speech is at once probably the most admired, most abused, and most difficult. To it, all that we have said about the entertaining speech applies with special force. *Hence our particular suggestions to the after-dinner speaker may serve to point up and to summarize the essence of our advice about speaking for entertainment.*

All postprandial speeches are not speeches of entertainment, and many of them are not even intended to be. The essentially serious informative or persuasive addresses delivered above dining tables need not occupy our time now. Most of this book is concerned with those speeches. We will only redirect the student's attention to the principle that such a speech will succeed best if it is adapted to the special conditions of audience and occasion which prevail after a meal in an atmosphere of disarrangement, cigar smoke, and tinkling water glasses and coffee cups.

Purpose

What is normally meant by after-dinner speaking is discourse providing *entertainment primarily,* usually after a meal of the banquet sort. The speaker is expected to present light stuff (though not exclusively frivolous) in an open, discursive, vivid style.

Demands

After-dinner speaking is difficult because it demands humor, because it must be interesting, and because the speaker is usually asked to *speak,* not to speak *about* anything in particular. After eating, people expect to be interested without giving much effort themselves except willingness to be entertained. They resent a speaker's imposing upon their good will by handling a heavy subject in a dry way; and, contrariwise, they are disgusted by a speaker's abusing their good will by pelting them with a string of pointless stories and anecdotes. The form requires wit, grace, charm, good humor, and at least some good sense.

Minimum essentials

The basic formula for an after-dinner speech is:

1. Have a single, simple idea which you state vividly and illustrate and develop good-naturedly.

2. Use humor if it can seem spontaneous and be germane to the subject.
3. Be brief.
4. Avoid making other persons ridiculous.

Materials

The after-dinner audience wants to be shown, not to be reasoned with; to watch, not to exert itself. Such concealed argument as there is must not be dry, heavy, or compact. It must be insinuated into the audience's minds, not loaded in or driven in. Hence the materials must be vivid; they must be capable of resting easily on a full stomach. *Illustrations,* humorous if humor is practicable, developed with perhaps more detail than would seem economical on more sober occasions, should occupy the largest portion of the time. *Analogies* which progress in a leisurely fashion rank with illustrations as basic material. Relief and change of pace can be attained by energetic *figures of speech* and *fresh turns of phrase.* A special type of illustration, the *imaginative sketch,* especially when it involves persons and their faults and foibles, is peculiarly appropriate to the after-dinner speech.

At the core of the speech, however, should be an idea or a sentiment which is worth the trouble. Ideas, for example, that serve to show us the absurdity or the folly of our ways—rather than the viciousness of our sins—or sentiments that make us aware of the possible charm or pleasure of our relations with our fellows may well be amplified in after-dinner speeches. Subject sentences for such speeches (stated or implied) may be exemplified by the following:

> It is far more important for the new Dean of the Law School to charm and please his students than to see that they are prepared for the Law. (*Ironic*)
>
> He who feeds the chickens deserves the egg.
>
> In many walks of life oversize decisions are frequently made by undersized brains.
>
> Men harass themselves unduly and plague their wives unnecessarily by wrongly supposing that women's hats are intended to be head coverings instead of ornaments.
>
> Our school (or our association) provides a basis for good fellowship which is worth all the expense and inconvenience of attending reunions (or conventions).
>
> The professor is, after all, the collegiate athlete's best friend.

Ideas and sentiments such as these, developed with fundamental insight as well as jocularity and good humor, can make, and have made, entertaining after-dinner speeches. Audiences have come away realizing, agreeably, that they had not only a glow of enjoyment but a feeling that something had been said.

Arrangement

In presentation, the normal forms and divisions of the speech are often eliminated in favor of an *apparently* casual and impromptu organization. The introduction and conclusion, however, are very important. The introduction *must* be interesting and in perfect harmony with the mood of the occasion. An anecdote is a good device for effecting an introduction. Sometimes the anecdote, however, is too good; it may set a pace which the speaker will find hard to keep up, and it may dominate rather than serve the *idea* of the speech. A speaker should beware of permitting himself to drag in a feeble excuse for an idea in order to have a plausible reason for telling a good story. His effort should be to find the story for the idea, not the idea for the story. In any event, his introduction must be graceful, because expression, graceful and charming, may often serve to avert the dismal consequences of weaknesses of idea in a speech, although stylistic excellence can never be an adequate substitute for substance.

The conclusion will be best if it is brief and if it leads to a real climax. At this point also an anecdote may be good if it is short and pointed. Some speakers find an apt and surprising quotation a good means of securing the effect of brevity and climax. The formal conclusion is effective only if it is obviously burlesqued. The conclusion must not, like the "lone and level sands," "stretch far away."

Some smart but unwary toastmaster once introduced a famous after-dinner speaker by likening him to an automatic vending machine. Said he, "Just put a dinner in the slot and up comes a speech." The speaker's retort, deadly but indelicate, paid the toastmaster amply for a personal slur and for misrepresenting the true genesis of a good after-dinner speech. Good after-dinner speeches are not prepared during the consumption of a meal at the speaker's table. They are carefully and thoroughly prepared on a foundation of knowledge of the audience and the occasion. One does not take lightly an invitation to "speak informally." He understands that to mean "Be so well prepared that you will be free to seem informal and casual." One can't debate extemporaneously with other speakers on the program, for argument and debate are not *in* the occasion. One cannot rely on commonplaces, for other speakers may have uttered them already. "If the known practice of many of the best speakers is worth anything," wrote Sears, "it may be inferred that very careful prevision and provision are needful: prevision to see what is likely to be timely and effective; provision to secure it and order it in effective sequence."[3] That is the lesson from successes and failures in after-dinner speaking.

[3] "After Dinner Speaking," *Modern Eloquence* (rev. ed., New York, 1929), III, xxi.

In the long run, we may agree that "good taste, generous sentiment, sober and fond recollection may be more needful than knowledge and zeal."[4] *Fitness* is the one great standard for the after-dinner speech.

FURTHER READING

The inclusion of many actual examples of whole speeches and portions of speeches in the preceding pages would, we realize, have some advantages. We believe, however, that they would not be worth the lengthening of the chapter and the interruption of the reading of the text which they would have cost. Though the speeches for special purposes have certain definable requisites, each speech is so much a function of the occasion which creates it that no one speech is truly illustrative of what another ought to be. For this reason we choose rather to refer the interested student or teacher to the collections of speeches listed below than to provide him with a selected anthology in these pages.

Baird, A. Craig, *American Public Addresses 1740–1952.* New York, 1954.
Brigance, W. H., *Classified Speech Models.* New York, 1928.
Lindgren, Homer D., *Modern Speeches.* New York, 1926, 1930.
Modern Eloquence. New York, 1929.
O'Neill, J. M., *Models of Speech Composition.* New York, 1921.
———, *Modern Short Speeches.* New York, 1924.
O'Neill, J. M., and Riley, F. K., *Contemporary Speeches.* New York, 1930.
Parrish, W. M., and Hochmuth, Marie, *American Speeches.* New York, 1954.
Sarett, Lew, and Foster, W. T., *Modern Speeches on Basic Issues.* New York, 1939.

[4] *Ibid.*, xxiii.

VIII
The Study of Speeches

23

Method in the Study of Speeches

Purposes

Speechmaking is a distinctive process in the operation of society, and speeches are living events or facts in the history of human affairs. They happen. Like any event, a speech comes about as part of a situation—of circumstances and movement prior to it and surrounding it—and it affects circumstances and movement subsequent to it. It draws upon and feeds the springs of decision and action. So speeches live in time and space, serving immediate or extended purposes and performing intended and unintended functions. In the broadest sense, then, a speech is material for the study of society in operation, either recent or remote.

Like any historical event, moreover, a speech can become an object of study so long as there is a record of it, whether in print, in manuscript, in typescript, on sound recording, on film or video tape, or in the recollection of witnesses. Since a speech, furthermore, is an organic embodiment of audience, speaker, subject, circumstances, and language, the record of a speech may furnish data on any of these elements at a given time, or on the relations among them. To speeches, therefore, we may go for biography, sociology, economics, linguistics, psychology, philosophy, politics, science, religion, literature, or almost any other matter which men in society discuss, think about, or exemplify.

Thus, speeches may be studied profitably for evidence relevant to many things outside speechmaking. We may learn from a speech of Oliver Cromwell, for example, how discipline was maintained in the army that subdued Ireland, or from a speech of Andrew Jackson what the idiom of the western territory was in the early nineteenth century. Speeches themselves, however, are distinctive phenomena, individual artifacts, which may be studied for what they are, rather than solely for the historical evidence which they contain. In this respect, of course, they are like poems and plays, paintings, scarabs, fossils, and the stumps of large trees.

Strictly speaking, a speech is not a speech in the fullest sense except when it is being presented to an audience at a time and a place and by a speaker. For practical purposes of study, however, we will speak of available records of speeches in whatever form as speeches. The text of a speech is only the basic material of study, of course, but it is the indispensable evidence. From it and around it we reconstruct, with the degree of completeness that suits our purposes, the context which was the speech—whether the Governor's address to the convention of the pharmacists, published in today's newspaper, or Pericles' Funeral Oration, recorded in Thucydides' *History of the Peloponnesian War.* In this chapter, as we have throughout the book, we write of the speech as a discrete object, as an individual verbal artifact. It should be evident, however, that we are considering the speech also as part of the pervasive phenomenon of *speaking,* of the process of intentional oral communication.

Nothing is so dull, we are told, as dead issues. Perhaps we are told rightly. Dead issues, however, have a way of not staying dead. Moreover, so long as men strive to form and control their collective destinies, they will probably go on trying, through public speaking and debate (and the equivalent in print), to diagnose the ailments of their times, to identify the remedies, and to persuade each other to take the cures. Perhaps the specific ideas presented in the debates over British parliamentary reform in the 1770's and 1780's are dull and have little relevance to problems in the United States today. Yet the ways in which men in the parliaments of George III went about attacking or defending the maladjustments in representation, which two hundred years of shifting population and social change had brought about, bear close resemblance to the ways men and women attacked and defended legislative reapportionment in the General Assembly of Iowa in 1965 and 1967.

Because many of the ways and methods of speechmaking are timeless, the serious student of speaking will include in his program the frequent and methodical study of speeches. No doubt, simply because he is living in the present, he will be most likely to get involved with current or recent speeches in which the unresolved issues of present politics, society, and the life of the human spirit are being worked over. He will wish to study also speeches from the past, even the distant past. Speeches at a distance are far enough removed from the passions and controversies of the present, so that one may view them and their circumstances with more objectivity, though with less intimacy, than those in which one's personal interests are actively concerned. Furthermore, any critic of human achievement, if he would understand and judge the present soundly, ought to know well that sort of achievement in the past.

To be most effective, the process of getting acquainted with speeches should be systematic rather than random, it should proceed according to method rather than caprice, and it should be consciously critical rather than merely absorbent. So-called gut reactions are often cues for judgment, but they must not be substituted for analysis. We shall undertake, therefore, to sketch briefly in this chapter purposes, methods, and procedures for the study of speeches by the student of speaking. The student of speaking, of course, will be also the critic or judge of speeches. The functions of maker and critic are closely related; yet the plan of study is designed chiefly to supplement the student's practice of speechmaking, not to qualify him as a professional critic. He is a critic, nevertheless, and we often refer to him thus in this chapter.

Four purposes, in brief, should guide the student in his study of speeches:

1. To gain the knowledge which comes of wide and intelligent acquaintance with the kind of product he wishes to learn to understand and to make.
2. To know from experience the practice of good speakers and poor ones, and hence, to understand, to test, and to modify the rules and principles of speechmaking which he finds in his textbook.
3. To observe analytically what a characteristic product of the human mind and ingenuity is, and from that observation to develop taste in speeches—that is, a reliable sense of the better and the worse in quality.
4. To understand, and hence be better able to cope with, one of the important factors in the functioning of organized society.

To the furtherance of these purposes, the student-critic may well direct attention first to what sorts of artifacts particular speeches are; second, to how those particular speeches might be expected to have functioned in their situations; and third, to how to approach the problems of appraisal and judgment.

Let us comment first, however, upon the relation of the study of speeches to the study of speechmaking. All the arts and skills of doing and making are learned first of all from unconscious imitation of makers and of works, and later from conscious imitation. In the long run, we learn *primarily* from practice and from observing the example of others. Intelligent practice and intelligent use of the example of others are guided by method, such method as is elaborated in this textbook. Art follows nature, however, and the product precedes the discovery and formulation of rules and principles governing it. Hence, the practice of speakers can be the only ultimate criterion for the soundness of the rules and the validity of the principles. As the architect must know houses; the poet, poems; the dramatist, plays; the tailor, clothes; so the speaker must know speeches and the process of speaking.

As rapidly as possible, therefore, the student of speechmaking should gain *familiarity with many and various speeches and many and various speakers.* Through familiarity he may gradually develop a sense of what sort of things speeches and speakers are, of what speeches are made of and how they function, and of the basic characteristics of a speech amidst the unlimited variety of speeches and speaking.

The Speech as Artifact

In proceeding to the study of a speech, one may begin with any of several considerations: (1) the speaker—who he is, what his purposes are, what his reputation is—in short, what in the speaker gave rise to the speech and contributed to its meaning; (2) the times and the circumstances, including the audience, and the conditions of the world into which the speech was born; (3) text of the speech, what the verbal creation actually is. Ultimately, for the full investigation of the speech, one must study all these aspects in relation to each other. The normal and natural place to begin, however, is at the text of the speech, what actually was said or was prepared for saying. Obviously, any particular speech is an element in a historical situation, and what is actually in the text is finally to be determined only through study of the situation. With that ultimate necessity always in mind, however, the critic may safely concentrate first upon the recorded verbal object, the text.

In one common view, the function of the literary critic—for example, the student of poetry—is to show how the poem is made; that is, to examine its contents, its form, its language, its imagery, its mood, and the interrelations of all these, in order to determine the total meaning which is potential in the poem. The first and crucial task of the critic of a speech is comparable. He will seek (1) to determine the foundations and framework of the thought; (2) to discover the pattern of development through which that basic thought comes to life in a structure of related statements and propositions; (3) to observe the methods and materials of amplification through which the statements and propositions find meaning in facts and values, and that meaning becomes clear, lively, and limited; and (4) to appreciate the qualities of style which make the whole into the particular speech of the particular speaker to the particular audience and arising out of the particular occasion to which it belongs.

How should one go about this study, this analysis? The essentials and much of the detail of procedure may be derived from our earlier chapters. Although composing and presenting a speech is not the same undertaking as analyzing and judging a speech that has already been made or is being made, the methods and principles for composing may readily become the guides for analysis, the working criteria for critical appraisal. The student of speeches, therefore, will, in effect, reverse the application of the principles he has learned for speechmaking and will use them to help him as a critic to look systematically inside and around a speech which he wishes to examine. For example, in the making of a speech there are in general certain principal purposes which govern the choice of subject, the selection of material, and the manner of handling material. In studying a speech which has been made, the discovery of the apparent principal purpose will begin to throw light on how the subject, material, and modes of handling were, may have been, or might have been controlled. Again, if there are so-and-so many kinds of amplifying and supporting material usually potentially available to a speaker, and if each of the kinds of material has certain characteristic uses (Chapters 7 and 21), then one who is studying a speech may apply his knowledge of these matters to guide him in identifying and describing the kinds of development which are there in a speech and how they probably worked.

In undertaking to use the principles, methods, and topics treated in a textbook on public speaking as his guides for the study of a speech, the student may slip unconsciously into the unsatisfactory practice of discovering in the speech merely examples of such relevant items as may appear in the textbook. This process may be useful as a method of getting under way, but the student should remind himself that he is attempting primarily to illuminate a speech—what it is and how it will work—not to illustrate the textbook or even Aristotle's *Rhetoric*. Hence he will use the reminders which the text provides as means of getting into the speech and seeing what is there and as suggestions of some of the things which he may discover. Chiefly what he wishes to know is the speech. Only secondarily is he concerned with how good a guide the textbook may be.

The student need not, perhaps should not, be concerned at first with whether a speaker has used the best materials and methods or whether he has used them with greater or lesser skill. He should first wish to know what the speech is made of and how it is constructed. In other words, with the principles of speechmaking as the basis of his inquiry and with any other relevant aid, including that of his own independent observation and common sense, the student of a speech should seek first to possess the speech, then later, perhaps, to judge it.

Establishing the text

To study a speech as a speech, therefore, the student will discover first what was actually said. That is, he will verify so far as is needful the printed or recorded text from which he is going to work. Normally, this problem need not delay him long. Speakers, and editors who publish speeches, however, are usually more interested in texts which will sustain the scrutiny of readers than in representing exactly the words and sentences as they were actually spoken. Hence there is always likely to be some problem of text in the study of any speech which has appeared in print. The problem is of most importance, usually, and presents most difficulty to the scholarly investigator of speeches from the more or less remote past. The problem exists, of course, for the student of contemporary and recent speeches—for anyone wishing to study speech in its spoken version. For the most part it will be sufficient if the student is on his guard and does his best to know the source, authenticity, and condition of the text which he is studying. Texts printed in the *Congressional Record* are likely to be notably different from what the speaker actually said, even when the speeches were actually delivered, for Congressmen and Senators have, and use, great freedom in revising and "extending" their remarks before printing.

For current speeches one should prefer the complete texts as published in such newspapers as *The New York Times* and the *St. Louis Post-Dispatch*. Whereas most newspapers summarize or abridge speeches, even key speeches of important persons, the *Times* and often the *Post-Dispatch* make a point of giving the complete text. Another ready source of full texts of some current speeches is the periodical, *Vital Speeches of the Day*. There the texts are very likely to have been reedited by the speakers. Good tape or disc recordings are likely to be available also for many speeches broadcast during the past thirty years or so. Even where confirmation or correction of the text is not possible or feasible, however, we may generally assume that what a speaker offers the readers of his speech is pretty close to what he presented to his listeners. We may profitably study the text, therefore, as that of a speech rather than of an editorial or an essay.

Beginning the analysis

Initial Impression of the Speech as a Whole. With a satisfactory text before him, it is perhaps best for the student-critic to begin by reading or listening to the entire speech two or three times without stopping to make any special notes and without concentrating any more sharply on what is going on than would a judicious listener to the original. This stage in the process will help the student get accustomed to the speaker's habits of language and, if the speech is on a recording, to his pronunciation and delivery. More important, this continuous reading or listening will give the observer an overall impression of the purpose, content, and import of the speech as a whole, with at least a sense of its form and pattern. Perhaps at the conclusion of each reading, or listening, he might jot down his impressions on these general matters and on any other elements which especially attract his attention, such as striking examples or impressive language.

Why the Speech was Made. The critic should direct some thought to why the speech was made. He examines the occasion, for it is the occasion and the circumstances which give birth to a speech. Knowledge of these enables him to determine the speaker's purpose as precisely as may be, and information about the circumstances illuminates, as nothing else can, the speaker's chief lines of thought and principal arguments. So the student inquires, Did the speaker confess to his purpose either in the speech or elsewhere? Most speakers will at least suggest what they want their hearers to believe or do, but they are often more explicit about their purposes later—in their biographies, letters, and memoirs. What was the audience most interested in at the time of delivery? Was it, for example, a specific motion in the Senate, such as prompted Webster's famous replies to Haynes on nullification and slavery? What prompted the minister's sermon last Sunday? or the President's television address? Sometimes, of course, the obvious occasion is not very illuminating; rather, the context of the audience's thought provides the clues. G. W. Curtis's speech on "The Puritan Principle" was not prompted by the mere fact of a banquet; rather, the kinds of people who were present and what was uppermost in their minds called forth a great speech whose purpose did not have to be announced. Huxley's "On a Piece of Chalk" was not designed primarily to explain the chalk beds underlying England. The situation, the context of the occasion, is especially important to the critic when he suspects he is dealing with a piece of propaganda. The history of the moment is most likely to yield the right slant on a speech.

Chief lines of thought

In the light of his initial impressions of the content and development of the speech and his conclusions about why the speech was made, the critic should formulate a provisional subject sentence or proposition embodying the governing thought. This formulation must be necessarily provisional, for the critic is always likely to modify and refine his initial judgments, even if he does not change them substantially, as he progresses with his analysis. The relations, however, between his first impressions and his later determinations will tell him something significant about himself as audience or about the speech.

As we have shown in our early chapters, the first stage in the composition of a speech—after the subject is chosen, the material is found, and the purpose is determined—is the establishment of a central idea and the working out of the principal lines of reasoning, patterns of thought, or imaginative conceptions to promote the purpose and control the material. Likewise, in the first step of his critical study of a speech the student had better outline in writing the lines of reasoning which underlie the speech, or the internal structure of the speaker's apparent thinking, including the important unspoken as well as spoken propositions upon which he appears to base his ideas. Booker T. Washington (see pages 543–546) argues, for example, that the South will prosper or come to grief depending on whether the Southern white man and the Negro take advantage of each other's economic potentialities. The critic should inquire what unspoken assumptions about political and social rights for the Negro lie behind his argument.

In short, the student wants to know what, stripped to the bare bones, supports the thought of the speech and holds it together—if, indeed, it is unified. In coming to grips with the basic reasoning behind a speech, the student will call upon his own best analytic and critical powers. He may, perhaps, gain some help from reviewing what he has learned about logical and imaginative processes (pages 304–312, 359–369). Through this analytical study he will arrive at a reformulation of the central idea and a speech outline showing the chronological pattern and the logical relations of the statements and the supporting statements of the several levels of generality. That outline will embody the principles and take the form which we have developed in Chapter 9.

No doubt most speeches which one studies, including one's own, fall short, sometimes more and sometimes less, of the ideal tidiness of outline, the schematic sharpness of structure, which in our chapters we present and exemplify. Since critical analysis, however, involves first what a given speech actually is, and only later, if at all, what it might have been, the outline should show the actual structure and organization, without forcing the speech into conformity with an outline which is neater, no doubt, but is not the outline of that speech. None of us (except a teacher!) is obligated to straighten out someone else's chaos—only to be sure that we ourselves are not deceived.

Methods and materials of development

Using the structural outline as his guide, the critic will seek to determine how the main lines of thought or argument are developed into the finished speech. Now he will bring to bear his knowledge of methods and materials of development—of amplifying and supporting the statements and propositions. He will observe, for example, which ideas in the speech are emphasized through enlargement, which through position. He will notice which ideas seem to be barely stated or suggested rather than developed. He will discover what kinds and qualities of amplification and support are brought to bear, and where and how they are employed. The principal materials of this sort for which he will be on the lookout are examples, comparisons, definition, factual material, values, testimony and authority, repetition and restatement, evidence of various sorts, logical reasoning (including deduction, generalization, analogy, cause and effect), and the other methods and materials which we have discussed for making ideas, information, and courses of action clear, strong, and attractive. From this phase of his investigation the student may draw some conclusions about the characteristic methods of amplification and of argument which belong to a particular speech or a particular speaker. Henry Van Dyke, for example, in his sermon called "Salt," leans heavily upon analogy. So does Huxley in the "Method of Scientific Investigation" and "On a Piece of Chalk." The student will wish to determine so far as he can what in the economy of the speech, or in the predispositions of the speaker, or in the nature of the occasion, for example, accounts for the characteristic kind of material. A recent critic of Edmund Burke finds that Burke, especially in his speeches and writings on the French Revolution, characteristically uses the argument from "circumstance," and on the basis of this discovery the critic comes to certain conclusions about the weakness of Burke's speaking.[1]

Arrangement of the speech

It will be especially enlightening to the student for improving his own practice to observe carefully where, in what relations to each other, and with what apparent effect on each other the several kinds of developing material occur in the speech. For instance, does an example placed after the presentation of a block of statistical information have the effect of enlightening the force of the statistics or of leaving the emphasis on the particular application? Is the resulting meaning different from the meaning if the example were to appear first and be followed by statistics?

These questions suggest a larger, more general question about the detailed arrangement of the speech, the disposition, as it is called traditionally. What meaning are influenced or effects produced by the order, the placing, the proportioning, and the sequence of the elements of the speech? Perhaps this question often cannot be answered with complete assurance; but the answer, if it is to be worth much, must be derived from a detailed and careful description of how the parts and ingredients of the speech are put together. Perhaps the structure of Bruce Barton's speech "Which Knew Not Joseph," in which two longish stories lead to three "very simple" points, suggests an informality which the speaker wished to establish and promotes a sense that he is not really telling his audience anything but is merely reminding them of what they know already.

Style

By this point in his analysis the critic will have achieved a pretty good description of the thought-and-idea-content, of the structure and organization the subject (both ostensible and real), and the purpose of the speech. He will have decided whether it is a speech primarily to inform and bring about understanding, or to persuade and influence belief or action, or to serve some formal or entertaining function. Furthermore, with the purpose especially in mind, he will have studied the kinds of developing material used and the way they are used, and he will have gained some sense of the mood of the speech, the tone, the particular flavor. Before he has finished his examination however, the critic must give careful and detailed attention to the style. As in Chapter 16, so here we mean by style the selection and management of language. Style gives a speech its most distinctive quality. It actually determines the exact shade of meaning that the speech will be able to communicate. In short, style gives a speech its final being, form, and meaning.

[1] Richard M. Weaver, *The Ethics of Rhetoric* (Chicago, 1953), Chapter 5.

In combination with the delivery, from which it is not really separable in its effect in the speech as presented, the style of a speech is probably the element most often commented on by listeners both amateur and professional. The language and the way that language is spoken create the first and most obvious impression which the speech conveys. Furthermore, a student or critic finds it easiest to make observations about the details of language, the structure of sentences, the use of figures of speech and picturesque vocabulary.

These items are directly before him in printed text or recording, and he may isolate them easily without complex analysis of the speech in its many other aspects. Even so, or perhaps in consequence, much comment on style is more impressionistic than critical and tends to be superficial rather than analytically descriptive. Full and penetrating characterization of the style of a speech, discovery of the special qualities which make it what it is and distinguish it from styles of other speeches, is perhaps the most difficult and elusive problem of the student or critic of speechmaking.

For the study of the structure of a speech we recommended recourse to one's knowledge of outlining, and for the study of the development and support of ideas we referred the student to the methods and materials of amplification and persuasion. Likewise, for the analysis of style we suggest a review of those elements that are likely to give style, clearness, appropriateness, liveliness, interest, strength, and movement. It should be profitable for the student to examine the style of any speech with those elements and qualities in mind.

Vocabulary, sentences, imagery

In examining the style of a particular speech, perhaps first the student-critic should describe the vocabulary, the choice of words, for familiarity, currency, and correctness. He should notice the propriety of the language to the speaker, subject, audience, and occasion. He will observe the sources of such vividness, imaginativeness, and vitality as may be evident. He will wish also to analyze the lengths, kinds, and qualities of the characteristic sentences of the speech and to notice the sources of variety and movement in them. He will analyze the imagery to discover what meanings, flavor, or atmosphere the images or figures of speech tend to create and how they harmonize or fail to harmonize with the other material. In a speech reviewing a certain political campaign, Adlai Stevenson suggested his disappointment at the unscrupulous methods which some persons had used, but he added, "Perhaps it was too much to hope that ambitious men would forswear low roads to high places." In that sentence the student-critic would notice especially two words and the metaphor. What are the implications and connotations, he would ask, of the word *ambitious* applied to one's opponents? Is it commendable? Dishonorable? Normal? Does the use of the word in its context possibly echo Antony's speech over the body of Caesar? What of *forswear*? Does it mean simply "swear not to use"? Or is there a suggestion of deception in it? What is the figure of speech, "low roads to high places," likely to mean and to imply? Whom or what will the audience be likely to visualize? Will there be a touch of lightness and irony in the image, deriving perhaps from the echo of the familiar Scottish song? Such questions as these the thorough student of the speech will ask and try to answer. Of course, he cannot answer them except in the context of the whole speech, but his answers will help determine what the style contributes to the total speech.

Striking expressions of ideas

The student, further, will look for turns of phrases and thought which might affect the memorableness of the speech and determine its pleasing or amazing or dull quality. He will observe, for example, the presence or absence of slogans, refrains, wit, humorous juxtapositions, and special effects of sound such as occur in those examples which we cite in the chapter on style (for example, see pages 209–215). Many other useful observations will occur to the sensitive critic if he lets himself respond freely to the language of the speech at the same time that, in so far as possible, he observes and records his early responses. After all, a speech is a communicative composition in words, and if we are to describe and assess that composition accurately, we must give full attention to the selection and management of language. In its language the speech lives.

Delivery

So far, the critic has considered those factors which may be studied in the printed or written text of the speech independently of the live presentation. From these factors a student-critic will be able to infer what sort of thing, potentially, the speech is. If he wishes further to know what it probably was like when it was presented, he must learn as accurately as possible how the speech was delivered, for the delivery confers the final actuality upon the speech.

In the first place, as we have said, style and delivery tend to become inseparable, especially in their movement and tone. Differences in pace and rhythm depend, of course, on choice of words and construction of sentences; but finally they depend on how the words and sentences are spoken. In his delivery, for example, a speaker may reinforce or he may counteract the movements implict in the language he is uttering. Thus he will create meanings and effects in the speech which exist only in the delivery. Likewise in the tone of voice and the whole audible and visible manner in which the speech is communicated, may lie, probably will lie, the clues to the subtleties and shades of interpretation which a listener will put upon the meanings potential in the material and language of the speech. Such an important quality as irony, jesting, or indignation, for example, may be detectable in a speech as the student reads it; but the principal source of that quality is likely to reside in the delivery. Hence, the student may miss it except in a live speech. Very largely through the delivery also the audience will gain its impression of the speaker's character—his honesty, his trustworthiness, his attitude toward his subject and his listeners. Such subtle elements, therefore, are evidences of what the speech was. Even to some of his admirers, the late Senator Robert Taft's delivery (especially his tone of voice) was likely to convey a coldness which was hard to overcome, though he usually sounded as if he were speaking frankly and meaning what he said. Another prominent senator, however, delivers his speeches with such unctuousness that many people who would like to take him at his word do not trust his statements.

Obviously, in a broader sense, also, the general comprehensibility of a speech will depend on qualities in the delivery. The ability of a listener to keep his attention on the speech will depend very much upon the assistance that the speaker gives him through audibility, intelligibility, pleasantness, and so on.

The distinctive qualities which make a speech the speech of a particular person and no other—that give it his individual "style"—are most obvious in the delivery, though they may derive also from most other aspects of the speech, especially from the selection and management of language. Voice and pronunciation, manifestly, enable us to identify most persons whom we know. So it is with public speakers, too. The late President Kennedy, for example, like Franklin D. Roosevelt before him, was easily identifiable, so many people thought, by his pronunciation and the special inflections and rhythms of his voice. The President spoke with a fragmented rhythm and a confined phrasing which seemed to be his own and (at least for persons who were inclined to be sympathetic) seemed to enhance the impression of thoughtfulness, of deliberation, in his speaking.

The critic of speaking, therefore, will wish to observe such evidences of the elements in the delivery as we have just mentioned and those others which we have discussed in our earlier chapters. He can secure the evidence directly if he hears the speech or a recording of it. But for speeches of the more remote past he will have had no way of observing these factors firsthand. He will look for them, therefore, in any accounts he can find of the speech or of the usual habits of the speaker: in newspapers of the time, in biographies, in comments of persons who heard the speaker, in the speaker's own accounts of himself. Seldom will these descriptions be altogether satisfactory. Often they will be couched in language which will be hard to interpret exactly. From them, however, the critic will go as far as he can toward reconstructing the live speech as it probably was heard.

The Speech in Context

Anyone studying a speech, who has proceeded conscientiously, carefully, and intelligently as we have indicated so far, is likely to have achieved a serviceable analytical description of the speech as artifact. The speech, however, like, to a lesser degree, a poem or a play or an essay, is not only a composition which has certain characteristics as an artifact. It is a dynamic discourse addressed by a speaker to an audience in circumstances of time and place.

Audience and speaker

The student must analyze the speech, therefore, as it functions to bring together speaker, message, audience, and circumstances. He must observe how the form and material of the speech might react with the knowledge, the tastes, the interests, the preoccupations, the motives, the prejudices, the feelings and emotions, the circumstances of the audience. He must seek also to determine what impressions and opinions the audience may have had of the speaker beforehand and may have gained through the speech, and how these opinions and impressions may have modified the effect of the speaker's message. Who the speaker is during the speech—that is, who the audience thinks him to be or unconsciously feels that he is—will usually go far toward determining the confidence they will put in his judgment and the credence which they will give to what he tells them. Richard M. Nixon, addressing the American people by television, as the Vice-President just returned from something like a triumph in Russia and Poland, was a quite different speaker from Richard M. Nixon explaining his finances to the American people by television as a candidate for the Vice-Presidency. His audience's suppositions about him and their potential responses to him were quite different each time, and they were handled quite differently.

The student of speech, therefore, will notice especially evidences of the mind, character, and personality of the speaker himself; his conception of himself and of his function, his attitude toward his audience, the reputation which he brings to the speech, his tone and manner in speaking, his direct, and especially his indirect, suggestions of honesty, friendliness, knowledge, understanding, and sympathy, his firmness and determination or his readiness to compromise, his humility or vanity. Anything in the speech which might suggest something to the audience on any of these matters, whether the speaker intends it so or not, will have an effect on the communication of his message.

Similarly, what the speaker thinks of the audience, what he knows of the audience—as men in general and as these men in particular—will determine to a very large extent the strategy, the material, the language, and the manner of delivery of the speech. It will determine, or strongly influence, what he will do and say to impress his listeners as a man of "good sense, good morals, and good will." He will seek in the minds and feelings of the audience available means of recommending his message.

Hence the student should undertake to know, as fully as time and resources permit, the speaker and the audience, and he will attempt to learn the particular events and circumstances which might have affected the susceptibilities and responses of speaker and audience at the time the speech was given. With this special knowledge freshly in mind and with the methods of general audience analysis at his disposal, the student will consider what he has found out about the constituents and form of the speech, with reference to speaker, audience, and circumstances. Thus he will be able to say how the speech would be likely to function. He will want to know what its meaning probably would be to the particular audience and what its probable effects on that audience would be. In this investigation he will be able to hazard opinions on why, presumably, the speaker made the kind of speech he did in the way he made it.

The student may find plenty of practical suggestions for this phase of his analysis in our earlier chapters touching on the adaptation of idea, purpose, materials, style, and delivery to an audience. He will ask questions about the relation of the elements of the speech to the audience's available knowledge, its interests, and its motives: How would the audience understand the language of the speech? Would the examples and comparisons touch the audience's general or special experience? How would the organization and emphasis affect clearness and force?

Certain books may be of assistance also. Aristotle's analysis of the emotions, his explanation of the "goods" which audiences accept as worth striving for, his list of the commonly accepted "constituents of happiness," may be. So may most of the checklists of items in audience analysis in any of the popular textbooks on public speaking, new and old. Nor will the serious critic neglect the results of research in communication being published more and more extensively by the behavioral scientists in communication. He may also make use, if he proceeds with caution, of popular works on advertising, salesmanship, and practical psychology. Nothing, however, will take the place of his own keenness and good sense. As Professor Parrish writes:

> Sometimes the "motivation" of a speech will be immediately clear. . . . But often the motive to which the orator appeals is hidden or obscure. It may nowhere be mentioned, and the emotions he seeks to arouse may not be named. One of the most rewarding tasks of the critic is to search them out and to determine from a study of them what kind of audience the orator presumes himself to be addressing. Does he assume that his hearers will respond to such motives as group loyalty, honor, courage, fair play, altruism, or does he appeal only to self-interest and personal security? Does he assume that they are progressive and forward-looking, or that they are timid, conservative, and fearful

> of anything new? Does he rely more on challenges to reason than on appeals to emotion? Does he attempt to arouse fear, anger, hatred, jealousy, or confidence, temperance, and love? And so on.[2]

The principal tasks of the student of a speech, we may conclude, are to learn what the speech was made of and how constructed, and to determine how the speech would function in the context. He will study, therefore, the occasion, the thought, the structure, the materials and methods of development, the style and the delivery in order to construct as full and accurate a description as possible of the great stimulus which is presented to the audience: what it is made of and how it is put together. Then he will analyze the audience with relation to the great stimulus and with relation to the speaker in order to discover how the audience is responding, or may be supposed to have responded, to speech and speaker; that is, what happens as speaker, subject, audience, and occasion meet and impinge upon each other. Of course, in the study of a particular speech the student would not maintain a strict separation of how the speech is made and how it works. Thoroughness suggests, however, that he should give primary attention first to the one and then to the other. Putting both together, finally, he will be able to say what, dynamically, the speech is or was.

Models for speechmaking

An intelligent person who pursues the study of speeches and develops taste in speeches will also find himself coming to practical conclusions about desirable and undesirable practices in speechmaking. These conclusions will suggest to him principles and methods which will serve to confirm, correct, or supplement the instruction which he receives from teachers and books. But more important, he will tend to experiment in his own speaking with methods and devices which he observes in good speakers, and he will be likely to steer away from those practices which strike him as unfortunate or ineffective in poor speakers. This is the process of imitation which is an important part of learning, and it is likely to be most economical and effective if it is carried on consciously and critically. The ancient writers on public speaking taught that besides a reasonable share of natural talent, a speaker needs theory, imitation, and practice. From his study of speeches the student develops a sound basis for imitation.

Appraisal and Judgment

When the student has assured himself through analysis and description of what the speech is or was, he will usually wish to go on to some comparative

[2] W. M. Parrish and Marie Hochmuth, *American Speeches* (New York, 1954), p. 16.

or absolute judgment of the quality of the speech, the skill of the speaker, and the public significance of the performance. He will wish to ask such questions as, Was this a good speech, a poor speech, a middling speech—according to the best criteria of speech composition? According to the possibilities of the situation? According to the consequence and importance of the subject? According to the quantity and value of the material presented? Ought this speech, on this subject, with this content, developed and presented as it was, to this audience, under these circumstances—to have been made by this man? In short, how socially valuable was this speech?

Did the speaker discover all the available resources of subject, audience, and occasion? Did he use them, or their appropriate substitutes, with skill and responsibility? What did he do which he might better not have done? What did he omit that he might well have done?

Some answers to most of these questions will appear during the analysis and description of the speech. We suggest special attention, however, to the implications for the critic of our comments on the ethics of persuasion (pages 284–298). For his ultimate judgment of the worth of the whole performance, however, the critic must undertake to know enough of the subject to appraise the speaker's knowledge, his judgment, his honesty and responsibility, and the extent of the potential public good or evil in the speech. It will be useful for him to know, as nearly as he can, the effects of the speech—the results and the response both immediate and more remote, both particular and more general and various; but he will realize that the quality of a speech is not to be measured primarily, sometimes not even significantly, by immediate measurable results. A man of wisdom and understanding may very well prefer the speech of practically no visible effect on the outcome of present decision to the one that "launched a thousand ships and burned the topless towers of Ilium." The total achievement of a speech or speaker may very well be much wider and deeper than the measurable share in the immediate countable vote. A speech, for example, may contribute significantly to a man's cumulative reputation and status, even though his audience does not vote with him on the current tax bill. A notable recent statement of the basic independence of *quality* from *effect* is Professor Parrish's, in the book listed at the end of this chapter.[3]

Speeches in society

We hear it said sometimes that the critic's legitimate task ends when he has determined what the speaker intended to accomplish and how and how well he accomplished it. We have already suggested further scope for the critic, however, in judging whether what the speaker sought to do and what he did were desirable and worth doing. If the student is to develop taste and

[3] *American Speeches,* p. 7.

judgment in speeches, he will wish to extend his study to include such large social questions.

For the person with active curiosity about the dynamics of society, still another field of study may grow out of his study of speeches: investigation of the actual workings of verbal communication, and especially the way public speaking operates in the formation of public opinion and the determination of public action. Such study is complex and difficult, and it may be pursued only in part with the equipment usually involved in the study of speechmaking. It requires, also, for example, the knowledge and techniques of the sociologist and the social psychologist, the political scientist and the statistician, the historian and the philosopher, as well as the rhetorician, whose business, according to I. A. Richards, is the study of how words work.

When we study how the speech functions, we are studying how words work. In its most thorough form, this study is the life work of the professional scholar; but within the resources of the educated citizen, it is his study also, and he may get at it as a by-product of his study of speeches. That is why we said earlier that the student of speeches will approach an undertanding of the functioning of speaking in society. It is beyond our province to construct a system covering the whole scope of that inquiry, but the methods which we have sketched in this chapter should see the curious student firmly on his way.

Since we have been writing in this chapter primarily for the student of speechmaking, we have omitted discussion of many of the factors and criteria which will come within the scope of one who is primarily the critic of speeches—often called the rhetorical critic. In the books and articles which we list at the end of the chapter, however, the student and teacher will find full discussions of many aspects of the study and criticism of speeches, and some few examples of the work of competent rhetorical critics. Every man, of course, is a rhetorical critic, even as every man is a literary critic, for we all try to understand, interpret, and judge speeches and speakers just as we express our interpretations and judgments of writers and their books. The craft of the trained, professional rhetorical critic is developing rapidly, however, and with his help we are coming to a better understanding and appreciation than we have had before of the speech as a distinctive phenomenon which is not only a source for other studies, but is itself a study.

Pattern for the Study of a Speech

The following scheme, based on the discussion in the previous pages, may provide a convenient guide for making a study of a speech and for writing up the results. The outline is suggestive in detail, not inclusive, and it does not follow exactly the sequence of items in the chapter. Modified to suit the limitations of classroom speaking, it should be useful to students and teachers in courses in speechmaking. The student will supplement and omit as the circumstances of the individual speech suggest, but he should probably give consideration to each of the principal items at least.

The Speech as Composition

I. Kind and Purpose
  A. General: informative, persuasive, or other
  B. Particular: purpose and reason for this speech
    1. In the occasion and circumstances
    2. In the audience
    3. In the speaker
    4. In the subject

II. Condition, Source, Authenticity, and Reliability of the Text

III. Thought and Idea Content
  A. The subject
    1. General—particular
    2. Ostensible—real
  B. Underlying assumptions and background reasoning
  C. Governing idea (subject sentence or proposition) and supporting ideas
    1. Explicitly stated
    2. Implicitly presented
  D. Overall plan and structure
    1. Pattern of organization: Time, space, topical, cause to effect, disease and remedy, etc.
    2. Logical-chronological outline
    3. Departures from consistent plan
      a. Introduction of extraneous matter, for what reason and with what effect
      b. Use of structural digressions, for what reason and with what effect
      c. Failure to follow through
    4. Establishing and maintaining unity
      a. Sustained mood or attitude
      b. Connective and transitional methods
      c. Structural emphasis
      d. Kind and function of introduction and conclusion

IV. Development: Amplification and Support
  A. Methods, techniques, and materials of amplification
    1. Methods: example, information, comparison, definition, etc.
    2. Techniques: restatement, repetition, quotation, etymology, etc.
    3. Use of laws and principles of interest: perennial interests, human

interest, humor, variety, activity, familiarity, novelty, laws of attention

B. Methods of argument and persuasion
   1. Evidence and logical support
   2. Motives and basic lines of thought
   3. Suggestion
   4. Involvement of feelings, desires, likes and dislikes of audience

C. Predominant or characteristic methods of development: reasons, effects

V. Style: The Use of Language

A. Qualities of the vocabulary
   1. Clearness, appropriateness, interest, impressiveness
   2. Size, sources of words, net effect

B. Qualities of the connected language
   1. Clearness: length of sentences, structures of sentences, coherence and emphasis, idiomatic usages
   2. Propriety
      a. To speaker, occasion, audience, subject
      b. Correctness, conventionality of forms
   3. Interest and attractiveness
      a. Movement and variety
      b. Strength and beauty
      c. Wit and humor
   4. Impressiveness
      a. Memorable coinages of phrases and slogans
      b. Vividness of images and figures
      c. Rhythms and harmonies

C. Apparent total effects or general characteristics; how achieved

VI. Delivery: Speech and Action

A. General characteristics
   1. Loud—weak
   2. Fast—slow
   3. Intelligible—unclear
   4. Pleasant—unpleasant
   5. Appropriate—inappropriate

B. Factors meriting special comment
   1. In voice
   2. In pronunciation
   3. In vocal rhythm and movement: phrasing, pause, changes of pace, inflection, etc.
   4. Gesture, facial expression, bodily movement

C. Basis of description of delivery
   1. Primary sources: face to face, recording, radio-TV, etc.
   2. Secondary sources: various accounts of witnesses and others

D. Apparent total effects or general characteristics; how achieved

The Speech in Context

I. Who the Audience Is
  A. As people in general
    1. Old—young
    2. Prosperous—unprosperous
    3. Urban—rural
    4. Educated—uneducated
    5. Men—women
    6. Business, professions, trades, etc.
  B. As people in particular
    1. Relation of audience to speaker's subject and particular purposes
      a. Special knowledge and interests
    2. Economic, political, racial, religious, geographical, domestic allegiances
    3. Special desires, needs, susceptibilities, preoccupations, prejudices, preferences
  C. As affected by the ideas, materials, methods, structure, style, etc. of the speech in
    1. Holding attention
    2. Informing
    3. Convincing
    4. Enlisting feelings, tastes, emotions
    5. Releasing motives and impulses to believe and to act
  D. Probable (or actual) responses of audience; how brought about

II. Who the Speaker is
  A. From outside the speech
    1. His family, educational, social, religious, economic, political, professional background so far as relevant to this occasion
    2. His habits of thought, opinions, knowledge, experience, temperament
    3. His relation to the subject, to the occasion, and to the audience
    4. His reputation as known to this audience at this time, especially as a man likely to speak truly and wisely
      a. As a man of intelligence, knowledge, and sound opinion
        (1) In general
        (2) On the current subject
      b. As a man of sound morality
        (1) Honesty
        (2) Truthfulness
        (3) Firmness
      c. As a man of good will
        (1) Friendliness
        (2) Regard for the welfare of his listeners
  B. From the speech
    1. What the speaker says and does that may affect the audience's

opinions of him as a man of "good sense, good morals, and good will"
   a. Explicitly in the material and language
   b. Implicitly in the content and style
   c. In the delivery
2. The speaker's conception of himself in relation to the audience and in relation to the picture of himself which he gives to the audience

C. Relation of what the speaker shows himself to be in the speech to what the audience "knows" him to be beforehand
D. Probable (or actual) responses of the audience to the speaker's character and personality; how brought about

Appraisal and Judgment

I. Quality of the Speech in Terms of the Speaker's Skill
   A. Value of the material presented
      1. Thoroughness and soundness of the speaker's knowledge
      2. Scope and quality of his thinking and judgment
      3. Significance of his purpose and governing idea
   B. Skill of the presentation
      1. Discovery of available resources of subject, audience and circumstances
      2. Use of resources discovered
         a. Speaker's special excellences
         b. Speaker's weaknesses
            (1) Seen in things done
            (2) Seen through omissions
         c. Sources of speaker's strengths
         d. Sources of speaker's weaknesses
            (1) Limitations of his capacities
            (2) Faults of ethics and sense of responsibility
   C. Determinable effects of speech
   D. Relation of quality of speech as speech to determinable results; reasons

II. Quality of Speech in Terms of its Social Consequence
   A. Value to this audience
      1. Because of ideas and information presented and opinions and actions sought
      2. Because of means and methods used to affect audience's minds and feelings
   B. Value to society generally
      1. At present
      2. In the future

III. Composite Estimate of the Worth of the Speech; Reasons
   A. "A good man speaking well" in the public interest
   B. Or something less

FURTHER READING

A History and Criticism of American Public Address. 3 vols. W. N. Brigance (ed.), Vols. I and II. New York, 1943. Marie Hochmuth (ed.), Vol. III. New York, 1955. Studies of American speeches and speakers. See "The Criticism of Rhetoric" by Marie Hochmuth. Vol. II, pp. 1–23.

Baird, A. Craig (ed.) *American Public Address, 1740–1952.* New York, 1956. Introduction, pp. 1–14.

———, and Thonssen, Lester. "Methodology in the Criticism of Public Address," *The Quarterly Journal of Speech,* 23 (1947), 134–138.

Black, Edwin. *Rhetorical Criticism: A Study in Method.* New York, 1965.

Bryant, Donald C. (ed.) *The Rhetorical Idiom.* Ithaca: Cornell University Press, 1958. See "The Literary Criticism of Oratory" by Herbert A. Wichelns.

Murphy, Richard. "The Speech as a Literary Genre," *The Quarterly Journal of Speech,* 44 (1959), 117–127.

Nichols, Marie Hochmuth. *Rhetoric and Criticism.* Baton Rouge: Louisiana State University Press, 1963.

Nilsen, Thomas R. (ed.) *Essays on Rhetorical Criticism.* New York, 1968.

Thonssen, Lester, and Baird, A. Craig. *Speech Criticism.* New York, 1948. A comprehensive treatment of the problems of studying speeches.

Wallace, Karl R. "On the Criticism of the MacArthur Speech," *The Quarterly Journal of Speech,* 39 (1953), 69–74.

Wrage, Ernest J. (ed.) "Symposium: Criticism and Public Address," *Western Speech,* 21 (1957), 69–118. See "Burkeian Criticism" by Marie Hochmuth and "Of Style" by Donald C. Bryant.

24

The Practice of Analysis and Criticism—John F. Kennedy's Inaugural Address

To exemplify in practice the application to a single speech of the principles and methods explained in Chapter 23 we present three different kinds of commentaries on the Inaugural Address of President John F. Kennedy. The Introduction, or headnote, to the address is adapted from a course paper written by Miss Sheryl Etling, a graduate student in Speech at The University of Iowa. This introduction supplies illuminating commentary on the political atmosphere surrounding the address, on the preparation of the address, and on the conditions of presentation.

Unlike plays, novels, and other works of literature, speeches as speeches rarely receive extended critical treatment in the newspapers or the periodical press. A notable exception is furnished by the critique of President Kennedy's Inaugural Address, published as the opening piece in *The New Yorker* magazine of February 4, 1961, less than two weeks after the speech was given. Written in an informal style by Susan Lardner, a young woman well read in ancient Greek and Roman rhetoric and oratory, it is indeed a worthy example for any student of speaking. That critique follows the text of the address below.

Finally Professor Bryant offers his extended critical analysis of the address. The treatments which we present are longer, more detailed, and more comprehensive, perhaps, than most teachers and most students will think feasible as frequent undertakings in the usual limited courses in public speaking. We wish, however, to illustrate the many resources for analysis available to the serious student of speaking and speeches, and to introduce him, through this chapter, to an interesting kind of humanistic study which is often not a part of courses in speech and is seldom available elsewhere in programs of liberal studies.

SHERYL ETLING

An Introductory Commentary on Kennedy's Inaugural Address

In the national election of November 8, 1960, one of the most closely contested in history, John Fitzgerald Kennedy was elected to the Presidency over Richard M. Nixon by a margin of less than 120,000 popular votes out of a total of more than 69,000,000. The electoral vote, however, was 303 to 219.

When Kennedy assumed the Presidency, he was not faced with a single major crisis as were Lincoln, Wilson, and Franklin Roosevelt. Instead, he faced the continuing tension of the Cold War. In all corners of the world, there were situations which at any moment might develop into major crises. In the year preceding Kennedy's inauguration India and China were involved in a border dispute, Sukarno was consolidating his power in Indonesia, the Congo was threatened with civil war, Israel was protesting alleged threats by the United Arab Republic, the U.S.S.R. and Cuba signed an economic pact, nuclear test ban talks were in progress but were not meeting with success, and proposed summit talks were cancelled after Russia accused the United States of conducting spy flights in Soviet air space. At home the economy was in a period of recession, and civil rights was becoming an ever more pressing issue.

Kennedy's inauguration took place on January 20, 1961. The day before, a blizzard had struck Washington, disrupting pre-inaugural festivities. Seven inches of snow had fallen before the storm ended shortly before dawn on inauguration day. By noon the sky had cleared. The temperature, however, remained in the low twenties, and a brisk wind whipped through the city.

A crowd of about 20,000 people gathered in the cold morning in front of the platform erected on the steps of the east portico of the Capitol. They watched silently as invited guests assumed their places on the platform: justices of the Supreme Court, members of the diplomatic corps, newly appointed Cabinet officers, the Joint Chiefs of Staff, and the Kennedy family. These guests were joined by outgoing President Dwight D. Eisenhower and Mrs. Eisenhower, Vice-President and Mrs. Richard Nixon, the Vice-President elect and Mrs. Lyndon Johnson, and Mrs. John Kennedy. Finally, at 12:20, the President-Elect entered, and the crowd applauded warmly.

The inaugural ceremonies began with an invocation by Richard Cardinal Cushing of Boston, followed by the singing of the national anthem by Marian Anderson. Robert Frost recited his poem, "The Gift Outright," although the glare of the sun prevented his reading the preface he had written for the occasion. Vice-President Johnson was sworn in by Speaker of the House Sam Rayburn, an old friend and political mentor. Then, at 12:51 P.M., John F. Kennedy stood, removed his top coat, and stepped forward to take the Presidential oath of office, administered by Earl Warren, Chief Justice of the Supreme Court. Kennedy stood with his right hand raised before the family Douay Bible as he spoke the oath in a clear, crisp voice.

After taking the oath, President Kennedy began his inaugural address. Eight Corinthian columns on the platform and the facades of government buildings formed the background. The President stood erect with both hands resting lightly on the podium throughout most of the speech. Like all men in the inaugural party, the President was dressed in formal morning attire.

The President spoke in a clear firm voice which carried well through the brisk, clear air, and through the radio and television networks to millions of persons throughout the world. A prepared manuscript of the address lay on the podium before him, but he had studied the speech so thoroughly that he had it practically memorized.

Following the address, the applause of the crowd was warm and sustained. After greeting platform guests, Kennedy returned to the Capitol before going to luncheon and then on to the reviewing stand near the White House to view the inaugural parade.

Preparation of the inaugural address had begun shortly after the election. Kennedy asked several of his aids for suggestions, emphasizing that he wanted the address short and wanted it focused on foreign policy.[1] In deciding to focus his speech on foreign policy, Kennedy was following a twentieth-century inaugural tradition. Presidents customarily focus their addresses on the principal issues of the day. Domestic issues were discussed most often in nineteenth-century inaugurals, but as the United States became more concerned with international affairs, twentieth-century inaugurals have tended to focus more on international issues.[2]

Kennedy indicated a purpose for his speech when he told his aids that he wanted the address to set a tone for the era about to begin. He hoped to "express the spirit of the postwar generation in politics, to summon America to new exertions and new initiatives, to summon the world to a new mood beyond the clichés of the cold war."[3] He wanted neither "cold war rhetoric about the Communist menace nor any weasel words that Khrushchev might misinterpret."[4] In the introduction to *To Turn the Tide,* a collection of his speeches published in 1962, Kennedy expressed a principle which he had probably applied to the inaugural address. He wrote: "Words can do more

[1] Theodore C. Sorenson, *Kennedy* (New York: Harper and Row, 1965), p. 240.

[2] Donald L. Wolfarth, "John F. Kennedy in the Tradition of Inaugural Speakers," *Quarterly Journal of Speech,* 48 (April 1961), 129.

[3] Arthur M. Schlesinger, Jr., *A Thousand Days* (Greenwich, Conn.: Fawcett Publications, Inc., 1967), p. 155. First published, Boston: Houghton Mifflin, 1965.

[4] Sorenson, p. 240.

than convey policy. They can also convey and create a mood, an attitude, an atmosphere, or an awakening."[5]

There is some indication that Kennedy purposely set out to create a classical inaugural. His aide Ted Sorenson was asked to read all previous inaugural addresses as background for the composition of the Kennedy inaugural. Sorenson was also asked to try to learn the secret that has made Abraham Lincoln's Gettysburg Address a classic in American public address.[6]

The influence of previous inaugurals on John F. Kennedy's address may be seen by comparing the opening paragraph of the Kennedy address with portions of the inaugural addresses of Lincoln, Wilson, and Franklin Roosevelt.

The Kennedy inaugural began:

> We observe today not a victory of party, but a celebration of freedom—symbolizing an end, as well as a beginning—symbolizing renewal, as well as change.[7]

The first two paragraphs and the closing paragraph of Woodrow Wilson's first inaugural address expressed a similar sentiment:

> There has been a change of government. . . . It means much more than the mere success of a party. . . . No one can mistake the purpose for which the Nation now seeks to use the Democratic Party. It seeks to use it to interpret a change in its own plans and point of view.
>
> This is not a day of triumph; it is a day of dedication. Here muster, not the forces of the party, but the forces of humanity.

Further, Kennedy referred to the inauguration tradition in the opening paragraph of his address:

> For I have sworn before you and Almighty God the same solemn oath our forebears prescribed nearly a century-and-three-quarters ago.

Lincoln had said:

> In compliance with a custom as old as the Government itself, I appear before you to address you briefly and to take in your presence the oath prescribed by the Constitution of the United States to be taken by the President before he enters on the execution of this office.

[5] John F. Kennedy, *To Turn the Tide*, ed. by John W. Gardner (New York: Harper and Brothers, 1962), quoted in Clifford Owsley, *Inaugural* (New York: Olympic Press, 1964), p. 70.

[6] Sorenson, p. 240.

[7] The source of this and other quotations from inaugural addresses is Clifford Owsley, *Inaugural* (New York: Olympic Press, 1964), pp. 65–90.

The third inaugural address of Franklin D. Roosevelt began:

> On each national day of inauguration since 1789, the people have renewed their sense of dedication to the United States.

The similarity of Kennedy's speech both in wording and in the thought to those of Lincoln, Wilson, and Roosevelt is striking.

Although numerous Kennedy aides contributed to the drafting of the speech, and though suggestions for inclusions, both solicited and unsolicited, were considered, the speech must be regarded as Kennedy's own work. He went over every detail himself, drafting and redrafting, adding and deleting. "However numerous the assistant artisans," Kennedy's major speech writer wrote, "the principal architect of the Inaugural Address was John Fitzgerald Kennedy."[8]

The inaugural address, as Kennedy had planned, was kept brief—1,355 words. Only five other inaugural addresses had been shorter.[9] Ted Sorenson's study of Lincoln's Gettysburg Address led to the conclusion that one of the things which had made it a classic was its conciseness in expression. Lincoln never used a two- or three-syllable word when a one-syllable word would do, and never used two or three words when only one word would express the same idea.[10] The same principle was applied to the Kennedy speech: of the first two hundred words seventy-five percent are of one syllable only, while only eight reach four syllables.[11] The search for expressive words continued to the last possible moment. Walter Lippmann, when shown one of the last drafts of the speech, suggested that references to the Soviet Union as the "enemy" should be replaced by the word "adversary." The suggestion expressed Kennedy's intention more precisely, so he adopted the suggestion and continued to use "adversary" throughout his term in office.[12]

Within a few days after the inauguration, newspapers and commentators both at home and abroad commented favorably on the inaugural address. It was described as "eloquent," "persuasive," "inspirational," and "universal." Striking phrases from the address were repeated again and again as the speech was reviewed. As an expression of spirit and as a summons to a new mood and new exertions, the speech must be counted a success.

[8] Sorenson, p. 241.
[9] Wolfarth, p. 130.
[10] Sorenson, p. 240.
[11] Owsley, p. 73.
[12] Schlesinger, p. 156.

JOHN F. KENNEDY

*Inaugural Address, January 20, 1961**

My fellow citizens:

We observe today not a victory of party but a celebration of freedom—symbolizing an end as well as a beginning—signifying renewal as well as change. For I have sworn before you and Almighty God the same solemn oath our forebears prescribed nearly a century and three-quarters ago.

The world is very different now. For man holds in his mortal hands the power to abolish all form of human poverty and all form of human life. And yet the same revolutionary beliefs for which our forebears fought are still at issue around the globe—the belief that the rights of man come not from the generosity of the state but from the hand of God.

We dare not forget today that we are the heirs of that first revolution. Let the word go forth from this time and place, to friend and foe alike, that the torch has been passed to a new generation of Americans—born in this century, tempered by war, disciplined by a hard and bitter peace, proud of our ancient heritage—and unwilling to witness or permit the slow undoing of those human rights to which this nation has always been committed, and to which we are committed today—at home and around the world.

Let every nation know, whether it wishes us well or ill, that we shall pay any price, bear any burden, meet any hardship, support any friend, oppose any foe to assure the survival and success of liberty.

This much we pledge—and more.

To those old allies whose cultural and spiritual origins we share, we pledge the loyalty of faithful friends. United, there is little we cannot do in a host of new co-operative ventures. Divided, there is little we can do—for we dare not meet a powerful challenge at odds and split asunder.

To those new states whom we welcome to the ranks of the free, we pledge our word that one form of colonial control shall not have passed away merely to be replaced by a far more iron tyranny. We shall not always expect to find them supporting our view. But we shall always hope to find them strongly supporting their own freedom—and to remember that, in the past, those who foolishly sought power by riding the back of the tiger ended up inside.

To those peoples in the huts and villages of half the globe struggling to break the bonds of mass misery, we pledge our best efforts to help them help

* Reprinted by permission of the White House.

themselves, for whatever period is required—not because the Communists may be doing it, not because we seek their votes, but because it is right. If a free society cannot help the many who are poor, it cannot save the few who are rich.

To our sister republics south of our border, we offer a special pledge—to convert our good words into good deeds—in a new alliance for progress—to assist free men and free governments in casting off the chains of poverty. But this peaceful revolution of hope cannot become the prey of hostile powers. Let all our neighbors know that we shall join with them to oppose aggression or subversion anywhere in the Americas. And let every other power know that this hemisphere intends to remain the master of its own house.

To that world assembly of sovereign states, the United Nations, our last best hope in an age where the instruments of war have far outpaced the instruments of peace, we renew our pledge of support—to prevent it from becoming merely a forum of invective—to strengthen its shield of the new and the weak—and to enlarge the area in which its writ may run.

Finally, to those nations who would make themselves our adversary, we offer not a pledge but a request: that both sides begin anew the quest for peace, before the dark powers of destruction unleashed by science engulf all humanity in planned or accidental self-destruction.

We dare not tempt them with weakness. For only when our arms are sufficient beyond doubt can we be certain beyond doubt that they will never be employed.

But neither can two great and powerful groups of nations take comfort from our present course—both sides overburdened by the cost of modern weapons, both rightly alarmed by the steady spread of the deadly atom, yet both racing to alter that uncertain balance of terror that stays the hand of mankind's final war.

So let us begin anew—remembering on both sides that civility is not a sign of weakness, and sincerity is always subject to proof. Let us never negotiate out of fear. But let us never fear to negotiate.

Let both sides explore what problems unite us instead of belaboring those problems which divide us.

Let both sides, for the first time, formulate serious and precise proposals for the inspection and control of arms—and bring the absolute power to destroy other nations under the absolute control of all nations.

Let both sides seek to invoke the wonders of science instead of its terrors. Together let us explore the stars, conquer the deserts, eradicate disease, tap the ocean depths and encourage the arts and commerce.

Let both sides unite to heed in all corners of the earth the command of Isaiah—to "undo the heavy burdens . . . [and] let the oppressed go free."

And if a beachhead of a co-operation may push back the jungles of suspicion, let both sides join in the next task: creating, not a new balance of power, but a new world of law, where the strong are just and the weak secure and the peace preserved.

All this will not be finished in the first one hundred days. Nor will it be finished in the first one thousand days, nor in the life of this Administration, nor even perhaps in our lifetime on this planet. But let us begin.

In your hands, my fellow citizens, more than mine, will rest the final success or failure of our course. Since this country was founded, each generation of Americans has been summoned to give testimony to its national loyalty. The graves of young Americans who answered the call to service surround the globe.

Now the trumpet summons us again—not as a call to bear arms, though arms we need—not as a call to battle, though embattled we are—but a call to bear the burden of a long twilight struggle, year in and year out, "rejoicing in hope, patient in tribulation"—a struggle against the common enemies of man: tyranny, poverty, disease, and war itself.

Can we forge against these enemies a grand and global alliance, north and south, east and west, that can assure a more fruitful life for all mankind? Will you join in that historic effort?

In the long history of the world, only a few generations have been granted the role of defending freedom in its hour of maximum danger. I do not shrink from this responsibility—I welcome it. I do not believe that any of us would exchange places with any other people or any other generation. The energy, the faith, the devotion which we bring to this endeavor will light our country and all who serve it—and the glow from that fire can truly light the world.

And so, my fellow Americans: Ask not what your country can do for you—ask what you can do for your country.

My fellow citizens of the world: Ask not what America will do for you, but what together we can do for the freedom of man.

Finally, whether you are citizens of America or citizens of the world, ask of us here the same high standards of strength and sacrifice which we ask of you. With a good conscience our only sure reward, with history the final judge of our deeds, let us go forth to lead the land we love, asking His blessing and His help, but knowing that here on earth God's work must truly be our own.

SUSAN LARDNER

*Notes and Comment on Kennedy's Inaugural Address**

As rhetoric has become an increasingly dispensable member of the liberal arts, people have abandoned the idea, held so firmly by the ancient Greeks and Romans, that eloquence is indispensable to politics. Perhaps President Kennedy's achievements in both spheres will revive a taste for good oratory—a taste that has been alternately frustrated by inarticulateness and dulled by bombast. There have been a few notable orators in our day—most recently, Adlai Stevenson—but they have been the exceptions, and it has taken Mr. Kennedy's success as a politician to suggest that the power to "enchant souls through words" (Socrates) may soon be at a premium once more. Whatever the impact of the Inaugural Address on contemporary New Frontiersmen, we find it hard to believe that an Athenian or Roman citizen could have listened to it unmoved, or that Cicero, however jealous of his own reputation, would have found reason to object to it.

We are all familiar by now with the generally high praise the President received for his first speech, but before the responsibility for the final judgment is yielded to Time it would be a shame not to seek the opinion of a couple of true professionals. Both Aristotle and Cicero, the one a theorist and the other a theorizing orator, believed that rhetoric could be an art to the extent that the orator was, first, a logician and, second, a psychologist with an appreciation and understanding of words. Cicero felt, further, that the ideal orator was the thoroughly educated man. (He would be pleased by Mr. Kennedy's background, with its strong emphasis on affairs of state: the philosopher-orator-statesman.) Of the three types of oratory defined by the ancients—political, forensic, and display (in which audience participation was limited to a judgment of style)—the political was esteemed most highly, because it dealt with the loftiest of issues; namely, the fate of peoples, rather than of individuals. ("Now the trumpet summons us again. . . against the common enemies of man. . . .") The ideal speech was thought to be one in which three kinds of persuasion were used by the speaker: logical, to present the facts of the case and construct an argument based on them; emotional, to reach the audience psychologically; and "ethical," to appeal to the audience by establishing one's own integrity and sincerity. The Inaugural Address, being a variation on the single theme of man's rights and obligations, is not primarily logical, although it contains no illogic; it is an appeal to men's souls rather than to their minds. During the Presidential campaign, Mr. Kennedy tested and patented an exercise in American psychology that proved to be all the emotional appeal he required for the inaugural speech: "And so, my fellow-Americans, ask not what your country can do for you, ask what you can do for your country." His ethical persuasion, or indication of his personal probity, consisted of an extension of that appeal: ". . . ask of us here the same high standards of strength and sacrifice which we ask of you."

Aristotle recognized only one (good) style, while Cicero thought that there were three styles—the plain, the middle, and the grand. To Aristotle, who considered it sufficient for a style to be clear and appropriate, avoiding undue elevation (whence bombast) and excessive lowliness, it would have seemed that Mr. Kennedy had achieved the Golden Mean. The formality of the Inaugural Address ("To that world assembly of sovereign states, the United Nations. . . .") is appropriate to the subject; the language ("In your hands, my fellow-citizens, more than mine, will rest the final success or failure of our course") is clear and direct. Cicero's ideal orator was able to speak in all three styles, in accordance with the demands of his subject, and in that respect Mr. Kennedy filled the role by speaking plainly on the practical ("All this will not be finished in the first one hundred days"), by speaking formally but directly on the purpose of national defense ("For only when our arms are sufficient beyond doubt can we be certain beyond doubt that they will never be employed"), and by speaking grandly on the potential accomplishments of the movement toward the New Frontier ("The energy, the faith, the devotion which we bring to this endeavor will light our country and all who serve it—and the glow from that fire can truly light the world").

The address, however, is largely in the grand style, which is characterized by Cicero as the ultimate source of emotional persuasion, through figures of speech and a certain degree of dignified periodic rhythm, not iambic ("The world is very different now. For man holds in his mortal hands the power to abolish all forms of human poverty, and all forms of human life"). The oration is so rich in figures of speech—the many metaphors include a torch, a beachhead, jungles, a trumpet, a tiger—that we can imagine students of the future studying it for examples of antithesis ("If a free society cannot help the many who are poor, it cannot save the few who are rich"), personification, (". . . . the hand of mankind's final war"), anaphora ("Not as a call to bear arms, though arms we need; not as a call to battle, though embattled we are. . . ."). "Battle" and "embattled"—an excellent example of paronomasia.

And so we leave the speech to the students of rhetoric, having invoked for Mr. Kennedy the blessings of Aristotle and Cicero, and for ourself the hope that he has reestablished the tradition of political eloquence.

DONALD C. BRYANT

Analysis of the Inaugural

John F. Kennedy's Inaugural Address as President of the United States is one of the distinguished speeches of our time. "Its impact upon members of both parties," wrote *Life* magazine, "and on people everywhere in the world was immediate and impressive." Subsequent regard for it, perhaps enhanced but certainly not sustained by the untimely death of the President, has grown as the ideals for America and for the world which President Kennedy asserted that day, and the image of leadership which he seemed to incarnate, have become more and more important and more and more difficult of achievement.

A totally dispassionate analysis may yet not be possible—or even desirable. Americans at home, and friends and antagonists all over the world, are still, perhaps, too closely and seriously embroiled in the problems and controversies of which Mr. Kennedy spoke. We think it not too soon, however, for the student of speaking to pay careful and detailed attention to a speech which, shortly after the event, *The New Yorker* magazine called a speech which an Athenian or a Roman of the eloquent ages of Demosthenes and Cicero could not have listened to unmoved. We undertake a technical analysis and criticism, therefore, following generally the suggestions for the study of speeches which we have presented in the preceding pages. Our analysis and criticism will be illustrative and suggestive rather than exhaustive. We invite the serious student to proceed in greater detail and greater depth and to arrive at appraisals of his own.

In certain of its important elements a President's Inaugural Address is a special kind of speech. It embodies by necessity and custom elements which belong to no other speech. It is the central feature of the most formal and most splendid public occasion in American life. There is a dignity, a sobriety, a ritual, perhaps even a sacredness in the occasion which the speaker is expected to recognize explicitly in what he says and the way he conducts himself. In the presence of the justices of the Supreme Court, of the retiring President, of the major personages of his new government and representatives of foreign governments from all over the world, of thousands of persons of position and importance from all states of the union, and of millions of others on radio and television, the President has just taken his solemn and traditional oath of office and has assumed the most difficult and important responsibility of any one man on this planet. He is no longer the political candidate seeking office or glowing with victory. He is the President of "all the American people" and nowadays the political leader of the "free world." With the scars, the extravagance, the bitterness, and alas the dirt of party strife only two short months gone by, the American people and much of the rest of the world expect the new President to show himself worthy of his victory. They require him to "bind up the nation's wounds" and to set the tone if not to describe in detail the program of the new Administration.

The Inaugural Address, therefore, will be in part ceremonial, in part hortatory, in part dedicatory, and in great part predictive. There is much in the occasion to invite reassurance; there is little to make appropriate either argumentation, political persuasion, or major ventures in exposition. These have been expended (for the moment, at least) in the campaign and in public discussion in the interim.

Except for the bare minimums of formality, however, no standard pattern for the Inaugural Address has emerged over the years. Some Presidents have undertaken in considerable detail and at length to review programs and to elaborate positions to which earlier they had committed themselves and now wished to commit their parties and their administrations. Others, like Lincoln in his Second Inaugural and perhaps Franklin D. Roosevelt in his First, have sought primarily to enunciate high ideals for the country and to move their fellow citizens toward renewed commitment to worthy principles and courageous action. President Kennedy's Inaugural Address belongs among the latter.

The Governing Purpose and Intention

A speech is to be examined and criticized, we have said, primarily as an instrument of the speaker's purposes and intentions. No critic, however, has direct access to the conscious and subconscious mind and feelings of a speaker. He must be content, usually, to infer purposes and intentions from the speech as given, and to assess from the total context of the circumstances the propriety of the purposes and intentions and the adequacy of the speech to them. True, a speaker or his associates and confidants may have testified, either before or after the fact, what the speaker intended to do or wished to accomplish; and the critic should take such testimony into account. Like the critic of a poem or a play, however, the critic of a speech will seek in the content and the circumstances the keys to purposes and intentions.

From Kennedy's Inaugural as we have it recorded, it is evident that he sought to stir in the American people and in the rest of the world a dynamic sense of the mission in foreign affairs of a young, active, imaginative, able American Administration—not a sense that the United States wished to run the world, but an assurance that we were ready and able to assist all peoples to achieve for themselves liberty and the good life. Through the speech there seems to sound anew and for a new day Franklin D. Roosevelt's promise of the "four freedoms" "everywhere in the world." Through the Presidential campaign had run the theme of youth—that no matter which candidate won, a young man of a new generation would be taking over the government of the United States and leadership in the world. That man and that generation faced problems of world revolution and cold war, bequeathed from their predecessors, which were as primary in 1960 as the domestic crisis in economics had been primary in 1932. As Roosevelt's governing purpose in his First Inaugural, therefore, had been to give the American people new faith in themselves and the strength of their society ("The only thing we have to fear is fear itself"), so, appropriately, in 1960 Kennedy's governing purpose was to reassure and inspire the American people in their new world role. To speak of affairs at home would have tended to renew the devisive issues of the campaign. Americans could unite most completely on a confident and generous posture towards their friends and adversaries in the rest of the world.

The Structure of Thought

Though John Kennedy's speech is not argumentative, though the traditional "logical proof" is not dominant in it, the line of thought is clear, firm, and relevant, as the following outline shows.

Introduction

A. Today we observe, not a party victory, but a celebration of freedom in renewal of the past and realization of change.
   1. From the past I have taken an oath prescribed by our distant forebears.
   2. The world is different now.
      1. Man can abolish all poverty.
      2. He can also destroy all life.
   3. Our forebears' revolutionary belief in human rights under God is still the same.
      We still believe that these rights do not come from the generosity of the state but from the hand of God.

B. A new generation of Americans is ready to reestablish at home and in the world the human rights to which this nation has always been committed and is still committed.
   1. It is a generation born in this century, tempered by war, and disciplined by a hard and bitter peace.
   2. It is a generation proud of our ancient heritage.

C. We are ready to do anything it takes to assure the survival and success of liberty.

Development

Proposition: [The new Administration commits itself and the United States to a renewal of our traditional quest for freedom, peace, and human welfare at home and abroad.]

I. We pledge our cooperation and support to the free world.
  A. To our old allies in the North Atlantic Community we pledge the loyalty of faithful friends in new cooperative ventures.
    1. United there is little we cannot do.
    2. Divided we dare not meet a powerful challenge.
  B. To the emerging nations we pledge our support in their efforts for their own true freedom.
    1. Old colonialism must not become new tyranny.
    2. We do not expect them always to agree with us.
    3. We warn them against riding the back of the tiger.
  C. To those peoples still struggling with poverty and oppression, we pledge our best efforts to help them help themselves.
    1. We will do so as long as necessary.
    2. We will do so because it is right.
      a. Not because the Communists are doing it.
      b. Not because we want their votes.
      c. If a free society cannot help the many who are poor, it cannot save the few who are rich.
  D. To Latin America we offer a special pledge—to convert good words to good deeds in a new alliance for progress.
    1. We will assist them to eliminate poverty.
    2. We will protect them from foreign aggression and subversion [in a new Monroe Doctrine].
  E. To the United Nations we renew our pledge of support.
    1. To keep it from becoming a "forum of invective."
    2. To strengthen its protection of new and weak nations.
    3. To enlarge its useful scope.

II. To our adversaries we propose that together we begin anew the quest for peace.
  A. We will remain strong enough to discourage aggression against us, but
  A′. We cannot accept the armaments race as satisfactory to either side.
  B. We urge that neither side ever fear to negotiate.
    1. To explore problems which unite us instead of belaboring those that divide us.
    2. To proceed seriously to real arms control and inspection.
    3. To use science cooperatively for peaceful purposes.
      a. Develop the exploration of space.
      b. Irrigate the deserts.
      c. Eradicate disease.

d. Tap the ocean depths.
e. Encourage the arts and commerce.
4. To relieve misery and oppression in the world.
5. To create, not a new balance of power in the world, but a new rule of law.

III. Though the task is long and hard, we must begin it.
A. It will not be done in the first hundred days, or a thousand days, or the life of this Administration or perhaps in our lifetime.
B. Like other generations of Americans, we are summoned to demonstrate our national loyalty.
1. Young Americans in graves all over the world have demonstrated theirs.
2. Our success depends more on you than on me.
3. We are called to struggle against the common enemies of man—tyranny, poverty, disease, and war itself.
a. We are not called to arms, though we need them.
b. We are not called to battle, though we are embattled.

IV. I challenge you to join me in the historic task of forging a global alliance to assure a more fruitful life for all mankind.
A. Few generations, like ours, have been granted the role of defending freedom in its hour of maximum danger.
B. I welcome the responsibility.
1. To Americans I say: "Ask not what your country can do for you—ask what you can do for your country."
2. To the rest of the world I say: "Ask not what America will do for you, but what together we can do for the freedom of man.
3. To all I say, "Ask of us the same high standards of strength and sacrifice which we ask of you."

Conclusion

Let us be assured that God's work on earth must be done by us.

Because of the circumstances, Mr. Kennedy needed little or no explicit bid for attention in the introduction to his Address, and he dispatched very quickly any special orientation of audience to subject. In fact, he moved almost imperceptibly from introduction into proposition or central theme. Starting from an explicit invocation of the best of America's traditional ideals of liberty and justice for all, the speech proceeds at once to the relevance of this inheritance of revolutionary ideas to the new world of massive antagonisms and of alternative possibilities of nuclear destruction and nuclear salvation. As we have phrased the proposition (in brackets), it never becomes explicit but is approximated several times. After setting his theme, that the United States "will pay any price, bear any burden, meet any hardship, support any friend, oppose any foe to assure the survival and success of liberty," the speaker gives principal attention in succession to those nations and peoples with whom we must strive for a better world. First, to those who wish or may come to wish us well he pledges our renewed support. Then to those—he does not call them our enemies, but "those . . . who would make themselves our adversaries"—to them he offers joint action for the mutual benefit of all.

The progression is quick and cumulative to the final invitation to Americans at home and to nations abroad to forge a global alliance that can assure a more fruitful life for all mankind. All is done with economy and force; nothing is elaborated; but something positive is said to and about each of the important nations and groups. The speech is short. We may observe the compactness by comparing the length with that of our bare outline. The structure is tight, but because of the selection and management of the language, the bare bones of the skeleton do not obtrude. In the central portion (our Roman numerals I and II), constituting nearly two pages of the less-than-three-page text, a sense of order, clarity, and progress is enhanced by simple verbal signals. In similar functional groups parallel matters are introduced in parallel phrases: *To those, To our,* or *To that;* and later *So let us begin, Let both sides* (five successive times). Thus the audience gets a sense of order without obvious enumeration or framework.

The conclusion seems an integral part of the structure of the thought, the fitting climax to the previous development. We consider the final challenge to Americans and the world, therefore, as the third major phase of the development. Other critics, following the traditional notion that exhortation is one function of the peroration, might wish to label it otherwise. In so short and homogeneous a speech, a sharp division of the classical parts is hardly very important. The major functions, however, are plain.

The Style and the Texture

Most commentators on President Kennedy's Inaugural—Miss Susan Lardner of *The New Yorker,* for example—and other perceptive persons who heard the speech or have since read it, give chief attention to the style—the selection and management of language. They observe its simplicity and dignity, its rhythm and force and harmony, its subtlety and its impressiveness, the aptness of the images and the figures of speech, the stately echoes in the structure of sentences and in the allusions and quotations, the overall economy of expression. Such attention is especially proper for that speech. Style, brought to life in delivery, we have said, gives to discourse the final elaboration and refinement of meaning. So it does in President Kennedy's Inaugural more fully than in others of his speeches, and perhaps more fully than in any other speeches of recent years. The qualities of the *texture* rather than the bare substance and structure make that speech especially worth analysis by the contemporary student of speaking.

An exhaustive analysis would lead us into greater detail and minuteness than present circumstances call for; but let us touch upon some of the sources and qualities of that texture.

The choice of words—selection of language—throughout is familiar and unpretentious. Only very rarely does the speaker use a word or expression infrequent in the common working vocabulary of educated Americans. The most uncommon words which we can find in the text are *forebears, engulf, tribulation,* and *forum of invective.* It is obvious that these words are easily understood, even by persons who do not use them. In part for that reason, they lend a subtle elevation to the language without rendering it pompous or inflated. On the other hand, never does Kennedy drop into popular jargon or indulge in the vocabulary of abuse.

We have seen that the ideas of conflict and battle in the cause of freedom and liberty for all men carry through the speech. So, also, words of war and freedom pervade the text. The enemies, however, are not the military antagonists of the United States but the universal foes of mankind. In the first sentence come both *victory* and *freedom,* and the interplay of words of battle and liberty colors the texture all the way through: *tempered by war, hard and bitter peace, human rights, success of liberty, bitter tyranny, their own freedom, arms, modern weapons, deadly atom, mankind's final war, negotiate, twilight struggle, bear arms, call to battle, common enemies of man: tyranny, poverty, disease, and war itself, peaceful revolution, quest for peace, the oppressed go free, strong are just, weak are secure, global alliance, more fruitful life, freedom in its hour of danger, freedom of man.*

Over the centuries, even the Christian centuries, the vocabulary of struggle and battle seems to have been the most popular vocabulary for talking about the quest for the good world ("Onward Christian soldiers," "Fight the good fight," "A mighty fortress is our God"). Kennedy and his audience would fall in with that vocabulary naturally, especially in a century consumed by two of the greatest of wars and by their "cold" and not-so-cold sequels. The present enemies of the "free world" and the opponents of the United States, of course, were before the minds of the audience throughout the speech, as those enemies had been on their tongues for the days and years before it. Kennedy, nevertheless, uses the word *Communists* only once, in connection with the exploitation of undeveloped countries. He does not mention Russia, the Soviets, or any other nation by name. He does not choose to perpetuate strife. Instead, the other side is made up of "those nations who would make themselves our adversary" and those who "wish us ill."

Imagery and figures of speech sustain the meaning of the speech and color and deepen the texture even more strongly than the vocabulary. These major instruments of impressiveness and potential sources of dignity weave through the whole text—subtly and delicately, for the most part, and sometimes almost imperceptibly. Seldom are they startling or obviously decorative. They are vehicles of thought and feeling, conveying hints and arousing meanings which explicit statement would distort or deform. The figures and images are almost always familiar, and sometimes hardly distinguishable from established vocabulary, but so used as not to be trite or commonplace. "Our ancient heritage" of "revolutionary beliefs," for instance, sets the tone of the opening. Heirs, we know, are receivers of benefits, not of misfortunes. The familiar image of passing the torch, suggests antiquity and a race, and races are run and won by the young—"a new generation of Americans." The old image in the limerick about the lady and the tiger, Kennedy recasts to warn the new countries against turning themselves over to unscrupulous (Russian? Chinese? Cuban?) exploiters. In "the dark powers of destruction unleashed by science" which could "engulf all mankind" there are echoes of satanic evil, of the "dogs of war," and of a vast flood. For some of President Kennedy's partisan listeners there might have been also an oblique thrust at Secretary of State John Foster Dulles's threat to "unleash" Chiang Kai-Shek.

Many other images and allusions coloring the texture and affecting the meaning will be evident to the analytical student. We will call attention to a few of them. The futility of the United Nations as a "forum of invective" stands in contrast to enlargement of "the area in which its writ may run." The figure of the writ suggests the happy goal of an international rule of law, which Kennedy makes explicit a little later. The "beachhead of cooperation" pushing back the "jungles of suspicion" raises recollections familiar to men like Kennedy who fought in World War II and sustains the theme of mankind's war for a good world. Also sustaining the theme of war, but the long doubtful war against the enemies of all men, is the "trumpet summons." And near the conclusion Kennedy turns to the beneficent images of fire and light for the promise of hope: "this endeavor will light our country . . . and the glow from that fire can truly light the world."

Explicit quotation occurs only twice in the text, each time to reinforce the prospect of the new world of freedom which can be. Both quotations come from the Bible. The first, from Isaiah 58:6, concludes the new President's invitation to our antagonists to join us in relieving the miseries of the world: "to undo the heavy burdens . . . [and] let the oppressed go free." The second, from Romans 12:12, offers strength for the long struggle: "rejoicing in hope, patient in tribulation." Submission to God and the Christian religion, normal and necessary in a Presidential Inaugural ceremony and address, is explicitly there in Kennedy's, at the beginning and at the end. It is there also in those two quotations, explicitly as Kennedy mentions the Old Testament prophet, and allusively in the words of St. Paul. Nowhere, however, does Kennedy call to his audience's mind the ugly issue of Protestant versus Catholic which had darkened much of the campaign. Perhaps there is a subtle suggestion of the basic irrelevance of the issue, for the words of the two quotations are those of the traditional Protestant King James translation, not the Douay translation, the official version of Mr. Kennedy's own church. Suggestions of the Biblical idiom appear often in the language and structure of Kennedy's sentences as they do in Lincoln's and in much of early American eloquence.

Besides the explicit quotations, giving depth to the feeling of the texture, are implicit allusions in the language, often hardly more than touches, but stirring a sense of the greatness and dignity of tradition. "Our *last best hope* in an age where instruments of war have far outstripped instruments of peace" includes words of Lincoln which have recently been invoked again and again to characterize the United Nations. *Master of its own house* echoes the ancient Anglo-American sense of individual independence. "All this will not be finished in the first hundred days" seems intended to remind some listeners of the remarkable achievements of Franklin D. Roosevelt's "first hundred days" and to connect the new President with his celebrated Democratic predecessor.

We do not imply that all or most of Kennedy's hearers or readers would be actively conscious of such quotations and allusions; nor do we know as we interpret them that they were specifically in the minds of Kennedy or his advisors. Such elements of style, however derived, help to create the texture of a speech and fuse cumulatively into the tone and quality of the meaning—the effect.

More important to the total effect, more obvious to the critic, and more actively at work in creating the texture of meaning are the order and structure—the parallelism, the balance, the inversion and antithesis—which make impressive many of Kennedy's principal statements.

> the power to abolish all form of human poverty and all form of human life
>
> the rights of man come not from the generosity of the state but from the hand of God
>
> born in this century, tempered by war, disciplined by a hard and bitter peace, proud of our ancient heritage
>
> United there is little we cannot do. . . . Divided, there is little we can do. [Echoing the "United we stand, divided we fall" of the Aesop fable and the slogan of the American Revolution, and suggesting Lincoln's "House Divided" speech.]
>
> If a free society cannot help the many who are poor, it cannot save the few who are rich.

> For only when our arms are sufficient beyond doubt can we be certain beyond doubt that they will never be used.

> civility is not a sign of weakness, and sincerity is always subject to proof.

> Let us never negotiate out of fear. But let us never fear to negotiate.

> not a new balance of power, but a new world of law, where the strong are just and the weak secure and the peace preserved

> —not as a call to arms, though arms we need—not as a call to battle, though embattled we are—but the call to bear the burden of a long twilight struggle

And the final trio of challenges:

> Ask not what your country can do for you—ask what you can do for your country.

> Ask not what America will do for you, but what together we can do for the freedom of man.

> Ask of us here the same high standards of strength and sacrifice which we ask of you.

The first of those challenges has lodged in the consciousness and the idiom of America, like Lincoln's "of the people, by the people, for the people," until, for many persons, it now lives as the whole meaning of the address. So powerful is the fine crystallization of a high ideal.

Little that is uncommon or remarkable, as we have observed earlier, marks the words in these passages. They are what most English-speaking people would expect to encounter in the language of their leaders. What raises all the passages out of the commonplace is the structure—the balance and the stately rhythm. In several, however, small departures from common word order add suggestions of the different, the ancient, even the Biblical. As we have shown in Chapter 12 on style, the order of the first two words of the "Ask not" sentences turns ordinary language into a call to patriotism which is touched with sacred dignity. *Ask not* and *Do not ask* convey roughly the same directive, but the textures of significance are distinctly different. A similar contribution to the texture follows from the structure of the opening words of Kennedy's original proclamation of the new order: "Let the word go forth from this time and place. . . ." So also the reversal of subject and verb in the second clauses of the "not a call" passages contributes that slight strangeness of idiom which Aristotle thought desirable and which we still find effective in the grander passages of rhetorical discourse—in eloquence. The striking play on words in "negotiate out of fear" and "fear to negotiate," turning *fear* from noun to verb, converts a standard doctrine of American policy into a memorable slogan.

Among the many catchwords and slogans which Kennedy launched that day, one came in more or less casually which has assumed much importance since that time. Absent from the address—perhaps remarkably absent—is any hint of the popular label "New Frontier," which the Kennedy party had already established as its successor to Roosevent's New Deal and Truman's Fair Deal. The Inaugural, however, was devoted to world affairs, and that label would have raised questions of domestic policy which the President had decided not to treat that day. Not so, however, with affairs south of the border. In his assurance to Latin America that "good words" should become "good deeds," he raised neighborliness to something much stronger as he turned the "Good Neighbor Policy" into "The Alliance for Progress."

It is important to observe that the concentration of stylistic resources brought to bear in these passages is not the normal characteristic of Kennedy's speaking. In a speech of the brevity and compactness of this Inaugural they occur often enough and in such multiplied combination that the cumulative effect is a sustained grandeur throughout. They generate their power, however, in part through contrast with more ordinary language:

> The world is very different now.
>
> We dare not forget that we are the heirs of that first revolution.
>
> We shall not always expect to find them supporting our view.
>
> But neither can two great and powerful groups of nations take comfort from our present course.

Kennedy seems to reserve his special stylistic strengths quite properly for the presentation of principal ideas, frequently for the concluding statements of such ideas. Style may serve more readily than any other aspect of speaking to display the prowess of the speaker, perhaps to the detriment of the substantive message. We find little hint of such intention or effect in Kennedy. Such passages as those we have been analyzing make memorable, impressive, and important what is central to the message. They focus the attention and stir the feelings of listeners in the interest of what the President wished to make powerful. Taken in sequence they carry the audience through the heart of the address.

We have now examined at some length President Kennedy's Inaugural Address for its purposes, its thought and structure, its style and texture, and its characteristics as the kind of speech it was—an Inaugural. A speech, however, is not fully a speech without the speaker as he delivered it. What the new President showed himself to be as he spoke, we think, was in harmony with the message he sought to convey.

The audience knew him as the youngest man ever elected to that high office; as a Congressman and Senator of good repute; as a fresh, vigorous, resourceful, buoyant, energetic, forthright campaign speaker; as a young man with a fine war record who had suffered long and serious physical disability and pain and had written a book called *Profiles in Courage;* as a highly intelligent and well-educated member of one of the wealthiest and most politically active families in the United States; as a Roman Catholic of immigrant Irish stock whose grandfather and father had built a great fortune in Boston politics and in business and finance; as the son of Franklin D. Roosevelt's ambassador to Great Britain and as the author of a book about the early disaster of World War II called *Why England Slept;* as a man whose political organization, managed by his brother, now to be his Attorney-General, had ridden over the popular favorite of the party, had commanded the convention, and had taken as his Vice-Presidential running mate his bitterest opponent; a man who had been elected with a popular majority of hardly more than 118,000 votes and was succeeding as President the country's most popular military hero.

In the staging and presentation of the address Kennedy accentuated those elements of the prevailing impression of him which would tend to give confidence and reassurance to the country and the world, and omitted or played down those features of the image which would perpetuate the residual sources of resentment, hostility, and doubt. As we have observed, at the outset he established his sense of tradition and his adherence to the ancient American ideals of liberty and revolution. There would be no discarding of the past—the immediate past of Eisenhower and Nixon, or the remoter past of our founders and ancestors. There would be a renewal, however, of youth and vigor, "a new generation of Americans—born in this century. . . ."

After he had taken the oath of office in a firm earnest voice, the new President moved to the podium and the banked microphones with the lively confident step which his audience had learned to expect. Amongst the dignitaries on the platform, bundled in their warm coats and hats against the cold penetrating January weather, the new President came before his audience and the television cameras hatless and coatless, as his audiences had been accustomed to seeing him—as if he were the equal even of the elements. He refrained from casting over the crowd his well-known ingratiating smile; but as he began to speak he looked out upon the listening and watching world with friendly responsible sobriety and earnestness. This, he no doubt wished to convey, was not the power politician, the versatile contestant in the "Great Debates," the genial and unruffled campaigner. This was the new leader of a free people, the friend of men of good will anywhere in the world, the determined adversary of those who would be oppressors and disturbers of the peace. That this image registered uncontaminated and unblurred throughout this country and throughout the world no one would be idolatrous enough to claim. The immediate responses to the speech, however, testify that in an uncommon measure Kennedy was successful.

As he proceeded through the short address, his voice and his manner of utterance, of course, sounded the John F. Kennedy to whom America had become accustomed—the tenor tones of youth; the pronunciation characteristic of New England, but of educated America as well; the short restrained gesture, shorter and more restrained than usual on that solemn occasion and behind that massive podium; the fragmented phrasing and confined rhythm which seemed to be his own, his hallmark. To some listeners, those who associated greatness of ideas and grandeur of language with rolling swells of voice and utterance, Kennedy's delivery tended perhaps to defeat the force of his message. For most hearers, however, his characteristic manner appears to have served to reduce the taint of conscious eloquence in his speaking and (at least for persons inclined to be sympathetic) to enhance the impression of thoughtfulness, of deliberation, in the speaker—so much is delivery part of the speaker and the speech.

We need not remark again the tone of strength, firm will, and modest confidence which sustained and were sustained by the substance and the language of Kennedy's address. Several times, however, and especially towards the end, the President explicitly showed himself counting on others as well as himself for the achievement of great goals, and ready to bear himself the burdens and the sacrifices that he was asking of others:

> In your hands, my fellow citizens, more than mine, will rest the final success or failure of our course.
>
> I do not shrink from this responsibility—I welcome it.
>
> Ask of us here the same high standards of strength and sacrifice which we ask of you.

To the cynic, the ethos of the speaker means little; to the idolater, it purifies all. Both are deceived. There can be little doubt, however, that after his Inaugural President Kennedy stood, for the time at least, higher in the regard and confidence of Americans and many peoples around the world than had before seemed possible.

That John F. Kennedy's Inaugural Address ranks or will rank among the ten greatest speeches of the western world or of modern times, any one at so near a date would be foolish to claim. Its high quality, however, and its appropriateness to the temper of the critical times and the mood and condition of the country can hardly be in doubt.

25
Speeches for Reading and Analysis

The speeches which make up the substance of this chapter should serve the student and the instructor in at least two important ways. They should help to interest and in a measure to involve a student in some of the problems and issues of our times; and they should provide practical examples of many of the techniques and methods by which competent speakers go about the business of adjusting ideas to people and people to ideas in the public arena. Not only may the student find in them much that he will wish to undertake in his own speaking (as well as some tactics and methods which he will wish to avoid), but also he may see through them into speechmaking as part of the historical record and as a significant factor in the dynamics of his society. So far as time and resources permit, we recommend that the study of speeches be made a substantial part of any college course in public speaking, and that the serious student apply to the study of these and other comparable speeches the methods of analysis and criticism which we have discussed and illustrated in the previous chapters.

The selection of speeches which is possible in such a book as this cannot purport to exemplify all significant aspects of public speaking or all the kinds of occasions and subjects in which significant speechmaking is involved. For practical reasons, for example, we do not include in this edition sermons, panel discussions, or examples of public interviews (see above, page 265) with which the television programs abound (especially on Sundays). We have attempted, however, to represent conveniently for classroom study and discussion kinds of occasions, types of subjects, and forms of speaking which the citizen is likely to encounter in either his own speaking, his role as an audience member, or his exploration as student of his society. We wish not only to exemplify as many as possible of the ways good speakers solve or try to solve the difficult problems of informing and persuading audiences of various sorts, but also to involve the student-reader in some of the interesting and disturbing political, social, and moral problems of our society. We intend the chapter, therefore, as a collection of examples and stimulating readings.

Students who become seriously interested in political and parliamentary discussion, in which speechmaking plays a part, will seek recourse to *The*

New York Times, to the local and metropolitan press in various parts of the country, and to the *Congressional Record* and *Hansard* respectively for speaking in the Congress of the United States and in the British Parliament. They will also become aware of collections of historic and contemporary speeches such as these:

BRYANT, Donald C., ARNOLD, Carroll C., HABERMAN, Frederick W., MURPHY, Richard, and WALLACE, Karl R. *An Historical Anthology of Select British Speeches.* New York: The Ronald Press, 1967.

PARRISH, Wayland Maxfield, and HOCHMUTH, Marie. *American Speeches.* New York, 1954.

Vital Speeches of the Day. A semimonthly periodical publishing the texts of current speeches in English.

Characteristic Speeches of Recent Times

ABBA EBAN

Address to the General Assembly of the United Nations, June 19, 1967*

The Chamber of the General Assembly of the United Nations in New York is the live public forum of the world. Whether at any particular moment the speaking which goes on there is in fact genuine give and take, genuine debate on the international crises which plague and threaten mankind, or, as some persons assert, the exhibition of nationalist propaganda for domestic and international consumption, what is said there, as well as what is done in the committees and the councils, is of great importance to all nations and peoples. Especially does the United Nations give the small nations and their statesmen opportunity to let their voices be heard and their strengths and weaknesses exhibited to the representatives and often, through radio and television, to the peoples of most nations of the earth.

Among the recent debates in the United Nations, those arising from the Israeli-Arab war of June 1967 received especially wide and close attention because of both the gravity of the issues and the talents and efforts of the speakers. For many years, and especially since the establishment of the new state of Israel in 1948, tensions and bitterness, erupting from time to time in fighting, had beset the Middle East. A history of those years, one-sided to be sure, may be gathered from the speech below. Finally, on June 5, 1967, a full-scale war broke out, in which Israel in five days totally routed and defeated her Arab foes, Egypt, Syria, Jordan, and their allies.

As soon as hostilities began, the problem came before the Security Council which, after much hard work behind the scenes, publicly passed a resolution ordering a cease-fire. There followed a long session, broadcast on radio and television, in which all interested parties discussed the decision from their particular situations. In effect, the

* We reprint, with permission, the text published by the Israeli Information Services, New York, June 1967. We have inserted in square brackets a few additional sentences from the partial text published in *The New York Times,* June 20, 1967, p. 17.

question was "debated" publicly after the decision had been made. In that debate, Abba Eban, Foreign Minister of Israel played a conspicuous part.

After the cease-fire was established and the war ended with Israel's total victory, the General Assembly of the United Nations, consisting of representatives of all the 120 member nations, was called into session by Israel's adversaries and the Soviet Union to press for the restoration by Israel of the conquered territory. To that debate the Foreign Minister of Israel contributed the speech below, certainly one of the most expert pieces of narrative argument of modern times. We present it as a superior example of present-day international public address, especially notable for Mr. Eban's impressive massing of documentary evidence, his facility of phrasing, and his infusion of patriotic and humanitarian emotion into his argumentative narrative.

Abba Eban, born in South Africa in 1915, lived and was educated in England, where he took the M.A. with honors in Hebrew, Arabic, and Persian languages and literatures in 1938. After teaching the Middle Eastern languages in England and serving during World War II as liaison officer between the British in Cairo and the Jews in Palestine, he took up residence in Palestine and continued his teaching and cultural work in Jerusalem. In 1946 he turned to politics and had an important part in the creation of the State of Israel. He has served Israel in various capacities in the United Nations and as Ambassador to the United States. He has been minister of Education in Israel and Deputy Prime Minister, and since early 1966 has been Minister of Foreign Affairs. Mr. Eban is perhaps the most fluent, literate, and copious speaker on the international scene today. He understands and speaks the major Western and Middle Eastern languages, and uses English for his public addresses in the United Nations.

In recent weeks the Middle East has passed through a crisis whose shadows darken the world. This crisis has many consequences but only one cause. Israel's right to peace, security, sovereignty, economic development and maritime freedom—indeed its very right to exist—has been forcibly denied and aggressively attacked. This is the true origin of the tension which torments the Middle East. All the other elements of the conflict are the consequences of this single cause. There has been danger, there is still peril in the Middle East because Israel's existence, sovereignty and vital interests have been and are being violently assailed.

The threat to Israel's existence, its peace, security, sovereignty and development has been directed against her in the first instance by the neighbouring Arab States. But all the conditions of tension, all the temptations to aggression in the Middle East have, to our deep regret, been aggravated by the one-sided policy of one of the Great Powers which under our Charter bear primary responsibility for the maintenance of international peace and security. I shall show how the Soviet Union has, for 15 years, been unfaithful to that trust. The burden of responsibility lies heavy upon her. Today's intemperate utterance illustrates the lack of equilibrium and objectivity which has contributed so much to the tension and agonies.

I come to this rostrum to speak for a united people which, having faced danger to their national survival, is unshakeably resolved to resist any course which would renew the perils from which it has emerged.

The General Assembly is chiefly preoccupied by the situation against which Israel defended itself on the morning of June 5. I shall invite every peace-loving state represented here to ask itself how it would have acted on that day if it faced similar dangers. But if our discussion is to have any weight or depth, we must understand that great events are not born in a single instant of time. It is beyond all honest doubt that between May 14 and June 5, Arab governments, led and directed by President Nasser, methodically prepared and mounted an aggressive assault designed to bring about Israel's immediate and total destruction. My authority for that conviction rests on the statements and actions of Arab governments themselves. There is every reason to believe what they say and to observe what they do.

During Israel's first decade the intention to work for her destruction by physical violence had always been part of the official doctrine and policy of Arab States. But many members of the United Nations hoped and some believed that relative stability would ensue from the arrangements discussed in the General Assembly in March, 1957. An attempt was then made to inaugurate a period of non-belligerency and co-existence in the relations between Egypt and Israel. A United Nations Emergency Force was to separate the armies in Sinai and Gaza. The maritime powers were to exercise free and innocent passage in the Gulf of Aqaba and the Straits of Tiran. Terrorist attacks against Israel were to cease. The Suez Canal was to be opened to Israeli shipping, as the Security Council had decided six years before.

In March, 1957, these hopes and expectations were endorsed in the General Assembly by the United States, France, the United Kingdom, Canada, and other states in Europe, the Americas, Africa, Asia and Australasia. These assurances, expressed with special solemnity by the four governments which I have mentioned, induced Israel to give up positions which she then held at Gaza and at the entrance to the Straits of Tiran and in Sinai. Non-belligerency, maritime freedom and immunity from terrorist attack were henceforth to be secured, not by Israel's own pressure but by the concerted will of the international community. Egypt expressed no opposition to these arrangements. Bright hopes for the future illuminated this hall ten years ago.

There were times during the past decade when it really seemed that a certain stability had been achieved. As we look back it becomes plain that the Arab governments regarded the 1957 arrangements merely as a breathing space enabling them to gather strength for a later assault. At the end of 1962, President Nasser began to prepare Arab opinion for an armed attack that was to take place within a few brief years. As his armaments grew his aggressive designs came more blatantly to light. On 23 December, 1962, Nasser said: "We feel that the soil of Palestine is the soil of Egypt, and of the whole Arab world. Why do we all mobilize? Because we feel that the land of Palestine is part of our land, and are ready to sacrifice ourselves for it."

The present Foreign Minister of Egypt, Mahmoud Riad, echoed his master's voice: "The sacred Arab struggle will not come to an end until Palestine is restored to its owners."

In March, 1963, the official Cairo radio continued the campaign of menace: "Arab unity is taking shape towards the great goal—i.e. the triumphant return to Palestine with the banner of unity flying high in front of the holy Arab march."

The newspaper *Al-Gumhuriya* published an official announcement on the same day: "The noose around Israel's neck is tightening gradually . . . Israel is no mightier than the empires which were vanquished by the Arab east and west . . . The Arab people will take possession of their full rights in their united homeland."

Egypt is not a country in which the press utters views and opinions independently of the official will. There is thus much significance in the statement of *Al-Akhbar* on 4 April, 1963: "The liquidation of Israel will not be realized through a declaration of war against Israel by Arab States, *but Arab unity and inter-Arab understanding will serve as a hangman's rope for Israel.*"

The Assembly will note that the imagery of a hangman's rope or of a tightening noose occurs frequently in the macabre vocabulary of Nasserism. He sees himself perpetually presiding over a scaffold. In June, 1967, in Israel's hour of solitude and danger, the metaphor of encirclement and strangulation was to come vividly to life.

In February, 1964, Nasser enunciated in simple terms what was to become his country's policy during the period of preparation: "The possibilities of the future will be war with Israel. It is we who will dictate the time; it is we who will dictate the place."

A similar chorus of threats arose during this period from other Arab capitals. President Aref of Iraq and President Ben-Bella of Algeria were especially emphatic and repetitive in their threat to liquidate Israel. They were then far away. The Syrian attitude was more ominous because it affected a neighbouring frontier. Syrian war propaganda has been particularly intense in the past few years. In 1964, the Syrian Defense Minister, General Abdulla Ziada, announced: "The Syrian army stands as a mountain to crush Israel and demolish her. This army knows how to crush its enemies."

Early last year Syria began to proclaim and carry out what it called a "popular war" against Israel. This was a terrorist compaign which expressed itself in the dispatch of trained terrorist groups into Israel territory to blow up installations and communications centers and to kill, maim, cripple and terrorize civilians in peaceful homes and farms. Often the terrorists, trained in Syria, were dispatched through Jordan or Lebanon. The terrorist war was formally declared by President Al-Atassi on 22 May, 1966, when he addressed soldiers on the Israel-Syrian front: "We raise the slogan of the people's liberation war. We want total war with no limits, a war that will destroy the Zionist base."

It is a strange experience in this hall of peace to be sitting with a delegate whose philosophy is: "We want total war with no limits."

The Syrian Defense Minister, Hafiz Asad, said two days later:

> We say: We shall never call for, nor accept peace. We shall only accept war and the restoration of the usurped land. We have resolved to drench this land with our blood, to oust you, aggressors, and throw you into the sea for good.
>
> We must meet as soon as possible and fight a single liberation war on the level of the whole area against Israel, imperialism and all the enemies of the people.

From that day to this not a week has passed without Syrian officials adding to this turgid stream of invective and hate. From that day to this, there has not been a single month without terrorist acts, offensive to every impulse of human compassion and international civility, being directed from Syria against Israeli citizens and territory. I would have no difficulty in swelling the General Assembly's records with a thousand official statements by Arab leaders in the past two years announcing their intention to destroy Israel by diverse forms of organized physical violence. The Arab populations have been conditioned by their leaders to the anticipation of a total war, preceded by the constant harassment of the prospective victim.

From 1948 to this very day there has not been one statement by any Arab representative of a neighbouring Arab State indicating readiness to respect existing agreements on the permanent renunciation of force; to recognize Israel's sovereign right to existence or to apply to Israel any of the central provisions of the United Nations Charter.

For some time Israel showed a stoic patience in her reaction to these words of menace. This was because the threats were not accompanied by a capacity to carry them into effect. But the inevitable result of this campaign of menace was the burden of a heavy race in arms. We strove to maintain an adequate deterrent strength; and the decade beginning in March, 1957, was not monopolized by security considerations alone. Behind the walls of a strong defense, with eyes vigilantly fixed on dangerous borders, we embarked on a constructive era in the national enterprise. These were years of swift expansion in our agriculture and industry; of intensive progress in the sciences and arts; of a widening international vocation, symbolized in the growth of strong links with the developing world. At the end of her first decade Israel had established relations of diplomacy, commerce and culture with all the Americas, and with most of the countries of Western, Central and Eastern Europe. In her second decade she was to build constructive links with the emerging countries of the developing world with whom we are tied by a common aspiration to translate national freedom into creative economic growth and progress.

Fortified by friendships in all five continents; inspired by its role in the great drama of development; intensely preoccupied by tasks of spiritual cooperation with kindred communities in various parts of the world, and in the effort to assure the Jewish survival after the disastrous blows of Nazi oppression; tenaciously involved in the development of original social ideas, Israel went on with its work. We could not concern ourselves exclusively with the torrent of hatred pouring in upon us from Arab governments. In the era of modern communications a nation is not entirely dependent on its regional context. The wide world is open to the voice of friendship. Arab hostility towards Israel became increasingly isolated, while our position in the international family became more deeply entrenched. Many in the world drew confidence from the fact that a very small nation could, by its exertion and example, rise to respected levels in social progress, scientific research and the humane arts. And so our policy was to deter the aggression of our neighbours so long as it was endurable; to resist it only when failure to resist would have invited its intensified renewal; to withstand Arab violence without being obsessed by it; and even to search patiently here and there for any glimmer of moderation and realism in the Arab mind. We also pursued the hope of bringing all the Great Powers to a harmonious policy in support of the security and sovereignty of Middle Eastern States.

It was not easy to take this course. The sacrifice imposed upon our population by Arab violence was cumulative in its effects. But as it piled up month by month the toll of death and bereavement was heavy. And in the last few years it was evident that this organized murder was directed by a central hand.

We were able to limit our response to this aggression so long as its own scope appeared to be limited. President Nasser seemed for some years to be accumulating inflammable material without an immediate desire to set it alight. He was heavily engaged in domination and conquest elsewhere. His speeches were strong against Israel. But his bullets, guns and poison gases were for the time being used to intimidate other Arab States and to maintain a colonial war against the villagers of the Yemen and the peoples of the Arabian Peninsula.

But Israel's danger was great. The military build-up in Egypt proceeded at an intensive rate. It was designed to enable Egypt to press its war plans against Israel while maintaining its violent adventures elsewhere. In the face of these developments Israel was forced to devote an increasing part of its resources to self-defense. With the declaration by Syria early in 1965 of the doctrine of a "day by day military confrontation" the situation in the Middle East grew darker. The Palestine Liberation Organization, the Palestine Liberation Army, the Unified Arab Command, the intensified expansion of military forces and equipment in Egypt, Syria, Lebanon, Jordan and more remote parts of the Arab continent—these were the signals of a growing danger to which we sought to alert the mind and conscience of the world.

In three tense weeks between 14 May and 5 June, Egypt, Syria and Jordan, assisted and incited by more distant Arab States, embarked on a policy of immediate and total aggression.

June, 1967, was to be the month of decision. The "final solution" was at hand.

There was no convincing motive for the aggressive design which was now unfolded. Egyptian and Soviet sources have claimed that a concentrated Israeli invasion of Syria was expected during the second or third week in May. No claim could be more frivolous or far-fetched. It is true that Syria was sending terrorists into Israel to lay mines on public roads and, on one occasion, to bombard the Israeli settlement at Manara from the Lebanese border. The accumulation of such actions had sometimes evoked Israeli responses limited in scope and time. All that Syria had to do to ensure perfect tranquility on her frontier with Israel was to discourage the terrorist war. Not only did she not discourage these actions. She encouraged them. She gave them every moral and practical support. But the picture of Israeli troop concentrations in strength for an invasion of Syria was a monstrous fiction. Twice Syria refused to cooperate with suggestions made by the UN authorities and accepted by Israel for a simultaneous and reciprocal inspection of the Israeli-Syrian frontier. On one occasion the Soviet Ambassador complained to my Prime Minister of heavy troop concentrations in the north of Israel. When invited to join the Prime Minister that very moment to a visit to any part of Israel which he would like to see the distinguished envoy brusquely refused. The prospect of finding out the truth at first hand seemed to fill him with a profound disquiet. [There is only one thing to be said about Prime Minister Kosygin's assertion this morning that there were heavy concentrations of Israeli troops on the Syrian frontier in mid-May. The only thing to say about the assertion is that it is completely untrue. There is only one thing to say about these descriptions of villages being burned and inhabitants being shot. These are false, inflammatory words of propaganda designed to inflame passions in an area already too hot with tension.] But by 9 May the Secretary General of the United Nations from his own sources on the ground had ascertained that no Israeli troop concentrations existed. This fact had been directly communicated to the Syrian and Egyptian governments. The excuse had been shattered, but the allegations still remained. The steps which I now describe could not possibly have any motive or justification in an Israeli troop concentration which both Egypt and Syria knew did not exist. Indeed the Egyptian build-up ceased [very quickly even] to be described by its authors as the result of any threat to Syria. [Let us now see how the design began to unfold.]

On 14 May, Egyptian forces began to move into Sinai.

On 16 May, the Egyptian Command ordered the United Nations Emergency Force to leave the border. The following morning the reason became clear. For on 17 May, 1967, at 6 in the morning, Radio Cairo broadcast that Field Marshal Amer had issued alert orders to the Egyptian armed forces. Nor did he mention Syria as the excuse.

This announcement reads:

1. The state of preparedness of the Egyptian Armed Forces will increase to the full level of preparedness for war, beginning 14.30 hours last Sunday.
2. Formations and units allocated in accordance with operational plans will advance from their present locations to the designated positions.
3. The armed forces are to be in full preparedness to carry out any combat tasks on the Israel front in accordance with developments.

On 18 May, Egypt called for the total removal of the United Nations Emergency Force. The Secretary-General of the United Nations acceded to this request and moved to carry it out, without reference to the Security Council or the General Assembly; without carrying out the procedures indicated by Secretary Hammarskjöld in the event of a request for a withdrawal being made; without heeding the protesting voices of some of the permanent members of the Security Council and of the Government at whose initiative the Force had been established; without consulting Israel on the consequent prejudice to her military security and her vital maritime freedom; and without seeking such delay as would enable alternative measures to be concerted for preventing belligerency by sea and a dangerous confrontation of forces by land.

It is often said that United Nations procedures are painfully slow. This decision was, in our view, disastrously swift. Its effect was to make Sinai safe for belligerency from north and to south; to create a sudden disruption of the local security balance; and to leave an international maritime interest exposed to almost certain threat. [I will not say anything of the compulsions which led to the decision.] I have already said that Israel's attitude to the peacekeeping functions of the United Nations has been traumatically affected by this experience. What is the use of a fire brigade which vanishes from the scene as soon as the first smoke and flames appear? Is it surprising that we are firmly resolved never again to allow a vital Israeli interest and our very security to rest on such a fragile foundation?

The clouds now gathered thick and fast. Between 14 May and 23 May, Egyptian concentrations in Sinai increased day by day. Israel took corresponding precautionary measures. In the absence of an agreement to the contrary, it is legal for any state to place its armies wherever it chooses in its territory. It is equally true that nothing could be more uncongenial to the prospect of peace than to have large armies facing each other across a narrow space with one of them clearly bent on an early assault. For the purpose of the concentration was not in doubt. On 18 May, at 24 hours, the Cairo Radio *Saut El Arab* published the following Order of the Day by Abdul Muhsin Murtagi, the General then commanding Sinai:

> The Egyptian forces have taken up positions in accordance with a definite plan.
>
> Our forces are definitely ready to carry the battle beyond the borders of Egypt.
>
> Morale is very high among the members of our armed forces because this is the day for which they have been waiting—to make a holy war in order to return the plundered land to its owners.
>
> In many meetings with army personnel they asked when the holy war will begin—the time has come to give them their wish.

On 21 May, General Amer gave the order to mobilize reserves.

Now came the decisive step. All doubt that Egypt had decided upon immediate or early war was now dispelled. Appearing at an air force base at 6 o'clock in the morning, President Nasser announced that he would blockade the Gulf of Aqaba to Israeli ships, adding: "The Jews threaten war and we say by all means we are ready for war."

On 25 May, Cairo Radio announced: "The Arab people is firmly resolved to wipe Israel off the map and to restore the honor of the Arabs of Palestine."

On the following day, 26 May, Nasser spoke again:

> The Arab people wants to fight. We have been waiting for the right time when we will be completely ready. Recently we have felt that our strength has been sufficient and that if we make battle with Israel we shall be able, with the help of God, to conquer. Sharm-el-Sheikh implies a confrontation with Israel. Taking this step makes it imperative that we be ready to undertake a total war with Israel.

Writing in *Al Ahram,* on 26 May, Nasser's mouthpiece, Hasanein Heykal, wrote, with engaging realism:

> I consider that there is no alternative to armed conflict between the United Arab Republic and the Israeli enemy. This is the first time that the Arab challenge to Israel attempts to change an existing fact in order to impose a different fact in its place.

On 28 May, Nasser had a press conference. He was having them every day. He said: "We will not accept any possibility of co-existence with Israel."

And on the following day: "If we have succeeded to restore the situation to what it was before 1956, there is no doubt that God will help us and will inspire us to restore the situation to what it was prior to 1948." There are various way of threatening Israel's liquidation. Few ways could be clearer than to ask to move the clock of history back to 1948.

The troop concentrations and blockade were now to be accompanied by encirclement. The noose was to be fitted around the victim's neck. Other Arab States were closing the ring. On 30 May, Nasser signed the defense agreement with Jordan; and described its purpose in these terms:

> The armies of Egypt, Jordan, Syria and Lebanon are stationed on the borders of Israel in order to face the challenge. Behind them stand the armies of Iraq, Algeria, Kuwait, Sudan and the whole of the Arab nation.
>
> This deed will astound the world. Today they will know that the Arabs are ready for the fray. The hour of decision has arrived.

On 4 June Nasser made a statement on Cairo Radio after signing the Protocol associating Iraq with the Egyptian-Jordanian Defense Pact. Here are his words: ". . . We are facing you in the battle and are burning with desire for it to start, in order to obtain revenge. This will make the world realize what the Arabs are and what Israel is . . ."

Nothing has been more startling in recent weeks than to read discussions about who planned, who organized, who initiated, who wanted and who launched this war. Here we have a series of statements, mounting in crescendo from vague warning through open threat to precise intention.

Here we have the vast mass of the Egyptian armies in Sinai with seven infantry and two armored divisions, the greatest force ever assembled in that peninsula in all its history. Here we have 40,000 regular Syrian troops poised to strike at the Jordan Valley from advantageous positions in the hills. Here we have the mobilized forces of Jordan with their artillery and mortars trained on Israel's population centers in Jerusalem and along the vulnerable narrow coastal plain. Troops from Iraq, Kuwait and Algeria converge towards the battlefront at Egypt's behest. 900 tanks face Israel on the Sinai border, while 200 more are poised to strike the isolated town of Elath at Israel's southern tip. The military dispositions tell their own story. The Southern Negev was to be sundered in a swift decisive blow. The Northern Negev was to be invaded by armour and bombarded from the Gaza Strip. From May 27 onward, Egyptian air squadrons in Sinai were equipped with operation orders, now in our hands, instructing them in detail on the manner in which Israeli airfields, pathetically few in number, were to be bombarded, thus exposing Israel's crowded cities to easy and merciless assault. Egyptian air sorties came in and out of Israel's southern desert to reconnoitre, inspect and prepare for the attack. An illicit blockade had cut Israel off from all her commerce with the eastern half of the world.

Now those who write this story in years to come will give a special place in their narrative to the blatant decision to close the Straits of Tiran in Israel's face. It is not difficult to understand why this outrage had such a drastic impact. In 1957 the maritime nations, within the framework of the United Nations General Assembly, correctly enunciated the doctrine of free and innocent passage through the Strait. Now, when that doctrine was proclaimed—and incidentally, not challenged at the time by the Egyptian representative—it was little more than an abstract principle for the maritime world. For Israel it was a great but still unfulfilled prospect; it was not yet a reality. But during the ten years in which we and the other States of the maritime community have relied upon that doctrine and upon established usage, the principle has become a reality consecrated by hundreds of sailings under dozens of flags and the establishment of a whole complex of commerce and industry and communication. A new dimension has been added to the map of the world's communications, and on that dimension we have constructed Israel's bridge towards the friendly States of Asia and Africa, a network of relationships which is the chief pride of Israel in the second decade of its independence and on which its economic future depends.

All this, then, had grown up as an effective usage under the United Nations flag. Does Mr. Nasser really think that he can come upon the scene in ten minutes and cancel the established legal usage and interests of ten years?

There was in this wanton act a quality of malice. For surely the closing of the Strait of Tiran gave no benefit whatever to Egypt except the perverse joy of inflicting injury on others. It was an anarchic act, because it showed a total disregard for the law of nations, the application of which in this specific case had not been challenged for ten years. And it was, in the literal sense, an act of arrogance, because there are other nations in Asia and East Africa that trade with the Port of Elath, as they have every right to do, through the Straits of Tiran and across the Gulf of Aqaba. Other sovereign States from Japan to Ethiopia, from Thailand to Uganda, from Cambodia to Madagascar, have a sovereign right to decide for themselves whether they wish or do not wish to trade with Israel. These countries are not colonies of Cairo. They can trade with Israel or not trade with Israel as they wish, and President Nasser is not the policeman of other African and Asian States.

When we examine, then, the implications of this act, we have no cause to wonder that the international shock was great. There was another reason too for that shock. Blockades have traditionally been regarded, in the pre-Charter parlance, as acts of war. To blockade, after all, is to attempt strangulation—and sovereign States are entitled not to have their trade strangled.

The blockade is by definition an act of war, imposed and enforced through armed violence. Never in history have blockade and peace existed side by side. From May 24 onward, the question who started the war or who fired the first shot became momentously irrelevant. There is no difference in civil law between murdering a man by slow strangulation or killing him by a shot in the head. From the moment at which the blockade was imposed, active hostilities had commenced and Israel owed Egypt nothing of her Charter rights. If a foreign power sought to close Odessa or Copenhagen or Marseilles or New York harbor by use of force, what would happen? Would there be any discussion about who had fired the first shot? Would anyone ask whether aggression had begun? Less than a decade ago the Soviet Union proposed a draft resolution in the General Assembly on the question of defining aggression. The resolution reads: "In an international conflict that state shall be declared an attacker which first commits one of the following acts: (*a*) Naval blockade of the coasts or ports of another State."

This act constituted in the Soviet view direct aggression as distinguished from other specified acts designated in the Soviet draft as indirect aggression. In this particular case the consequences of Nasser's action had been fully announced in advance. On March 1, 1957, my predecessor announced that:

> Interference, by armed force, with ships of Israeli flag exercising free and innocent passage in the Gulf of Aqaba and through the Straits of Tiran, will be regarded by Israel as an attack entitling it to exercise its inherent right of self-defence under Article 51 of the United Nations Charter and to take all such measures as are necessary to ensure the free and innocent passage of its ships in the Gulf and in the Straits.

The representative of France, declared that any obstruction of free passage in the Straits or Gulf was contrary to international law "entailing a possible resort to the measures authorized by Article 51 of the Charter."

The United States, inside and outside of the United Nations gave specific endorsement to Israel's right to invoke her inherent right of self-defence against any attempt to blockade the Gulf. Nasser was speaking with acute precision, therefore, when he stated that Israel now faced the choice of either to be choked to death in her southern maritime approaches or to await the death blow from northern Sinai.

Nobody who lived those days in Israel between May 23 and June 5 will ever forget the air of heavy foreboding that hovered over our country. Hemmed in by hostile armies ready to strike, affronted and beset by a flagrant act of war, bombarded day and night by predictions of our approaching extinction, forced into a total mobilization of all her manpower, her economy and commerce beating with feeble pulse, her main supplies of vital fuel choked by a belligerent act, Israel faced the greatest peril to her existence that she had known since her resistance against aggression nineteen years before, at the hour of her birth. There was peril wherever she looked and she faced it in deepening solitude. On May 24 and on succeeding days, the Security Council conducted a desultory debate which sometimes reached a point of levity. Russian and Oriental proverbs were wittily exchanged. The Soviet representative asserted that he saw no reason for discussing the Middle Eastern situation at all. The distinguished Bulgarian Delegate uttered these unbelievable words: "At the present moment there is really no need for an urgent meeting of the Security Council." This was the day after the imposition of the blockade!

A crushing siege bore down upon us. Multitudes throughout the world began to tremble for Israel's fate. The single consolation lay in the surge of public opinion which rose up in Israel's defense. From Paris to Montevideo, from New York to Amsterdam, tens of thousands of people of all ages, parties and affiliations marched in horrified protest at the approaching stage of politicide—the murder of a State. Writers and scientists, religious leaders, trade union movements and even the Communist parties in France, Holland, Switzerland, Norway, Austria and Finland asserted their view that Israel was a peace-loving State, whose peace was being wantonly denied. In the history of our generation it is difficult to think of any other hour in which progressive world opinion has rallied in such tension and agony of spirit to any cause.

To understand the full depth of pain and shock, it is necessary to grasp the full significance of what Israel's danger meant. A small sovereign state had its existence threatened by lawless violence. The threat to Israel was a menace to the very foundations of the international order. The state thus threatened bore a name which stirred the deepest memories of civilized mankind, and the people of the threatened state were the surviving remnant of millions, who in living memory had been wiped out by a dictatorship more powerful, though scarcely more malicious, than Nasser's Egypt. What Nasser had predicted, what he had worked for with undeflecting purpose had come to pass—the noose was tightly drawn.

[And so] on the fateful morning of June 5, when Egyptian forces moved by air and land against Israel's western coast and southern territory, our country's choice was plain. The choice was to live or perish, to defend the national existence or to forfeit it for all time. [I will not narrate what then transpired.]

From these dire moments Israel emerged in five heroic days from awful peril to successful and glorious resistance. Alone, unaided, neither seeking nor receiving help, our nation rose in self-defense. So long as men cherish freedom, so long as small states strive for the dignity of survival, the exploits of Israel's armies will be told from one generation to another with the deepest pride. The Soviet Union has described our resistance as aggression and sought to have it condemned. We reject this accusation with all our might. Here was armed force employed in a just and righteous cause; as righteous as the defence of freedom at Valley Forge; as just as the expulsion of Hitler's bombers from the British skies; as noble as the protection of Stalingrad against the Nazi hordes, so was the defence of Israel's security and existence against those who sought our nation's destruction. What should be condemned is not Israel's action, but the attempt to condemn it. Never have freedom, honor, justice, national interest and international morality been so righteously protected.

While fighting raged on the Egyptian-Israel frontier and on the Syrian front, we still hoped to contain the conflict. Jordan was given every chance to remain outside the struggle. Even after Jordan had bombarded and bombed Israel territory at several points we still proposed to the Jordanian monarch that he abstain from general hostilities. A message to this effect reached him several hours after the outbreak of hostilities on the southern front on June 5.

Jordan answered tragically not with words but with shells. Artillery opened fire fiercely along the whole front with special emphasis on the Jerusalem area. Thus, Jordan's responsibility for the second phase of the concerted aggression is established beyond doubt. This responsibility cannot fail to have its consequences in the peace settlement. As death and injury rained on the city, Jordan had become the source and origin of Jerusalem's fierce ordeal. The inhabitants of the city can never forget this fact, or fail to draw its conclusions.

[Mr. President,] I have spoken of Israel's defence against the assaults of neighbouring states. This is not the entire story. Whatever happens in the Middle East for good or ill, for peace or conflict, is powerfully affected by what the Great Powers do or omit to do. When the Soviet Union initiates a discussion here our gaze is inexorably drawn to the story of its role in recent Middle Eastern history. It is a sad and shocking story; it must be frankly told.

There was in Soviet policy a brief but important episode of balanced friendship. In 1948, the USSR condemned what she called "Arab aggression."

Since 1955 the Soviet Union has supplied the Arab States with 2000 tanks, of which more than 1000 have gone to Egypt. The Soviet Union has supplied the Arab States with 700 modern fighter aircraft and bombers, more recently with ground missiles; and Egypt alone has received from the USSR 540 field guns, 130 medium guns, 200 120 mm. mortars, 695 anti-aircraft guns, 175 rocket launchers, 650 anti-tank guns, 7 destroyers; a number of Luna M and Sopka 2 ground to ground missiles, 14 submarines and 46 torpedo boats of various types including missile carrying boats. The Egyptian army has been trained by Soviet experts. This has been attested by Egyptian officers captured by Israel. Most of this equipment was supplied to the Arab States after the Cairo Summit Conference of Arab leaders in January 1964 had agreed on a specific program for the destruction of Israel; after they had announced and hastened to fulfil this plan by accelerating their arms purchases from the Soviet Union. The proportions of Soviet assistance are attested to by the startling fact that in Sinai alone the Egyptians abandoned equipment and offensive weapons of Soviet manufacture whose value is estimated at two billion dollars.

Together with the supply of offensive weapons the Soviet Union has encouraged the military preparations of the Arab States.

Since 1961 the Soviet armaments have assisted Egypt in its desire to conquer Israel. The great amount of offensive equipment supplied to the Arab States strengthens this assessment.

Thus, a Great Power which professes its devotion to peaceful settlement and the rights of States has for fourteen years afflicted the Middle East with a headlong armaments race; with the paralysis of the United Nations as an instrument of security; and with an attitude of blind identification with those who threaten peace against those who defend it.

The constant increase and escalation of Soviet armaments in Arab countries has driven Israel to a corresponding though far smaller procurement program. Israel's arms purchases were precisely geared to the successive phases of Arab, and especially Egyptian rearmament. On many occasions in recent months we and others have vainly sought to secure Soviet agreement for a reciprocal reduction of arms supplies in our region. These efforts have borne no fruit. The expenditure on social and economic progress of one half of what has been put into the purchase of Soviet arms would have been sufficient to redeem Egypt from its social and economic ills. A corresponding diversion of resources from military to social expenditure would have taken place in Israel. A viable balance of forces could have been achieved at a lower level of armaments, while our region could have moved forward to higher standards of human and social welfare. For Israel's attitude is clear. We should like to see the arms race slowed down. But if the race is joined, we are determined not to lose it. A fearful waste of economic energy in the Middle East is the direct result of the Soviet role in the constant stimulation of the race in arms.

It is clear from Arab sources that the Soviet Union has played a provocative role in spreading alarmist and incendiary reports of Israeli intentions amongst Arab governments.

On 9 June, President Nasser said: "Our friends in the USSR warned the visiting parliamentary delegation in Moscow at the beginning of last month, that there exists a plan of attack against Syria."

Similarly an announcement by TASS of 23 May states:

> The Foreign Affairs and Security Committee of the Knesset have accorded the Cabinet on 9 May, special powers to carry out war operations against Syria. Israeli forces concentrating on the Syrian border have been put in a state of alert for war. General mobilization has also been proclaimed in the country.

There was not one word of truth in this story. But its diffusion in the Arab countries could only have an incendiary result.

Cairo Radio broadcast on 28 May (0500 hours) an address by Marshal Gretchko at a farewell party in honour of the former Egyptian Minister of Defense Shams ed-Din Badran:

> The USSR, her armed forces, her people and government will stand by the Arabs and will continue to encourage and support them. We are your faithful friends and we shall continue aiding you because this is the policy of the Soviet nation, its party and government. On behalf of the Ministry of Defense and in the name of the Soviet nation we wish you success and victory.

This promise of military support came less than a week after the illicit closing of the Tiran Straits, an act which the USSR has done nothing to condemn.

The USSR has exercised her veto right in the Security Council five times. Each time a just and constructive judgment has been frustrated. On 22 January 1954 France, the United Kingdom and the United States presented a draft resolution to facilitate work on the West Bank of the River Jordan in the Bnot Yaakov Canal project. The Soviet veto paralyzed regional water development for several years. On 29 March 1954, a New Zealand resolution simply reiterating UN policy on blockade on the Suez Canal was frustrated by Soviet dissent. On 19 August 1963, a United Kingdom and United States resolution on the murder of two Israelis at Almagor was denied adoption by Soviet opposition. On 21 December 1964, the USSR vetoed a United Kingdom and United States resolution on incidents at Tel Dan, including the shelling of Dan, Dafne, Shaar Yashuv. On 2 November 1966, Argentina, Japan, Netherlands, New Zealand, Nigeria joined to express regret at "infiltration from Syria and loss of human life caused by the incidents in October, November 1966." This was one of the few resolutions sponsored by member States from five continents.

The Soviet use of the veto has had a dual effect. First, it prevented any resolution to which an Arab State was opposed from being adopted by the Council. Secondly, it has inhibited the Security Council from taking constructive action in disputes between an Arab State and Israel because of the certain knowledge that that veto would be applied in what was deemed to be the Arab interest. The consequences of the Soviet veto policy have been to deny Israel any possibility of just and equitable treatment in the Security Council, and to nullify the Council as a constructive factor in the affairs of the Middle East.

Does all this really add up to a constructive intervention by the USSR in the Arab-Israel tension? The position becomes graver when we recall the unbridled invective against the Permanent Representative of Israel in the Security Council. In its words and in a letter to the Israeli Government the USSR has formulated an obscene comparison between the Israeli Defense

Forces and the Hitlerite hordes which overran Europe in the Second World War. There is a flagrant breach of international morality and human decency in this comparison. Our nation never compromised with Hitler Germany. It never signed a pact with it as did the USSR in 1939. To associate the name of Israel with the accursed tyrant who engulfed the Jewish people in a tidal wave of slaughter is to violate every canon of elementary taste and fundamental truth.

In the light of this history, the General Assembly will easily understand Israel's reaction to the Soviet initiative in convening this special session for the purpose of condemning our country and recommending a withdrawal to the position that existed before June 5.

In respect to the request for a condemnation, I give a simple answer to the Soviet Representative. Your Government's record in the stimulation of the arms race, in the encouragement throughout the Arab world of unfounded suspicion concerning Israel's intentions, your constant refusal to say a single word of criticism at any time of declarations threatening the violent overthrow of Israel's sovereignty and existence—all this gravely undermines your claims to objectivity. You come here in our eyes not as a judge or as a prosecutor, but rather as a legitimate object of international criticism for the part that you have played in the somber events which have brought our region to a point of explosive tension. If the Soviet Union had made an equal distribution of its friendship amongst the peoples of the Middle East, if it had refrained from exploiting regional rancors and tensions for the purpose of its own global policy, if it had stood in evenhanded devotion to the legitimate interests of all states, the crisis which now commands our attention and anxiety would never have occurred. To the charge of aggression I answer that Israel's resistance at the lowest ebb of its fortunes will resound across history, together with the uprising of our battered remnants in the Warsaw Ghetto, as a triumphant assertion of human freedom. From the dawn of its history the people now rebuilding a state in Israel has struggled often in desperate conditions against tyranny and aggression. Our action on the 5th of June falls nobly within that tradition. We have tried to show that even a small state and a small people have the right to live. I believe that we shall not be found alone in the assertion of that right which is the very essence of the Charter of the United Nations.

Similarly, the suggestion that everything goes back to where it was before the 5th of June is totally unacceptable. The General Assembly cannot ignore the fact that the Security Council, where the primary responsibility lies, has emphatically rejected such a course. It was not Israel, but Syria, Egypt and Jordan, who violently shattered the whole fabric and texture of interstate relations which existed for a decade since 1957. That situation has been shattered to smithereens. It cannot be recaptured. It is a fact of technology that it is easier to fly to the moon than to reconstruct a broken egg.

The Security Council acted wisely in rejecting the backward step, now advocated by the Soviet Union. To go back to the situation out of which the conflict arose would mean that all the conditions for renewed hostilities would be brought together again. I repeat what I said to the Security Council. Our watchword is not backward to belligerency—but forward to peace.

What the Assembly should prescribe is not a formula for renewed hostilities, but a series of principles for the construction of a new future in the Middle East. With the cease-fire established, our progress must be not backward to an armistice regime which has collapsed under the weight of years and the brunt of hostility. History summons us forward to permanent peace and the peace that we envisage can only be elaborated in frank and lucid dialogue between Israel and each of the States which have participated in the attempt to overthrow her sovereignty and undermine her existence. We dare not be satisfied with intermediate arrangements which are neither war nor peace. Such patchwork ideas carry within themselves the seeds of future tragedy. Free from external pressures and interventions, imbued with a common love for a region which they are destined to share, the Arab and Jewish nations must now transcend their conflicts in dedication to a new Mediterranean future in concert with a renaissant Europe and an Africa and Asia which have emerged at last to their independent role on the stage of history.

In free negotiation with each of our neighbours we shall offer durable and just solutions redounding to our mutual advantage and honour. The Arab States can no longer be permitted to recognize Israel's existence only for the purpose of plotting its elimination. They have come face to face with us in conflict. Let them now come face to face with us in peace.

In peaceful conditions we could imagine communications running from Haifa to Beirut and Damascus in the north; to Amman and beyond in the east; and to Cairo in the south. The opening of these blocked arteries would stimulate the life, thought and commerce of the region beyond any level otherwise conceivable. Across the Southern Negev communication between the Nile Valley and the Fertile Crescent could be resumed without any change in political jurisdiction. What is now often described as a wedge between Arab lands would become a bridge. The Kingdom of Jordan, now cut off from its natural maritime outlet, could freely import and export its goods on the Israeli coast. On the Red Sea, cooperative action could expedite the port developments at Elath and Aqaba which give Israel and Jordan their contact with a resurgent East Africa and a developing Asia.

The Middle East, lying athwart three continents, could become a busy center of air communications, which are now impeded by boycotts and the necessity to take circuitous routes. Radio, telephone and postal communications which now end abruptly in mid-air would unite a divided region. The Middle East with its historic monuments and scenic beauty could attract a vast movement of travellers and pilgrims if existing impediments were removed. Resources which lie across national frontiers—the minerals of the Dead Sea and the phosphates of the Negev and the Aqaba—could be developed in mutual interchange of technical knowledge.

Economic cooperation in agricultural and industrial development could lead to supranational arrangements like those which mark the European Community. The United Nations could establish an Economic Commission for the Middle East, similar to the Commissions now at work in Europe, Latin America and the Far East. The specialized agencies could intensify their support of health and educational development with greater efficiency if a regional harmony were attained. The development of arid zones, the desalination of water and the conquest of tropical disease are common interests of the entire region, congenial to a sharing of knowledge and experience.

In the institutions of scientific research and higher education on both sides of the frontiers, young Israelis and Arabs could join in a mutual discourse of learning. The old prejudices could be replaced by a new comprehension and respect, born of a reciprocal dialogue in the intellectual domain. In such a Middle East, military budgets would spontaneously find a less exacting point of equilibrium. Excessive sums devoted to security could be diverted to development projects.

Thus, in full respect of the region's diversity, an entirely new story, never known or told before, would unfold across the Eastern Mediterranean. For the first time in history, no Mediterranean nation is in subjection. All are endowed with sovereign freedom. The challenge now is to use this freedom for creative growth. There is only one road to that end. It is the road of recognition, of direct contact, of true cooperation. It is the road of peaceful co-existence. This road, as the ancient Prophets of Israel foretold, leads to Jerusalem.

Jerusalem, now united after her tragic division, is no longer an arena for gun emplacements and barbed wire. In our nation's long history there have been few hours more intensely moving than the hour of our reunion with the Western Wall. A people had come back to the cradle of its birth. It has renewed its link with the mystery of its origin and continuity. How long and deep are the memories which that reunion evokes.

For twenty years there has not been free access by men of all faiths to the shrines which they hold in unique reverence. This access now exists. Israel is resolved to give effective expression, in cooperation with the world's great religions, to the immunity and sanctity of all the Holy Places.

The prospect of a negotiated peace is less remote than it may seem. Israel waged her defensive struggle in pursuit of two objectives—security and peace. Peace and security, with their juridical, territorial, economic and social implications, can only be built by the free negotiation which is the true essence of sovereign responsibility. A call to the recent combatants to negotiate the conditions of their future co-existence is the only constructive course which this Assembly could take.

We ask the Great Powers to remove our tormented region from the scope of global rivalries; to summon its governments to build their common future themselves; to assist it, if they will, to develop social and cultural levels worthy of its past.

We ask the developing countries to support a dynamic and forward-looking policy and not to drag the new future back into the outworn past.

To the small nations which form the bulk of the international family we offer the experience which teaches us that small communities can best secure their interests by maximal self-reliance. Nobody will help those who will not help themselves. We ask the small nations, in the solidarity of our smallness, to help us stand firm against intimidation and threat such as those by which we are now assailed.

We ask world opinion which rallied to us in our plight to accompany us faithfully in our new opportunity.

We ask the United Nations, which was prevented from offering us security in our recent peril, to respect our independent quest for the peace and security which are the Charter's higher ends. We [are going to] do what the Security Council decided should be done—[maintain the cease-fire] and reject the course which the Security Council emphatically and wisely rejected [but a few days ago—it rejected the concept of returning to the situation of belligerency out of which the crisis arose, back to the old situation.]

[Now] it may seem that Israel stands alone against numerous and powerful adversaries. But we [have faith in] the undying forces in our nation's history which have so often given the final victory to spirit over matter, to inner truth over quantity. We believe in the vigilance of history which has guarded our steps.

The Middle East, tired of wars, is ripe for a new emergence of human vitality. Let the opportunity not fall again from our hands.

JULIA DAVIS STUART

What Can I Do That Matters?*

This speech was delivered at a meeting of the League of Women Voters in Detroit, Michigan, on September 19, 1967, at the close of a long summer of racial unrest and destructive violence in many of the cities of the nation. The speaker, Mrs. Robert J. Stuart, was the national President of the League, a strong, nonpartisan organization

* By permission of Mrs. Stuart.

working locally, statewide, and nationally to develop informed, thoughtful, effective participation in public affairs by the women of America. When, by the ratification of the Nineteenth Amendment in 1920, women finally achieved the vote throughout the nation, the leaders who had worked to win suffrage turned their energies to making that suffrage as effective as possible for good government. To that end they founded the League of Women Voters, which since then has been in the forefront of the forces working for the political and social improvement of this country. One would expect, therefore, the League and its national president to be deeply involved with the sober issues treated in this speech.

Mrs. Stuart, a native of Missouri and for some years past a citizen of the State of Washington, has been active in the League since 1950. She has sat on the state and national boards, been president in her home state, and served as president of the national League from 1964 to 1968. Among her many important assignments outside the League was, as she notes in this speech, membership on President Johnson's Crime Commission, which enabled her to speak with special authority on the problems of poverty, the Negro, and the cities.

We include Mrs. Stuart's speech as a good example of the kind of venture in public address which, more and more, will enable educated men and women to exercise, through the organizations to which they belong, effective political and social leadership in their communities and in the nation. This speech is notable for the frank, realistic, forthright, unpretentious but urgent way in which the speaker seeks to bring knowledge, reason, and goodwill to some of the very explosive matters from which, if possible, many comfortable people would like to look away.

I am very much pleased to be here in Detroit today and to talk to you about big cities and crime and urban-suburban relations and the League of Women Voters. The problems of big cities are ones that are almost constantly on my mind these days—and I know they are on yours.

The title of my talk to you is "What Can I Do That Matters?" It is taken from a poem in the form of a prayer written by Stephen Spender thirty years ago. "Living," he said, "in the shadow of a war, what can I do that matters?" In his day the shadow was the depression and the growing edge of Fascism. In our day we wage war against crime and poverty and for a more orderly world, but the cry, "What can I do that matters?" is still relevant.

If in moments of despair those of us who are middle-class, fairly well educated, and knowledgeable about our communities, and have at least a bowing acquaintance with the "establishment" and the "power structure"—if we question whether what we do makes a difference, it is little wonder that those who have been excluded from the mainstream of American life for centuries and whose hopes have been raised time after time only to be dashed down, are expressing themselves through anti-social means such as riots.

The President's Crime Commission said months ago that "there is no sense to the idea—in the doubtful event that anyone entertains it—that sporadic outbursts of frenzy and violence can solve complicated social problems." I am sure you would agree, but perhaps you would agree too that we *should* be able to understand the message which the riots—unplanned, undisciplined, unled, and incoherent as they are—express. The President's Commission said further: "They [the riots] expressed the general hostility many Negroes feel toward white people. They expressed the particular hostility many Negroes feel toward the police and ghetto merchants and businessmen. They expressed the outrage many Negroes feel at the conditions in which they must live. They expressed the increasing refusal by Negroes to accept further delay in being granted full participation in the social, economic, and political development of the Nation. They expressed the increasing conviction of Negroes that legal methods of protest have not accomplished enough fast enough. They signified that the ghettos of American cities are a threat to the peace and safety of all America. They signified that the need to abolish ghettos is urgent and the time is short." The Report of the Crime Commission was written before the riots in Detroit or Newark or New Haven, so this is the message that we *should* have received from the riots in 1965 and from 1966 and which we most surely should have understood in 1967. But it is not the message everyone received, including a great many members of the Congress of the United States.

At this moment, millions of Americans are reacting to the riots in a way that could stop progress dead in its tracks: the home-owner who vows to shoot the next suspicious character he sees in his neighborhood; the businessman who decides to get out of the slums; the labor leader who determines to keep minorities out of the union; the Negro or white who goes out to take whatever he can get his hands on; the legislator who fails to meet his public responsibilities.[1] So we ask again, "What can we do that matters?"

No one can become an "instant expert" on race relations; we cannot become trained teachers overnight; we cannot single-handedly persuade Congress to find the funds for increased training programs and increased jobs; we cannot offer a million jobs or job training for thousands; we cannot with our own hands rebuild sections of our cities that need rebuilding. But there are things each of us can do. For some of us it may be the actual *doing;* for others, "what we can do that matters" may be giving financial and moral support to efforts of which we approve.

Before I go into the kinds of things we can do that matter, I should like to put forth some assumptions on which I hope we can all agree.

[1] Adapted from the Preamble issued by the Urban Coalition.

First, I think we are agreed that the city is here to stay. We may not like everything about every city we know, but for most of us the city is an exciting place not only to visit but to live in. We understand the significance of the city as a place where important transactions are carried out, where things happen in business and commerce and the arts and education—the place where ideas hatch and are discussed and developed.

Second, I believe we are agreed that the ultimate answer to political problems, and some social and economic problems as well, is through the political process. Certainly in the League of Women Voters we believe in the give and take of discussion and debate, the forming of a consensus, the power of persuasion, and the use of the vote to bring about the ends we seek.

Third, we are aware that those who live in the cities cannot achieve political results all by themselves. Even with newly apportioned legislatures we find that the suburbs rather than the cities have been the biggest beneficiaries in the state legislative bodies and that the United States Congress itself reflects suburban and rural areas in greater proportion than is comfortable for city dwellers. Therefore, in order to achieve political results the city is going to have to find allies in the suburbs and elsewhere. Because those who have been most successful in the inner city—Saul Alinsky, Nathan Wright, James Gibson of the Potomac Institute—say that self help alone is not enough. Those in the inner city must have allies outside.

Fourth, I think we are aware, too, of the enormous complexity of all that goes to make up the so-called urban problems, and of the enormous complexity of the solution. In truth, there *is* no one *big* overall solution. Instead the solution is made up of a complex of solutions—big, small, and intermediate. We don't deal with the problem all at once. We deal with only portions of it; we find only partial solutions.

Fifth, there is no absolute power structure or establishment that can wave a wand and command solutions. The truth is that all of us make up a highly pluralistic, highly diverse, highly diffused establishment. It is too easy to search for scapegoats or to tell each other, "If we had only had this or that or the other thing, . . ." Instead we need to recognize that we all stand indicted because none of us has used all the power that each of us commands.

On the basis of these five assumptions which I hope we share, let me go on to delineate a few of the problems implicit in these assumptions.

While all of *us* are aware that the city is here to stay and we share a respect for and an attachment to the city, not everyone shares our enthusiasm. There are many people who are downright hostile to the city and think of it as a place they wish to avoid except for an occasional "evening on the town" or day of shopping. In some ways they are right. The city *is* where a good part of the crime takes place. As the President's Commission said: "One of the most fully documented facts about crime is that the common serious crimes that worry people most—murder, forcible rape, robbery, aggravated assault and burglary—happen most often in the slums of large cities." And those who live in the slums are most often the victims—a point we very often forget.

Violence and rioting have always been part of the city's pattern. When the Irish and the Italians and the Poles and other newcomers to this country lived in the ghettos of the big cities, they too expressed their frustrations through violence and riots. Wave after wave of those earlier slum dwellers were able to leave the ghetto, an escape denied most Negroes.

Along with the unfriendly attitude toward cities of some who live in the suburbs we have an equal problem of communication and of finding rapport between different elements within the city. Those of us who believe in working through the political process feel that others should do so as well. We are used to political set-backs; we realize that it sometimes takes years to inch forward just a little; but "this is the way it works," we say, "and we'll have to keep at it."

This is fine for us and very often we do achieve success eventually. But the people in the inner city aren't so keen about the method. In our middle-class society we often speak of motivation and we wonder, sometimes aloud, why "those people" have so little of it. Daniel Fullmer of Oregon may have the answer. "We professionals," he said, "have been playing with the word 'motivation' for years. We have been treating it as an antecedent. Motivation is not an antecedent; it is a consequence. I am motivated because of experiences I have had; I am not motivated to have experiences." This concept explains a great deal, I think, of the attitude of those whose attempts to get ahead, to improve, have been met with frustration. As someone said recently: "Power may corrupt, but powerlessness can corrupt too, and absolute powerlessness corrupts absolutely."

To work through the political process, what the inner city needs is a coalition with those in other parts of the city who share their aims, or whose aims coincide with theirs for particular objectives. But this coalition isn't as easy to achieve, on either side, as it is to enunciate. My experience on the Crime Commission brought home to me the great gaps there are in understanding between segments of the community.

One block to communication is the real disinclination of some of us to share power. We want to be "helpful" we say, but we really don't want to share in the decision-making process. We have a "mother or father knows best" philosophy. We want to superimpose our ideas; we want to work "for" not "with." There are analogies here between the role of women and the role of the disadvantaged citizen in the ghetto. Back when women were trying to get the vote, a favorite argument of those against such a move was that the men in their families could "represent" their wishes at the polls and in other places. Women, quite naturally, didn't care much about this arrangement, especially when the decisions made had a direct effect on their lives.* The people in the inner city don't care much for this system either.

Many people in the inner city have both sophistication and cynicism. James Gibson tells the "why" of the cynicism. "There have been agencies and social workers and programs and thrusts and target areas for years," he says. "Probably more services, or people related to services, walk in and out of the houses in the inner city than have ever touched your doorstep. They are aware of it all. Every agency has somebody who's got something that they want to contact these people about. And yet the people are unemployed, the kids are dropping out of school. The conditions remain. So there is a shell, a callus you've got to get through." And yet the sophistication Mr. Gibson speaks about and the demand for a part in decision making—for power, if you will—is one of the hopeful signs on the horizon as I see it.

There are other hopeful signs. One of them is the Urban Coalition to mobilize the nation's public and private resources in a concerted attack on urban problems. I had the privilege of being one of the 1000 people invited to attend an Emergency Convocation in Washington. Your Mayor was there; and Henry Ford; and Andrew Heiskel, Chairman of the Board of Time, Inc.; A. Philip Randolph, President of the Brotherhood of Sleeping Car Porters; Frederick J. Close, Chairman of the Board of the Aluminum Company of America; Walter Reuther; Mayor John F. Collins of Boston; and so on. The list read like a list of the "establishment" of business, labor, religious, civic, and civil rights groups. At the meeting David Rockefeller argued that business can't ask government to spend a lot of money unless it is making its own effort. His proposal for "Earn and Learn" centers was only one of the many ideas put forth that deserve follow-up. I understand local coalitions are springing up at the grass roots. Perhaps you have one here in Detroit. I am encouraged by the potential of the Urban Coalition.

I am encouraged, too, by reports of programs already in being. At the Urban League convention which I attended I heard Mr. C. S. Gross, former board chairman and now director and finance committee chairman of Lockheed, describe their program of hiring and training on the job a group of hard core, unemployed Negro youths with criminal records. I am impressed with reports Leagues have sent us of the Job Corps Centers they have visited and worked with; and of course I am impressed by Vista, and Head Start, and Upward Bound.

And still another encouraging sign is what I see in the on-coming generation. I am impressed with the young people who have been interns in the nation's capital this summer, and I am impressed with the twenty-year-old Negro leader, Rufus Mayfield, who organized project PRIDE in Washington. I am impressed with what the Girl Scouts are doing in the inner city. Many young people are both realistic and idealistic. As *Look* magazine has said of what it terms the "open generation": "The world of the poor is real

* [See the speech by Emmeline Pankhurst in this book.]

to them, not academic. The Negroes' struggle is a fact the younger generation experiences and will continue to experience as today's adults never did."

Another plus I find is in the women of this country, those working as volunteers in Head Start Programs, WICKS, and all the rest.

And last, but not least, I find encouragement in what Leagues are doing all over the country. When you get right down to it, the League of Women Voters is a middle-class organization. Our husbands are mostly business and professional men; the great majority of our members live in the suburbs. We are the kind of women who, someone has said, in another era would have been members of the Browning society. And yet our members are concerned—deeply concerned—over the plight of the cities; we are concerned—deeply concerned—about the people in the *inner* city. We seek equality of opportunity in education and employment for all of the citizens of this nation; and we do not do this in Lady Bountiful mood because we also believe in the concept of participation. Indeed, to achieve informed and active participation of citizens in government is our stated purpose. And having been left out of the decision-making process ourselves for 150 years in this country, we are perhaps more aware of what it is like to be ignored.

We have been working on problems of equality of opportunity in education and employment intensively for over three years. We have learned not only through reading and theory but through personal observation and participation in our own communities. The issues we are addressing ourselves to are of prime importance to our communities and to the country as a whole. They are closely connected to urban problems and the problem of crime.

We support compensatory education. We are supporting amendments to the Economic Opportunity Act and are working hard to build support for the Community Action Program. We believe in it. The principle carried out by the Community Action Program that the poor participate in its decision-making is part of the basic philosophy, indeed part of the purpose, of the League of Women Voters. When we speak of the "informed and active participation of citizens in government," CAP is part of what we mean. We are strengthening our statements of support by telling our Congressmen what we know from our own experiences in these programs.

Other Leagues are working as you are here in Detroit on local and state programs that are relevant. And all over the country Leagues are, hopefully, helping to arouse people to the need for greater effort.

There is something else we are doing. Warren Christopher of the United States Department of Justice, who was formerly a Los Angeles attorney and vice chairman of a commission that investigated the Watts riots, has said that the solution to problems that sparked summer riots in Negro slums lies in the nation's overwhelmingly white suburbs, but suburbanites aren't likely to help right now. He feels that white suburbanites may show their anger over the riots by blocking efforts to clear up big-city problems. This must not happen. As I said earlier most League members are located in the suburbs. Thus the League is truly in a position to help bridge the gap between city and suburb. In the first place, by the very nature of our work in the field of human resources, League members in the suburbs and the small towns of America are becoming informed and involved in urban problems. And League members in the suburbs and in the small towns are letting their Congressmen know how they feel. During the recent Labor Day recess Congressmen in many League communities were reached by League members telling them of their concern for the fate of present legislation in the field of equality of opportunity. The League is taking part in the political process. The League is engaged in creating public opinion.

Communication with the inner city is also important, and more than that it is important that we learn to listen as well as learn how to get our messages across. James Gibson has said that inner city people have a good deal of sophistication. They do indeed. What is more, they have a great deal to contribute to self-government U.S.A. Once more I should like to go back to the analogy with women and the vote. Carrie Chapman Catt, the founder of the League of Women Voters, believed that when women got the vote, if they were properly trained and sufficiently motivated, they could act as the agent that would lift the entire electorate to a new level. By the infusion of 20 million new voters into the political process, not one by one but all at once, the whole system would get a shot in the arm.

A case can be made that indeed women have imparted a new dimension to democracy—but that is another speech. My point here is that another new element—the men and women (mostly Negroes) who heretofore have either been deprived of the vote or have not seen its significance in relation to their own lives—is being added to the democratic process. In a recent article in *The New Yorker* magazine, Richard Rovere had this to say:

> It is widely believed here [in Washington] that the civil rights and Negro movement of recent years have been more ably led and more eloquently spoken for than any similar movements in American history. If "black nationalism" were to lead to the founding of a black nation within the white one—an aim generally viewed as irresponsible and undesirable, as well as impossible, by even the most militant of Negro spokesmen—it might be able to start its life with leaders of more sophistication and ability than most of their counterparts in the white society.

Leagues working in the inner city know this to be true as well.

Thus it seems to me we should not fear the demands for power from Negroes, but as Nathan Wright suggested "foster black men's intuitions and insights to add their actual and potentially rich gifts to American life as a whole." "Every effort must be made," he said, "to convince every American that the immediate establishment of equitable power relationships for black people is in both the short and long-range self interest of every man, woman, and child in America." And he goes on to say, "By far the greatest area of potentially productive white involvement in a race-related problem area is in converting and alerting white people themselves to the need for enabling every part of America to come to flower." Interestingly enough, Mr. Wright believes that middle-class women will be a most effective force in getting this message across.

I wish I had time to mention the examples of what the League is doing not only in work with Community Action Programs but in our various Voters Service efforts in the inner city. I will speak of only two.

In Indiana through several projects the League had established good rapport with some of the groups in the inner city in Indianapolis. Came a time last winter when the mothers of children receiving Aid to Dependent Children decided they wanted to take effective action before the state legislature to get their allotments increased. The League was asked to help brief them on approaching their legislators, drafting effective letters, and preparing good testimony. Leagues in several communities met with the women and did help. They briefed them on what to expect at a legislative hearing, how to get their statements mimeographed and passed around, and other pointers they would give to a League group taking action for the first time. The women went to the Capitol, testified, and got a favorable vote from the committee and later from the legislators. The political process worked!

Another instance was on the West Coast. There a League started cooperative efforts through work on a registration drive. When the project began there were very few registrars in the Negro community, and it was decided to increase the number. The problem was that these people work and find it difficult to travel the great distance necessary to attend classes. The committee had received a promise that if 20 people were signed up for the class, it would be conducted nearer to home. Without any difficulty 25 people were rounded up only to find that the Registrar's office had changed its mind about conducting a class locally. Now here was where "the middle-class friends with access to the centers of power" (that is, the Registrar's office!) came in. The League reminded the Registrar's office of past favors the League had done for it, and the problem dissolved and the class was conducted, the registration drive went on, and hundreds of people were added to the lists.

But perhaps the most important part of the project was this (and here I should like to quote from the report):

> We held a number of planning meetings before we ever swung into action. The meetings started in summer, continued all through the fall and winter and our registration drive didn't begin until the end of January. The primary was May 10. We were meeting so often, doing so much talking, and there was so little action that our League women were beginning to feel very doubtful about the whole project. We didn't realize at the time that the real value of all

> these meetings was that we were getting to know each other on a very basic level. There was some hostility and I'm sure widespread doubt on the part of the Negro members of the committee as to the motives of the white committee members. Some of the meetings deteriorated into bull sessions, but in the process a lot of chips got knocked off shoulders and were replaced by a much more realistic understanding of the motives and attitudes of committee members.
>
> As a result of this "getting to know you" business, a Negro member is now serving on the Board of the Community Welfare Council and the League has been asked by Negro leaders to serve on committees sponsored by the Negro community.

Many of the examples we can mention appear to be rather small steps in the right direction; but I am convinced that if we are to achieve communication and solve urban problems, we are going to have to do it by *seeking* big goals and achieving them by taking many and simultaneous *actions* and taking them now.

Setting a goal of a million jobs is a big step. To achieve it businessmen are going to have to think in terms of thousands or hundreds or tens or twos and threes in their own plants or establishments. Seeking a billion dollars in federal appropriations is a big step. To see that action is going to take thousands of individual acts of commitment; and to see that the money is spent well is going to take thousands more. The Urban Coalition is a big step forward. To make it work hundreds—no, thousands—of little and big and middle-sized acts will be needed.

Getting communication and understanding and trust established between the cities and the suburbs and the city dweller and those in the inner city is a big goal. To bring it about will take thousands of small confrontations, small meetings of minds, small acts of faith. Building public opinion is a big goal. To bring it about will take more than editorials and magazine articles and speeches like this. We can all build public opinion by expressing personal concern person-to-person. We can spread the word of programs we know to be successful. We can encourage those who are doing a good job. We can give moral and financial support to churches and organizations and individuals who are seeking solutions to our urban problems.

And among the organizations that deserve support for this very reason is the League of Women Voters. The League has tenacity; we have steadiness. We are not daunted by complexity. We are a partnership of suburb and city; we know our way around in Washington, in state capitals, and in city halls; we are convinced that only as each citizen believes in self-government so strongly that he is willing to make a personal effort to use political power can self-government succeed. But just as the people in the inner city need help, so do we. We need more members and we need more money. I think the time is ripe for us to get both.

I believe there are many women who are asking, "What can I do that matters?" I believe there are many men who see in the present crisis in urban affairs an urgent reason for giving financial and moral support to the League of Women Voters, who need the League to help create the kind of climate in which *they* can move ahead to pursue goals they know to be right. Whitney Young has said that if the moderates among Negroes are to have a voice and an influence "you will have to give us some victories." The League can be part of a partnership to achieve these victories. Its place is indeed right in the middle where the action is—now, next year, for the next ten years, if need be.

"What can I do that matters?" I believe I know, and I think that you do too.

HOWARD K. SMITH

*Television in the Nation's Service —Where Do We Go From Here?**

Howard K. Smith, one of a distinguished few American newspaper, radio, and television reporters and commentators whose national and international experience spans the time from the years immediately prior to World War II to the present, is the senior news analyst and commentator for the American Broadcasting Company in Washington, D.C. From 1939 to 1941 he was on the staff of the United Press in Europe; and from 1941 to 1962 he served the Columbia Broadcasting System in Europe and in Washington. The speech printed here was the keynote address at the National Conference on Broadcasting and Election Campaigns in Washington, D.C., on October 13, 1965.

We include this speech because it affords a penetrating view of the functioning, for good and for ill, of American public address at the present time; because the subject-matter is immediately relevant to all those persons who would engage in public affairs; and because of Smith's cogent use of specific reference, specific example, and comparison. Broadly speaking, Smith's address concerns the application of rhetoric—how best to inform and persuade the American audience —to the resources of the electronic media of mass communication.

Mr. Taft, Distinguished Guests, Ladies and Gentlemen:

I am honored to be among the first to welcome this Conference to Washington. I think it is fitting that I begin by denying with all the vigor I can

* By permission of Howard K. and Benedicte Smith.

command the impression created by the little girl in the Middle West, the little girl whose father was elected to Congress, and who said in her prayers that night: "God Bless Mummy and Daddy, and Brother and Sister; and this is goodbye, God. We are moving to Washington." Ladies and Gentlemen: We *do* have God in Washington. He spends some time at the Ranch—but mostly he is here.

This conference is a timely venture. Recently, when His Holiness, Pope Paul, visited America, I had occasion to point out that his Church not long ago designated a patron saint for television. She was Saint Clara, a thirteenth-century nun who once saw before her eyes actual events that were transpiring at a great distance. When I made the remark that the medium had been given a patron saint, a colleague of mine was heard to mutter, "And not a moment too soon!"

I am prompted to say the same thing about your conference. If I have any message today it is the simple one that broadcasting and the democratic process were made for each other. The system whereby people govern themselves by intelligent choice, and the medium which can most vividly and absorbingly present the elements for making a choice, should keep steady company. It is high time an influential group of Americans devoted serious attention to making their alliance a stronger one.

May I say that I am honored to be called on to make these remarks, which are called a keynote address. But I think I should say immediately that I am typical of nothing and I represent nobody. I am only sporadically on television; and I am not on radio at all. That is a disadvantage in some respects. But in one respect my tenuous relation to the medium, after years of doing everything within it from being an executive to field reporting, allows me a kind of objectivity about it that is not easy to acquire.

My completely dispassionate view is that television has performed a unique service to the democratic process, particularly the daily, half-hour news programs. My friend Walter Cronkite expressed an opposite view the other day, according to *Newsweek* magazine. He said that TV news was deceiving the public. It is, he said, creating an impression that TV gives the public all the information it needs, and that is not true. I do not know where Walter got that notion. I have never seen or heard of any network or station saying, indicating, hinting, or implying that it was providing all the information the public needs. Members of the public who believe that TV provides a whole diet of information are probably the kind of people who previously depended on the average American daily newspaper for their information. In contrast to the meager diet of information and the dull and stereotyped presentation of reporting in the average daily paper, TV news programs must seem illuminating and absorbing indeed.

Let me state to you, in its proper context, the special service I think the daily news programs are performing. In the twenty years since World War

II, our nation has accumulated wealth faster than any nation in history. But, while growing exceedingly rich, it also, curiously, neglected itself as few nations have. In that long period it has been possible to persuade Congress to appropriate fabulous sums for military projects and foreign affairs. But until this year Congress could rarely be persuaded to appropriate anything to meet our domestic problems. As a result the domestic problems grew to huge and frightening proportions.

The signs of this neglect are familiar: Crime is rising five times as fast as our population is increasing. Our cities, which should be the show-places for the best that our nation has to display, are decaying and dangerous. It is safer to walk some trails in the jungles of Africa and Asia at night than to walk the streets of some of our cities. We suffer in our midst what can only be called by the ancient name of a proletariat—an undigested, un-integrated minority, without rights and in a condition of oppression—which in pure frustration has simply begun exploding. I refer to our Negro population. In the longest and highest boom ever, we countenance the second highest rate of unemployment in the Western world. In the richest nation of all time, we have between 25 and 35 million Americans living in poverty. These are but a few signs of our monumental national neglect.

There are many reasons why this happened. One reason certainly is that articulate, middle-class Americans, who create pressure for action, have tended to lose contact with their country. The creation since World War II of the Freeway, which whisks people from their place of business and out of town without ever coming into contact with the sight of the way millions live, has hidden America from us. The growth of the self-contained, well-off suburb, where you can live, shop, play golf, and go to the movies without ever seeing the way people live, has hidden America from us. The decline of rail travel, which used to keep us in some contact with the way people live, and the increase in air travel, which does not, have hidden America from us. Developments of that nature have made much of our country invisible to the very classes we depend on for political action.

The service that television news performs is the function that Saint Clara achieved: it has made visible things that had become invisible. I am absolutely sure that the presentation on television of what was happening in Birmingham and Selma caused Americans—even those afflicted with racial prejudice—to say: "That cannot be permitted to continue." That feeling, articulated into political pressure, largely caused Congress to pass the landmark rights bill last year, and the more remarkable voting bill this year. The vivid presentation of poverty in our affluent midst had an effect. So did the vivid presentation of the uglification that has taken place in our country.

I know that in your Conference you are primarily interested in broadcasting in relation to elections. The matters I have mentioned are a stage removed from actual elections. But the connection is powerful and possibly decisive. In that sense, television news has been a mighty force in making democracy a more meaningful thing than it was.

Now I must admit that there are ways in which broadcasting has not done its duty, or has even neglected or abused it. One of the sad developments of recent years has been the decline of the TV documentary program, the in-depth treatment of subjects. Some people argue that television is not suited to in-depth treatment of topics. That is not so. Any of you who saw the program memorializing Ed Murrow on the occasion of his death—a series of excerpts from some of his documentary programs—will know that television is well suited to that kind of treatment. Some fine documentaries have been done since Murrow quit. One of the last truly fine practitioners was David Lowe, the producer, whose death we mourned last month. But in its present form, the TV documentary was virtually invented by Murrow and Fred Friendly. Nobody has added much.

The trouble is that while present practitioners use the form, they overlook the fact that what made the products of Murrow and Friendly outstanding was not form; it was boldness and imagination—two qualities that seem almost taboo in documentary production today. Basically, the standard TV documentary today misunderstands the meaning of the word *objectivity*. Objectivity means judging each case or story or situation on its own merits, applying a powerfully schooled and disciplined judgment. Objectivity does not mean what present documentarians think it does: balancing each thought or statement with its opposite. That brand of objectivity is really simply a respectable name for playing it safe. With each fact or view that is presented cancelled out by its opposite, the documentary ends with meaning vanished like the Wicked Witch of the West and a puff of nothing left.

The programs are as a result exceedingly dull. And the public finds it possible to stay away in millions. I was a judge for the Emmy awards this year. I sat through six solid hours of watching what were called documentaries. They were all very elaborate, and in beautiful color and must have cost a fortune to produce. But not one dealt with the untidy but fascinating world we live in. Most were a good two or three safe centuries away from today. I protested that I had been given no documentaries to judge. I was told, there weren't any.

I could cite innumerable examples. CBS's documentary on TV ratings was a careful, mutual cancellation of facts and views signifying, in the end, nothing. My network mass produces that kind of documentary. NBC recently displayed the typical reaction of a declining form of expression; it sought to meet what is really a question of quality by heaping on quantity. Just as movies met their problem by making their screens three times bigger, they made their documentary three times longer. Truly you can say of documentary reporting what Mark Twain said of Christianity: the only thing wrong with it is that nobody practices it.

Our other main dereliction, and in some ways it is sadder, is the decline—nay, the death—of radio as a medium for making democracy more real. When TV took away the job of entertainment, radio had its great opportunity to do things with words. Except for the work of my colleague Ed Morgan, radio has failed. The DuPont Award for broadcast commentary was not made last year; there was no one to give it to. The Peabody awards were given, but with a comment that the year was a poor one.

But, enough of our faults. The world of politics has let down broadcasting quite as much as we have let it down. That was never so evident as during the last presidential conventions. There is a legend that conventions have been re-shaped and re-formed to suit television. It is not so. Speeches remain uninspired and too long. Demonstrations remain ridiculous and tiresome. Schedules and agenda remain un-observed and un-policed by chairmen and those who organize conventions. Our politicians are guilty of boring people to death in a realm in which boredom means less effective democracy.

Let me tell you something about television which few people in it realize. Executives and producers and editors are easily dazzled by pictures. I have had to listen to innumerable executives lecturing reporters about the way in which words have been rendered out of date in journalism by pictures. Periodicals that believed that juvenile notion have paid dearly for it. The New York picture tabloids founded on the principle that a picture is worth a thousand words have not prospered. *Life,* which followed the same principle, began to decline, while *Look,* which kept its textual material bright, ascended. Now, *Life* is reverting to filling pages with columns of comment, and the magazine is better for it.

Words are the vital matter of television. Fred Friendly has said that the best thing you can put in front of a television camera is still a human being anxious to say something and who can say it compellingly. The best thing on the Huntley-Brinkley program is David Brinkley reporting or explaining some event—not because of his celebrated wry wit but because of his impeccable, economic, clear prose, utterly devoid of cliché. As a picture Walter Cronkite is nothing compared to Anne Francis. But by words he conveys an assurance and an authority which keep his audiences large and—his own statement to the contrary notwithstanding—well informed.

Words are still the best means of communication between human beings. But our politicians rarely give us words worth communicating. The number of speeches really worth listening to or watching in the last four conventions can be numbered on the fingers of one hand. Election campaigns tend to be dull for the same reason. Some politicians say speeches are the same as they always were; the trouble is that the public now has so many alternate ways of amusing itself that it won't listen to a speech. That is only partially true. Recently I had occasion to go over speeches made in the U.S. Senate between the age of Jackson and the Civil War. Those men knew the value of language. Their words compelled attention. I am afraid that the decline of floor debate in Congress and the increasing importance of committee work has damaged the ability of our public men to communicate. Language has to fit realities like a stocking—not like a pair of baggy pants. But that is the manner of most politicians today.

If human beings talking are interesting matter for television, human beings speaking in conflict are doubly or triply interesting. I had the honor of being the chairman for the first Kennedy-Nixon debate. I felt the electric thrill of the conflict. The campaign attained a rather higher level because men who must face one another cannot quite indulge in schoolboy invective the way men can when apart. It certainly engaged public interest as few recent campaigns have.

I know that many politicians fear and oppose direct debate or confrontation on television. The objection is made that an ability to perform on TV is a bad criterion for judging a candidate for office. I disagree. At present we judge by a host of qualifications from the cut of a man's hair to the cleverness of the slogans invented for him by a public relations firm. I think it would be far better to judge candidates by their ability to explain and argue and answer under pressure of their opponents' presence while a large public is watching.

Some politicians have argued against the idea by going down the list of our past Presidents and alleging that all the good ones would have been failures on TV. George Washington had imperfect dentures and would have looked and sounded ridiculous. Thomas Jefferson had shifty eyes and would have appeared insincere and sneaky. Abraham Lincoln was physically awkward and had a high-pitched voice and would have seemed a man of no depth. On this scale, the only President who would really have displayed the aspect of greatness would have been Warren G. Harding!

Well, I disagree with that, too. TV has a kind of spiritual X-ray built into it. Phoniness shines through. That is why so many non-news dramatic productions on TV fail, except with the very young and undiscriminating viewer. I recall the candidate of recent times who was nominated by his convention and went out to the podium and looked up at the cameras and said, "I accept . . . in all humility," and there was no trace of humility on that face, and that candidate was beaten then and there.

In our imperfectible world I think that debate, personal confrontation, on the broadcast media is far the best way for the public to assay a candidate. I wish it could be made a constitutional requirement.

Ladies and Gentlemen, I wish that I could now make some constructive proposals. But I do not know clearly what to do about quality in television. I used to be an environmentalist in interpreting history—one who believes great impersonal trends sweep people along. In respect to television I have become the opposite, a Carlylean. I believe that accidental and individual heroes make good TV. I believe that CBS's long ascendancy in reporting the real world was due to the accident of Ed Murrow who chose a staff by disregarding all the rules of baritone delivery and cliché reporting. NBC became supreme when the newsman, Robert Kintner, became head of the network and allegedly called in his news executives and said: "I want us to be first. Do what you have to and send the bills to me." It may not have happened that way literally, but it certainly happened that way in spirit.

Unfortunately, television does not normally create many heroes. Probably that is because the stakes are huge and millions of dollars in income and great reputations rise and fall because of flighty little percentages of indubitably inaccurate ratings.

Nor do I know what to do to make politicians aware of their deep responsibility to make their fascinating profession appear as fascinating as in fact it is. How you make them develop the respect for language and utterance that used to be essential to an American politician I do not know. I had rather hoped that the lash of a disastrous defeat would cause the Republicans to do some creative thing about it; but so far signs of change are nowhere in evidence. So far, only the President seems to understand what the medium is for. His use of it could make him in the end the most effective President we have had.

However, there is no good reason why I should both state the problems and resolve them. That is what you are gathered for. The medium of expression—vivid and sensitive—is there. The democratic process—dramatic and sensitive—is there. May you discover the right ways to marry them. I thank you for your attention.

JAMES B. RESTON

*The Rest of the Sixties**

As in the past, so today also, built into our social, political, intellectual, and educational framework are hundreds of more or less formal and regular occasions requiring talks, speeches, even "addresses": regular Sunday church services, weekly luncheons of innumerable business and professional service clubs all over the country, school and college commencements, annual conventions of organizations from federations of labor to associated garden clubs. On such occasions we expect speeches as a matter of course; we feel deprived or cheated if for some reason we do not get them; but at the same

* Reprinted with the permission of James B. Reston and the *Illinois Alumni News.*

time we are uneasy at the prospect of what we may have to sit through before the program is completed. The captive audience is long-suffering; but every now and then its patience is rewarded with a speech worth the cost.

Such a speech was delivered in 1965 at the Fall Convocation for new students in the vast new Assembly Hall at the University of Illinois. The speaker was the eminent political commentator and associate editor of The New York Times *James B. Reston, alumnus of Illinois, two-time Pulitzer Prize winner, and recipient of various honorary degrees including one from his alma mater in 1962. Because he is a journalist rather than a radio and television commentator, he was perhaps less generally known to the public than, for example, Howard K. Smith (see the previous speech). To readers of newspapers and magazines, however, he would be well known as one of the most reasonable and respected interpreters of the world today.*

The student of speaking should observe especially the clear, realistic, unexcited but emphatic way Mr. Reston set forth the opportunities, challenges, and obligations of college students of the present generation. Worth observing also are the speaker's reference to immediate circumstances and his friendly though not frivolous or irreverent use of his own connection with the university in establishing and maintaining a common ground with his audience. One may compare this speech usefully with Adlai E. Stevenson's to the Princeton seniors a decade earlier (see below, pages 508–516) as examples of interpretive, advisory speechmaking. The text is taken from the Illinois Alumni News *(November 1965), page* 3.

Dr. Lanier, President Henry, Members of the Class of 1969, Ladies and Gentlemen:

This is quite a place for a quiet heart-to-heart talk. As Bob Hope said when he saw it: Some barn! However, part of the discipline of university life is to listen patiently to middle-aged bores, and you might as well start now.

I was here as a freshman in the latter part of the Middle Ages. This was away back in the days when women wore skirts. The president of the University then was David Kinley. He was a Scot with a strong conviction that all men and some women shared the burden of original sin—especially college undergraduates. He assumed that the students of that day were willful, and potentially wicked, children—particularly when gathered together as males and females—so he believed they had to be policed like prospective criminals. This task he assigned to the dean of men, Mr. Thomas Arkle Clark, who looked like Mr. Chips and acted like J. Edgar Hoover. Dean Clark was assisted by the dean of women, Miss Leonard, who warned the girls that wearing red might arouse the passions of the men.

I should say in passing that I myself married a recklessly beautiful girl whom I first saw on Wright Street wearing a scarlet coat. I will spare you the happy story of my life, but in any event, we got a new president at the end of my sophomore year, who ran the place on the totally opposite theory that all undergraduates were mature ladies and gentlemen, who needed very little supervision or discipline. I have often wondered since then who was right, but the contrast between presidents Kinley and Chase was so striking that it illustrates really the only point I want to make to you about University life.

This is that the approach to a new experience or problem is fundamental. What assumptions you bring here with you at the beginning may be more important than what you take away at the end, for your approach to the beginning often determines the end. What I want to talk about, therefore, as frankly as I can, is how to approach university life at a time of great upheaval and convulsion in the world.

When Gilbert Keith Chesterton, one of the great Victorians, wrote his autobiography at the end of a long and useful life, he set himself the task of defining in a single sentence the most important lesson he had learned. And he concluded that the critical thing was whether one took things for granted or took them with gratitude. This, I think, is a good place to begin, and it has a special reference to the Class of 1969.

This country is at war. My generation may have staggered into it, but yours is fighting it. I have just come from the battle of Chu Lai up near the 17th parallel in South Vietnam. Americans who by the accident of birth, happen to be a little older than you are, fought and won that critical opening test of strength with the Vietcong. Other Americans of your own age, most of them probably a little poorer than your parents, are now registering not for classes but for uniforms. I don't want to make too much of the point, for all wars are unequal, but the fact that you are here and they are there is not the sort of thing that should be taken for granted, but should be regarded, perhaps, with a little gratitude.

I leave aside the people of Vietnam, who have a life expectancy of 38 years, and have been at war for over 20 years. The theory of our public policy on the draft is that you will do more for the development and security of your country by studying here than fighting there. I think it is a good, if often an unfair policy, but it does place upon you an obligation to do your best and at some time to repay the nation for the opportunities provided for you in this place.

A respect for fact is another useful companion at the beginning of your journey. You are not obliged to be grateful for the present tumult of the world, but you have to live in it. You may have any opinion you like about Lyndon Johnson, but he's the only President we have. He is a fact—and some fact! You may not like the war in Vietnam, but it is also a fact. You may not like the size of this University—it is certainly not a small monastery—but you have to deal with the world as it is and not with the world of your desires and dreams.

It may be a significant fact that you entered this university in the week when one-fifth of the human race on the sub-Indian continent started bombing one another, and China, which contains one fourth of the human family, gave India a 72-hour ultimatum to abandon her military bases in the disputed areas of the Himalayas. We all have our thoughts about this madness. China is undoubtedly a nuisance, but even though we do not recognize China, it will not accommodate us by going away.

I have to tell you bluntly that the outlook for the rest of the Sixties is not entirely rosy. My generation has had to deal with its share of moral monsters and staggering and blundering governments, but there is an important difference. Our problems were primarily in Europe and in Russia, which to some extent has come under the influence of a civilization we know something about. But your generation will be dealing with Asia, which comes from a much different culture and has a majestic disregard and even contempt for many of the fundamental things we proclaim in the Declaration of Independence to be "self-evident."

Our assumptions are not self-evident to the turbulent peoples who live between the Yellow Sea off Korea and the Black Sea between Russia and the Balkans. In fact, our assumptions are being challenged even by many of our allies, let alone our enemies.

General Ky, who is prime minister of South Vietnam—or anyway he was when this meeting started—said to me the other day in Saigon: "Don't talk to us about individual responsibility. Talk to us about rice and schools. We don't believe in individual responsibility. We believe the individual is precious only when he is part of the family, only when he sublimates himself to his parents and grandparents, and loses himself in the larger concerns of the people of his own blood."

It is, then, going to be difficult to deal with this kind of world. I do not think the big war is going to start or that the little wars are going to end in this decade or maybe even in this century. But different habits of thought are facts too, and we are going to have to learn to think as steadfastly about them as those boys think when they bring down a jet at 135 miles an hour onto 200 feet of the deck of an aircraft carrier. In short, we are going to have to learn to live with disagreeable facts. After all, we couldn't even beat Oregon State.

You may ask what all this has to do with you. What can you do about the distracting tumult of the world when you haven't yet adjusted to the distracting tumult of the campus? There are, I believe, a great many simple things you can do. You can park your prejudices at the door, or maybe even better, examine them and see where they came from, and whether they make any sense in the face of the stubborn facts of the present day.

You can put aside 15 minutes a day to read a newspaper and get some idea of what's going on. I will not presume to tell you what newspaper to read.

You can listen: that would be a remarkable innovation, and ask questions. I have learned in over 30 years of reporting that by far the most effective device is what I call the "dumb-boy technique," which is nothing more than refusing to pretend you know what you obviously don't know and saying honestly: "Sorry, I don't get it. I want to understand but I don't." You will, I think, be amazed at the possibilities of candid stupidity.

It is easy, of course, not to think consciously at all about these things, but simply relax and be carried along the Boardwalk by the stream of others who seem to know where they are going. This is natural at first, but it would be a pity to let it go on for long. A University is not a few classes and teachers and a place to eat and sleep, with trees and pleasant walks in between. All the wisdom of the past has been gathered here on this fertile prairie. It can supply all the answers to all your questions except why a football bounces into the arms of the wrong man. But you have to know what is going on. A University is a vast catalogue of interesting events on the side: lectures, concerts, political, religious and dramatic societies to suit every interest and taste. You cannot digest this whole smorgasbord. You will find that every teacher thinks you have nothing else to do except produce for him. But even so, you can look at the intellectual menu every morning in the Calendar of Events in the *Daily Illini,* and taste the fare from time to time.

Also, you can take a walk. This is a big place, but you can beat the bounds in an afternoon, and there's no telling what or whom you may run into by suppertime. You may see somebody with a certain expression or a certain wistful smile that takes your fancy, and you may be pleasantly surprised to find out how easy it is to discover who she is and where she lives. I did, and it was the most important discovery of my life.

It is in these simple ways, by these practical small initiatives that you come upon windows and doors into the wider world of the mind. Much more than my generation, most of you are going to live in the great clattering world of cities, where the enduring things of the human spirit—love and friendship and the association of lively minds—are not so easy to come by without an effort.

For a time here in this place, a comparatively brief intermission between leaving your father's home and starting your own, you will be free to discover who you are, and where you are, and what way you are going and who's going with you. But it is a much more ambiguous world, much more complicated than following or defying the old man's orders at home. And it is, I think, better to paddle around and explore than just to drift, for if the privileged generation of educated young Americans does not learn to influence the revolutions of our time at home and abroad, the world is going to be in even worse trouble than it is.

The United States is now the most powerful nation-state, the latest, and if we falter, perhaps the last inheritor of Western civilization. We have avoided a big war for over 20 years, but we are still very new at the business, and we have to look to the men and women trained in these university repositories of our civilization, to understand what is at stake and how we can approach our problems.

For a long time, we denied that the disorder of the world was any of our business; for another period we thought that maybe it was our business but that we couldn't do anything about it; then in a spasm of presumption, we seemed to think that nobody else could do anything and that we could do everything. But now we are passing through a phase of intellectual revision, in which we see more clearly that we are neither helpless nor omnipotent, but that we need friends and allies, and above all clarity in ourselves about what we can do and what we cannot do.

In this situation, a bawling patriotism, relieved only by a whining moralistic criticism of other nations, is not very helpful. We need watchful minds and steady nerves to get through this period, and nothing, we may be sure, will come out as we would like or even fit into those tidy intellectual patterns we adore. Nationalism is wrecking our policy of interdependence in Europe, but Nationalism is the strongest force against Communism in Asia and Africa, and may very well be our greatest hope on these two continents.

Above all, we must not be afraid of our enemies or make them so afraid of us that they will pull down the world. We thought there could never be an aggressor so wicked as Germany under the Kaiser, so we fought the first world war to the point of total surrender and in the process helped build up those two other more formidable enemies: Fascism and Communism. Fear and presumption are the great dangers to a steady course. The fear that Hobbes had in mind concerned men who were not absolutely brutish, and did not even want to be brutish, but were made brutish by fear and suspicion of one another and thus lurched into war.

Your generation did not invent anxiety. The world has always been unsafe and undoubtedly will be when your children are sitting where you now are. As Herbert Butterfield has pointed out, no nation can ever achieve the perfect security it desires without so tipping the power balance that it becomes or at least seems to become a menace to its neighbors.

The problem of this age is not so much insecurity as it is ambiguity. We are living in a time when change is the order of the day, when nobody but a fraud or a fool would pretend he had any perfect solutions, and when, above all, we need great integrity and flexibility of mind, not only to understand but to endure all this complexity.

This, at least, is my approach, my way of looking at this great University and the world. We shall have to develop a League of Minds, free and enquiring and respectful of fact, before we shall ever develop an effective League of Nations. And if we cannot look to the universities for this, I don't know where we can turn.

ROBERT W. ROGERS

The American Scholar—Then and Now*

As Dean of the College of Arts and Sciences at the University of Illinois, former teacher at Harvard and Illinois, and author of The Major Satires of Alexander Pope, *Robert W. Rogers combines in himself the scholar and educator. He holds three degrees from the University of Michigan and Harvard University and is a member of Phi Beta Kappa and Phi Kappa Phi. He has held a Guggenheim Fellowship, has been active in the affairs of the National Council of Teachers of English, and is a former president of the Midwest Modern Language Association. Before assuming the deanship, for many years he was first professor of English at Illinois and then head of the department.*

The occasion of this address was the Phi Beta Kappa initiation and banquet at the University of Illinois in May, 1967. Some 150 persons were in attendance—the initiates, their parents, and a few faculty. Dean Rogers, president of the local chapter of the society, directed attention to the timeless traits of the true scholar: the man of large vision, clear understanding, and high purpose. Reminding his hearers of Emerson's portrait of the scholar as "man thinking," he largely repeated Emerson's own words, through which gleam imagery both philosophic and poetic, and the serene cadences of the large and confident mind. The idea and tone thus established, Dean Rogers focused on the modern scholar, touching on his segmental knowledge, his prestige, and the political and moral forces, created by his own specialized knowledge, that keep him from seeing modern life as it is. Readers will want to compare Emerson's scholar and today's scholar, particularly their ideals and their styles of utterance.

When the University of Illinois was founded in 1867, the aims of scholarship in America were becoming those that had been eloquently set forth by Ralph Waldo Emerson before the Harvard Chapter of this society in 1837. Emerson's address, now known as "The American Scholar," has been so widely read and so readily available that it hardly requires extensive summary here; but, by way of introduction, let me mention a few of its main points. Emerson defined the scholar as "man thinking"; his concern was not just the professor in the university or the teacher. He was describing certain aspects and duties of the inquiring, reflective mind, wherever that mind might be found. The scholar, Emerson asserts, is shaped by Nature, by the

* Printed by permission of Robert W. Rogers.

Past, and by action or direct participation in life. His principal quality is self-trust, the kind of confidence that arises from the conviction that "he, and he only, knows the world." The duty of the scholar is to cheer, to raise, and to guide men by showing them facts amidst appearance. Knowing truth, things as they truly are, the scholar can move and shape his world:

> As the world was plastic and fluid in the hands of God, so it is ever to so much of his attributes as we bring to it. To ignorance and sin, it is flint. They adapt themselves to it as they may; but in proportion as a man has anything in him divine, the firmament flows before him and takes his signet and form. Not he is great who can alter matter, but he who can alter my state of mind. They are the kings of the world who give the color of their present thought to all nature and all art, and persuade men by the cheerful serenity of their carrying the matter, that this thing which they do, is the apple which the ages have desired to pluck, now at last ripe, and inviting nations to the harvest. The great man makes the great thing. Wherever Macdonald sits, there is the head of the table. Linnaeus makes botany the most alluring of studies, and wins it from the farmer and the herd-woman; Davy, chemistry; and Cuvier, fossils. The day is always his, who works in it with serenity and great aims. The unstable estimates of men crowd to him whose mind is filled with a truth, as the heaped waves of the Atlantic follow the moon.

Emerson's views were, of course, influenced by the situation of his contemporary society. He was aware that myth and illusion frequently dictated, as they do now, national decisions; and he was also attempting to define a role for the scholar, one that would satisfy American needs and purposes and one that would be different from the role of the scholar in Europe. As he himself put it, "Our long apprenticeship to the learning of other lands draws to a close." What he contributed was not a faith that knowledge is power but a conviction that the scholar should use his knowledge by action, by direct participation in the affairs of his society. He emphasizes the importance of action in the training of the scholar:

> The world,—this shadow of the soul, or *other me,*—lies wide around. Its attractions are the keys which unlock my thoughts and make me acquainted with myself. I run eagerly into this resounding tumult. I grasp the hands of those next me, and take my place in the ring to suffer and to work, taught by an instinct, that so shall the dumb abyss be vocal with speech. I pierce its order; I dissipate its fear; I dispose of it within the circuit of my expanding life. So much only of life as I know by experience, so much of the wilderness have I vanquished and planted, or so far have I extended my being, my dominion. I do not see how any man can afford, for the sake of his nerves and his nap, to spare any action in which he can partake. It is pearls and rubies to his discourse. Drudgery, calamity, exasperation, want, are instructors in eloquence and wisdom. The true scholar grudges every opportunity of action past by, as a loss of power.

He stresses the need for using knowledge once it is achieved:

> The scholar is that man who must take up into himself all the ability of the time, all the contributions of the past, all the hopes of the future. He must be an university of knowledges. If there be one lesson more than another, which should pierce his ear, it is, The world is nothing, the man is all; in yourself is the law of all nature, and you know not yet how a globule of sap ascends; in yourself slumbers the whole of Reason; it is for you to know all, it is for you to dare all.

Emerson's essay is an application of his faith, so well put by Matthew Arnold in his sonnet, "Written on Emerson's *Essays*":

> Yet the Will is free:
> Strong is the Soul, and wise, and beautiful:
> The seeds of godlike power are in us still:
> Gods are we, Bards, saints, heroes if we will.

The force of Emerson's rhetoric and the congeniality of his ideas to American needs and aspirations have given his essay a wide currency; and the conceptual model of a scholar that he developed has had a profound influence upon the academic community, its view of itself and the curricula by which it hopes to produce other thinking men. Much has also happened in America since 1837 to push the scholar to a central position in American life. The development of the land-grant college made the university, and its scholars, an integral part of the processes of progress. Emerson sought a place of great influence for the scholar in the life of this nation—this was to be the distinctive quality of American life;—and his vision has been achieved beyond his wildest dreams. We have seen society turn to scholars for help in understanding social, economic, political, psychological, and educational problems—and for the knowledge capable of solving them.

No longer does the scholar need to fear the poverty, scorn, isolation, and solitude that Emerson thought were part of his existence; he needs fear rather affluence and praise. From the time a young man now shows a capacity for scholarship, he is courted by society, an object of anxious solicitude. Encouragement and subsidy are his; and, once having assumed a place in the company of confirmed scholars, his counsel is eagerly sought and fastidiously followed. He must spend his time flying from airport to airport, a harried participant in committees, panels, and symposia. Money to support his quest is available in sums that far exceed the cost of government in the mid-nineteenth century.

It requires no great insight, however, to remark that the scholar of the 1960's is often not the scholar of Emerson's essay. Emerson could still believe that mastery of all learning—or at least of all useful learning—was an attainable objective. Much has happened to the character of knowledge since 1837. The scholarly community has accepted the view that effective knowledge is organized knowledge—or science—in both natural philosophy and the humanities. The result of this acceptance has been a vast extension of what the scholar must understand: we now know more about man and his past, and are more sensitive to his aspirations, than ever before. This extension of intellectual boundaries has rendered difficult for individuals the kind of comprehensive understanding advocated by Emerson. Scholarship capable of achieving the social contributions Emerson proposed has seemed to require a focus upon limited segments. The limitations thus imposed upon our areas of comprehension and understanding require that in the solution of problems we bring together groups of experts, each with his own specialty, for a collective attack upon major problems. In instruction we offer "interdisciplinary" courses; but we require three or four teachers, each with his own brand of specialization, for a single course. All too rarely can the individual scholar of today give life and experience his own signet and form. The American scholar is in real danger of losing his individuality, which Emerson thought so important, to a kind of collegial authority to which he can make but a limited or partial contribution.

The present position of the American scholar, so enviable in many ways, carries with it many difficulties and dangers. That he is asked so frequently to help solve America's ills creates a pressure to address himself to the solution of pressing and direct problems while neglecting fundamental and basic issues that should also be the concern of the inquiring mind. He is asked to find improvisations that will cut down crime in the street, or mitigate the effects of poverty, or provide immunity from disease. To the extent that our American scholar succeeds he has performed valuable service; but his *ad hoc* efforts have created many now inexplicable paradoxes and moral ambiguities which the adolescent generation today seems to be uneasy with. We have the bomb but can control it with great difficulty. We are putting a man on the moon and yet neglect the problems relating to human survival. We preach equality, yet our solutions perpetuate elementary injustice. We need constantly to remind ourselves that the highest employment of the scholarly mind is the development of seminal ideas, concepts and paradigms that make a difference by changing our way of regarding and interpreting large segments of experience, that will give order, coherence, and purpose to our efforts. Too much of our scholarly energy seems to be wasted on the trivial, in documenting the obvious, which is pedantry, or on the manipulations of events, institutions, and people, which is administration.

In spite of the many triumphs of American scholarship, and in spite of the vast quantity of energy that has been devoted to scholarly pursuits, we get humilitating answers when we ask ourselves how many new, truly basic concepts have been generated by it. One can think of many reasons for this failure; the traditional pragmatic cast of our society, which is not much given to sophisticated abstraction and which evaluates the expenditure of effort in terms of its immediate, observable result. Too often, I fear, in academic societies this pragmatic view operates to affect matters of status and recognition. How often do promotions come to those whose credentials include long bibliographies composed of trivial notes on trivial themes; and how often is recognition denied to those who are working on large and significant subjects that require years of preparation through patient research, extended reflection, and careful composition? We all say that we make the necessary distinctions; and I believe we make a genuine effort to do so. Nevertheless, we sometimes fail; and our failures do encourage busy-work and the outflow of half-digested, immature, or inchoate lumps with which our learned journals seem to be loaded.

A part of the explanation also lies in the absence of the leisure that is a pre-condition for contemplation. The role of the scholar in national affairs, beset as we are with challenges that press for responses, makes it difficult for him to do more than hope for those hours when reflection may be possible. Moreover, American society has in recent decades committed itself to a program of mass education beyond the high school, a commitment that has complicated the responsibilities and duties of the scholar. Scholarly talent, real talent, is rare enough; and what exists must be exploited in carrying on the mission of the university that involves the transmission of knowledge.

What I should like to say is that the American scholar, and consequently American scholarship, is facing great challenges today in spite of—or perhaps because of—the great prestige that he enjoys. The greatest danger is, I think, a misinterpretation of the scholar's proper role. That role is, as I have already suggested, the development of new and fresh comprehensive hypotheses or abstractions by which it becomes possible to interpret human experience in fresh and vital ways. The role includes a large effort at seeing life steadily and seeing it whole, in the face of all the pressures to specialize and concentrate. We cannot make large gains in one area at the expense of another: it requires no great insight to note that our technological advances have far outstripped our moral, spiritual, and physical capacity to adapt to them. Riots in the streets, sensuality, rock and roll, LSD, protests on the campus, tranquillizers, sedatives, psychiatry, shortages of doctors and nurses are not signs of original sin or a degenerate race; they are symptoms of an inability to accommodate to an environment. The development of scholarship in ways not anticipated by Emerson has made it difficult for the individual scholar to exercise the kind of moral and spiritual leadership that our situation demands.

A new direction for the American scholar is suggested by Arthur Schlesinger, Jr., in the April (1967) *Progressive.* Professor Schlesinger's immediate concern is the present state of liberalism in politics; but his remarks have implications for scholarship. He argues that the 1930's "tackled the elemental needs of the American people—a job, a suit of clothing, three meals a day, a roof over one's head, and a measure of security for old age." Now, however, we are moving on "to qualitative tasks—to measures, in other words, designed to improve the quality of life in an industrial society. These are the issues of civil rights, of civil liberties, of education, of urban planning, of the state of the arts, and the beauty of the environment." These issues, he concludes, "are no longer social and economic, so much as they are cultural and moral." If Professor Schlesinger has read the tendencies of our time correctly—and there is little evidence that he has not,—then new demands are going to be made upon the scholar, for which the kinds of specialized knowledge he has been seeking will be largely inadequate. The cultural and moral issues of our time call not for expertise or specialization; they call for comprehensive understanding, great insight, and broad vision. Above all, they call for that ability so emphasized by Emerson, the ability to see things as they really are. One may conjecture that few large societies have demonstrated the enormous capacity for cant, self-deception, illusion, and myth which we find among our countrymen, including our scholars. We argue that a man should not be president because he is too much a politician. Where, if not in the White House, is there a better place for a politician? We have an enormous faith that a youth who has sat in a class for a period of time is educated. We talk of rights and privileges as though they had an existence in something other than a context of responsibility. We cannot be unmindful of the horrendous instances of suppression that have been carried on in the name of free speech. With scarcely a murmur of complaint we seem to accept outrageous semantic distortions of the true nature of things: a bitter and bloody intensification of military action is called escalation; outrageous slums that should shock the sensibilities of any human being are described as economically deprived neighborhoods.

"Clear your mind of cant," was Samuel Johnson's most frequent advice to his friends and protégés; and it is the timely advice which the American scholar today needs constantly to give his contemporaries. It is in his capacity as guide, philosopher, and teacher, rather than as expert and specialist, that he can make his greatest contribution at this juncture in our history. I do not believe expertise in either the sciences or the humanities is going to carry us much further in the pursuit of perfection, even though faith in it will die hard; we have a naive belief that we can be engineered out of our troubles, that there is no problem that cannot be solved with a little knowledge and skill. I believe (perhaps with comparable naiveté) that history is determined by great men, reflective men, who are capable of giving their societies a purpose and an aim. No form of government that human reason can provide will in itself guarantee perfection; certainly committees and panels will not. Perhaps what I advocate is a government of true scholars, or philosophers (if you will) which brings us back to Emerson, and ultimately to Plato!

DORA E. DAMRIN

The James Scholars and the University*

Educated at Ohio Wesleyan (B.A.) and at the University of Illinois (Ph.D.), Dora E. Damrin spent five years with the Educational Testing Service at Princeton, New Jersey, where she was instrumental in developing the Medical Aptitude Test, now in wide use. For five years until her death she was Assistant Director of the James Scholar Program for superior student at Illinois. A vivid, dynamic person, she was deeply interested in education and in all kinds of students, those of normal intellect as well as those with superior abilities.

After a comforting luncheon in the University of Illinois Union Building, December 4, 1964, Dr. Damrin addressed about three hundred high school principals, teachers, university faculty and administrators who gather annually to confer on their common problem, the education of young men and women. How fared the high school student who went on to the university? Past occasions of this kind were usually marked by school and college teachers generously congratulating each other on their successes and admitting their shortcomings, if at all, in private conversations later. So there was immediate attention and some astonishment when Professor Damrin announced clearly and firmly that she proposed to concentrate on "our failures." The speech was an impressive one, marked by the use of essential and telling facts, refutation of the stock excuses for poor student performance in college, specific illustration and clear characterization of the types of student failures, and a pointed plea for the kind of academic freedom she thought that talented, high-minded students wanted and deserved. Readers should take note of the dominant tone—intellectual and factual—and the clear undertone of accusation and indignation.

In previous talks which I have prepared for these articulation conferences I have spoken at length about the success of the James Scholar Program and its participants. Today I wish to present the other side of the coin and talk about our failures.

A strange phenomenon has been occurring since the start of the James Program in 1959. Each year we have raised and tightened our standards for admitting high school students to the Program, and each year—with only one minor exception—the percent of students who are dropped at the end of their freshman year for their failure to achieve good grades has steadily increased.

* Printed by permission of Professor Robert E. Johnson, first Director of the James Scholar Program.

Let me give you some specific data. In 1959 we admitted 137 students. This group had a mean high school rank of 93.8. By the end of their freshman year 36 percent—or one out of every three students—had been dropped. Last year, September 1963, we admitted 289 students. The mean high school rank for this group hit an all-time high of 94.7. By the end of their freshman year 49 percent—or one out of every *two* students—had been dropped. This fall our new class of freshman numbered 473 students. The mean high school rank for *this* group was a fantastic 96.2. One out of every four of these Scholars was the valedictorian or salutatorian of his high school. One out of every two Scholars had received a letter of commendation or a finalist rating of the National Merit Scholarship Tests. Without even looking at these students' mid-semester grades I can predict with unhappy certainty that one out of three will be dropped at the end of this, their first semester, and that by the end of next semester the attrition rate will approach the 50 percent level.

From 1959 through 1961 the attrition rate for the 284 valedictorians and salutatorians in the Program was 16 percent. For the 1963 class the rate for valedictorians and salutatorians had jumped to 39 percent. These same findings hold true for Illinois State Scholarship winners, National Merit finalists, and National Merit Scholars. And so we must ask the question, "What is happening to these eminently capable and highly qualified students?" "Why is it that they are not achieving grades commensurate with their developed abilities?" As most of you know, the James Scholar needs to maintain only a B average to remain in the program—and certainly these students are *more than* qualified to do this.

When I present these data to my colleagues at the University the typical reaction is, "The kids come from small high schools." There is absolutely no evidence that this is true. The correlation of size of high school with James Scholar grades is *zero.* The University's first Rhodes Scholar in many years was a James Scholar who graduated in a class of 64 students. One of the most brilliant young women we have ever had in the program—a student who graduated as a valedictorian at the University—came from a high school class of 34 students. The pat answer of "the small high schoool" simply is not true.

When I present these data to high school teachers and counselors the typical reaction is, "The University grades too hard—*especially* in the honors classes which all James Scholars are required to take." This is equally untrue. Our research shows that James Scholars in good standing, as well as James Scholars who have been dropped from the honors programs for low grades, obtain significantly *higher* grades in their honors courses than they do in the regular courses taken by the average University student. The rumor that "honors courses are graded on the curve" is sheer myth.

Still another hypothesis that we have tested concerns the students' preparation for college honors work. We compared the records of Scholars who reported that they had participated in honors courses in high school with the records of Scholars who said they had *no* honors work in high school. There was no significant difference in the drop-out rate for the two groups.

In due time we turned our attention to students' attitudes and values in regard to their high school work. Many of you have participated in this research—as you will recognize when I mention the Student Record Form. This is a short, 20-item questionnaire which a teacher who is selected by the student in question completes and sends to us. Those of you who are familiar with this Form have perhaps recognized the many revisions it has undergone. This instrument presently has been developed to the point where it is more predictive of students' success in the James Scholar program than are high school rank and standardized test scores. As such it has provided us with some interesting clues about why so many of our eminently qualified high school valedictorians, salutatorians, National Merit winners, and others drop out of the program. The answer is not a very happy one—for either high school teachers or, and most especially, for University faculty members.

James Scholars who make high scores on the Student Record Form are more successful than those who make low scores. What is the high-scoring student like? He is a veritable paragon of academic virtue. He is conscientious, interested, docile, well-adjusted, well-mannered. He studies hard—*regardless* of the assignment and *regardless* of his interest in it. His papers are neat and handed in on time. He thoroughly enjoys his high school work. He participates heavily in the extracurricular program of the school. In short, he is a joy to his high school teachers and later will become a joy to his college professors. He has accepted and internalized *our* values and *our* standards—he performs as *we* wish him to perform—and from us he receives our accolade of merit, the golden A. It is practically impossible for this student to fail.

What about the students who make low scores on the Student Record Form? These students are not such paragons. In high school they subject themselves to the rules of grade-getting, they play the game, but they do this primarily for the sake of getting into the University where—they believe—they will find the freedom to develop along lines which are of interest *to them.* At the University they will be able to express themselves, they will be able to pursue fascinating subjects taught by masters, they will meet other students as enamored of "real" learning as they themselves are, in short—they will have arrived, at long last, at a place where they can be themselves.

It is precisely at this point that their academic downfall begins, because the University—like the high school—rewards only those students who conform to its rules. Disillusionment comes quickly. Having spent four years in high school conforming—consciously or unconsciously—to a set of alien values for the sake of obtaining the grades necessary for college admission, these students literally "give up" when they discover that the University—in the words of one of our drop-outs—"is nothing more than a warmed-over high school." For some students, on the order of 10 percent of each entering class, the shock is so great and the disappointment so bitter that they quit altogether, leaving the campus to take menial jobs in business and industry. The common complaint of these students is that they "can't find themselves" and our common diagnosis of their trouble is that they are "maladjusted."

The majority of the honors program drop-outs, however, remain in school and graduate—often with close to the minimum grade average required, and frequently having been placed on academic probation for one or more semesters.

You will notice that the University says that "they"—the students—are maladjusted; it takes no part of the blame itself. Perhaps it should. You must keep clearly in mind that I am talking about a group of students who are among the brightest and most competent young people in the nation—half of whom fail to achieve at capacity level. Are all of these young people "maladjusted"—or are they registering their protest against an environment which forces them, in Paul Goodman's terms, to "grow up absurd"?

This is not to say that there are no instances of severe psychological maladjustment among James Scholars, because there are. I am saying, however, that by rewarding conformity and punishing all forms of erratic behavior the University is doing nothing to mitigate these students' problems and everything to compound them. I am suggesting that the University—despite the administrative headaches it will cause—should relax some of its academic rules and should permit these students greater freedom in the pursuit of the things that interest them.

In talking and working with honors students over the past five years I have come to recognize three rather distinct types. Not all drop-outs fit into one of these categories, but enough do to make some consideration of them worthwhile. I shall describe them in turn.

First is the student I refer to as the intellectual rebel. This student has the audacity to believe that he knows more than we do about what a good education consists of. Let me give you a few cases in point.

At present I am involved in what I believe will prove to be a futile attempt to get a National Merit Scholar re-admitted to the University. As a sophomore this student was doing A and B work in college courses designed for advanced undergraduates and graduates. Even so, he found the majority of his classes boring, irrelevant, and lacking in the kind of intellectual challenge he was seeking. One day he received a B+ on a mid-semester examination for which he had not opened a book. This did it. He cut classes for the remainder of the semester, appeared for none of his final examinations, and deliberately failed himself out of the University. Now he has reached the point where he thinks he can stand us again—especially if we will let him do a lot of independent study. In his petition for re-admission he wrote, "Society requires this silly piece of paper called a diploma and I have found that I need it for what I want to do with my life." Such a statement is not one to endear this young man to the faculty. Unless he recants I doubt that he will be admitted. Honesty—for these students at least—is *never* a good policy.

Another example is a brilliant young science major who will not graduate because of his refusal to take some required laboratory courses in his curriculum. He refuses on the grounds that the courses are a waste of his time and he has too many other important things to do. He says—and truthfully—that he could gain proficiency in the courses by spending a couple of nights reading the book and that if he ever needs the lab technique he can pick it up in a week—although in his field of interest he won't ever need it anyway—so why should he bother?

Then there is the young woman who came to my office in a rage over not being permitted to take the unheard of conglomeration of courses which interested her. She said she had no intention of getting a *degree,* she wanted only an *education,* and that she was a much better judge of her needs and interests than anyone else. She said she planned to marry in two years, but that if she changed her mind she could always go back and pick up the requirements. A college dean informed her in no uncertain terms that her schedule would *not* be approved for the rather strange reason that—quote—"the University is interested only in students who really want to learn something." She conformed for one semester, then quit.

A second type of James Scholar drop-out is the social reformer. These students, when not in jail for violating the draft laws or for participating in civil rights demonstrations, give first place to "the cause" and study only when they have the time and energy. Their transcripts show a weird assortment of A's and E's, and of A's and "Absents"—indicating that on more than one occasion they did not bother to appear for a final examination. Unlike the intellectual rebel who insults and angers us, the social reformer tends to be a gentle and reasonable young person over whom we weep because of what we regard as the waste of his or her talents. But these students, convinced of the rightness of their belief, pity *us* for our ignorance and lack of social conscience. There is little communication between them and the faculty; there is a great deal between them and the administration; and administrators are notoriously unsympathetic toward such students.

The third, and perhaps most tragic, type of academic failure is the one I have termed the socially-conditioned misfit. This is the talented student who tries to break free of the social conditioning he has been subjected to during the years prior to his enrollment in the University. He is the son of a doctor who doesn't want to *become* a doctor, the daughter of a family who insists that her education must be "useful" yet who doesn't want to become a public school teacher, or the bright young man of artistic bent who has for years been conditioned to the idea that the only worthwhile career today is the career of the scientist or engineer. These students find themselves in University curricula which are anathema to them. Their lack of genuine interest in a field subtly chosen for them by others leads to mediocre or failing grades, loss of their scholarships, severe harassment from their families, and bitter disappointment in themselves.

These are the students with whom the University has the least patience. It just doesn't make sense for a boy with a college board math score in the 700's to make C's and D's in the calculus and in elementary science courses. Transferring out of the hated curriculum rarely proves to be a satisfactory solution because the student seldom has any clear idea of what he wants to do. He lacks the strength of the intellectual rebel and possesses none of the dedication of the social reformer. He is trapped in a morass of self-doubt which destroys his chance for academic success in *any* field.

Now what is it that I would have the University do for the rebels, the reformers, and the misfits? It seems to me that we—as a University—should have greater faith in these, our most capable students. Give the rebels freedom, let them pursue independent work with the best teachers on the campus, forget our sacred course, curriculum, and degree requirements. Give the reformers greater support and deeper understanding—our rebuff merely drives them deeper into themselves and farther out of contact with the mature intellectual world. Have patience with the misfits, give them time to re-orient and re-establish themselves, let them keep their scholarships, bear with them during the painful process of change. Most important of all, I believe, is for us to adopt the attitude that when a James Scholar fails the fault may lie not in *his* stars but in ourselves.

DONALD C. BRYANT

Professional and Amateur

Students of this textbook and readers of the analysis of John F. Kennedy's Inaugural Address, pages 425–437, already know a good deal about Professor Bryant. He has taught the history of rhetoric and public address at the University of the State of New York at Albany and at Washington University, St. Louis, as well as at The University of Iowa. His articles on the rhetorical tradition appearing in The Quarterly Journal of Speech *have been much praised and one of them widely reprinted. Interested especially in English public address, he has published extensively on Edmund Burke. Now the First Vice-President of the Speech Association of America, he becomes its President in 1970.*

This speech was given May 4, 1968, at The University of Iowa at the annual Honors Assembly, an occasion emphasizing the significance of the superior student. The address is a clear indication that some professors can speak well. Readers will want to observe the deft allusion to the experience of professor and student, and to the conditions said to account for the generation gap. Allusive, also, are the touches of humor. Perceptive readers will note the progressive sharpening of purpose and idea, emerging from a relaxed introduction and concrete illustration, and managed in part through an apparent reversal of direction. Over all is the dominant tone—that of an unpretentious discourse of reason whose broad appeal rests on a set of values stated as paradoxes and phrased in symmetry. Students interested in drawing comparisons will be repaid by placing this speech beside that of Robert W. Rogers.

Honor Students, Ladies, and Gentlemen:

Congratulations! This is indeed a gratifying occasion for all of you and for us, and I shall try to speak accordingly. It is not difficult, however, to praise Athens to the Athenians, as Aristotle remarked long ago. Nor is it now necessary, though indeed it is pleasant, to expend praise upon academic distinction before an audience gathered together totally for the purpose of reminding itself that excellence is excellent and greatly to be praised.

Over the years I have initiated many juniors and seniors and graduate students (and even certain colleagues who had been overlooked at the usual time) into that oldest of American honor societies, Phi Beta Kappa. On those occasions I have spoken, or have caused to be spoken, words of praise and sanguine prediction which my audiences of initiates and their families and friends were little inclined to protest. I now declare those words, or words like them, uttered again to you here and now. So—may I go on to something else, no less relevant, I think, but perhaps appearing more current and popular.

I am going, with your permission, to presume to speak of a "gap." Not the famous "generation gap," for then, I should have to say, "I don't know for sure what it is, this conflict of the generations; but I do know that it is more than thirty years old, and therefore not to be believed or trusted." Nor will I speak of that other gap known as *alienation,* for the real "alienated generation" is my own, and it would be indecorous to speak of oneself on an occasion like this. The gap I mean; no one has seen it made or heard it made, but (as Robert Frost might have said and didn't) at political-action time we find it there. It is the gap between professional and amateur.

Often when I think of the plight of the young intellectual today—of his admirable impatience and his just frustration—I am reminded of some verses by that genial satirist, Charlotte Perkins Gilman, written, I am afraid, more than half a century ago. They are called "Similar Cases," and one of them is about a very bright young ape who was on the way up. He felt the impulses of evolution pounding through his system; but he had a very hard time getting any appropriate action out of the establishment:

> There was once an Anthropoidal Ape
> Far smarter than the rest,
> And everything that they could do
> He always did the best
> [He was an honor student];
> So, they *naturally* disliked him
> And gave him shoulders cool,
> And when they *had* to mention him,
> They said he was a fool.

Unrepressed by his honorable unpopularity, however, he went ahead agitating for change, deploring the in*humanity* of current anthropoidal society, and proclaiming that he, at least, was out to become a MAN.

Opposition, of course, was immediate and predictively human. The elders attacked him in the conventional three stages—first ridicule and verbal abuse:

> So, they yelled at him in chorus,
> Which he minded not a whit;

then violence:

> And pelted him with coconuts,
> Which didn't seem to hit;

and finally the last resort:

> And *then,* they gave him *reasons.* . . .

Yes, that's it—what Hamlet called "discourse of reason." Remote, it seems, inaccessible, slow to operate, easy to break off and abandon, seldom clear and self-evident, always precarious, yielding doubtful and uncertain glory, but in the long run the *only reliable way in the human condition.* At least, it seems so to me, or I should have little call to be devoting my life to that study in education concerned with how the processes of the discourse of reason (and of necessity also of unreason) have functioned, do function, and may perhaps be made to function in society, and especially democratic society.

And to whom do we turn for power and leadership in this discourse of reason and for the action which must be the fruition of it? We can turn with hope, it seems to me, only to those brightest of our race who have made themselves both professional and amateur, both specialist and generalist.

Perhaps I am just thinking those old thoughts about a liberal education and a liberal life, which, as John Milton wrote, "fits a man to perform justly, skillfully, and magnanimously all the offices, both public and private, of peace and war." If so, I refer you to a little book written by a wise professor of English about twenty-five years ago, Hoyt Hudson. It is called *Educating Liberally,* and is the best thing on the subject since Quintilian.

But I am not speaking of a liberal education, at least in the usual way. The late physicist and educational leader, Arthur Holly Compton, who was Chancellor of the university where I used to be employed before I was elevated to The University of Iowa, liked to tell a story which goes close to the heart of what I would wish you to consider this morning. Mr. Compton's sister, living in India, employed a carpenter to replace or alter a window. After leaving him with what she thought adequate instructions, she returned later to find the job completed and the carpenter eager for praise and pay. In some way, however, the new window was clearly unsatisfactory. The lady of the house protested: "If you couldn't remember my suggestions, you could at least have used your common sense." In response the disappointed carpenter explained: "Perhaps you are right, madam, but common sense is a rare and precious gift bestowed upon very few. *I* have only technical competence."

I do not repeat Chancellor Compton's story in order to belittle technical competence. That would be to deny the modern world. I repeat it to illustrate the "gap" which I want you to consider. All of us as specialists, as *pros,* are indispensable, crucial to ourselves and to our complex, sophisticated, fast-moving world. Milton's man totally competent in "all the offices, both private and public, of peace and war" was always unlikely and is now incredible.

The expert, the authority, the highly skilled operator, the master of a branch of knowledge or a way of doing things (including thinking) special to him and a few like him, is the foundation and the pride of our civilization. He it is who makes the nuclear power station, the communications satellite, the great university, the play or the painting or the sonata which brings new eminence in the life of the spirit. It is he who searches the astro-spaces, who explores the past, who penetrates the human soul for those seminal ideas which make man great—or perhaps destroy him. This is the man or woman we must nurture in greater and greater abundance and in higher and higher perfection, and he it is that we honor and reward and distinguish.

He it is that you were preparing yourself to be when you chose (or let yourself be guided into) a major study in the university, or when you settled upon a calling or a vocation. He it is whom you began to create when you left your friend to his Elizabethan literature and set yourself to knowing more than anyone else about the theory of electronic memory systems. That is good, that is the way it should be—the way it must be. You began to become a specialist, an expert; and if you intend to derive your livelihood from your expertise—whether in computer-science, philosophy, social organization, or football—you are setting out to become professional, a *pro.*

Meanwhile your friend is also becoming a *pro,* no more and no less than you. His Elizabethan literature has narrowed to Elizabethan sonnets, and he is heading for graduate school, a Ph.D., and perhaps a single Elizabethan sonneteer.

And why not? "It takes all kinds . . . ," we say to ourselves, when we cannot possibly understand the curious, inconsequential specialities of our colleagues and classmates! But it *does* take all kinds, of course; and our world demands ever more specialists, more *pros,* in studies and occupations ever more confined, ever more refined, ever more unlikely (and sometimes it seems more occult). In each of these, excellence of mind and skill gets more important all the time, and achieving that quality becomes a more and more totally consuming preoccupation.

Of course it does, and hence the justice of the familiar protest, "I'd like to be a whole man as well as a specialist, but I just haven't time. Breadth with depth is the ideal, in school and out; but if I can't have both, then I'll go for depth and let breadth blow in with the vacation breezes." Yes, the person who majors in things general, in school or in his career, majors in nothing. We can't afford to have amateurish professionals (though we get a good many such). We must have *pros.*

But that cannot be our choice—completely. And especially can it not be the choice of the brightest and most capable of all, the honor students of the University.

We today *must* find ways to live as a congregation of specialists, you in your small corner and I in mine, without having to trust blindly to some high command in the universe to make sense of it all and to see that it all does not destroy itself. That resource must be ourselves.

All of us recognize the necessity of the amateur to keep the professional in balance. Do we not pick up and cherish, in humor and in seriousness, the paradox that war is too serious a business to be left to the generals? Perhaps we think also of some parallel paradoxes: Education is too vast a business to be left to the school men. Politics is too vital a calling to be left to the politicians. Youth is far too grand an experience to be left altogether to the young. And finally, life is far too fine a venture to be guided wholly by the living.

So what do I conclude? What does the title of my talk mean? That each of us according to his talents—and especially the most academically distinguished of us—must see to it that he becomes both professional *and amateur.* In the University and out we must really work seriously at both, not merely at the *pro* side. We dare not leave the amateur side to required core courses and conversation over beer and bridge. Perhaps the reason that alumni of some universities (not Iowa, of course!) find little except the football teams to excite them about their alma maters when they gather for old times' sake is that when they were students, football was about all they understood in common.

It is my obligation to know my society, its ways and its needs, its possibilities and its inadequacies, and to take earnest part in it, not casually like a dilettante, but seriously like an inquirer. A current term does very well for what I mean—"involvement"—though I fear that that label is sometimes applied to give status to what is little more than casual fiddling. Professional we are, but involved amateur we must be also, beyond our specialties in the society that our specialties make possible.

In the *Iowa City Press-Citizen* last month a headline spread across the foot of page one inquired, "Can Amateurs Find Happiness Among Pros at Iowa Demo Parley?" Yes they can, I should answer, and not only happiness but proper consequence—if they go not as one-shot missionaries but as involved and attentive citizens. And at about the same time an editorial in the *Des Moines Register* read: "Most Americans are inexperienced in politics. They leave the political process to a handful of full-time professionals and to odd moments in their own lives, when a war or a depression or some personal friend or experience galvanizes them into unaccustomed action. Then they charge in like men possessed and make mistakes professionals would avoid. The man who hardly ever votes is likely to vote one day, but more out of prejudice than knowledge or intent. The man who never writes a letter to the editor may write one some day, but it may be intemperate and contain errors of fact. The man who never writes his congressman may do so some day, but like as not he will 'tell' his congressman how to vote and threaten not to vote for him if he doesn't vote 'right'—hardly the most persuasive approach. We are all like that. But we can learn."

Yes, my friends, all of us *pros,* if we will, can learn (and we had better) to be amateurs too, not mere dabblers—in politics, in community service, in education; in music, in literature, in art, in science, in political action. But it isn't amateurishness which we should covet. That is another name for clumsy ignorance, and we've too much of that even among the *pros.* We must seek what, if you will permit me, I shall call *amateurity.* That means sound working knowledge, involvement, and seriousness in those basics which matter in our society and underlie all specialties; that means commitment, integrity, and responsibility with humility in the world of which we are parts.

I need not try to remind you of the ready resources for advancing that amateurity which your university and community afford—both in courses and out, both above ground and "underground," in both the "free university" and the other kind! They are there for the using. Beyond the University (and I suggest that neither life nor the best part of it ends with commencement!), beyond the University you can find, if you will, ready sources, besides the television screen and the golf club, for enhancing the professional and the amateur in you—that is if you have the commitment and the energy to work them with intelligence.

In the interests of time, I shall hazard but a single example which must stand for many. I am led to it by the editorial from the *Register*. I can think of no better post-graduate school of political and social amateurity, for example, than the League of Women Voters. I've been married to it for years, to my perpetual profit! It's available to the young women of this country—and to the men whom they guide and educate. In that organization they're not political *pros*, but the dilettante and the busybody among them does not long survive.

And now I come back to my brilliant young ape and the discourse of reason. Let him automate and unify the telephonic communication of the whole world and be proud of his feat. But let him apply his other genius, his other talent, his other will to the broad human discourse of head and heart which can keep his world worth his special expertise.

Let them whose names crowd the columns of this Honors Day Program take as their slogan "Professional and Amateur—the Best in Both the Worlds."

FRANK STANTON

Mass Media and Mass Culture*

The following speech is a lecture by the President of the Columbia Broadcasting System, addressed specifically to the academic community of Dartmouth College at the Hopkins Center in Hanover, New Hampshire, on November 26, 1962. It is so developed, however, as to be appropriate, with few changes, to any audience of educated Americans. The lecture was part of the Great Issues Course, inaugurated by President John Sloan Dickey in 1947 as a series of weekly lectures to Dartmouth seniors, given through the college year by distinguished visitors to the campus.

A native of Michigan, Dr. Stanton was educated at Ohio Wesleyan and Ohio State universities, from the latter of which he received the Ph.D. degree. He has been President of CBS since 1946 and is intimately connected with many other business and cultural enterprises, both national and international, especially those related to the arts and sciences.

Dr. Stanton has established himself as one of the most articulate of American businessmen and as a public speaker of distinction. We

* Reprinted by permission of Dr. Stanton from *Mass Media and Mass Culture,* New York: The Columbia Broadcasting System, Inc., n.d.

include the speech below as a skillful academic and popular lecture on some of the important present and future problems of American life with which college students of today will have to be concerned for years to come. We call the attention of the student of public speaking especially to how Dr. Stanton effectively manages large amounts of statistical information without seeming to oppress his audience with figures.

The subject of your deliberations this week is highly appropriate to the chapter in Dartmouth's history marked by the opening of this promising Center. It is one of the most hopeful signs of our times, I think, that academic institutions all over America are becoming more and more concerned with the arts, both visual and performing. Certainly this enlarged concern, of which this building is a characteristic symbol, is central to any deeper understanding of American culture and of the culture of the twentieth century.

But if you have been apt in your choice of a subject, I am afraid that you have not been unique. There is a great stir going on everywhere about what feature writers like to call the "cultural explosion"—an expression that leaves something to be desired in view of the dictionary definitions of "explosion." Financial pages have probed the commercial implications of increased cultural activity. Philosophers have explored the moral aspects in learned and spirited seminars. Sociologists, psychologists, historians have given lectures, written books, advanced and attacked theories. Writers have had a field day visiting new deformities upon the English language in such coined words as "masscult," "midcult" and "highcult" that threaten to survive more for their ugliness than for their relevance.

I think that I have followed most of this discussion—responsible and otherwise—fairly faithfully. It will be no news to you that in my line of work we have not suffered from a shortage of critical attention. And with whatever grace we may appear to accept and—some would say—ignore it, we do occasionally ask ourselves questions about what is happening to our culture and the nature of the effect that the mass media have upon it. I thought I might share with you tonight my own reflections on some of these questions, although you will quickly discover that I do not necessarily have the answers. Here among these silent hills you, who are blessed with more time and more salubrity for pure thought, will, I trust, no later than the end of the academic year, arrive at your own conclusions.

A first and fundamental question is: What is the true extent to which there is an acceleration in cultural activity in this country?

The tools of measurement that we have are far from perfect, but we do have some statistical evidence that is impressive. I am sure that I do not need to warn you that statistics alone do not tell the whole story. But as my predecessor on this platform, Mr. Heckscher, wrote recently, "Yet when all has been said in the way of caution or disparagement, the fact remains that numbers *are* important."

Our population is now growing at an average annual rate of some 1.5 per cent, and of our present population of 186 million, over 70 per cent are 14 years old or older. These figures ought to be kept in mind when considering statistics on cultural activity, for it will be apparent that the increasing rate at which Americans are listening to serious music, looking at fine art, and reading significant books far outpaces the population increase.

The number of symphony orchestras in the United States has increased from 800 in 1952, to 1252 in 1962. Two hundred of these are solidly professional, and nearly 50 of them operate on annual budgets ranging upwards of $100,000. Nor is this limited to big cities or urban centers; 30 per cent of U.S. symphony orchestras are in communities of no more than 25,000. Attendance at concerts has also risen until today more people attend concerts in America than go to all major and minor league baseball games including the World Series. The audience of the Detroit Symphony Orchestra, for example, rose 130 per cent in the past decade. And when the New York Philharmonic went on a two-month tour in 1960, 100,000 jammed concert halls to hear it.

A survey by Broadcast Music, Inc. reveals that, in March 1962, 1255 AM and 126 FM radio stations, nearly a third of all commercial radio stations in the U.S., programmed a weekly total of 16,748 hours of concert music—an average of 12.1 hours a week. The 1955 survey showed a weekly average of only 6.5 hours.

Ten years ago there were a little over 300 performing opera groups in the U.S.; today there are over 780, both professional and amateur, whose 3700 performances play to capacity audiences each year. Larger communities are building new opera houses at musical centers, largely through popular subscriptions.

Sales of long-playing recordings of serious music have increased 80 per cent in three years, and according to *Fortune,* now reach 25 million sales a year. The public spends some $100 million annually on this recorded music —not to mention $300 million for high fidelity equipment on which to play it. This $400 million total compares to a Department of Commerce estimate of $280 million spent a year on admissions to *all* spectator sports in America.

In the visual arts, such evidences of popular interest as museum attendance is extremely persuasive. In New York, attendance at the Metropolitan Museum of Art has risen 200 per cent since 1950. Translated into numbers, this means that people are going to the Metropolitan Museum at an annual rate of 5 million visits. The Metropolitan's experience is being duplicated and even surpassed all over the country, with some 60 million visits to our museums and galleries yearly. And since government funds for the fine arts are very limited, these people are also providing the lion's share of the $300 million necessary to maintain these institutions.

Nor has reading become a lost pursuit in our country. Over a billion books are now bought each year, and 800 million are borrowed from public libraries as compared to 500 million in 1956. Paperbacks, which sold over 300 million copies in 1961, will number 21,000 titles in 1962 as compared to 15,000 in 1961, and these include not only the classics of literature, history and philosophy but also virtually every book of serious creative effort and comment that has been published in recent years in hardbacks.

To supplement all these statistics, and to refute the charge, that, like raspberry jam, the farther culture is spread the thinner it gets, we should take a brief look at some other data. Harold Lasswell, a pioneer student of communications, has said there are five stages in communication: attention, comprehension, enjoyment, evaluation and action. The statistics we have been using reveal no more than attention. Let us now move to the other end of Mr. Lasswell's spectrum, to action.

In the field of music, there were in 1950, the American Music Conference reports, 21 million musical instruments owned and presumably played by Americans. Today there are about 37.5 million—an increase of over 76 per cent. The number of amateur musicians in the same period has risen from 19 million to 33 million—a rise of 73 per cent compared to a population rise of 22 per cent. This means that one out of five Americans plays a musical instrument. And although some of it may be at times an assault on the ear, that the instrumentalists are presumably competent enough to participate in combinations seems to me apparent from the fact that school bands and orchestras alone have doubled in number since World War II. And it *is* action: it involves spending time, money and effort.

Similarly, in the visual arts, members of the Metropolitan Museum—as distinguished from those who only visit it—have increased 100 per cent over the last decade. Substantially more slides are borrowed; more photographs and photostats are sold; more lectures are attended.

In books, the persistence with which canny publishers put out competing paperback editions of Plato and Homer, Shakespeare and Milton, and sell them in drug stores, variety stores and at airport newsstands shows that somebody is buying them. No one has ever claimed there is much snobbery in buying paperback books—they are hardly designed for conspicuous or impressive display—but I am thoroughly convinced too that few expensive books are bought as cocktail table furniture. There may be an occasional purchase with such a purpose, but that kind of market would soon be glutted. Last year there were 539 new titles in art books, as against 317 in 1950. One publisher a few seasons ago was astonished to find that his $30 volume on the Robert Woods Bliss collection of pre-Columbian art was sold out within a week of publication.

Although all of this may not be final proof that we are on the verge of a new renaissance, I think that it at least establishes the premise that we live in a period of increasing cultural interest that is not mere lip service but genuine and active.

Let me raise the point of the effect of the mass media on our cultural life and, the opposite side of the coin which is less often examined, the effect of our cultural life on our mass media. I will be the first to admit that we don't know enough about either side of this matter. I see several questions here. One is this: Is the increased attention directed to the appreciation of the arts and to the acquisition of knowledge due, to any considerable degree, to the mass media?

The answer is to some extent implicit in the premises. The mass media must by definition deal with very large and inclusive groups of our population, and all of them together reach virtually all groups. If on any very broad front there is a great increase in popular attention to any aspect of life or increased activity in it, there is inevitably some relation to the mass media. With regard to the arts and knowledge specifically, it is the mass media that have brought an intensified awareness of the art or knowledge, made it more generally available and usually done both. And these are the minimum essentials of any widespread cultural activity: awareness and availability.

If we consider music, it seems to me obvious that both radio and, to a lesser extent, television, have brought an awareness of fine music into millions of homes. The proliferation of standard radio stations, the increase of FM operations, the economic revolution in radio—all these factors have put music back into radio; and the fragmentation of the audience has made it possible for many stations, particularly FM, to devote the major segments of their schedules to serious music, creating and broadening public awareness of it. Television, though more sporadically, has also made the public aware of the pleasures of listening.

When Leonard Bernstein reported the reception that the Philharmonic got on its tour, he said that there was "an explanation other than musicianship to explain the extraordinary enthusiasm" of the audience. "You can't imagine," he said, "how we have been gathered in by audiences that obviously knew about us through television." In some places the audiences stood and cheered for minutes before the orchestra had played a note. In Las Vegas, whose cultural opulence doesn't always run in traditional channels, and where no major symphony had performed before, a hall holding 7000 was jammed. I do not know that the highest level of musical discrimination has been reached by audiences that silence an orchestra with their cheers before hearing it play; but we are talking of awareness here, and these people were well aware of the Philharmonic. I doubt if awareness of the Philharmonic extended much beyond the Hudson fifty years ago.

The opening of Lincoln Center for the Performing Arts last September provides another revealing example of how television can increase the awareness of a vast public. Some 25.6 million television viewers in America saw and heard some part of the two-hour concert, in contrast to the 2600 who attended the concert that night in Philharmonic Hall. During the 1961–62 season, the CBS Television Network broadcast six special programs of the Philharmonic during prime evening hours with an average rating for the six hours of 8.9, which means that some 4.3 million sets were tuned in to the concert during the average minute. Just as, according to Leonard Bernstein, television must be credited for the popular reception of the Philharmonic on tour, it seems probable that the television appearances of the orchestra have helped stimulate the popular interest that has led to the more than one million sales of Philharmonic record albums.

The availability of fine music has been immeasurably increased by the long-playing, high fidelity record. The average cost, per minute of playing time, to a member of the Dartmouth Class of 1939, for a recording of Beethoven's "Eroica" Symphony was 25.2 cents. Since that symphony takes 50 minutes, your hard-pressed predecessors paid something like $14 for a cumbersome album of the entire symphony. The cost to you for the same symphony, by the same orchestra, is about eight cents per minute of playing time. And it is now possible to get an LP recording of the whole symphony for around $4.

It is an incomparably better recording, with a far longer, useful life. Your fathers listened to mechanical approximations of an orchestra playing a symphony. You listen to a faithful play back of the actual performance. Moreover, the weight and bulk of your records are not so great that you have to limit your collections, neither will they crack on the slightest pressure nor melt like one of Dali's timepieces if left in the sun.

Long-playing records not only make fine musical performances available to great numbers of people wherever they live, but they also furnish wider audiences to new composers. In April 1962, the inclusive *Schwann Long Playing Record Catalog* listed 1878 works of 483 contemporary composers, as compared to 504 works of 49 composers of the age of Beethoven. There is an hospitable enthusiasm for contemporary composers, and the last generation's avant-garde is today's historic survival.

The nature of the visual arts does not permit a wholly comparable experience. It does not seem to me that the reproduction of a great painting can yet come as close to the original as do the high fidelity recordings of great musical performances. Nevertheless, such innovations in printing techniques as the electronic scanning of color values has brought about a kind of visual high fidelity that has made possible far more exact reproductions of paintings. *Life* publishes some 500 art pictures a year, many in very faithful color reproductions. In most cases these are based on current exhibits, special shows or the permanent collections of American museums—as, for example, the 400-

artist collection of the Carnegie International Exhibition of Art, the traveling exhibition of the national treasures of Thailand, and the Detroit Institute of Art's memorable Flemish masterpieces exhibit, which was seen by some 100,000 visitors.

I don't think that looking at reproductions in the pages of a book or magazine can ever equal looking at an original painting. There are too many matters of texture and scale involved. But it can open up new awarenesses. If millions of people see a painting in *Life,* hundreds of thousands are going to seek out originals in museums and galleries. Prominent accounts in the mass media of the purchase of Rembrandt's "Aristotle Contemplating the Bust of Homer," for $2.3 million, brought scores of thousands into the Metropolitan Museum in New York, probably out of curiosity; but long after the sensationalism had worn off, the increased attendance held up. Attendance at the Museum has soared 40.7 per cent since the acquisition, and *The New York Times* reports, "Books about Rembrandt are selling furiously." Visitors may have come to stare, but they stayed to appreciate and to learn.

The part that television plays in this process of increasing cultural awareness is still the subject of tentative probings by the social scientists. The bills of particulars range all the way from a determining effect to a deterring effect to no effect at all. I have put myself in the enviable position of raising questions tonight rather than answering them, and I will make no claims for television. On the other hand, it may be useful to you to consider with me some factors that I hope will help you arrive at your own answers.

The chairman of the American Library Association's broadcasting committee has said, "Dramatization of classics on TV inspires people to read or re-read the classics. And public affairs documentaries have been sending people back to history books. . . . We look upon television as a tremendous motivational force. And we haven't even scratched the surface." A monthly bulletin of the New York Board of Education published the results of a survey of 73 library systems across the country and concluded, "Television encourages more reading . . . any story which appears on television creates a demand for the book."

These findings fly in the face of the argument that the reason why better books are being bought and borrowed is that television provides all the escape that cheap reading matter once provided. The Modern Library edition of James's *The Turn of the Screw* was sold out because of a television play based on it—not in spite of it. Stendhal's *The Red and the Black* reached unheard of sales during the first week of SUNRISE SEMESTER's program on comparative literature. An hour-long reading of the works of 23 American poets on the CBS Television Network in August this year brought 34,000 requests for bibliographies.

Television is, to be sure, escape entertainment for millions just as circulating library romances and magazine fiction once were to a greater extent than at present. But the customer who went out for a copy of Ethel M. Dell did not pick up a copy of Proust at the same time. On the other hand, millions who look at a situation comedy on television have frequent access also to such experiences as a Shakespearean play, a ballet, and a discussion of economic warfare. In the New York area alone last June, over 1.6 million people saw a two-and-a-half hour production of *The Merchant of Venice* on WCBS-TV.

But culture is not a matter only of the arts. It also involves knowledge—and this is an age when new areas of knowledge are opening up at an unprecedented pace. At CBS, the range of news and public affairs broadcasts is constantly broadening. We are no longer satisfied with only front page stories—virtually the whole range of the human experience is now included. Early in 1963, for example, an insight into the character of the Russian people will be provided our audiences through an hour-long prime time special broadcast of dramatized excerpts from five great Russian works of fiction ranging chronologically from Gogol to Pasternak.

Also early next year, CBS REPORTS will present, in two hour-long broadcasts, an account of the development of the United States Supreme Court, with extensive excerpts from its most significant decisions.

I am aware that some of these remarks on mass media and culture may have been overburdened with specifics and not enough concerned with general principles. I share with you the desire to raise more general questions and also the inability fully to answer them.

Paramount among them is this: Are we not in this age encountering a whole new kind of cultural activity—unique to our times and to the conditions of life today? Historically, there have been—since ancient times—two audiences for the arts. One has been the patron—a rich individual or institution that supported the arts and also, frequently in the least attractive sense, patronized them. The other was the simple folk art, to a great extent functional, that grew out of the ordinary daily requirements of life—pottery, work chants, artifacts. The first was a sparse world, rare in artists and rare in audiences. The second was large, but slow in progress and limited in range. And there was nothing between.

Cultural activity is no longer split into two isolated levels of the population. There was the great art, access to which was generally restricted to the few at the top, and there was the minor art for the many at the bottom. The void between began to fill only when progress in universal education, in economic feasibility, and in technical innovations made great art interesting and accessible to the many. Now cultural activity of variety and depth has become the common heritage and the common quest of all the people. Millions of people become acquainted with a new painter in the pages of a magazine. Millions hear a new composition on radio. Millions meet a new author on television. Although it is by now a commonplace, or regarded as "unknowable," it is still significant to recall that more people in a single night saw *Hamlet* on television than it is estimated had seen it in live performances since it was written.

The very dimensions of what we are witnessing have dislocated, I think, all our old standards. We have not had the time yet to produce the artists—writers, composers, and painters—necessary to feed this gargantuan appetite. We have not yet worked out patterns of exposure for many of those we do have. We are restless because television has not yet achieved as consistent a flow of programs of high cultural level in the arts as it has achieved in information, just as we have sometimes been restless because the printing press has produced a greater volume of passing trivia than of works of high and lasting merit.

There are, of course, some practical work-a-day factors that help to account for this situation. The processing of the raw materials of news broadcasts is responsive to organizational efforts: we can set up procedures, devise techniques and assemble staffs to provide a steady flow of top informational broadcasts. It is an intellectual process. But the top level program in the arts—the absorbing drama, the inspired comedy, the moving composition—cannot be brought about by organizing or planning or devising. They have to come from the vision, the flash of light, the wild surmise of the individual artist. You don't know where he is, what he is doing, or even if he exists.

But I think that we have a more essential, more basic dilemma even than this. Compared to the total human experience and the long chronicles of the arts and human culture, the mass media are very, very young. And mass communications are much more advanced as mass transmission than as mass interchange. For the major extent of civilized history the artist was in the company of his audience. The artist and his patron, the minstrel and his circle of listeners, the players and their little audiences, even the news criers and those who gathered in the town squares to hear—all these represented opportunities for the originators and transmitters of material to establish a rapprochement with their audiences, to pace themselves, to see what interested and what paled, to note when a phase was over and there was a need to move on to something else.

There have always been two ends to communication—the sender and the receiver; otherwise there is no communication. The painting of pictures that no one sees may be expression but it is not communication. "To have great poets," said Whitman, "there must be great audiences, too." We must know also whether we are reaching them, are in league with them and not so far ahead or so far behind that no one is paying any attention.

From their very nature, the mass media suffer from an indirectness and a lack of immediacy in getting audience response. A greater degree and a longer period of trial and error are involved in learning about audiences than has been the case over the ages when sender and receiver were at the same spot and usually in the same room. Those of you interested in the performing arts are well aware, I am sure, that there are great performances and lack-luster performances of the same play by the same performers in the same theatre the same week. This is generally the result of the spark that is struck between the performer and his audience. Nightclub performers handle their material as they go along to match the mood and responsiveness of their audiences. The improvised theatre, which has attained a considerable following both here and abroad, carries this performer-audience relationship back to the directness that was once the basis for all theatrics.

What we in the mass media have to work with, in gaging the responsiveness of audiences, is still far from perfect. We can make some assumptions from statistics. Obviously, if only a few viewers are looking at your program and many more at someone else's or not at any, there is something wrong. The broadcaster—not the audience—is out of step. And the realities of the mass media are not such that you can say that it is good enough to speak to an interested few. The whole structure of mass communications is based on the unit cost of bringing great art, great entertainment and great informational material to millions. If you reduce your audience from the many to the few, then the structure collapses. Moreover, in television, we occupy a limited number of channels and we must respect our obligation to the majority even though we cannot ignore minorities.

Like Whitman's poetry, then, mass media must have responsive audiences. To support the media's necessarily giant costs and, in the case of television, to justify the occupation of scarce commercial channels, they must be large audiences. And yet there is all the need for movement, for flexibility, for rapprochement in the relationship of mass media to their audiences as there was in the case of the minstrel or the crier. Indeed the penalty for consistent failure is far more devastating.

I suggest that the great challenge to the whole advancement of the mass media's contribution to our cultural life lies in the inroads that your generation can make on this problem of the relationship between the media and the audience. Of all the questions I have put tonight, this is by far the most perplexing.

There is, for example, the problem of pacing the interpolation of serious and minority interest programs in a schedule that must on the whole appeal to much greater numbers. One program in the schedule affects adjacent programs, and if we broadcast a program of high cultural value but limited interest, our audiences do not shrink just for that one program but for those following it. And they do not come all the way back during the same period the next week. Unless we handle this phenomenon with great caution, we could get into sufficient economic trouble to discourage us from doing any experimental or limited interest programs.

There is also the problem of understanding better the variety, the intensity and steadfastness of the motives of the audience in looking at television. How much are they really creatures of habit? How firmly are they really attached to their surface interests? How venturesome are they, how often ready for something new, under what circumstances, and at what times?

We do not have a sufficiently clear understanding of all this. Nor, for that matter, do we have a sufficiently clear understanding of the origins of tastes and the mechanisms by which they may be developed. Some researchers have claimed that the intellectual and cultural tastes of the majority are relatively limited, and that this majority is not likely to expose itself to material on the higher aesthetic and intellectual levels, or, if it is so exposed, that it is unlikely to develop tastes for such material merely as a result of exposure. To whatever degree this is true, mass media must look for assistance to other institutions where tastes are born—to the family, to the school, and to other primary groups. This whole question of how tastes are created and developed is one of the topics to which we at CBS plan to devote considerable research attention. And this is one of the reasons why we recently established within CBS a department of social research.

We are constantly striving to improve quantitative measurement of audience reactions. We are trying to understand trends better, and to determine their meaning and their depth. We want to know more, with more certainty. We need to know—with less costly trial and error, if it's possible—how far and how fast we can go in doing new things in new ways.

I hope very much that those of you whose imaginations are fired by the unlimited possibilities of the mass media in enriching our cultural life will, in the years to come, address your minds and ingenuity to these problems. There seems to me no area in which you can spend your time, your talents and your energies with more promise.

And now that I have given you an assignment that surpasses anything, I am sure, with which your faculty has afflicted you, I will not detain you further. You haven't a minute to lose if you are going to tackle it successfully.

ADLAI E. STEVENSON

The Educated Citizen*

The graduating classes of colleges and universities are perhaps the most abundantly advised and the most ideally delineated segment of our citizenry. In describing the educated citizen in the following speech, therefore, and in urging the Princeton senior to be that citizen, Adlai E. Stevenson was making his contribution to a long tradition. In this respect both his ideas and his methods may be compared profitably with those of James B. Reston, whose speech appears on pages 475–480. Stevenson, who, when he made his speech, was midway between two unsuccessful campaigns for the Presidency as the Democratic candidate, was perhaps the most literate, most thoughtful, and least commonplace political speaker in this country in recent years. His handling of the old themes, therefore, has elements of novelty and freshness and surprise whose sources are worthy of study. The theme of intellectual freedom had a special cogency at the time, for the unfortunate frenzy over "disloyalty" and "subversives" was about to culminate in the so-called Army-McCarthy hearings. Stevenson made use of the current atmosphere to point his meaning, but without rubbing it in or seeking to make it into political capital. One may observe in this speech evidences of two qualities for which Stevenson has been both praised and condemned—phrase-making and humor.

The speech was delivered at the Senior Class Banquet at Princeton University, March 22, 1954.

I am informed that this senior class banquet is being held at the expense of your accumulated reserves. I suggest that inviting me here is a very perilous thing to do because certainly within a few hours the Republicans will ask for equivalent time.

I was delighted to witness a moment ago your emphatic approval of my program for Princeton some thirty-two years ago—unlimited cuts, non-compulsory Chapel, and student firing of the Dean. I always considered that it was wise in politics to have—shall we say—a popular program. The trouble is that when I went into politics it appears that I changed my views.

I feel as though I were opening the hunting season on college seniors. From now until mid-June, college seniors are fair game for all of us uplifters, viewers with alarm, Chautauqua-style orators, even for occasional unemployed politicians. From now until mid-June college seniors are to be repeatedly reminded how fortunate they are and what they should do with their hard-won educational disciplines; they are to be warned repeatedly that the old order is changing, that the sky is overcast, visibility low; and they are to be urged and goaded and implored to accept the challenge to remake the future.

Thirty-two years ago—and I might say quite a number of pounds and a good many inches around the waist ago—when I graduated I believe I listened to these same challenges flung down by orators whose names I have completely forgotten. Now it is my turn to be forgotten. In doing my homework this morning on this evening's oration, I not only let my mind run back to the state of the world thirty-two years ago when I graduated from Princeton but I also glanced at the *Nassau Herald* of 1922 in the hope that I could find something about myself that would impress you. I discovered that when my senior class voted to bestow the sobriquet of "biggest politician" upon one of its members I received only eight votes—but when it voted on "thinks he is biggest politician" I won second place, and that was due to a conspiracy among my roommates.

Thirty-two years ago my classmates and I graduated into a world that was quite different from the one you enter in 1954. Before settling down to the business of trying to earn a living, I did some more traveling. It was a happier, more hopeful world than the one I saw on a recent journey around the globe. A terrible war to make the world safe for democracy had just ended victoriously. A noble concept, the League of Nations, had emerged from the chaotic aftermath of that elemental struggle. It was the twilight of kings, the dawn of world-wide democracy. Optimism was boundless and people proclaimed that we were on the threshold of the new era of universal and perpetual peace and prosperity.

It didn't turn out that way. It wasn't a threshold after all. Ernest Hemingway soon wrote,

> I was always embarrassed by the words sacred, glorious, and sacrifice and the expression in vain. We had heard them, sometimes standing in the rain almost out of earshot, so that only the shouted words came through, and had read them, on proclamations that were slapped up by billposters over other proclamations, now for a long time, and I had seen nothing sacred, and the sacrifices were like the stockyards at Chicago if nothing was done with the meat except to bury it.

But I don't need to tell you, a generation that was born and nurtured in the depths of depression and came to consciousness in war and to maturity in the confusion of world revolution—I don't need to tell you that your elders have made something of a mess of things. Things didn't turn out as we had thought they would in 1922, and somehow the hope and easy confidence we felt dissolved as more and more the articulate and vocal among us doubted their beliefs and believed their doubts.

Nor do I need to enumerate for you in sepulchral tone the problems that you face. You know them only too well. Perhaps you can solve them. I would not presume to tell you how to do it. This university has given you the tools with which to try. Moreover, even if I would guide you, I could not. What a man knows at fifty that he did not know at twenty is, for the most part, incommunicable. The laws, the aphorisms, the generalizations, the universal truths, the parables and the old saws—all of the observations about life which can be communicated handily in ready, verbal packages—are as well known to a man at twenty who has been attentive as to a man at fifty. He has been told them all, he has read them all, and he has probably repeated them all before he graduates from college; but he has not lived them all.

What he knows at fifty that he did not know at twenty boils down to something like this: The knowledge he has acquired with age is not the knowledge of formulas, or forms of words, but of people, places, actions—a knowledge not gained by words but by touch, sight, sound, victories, failures, sleeplessness, devotion, love—the human experiences and emotions of this earth and of oneself and other men; and perhaps too, a little faith, and a little reverence for things you cannot see.

Nonetheless, I would speak to you not of the past, when my generation held its hopes so high, but rather of the future. And if I cannot advise you on how to solve the momentous problems of your future, perhaps I can venture to suggest some duties and, if you please, some rules of conduct that, it seems to me, devolve upon the educated man. I would speak, then, about the educated man and his government, and about the educated man and his university.

The political organization that goes by the name of the United States of America consists of no fewer than 155,000 governing units, school boards, conservation districts, municipalities, states, the nation, etc. It is operated by some one million elected officials, ranging from mosquito district trustee to President, and by some six million full-time employees. Our government is so large and so complicated that few understand it well and others barely understand it at all. Yet we must try to understand it and to make it function better.

For the power, for good or evil, of this American political organization is virtually beyond measurement. The decisions which it makes, the uses to which it devotes its immense resources, the leadership which it provides on moral as well as material questions, all appear likely to determine the fate of the modern world.

All this is to say that your power is virtually beyond measurement. For it is to you, to your enlightened attention, that American government must look for the sources of its power. You dare not, if I may say so, withhold your attention. For if you do, if those young Americans who have the advantage of education, perspective, and self-discipline do not participate to the fullest extent of their ability, America will stumble, and if America stumbles the world falls.

You know that our record as citizens in recent years has been something less than perfect. Too often our citizens have ignored their duty to their government. Too often they have not even bothered to vote. But this is not all. Participating in government in a democracy does not mean merely casting a ballot on election day. It means much more than that. It means an attitude, a moral view, and a willingness to assume a day-to-day responsibility. How many good citizens do you know who constantly deplore waste, inefficiency, and corruption in government, and who also go out and ring doorbells for candidates they believe in? Not very many. Far more say, "Politics is dirty"—and that is about their only protest about the quality of government, and far more use the word "politician" as a term of opprobrium, disrespect, and dishonor—and this in the land of Washington, Jefferson, and Lincoln. How many respectable citizens do you know who protest loudly about the lawlessness and venality but don't hesitate to fix a traffic ticket? And then there are the unscrupulous for whom anything goes if it is within the letter of the law, or at least not too far outside; the numerous kind for whom *legality* and *morality* are synonyms. "The Fix" has become endemic in our political life.

I would remind you of an axiom of political science: People get the kind of government they deserve. Your public servants serve you right. Our American government may be defined, perhaps, as the government that really cares about the people. Just so, our government demands, it depends upon, the care and the devotion of the people.

Now it is sadly true that there are corrupt officials that don't get caught, if not as many perhaps as the cynical suspect. It is also true that there are at every level of our government able, patient, patriotic, devoted public servants, but all too often their reward is ingratitude, contumely, and lately even investigation. In years gone by we required only of our career servants, upon whom the successful operation of this huge mechanism of government depends, that they serve at a financial sacrifice and that they serve with little glory or public recognition. Increasingly, it appears, we also require them to run the risk of being branded as "subversive," "undesirable," as "security risks." It becomes increasingly hard to attract good men to government, and no wonder. Thoughtful men do not enjoy living in an atmosphere of constant guerrilla warfare and suspicion.

You who have spent four years on this campus know better than most people that your greatest satisfactions, your greatest rewards, resulted from the free interplay of ideas. You know that your most penetrating insights resulted from the exchange and the interchange and clash of ideas. And I would remind you that just as a great university cannot operate in any but an atmosphere of intellectual freedom, neither can a great government. It is the function of the democratic form of government to nurture freedom. No less does the democratic form of government require freedom as the condition in which it can function at all.

I would suggest, then, that it is the duty of an educated man in America today to work actively to put good men into public office—and to defend them there against abuse and the ugly inclination we as human beings have to believe the worst. I would suggest that it is not enough merely to vote but that we, all of us, have the further obligation to think, and to maintain steadfastly the rights of all men to think freely. It is always true that when the citizens of a democracy become apathetic, a power vacuum is created, and corrupt men, or incompetents or worse, rush in to fill it. But today our situation is even more dangerous than that. In ordinary times the corrupt or the incompetent can be suffered for a while and then ejected. But these are no ordinary times. The world's fate now hangs upon how well or how ill we in

America conduct our affairs. And if a bad man is elected trustee of a sanitary district, or if an able man in Washington is left to shift for himself in the face of unjustified attack, then our government is diminished by that much—and even more because others will lose heart from his example. So you as educated, privileged people have a broad responsibility to protect and improve what you have inherited and what you would die to preserve—the concept of government by consent of the governed as the only tolerable way of life.

We in our country have, indeed, placed all of our faith, we have placed all of our hopes, upon the education, the intelligence, and the understanding of our people. We have said that ours is a government conducted by its citizens, and from this it follows that the government will be better conducted if its citizens are educated. It's as simple as that. We believe that the people will find their way to the right solutions, given sufficient information. We believe with Lincoln, "Why should there not be a patient confidence in the ultimate justice of the people?" (although I must confess to having entertained certain private, fleeting doubts upon occasion). We have bet all our chips, if you please, on the intellectual improvement of our people. This is a magnificent gamble—but it is a gamble, for it raises the question whether we have reached the awesome pinnacle of world power we now occupy too soon, before we have sufficiently elevated our national mind to lead the world wisely. Only the educated man entertains doubts, and doubt is the beginning of wisdom; but doubt is not wisdom's fulfillment, and in a time of crisis the man who doubts may fall prey to the strong dumb brute—to the man on horseback.

There is in the moiling masses of Asia a tremendous power, potentially the greatest power on earth, and today our enemies conspire to gain the mastery of this power. They have at their disposal, as we all know, a powerful weapon, for Communism is a perversion of the dream of justice. And while we see its leading attribute as the perversion, the illiterate, the toiling masses still have their eyes fixed on the dream.

We, too, have a powerful weapon, truth, and we gain our strength from our thoughtful citizenry, which seeks and holds the truth with both its heart and its mind. The question is, however, whether we have come to decisive responsibility too early, before we were ready, before we had matured sufficiently. No man can say with certainty. Personally I am optimistic and confident, but this question will not be answered tomorrow; it will be answered in your lifetime, and it will be answered in large part by you, the privileged American.

If I have made your tasks and your responsibilities sound formidable, which indeed they are, may I also remind you that this is what makes the prospects of your careers so exciting. There is a wonderful passage in Emerson—and happily I couldn't lay my hands on it—I'll spare you from it. I hope sometime you will read that essay. It says the time to live is not when everything is serene, but when all is tumult—when the old admits being compared with the new. This is the time of early morning, when it is fresh and exciting. I think this is your generation, I cannot be sure. Change is the order of life and difficulties its meat. You live in a time of historic change and of infinite difficulty. But do not let the difficulties distract you. Face the problems of your time you must, deal with them you must. But do not allow the alarms and excursions and partisanship of our political scene to distract you, do not let even the awful problems of the Atomic Age claim all your attention. Dare, rather, to live your lives fully, boldly; dare to study and to learn, to cultivate the mind and the spirit, even though it isn't fashionable in your community. For though our people become prosperous as never before and though our foreign policy triumphs, these things are but instruments of the proper purpose, the higher purpose, of Western man—the cultivation of the mind and of the spirit.

It would be presumptuous, and out of character, for me to lecture you about your spirit. That I must leave to wiser, and to better men. But perhaps you'll forgive me if I draw on what experiences I have had—I have not always been an unemployed politician, you know—to say a word about intelligence and experience as attributes of the good judgment you will need—the good sense, if you please.

Don't be afraid to learn; to read, to study, to work, to try to know, because at the very best you can know very little. And don't above all things be afraid to think for yourself. Nothing has been, in my judgment, more disheartening about the contemporary scene the last several years in America than the growth of the popularity of unreason—of anti-intellectualism. One thinks of those chanting, screaming crowds that walked over precipices in Germany—and not so long ago. The conformists abominate thought. Thinking implies disagreement and disagreement implies non-conformity and non-conformity implies heresy and heresy implies disloyalty. So obviously thinking must be stopped. This is the routine. But I say to you that bawling is not a substitute for thinking and that reason is not the subversion but the salvation of freedom. And don't be afraid of unpopular positions, of driving upstream. All progress has resulted from people who took unpopular positions. All change is the result of a change in the contemporary state of mind. Don't be afraid of being out of tune with your environment, and above all pray God that you are not afraid to live, to live hard and fast. To my way of thinking it is not the years in your life but the life in your years that count in the long run. You'll have more fun, you'll do more and you'll get more, you'll give more satisfaction the more you know, the more you have worked, and the more you have lived. For yours is a great adventure at a stirring time in the annals of men.

University is a proud, noble and ancient word. Around it cluster all of the values and the traditions which civilized people have for centuries prized more highly. The idea which underlies this university—any university—is greater than any of its physical manifestations; its classrooms, its laboratories, its clubs, its athletic plant, even the particular groups of faculty and students who make up its human element as of any given time. What is this idea? It is that the highest condition of man in this mysterious universe is the freedom of the spirit. And it is only truth that can set the spirit free.

The function of a university is, then, the search for truth and its communication to succeeding generations. Only as that function is performed steadfastly, conscientiously, and without interference, does the university realize its underlying purpose. Only so does the university keep faith with the great humanist tradition of which it is a part. Only so does it merit the honorable name that it bears.

When you depart, think occasionally upon your university's inherent ideas and purposes, as its outward trappings recede. Don't forget that Princeton is a university, as well as *your* university; and that it has obligations to the whole of mankind not just to you—obligations which it can neither ignore nor shirk, and which cannot, consistently with its honorable name and its place in the community of scholarship, be sacrificed to passing passions and prejudices.

The right to the serene pursuit of truth did not descend like manna from heaven; it was won by hard fighting, and the fight goes on and on to the end of time—even as the struggle between good and evil. In this continuing battle for freedom, Princeton and her sister universities are at the farthest front, and so should you be who are Princeton's children. As the archive of the Western mind, as the keeper of Western culture, the university has an obligation to transmit from one generation to the next the heritage of freedom—for freedom is the foundation of Western culture. As graduates of this university, as individuals who have made in it an investment of the golden, irretrievable years of your lives, you have an obligation to oppose the efforts of anyone, for whatever reason or in the service of whatever interest, to divert Princeton or any sister institution from her classic objective. If you are to be true to your democratic traditions and realize your own best selves you cannot, I suggest, do less.

And I hope you will carry away with you some of the wise serenity of the timeless courage, the unhurried objectivity which is the atmosphere of Princeton and which represents the collective imprint of its founders, students, and teachers who have gone before you.

I came here last night in darkness, after an absence of four or five years. I came with an old friend, an old classmate. We drove a little through the campus, after dusk. It was soft, the air fresh with the beginning of spring. I thought of some words that I read here long ago, written by the English poet, Alfred Noyes, who stayed for a time on the Princeton campus. They went something like this if I am not mistaken:

Now lamp-lit gardens in the blue dusk shine
Through dog-wood red and white,
And round the gray quadrangles, line by line,
The windows fill with light,
Where Princeton calls to Magdalen, tower to tower,
Twin lanthorns of the law,
And those cream-white magnolia boughs embower
The halls of old Nassau.[7]

Sentimental? Yes. Nostalgic? Perhaps. Yet beautiful, true. Your days are short here; this is the last of your springs. And now in the serenity and quiet of this lovely place, touch the depths of truth, feel the hem of Heaven. You will go away with old, good friends. And don't forget when you leave why you came.

FRANKLIN D. ROOSEVELT

The "Quarantine" Speech*

The use of a formal, ceremonial occasion as setting for a speech of wide and general public significance is as old, at least, as Pericles' Funeral Oration. The statesman tries to time significant policy statements strategically, but unless he wishes to emphasize an element of crisis, he is likely to choose for his speech an occasion already established. Thus, in the speech reprinted below, President Roosevelt chose the ceremonies dedicating the Outer Drive Bridge in Chicago, October 5, 1937, for making the first public statement, prior to World War II, that the United States was not entirely neutral in affairs outside this hemisphere.

A statement such as this is usually worded so as to permit, or to encourage, those for whom it is intended to understand the significance, but so as not to assert more, specifically, than is appropriate and can be supported at the moment. The student will observe the means, especially the selection and management of language, through which President Roosevelt sought to make a firm statement and yet not an arbitrary one, and the oblique yet relevant terms in which the speaker connected his speech with the formal occasion.

[7] From *Collected Poems,* Vol. III, by Alfred Noyes. Copyright 1913, 1941, by Alfred Noyes. Published by J. B. Lippincott Company.

* Reprinted by permission from *Nothing to Fear; the Selected Addresses of Franklin D. Roosevelt, 1932–1945,* edited with an introduction and historical notes by B. D. Zevin, Foreword by Harry L. Hopkins (Boston, Houghton Mifflin Co., 1946), pp. 111–115.

I am glad to come once again to Chicago and especially to have the opportunity of taking part in the dedication of this important project of civic betterment.

On my trip across the continent and back I have been shown many evidences of the result of common sense co-operation between municipalities and the Federal Government and I have been greeted by tens of thousands of Americans who have told me in every look and word that their material and spiritual well-being has made great strides forward in the past few years.

And yet, as I have seen with my own eyes, the prosperous farms, the thriving factories and the busy railroads, as I have seen the happiness and security and peace which cover our wide land, almost inevitably I have been compelled to contrast our peace with very different scenes being enacted in other parts of the world.

It is because the people of the United States under modern conditions must, for the sake of their own future, give thought to the rest of the world, that I, as the responsible executive head of the Nation, have chosen this great inland city and this gala occasion to speak to you on a subject of definite national importance.

The political situation in the world, which of late has been growing progressively worse, is such as to cause grave concern and anxiety to all the peoples and nations who wish to live in peace and amity with their neighbors.

Some fifteen years ago the hopes of mankind for a continuing era of international peace were raised to great heights when more than sixty nations solemnly pledged themselves not to resort to arms in furtherance of their national aims and policies. The high aspirations expressed in the Briand-Kellogg Peace Pact and the hopes for peace thus raised have of late given way to a haunting fear of calamity. The present reign of terror and international lawlessness began a few years ago.

It began through unjustified interference in the internal affairs of other nations or the invasion of alien territory in violation of treaties; and has now reached a stage where the very foundations of civilization are seriously threatened. The landmarks and traditions which have marked the progress of civilization toward a condition of law, order and justice are being wiped away.

Without a declaration of war and without warning or justification of any kind, civilians, including vast numbers of women and children, are being ruthlessly murdered with bombs from the air. In times of so-called peace, ships are being attacked and sunk by submarines without cause or notice. Nations are fomenting and taking sides in civil warfare in nations that have never done them any harm. Nations claiming freedom for themselves deny it to others.

Innocent peoples, innocent nations, are being cruelly sacrificed to a greed for power and supremacy which is devoid of all sense of justice and humane considerations.

To paraphrase a recent author, "perhaps we foresee a time when men, exultant in the technique of homicide, will rage so hotly over the world that every precious thing will be in danger, every book and picture and harmony, every treasure garnered through two millenniums, the small, the delicate, the defenseless—all will be lost or wrecked or utterly destroyed."

If those things come to pass in other parts of the world, let no one imagine that America will escape, that America may expect mercy, that this Western Hemisphere will not be attacked and that it will continue tranquilly and peacefully to carry on the ethics and the arts of civilization.

If those days come, "there will be no safety by arms, no help from authority, no answer in science. The storm will rage till every flower of culture is trampled and all human beings are leveled in a vast chaos."

If those days are not to come to pass—if we are to have a world in which we can breathe freely and live in amity without fear—the peace-loving nations must make a concerted effort to uphold laws and principles on which alone peace can rest secure.

The peace-loving nations must make a concerted effort in opposition to those violations of treaties and those ignorings of humane instincts which today are creating a state of international anarchy and instability from which there is no escape through mere isolation or neutrality.

Those who cherish their freedom and recognize and respect the equal right of their neighbors to be free and live in peace must work together for the triumph of law and moral principles in order that peace, justice, and confidence may prevail in the world. There must be a return to a belief in the pledged word, in the value of a signed treaty. There must be recognition of the fact that national morality is as vital as private morality.

A bishop wrote me the other day:

> It seems to me that something greatly needs to be said in behalf of ordinary humanity against the present practice of carrying the horrors of war to helpless civilians, especially women and children. It may be that such a protest might be regarded by many, who claim to be realists, as futile, but may it not be that the heart of mankind is so filled with horror at the present needless suffering that that force could be mobilized in sufficient volume to lessen such cruelty in the days ahead. Even though it may take twenty years, which God forbid, for civilization to make effective its corporate protest against this barbarism, surely strong voices may hasten the day.

There is a solidarity and interdependence about the modern world, both technically and morally, which makes its impossible for any nation completely to isolate itself from economic and political upheavals in the rest of the world, especially when such upheavals appear to be spreading and not declining. There can be no stability or peace either within nations or between nations except under laws and moral standards adhered to by all. International anarchy destroys every foundation for peace. It jeopardizes either the immediate or the future security of every nation, large or small. It is, therefore, a matter of vital interest and concern to the people of the United States that the sanctity of international treaties and the maintenance of international morality be restored.

The overwhelming majority of the peoples and nations of the world today want to live in peace. They seek the removal of barriers against trade. They want to exert themselves in industry, in agriculture and in business, that they may increase their wealth through the production of wealth-producing goods rather than striving to produce military planes and bombs and machine guns and cannon for the destruction of human lives and useful property.

In those nations of the world which seem to be piling armament on armament for purposes of aggression, and those other nations which fear acts of aggression against them and their security, a very high proportion of their national income is being spent directly for armaments. It runs from thirty to as high as fifty per cent. We are fortunate. The proportion that we in the United States spend is far less—eleven or twelve per cent.

How happy we are that the circumstances of the moment permit us to put our money into bridges and boulevards, dams and reforestation, the conservation of our soil and many other kinds of useful works rather than into huge standing armies and vast supplies of implements of war.

I am compelled and you are compelled, nevertheless, to look ahead. The peace, the freedom and the security of ninety per cent of the population of the world is being jeopardized by the remaining ten per cent who are threatening a breakdown of all international order and law. Surely the ninety per cent who want to live in peace under law and in accordance with moral standards that have received almost universal acceptance through the centuries, can and must find some way to make their will prevail.

The situation is definitely of universal concern. The questions involved relate not merely to violations of specific provisions of particular treaties; they are questions of war and of peace, of international law and especially of principles of humanity. It is true that they involve definite violations of agreements, and especially of the Covenant of the League of Nations, the Briand-Kellog Pact and the Nine Power Treaty. But they also involve problems of world economy, world security, and world humanity.

It is true that the moral consciousness of the world must recognize the importance of removing injustices and well-founded grievances; but at the same time it must be aroused to the cardinal necessity of honoring sanctity of treaties, of respecting the rights and liberties of others and of putting an end to acts of international aggression.

It seems to be unfortunately true that the epidemic of world lawlessness is spreading.

When an epidemic of physical disease starts to spread, the community approves and joins in a quarantine of the patients in order to protect the health of the community against the spread of the disease.

It is my determination to pursue a policy of peace. It is my determination to adopt every practicable measure to avoid involvement in war. It ought to be inconceivable that in this modern era, and in the face of experience, any nation could be so foolish and ruthless as to run the risk of plunging the whole world into war by invading and violating, in contravention of solemn treaties, the territory of other nations that have done them no real harm and are too weak to protect themselves adequately. Yet the peace of the world and the welfare and security of every nation, including our own, is today being threatened by that very thing.

No nation which refuses to exercise forbearance and to respect the freedom and rights of others can long remain strong and retain the confidence and respect of other nations. No nation ever loses its dignity or its good standing by conciliating its differences, and by exercising great patience with, and consideration for, the rights of other nations.

War is a contagion, whether it be declared or undeclared. It can engulf states and peoples remote from the original scene of hostilities. We are determined to keep out of war, yet we cannot insure ourselves against the disastrous effects of war and the dangers of involvement. We are adopting such measures as will minimize our risk of involvement, but we cannot have complete protection in a world of disorder in which confidence and security have broken down.

If civilization is to survive, the principles of the Prince of Peace must be restored. Trust between nations must be revived.

Most important of all, the will for peace on the part of peace-loving nations must express itself to the end that nations that may be tempted to violate their agreements and the rights of others will desist from such a course. There must be positive endeavors to preserve peace.

America hates war. America hopes for peace. Therefore, America actively engages in the search for peace.

ALFRED E. SMITH

The Cooing Dove*

This speech was given by the Governor of New York in Albany on October 23, 1926, in his fourth successful campaign for the office.

* The text is from *Progressive Democracy,* Henry Moskowitz, ed. (New York, Harcourt, Brace and Company, 1928).

His Republican opponent was Ogden Mills, a man of wealth who was then Congressman from New York. Governor Smith (1873–1944), a son of "the sidewalks of New York," had held public office almost since the beginning of the century in New York City and New York State. He was distinguished by great energy, unsurpassed knowledge of the business of the state, the ability to select excellent advisors, and great skill as a popular speaker. One of his favorite expressions was "Let's look at the record," and he knew the record. What distinguishes this from the usual campaign speech, in which one deplores one's opponent's record and praises one's own, is perhaps Governor Smith's abundant and specific evidence enlivened by the deft use of a catch refrain, taken from his opponent, to give emphasis and structure to the speech.

I will take for my text tonight an extract from a speech recently made by Congressman Mills in which he said, "If I am elected Governor, I will get along with the Legislature like a cooing dove."

Let us look back a little into the history of the State and see how many Governors played the part of a cooing dove in their dealings with the Legislature; see what happened to the State when they did and when they did not.

Theodore Roosevelt did not play the part of the cooing dove. He played the part of the chief executive of the State. He laid his requests before the Legislature and backed them up with all the force and power that he could bring to his command. Had he been the cooing dove, the legislative leaders would have forced upon him the appointment of incompetent people. Had he played the part of the cooing dove, he would have sat quietly by and permitted the Legislature to defeat his proposal for the taxation of special franchises. His fight with the Legislature on that subject is a matter of State history.

Let us look into the administration of Governor Hughes. Surely, the Congressman would not hold that Governor Hughes played the part of a cooing dove. If he had, there would have been no legislation setting up the Public Service Commission and, consequently, no control over the public-utility corporations. It is a matter of history that Governor Hughes, far from playing the part of the cooing dove, went around the State and appealed to the people to sustain him in his argument with the Legislature for the suppression of gambling and called extraordinary sessions of the Legislature for the purpose of compelling the Legislature to act upon his suggestion. He was not playing the part of the cooing dove when he bitterly fought both houses of the Legislature, under the control of his own party, in the interest of primary ballot reform and short ballot. He was not playing the part of the cooing dove when he called on the Senate for the removal of a man whom he deemed to be unfitted for the post of superintendent of insurance, only to be defeated by a Senate, the majority of which belonged to his own party. It was because he did not play the part of the cooing dove that the people of this State in 1910 were so thoroughly disgusted with Republican misrule in the Legislature that the State went overwhelmingly Democratic, electing not only a Democratic Governor but a Democratic Legislature in both branches.

Governor Whitman did not always play the part of the cooing dove. He did not play it when he sought to eliminate useless patronage in the various taxing departments of the State and to consolidate them into one. In this attempted reform he was defeated by the Legislature of his own party, who desired to keep the patronage in the hands of the comptroller. However, when he did play the part of the cooing dove, think of what happened to the State. While in that role, the Legislature put over the direct-settlement clause in the Compensation Law, which gave the insurance companies the power to deal directly with injured men and women; and Congressman Mills himself was the great driving force behind that amendment in the State Senate. While playing the role of the cooing dove, the Legislature succeeded in ripping and tearing apart all the great departments of the State government for patronage purposes and, not content with that, created numerous new boards and commissions for the same purpose. While Governor Whitman acted the role of the cooing dove, the Legislature destroyed the Hughes Water Power Act and made it ineffective for the purposes for which it was originally designed.

In 1919 and 1920, I was Governor. It is a matter of history that I did not play the part of a cooing dove. If I had, there would have been no amendment to the Constitution for the reorganization of the government. There would have been no rent laws for the protection of tenants threatened with dispossess during the housing shortage throughout the State. There would have been no repeal of the direct-settlement clause in the Workmen's Compensation Act that was defrauding injured men and women out of half a million dollars a year, according to the report of a special commissioner appointed to investigate the whole question. Had I gotten along with the Legislature like a cooing dove, I would have written my name on the infamous Lusk Laws that questioned the devotion to this country of our great army of school teachers and subjected our private schools to examinations for license before they could operate. Had I played the role of the cooing dove, I would have agreed to the repeal of the Direct Primary Law and I would have signed, instead of vetoing, millions of dollars of local appropriations not made in the interest of, for the benefit of, the State but made for the benefit of prominent legislators in the localities from which they came.

Governor Miller arrived in the Capital city in 1921. He played the role of the cooing dove, and the infamous Lusk bills became law. The Labor Department was again thrown into chaos by a ripper bill intended to secure for the Republican organization the patronage of that great department. The Public Service Commission Law was amended so as to take away from localities all control over their own contracts with their public-service corporations.

Governor Miller got along with the Legislature like a cooing dove, and certain members of the Legislature received large fees as a result of selling to the State the Black Lake Bridge in St. Lawrence County for $68,000, when the supervisors of the county ten years before had refused to give $18,000 for it and were sustained in their decision by the Court of Appeals. Governor Miller played the role of the cooing dove when he let the Assemblyman from Wayne County dip into the highway maintenance funds for the construction of a bridge over Great Sodus Bay against the policy of the State as defined by law. The cooing-dove act was played overtime when the superintendent of public works let a contract for the construction of the power houses on the canal on a cost-plus basis, which meant that the contractor could not lose.

The Governor and the Legislature were like cooing doves in their desire to get political credit for a low appropriation bill, although to accomplish it they were compelled to neglect the known wants of the State. They neglected to make any appropriation whatever in 1922 for indemnities to the owners of slaughtered tuberculosis cattle. They made inadequate appropriation for the repair and maintenance of existing improved highways. In the interest of a so-called economy, they continued paying rental of $45,000 a year for the State Police Barracks which could have been purchased, and were afterwards, for $480,000. They purchased a piece of land adjoining the State camp at Peekskill on the installment plan, and, spread over a period of years, they were to pay $44,000 more than the land could have been purchased for in cash. They neglected to the tune of more than half a million dollars to make adequate appropriation for the repair and maintenance of the State's equipment on the canal system. They crippled the Labor Department by cutting its appropriations in half. They neglected to the sum of $710,000 to make adequate appropriation for the construction of the hydroelectric plants at Crescent Dam and Visscher's Ferry. They made absolutely no appropriation for grade-crossing removal but did, contrary to accepted custom, appropriate $175,000 for a special grade-crossing elimination in the city of Jamestown. It is impossible to escape the conclusion that this was done as a matter of local favor.

As a result of the cooing-dove performance, the hospitals of the State were neglected to such an extent that two of the hospital commissioners were compelled to resign because according to their statement, the amount of money appropriated for the care, comfort, and cure of the unfortunate insane was totally inadequate. As a result of the cooing-dove performance, the appropriation for the Soldiers' Memorial Hospital at Kings Park was transferred and the Memorial Hospital delayed until I returned to Albany in 1923.

Had I played the role of the cooing dove for the last four years in Albany, what would have happened? There would have been no reorganization of the State government brought to a successful conclusion, after the Legislature and its Republican leaders did every human thing they could to stop it. Had I gotten along with the Legislature like a cooing dove, there would have been no rehabilitation of the Workmen's Compensation Commission and the Department of Labor. There would have been no amendments to the Medical Practice Act in the interest of the public health, because I had to fight for them for four years before they were finally written into the statute books in 1926. There would be less generous support for the public school system of the State were it not for my fight with the Legislature on the Rural School Bill, which brought about the recommendation of the legislative committee for larger quotas to the school districts of the State to provide better salaries for school teachers. If I had pursued the cooing-dove policy, nothing would have happened in the housing situation. Had I gotten along with the Legislature like a cooing dove, the Adirondack power grab would in all human probability have become law. Had I gotten along with the Legislature like a cooing dove, there would have been no automobile regulation. The Republican Assembly defeated it in 1923 and under the force of strong public opinion was compelled to enact it in 1924, but they left the State without its protection for a full year.

When the Legislature convened on the first Wednesday in January 1925, it was made apparent to the people all over the State that the leaders intended to fight. They regarded my election in the fall of 1924 by an overwhelming plurality as something of an accident. It must be fresh in the minds of the people that the Lieutenant Governor himself made the statement that I dared not leave the State. They started in before the Legislature convened in a spirit of open hostility to the executive and continued that hostility in spite of my public invitation to them to co-operate with me in the interest of the great reforms in the government for which I was fighting. Had I been a cooing dove, there would have been no tax reduction, although the platform adopted by the Republican Party at Rochester in 1924 specifically promised it. It must be fresh in the minds of everybody that the Republican leaders on Capitol Hill in the spring of 1925 fought to the death to prevent tax reduction and did it upon the senseless ground that they did not desire a Democratic Governor to have the credit for carrying out their own platform pledge.

Were it not for my vigorous stand, there would be no provision for grade-crossing elimination looking to a speedy elimination of death traps throughout the State. There would be no provision for bond issue to complete uncompleted construction and to give the State the necessary funds to rehabilitate the State hospitals and charitable institutions. This was fought, even after it passed the Legislature under the fire of well-directed public opinion, by the leaders of the Republican party throughout the State. In every Republican county it was overwhelmingly defeated. Congressman Mills and former Governor Miller, challenging me to debate it in New York and Buffalo, turned all the strength of the Republican machine against it.

Had I gotten along with the Legislature like a cooing dove, the State would have no office building and would have to wait years and years for the completion of the Teachers' College and the State Laboratory. Had I gotten along like a cooing dove in 1924, the government of this State would have cost the people upwards of eleven million dollars more as a result of pork-barrel bills passed by the Republican Assembly tending to extend the influence of the party in various sections of the State.

In 1925 we would have lost $10,826,781.04 by the same process. What has Congressman Mills to say about these figures? This is not the first time I have given them out since the campaign opened. He is strangely silent about them. All over the State he is talking the economy of the Republican party and the extravagance of Governor Smith. How does he get away from the clear fact, the figures of which can be found in the office of the comptroller, that had it not been for me in one year alone the Republican majority in the Legislature would have increased the cost of this government by more than ten million dollars, all for purposes not needed for the actual operation of the government? Until he makes some definite explanation of what I here set forth, he ought to stop talking about Republican economy. There is no such thing. They do not know what it means—and those that have any knowledge of it hate it.

One of the greatest reforms in the government of this State now pending is the executive budget. I had to fight the Republican Legislature to the death for that reform. The legislative leaders followed me all over the State making misstatements and false representations. There was no cooing-dove performance about that—if there had been, the people of the State would be denied indefinitely the benefits that will flow from its enactment into constitutional law.

In order to provide proper nursing service and number of attendants in the State hospitals, I had to use all the force that I could bring to my command to put into action the report that came from Dr. Pierce Bailey and Dr. Biggs, who said among other things that the ward-service shortage in the State hospitals was due in great part to the low wages paid by the State; and both of these eminent authorities said that if the State is to give the service it should to the unfortunate wards of the State, the salaries of the nurses and attendants should be made adequate. The work of caring for the insane requires such patience and skill that it should be sufficiently paid for. Carrying out that recommendation cost the State $1,120,000. Had I got along with the Legislature like a cooing dove, the right kind of nurses and attendants for the proper care of the unfortunate insane would not be forthcoming.

It is a matter of history, because I spoke of it at great length over the radio from the Assembly chamber, that had it not been for the vigorous fight that I put up the State of New York would be deprived of some very advantageous spots for parks and parkways. Had I pursued the role of the cooing dove, the owners of the wealthy estates on Long Island would have driven what they call the rabble of New York into the middle of the island and deprived them of the advantage to get near the water. As matters stand, they succeeded with the help of the Republican leaders in delaying, at great cost and inconvenience to the State, the fulfillment of the park program by one full year, thereby defeating the will of the people expressed by over a million majority when they voted the bonds for park purposes.

Had I played the role of the cooing dove there would have been no statutory consolidation of the scattered activities of the State pending the submission of the constitutional amendment. As it was, the Republican leaders by the brute strength of majority control in the Assembly in 1923 and 1924 and in both houses in 1925 and 1926 defeated, as they said they would, every proposal to consolidate departments when it interfered with Republican patronage.

It is known to everybody in the State of New York from Montauk Point to Niagara Falls that I am no cooing dove, and what is more I never will be. Everything I ever got in this world I had to fight for. I did not have it handed to me on a gold platter. Congressman Mills' Campaign Committee classed me with the great majority of the people in the State who had to either work or starve. The same advertisement says that Mills did not have to work. He can essay the cooing-dove role if he likes; I am unable to do it. While I am at the head of the government in this State, I will continue to fight for what I think will be in the best interests of the State and all of her people. I fought with the Congressman a year ago and licked him and all those he was able to muster to aid in his campaign. I think I am entirely within the truth when I say that it is because I have vigorously fought for the betterment of the State government, for the protection of our wards, and for the benefit of all our people that I have spent more years in the executive office than any Governor since the days of Dewitt Clinton. The people of the State of New York want clear-headed, strong-minded fighting men at the head of the government and not doves. Let the doves roost in the eaves of the Capitol—not in the Executive Chamber. So much for the doves, let us pass them up.

BRUCE BARTON

*Which Knew Not Joseph**

Bruce Barton, when he died in 1967, was Honorary Chairman of the Board of the advertising agency Batten, Barton, Durstine and Osborn, with which he had been associated for many years. He had been an

* By permission of the author. The text followed is that in *Modern Speeches*, rev. ed., comp. by Homer D. Lindgren (New York, 1930), pp. 358–364.

editor of two magazines and was an author of a number of books. For four years (1937–1941) he was Republican member of Congress from the Seventeenth New York District. Bruce Barton is regarded as one of the ablest business and political speakers of the 1920's and 1930's.

This speech was delivered to the Public Relations Section of the National Electric Light Association at New York in 1923. The controlling idea of the speech may be phrased as "You must advertise persistently and wisely." To the audience this message was not exactly news. Accordingly, the speaker's task was to present the old idea in a fresh manner and to impart new life and strength to a credo his hearers already regarded with favor. The student should note the methods of arousing and sustaining interest employed and should observe how Mr. Barton handled his partisan audience.

There are two stories—and neither of them is new—which I desire to tell you, because they have a direct application to everyone's business. The first concerns a member of my profession, an advertising man, who was in the employ of a circus. It was his function to precede the circus into various communities, distribute tickets to the editor, put up on the barns pictures of the bearded lady and the man-eating snakes, and finally to get in touch with the proprietor of some store and persuade him to purchase the space on either side of the elephant for his advertisement in the parade.

Coming one day to a crossroads town our friend found that there was only one store. The proprietor did not receive him enthusiastically. "Why should I advertise?" he demanded. "I have been here for twenty years. There isn't a man, woman or child around these parts that doesn't know where I am and what I sell." The advertising man answered very promptly (because in our business if we hesitate we are lost), and he said to the proprietor, pointing across the street, "What is that building over there?" The proprietor answered, "That is the Methodist Episcopal Church." The advertising man said, "How long has that been there?" The proprietor said, "Oh, I don't know; seventy-five years probably." "And yet," exclaimed the advertising man, "they ring the church bell every Sunday morning."

My second story has also a religious flavor. It relates to a gentleman named Joseph, who is now deceased.

Those of you who were brought up on the Bible may have found there some account of his very remarkable business career. Those of you who have not read that book may have heard of Joseph through the works of Rudyard Kipling.

Said Mr. Kipling:

> Who shall doubt the secret hid
> Under Cheops' pyramid
> Was that the contractor did
> Cheops out of several millions.

And that Joseph's sudden rise
To comptroller of supplies
Was a graft of monstrous size
Worked on Pharaoh's swart civilians.

The account of Joseph in the Old Testament is much more complete and to his credit. It tells how he left his country under difficulties and, coming into a strange country, he arose, through his diligence, to become the principal person in the state, second only to the King. Now, gentlemen, the Biblical narrative brings us to that point—the point where Joseph had public relations with all the best-paying jobs—it brings us up to the climax of his career and then it hands us an awful jolt. Without any words of preparation or explanation, it says bluntly:

> And Joseph died, and there arose a new king in Egypt which knew not Joseph.

I submit, gentlemen, that this is one of the most staggering lines which has ever been written in a business biography. Here was a man so famous that everybody knew him and presto, a few people die, a few new ones are born, and *nobody* knows him. The tide of human life has moved on; the king who exalted the friends of Joseph is followed by a king who makes them slaves; all the advertising that the name "Joseph" had enjoyed in one generation is futile and of no avail, because that generation has gone.

Now what has all that to do with you? Very much indeed. When we gathered in this room this afternoon, there were in this country, in bed, sick, several thousand old men. It perhaps is indelicate for me to refer to that fact, but it is a fact, and we are grown up and we have to face these things. On those old men you gentlemen collectively have spent a considerable amount of time and a considerable amount of money. It is to be supposed that you have made some impression upon them regarding your service and your purposes and your necessities. But in this interval, while we have been sitting here, those old men have died and all your time and all your money and whatever you have built up in the way of good will in their minds—*all* your labor and investment have passed out with them.

In the same brief interval, there have been born in this country several thousand lusty boys and girls to whom you gentlemen mean no more than the Einstein theory. They do not know the difference between a Mazda lamp and a stick of Wrigley's chewing gum. Nobody has ever told them that Ivory Soap floats or that children cry for Castoria, or what sort of soap you ought to use if you want to have a skin that people would like to touch. The whole job of giving them the information they are going to need in order to form an intelligent public opinion and to exercise an intelligent influence in the community has to be started from the beginning and done over again.

So the first very simple thing that I would say to you (and it is so simple that it seems to me it ought to be said at every convention of this kind) is that this business of public relations is a very constant business, that the fact that you told your story yesterday should not lead you into the delusion of supposing that you have ever told it. There is probably no fact in the United States that is easier to impress upon people's minds than that Ivory Soap floats, and yet the manufacturers of Ivory Soap think it is not inconsistent or wasteful to spend more than a million dollars a year in repeating that truth over and over again.

Cultivating good will is a day-by-day and hour-by-hour business, gentlemen. Every day and every hour the "king" dies and there arises a new "king" to whom you and all your works mean absolutely nothing.

Now the second very simple thing which I might say to you is that in your dealings with the public, in what you write and say, you must be genuine.

When I came to New York a great many years ago I had a lot of trouble with banks. It was very hard to find any bank that would be willing to accept the very paltry weekly deposit that I wanted to make. Finally I discovered one which was not as closely guarded as the others, and I succeeded for a period of three years in being insulted by the teller every Saturday. At the end of three years when I came to draw out my money I had an audience with the vice-president who wanted personally to insult me. I said to myself, if I live and grow old in this town, some day I think I would like to take a crack at this situation.

And so as the years passed (as they have the habit of doing), and I lived and grew old, one day a bank official came in to us and said he would like to have us do some advertising for him. I said to this banker, "Now you go back to your office and shave off all the side-whiskers that there are in your bank and you take all the high hats and carry them out into the back yard of the bank and put them in a pile and light a match to the pile and burn them up, because I am going to advertise to people that you're human, and it may be a shock to have them come in and find you as you are."

So he went back to his bank and I wrote an advertisement which said:

> There is a young man in this town who is looking for a friendly bank; a bank where the officers will remember his name and where some interest will be shown when he comes in, etc.

It was very successful. It was too successful. It was so successful that we could not control it, and all over the country there broke out a perfect epidemic, a kind of measles, of "friendly banks." Bankers who had not smiled since infancy and who never had or needed an electric fan in their offices suddenly sat up and said, "Why, we are friendly."

Well, our bank dropped out. The competition was too keen. But it culminated, I think, in a letter which I saw and which was mailed by the president of a really very important bank in a large city. I won't attempt to quote it verbatim, but it was to this effect:

> Dear Customer: As I sit here all alone in my office on Christmas Eve thinking of you and how much we love you, I really wish that you and every other customer could come in here personally so I could give you a good sound kiss.

Well, that is a trifle exaggerated, but the fact is this—if you don't feel these things you can't make other people feel them. Emerson said, as you will remember, "What you are thunders so loud I cannot hear what you say." Unless there is back of this desire for better public relations a real conviction, a real genuine feeling that you are in business as a matter of service, not merely as a matter of advertising service—unless there is that, then it is very dangerous, indeed, to attempt to talk to the public. For as sure as you live the public will find you out.

The third very simple thing, and the last thing that I suggest, is this: in dealing with the public the great thing is to deal with them simply, briefly, and in language that they can understand.

Two men delivered speeches about sixty years ago at Gettysburg. One man was the greatest orator of his day, and he spoke for two hours and a half, and probably nobody in the room can remember a single word that he said. The other man spoke for considerably less than five minutes, and every school child has at some time learned Lincoln's Gettysburg Address, and remembers it more or less all his life. Many prayers have been uttered in the world—many long, fine-sounding prayers—but the only prayer that any large majority of people have ever learned is the Lord's Prayer, and it is less than two hundred words long. The same thing is true of the Twenty-third Psalm, and there is hardly a Latin word in it. They are short, simple, easily understood words.

You electric light people have one difficulty. I was in Europe this spring, and I rode a great deal in taxicabs. In England I sat in a taxicab and watched the little clock go around in terms of shillings. Then I flew over to Amsterdam and watched it go around in terms of guilders. Then I went down to Brussels and it went around in terms of francs. Then I went to France and it went around in terms of francs of a different value.

I would sit there trying to divide fifteen into one hundred and multiply it by seven, and wonder just where I was getting off, and I have no doubt now that really I was transported in Europe at a very reasonable cost, but because those meters talked to me in terms that were unfamiliar I never stepped out of a taxicab without having a haunting suspicion that probably I had been "gypped."

In a degree you suffer like those taxicab men. You come to Mrs. Barton and you say, "Buy this washing machine and it will do your washing for just a few cents an hour." She says, "Isn't that wonderful!" She buys it, and at the end of the month she sits with your bill in her hands and she says, "We have run this five hours and that will probably be so and so." Then she opens the bill and finds that she has not run it five hours; that she has run it 41 kws. and 11 amp. and 32 volts, and that amount is not so-and-so but it is $2.67.

Well, that is a matter that I suppose you will eventually straighten out.

Asking an advertising man to talk about advertising at a convention like this is a good deal like asking the doctor to talk about health. I have listened to many such addresses and they are all about the same. The eminent physician says, "Drink plenty of water. Stay outdoors as much as you can. Eat good food. Don't worry. Get eight hours' sleep. And if you have anything the matter with you, call a doctor."

So I say to you that there is a certain technique about this matter of dealing with the public, and if you have anything seriously the matter with you—whether it be a big advertising problem or merely a bad letterhead (and some of you have wretched letterheads)—there probably is some advertising doctor in your town who has made a business of the thing, and it may be worth your while to call him in. But in the meantime, and in this very informal and necessarily general talk, I say to you, "Be genuine, be simple, be brief; talk to people in language that they understand; and finally and most of all, be persistent." You can't expect to advertise in flush times and live on the memory of it when you are hard up. You can't expect to advertise when you are in trouble, or about to be in trouble, and expect to get anything in that direction. It is a day-by-day and hour-by-hour business. If the money that has been thrown away by people who advertised spasmodically was all gathered together it would found and endow the most wonderful home in the world for aged advertising men and their widows. Don't throw any more of that money away. If advertising is worth doing at all, it is worth doing all the time. For every day, gentlemen, the "king" dies, and there arises a new "king" who knows not Joseph.

Notable Speeches from History

EMMELINE G. PANKHURST

The Importance of the Vote*

The long hard struggle for the enfranchisement of women ended successfully in England in 1918 with the passage of legislation giving almost all women the vote, and in this country in 1920 with the ratification of the Nineteenth Amendment to the Constitution. In both countries the achievement was the culmination of years of agitation, in which many women developed conspicuous talents as public speakers. Probably the best of these speakers in England, and the leader of the militant Suffrage movement in its final stages, was Emmeline Pankhurst. Her position and her talents were comparable to those of Susan B. Anthony and Carrie Chapman Catt in this country.

The speech printed below is a characteristic example of the direct appeal to women to help themselves. It was given on March 24, 1908, at one of the regular weekly programs put on by Mrs. Pankhurst's organization, the Women's Social and Political Union, to overflow crowds of London women and visitors from abroad. The speech was subsequently published by the WSPU and distributed widely as a pamphlet.

The student of speaking should observe especially the clear organization which the speaker announces very early and then carries through; the straightforward use of clear specific evidence of the injustices perpetrated against women by man's government and man's laws; and the effective ways in which Mrs. Pankhurst, especially through the development of contrast, establishes a strong sense of the absurdity of woman's situation.

It seems to me a very strange thing that large numbers of women should have met together to-night to consider whether the vote is of importance, while all day long, across the water, in the Peckham Bye-election, men, whether they realise the importance of the vote or not, have been exercising

* Reprinted by permission of Grace Roe, Executrix of Dame Christobel Pankhurst, from *The Importance of the Vote,* published by the Women's Press, 156 Charing Cross Road, London, [1908].

it, and in exercising it settling for women as well as for themselves great questions of public importance.

What, then, is this vote that we are hearing so much about just now, so much more than people have heard in discussion at least, for a great many years? I think we may give the vote a threefold description. We may describe the vote as, first of all, a symbol, secondly, a safeguard, and thirdly, an instrument. It is a symbol of freedom, a symbol of citizenship, a symbol of liberty. It is a safeguard of all those liberties which it symbolises. And in these later days it has come to be regarded more than anything else as an instrument, something with which you can get a great many more things than our forefathers who fought for the vote ever realised as possible to get with it. It seems to me that such a thing is worth fighting for, and women to-day are fighting very strenuously in order to get it.

Wherever masses of people are gathered together there must be government. Government without the vote is more or less a form of tyranny. Government with the vote is more or less representative according to the extent to which the vote is given. In this country they tell us we have representative government. So far as women are concerned, while you have representative government for men, you have despotic government for women. So it is in order that the government of the country may be made really representative, may represent not only all classes of the community, but both sexes of the community, that this struggle for the vote is going on on the part of women.

To-day, women are working very hard for it. And there is no doubt whatever that very, very soon the fight will be over, and victory will be won. Even a Liberal Government will be forced to give votes to women. Gentlemen with Liberal principles have talked about those principles for a very long time, but it is only just lately that women have realised that so far as they are concerned, it began in talk and ended in talk, and that there was absolutely no intention of performance. To-day, we have taken off the mask, and we have made these gentlemen realise that, whether they like it or not, they will have to yield. People ask us, "Why force it on just now? Why give all this trouble to the Liberals, with their great and splendid programme of reform?" Well, we say, after all, they are just the people to whom we ought to give trouble, and who, if they are sincere, ought to be very glad that we are giving them trouble, and forcing them to put their great principles into practice.

To-night, it is not for me to talk to you very much about the agitation. I have to talk to you about what the vote will do for women, and what being deprived of the vote has caused women to suffer. And so I mean to devote most of the time at my disposal to this side of the question. What I am going to say to you to-night is not new. It is what we have been saying at every street corner, at every bye-election during the last eighteen months. It is perfectly well known to many members of my audience, but they will not mind if I repeat for the benefit of those who are here for the first time to-night, those arguments and illustrations with which many of us are so very familiar.

In the first place it is important that women should have the vote in order that in the government of the country the women's point of view should be put forward. It is important for women that in any legislation that affects women equally with men, those who make the laws should be responsible to women in order that they may be forced to consult women and learn women's views when they are contemplating the making or the altering of laws. Very little has been done by legislation for women for many years—for obvious reasons. More and more of the time of Members of Parliament is occupied by the claims which are made on behalf of the people who are organised in various ways in order to promote the interests of their industrial organisations or their political or social organisations. So the Member of Parliament, if he does dimly realise that women have needs, has no time to attend to them, no time to give to the consideration of those needs. His time is fully taken up by attending to the needs of the people who have sent him to Parliament. While a great deal has been done, and a great deal more has been talked about for the benefit of the workers who have votes, yet so far as women are concerned, legislation relating to them has been practically at a standstill. Yet it is not because women have no need, or because their need is not very urgent. There are many laws on the Statute-book to-day which are admittedly out of date, and call for reformation; laws which inflict very grave injustices on women. I want to call the attention of women who are here to-night to a few Acts on the Statue-book which press very hardly and very injuriously on women.

Men politicians are in the habit of talking to women as if there were no laws that affect women. "The fact is," they say, "the home is the place for women. Their interests are the rearing and training of children. These are the things that interest women. Politics have nothing to do with these things, and therefore politics do not concern women." Yet the laws decide how women are to live in marriage, how their children are to be trained and educated, and what the future of their children is to be. All that is decided by Act of Parliament. Let us take a few of these laws, and see what there is to say about them from the women's point of view.

First of all, let us take the marriage laws. They are made by men for women. Let us consider whether they are equal, whether they are just, whether they are wise. What security of maintenance has the married woman? Many a married woman having given up her economic independence in order to marry, how is she compensated for that loss? What security does she get in that marriage for which she gave up economic independence? Take the case of a woman who has been earning a good income. She is told that she ought to give up her employment when she becomes a wife and mother. What does she get in return? All that a married man is obliged by law to do for his wife is to provide for her shelter of some kind, food of some kind, and clothing of some kind. It is left to his good pleasure to decide what the shelter shall be, what the food shall be, what the clothing shall be. It is left to him to decide what money shall be spent on the home, and how it shall be spent; the wife has no voice legally in deciding any of these things. She has no legal claim upon any definite portion of his income. If he is a good man, a conscientious man, he does the right thing. If he is not, if he chooses almost to starve his wife, she has no remedy. What he thinks sufficient is what she has to be content with.

I quite agree, in all these illustrations, that the majority of men are considerably better than the law compels them to be, so the majority of women do not suffer as much as they might suffer if men were all as bad as they might be, but since there are some bad men, some unjust men, don't you agree with me that the law ought to be altered so that those men could be dealt with?

Take what happens to the woman if her husband dies and leaves her a widow, sometimes with little children. If a man is so insensible to his duties as a husband and father when he makes his will, as to leave all his property away from his wife and children, the law allows him to do it. That will is a valid one. So you see that the married woman's position is not a very secure one. It depends entirely on her getting a good ticket in the lottery. If she has a good husband, well and good: if she has a bad one, she has to suffer, and she has no remedy. That is her position as a wife, and it is far from satisfactory.

Now let us look at her position if she has been very unfortunate in marriage, so unfortunate as to get a bad husband, an immoral husband, a vicious husband, a husband unfit to be the father of little children. We turn to the Divorce Court. How is she to get rid of such a man? If a man has got married to a bad wife, and he wants to get rid of her, he has but to prove against her one act of infidelity. But if a woman who is married to a vicious husband wants to get rid of him, not one act nor a thousand acts of infidelity entitle her to a divorce; she must prove either bigamy, desertion, or gross cruelty, in addition to immorality before she can get rid of that man.

Let us consider her position as a mother. We have repeated this so often at our meetings that I think the echo of what we have said must have reached many. By English law no married woman exists as the mother of the child she brings into the world. In the eyes of the law she is not the parent of her child. The child, according to our marriage laws, has only one parent, who can decide the future of the child, who can decide where it shall live, how it shall live, how much shall be spent upon it, how it shall be educated, and what religion it shall profess. That parent is the father.

These are examples of some of the laws that men have made, laws that concern women. I ask you, if women had had the vote, should we have had such laws? If women had had the vote, as men have the vote, we should have had equal laws. We should have had equal laws for divorce, and the law would have said that as Nature has given the children two parents, so the law should recognise that they have two parents.

I have spoken to you about the position of the married woman who does not exist legally as a parent, the parent of her own child. In marriage, children have one parent. Out of marriage children have also one parent. That parent is the mother—the unfortunate mother. She alone is responsible for the future of her child; she alone is punished if her child is neglected and suffers from neglect. But let me give you one illustration. I was in Herefordshire during the bye-election. While I was there, an unmarried mother was brought before the bench of magistrates charged with having neglected her illegitimate child. She was a domestic servant, and had put the child out to nurse. The magistrates—there were colonels and landowners on that bench—did not ask what wages the mother got; they did not ask who the father was or whether he contributed to the support of the child. They sent that woman to prison for three months for having neglected her child. I ask you women here to-night, if women had had some share in the making of laws, don't you think they would have found a way of making all fathers of such children equally responsible with the mothers for the welfare of those children?

Let us take the law of inheritance. Often in this agitation for the vote, we have been told by advanced members of the Liberal Party that to give votes to women on the same terms as those on which men now have the vote, would be to strengthen the influence of property, and to help to continue the existing laws of property.

When you look at the laws of inheritance in this country, it makes you smile to hear that argument. Men have taken very good care that women do not inherit until all male heirs are exhausted. So I do not think these democratic gentlemen are quite sincere in the fears they express lest the influence of property should be very much strengthened if women got the Parliamentary franchise. I do not think it is time yet for women to consider whether the law that the eldest son shall inherit the estate is a just law. I think we should put it in this way: if it is to be the eldest child, let it be the eldest child, whether that child is a man or a woman. I am perfectly certain that if women had had the vote when that law was made, that that is how it would have been settled, if they had decided to have a law of primogeniture.

Well, one could go on giving you many more of these examples. I want now to deal with an objection which may be in the minds of some people here. They say, you are talking about laws made a long time ago. Laws would not now be made like that. If a new law were made, it would of course be equal between the sexes. But as a matter of fact, it seems almost impossible for men, when making new laws that will affect both sexes, to recognise that there is any woman's side at all. Let us take an illustration from the last session of Parliament. For many years we have been accustomed to see pass through the House of Commons and go up to the House of Lords that hardy evergreen, the Deceased Wife's Sister Bill. I used—it is many years since I began reading the debates on that measure—I used to read the speeches carefully through to see if I could find one speech from a man which showed any kind of realisation of the women's side of that Bill. You read eloquent appeals to make it possible for a man who had lost his wife to give to the children the best kind of step-mother that they could have. Who could make a better step-mother, it was asked, than the sister of their deceased mother? By natural ties, by old associations, by her knowledge of the children, she was better fitted than anybody else to take the mother's place. But you never heard of a man who thought there might be another side to the picture. So you have on the Statute-book a piece of legislation which gives relief to the widower who would like to provide a kind step-mother for his children, but does not give relief to the widow who would like to give a kind step-father to her children. I do not think it ever entered into the minds of these legislators that there might be a widow who would like to fulfil the behest of the Old Testament that the living brother should take up his deceased brother's burden and do his duty to his brother's family. So you see, even in this twentieth century, you have got the same spirit.

The man voter and the man legislator see the man's needs first, and do not see the woman's needs. And so it will be until women get the vote. It is well to remember that, in view of what we have been told of what is the value of women's influence. Woman's influence is only effective when men want to do the thing that her influence is supporting.

Now let us look a little to the future. If it ever was important for women to have the vote, it is ten times more important to-day, because you cannot take up a newspaper, you cannot go to a conference, you cannot even go to church, without hearing a great deal of talk about social reform and a demand for social legislation. Of course, it is obvious that that kind of legislation—and the Liberal Government tell us that if they remain in office long enough we are going to have a great deal of it—is of vital importance to women. If we have the right kind of social legislation it will be a very good thing for women and children. If we have the wrong kind of social legislation, we may have the worst kind of tyranny that women have ever known since the world began.

We are hearing about legislation to decide what kind of homes people are to live in. That surely is a question for women. Surely every woman, when she seriously thinks about it, will wonder how men by themselves can have the audacity to think that they can say what homes ought to be without consulting women. Then take education. Since 1870 men have been trying to find out how to educate children. I think that they have not yet realised that if they are ever to find out how to educate children, they will have to take women into their confidence, and try to learn from women some of those lessons that the long experience of ages has taught to them. One cannot wonder that whole sessions of Parliament should be wasted on Education Bills. For, you see, it is only just lately that men have begun to consider education, or to try to learn what the word means. So as we are going to have a great deal more time devoted to education, I think it will be a great economy of time if we get the vote, if only that we may have an opportunity of deciding how girls are to be trained, even in those domestic duties which gentlemen are so fond of reminding us we ought to attend to.

I suppose you all read your newspapers this morning. You saw that a great statesman was pouring out words of wisdom on a subject which one may think might well be regarded as women's business, and which they might at all events have some share in deciding. How it makes one smile to hear a statesman comparing whisky and milk, and discussing whether babies should have natural mother's milk, or humanised milk, or sterilised milk, or what is a sufficient quantity of milk. All these things Cabinet Ministers have discovered that they are quite competent to decide without us. And when a few women ventured to make a small protest and suggested that perhaps it would be best to give to women, the mothers of the race, an opportunity of expressing themselves on the subject, they were characterised as disgraceful, and turned out of the meeting for daring to raise their voices in protest.

Well, we cannot wonder that they are deciding what sort of milk the babies are to have, for it is only a few months ago that they decided how babies should be brought into the world, and who should officiate on the occasion. The Midwives Act, owing to the extreme difficulty and slowness with which, during twelve years of ceaseless agitation, it was carried through Parliament, has made of the women who agitated for it convinced suffragists, since, if they had had votes the measure could have been passed in a couple of years. Even when carried, it was at the expense of many concessions, which, had the women promoting the Bill possessed the franchise, they would certainly have been able to avoid. To this day the midwives have no direct representation on the Central Board which administers the Act. Still, in spite of legislation like that, we find politicians, responsible members of the Government, saying that women ought to have nothing to do with politics, and that they ought not to ask for the vote.

What limits are there to be to this? The same gentleman who thinks himself quite competent to say how babies ought to be fed tells us that he is going to interfere not only with babies, but with their mothers as well. He is going to decide by Act of Parliament whether married women are to be allowed to earn an economic independence, or are to be prevented from doing so. He thinks married women who are earning their living are going to submit to a virtual repeal of the Married Women's Property Act, and to leave it to their husbands to decide whether they shall have any money to spend as they please. To deprive married women of the right to go out to work, to decide this for them without consulting women voters whether they are to earn wages or not, is an act of tyranny to which, I believe, women, patient and long-suffering as they are, will not submit. I hope that even the Liberal women will revolt when it comes to that. But I am not over hopeful about them, because, unfortunately for poor married women who know what it is to need to earn a living, those who decide what the policy of the Liberal women shall be are women who have never had to earn a living, and do not know what it is to have little children dependent upon them and liable to be starved if their mothers are prevented from going out to work. But fortunately the women who are going to be interfered with are not the kind of women who will submit to be interfered with quietly. Women who belong to the aristocracy of industry, women such as the cotton workers in the Lancashire mills, are not likely to be driven into the ranks of the sweated without protest.

What is the reason for the proposal? We are told it is to set these women free, to let them stay at home. I do not see that Mr. John Burns proposes to compensate women for the loss of their earnings. I do not see that he proposes to compel husbands to give to their wives a definite portion of their income for house-keeping purposes. All he proposes is that women, who are earning from ten shillings to thirty shillings a week shall be prevented from earning that income for themselves. He does not propose if the husband is sick or weakly and unable to earn enough to keep the home, to supplement that income by a grant from the State. All he proposes to do is to take away from the married woman the right to earn an income for herself. This, he says, will stop infantile mortality and put an end to race degeneracy. Could you have a greater example of ignorance of the real facts of the situation? I come from Lancashire. I was born in Lancashire. I think I know more about Lancashire than Mr. John Burns. I can tell you this, that infantile mortality and physical degeneration are not found in the homes of the well-paid factory operatives, but they are found in the home of the slum-dweller, the home of the casual labourer, where the mother does not go out to work, but where there is never sufficient income to provide proper food for the child after it is born. That is where babies die—in those horrible slum districts, where families have to be maintained on incomes of from sixteen shillings to eighteen shillings per week, and where you have rents from five shillings to eight shillings per week to pay. What woman can feed her children on an income like that, even if her husband brings the whole of it home?

I know the cotton workers of Lancashire. Not long ago, we were in the Rosendale Valley, Mr. Harcourt's constituency. In that constituency more women earn wages than men. You find daughters earning more money than their fathers. You find wives earning more money than their husbands. They do piece work, and they often earn better wages than the men. I was talking one day to one—a married woman worker whom I met in the train. She was going home from the mill. She had a child three or four years of age, well dressed, very blithe, and looking well fed. I asked her if she worked in the mill. She said, "Yes." I asked her what wages she earned. She said, "Thirty shillings a week." She told me she had other children. "Who looks after the children while you are at work?" "I have a housekeeper," she answered. I said to her, "You are not going to be allowed to work much longer. Mr. John Burns is going to make you stay at home and look after the children." And she said, "I don't know what we shall do then. I suppose we shall have to clem." I don't know whether you all know our Lancashire word "clem." When we say clem, we mean starve. In thousands of homes in Lancashire, if we get Mr. John Burns' proposal carried into law, little children, now well clothed and well fed and well cared for, will have clemmed before many months are over. These women say a shilling that they earn themselves is worth two shillings of their husbands' money, for it is their own. They know far better than their husbands how much money is needed for food, how much is needed to be spent on the home. I do not think there is a woman in Lancashire who does not realise that it is better to earn an income of her own than to be dependent on her husband. They realise it better than women of the upper classes who provide nurses and governesses for their children. I put it to you whether the woman of the working class, so long as she sees that her children are well fed and are well enough cared for, has not as much right as her well-off sister to provide a nurse for her children. We should like to say this to Mr. John Burns, that when women get the vote, they will take very much better care of babies than men have been able to do.

There may be many women in this room to-night who do not know much about the industrial women from practical experience. I want to say something about them. Here in London last year there was the Sweated Industries Exhibition. That Exhibition went to Manchester. It went to Birmingham. The papers were full of it. After it was held there were conferences in the Guildhall, conferences in the large centres of population, and resolutions were carried demanding legislation to deal with the sweating evil. Nothing has come of it all. If any of you women are doubtful about the value of the vote to women, that example ought to be enough. Look at the Government's proposals. What do you get in the forefront of their programme? You get an eight hours' day for miners. But you get nothing for the sweated women. Why is the miner being attended to rather than the sweated worker? The miner is being attended to because he, the miner, has got a vote. You see what the vote will do. You see what political power will do. If women had had the vote there would have been proposals to help the sweated woman worker in the Government programme of this session. I think that women, realising the horrible degradation of these workers, the degradation not only to themselves, but to all of us, caused by that evil of sweating, ought to be eager to get political freedom, in order that something may be done to get for the sweated woman labourer some kind of pay that would enable her to live at least a moral and a decent life.

Now let me say something on another point. Among those here are some professional women. You know what a long and a weary struggle it has been for women to get into the professions, some of which are now open to women. But you all know that the position of women in those professions is not what it ought to be, and is certainly not what it will be when women get the franchise. How difficult it is for women to get posts after they have qualified for them. I know this from practical experience on a public body. Every time we had applications from women for posts open to them, we had applications also from men. Usually the standing of the women was very much higher than that of the men. And yet the women did not get those appointments. The men got them. That would all be altered if we got political equality. It is the political key that is needed to unlock the door.

Again, in all grades of education, certainly in elementary education, women are better qualified for the work than the men. You get a better type of woman. Yet for work equal to that of men, she cannot get equal pay. If women teachers had the Parliamentary vote, those men who go to the House of Commons to represent the interests of teachers would have to represent the interests of women teachers as well as the interests of the men. I think that the gentleman who made the teachers the stepping-stone to office, and who talks at bye-elections about manhood suffrage would have taken up the interests of the women who have paid his wages if he felt that he was responsible to women voters.

Almost everywhere the well-paid posts are given to men. Take the College of Arts. Women art students do quite as well as the men students. And yet after their training is over, women never get any of the posts. All the professorships, all the well-paid posts in the colleges and Universities are given to men. I knew the Head of one of the training colleges in one of our great cities. She said to me: "It makes me feel quite sad to see bright young girls expecting to get their living, and finding after their training is over that they can get nothing to do." The Parliamentary vote will settle that. There is no department of life that you can think of in which the possession of the Parliamentary vote will not make things easier for women than they are to-day.

Then there is the administrative side of public life. We want the vote not merely to get laws made. I think the possession of the Parliamentary vote is very important on the administrative side of politics. I have every reason to think that, because I have just come out of prison. We may congratulate ourselves that the Militant Suffragists, of whom I am one, have at least succeeded in forcing the Government to appoint the first woman inspector of prisons. Of course, it is a very small thing, but it means a very great deal. It means the beginning of prison reform, reform in prison discipline and prison treatment that have been needed for a very long time. Well, when we get the vote, it won't take many years talking about things to get one woman inspector appointed. The immediate result of our getting the vote will be the appointment of many more women inspectors of factories. When I last made inquiries there was only one woman inspector of factories in all Ireland. Yet in Belfast alone, more women and girls are working in factories than men and boys. The need there for inspection is enormous in those linen and jute factories. It is perfectly obvious that when you have women and girls working in factories, if they are to be properly inspected, you must have women inspectors. We shall get them as soon as we are able to get women's interests properly attended to, which we shall only be able to do when we are in possession of the vote.

There is the same thing with regard to education. Women inspectors of schools are greatly needed. Moreover, there is not a single woman Poor Law inspector, nor a woman inspector of workhouses and workhouse hospitals. And yet it is to the workhouses and the workhouse hospitals that we send old people, sick people, and little children. We need to get women relieving officers appointed. I cannot get away from Mr. John Burns. You would think that a working man by origin, and the son of working people, might have been able to realise that it would have been a good thing to have women as relieving officers. And yet when Mr. John Burns, shortly after his appointment, was asked whether he would sanction the appointment of a woman relieving officer in a large Union in the North of England, he said it was not illegal, but it was a practice not to be encouraged. We shall get that position for women. We shall get it made possible for women to manage the business which men have always conceded is the business of women, the care of the sick, the care of the aged, the care of little children.

Well, I could go on giving you many, many more of these illustrations. In fact, the more one thinks about the importance of the vote for women, the more one realises how vital it is. We are finding out new reasons for the vote, new needs for the vote every day in carrying on our agitation.

I hope that there may be a few men and women here who will go away determined at least to give this question more consideration than they have in the past. They will see that we women who are doing so much to get the vote, want it because we realise how much good we can do with it when we have got it. We do not want it in order to boast of how much we have got. We do not want it because we want to imitate men or to be like men. We want it because without it we cannot do that work which it is necessary and right and proper that every man and woman should be ready and willing to undertake in the interests of the community of which they form a part. It has always been the business of women to care for these things, to think of these home questions. I assure you that no woman who enters into this agitation need feel that she has got to give up a single one of her woman's duties in the home. She learns to feel that she is attaching a larger meaning to those duties which have been woman's duties since the race began, and will be till the race has ceased to be. After all, home is a very, very big thing indeed. It is not just your own little home, with its four walls, and your own little private and personal interests that are looked after there. The home is the home of everybody of the nation. No nation can have a proper home unless women as well as men give their best to its building up and to making it what a home ought to be, a place where every single child born into it shall have a fair chance of growing up to be a fit, and a happy, and a useful member of the community.

BOOKER T. WASHINGTON

Atlanta Address*

Booker T. Washington, principal of the Tuskeegee Normal and Industrial Institute, Alabama, from 1881 until his death in 1915, was born a Negro slave and became the leading spokesman of the Negro cause in America. Because of his position and his high reputation, he was invited to speak at the Cotton States Exposition at Atlanta, September 18, 1895. His speech on that occasion is a distinguished example of successful adaptation to a very ticklish situation. He had to gain or hold the respect of the white men and avoid offending their prejudices at the same time that he asserted the dignity and humanity of the Negro. The speech is firm but not belligerent, self-respecting but not aggressive, modest but not fawning, warning but not threatening, fair alike to the white and the Negro. The structure is marked by a refrain drawn from a highly effective but brief story. The student might consider what in the speech would be more appropriate or less appropriate today; and what in it might be received well or ill today by Negroes or by whites.

One-third of the population of the South is of the Negro race. No enterprise seeking the material, civil, or moral welfare of this section can disregard this element of our population and reach the highest success. I but convey to you, Mr. President and Directors, the sentiment of the masses of my race when I say that in no way have the value and manhood of the American Negro been more fittingly and generously recognized than by the managers of this magnificent Exposition at every stage of its progress. It is a recognition

* The text is from *The Negro and the Exposition,* by Alice M. Bacon, Occasional Papers of the Trustees of the John F. Slater Fund, No. 7 (Baltimore, 1896).

that will do more to cement the friendship of the two races than any occurrence since the dawn of our freedom.

Not only this, but the opportunity here afforded will awaken among us a new era of industrial progress. Ignorant and inexperienced, it is not strange that in the first years of our new life we began at the top instead of at the bottom; that a seat in Congress or the state legislature was more sought than real estate or industrial skill; that the political convention or stump speaking had more attractions than starting a dairy farm or truck garden.

A ship lost at sea for many days suddenly sighted a friendly vessel. From the mast of the unfortunate vessel was seen a signal. "Water, water; we die of thirst!" The answer from the friendly vessel at once came back, "Cast down your bucket where you are." A second time the signal, "Water, water; send us water!" ran up from the distressed vessel, and was answered, "Cast down your bucket where you are." And a third and fourth signal for water was answered, "Cast down your bucket where you are." The captain of the distressed vessel, at last heeding the injunction, cast down his bucket, and it came up full of fresh, sparkling water from the mouth of the Amazon River. To those of my race who depend on bettering their condition in a foreign land or who underestimate the importance of cultivating friendly relations with the Southern white man, who is their next-door neighbour, I would say: "Cast down your bucket where you are"—cast it down in making friends in every manly way of the people of all races by whom we are surrounded. Cast it down in agriculture, mechanics, in commerce, in domestic service, and in the professions. And in this connection it is well to bear in mind that whatever other sins the South may be called to bear, when it comes to business, pure and simple, it is in the South that the Negro is given a man's chance in the commercial world, and in nothing is this Exposition more eloquent than in emphasizing this chance. Our greatest danger is that in the great leap from slavery to freedom we may overlook the fact that the masses of us are to live by the productions of our hands, and fail to keep in mind that we shall prosper in proportion as we learn to dignify and glorify common labour and put brains and skill into the common occupations of life; shall prosper in proportion as we learn to draw the line between the superficial and the substantial, the ornamental gewgaws of life and the useful. No race can prosper till it learns that there is as much dignity in tilling a field as in writing a poem. It is at the bottom of life we must begin, and not at the top. Nor should we permit our grievances to overshadow our opportunities.

To those of the white race who look to the incoming of those of foreign birth and strange tongue and habits for the prosperity of the South, were I permitted, I would repeat what I say to my own race, "Cast down your bucket where you are." Cast it down among the eight millions of Negroes whose habits you know, whose fidelity and love you have tested in days when to have proved treacherous meant the ruin of your firesides. Cast down your bucket among these people who have, without strikes and labour wars, tilled your fields, cleared your forests, builded your railroads and cities, brought forth treasures from the bowels of the earth, and helped make possible this magnificent representation of the progress of the South. Casting down your bucket among my people, helping and encouraging them as you are doing on these grounds, and to education of head, hand, and heart, you will find that they will buy your surplus land, make blossom the waste places in your fields, and run your factories. While doing this, you can be sure in the future, as in the past, that you and your families will be surrounded by the most patient, faithful, law-abiding, and unresentful people that the world has seen. As we have proved our loyalty to you in the past, in nursing your children, watching by the sick-bed of your mothers and fathers, and often following them with tear-dimmed eyes to their graves, so in the future, in our humble way, we shall stand by you with a devotion that no foreigner can approach, ready to lay down our lives, if need be, in defence of yours, interlacing our industrial, commercial, civil, and religious life with yours in a way that shall make the interests of both races one. In all things that are purely social we can be as separate as the fingers, yet one as the hand in all things essential to mutual progress.

There is no defence or security for any of us except in the highest intelligence and development of all. If anywhere there are efforts tending to curtail the fullest growth of the Negro, let these efforts be turned into stimulating, encouraging, and making him the most useful and intelligent citizen. Effort or means so invested will pay a thousand per cent. interest. These efforts will be twice blessed—"blessing him that gives and him that takes."

There is no escape, through law of man or God, from the inevitable:

> The laws of changeless justice bind
>   Oppressor with oppressed;
> And close as sin and suffering joined
>   We march to fate abreast.

Nearly sixteen millions of hands will aid you in pulling the load upward, or they will pull against you the load downward. We shall constitute one-third and more of the ignorance and crime of the South, or one-third its intelligence and progress; we shall contribute one-third to the business and industrial prosperity of the South, or we shall prove a veritable body of death, stagnating, depressing, retarding every effort to advance the body politic.

Gentlemen of the Exposition: As we present to you our humble effort at an exhibition of our progress, you must not expect overmuch. Starting thirty years ago with ownership here and there in a few quilts and pumpkins and chickens (gathered from miscellaneous sources), remember the path that has led from these to the inventions and production of agricultural implements, buggies, steam-engines, newspapers, books, statuary, carving, paintings, the management of drug-stores and banks, has not been trodden without contact with thorns and thistles. While we take pride in what we exhibit as a result of our independent efforts, we do not for a moment forget that our part in this exhibition would fall far short of your expectations but for the constant help that has come to our educational life, not only from the Southern states, but especially from Northern philanthropists who have made their gifts a constant stream of blessing and encouragement.

The wisest among my race understand that the agitation of questions of social equality is the extremest folly, and that progress in the enjoyment of all the priviliges that will come to us must be the result of severe and constant struggle rather than of artificial forcing. No race that has anything to contribute to the markets of the world is long in any degree ostracized. It is important and right that all privileges of the law be ours, but it is vastly more important that we be prepared for the exercises of these privileges. The opportunity to earn a dollar in a factory just now is worth infinitely more than the opportunity to spend a dollar in an opera-house.

In conclusion, may I repeat that nothing in thirty years has given us more hope and encouragement, and drawn us so near to you of the white race, as the opportunity offered by this Exposition; and here bending, as it were, over the altar that represents the results of the struggles of your race and mine, both starting practically empty-handed three decades ago, I pledge that, in your effort to work out the great and intricate problem which God has laid at the doors of the South, you shall have at all times the patient, sympathetic help of my race. Only let this be constantly in mind, that while, from representations in these buildings of the product of field, of forest, of mine, of factory, letters, and art, much good will come—yet, far above and beyond material benefits will be that higher good, that let us pray God will come, in a blotting out of sectional differences and racial animosities and suspicions, in a determination, even in the remotest corner, to administer absolute justice; in a willing obedience among all classes to the mandates of law, and in a spirit that will tolerate nothing but the highest equity in the enforcement of law. This, this, coupled with our material prosperity, will bring into our beloved South a new heaven and a new earth.

GEORGE W. CURTIS

The Puritan Principle: Liberty under the Law*

George William Curtis (1824–1892) was one of the most notable American speakers of the last half of the nineteenth century. Always active in public life, he brought to politics ideals and high principles. He always urged that the educated man had a special duty in public life; late in his career, he fought for the enfranchisement of women and for civil service reform.

The speech was made at a dinner at the New England Society of the City of New York, December 22, 1876. Some of the circumstances of the occasion and the effect of the speech were reported by Edward Everett Hale for the Boston Transcript *and printed by G. P. Baker in his* Forms of Public Address, *pp. 430–431.*

About three hundred people attended the dinner, an occasion for which the Society had assembled many men who represented influential interests in New York and in the nation. The country was torn into hostile factions over the outcome of the Hayes-Tilden election controversy. Certain election frauds cast some doubt on whether Hayes had been properly elected. Feeling ran high, and some newspapers even spoke of settling the controversy by civil war. Hale believed that the diners, reflecting the country's intense partisanship, were divided almost equally over the issue; about half were for the Republican candidate, Hayes, and the other half were for the Democratic candidate, Tilden.

Curtis's words made a deep impression on the audience. "Those three hundred men of mark in New York," so Hale related, "went home that night, and went to their business the next day, to say that a court of arbitration must be established to settle that controversy. In that moment of Mr. Curtis's triumph, as I believe, it was settled. This is certain: that from that moment, as every careful reader may find today, the whole tone of the press of all parties in the city of New York expressed the belief which he expressed then, and which that assembly of leaders approved by their cheers. And from that moment to this moment there has been no more talk of civil war."

The student should give special attention to the means Curtis used to sidestep the intense rivalry of the opposing groups, and observe carefully the methods of suggestion employed.

Mr. President and Gentlemen of the New England Society:
It was Izaak Walton in his "Angler" who said that Dr. Botelier was accus-

* The text is from *Orations and Addresses,* by G. W. Curtis (New York, 1894), I.

tomed to remark "that doubtless God might have made a better berry than the strawberry, but doubtless He never did." And I suppose I speak the secret feeling of this festive company when I say that doubtless there might have been a better place to be born in than New England, but doubtless no such place exists. And if any skeptic should reply that our very presence here would seem to indicate that doubtless, also, New England is as good a place to leave as to stay in, I should reply to him that, on the contrary, our presence is but an added glory of our mother. It is an illustration of that devout, missionary spirit, of the willingness in which she has trained us to share with others the blessings that we have received, and to circle the continent, to girdle the globe, with the strength of New England character and the purity of New England principles. Even the Knickerbockers, Mr. President—in whose stately and splendid city we are at this moment assembled, and assembled of right because it is our home—even they would doubtless concede that much of the state and splendor of this city is due to the enterprise, the industry, and the genius of those whom their first historian describes as "losel Yankees." Sir, they grace our feast with their presence; they will enliven it, I am sure, with their eloquence and wit. Our tables are rich with the flowers grown in their soil; but there is one flower that we do not see, one flower whose perfume fills a continent, which has blossomed for more than two centuries and a half with ever-increasing and deepening beauty—a flower which blooms at this moment, on this wintry night, in never-fading freshness in a million of true hearts, from the snow-clad Katahdin to the warm Golden Gate of the South Sea, and over its waters to the isles of the East and the land of Prester John—the flower of flowers, the Pilgrim's "Mayflower."

Well, sir, holding that flower in my hand at this moment, I say that the day we celebrate commemorates the introduction upon this continent of the master principle of its civilization. I do not forget that we are a nation of many nationalities. I do not forget that there are gentlemen at this board who wear the flower of other nations close upon their hearts. I remember the forget-me-nots of Germany, and I know that the race which keeps "watch upon the Rhine" keeps watch also upon the Mississippi and the Lakes. I recall—how could I forget?—the delicate shamrock; for there "came to this beach a poor exile of Erin," and on this beach, with his native modesty, "he still sings his bold anthem of Erin go Bragh." I remember surely, sir, the lily—too often the tiger-lily—of France and the thistle of Scotland; I recall the daisy and the rose of England; and, sir, in Switzerland, high upon the Alps, on the very edge of the glacier, the highest flower that grows in Europe, is the rare *edelweiss*. It is in Europe; we are in America. And here in America, higher than shamrock or thistle, higher than rose, lily or daisy, higher than the highest, blooms the perennial Mayflower. For, sir and gentlemen, it is the English-speaking race that has molded the destiny of this continent; and the Puritan influence is the strongest influence that has acted upon it.

I am surely not here to assert that the men who have represented that influence have always been men whose spirit was blended of sweetness and light. I confess truly their hardness, their prejudice, their narrowness. All this I know: Charles Stuart could bow more blandly, could dance more gracefully than John Milton; and the cavalier King looks out from the canvas of Vandyke with a more romantic beauty of flowing lovelocks than hung upon the brows of Edward Winslow, the only Pilgrim father whose portrait comes down to us. But, sir, we estimate the cause beyond the man. Not even is the gracious spirit of Christianity itself measured by its confessors. If we would see the actual force, the creative power of the Pilgrim principle, we are not to look at the company who came over in the cabin of the *Mayflower;* we are to look upon the forty millions who fill this continent from sea to sea. The *Mayflower,* sir, brought seed and not a harvest. In a century and a half, the religious restrictions of the Puritans had grown into absolute religious liberty, and in two centuries it had burst beyond the limits of New England, and John Carver of the *Mayflower,* had ripened into Abraham Lincoln, of the Illinois prairie. Why, gentlemen, if you would see the most conclusive proof of the power of this principle, you have but to observe that the local distinctive title of New-Englanders has now become that of every man in the country. Every man who hears me, from whatever State in the Union, is, to Europe, a Yankee, and today the United States are but the "Universal Yankee Nation."

Do you ask me, then, what is this Puritan principle? Do you ask me whether it is as good for today as for yesterday; whether it is good for every national emergency; whether it is good for the situation of this hour? I think we need neither doubt nor fear. The Puritan principle in its essence is simply individual freedom. From that spring religious liberty and political equality. The free State, the free Church, the free School— these are the triple armor of American nationality, of American security. But the Pilgrims, while they have stood above all men for their idea of liberty, have always asserted liberty *under law* and never separated it from law. John Robinson, in the letter that he wrote the Pilgrims when they sailed, said these words, that well, sir, might be written in gold around the cornice of that future banqueting-hall to which you have alluded, "You know that the image of the Lord's dignity and authority which the magistry beareth is honorable in how mean person soever." This is the Puritan principle. Those men stood for liberty under the law. They had tossed long upon a wintry sea; their minds were full of images derived from their voyages; they knew that the will of the people alone is but a gale smiting a rudderless and sailless ship, and hurling it, a mass of wreck, upon the rocks. But the will of the people, subject to law, is the same gale filling the trim canvas of a ship that minds the helm, bearing it over yawning and awful abysses of ocean safely to port.

Now, gentlemen, in this country the Puritan principle in its development has advanced to this point, that it provides us a lawful remedy for every emergency that may arise. I stand here as a son of New England. In every fiber of my being am I child of the Pilgrims. The most knightly of all the gentlemen at Elizabeth's court said to the young poet, when he would write an immortal song, "Look into thy heart and write." And I, sir and brothers, if, looking into my own heart at this moment, I might dare to think that what I find written there is written also upon the heart of my mother, clad in her snows at home, her voice in this hour would be a message spoken from the land of the Pilgrims to the capital of this nation—a message like that which Patrick Henry sent from Virginia to Massachusetts when he heard of Concord and Lexington: "I am not a Virginian, I am an American." And so, gentlemen, at this hour, we are not Republicans, we are not Democrats, we are Americans.

The voice of New England, I believe, going to the capital, would be this, that neither is the Republican Senate to insist upon its exclusive partisan way, nor is the Democratic House to insist upon its exclusive partisan way, but Senate and House, representing the American people and the American people only, in the light of the Constitution and by the authority of the law, are to provide a way over which a President, be he Republican or be he Democrat, shall pass unchallenged to his chair. Ah! gentlemen—think not, Mr. President, that I am forgetting the occasion or its amenities. I am remembering the Puritans; I am remembering Plymouth Rock, and the virtues that made it illustrious. But we, gentlemen, are to imitate those virtues, as our toast says, only by being greater than the men who stood upon that rock. As this gay and luxurious banquet to their scant and severe fare, so must our virtues, to be worthy of them, be greater and richer than theirs. And as we are three centuries older, so should we be three centuries wiser than they.

Sons of the Pilgrims, you are not to level forests, you are not to war with savage men and savage beasts, you are not to tame a continent, nor even found a State. Our task is nobler, is diviner. Our task, sir, is to reconcile a nation. It is to curb the fury of party spirit. It is to introduce a loftier and manlier tone everywhere into our political life. It is to educate every boy and every girl, and then leave them perfectly free to go from any schoolhouse to any church. Above all, sir, it is to protect absolutely the equal rights of the poorest and the richest, of the most ignorant and the most intelligent citizen, and it is to stand forth, brethren, as a triple wall of brass, around our native land, against the mad blows of violence or the fatal dry-rot of fraud. And at this moment, sir, the grave and august shades of the forefathers whom we invoke bend over us in benediction as they call us to this sublime task. This, brothers and friends, this is to imitate the virtues of our forefathers; this is to make our day as glorious as theirs.

THOMAS HENRY HUXLEY

The Method of Scientific Investigation

Thomas Henry Huxley (1825–1895), a graduate of the University of London, one of the great biologists of Darwin's time, and a potent figure in securing educational reforms, is usually regarded as a master of expository methods.

This speech is one of a number of lectures addressed to English workingmen in the 1860's. Reported in shorthand, the lecture stands, so Huxley tells us, as it was delivered.

Lecture I was entitled "The Present Condition of Organic Nature"; Lecture II was called "The Past Condition of Organic Nature." Huxley's special title of Lecture III shows its relation to the preceding addresses: "The Method by Which the Causes of the Present and the Past Conditions of Organic Nature Are to be Discovered."

In the two preceding lectures I have endeavoured to indicate to you the extent of the subject matter of the inquiry upon which we are engaged; and having thus acquired some conception of the past and present phenomena of organic nature, I must now turn to that which constitutes the great problem which we have set before ourselves;—I mean, the question of what knowledge we have of the causes of these phenomena of organic nature, and how such knowledge is obtainable.

Here, on the threshold of the inquiry, an objection meets us. There are in the world a number of extremely worthy, well-meaning persons, whose judgments and opinions are entitled to the utmost respect on account of their sincerity, who are of the opinion that vital phenomena and especially all questions relating to the origin of vital phenomena, are questions quite apart from the ordinary run of inquiry, and are, by their very nature, placed out of our reach. They say that all these phenomena originated miraculously, or in some way totally different from the ordinary course of nature, and that therefore they conceive it to be futile, not to say presumptuous, to attempt to inquire into them.

To such sincere and earnest persons, I would only say, that a question of this kind is not to be shelved upon theoretical or speculative grounds. You may remember the story of the Sophist who demonstrated to Diogenes in the most complete and satisfactory manner that he could not walk; that, in fact, all motion was an impossibility; and that Diogenes refuted him by simply getting up and walking round his tub. So, in the same way, the man of science replies to objections of this kind, by simply getting up and walking onward, and showing what science has done and is doing—by pointing to that immense mass of facts which have been ascertained as systematized under the forms of the great doctrines of morphology, of development, or distribution, and the like. He sees an enormous mass of facts and laws relating to organic beings, which stand on the same good sound foundation as every other natural law. With this mass of facts and laws before us, therefore, seeing that, as far as organic matters have hitherto been accessible and studied, they have shown themselves capable of yielding to scientific investigation, we may accept this as proof that order and law reign there as well as in the rest of Nature. The man of science says nothing to objectors of this sort, but supposes that we can and shall walk to a knowledge of the origin of organic nature, in the same way that we have walked to knowledge of the laws and principles of the inorganic world.

But there are objectors who say the same from ignorance and ill-will. To such I would reply that the objection comes ill from them, and that the real presumption, I may almost say the real blasphemy, in this matter, is in the attempt to limit that inquiry into the causes of phenomena, which is the source of all human blessings, and from which has sprung all human prosperity and progress; for, after all, we can accomplish comparatively little; the limited range of our own faculties bounds us on every side,—the field of our powers of observation is small enough, and he who endeavours to narrow the sphere of our inquiries is only pursuing a course that is likely to produce the greatest harm to his fellow men.

But now, assuming, as we all do, I hope, that these phenomena are properly accessible to inquiry, and setting out upon our search into the causes of the phenomena of organic nature, or at any rate, setting out to discover how much we at present know upon these abstruse matters, the question arises as to what is to be our course of proceeding, and what method we must lay down for our guidance. I reply to that question, that our method must be exactly the same as that which is pursued in any other scientific inquiry, the method of scientific investigation being the same for all orders of facts and phenomena whatsoever. . . .

The method of scientific investigation is nothing but the expression of the necessary mode of working of the human mind. It is simply the mode in which all phenomena are reasoned about, rendered precise and exact. There is no more difference, but there is just the same kind of difference, between the mental operations of a man of science and those of an ordinary person, as there is between the operations and methods of a baker or of a butcher weighing out his goods in common scales, and the operations of a chemist in performing a difficult and complex analysis by means of his balance and finely-graduated weights. It is not that the action of the scales in the one case, and the balance of the other, differ in the principles of their construction or manner of working; but the beam of one is set on an infinitely finer axis than the other, and of course turns by the addition of a much smaller weight.

You will understand this better, perhaps, if I give you some familiar example. You have all heard it repeated, I dare say, that men of science work by means of induction and deduction, and that by the help of these operations, they, in a sort of sense, wring from Nature certain other things, which are called natural laws, and causes, and that out of these, by some cunning skill of their own, they build up hypotheses and theories. And it is imagined by many, that the operations of the common mind can be by no means compared with these processes, and that they have to be acquired by a sort of special apprenticeship to the craft. To hear all these large words, you would think that the mind of a man of science must be constituted differently from that of his fellow men; but if you will not be frightened by terms, you will discover that you are quite wrong, and that all these terrible apparatus are being used by yourselves every day and every hour of your lives.

There is a well-known incident in one of Molière's plays, where the author makes the hero express unbounded delight on being told that he had been talking prose during the whole of his life. In the same way, I trust that you will take comfort, and be delighted with yourselves, on the discovery that you have been acting on the principles of inductive and deductive philosophy during the same period. Probably there is not one here who has not in the course of the day had occasion to set in motion a complex train of reasoning, of the very same kind, though differing of course in degree, as that which a scientific man goes through in tracing the causes of natural phenomena.

A very trivial circumstance will serve to exemplify this. Suppose you go into a fruiterer's shop, wanting an apple,—you take up one, and on biting it, you find it is sour; you look at it, and see that it is hard and green. You take up another one, and that too is hard, green, and sour. The shopman offers you a third; but, before biting it, you examine it, and find that it is hard and green, and you immediately say that you will not have it, as it must be sour, like those that you have already tried.

Nothing can be more simple than that, you think; but if you will take the trouble to analyse and trace out into its logical elements what has been done by the mind, you will be greatly surprised. In the first place, you have performed the operation of induction. You found that, in two experiences, hardness and greenness in apples went together with sourness. It was so in the first case, and it was confirmed by the second. True, it is a very small basis, but still is enough to make an induction from; you generalise the facts, and you expect to find sourness in apples where you get hardness and greenness. You found that a general law, that all hard and green apples are sour; and that, so far as it goes, is a perfect induction. Well, having got your natural law in this way, when you are offered another apple which you find is hard and green, you say, "All hard and green apples are sour; this apple is hard and green, therefore this apple is sour." The train of reasoning is what logicians call a syllogism, and has all its various parts and terms,—its major premises, its minor premises, and its conclusion. And, by the help of further reasoning, which, if drawn out, would have to be exhibited in two or three other syllogisms, you arrive at your final determination, "I will not have that apple." So that, you see, you have, in the first place, established a law by induction, and upon that you have founded a deduction, and reasoned out the special conclusion of the particular case. Well now, suppose, having got your law, that at some time afterwards, you are discussing the qualities of apples with a friend: you will say to him, "It is a very curious thing,—but I find that all hard and green apples are sour!" Your friend says to you, "But how do you know that?" You at once reply, "Oh, because I have tried them over and over again, and have always found them to be so." Well, if we were talking science instead of common sense, we should call that an experimental verification. And, if still opposed, you go further, and say, "I have heard from the people in Somersetshire and Devonshire, where a large number of apples are grown, that they have observed the same thing. It is also found to be the case in Normandy, and in North America. In short, I find it to be the universal experience of mankind wherever attention has been directed to the subject." Whereupon, your friend, unless he is a very unreasonable man, agrees with you, and is convinced that you are quite right in the conclusion you have drawn. He believes, although perhaps he does not know he believes it, that the more extensive verifications are,—that the more frequently experiments have been made, and results of the same kind arrived at,—that the more varied the conditions under which the same results are attained, the more certain is the ultimate conclusion, and he disputes the question no further. He sees that the experiment has been tried under all sorts of conditions, as to time, place, and people, with the same result; and he says with you, therefore, that the law you have laid down must be a good one, and he must believe it.

In science we do the same thing; the philosopher exercises precisely the same faculties, though in a much more delicate manner. In scientific inquiry it becomes a matter of duty to expose a supposed law to every possible kind of verification, and to take care, moreover, that this is done intentionally, and not left to a mere accident, as in the case of the apples. And in science, as in common life, our confidence in a law is in exact proportion to the absence of variation in the results of our experimental verifications. For instance, if you let go your grasp of an article you may have in your hand, it will immediately fall to the ground. That is a very common verification of one of the best established laws of nature—that of gravitation. The method by which men of science establish the existence of that law is exactly the same as that by which we have established the trivial proposition about the sourness of hard and green apples. But we believe it in such an extensive, thorough, and unhesitating manner because the universal experience of mankind verifies it, and we can verify it ourselves at any time; and that is the strongest possible foundation on which any natural law can rest.

So much, then, by way of proof that the method of establishing laws in science is exactly the same as that pursued in common life. Let us now turn to another matter (though really it is but another phase of the same question), and that is the method by which, from the relations of certain phenomena, we prove that some stand in the position of causes towards the others.

I want to put the case clearly before you, and I will therefore show you what I mean by another familiar example. I will suppose that one of you, on coming down in the morning to the parlour of your house, finds that a tea-pot and some spoons which had been left in the room on the previous evening are gone—the window is open, and you observe the mark of a dirty hand on the window-frame, and perhaps, in addition to that, you notice the impress of a hob-nailed shoe on the gravel outside. All these phenomena have struck your attention instantly, and before two seconds have passed you say, "Oh, somebody has broken open the window, entered the room, and run off with the spoons and the tea-pot!" That speech is out of your mouth in a moment. And you will probably add, "I know there has; I am quite sure of it!" You mean to say exactly what you know; but in reality you are giving expression to what is, in all essential particulars, an hypothesis. You do not *know* it at all; it is nothing but an hypothesis rapidly framed in your own mind. And it is an hypothesis founded on a long train of inductions and deductions.

What are those inductions and deductions, and how have you got at this hypothesis? You have observed, in the first place, that the window is open; but by a train of reasoning involving many inductions and deductions, you have probably arrived long before at the general law—and a very good one it is—that windows do not open of themselves; and you therefore concluded that something has opened the window. A second general law that you have arrived at in the same way is, that tea-pots and spoons do not go out of windows spontaneously, and you are satisfied that, as they are not now where you left them, they have been removed. In the third place, you look at the marks on the window-sill, and the shoe-marks outside, and you say that in all previous experience the former kind of mark has never been produced by anything else but the hand of a human being; and the same experience shows that no other animal but man at present wears shoes with hob-nails in them such as would produce the marks on the gravel. I do not know, even if we could discover any of those "missing links" that are talked about, that they would help us to any other conclusion! At any rate the law which states our present experience is strong enough for my present purpose. You next reach the conclusion, that as these kinds of marks have not been left by any other animals than men, or are liable to be formed in any other way than by a man's hand and shoe, the marks in question have been formed by a man in that way. You have, further, a general law, founded on observation and experience, and that, too, is, I am sorry to say, a very universal and unimpeachable one—that some men are thieves; and you assume at once from all these premises—

and that is what constitutes your hypothesis—that the man who made the marks outside and on the window-sill, opened the window, got into the room, and stole your tea-pot and spoons. You have now arrived at a *vera causa*—you have assumed a cause which, it is plain, is competent to produce all the phenomena you have observed. You can explained all these phenomena only by the hypothesis of a thief. But that is a hypothetical conclusion, of the justice of which you have no absolute proof at all; it is only rendered highly probable by a series of inductive and deductive reasonings.

I suppose your first action, assuming that you are a man of ordinary common sense, and that you have established this hypothesis to your own satisfaction, will very likely be to go off for the police, and set them on the track of the burglar, with the view to the recovery of your property. But just as you are starting with this object, some person comes in, and on learning what you are about, says, "My good friend, you are going on a great deal too fast. How do you know that the man who really made the marks took the spoons? It might have been a monkey that took them, and the man may have merely looked in afterwards." You would probably reply, "Well, that is all very well, but you see it is contrary to all experience of the way tea-pots and spoons are abstracted; so that, at any rate, your hypothesis is less probable than mine." While you are talking the thing over in this way, another friend arrives, one of that good kind of people that I was talking of a little while ago. And he might say, "Oh, my dear sir, you are certainly going on a great deal too fast. You are most presumptuous. You admit that all these occurrences took place when you were fast asleep, at a time when you could not possibly have known anything about what was taking place. How do you know that the laws of Nature are not suspended during the night? It may be that there has been some kind of supernatural interference in this case." In point of fact, he declares that your hypothesis is one of which you cannot at all demonstrate the truth, and that you are by no means sure that the laws of Nature are the same when you are asleep as when you are awake.

Well, now, you cannot at the moment answer that kind of reasoning. You feel that your worthy friend has you somewhat at a disadvantage. You will feel perfectly convinced in your own mind, however, that you are quite right, and you say to him, "My good friend, I can only be guided by the natural probabilities of the case, and if you will be kind enough to stand aside and permit me to pass, I will go and fetch the police." Well, we will suppose that your journey is successful, and that by good luck you meet with a policeman; that eventually the burglar is found with your property on his person, and the marks correspond to his hand and to his boots. Probably any jury would consider those facts a very good experimental verification of your hypothesis, touching the cause of the abnormal phenomena observed in your parlour, and would act accordingly.

Now in this suppositious case, I have taken phenomena of a very common kind, in order that you might see what are the different steps in an ordinary process of reasoning, if you will only take the trouble to analyze it carefully. All the operations I have described, you will see, are involved in the mind of any man of sense in leading him to a conclusion as to the course he should take in order to make good a robbery and punish the offender. I say that you are led, in that case, to your conclusion by exactly the same train of reasoning as that which a man of science pursues when he is endeavouring to discover the origin and laws of the most occult phenomena. The process is, and always must be, the same; and precisely the same mode of reasoning was employed by Newton and Laplace in their endeavours to discover and define the causes of the movements of the heavenly bodies, as you, with your own common sense, would employ to detect a burglar. The only difference is, that the nature of the inquiry being more abstruse, every step has to be most carefully watched, so that there may not be a single crack or flaw in your hypothesis. A flaw or crack in many of the hypotheses of daily life may be of little or no moment as affecting the general correctness of the conclusions at which we may arrive; but, in a scientific inquiry, a fallacy, great or small, is always of importance, and is sure to be in the long run constantly productive of mischievous, if not fatal, results.

Do not allow yourselves to be misled by the common notion that an hypothesis is untrustworthy simply because it is an hypothesis. It is often urged, in respect to some scientific conclusion, that, after all, it is only an hypothesis. But what more have we to guide us in nine-tenths of the most important affairs of daily life than hypotheses, and often very ill-based ones? So that in science, where the evidence of an hypothesis is subjected to the most rigid examination, we may rightly pursue the same course. You have hypotheses and hypotheses. A man may say, if he likes, that the moon is made of green cheese: that is an hypothesis. But another man, who has devoted a great deal of time and attention to the subject, and availed himself of the most powerful telescopes and the results of the observations of others, declares that in his opinion it is probably composed of materials very similar to those of which our own earth is made up: and that is also only an hypothesis. But I need not tell you that there is an enormous difference in the value of the two hypotheses. That one which is based on sound scientific knowledge is sure to have a corresponding value; and that which is a mere hasty random guess is likely to have but little value. Every great step in our progress in discovering causes has been made in exactly the same way as that which I have detailed to you. A person observing the occurrence of certain facts and phenomena asks, naturally enough, what process, what kind of operation known to occur in Nature applied to the particular case, will unravel and explain the mystery? Hence you have the scientific hypothesis; and its value will be proportionate to the care and completeness with which its basis has been tested and verified. It is in these matters as in the commonest affairs of practical life: the guess of the fool will be folly, while the guess of the wise man will contain wisdom. In all cases, you see that the value of the result depends on the patience and faithfulness with which the investigator applies to his hypothesis every possible kind of verification.

. . . In reality there are but few things that can be more important for you to understand than the mental processes and the means by which we obtain scientific conclusions and theories.

PERICLES

Funeral Oration for the Athenian Soldiers*

Thucydides, the Greek historian, in his History of the Peloponnesian War, *that thirty-year life-and-death struggle between Athens and Sparta, included many speeches to liven up his story and to reveal the motivations and political purposes bearing on the war. Of them he wrote, "With reference to the speeches in this history, . . . some I heard myself, others I got from various quarters; it was in all cases difficult to carry them word for word in one's memory, so my habit has been to make the speakers say what was in my opinion demanded of them by the various occasions, of course adhering as closely as possible to the general sense of what they really said." The reader of Pericles' Funeral Oration as reported by the historian will probably wish to suppose that it was one of the speeches which Thucydides heard in person, for it does justice to Pericles' reputation for surpassing eloquence and leadership. It has become the archetype of eulogistic orations in both its praise of the dead and its inspiration to the living. What Pericles says of free democratic Athens, free democratic America, for the most part, would choose to have said of her; and what he praises in Athens' fallen soldiers would do appropriate credit to the honored dead in any free land in any age. We present Thucydides' account of the occasion, followed by the text of the speech.*

In the same winter the Athenians gave a funeral at the public cost to those who had first fallen in this war. It was a custom of their ancestors, and the manner of it is as follows. Three days before the ceremony, the bones of the dead are laid out in a tent which has been erected; and their friends bring to their relatives such offerings as they please. In the funeral procession

* The translation is the one by Richard Crawley, first published in 1876, revised by R. Feltham in 1903, and now available in Everyman and Modern Library editions.

cypress coffins are borne in cars, one for each tribe; the bones of the deceased being placed in the coffin of their tribe. Among these is carried one empty bier decked for the missing, that is, for those whose bodies could not be recovered. Any citizen or stranger who pleases, joins in the procession; and the female relatives are there to wail at the burial. The dead are laid in the public sepulchre in the beautiful suburb of the city, in which those who fall in war are always buried; with the exception of those slain at Marathon, who for their singular and extraordinary valour were interred on the spot where they fell. After the bodies have been laid in the earth, a man chosen by the state, of approved wisdom and eminent reputation, pronounces over them an appropriate panegyric; after which all retire. Such is the manner of the burying; and throughout the whole of the war, whenever the occasion arose, the established custom was observed. Meanwhile these were the first that had fallen, and Pericles, son of Xanthippus, was chosen to pronounce their eulogium. When the proper time arrived, he advanced from the sepulchre to an elevated platform in order to be heard by as many of the crowd as possible, and spoke as follows:

Most of my predecessors in this place have commended him who made this speech part of the law, telling us that it is well that it should be delivered at the burial of those who fall in battle. For myself, I should have thought that the worth which had displayed itself in deeds, would be sufficiently rewarded by honours also shown by deeds; such as you now see in this funeral prepared at the people's cost. And I could have wished that the reputations of many brave men were not to be imperilled in the mouth of a single individual, to stand or fall according as he spoke well or ill. For it is hard to speak properly upon a subject where it is even difficult to convince your hearers that you are speaking the truth. On the one hand, the friend who is familiar with every fact of the story may think that some point has not been set forth with that fulness which he wishes and knows it to deserve; on the other, he who is a stranger to the matter may be led by envy to suspect exaggeration if he hears anything above his own nature. For men can endure to hear others praised only so long as they can severally persuade themselves of their own ability to equal the actions recounted: when this point is passed, envy comes in and with it incredulity. However, since our ancestors have stamped this custom with their approval, it becomes my duty to obey the law and to try to satisfy your several wishes and opinions as best I may.

I shall begin with our ancestors: it is both just and proper that they should have the honour of the first mention on an occasion like the present. They dwelt in the country without break in the succession from generation to generation, and handed it down free to the present time by their valour. And if our more remote ancestors deserve praise, much more do our own fathers, who added to their inheritance the empire which we now possess, and spared no pains to be able to leave their acquisitions to us of the present generation. Lastly, there are few parts of our dominions that have not been augmented by those of us here, who are still more or less in the vigour of life; while the mother country has been furnished by us with everything that can enable her to depend on her own resources whether for war or for peace. That part of our history which tells of the military achievements which gave us our several possessions, or of the ready valour with which either we or our fathers stemmed the tide of Hellenic or foreign aggression, is a theme too familiar to my hearers for me to dilate on, and I shall therefore pass it by. But what was the road by which we reached our position, what the form of government under which our greatness grew, what the national habits out of which it sprang; these are questions which I may try to solve before I proceed to my panegyric upon these men; since I think this to be a subject upon which on the present occasion a speaker may properly dwell, and to which the whole assemblage, whether citizens or foreigners, may listen with advantage.

Our constitution does not copy the laws of neighbouring states; we are rather a pattern to others than imitators ourselves. Its administration favours the many instead of the few; this is why it is called a democracy. If we look to the laws, they afford equal justice to all in their private differences; if to social standing, advancement in public life falls to reputation for capacity, class considerations not being allowed to interfere with merit; nor again does poverty bar the way, if a man is able to serve the state, he is not hindered by the obscurity of his condition. The freedom which we enjoy in our government extends also to our ordinary life. There, far from exercising a jealous surveillance over each other, we do not feel called upon to be angry with our neighbour for doing what he likes, or even to indulge in those injurious looks which cannot fail to be offensive, although they inflict no positive penalty. But all this ease in our private relations does not make us lawless as citizens. Against this, fear is our chief safeguard, teaching us to obey the magistrates and the laws, particularly such as regard the protection of the injured, whether they are actually on the statute book, or belong to that code which, although unwritten, yet cannot be broken without acknowledged disgrace.

Further, we provide plenty of means for the mind to refresh itself from business. We celebrate games and sacrifices all the year round, and the elegance of our private establishments forms a daily source of pleasure and helps to banish the spleen; while the magnitude of our city draws the produce of the world into our harbour, so that to the Athenian the fruits of other countries are as familiar a luxury as those of his own.

If we turn to our military policy, there also we differ from our antagonists. We throw open our city to the world, and never by alien acts exclude foreigners from any opportunity of learning or observing, although the eyes of an enemy may occasionally profit by our liberality; trusting less in system and policy than to the native spirit of our citizens; while in education, where our rivals from their very cradles by a painful discipline seek after manliness, at Athens we live exactly as we please, and yet are just as ready to encounter every legitimate danger. In proof of this it may be noticed that the Lacedaemonians do not invade our country alone, but bring with them all their confederates; while we Athenians advance unsupported into the territory of a neighbour, and fighting upon a foreign soil usually vanquish with ease men who are defending their homes. Our united force was never yet encountered by any enemy, because we have at once to attend to our marine and to despatch our citizens by land upon a hundred different services; so that, wherever they engage with some such fraction of our strength, a success against a detachment is magnified into a victory over the nation, and a defeat into a reverse suffered at the hands of our entire people. And yet if with habits not of labour but of ease, and courage not of art but of nature, we are still willing to encounter danger, we have the double advantage of escaping the experience of hardships in anticipation and of facing them in the hour of need as fearlessly as those who are never free from them.

Nor are these the only points in which our city is worthy of admiration. We cultivate refinement without extravagance and knowledge without effeminancy; wealth we employ more for use than for show, and place the real disgrace of poverty not in owning to the fact but in declining the struggle against it. Our public men have, besides politics, their private affairs to attend to, and our ordinary citizens, though occupied with the pursuits of industry, are still fair judges of public matters; for, unlike any other nation, regarding him who takes no part in these duties not as unambitious but as useless, we Athenians are able to judge at all events if we cannot originate, and instead of looking on discussion as a stumbling-block in the way of action, we think it an indispensable preliminary to any wise action at all. Again, in our enterprises we present the singular spectacle of daring and deliberation, each carried to its highest point, and both united in the same persons; although usually decision is the fruit of ignorance, hesitation of reflexion. But the palm of courage will surely be adjudged most justly to those, who best know the difference between hardship and pleasure and yet are never tempted to shrink from danger. In generosity we are equally singular, acquiring our friends by conferring not by receiving favours. Yet, of course, the doer of the favour is the firmer friend of the two, in order by continued kindness to keep the recipient in his debt; while the debtor feels less keenly from the very consciousness that the return he makes will be a payment, not a free gift. And it is only the Athenians who, fearless of consequences, confer their benefits not from calculations of expediency, but in the confidence of liberality.

In short, I say that as a city we are the school of Hellas; while I doubt if the world can produce a man, who where he has only himself to depend upon, is equal to so many emergencies, and graced by so happy a versatility as the Athenian. And that this is no mere boast thrown out for the occasion, but plain matter of fact, the power of the state acquired by these habits proves. For Athens alone of her contemporaries is found when tested to be greater than her reputation, and alone gives no occasion to her assailants to blush at the antagonist by whom they have been worsted, or to her subjects to question her title by merit to rule. Rather, the admiration of the present and succeeding ages will be ours, since we have not left our power without witness, but have shown it by mighty proofs; and far from needing a Homer for our panegyrist, or other of his craft whose verses might charm for the moment only for the impression which they gave to melt at the touch of fact, we have forced every sea and land to be the highway of our daring, and everywhere, whether for evil or for good, have left imperishable monuments behind us. Such is the Athens for which these men, in the assertion of their resolve not to lose her, nobly fought and died; and well may every one of their survivors be ready to suffer in her cause.

Indeed if I have dwelt at some length upon the character of our country, it has been to show that our stake in the struggle is not the same as theirs who have no such blessings to lose, and also that the panegyric of the men over whom I am now speaking might be by definite proofs established. That panegyric is now in a great measure complete; for the Athens that I have celebrated is only what the heroism of these and their like have made her, men whose fame, unlike that of most Hellenes, will be found to be only commensurate with their deserts. And if a test of worth be wanted, it is to be found in their closing scene, and this not only in the cases in which it set the final seal upon their merit, but also in those in which it gave the first intimation of their having any. For there is justice in the claim that steadfastness in his country's battles should be as a cloak to cover a man's other imperfections; since the good action has blotted out the bad, and his merit as a citizen more than outweighed his demerits as an individual. But none of these allowed either wealth with its prospect of future enjoyment to unnerve his spirit, or poverty with its hope of a day of freedom and riches to tempt him to shrink from danger. No, holding that vengeance upon their enemies was more to be desired than any personal blessings, and reckoning this to be the most glorious of hazards, they joyfully determined to accept the risk, to make sure of their vengeance and to let their wishes wait; and while committing to hope the uncertainty of final success, in the business before them they thought fit to act boldly and trust in themselves. Thus choosing to die resisting, rather than to live submitting, they fled only from dishonour, but met danger face to face, and after one brief moment, while at the summit of their fortune, escaped, not from their fear, but from their glory.

So died these men as became Athenians. You, their survivors, must determine to have as unfaltering a resolution in the field, though you may pray that it may have a happier issue. And not contented with ideas derived only from words of the advantages which are bound up with the defence of your country, though these would furnish a valuable text to a speaker even before an audience so alive to them as the present, you must yourselves realize the power of Athens, and feed your eyes upon her from day to day, till love of her fills your hearts; and then when all her greatness shall break upon you, you must reflect that it was by courage, sense of duty, and a keen feeling of honour in action that men were enabled to win all this, and that no personal failure in an enterprise could make them consent to deprive their country of their valour, but they laid it at her feet as the most glorious contribution that they could offer. For this offering of their lives made in common by them all they each of them individually received that renown which never grows old, and for a sepulchre, not so much that in which their bones have been deposited, but that noblest of shrines wherein their glory is laid up to be eternally remembered upon every occasion on which deed or story shall call for its commemoration. For heroes have the whole earth for their tomb; and in lands far from their own, where the column with its epitaph declares it, there is enshrined in every breast a record unwritten with no tablet to preserve it, except that of the heart. These take as your model, and judging happiness to be the fruit of freedom and freedom of valour, never decline the dangers of war. For it is not the miserable that would most justly be unsparing of their lives; these have nothing to hope for: it is rather they to whom continued life may bring reverses as yet unknown, and to whom a fall, if it came, would be most tremendous in its consequences. And surely, to a man of spirit, the degradation of cowardice must be immeasurably more grievous than the unfelt death which strikes him in the midst of his strength and patriotism!

Comfort, therefore, not condolence, is what I have to offer to the parents of the dead who may be here. Numberless are the chances to which, as they know, the life of man is subject; but fortunate indeed are they who draw for their lot a death so glorious as that which has caused your mourning, and to whom life has been so exactly measured as to terminate in the happiness in which it has been passed. Still I know that this is a hard saying, especially when those are in question of whom you will constantly be reminded by seeing in the homes of others blessings of which once you also boasted: for grief is felt not so much for the want of what we have never known, as for the loss of that to which we have been long accustomed. Yet you who are still of an age to beget children must bear up in the hope of having others in their stead; not only will they help you to forget those whom you have lost, but will be to the state at once a reinforcement and a security; for never can a fair or just policy be expected of the citizen who does not, like his fellows, bring to the decision the interests and apprehensions of a father. While those of you who have passed your prime must congratulate yourselves with the thought that the best part of your life was fortunate, and that the brief span that remains will be cheered by the fame of the departed. For it is only the love of honour that never grows old; and honour it is, not gain, as some would have it, that rejoices the heart of age and helplessness.

Turning to the sons or brothers of the dead, I see an arduous struggle before you. When a man is gone, all are wont to praise him, and should your merit be ever so transcendent, you will still find it difficult not merely to overtake, but even to approach their renown. The living have envy to contend with, while those who are no longer in our path are honoured with a goodwill into which rivalry does not enter. On the other hand, if I must say anything on the subject of female excellence to those of you who will now be in widowhood, it will be all comprised in this brief exhortation. Great will be your glory in not falling short of your natural character; and greatest will be hers who is least talked of among the men whether for good or for bad.

My task is now finished. I have performed it to the best of my ability, and in word, at least, the requirements of the law are now satisfied. If deeds be in question, those who are here interred have received part of their honours already, and for the rest, their children will be brought up till manhood at the public expense: the state thus offers a valuable prize, as the garland of victory in this race of valour, for the reward both of those who have fallen and their survivors. And where the rewards for merit are greatest, there are found the best citizens.

And now that you have brought to a close your lamentations for your relatives, you may depart.

Appendices

APPENDIX A

Library Reference Materials Available to Speakers

We include here a brief review of reference materials which speakers can find readily available in libraries.

The card catalogue

As most students doubtless know, the card catalogue in a library lists all the books in that library alphabetically. For each book there are usually cards in three places in the catalogue, one filed under author, another by title, and a third by subject matter. Either of the first two will locate the specific book. If one has only a subject in mind, say *plastics, advertising, vitamins,* he may start with it, and after the card bearing the subject name, he will find the books related to it.

Each catalogue card for a book not only lists the book's publication date and its contents but notes whether the book contains a bibliography or reference list, which could be helpful in spotting related books. At the bottom of the card appear two or three subjects, under which to look for other books of related scope.

In general, the latest book on the subject is preferable. To discover it consult the *Cumulative Book Index.* This work lists all books printed in the United States since 1928 and is kept up to the month.

Encyclopedias

Encyclopaedia Britannica *Encyclopedia Americana* *Collier's Encyclopedia*

These sources try to keep their materials up to date by regularly publishing supplements, some of which appear annually. See *Britannica Book of the Year,* 1938 to date. The encyclopedias are valuable not only for their general articles on a variety of subjects but for the short reference lists usually given at the end of the principal articles.

Articles and pamphlets

Indexes General in Scope. The *Readers' Guide to Periodical Literature,* subscribed to by most libraries, is an up-to-date listing of many popular and general magazines in America which are largely nontechnical in nature. Articles are listed alphabetically by author, title, and subject, as books are listed in the card catalogue. In looking for articles on a subject, a searcher should not limit himself to looking only under the name that he happens to have in mind for that subject, for example, *taxes.* He should look also under other possible names for the same general subject, such as *taxation, revenue, finance.* The *Readers' Guide* is published monthly and the monthly installments are assembled into quarterly and yearly volumes. *Poole's Index to Periodical Literature* is useful similarly, especially for articles published before the *Readers' Guide* was begun (1900). The *Nineteenth Century Readers' Guide,* 1890–1899, published in 1944, covers some of the same material within *Poole's Index* but arranges the entries according to the same system used in the current *Reader's Guide.*

The *Social Sciences and Humanities Index,* formerly *The International Index to Periodicals,* covers periodicals not usually indexed in *The Readers' Guide,* including scholarly journals in the humanities and social sciences.

The Public Affairs Information Service, similar to the *Readers' Guide* in form and method of listing, includes not only periodical articles but books, pamphlets, and documents related to all subjects connected with public affairs.

The New York Times Index lists by subject (and author, if any) all articles that have appeared in *The New York Times.* The *Index* will also help to locate material in other newspapers to which there is no index. In *The Times Index* the date of an event or material is a guide for finding things in other newspapers.

The Vertical File Index is especially useful for locating valuable pamphlet material published by a variety of organizations. It is issued monthly. Users should realize that most libararies cannot acquire all the pamphlets listed in this catalogue. The General Reference Room in a library usually keeps the current pamphlets on hand, and the quickest way to find out what may be available on a subject is to ask the reference room attendant. Large colleges maintain departmental libraries housed in special rooms in the main library or elsewhere on the campus; these include collections of materials devoted to journalism, engineering, social sciences, education, and the like. Inquire at such places for pamphlet material. Consult also the Card Catalogue, for libraries keep the most important pamphlets permanently.

The Monthly Catalog of United States Government Publications lists all publications issued by the various departments and agencies of the government. The entries are arranged by subject and title. The *Catalog* is extensive

PHOTOMETRY
Flame-photometric determination of chlorine by indium chloride band emission. P. T. Gilbert. bibliog diag Anal Chem 38:1920-2 D '66
Gas chrometographic determination of compound 4072 and Shell SD-8447 by electron-capture and flame-photometric detection, M. Beroza and M. C. Bowman. bibliog J Agri & Food Chem 14:625-7 N '66
Photometric method determines fat in milk; abstract. Food Eng 38:115 D '66
See also
Measuring instruments, Optical
Optical instruments
Reflectometers

PHYSICIANS
Alcoholic and the physician. R. S. Cook. Ind Med 35:857-61 O '66
Position of the medically trained person in the administration of health services. K. Evang. Am J Pub Health 56:1722-33 O '66
Problem from the standpoint of the physician. D. J. Ansfield. Ind Med 35:946-9 N '66
Responsibilities of the physician in workmen's compensation cases. H. F. Howe. Ind Med 35:984-7 N '66
Some approaches to family planning counseling in local health departments; a survey of public health nurses and physicians. E. Siegel and R. C. Dillehay. bibliog Am J Pub Health 56:1840-6 N '66

Fig. 14. SAMPLE INDEX ENTRIES
Specific Headings and References to Specific Articles

PHYSICS
See also
American institute of physics
Cyclotron
Diffusion
Dimensional analysis
Dynamics
Elasticity
Electrons
Evaporation
Fluids
Fluorescence
Force and energy
Free energy
Friction
Gravitation
Gravity
Heat transmission
Ionization, Gaseous
Ions
Light
Liquids
Magnetism
Meteorology
Molecules
Nuclear physics
Particles, Elementary
Photoelasticity
Plasma (physics)
Plasticity
Porosity
Pressure
Quantum theory
Radiation
Reflection (optics)
Relaxation time (physics)
Sound
Space and time
Statistical mechanics
Steam
Temperature
Thermodynamics
Turbulence
Uncertainty principle
Velocity
Vibration
Viscosity
Vortex motion
Wave mechanics

Bibliography
Publications of the National bureau of standards. Phys & Chem 70A:447-52, 557-63 S-N '66
Resource letter PP-2 on plasma physics; waves and radiation processes in plasmas. G. Bekefi and S. C. Brown. bibliog Am J Phys 34:1001-5 N '66
Your child's physics books. M. Freeman. il Phys Today 19:67-70+ D '66

Figure 15. SAMPLE INDEX ENTRIES
Topics Related to a Specific Subject Heading, and Related Bibliography

and rather complicated, but it is probably the best single source of authoritative government information. When one uses it for the first time, he may need to ask the librarian for guidance.

Indexes Restricted in Scope. The range of the specialized indexes is indicated fairly accurately by their titles. They concentrate on materials appearing in publications dealing with particular fields. Each aims to cover everything in its field. Hence one discovers more articles related to farming in the *Biological* *and Agricultural Index* than he does in the *Readers' Guide.* Similarly, the *Readers' Guide* lists fewer articles on education than the *Education Index* does. The more specialized the subject is, the more useful is the appropriate special index.

Applied Science and Technology Index
Art Index
Biological and Agricultural Index
Business Periodicals Index
Cumulative Dramatic Index
Education Index
Engineering Index
Speech Index

The last named source is an index to collections of famous speeches, by subject and speaker.

Most of the more specialized encyclopedias are out of date. Nevertheless, attention should be called to two of them, for sudents still find their short historical articles useful:

Encyclopaedia of the Social Sciences (1930–1935)
Encyclopaedia of Religion and Ethics (1908–1927)

Statistical information

The sources below collect a vast amount of miscellaneous information concerning business, labor, industry, and social welfare. They are mines of facts.

World Almanac, and Book of Facts (1868 to date)
Information Please Almanac (1947 to date)
Statistical Abstract of the United States (1878 to date)
Statesman's Yearbook: Statistical and Historical Annual of the States of the World (1864 to date)
Monthly Labor Review (Reports on employment, payrolls, industrial disputes, retail prices, cost of living)
Survey of Current Business (Statistics on domestic and foreign trade, exports and imports, etc.)

Biographical information

Who's Who
Who's Who in America
International Who's Who
Current Biography
Webster's Biographical Dictionary (Includes pronunciation)
Twentieth Century Authors (See also its *First Supplement*)
Directory of American Scholars
American Men of Science: Physical and Biological Sciences; Social and Behavioral Sciences

For the most part, the sources above contain information about living persons, although *Webster's* lists famous persons of all time. The two publications below contain only the noteworthy dead. They are highly authoritative.

Dictionary of American Biography (Americans)
Dictionary of National Biography (United Kingdom)

Both works have supplements which bring them up to date.

VISITS TO NATIONAL FORESTS

table 250

In thousands.

Use and purpose	1950	1955	1960	1964
Total	27,368	45,713	92,595	133,762
General enjoyment of forest areas	7,969	12,444	30,181	49,145
Picnicking	6,326	10,883	19,497	20,664
Fishing	4,885	8,278	14,535	19,358
Hunting	2,285	4,064	7,591	10,817
Big-game take	358	518	682	(NA)
Camping	1,534	2,723	6,579	10,420
Winter sports	1,517	2,769	4,499	7,773
Swimming	902	1,368	2,801	3,749
Hiking and riding	635	1,053	2,018	3,263
Other	1,315	2,130	4,894	8,573

NA Not available.

Source: U.S. Forest Service.

No. 209. Grievances in Cities Where Civil Disorders Occurred, by Level of Intensity: 1967

[Based on surveys made in 20 cities where civil disorders occurred. Grievances evaluated as to significance in each city and rank and points assigned to the 4 most serious, as follows: 4 points for 1st place, 3 for 2d, 2 for 3d, and 1 for 4th. Total points for each grievance category represents number of cities in which it was ranked among the top 4 multiplied by the number of points. Thus, a 4-point grievance assigned to 2 cities amounted to 8 points. Judgments of severity based on frequency of mention of a particular grievance, relative intensity with which it was discussed, references to incidents exemplifying it, and estimates of severity]

Grievance category	Cities[1]	Points[2]
Police practices	14	45.5
Unemployment and underemployment	17	42.0
Inadequate housing	14	36.0
Inadequate education	9	21.0
Poor recreation facilities and programs	8	21.0
Ineffective political structure and grievance mechanisms	5	14.0
Disrespectful white attitudes	4	6.5
Discriminatory administration of justice	3	4.5
Inadequate Federal programs	1	2.5
Inadequate municipal services	1	2.0
Discriminatory consumer and credit practices	2	2.0
Inadequate welfare programs	—	—

Represents zero.
[1] Where grievances were mentioned as significant.
[2] Where 2 grievances were judged equally serious, points for the 2 rankings were divided equally.

Source: The National Advisory Commission on Civil Disorders; *Report,* March 1968.

Figure 16. TYPICAL REFERENCE TABLES

Collections of noteworthy quotations

Probably the best and the most available is John Bartlett's *Familiar Quotations,* the thirteenth and centennial edition, completely revised. Here the speechmaker can often find some of his ideas superbly and tellingly expressed. Even the novice speaker should be conversant with it.

APPENDIX B

Exercises and Drills for Improving Delivery

The procedures described below are designed to help the learning speaker to handle his body and gesture without distracting himself or his hearers; to help him secure poise, and as a consequence to be physically free to gesture spontaneously; to help him concentrate on the ideas of the speech he has prepared; and to aid him in acquiring a sense of communication.

Securing poise and freedom of action

The suggestions offered here may seem extremely elementary. They are. Nevertheless, they are basic to gesture and to efficient, unobtrusive platform behavior.

Posture and Carriage. The first step is learning to *stand* quietly and at ease. One finds his basic position.

Stand with the feet not more than six inches apart, with one foot somewhat behind the other. Observe that in this position the weight is not evenly distributed on both feet. (Avoid standing with toes in line and with feet tight together, for this tends toward stiffness.) Try to get the sensation of the floor being solidly yet comfortably beneath you; if necessary bend the knees and come back into position sharply, thus driving the toes into the floor. Finding and learning a basic stance is necessary for freedom of movement about the platform.

Body. The chest should be up, without being thrust out. The shoulders should be erect, without sagging and without being pushed back. Avoid a military, at-attention position, for this feels stiff and looks stiff to an audience. To help loosen the shoulders so that they will rest easily, rotate each shoulder, then raise the arms and let them fall like dead weights. When the torso is well poised, one feels as if the shoulders and upper body were suspended, rather than borne up laboriously from below. One is then free to respond readily with gesture.

Legs. The chief directions here are negative. Don't stand with the legs far apart, thus giving a planted or propped-up position. Don't let one leg bend or sag so much that the body is thrown out of line. Don't stick one leg out in front, for this also twists the body and breaks its general smoothness of line. All such positions attract attention to stance; no matter how natural and comfortable they may seem or how acceptable they are in everyday life, they don't look natural on the platform. If in avoiding such positions, one feels strange and stiff, he should practice in private until the stance becomes easy and comfortable.

Arms and Hands. The arms and hands must be ready to act, so that impulses to gesture are instantly translated into spontaneous movement. Accordingly, one should find a position that he can become comfortable in, and make it the basic, or *rest,* position from which he gestures.

One good position is with arms hanging freely—not stiffly or rigidly—at the sides. To find the position, raise the arms to shoulder height, relax, and let them fall. Another easy position, especially when a lectern is available, is to rest one forearm and hand on the lectern, with the other arm hanging free, or brought up to waist level. Guard against leaning or otherwise propping yourself on the stand.

Still another position is with both forearms up to waist level, the palms of the hands up and the fingers partially extended (avoid clenched fists and fingers rigidly extended). In this position the hands will just about meet at mid-body. Practice this position until you feel as if your forearms were resting on chair arms. This position is probably the easiest of all from which to gesture. (Caution: Don't clasp the hands in front or behind you, keep them out of the pockets, and in general avoid any position that inhibits instant movement.)

Stand Still, At Ease. After you have checked these positions carefully, stand still until the new position no longer seems new and strange. Stiffness won't depart instantly and magically; only practice and experience will bring results. Many students have used a watch to advantage. If one can stand still and like it for three minutes, he has a base of operations from which he can move when the spirit impels.

Movement on the platform

The next step is learning to move about the platform with ease and without attracting the listener's attention to movement as such. One cannot say flatly how often a speaker should move, or how much. All one can say with assurance is that any speaker who is keenly alive to his task doesn't remain stock-still in one position. Nor can one state at precisely what places in a speech a speaker should move. When his own body and his ideas demand action, he will be impelled to shift position—often without realizing it. What the beginner should do is to learn to handle his legs with ease and grace so that he moves when the impulse hits him.

From a standing position, move first to one side and then to the other two or three paces, observing these conditions:

1. Move on an angle, rather than directly sideways.
2. Lead with the right foot in going right; lead with the left foot in going left.
3. Initiate the movement lazily (sudden movement attracts attention) and cease it lazily.
4. Keep the shoulders on a level; avoid the sailor's roll.
5. Keep eyes on the audience.
6. After learning to move unobtrusively, learn to move about a speaker's stand or lectern. (At home substitute a straight-backed chair or a small table for the lectern.)
7. Stand behind the lectern; move far enough to the side to clear the stand, and then ease forward, keeping eyes on hearers.
8. Keep a hand on the stand during movement; the hand is a guide, and one appears to the observer like a normal human being, because human beings normally use furniture in this way, rather than avoid it.
9. Stand beside the lectern. In moving to a spot behind it, first back up a half-step or two and clear the back corner; then turn and continue to your destination. (Caution: Avoid dragging or scuffing the feet.) Keep a hand on the lectern, even though in this maneuver you will be shifting hands at the back corner of the stand as you turn. Keep eyes on the listeners.

If one is willing to work conscientiously for twenty to thirty minutes on these initial positions and movements as part of the preparation for his first speeches, he will see considerable improvement in platform behavior at once. But unless he is unusually skillful, he will not acquire acceptable platform behavior in a single, thirty-minute practice period. Remember that no habit is acquired magically, it is built in through directed practice and the desire to establish the habit firmly. If, then, after the delivery of a speech, the audience or the instructor points out inadequacies of behavior, jot them down and as a preliminary to the next speech, practice the positions and movements again, giving special attention to inadequacies. Repeat this procedure on subsequent speeches. Not until an audience ceases to be aware of a speaker's behavior can it be called adequate.

Securing vivid-realization-of-idea-at-the-moment-of-utterance

Rehearse Aloud. The emphasis is on practice *aloud*. Reading over the outline or the manuscript a dozen times is not so beneficial as speaking two or three times. The stimuli that control attention during utterance are not on a page; they are in the mind, and one needs to gain facility in controlling them.

The first oral rehearsal may not be very satisfactory. There's no audience, no real stimulus. The next trial should be easier, and so on. Frequently one can overcome the absence of an audience by imagining one. Many students pair off and practice on each other. When possible, use a classroom for rehearsal.

How Often to Rehearse. No one can say accurately. This is an individual problem. Some few students may need to rehearse very little, if at all. But do not let your ego rush forward here and put you into this rare group. Our years of teaching public speaking to hundreds of college students (a teacher hears no less than seven hundred student speeches a year) have shown us that 19 out of 20 students prosper by rehearsal. Some rehearse three times; some practice as many as twelve times. On this point especially, as we have said in Chapter 13, there is sound advice in the three old rules for public speaking: Practice, practice, practice.

When to Rehearse. Rehearsal should begin after the speech outline has been completed, for not until then is your sequence of ideas clear and complete. For speeches 3–7 minutes long, the first rehearsal should be no later than 24 hours before final delivery. This gives a chance to do some last-minute tinkering if first rehearsals suggest minor improvements to the outline. (Caution: It is unwise to make major changes in the outline the day before, particularly such a drastic change as abandoning an outline and making an entirely new one.) Later rehearsals may well come the night before the speech. Some students prefer to practice early in the evening before they undertake other studying, others prefer to practice after all other study is behind them and thus leave the speech as the last thing in mind.

Where to Rehearse. For the first few speeches it is wise to pick a place free of interruption. If possible rehearse once in the place where final delivery will take place and thus get adjusted to the sound of the speech there. The important thing in first practice is to avoid having one's attention diverted by distracting stimuli.

How to Rehearse. Although there is no single procedure that will fit everyone's needs, try the procedure below, following it meticulously for the first speeches and later changing it if necessary to fit individual requirements. The scheme is based on this psychological fact: the mind gives preference to a whole over its parts, to the stream of ideas in a sequence rather than the eddies. To use this procedure is to provide good insurance against omitting the main logical items and forgetting at joints and transitions. The procedure is designed, also, to keep attention on ideas, not on language and phraseology.

1. Get acquainted with the general pattern of ideas.
2. Read through the speech outline silently, slowly, thoughtfully, from beginning to end. Repeat. (Caution: Don't backtrack for any reason; and don't go back for details.)
3. Read the outline aloud, thoughtfully and deliberately; don't hurry.
   Abandoning the outline, go through the speech aloud from beginning to end. Don't back up for any reason, even if you know that you have forgotten a major item, and even if what is to be a 5-minute speech takes only a minute.
4. Reread the speech outline silently once again.
5. Practice aloud, again going through from start to finish without backing up.
6. If by this time the speech isn't running pretty well, continue to alternate silent study with oral practice.
7. Present an oral abstract of the speech. Include items in the abstract in this order: the purpose of the speech, the subject sentence or proposition, and the main heads. Ability to whip through an abstract should mean that the mind is in charge of the chief parts of a patterned sequence.

Polish the Details. Once control over the speech as a whole has been established, one can afford to pay attention to details that he has been omitting or to parts that he has been stumbling over. Give special attention to transitions. These are the hardest details for most speakers—even experienced ones—to manage well. Practice on them helps in keeping attention on the relationship of one part of the speech to the next part, and hence strengthens one's grasp on the path and structure of ideas.

The following suggestions may help in determining at what point in rehearsal one has satisfactorily assimilated ideas.

Do you have to struggle to remember the principal ideas? Are you afraid you will forget? Although no human being can be utterly sure that he will say everything he wants to and at the proper place, he can work over his ideas orally—in rehearsal and in conversation—to the point where he feels reasonably certain that he can make clear his essential ideas.

After planning the speech thoroughly, try this test of understanding and assimilation: Draw some acquaintance into conversation on the subject or a closely related subject. As the conversation develops, work into the dialogue at various times the ideas of the speech. Probably the best person for this purpose is someone else who is studying public speaking. Students are always inquiring of each other what they are going to speak on. Seize the opportunity. It will not only give you a chance to talk and think freely; you may pick up an idea or an illustration; or you may be asked a question that suggests what your audience would like to hear and what you hadn't provided for.

Can you change the order of the speech and still present the chief ideas so that they remain a unit? Try starting out with your best illustration; go from this to the head it illustrates, and thence to the next broader head until you have completed one logical unit. Then proceed to the next head that pops into mind, and so on. Summarize fully at the end.

Memorization. Should one memorize a speech? If the word memorize means verbatim recall, the answer is no. One should aim through rehearsal to stamp in, to assimilate, a sequence of ideas. What one memorizes and learns to handle through controlled association of ideas is a pattern of meanings. Phraseology will vary from one rehearsal to the next, and from last rehearsal to delivery on the platform. Remember that the most important task in acquiring good delivery is learning to think and talk as one does in good conversation. Of course, if rehearsal has been thorough, one may be repeating some phrases, sentences, and perhaps even chains of sentences, in the same words. This is well and good, and it means only that ideas and their word-symbols have become so completely associated in the mind that they are inseparable. One reacts to an idea, and its verbal counterpart springs into being automatically. What should be avoided during practice is any attempt to memorize words, deliberately and consciously. If one tries to memorize by rote, attention is on language, not on the ideas carried by language.

A very few individuals may find some verbatim memorization helpful at first. Those whose opening sentences are excessively slow, halting, and uncertain may find it advantageous to memorize the initial sentence or two. By having language definite and fixed, they are certain that they can get off to a good start. But if the device works, there is a temptation to repeat it and even to memorize verbatim more and more of the speech until one finds oneself wedded to words. Intending originally to develop a habit of extempore phraseology, the speaker falls into the opposite habit, a habit that is next to useless in discussion and conference and in the political and legal debates outside the classroom. It may be wiser to bear with the awkwardness and hazards of phraseology than to adopt hastily what looks like a speedy shortcut. In the long run, it will be best to plan and practice and let one's ideas find their own words.

Remember that there is no essential difference between the way the mind should work on the platform and the way it operates in conversation. Public utterance is an enlarged conversation.

Suggestions for reducing nervousness

There are a few practical expedients for minimizing the emotional disturbances that inhibit a speaker's giving full attention to idea and meaning.

Some of the expedients rest on the theory that bodily activity directly influences emotional behavior. One takes advantage of positive bodily sets and movements that are associated with feelings of assurance and confidence; one avoids running-away muscular sets and activity that accompany worry and fear. So in the classroom one volunteers to speak, moves positively to the platform, takes a step or two toward the audience as he starts his speech, and the like. He may use materials and visual demonstrations that require movement on the platform and movement of hands and arms. Blackboard diagrams require sketching, moving to and from the board at intervals, and pointing out special features as the speech develops. A model, and sometimes a chart, requires handling. Even the expedient of displaying a book and quoting from it demands activity. If the body is responding freely and appropriately, there is a good chance that the mind is also.

Another expedient is grounded on the fact that emotion once started becomes its own stimulus, feeds on itself, and pyramids. So if one "forgets" during delivery, he does not allow himself to get panicky. He immediately reviews aloud something he has already said. He may remind his hearers of his purpose, his subject sentence or proposal, or a main head. He may summarize swiftly, beginning a statement with, "Up to this point I have been trying to. . . ." Devices of this sort direct attention to where it belongs—on meanings. Furthermore, if the speech is well organized such expedients will almost invariably bring to mind what one has forgotten. One takes over his mind, so to speak, and directs it to what it should be doing.

Securing a lively sense of communication

Enhancing the Desire to Speak. The influence of emotion and feeling on a speaker's delivery can hardly be overvalued. Wanting to speak will give to presentation, first, an earnestness (earnestness is sincerity plus ardor) that any good speech should have. Second, it is a powerful source of vocal variety and of genuine gesture. Third, it helps overcome self-consciousness, because the desire to talk to others tends to take attention off one's self and to direct it to the task. Finally, it helps in remembering the pattern of ideas. Emotion holds together the data of experience as effectively as—perhaps more effectively than—formal logic. Hence, if the plan of ideas is dominated by and is shot through with the desire to speak, the desire will do much of one's remembering for him.

To promote a genuine desire to talk to others, observe the following suggestions:

1. Settle upon a specific purpose for the speech that really fits the audience.
2. Remember that all speech is provoked by and is directed to others. A speech isn't a performance. How one regards himself is not nearly so important as how his ideas affect his hearers.

3. State clearly and precisely why your audience should be interested in what you are going to say. This may give some sense that the speech is going to be worth the time and attention of your hearers, and if worthwhile to them, it should be worthwhile to you.

4. Be bodily alert, both during rehearsal and on the platform. In rehearsal, stir yourself up. Perhaps pace about some, throw in some gratuitous gestures, engage in a minute of calisthenics. In private one can overstep the modesty of conventional conduct in ways which in public would detract from the purpose of the speech. What would offend judicious persons if it were seen need not bother the speaker in private.

Keeping Eyes on the Audience. One can't expect to feel attached to his listeners, nor they to him, if he ignores them. Looking in their general direction is not enough. Look at individuals and see them.

Using the Style of Direct Address. Use the pronouns *we* and *you* in talking. They help tie speaker and audience together.

Use an occasional question, especially in introducing a new point. Questions obviously enough, are directed to others, and a speaker cannot use them without becoming somewhat aware that he has business, not with himself, but with the listeners. Particularly helpful are those questions that he thinks his audience would like to ask if it saw fit to interrupt. Anticipate these questions, state them, and answer them.

At the start of a speech employ salutations such as "Mr. Chairman, Ladies and Gentlemen," "Gentlemen," "Friends," "Classmates," or any other method of address that is appropriate and easy. A salutation is not only good manners, it makes the speaker become definitely aware of his hearers, and they of him.

Recognizing Persons by Name. If after one or two speeches one is still having difficulty in establishing direct contact, try an expedient that is permissible in the classroom, although inadvisable elsewhere. Recognize three or four individuals by name in as many different places in the speech. Perhaps something like this: "Now, Mr. Richards, as a student of biology, you may be interested in learning that this improvement to the microscope will. . . ." Or, "Mr. Wilson, if this plan for a simplified rushing procedure is workable, would you be willing to support it?"

Getting "Set" Before Speaking. The following suggestions may not only aid in heightening a speaker's sense of his purpose, but will also help in minimizing self-consciousness and nervousness:

Just before being called on to speak, try to recover that desire or impulse to communicate. In effect, say to yourself, "Here's my chance to do a real job for these people. I believe I can make them understand; I think I can claim their attention and interest. Let's see how they react." In other words, try to make the audience the essential stimulus that prompts you to action and speech. Instead of reviewing mentally what you want to say, appreciate and heighten the stimulus that should make you say it.

Adopt a positive physical approach to the platform; proceed directly to meet the task, rather than evade it. After facing your hearers, look at them for perhaps five seconds until they are for the most part paying attention.

Improving gesture

Once a speaker discovers that he is moving freely on the platform and is gesturing spontaneously and unself-consciously, he should consider two questions: (1) Are hand and arm gestures sufficient in number and in variety? (2) Are gestures graceful, free of ungainly, awkward, and jerky movements? On these questions the speechmaker will do well to consult his teacher or some candid critic who will tell him the plain truth. If the time has come to develop gesture in variety, number, and smoothness, the suggestions below will serve as guides. They should receive attention relatively late in the private rehearsal period, at about the time when the speaker can move along the main ideas of his speech without breaks.

Chief Kinds of Gesture. Recognizing the main kinds of gesture helps one see greater possibilities for gesture. One reviews his speech and see an opportunity to use a gesture where he hasn't done so before.

Gestures suggesting the relationship between ideas. *Contrasting ideas.* One hand marks one idea, the other hand the other, the hands moving away from each other and implying the notion of difference. In expressing a contrast, one often says, "On the one hand. . . . On the other hand. . . ."

Comparing ideas. Each hand marks one half of the comparison; then the hands approach each other to suggest that similar ideas belong together.

One idea subordinate to another. An example, an illustration, or a statistic which follows and amplies a general statement is often ushered in with a hand gesture which says, "Let me show you." A similar gesture is natural to use when offering a hypothetical illustration or a conditional statement such as "Suppose it were. . . ." or "Now if it is true that. . . ."

Gestures that describe. These suggest the size, shape, position, and movement of objects. They are perhaps the easiest for a speaker to learn to manage. They are natural, indeed virtually inevitable, in the informative speech. To illustrate their possibilities, gesture your way through this passage:

> Out in front of me was a large table. On one side of it was a round ball about two feet in diameter. On the other side was a rectangular column, about a foot across and three feet high. From it to the ball was stretched a wire. Just under the wire and at the half-way point was a small monkey who was rhythmically plucking it. Two feet in front of the monkey was a steel ball, about the size of a baseball. The ball would move back and forth in time with the monkey's plucking of the wire. With one pluck, the ball would roll to the right six inches; with the next pluck, it would roll back to the left, and so on.

Gestures that suggest emotion and feeling. To illustrate these gestures get into the mood of the following ideas and speak them.

> I shall have absolutely nothing to do with the proposal.
>
> I am quite willing to admit that I was wrong.
>
> I'm sorry, but it can't be helped.
>
> What's the difference; we may as well give up.
>
> No, no, it won't work. I'm warning you.
>
> Put the idea out of your mind.

Gestures that give force and emphasis. These gestures can be illustrated by the following ideas:

> We shall fight and struggle and toil on to the bitter end.
>
> Perjury and infamy on one hand; truth and honor on the other.
>
> Some may choose subjection and slavery, but as for me, give me liberty or give me death!
>
> Can you say that we should avoid the issue? I believe we should face it, now, once and for all.
>
> There's not a word of truth in it.

In working additional gestures into the speech during rehearsal, the speaker should practice them enough so that they spontaneously accompany ideas. If they don't become second nature to him, they may strike his audience as being planted and artificial. But the risk of looking a bit artful at times should not deter a speaker from gesturing more, if he needs to. Indeed, his speech class may well be the only place he will ever be able to improve his action.

We shall hazard the opinion that the modern speaker does not gesture enough. He seems to be made of clay or to be tied into a bag. The body-mind complex is a functional *whole.* To a remarkable degree in delivery, action sharpens thinking and gives force and variety to the voice. Gesture amplifies meanings and their expression. The student speaker scorns gesture to his disadvantage.

Smoothing Out Gesture. In working for smooth and graceful action, ones tries to attain, first of all, a feeling of easy limberness in the shoulders and arms. Then one proceeds to iron out any awkwardness of arm movement. The exercises and directions below should prove helpful.

Shoulders and arms. Roll the shoulders, first one shoulder and then the other. Roll both simultaneously. Loose and ready shoulders encourage arm movement.

Practice to secure a relaxed feeling in the arms. Lift the arms, extended in front (but not stretched), to shoulder height and *let them drop of their own weight*—simply *relax.* Then lift the extended arms to shoulder height at the sides; let them drop. Continue practice until you feel your arms *hang.* They should be loose as a rag doll's.

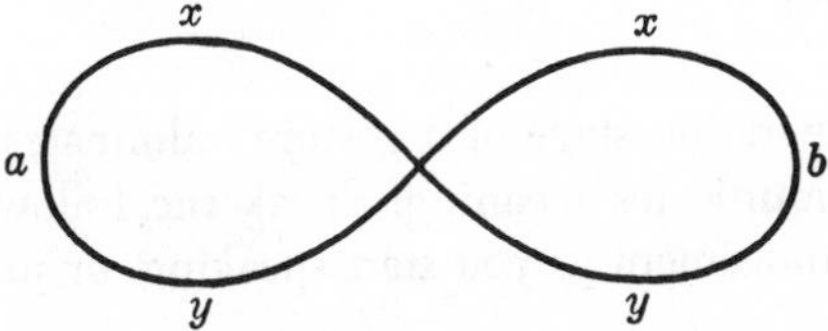

With the arms and shoulders loose and easy, practice the ancient double loop exercise. It is perhaps the best single exercise to secure graceful arm movements. First, go through the movement with one arm almost completely, though not entirely, extended in front of the body. The points of the loop, *a* and *b,* should be well beyond the sides of the body; the points marked *x* should be somewhat above the shoulder height; and the points marked *y* should be at about waist level. This gives a large figure 8, and the arm moves through most of the planes on which gesture takes place. Second, repeat the figure with the left arm. Finally, perform the figure with both arms simultaneously. (Caution: At no time must the arms be fully extended nor must they become rigid. It is the easy swing you are after.)

Arm movement. First, make sure that both arms are in the arm-rest position, that the forearms are horizontal. See that the hands, almost touching each other in front, are palm uppermost and that the fingers are in the position they would take if you were holding a large apple or orange. Rigid, extended fingers look unnatural and awkward. See, also, that the elbows lightly touch the sides of the body; to let them stick out looks ungainly. With the arms in this position and resting easily, one is ready for the three stages of arm movement.

Beginning. A gesture has a beginning, middle, and end. Neither the beginning movement nor the end carries meaning. The beginning movement is called the preparation, because it takes the arm and hand to the point where the meaningful action, called the climax, takes place. The concluding movement, the return, simply brings the arm back to a position of rest, ready to respond again to an idea.

With the arms in position, start a movement with the right arm to the right, observing these instructions.

1. Keep the elbow at the side of the body until the movement is well started. Leading with the elbow is awkward.
2. Start the movement by letting the wrist lead; the hand follows at first and gradually catches up by the time the climax is reached. Start the movement rather slowly, for sudden movement attracts attention to itself. Vigorous, swift activity—if any—takes place at the climax.
3. Practice the preparation first with one arm, then with the other arm, and finally with both.

Middle. The preparation stage of a gesture culminates in a rather sudden movement that communicates meaning. Speak the following sentence, starting the preparation movement as you start speaking, or just before utterance:

The plan is extremely dangerous.

Remember the actor's old rule: action always precedes speech unless one desires a comic effect. As you make the point, dangerous, hand and arm will execute a short, swift movement that marks and gives emphasis to the idea. With good preparation, the climax of a gesture will almost invariably take care of itself. What happens at the climax will depend entirely on the idea expressed. Use each arm alone and then both arms in saying the sentence above.

Ending. After the climax the arm should come to rest. Sometimes it will come back to the starting point of the cycle; sometimes it will return only slightly, especially if another gesture is to follow immediately. For example, experiment with the following sentence:

The plan is extremely dangerous, vicious, and altogether reprehensible.

After making the idea dangerous, the arm will remain where it is and from that point will emphasize the next two ideas, vicious and reprehensible. When the series is complete, the arm may return to mid-body, or drop lightly to the side. The arm should return rather slowly; if the action is swift the observer's attention will be attracted.

The student should not watch gestures—unless he wants to appear ridiculous.

In encouraging student speakers to improve the quantity and quality of their gestures, we are not implying that the speaker should be as active as the actor. Obviously, the speaker is not an actor, and accordingly his gestures, as a rule, are neither so numerous nor as extensive as the actor's. Nevertheless, gesture is to the speaker what gesture is to the actor: an aid in describing ideas, suggesting emotion and attitudes, and providing emphasis.

Index